Social Currents in Eastern Europe

D1382651

Social Currents in Eastern Europe

//

The Sources and Consequences

of the Great Transformation

Second Edition

Sabrina Petra Ramet

///

DUKE UNIVERSITY PRESS   *Durham and London 1995*

© 1995 Duke University Press   All rights reserved
Printed in the United States on acid-free paper
Typeset in Trump Mediaevel by Tseng Information Systems.
Library of Congress Cataloging-in-Publication Data
appear on the last printed page of this book.

Seid umschlungen, Millionen.
Dieser Kuss der ganzen Welt . . .
—Friedrich Schiller

To all who practice tolerance
To all who advocate tolerance
To all who fight for tolerance
To all who suffer in the fight,
For without tolerance,
There is no such thing
As civilized society.

Contents

V. Collapse of the Old Order

12. Bulgaria: A Weak Society   279
13. Strong Societies: Hungary, Poland, and Yugoslavia   288
14. Dominoes: East Germany, Czechoslovakia, and
the Future of Europe   313
15. The Great Transformation   338

VI. Building New Systems

16. Core Tasks for a Pluralist Order   371
17. Yugoslav Breakup and Ethnic War   401
18. Civil Society and Uncivil Chauvinism   431
19. Propositions About the Future   455

Appendixes: Public Opinion Polls   461
Notes   483
Selected Bibliography   565
Index   569

Tables

Preface to the Second Edition

This new edition contains five new chapters: 1 and 16–19. In these I have extended and developed the theory of social change upon which this book is based, added a theory of democratic politics based on recent cross-cultural literature, and surveyed the principal challenges presently confronting the region. Chapters 4 and 6 have been considerably revised to take into account recent scholarship and new data, as well as some revelations by the Russian government and by former President Wojciech Jaruzelski. I have also made modest revisions to the book's other chapters. As in the first edition, I have given minimal attention to Albania—this time largely for reasons of space.

Work on this second edition was accomplished while at the Slavic Research Center, Hokkaido University, Sapporo, Japan. I am grateful to the Center and to Hokkaido University for the support that has made this work possible. I am also grateful to Reynolds Smith of Duke University Press for encouraging me to carry out these revisions.

I also wish to thank John Löwenhardt for his helpful comments on an earlier draft of chapter 1. And special thanks to Chris Hassenstab for generous assistance in assembling a new index for this edition.

Sabrina Petra Ramet

Sapporo, 12 October 1993

Preface to the First Edition

This book is concerned with social change in seven communist countries of Eastern Europe—East Germany, Poland, Czechoslovakia, Hungary, Yugoslavia, Romania, and Bulgaria—and with their transformation into pluralist or pseudopluralist systems. I decided largely to exclude Albania from examination because until the latter half of 1990 it did not share for the most part in the patterns of change sweeping the rest of the area and because it has been largely cut off from any interaction with the other countries of the region. Some brief comments on Albania appear in chapter 15.

My idea in writing this book was that diverse social currents (mainly ethnic, religious, trade unionist, civic, feminist, musical-cultural, and youth) do not exist in isolation; on the contrary, they overlap, interact, and often follow parallel lines of development. I wanted to bring out this interrelationship and to show how changing social currents present political authorities with policy challenges, indeed with challenges that may bear on the fundamental questions of governance: system legitimacy and system stability. The phenomena described herein are of different levels of significance. To take the extremes, Solidarity has been a force for major system change in Poland, while Yugoslav feminists are relatively marginal. Both, however, are symptomatic of changing attitudes and changing behaviors.

Interviews have been important for the research for several chapters, in particular, chapters 3, 4, 6, 9, and 10. Interviews were conducted over an eight-year period, from 1982 through 1989: in Belgrade (1982, 1987, 1988, 1989), Ljubljana (1982, 1987, 1989), Zagreb (1982, 1987, 1989), Sarajevo (1982, 1989), Munich (1987), Rome (1987), Vienna (1987), East Berlin

(1988), Leipzig (1988), Dresden (1988), Halle (1988), Erfurt (1988), Eisenach (1988), and Skopje (1989). I am indebted to the American Council of Learned Societies and to the International Research Exchanges Board (IREX) for providing funding for the 1982 and 1988 research trips, and to IREX and the Graduate School Research Fund of the University of Washington for providing funding for the 1989 research trip.

I am deeply indebted to László Kürti, who read the entire manuscript and provided helpful suggestions for its improvement. I am also indebted to Chris Bettinger, my research assistant, who assisted with the research for chapter 4, and to Robin Alison Remington, Darko Glavan, and Lawrence W. Lerner for their comments on earlier drafts of chapters 7, 10, and 14, respectively. I am also very grateful to Dan Beck and Clark Sorensen, who translated some material from Czech and Korean sources, cited in chapter 6. I also wish to thank Helena Ott, Piotr Jankowski, Carolyn Kadas, and Michelle Arneaux for checking the diacritical marks for Czech, Polish, Hungarian, and Romanian names, and to the Henry M. Jackson School of International Studies of the University of Washington for providing a small grant for that purpose. Finally, I would like to thank Whit Mason, who helped to proofread the final page proofs.

Earlier versions of chapters 3, 8, and 10 were previously published in *World Politics,* the *Canadian Review of Studies in Nationalism,* and *Survey,* respectively. A portion of chapter 9 was previously published as part of a study appearing in *Osteuropa.* I am grateful to the editors of these journals for their permission to reuse this material.

This has been a difficult book to write insofar as events in Eastern Europe have been moving at a breakneck pace recently. The initial drafts of chapters 2–11 and 14 were completed in October 1988 and pointed to the building pressures for regionwide political change, but of necessity they had to be updated and revised. Chapters 12 and 13 were added in November 1989. When the book was finally cleared for publication in June 1990, I decided to update much of the text but to make only the slightest changes in chapter 2. Chapter 14 had to be substantially rewritten at that time, while chapter 15 is new.

Finally, a personal note: While working on this book, I have been wrestling with issues of my own. In December 1989, after years of recurrent depression and crisis, which reached a particular intensity at that time, I decided to begin the slow process of changing my physical sex in order to bring it into harmony with my psychic gender. While this has opened up feelings of euphoria and self-contentment surpassing anything I had ever experienced before, it has also presented me with continued challenges. Readers acquainted with the earlier incarnations of some of these chapters will associate them with the authorship of Pedro Ramet: Pedro and Sabrina are one and the same person.

Sabrina P. Ramet

Seattle, 12 June 1990

Abbreviations

CDU	Christian Democratic Union (West Germany)
CDU-EAST	Christian Democratic Union (East Germany)
CP	Communist Party
CPP	Czech People's Party
CPSU	Communist Party of the Soviet Union
FGY	Free German Youth (East Germany)
HDF	Hungarian Democratic Forum
HSWP	Hungarian Socialist Workers' Party
IPA	Independent Peace Association (Hungary)
KKS	National Strike Committee (Poland)
KOPP	Citizens' Committee Against Violence (Poland)
KOR	Committee for the Defense of the Workers (Poland)
KOS	Committee for Social Resistance (Poland)
KPN	Confederacy for an Independent Poland
LC	League of Communists
LCY	League of Communists of Yugoslavia
LDP	Liberal Democratic Party (Slovenia)
MKO	Interregional Commission for the Defense of Solidarity (Poland)
NOB	National Liberation Struggle (Yugoslavia)
NSF	National Salvation Front (Romania)
NVA	National People's Army (East Germany)
OKO	National Resistance Committee (Poland)
PPF	Patriotic People's Front (Hungary)
PRON	Patriotic Movement for National Renewal (Poland)
PUWP	Polish United Workers' Party
SAWP	Socialist Alliance of Working People (Yugoslavia)

SAWPY	Socialist Alliance of Working People of Yugoslavia
SD	Democratic Party (Poland)
SED	Socialist Unity Party (East Germany)
SSOJ	League of Socialist Youth of Yugoslavia
TKK	Interim Coordinating Committee (Solidarity, Poland)
UDF	Union of Democratic Forces (Bulgaria)
VONS	Committee for the Unjustly Persecuted (Czechoslovakia)
WSN	Freedom-Justice-Independence (Poland)
ZSL	United Peasant Party (Poland)

Part I
Introduction

1. Aspects of the Transition
from Authoritarianism to Pluralism

*Where the law is subject to some other authority and has none of its
own, the collapse of the state is not far off; but if the law is the master
of the government and the government is its slave, then the situation is
full of promise and men enjoy all the blessings that the gods shower on
a state.*—PLATO, *The Laws, 715d*

This book is about change and the forces of change. At the most basic
level it takes one side in a long-standing but rarely conceded covert
debate between, on the one hand, those who take a mechanistic approach, lodging the causes of change primarily (or in some cases, even
exclusively) in statistically measurable increases in popular political participation, declines in industrial production, changes in the number of
people existing below the poverty line, and so forth, and, on the other
hand, those who take a more phenomenological approach—in the sense
in which Jean-Paul Sartre and Maurice Merleau-Ponty use the term—
and who trace social changes ultimately, and in the first place, to changes
in people's thinking, recognizing that such changes may be produced
either by substantive changes in real terms or by elite manipulation of
media images or by religious conversion or by other factors or by a combination of these. For the phenomenological school, thus, if a population
is completely unaware of any change in its material well-being, then statistical indicators of "real" economic decline will not point to any drift
toward social chaos or protest, all other things being equal. This book is
firmly phenomenological in thrust (in the sense indicated), despite the
citation of extensive statistical indices of economic decline in chapter 2.

The book's central arguments may be stated as such: (1) The pressures
for change in Eastern Europe built up over years because of the com-

munist regimes' inability to solve the central problem of legitimation, and these pressures found multivarious outlets—in culture, in religious organizations, even in rock music, while simultaneously exciting tensions along latent axes such as those of an ethnic nature (as in Kosovo) or of a class nature (the Polish trade union Solidarity being a case in point). (2) The regimes' inability to quash incipient reflections of these pressures led to a proliferation of such pressures, as one success (even if only temporary) in dissident activity encouraged other efforts. (3) Because of this relationship among social forces, serious political complaints and demands could be read first in more "sanguine" contexts, allowing political observers to predict the ultimate upheaval without being able to determine its exact timing. (Among those who predicted the ultimate collapse of communism in the region were Ernst Kux in 1980,[1] George Schöpflin repeatedly in the early 1980s,[2] Dimitry Pospielovsky in 1987,[3] Ivan Volgyes in 1987,[4] and William C. Fletcher,[5] while this book was itself undertaken in early 1988 with the original purpose of demonstrating that dramatic political change had become unavoidable.) And (4) although often described as a revolution for democracy, the political shift that became explicit in 1989 and that resulted in the removal of the old communist elites everywhere but in Serbia, was a revolution—and I shall insist on that word—*against communism*, but not necessarily with the same understanding throughout the region and among different actors as to what programs and institutions should be established;[6] it also has opened a Pandora's Box of troubles, ranging from the challenges of institution-building, to the perils of privatization, to a new strength for chauvinism—whether of an ethnic, religious, or sexist stripe—to the disintegration of the preexisting state community, as in the cases of the German Democratic Republic (GDR), Czechoslovakia, and Yugoslavia. These "troubles" directly threaten aspirations to create and legitimate a stable democratic order anywhere in the region.

Although I have been emphasizing the impact that social and economic pressures may have on political outcomes, and the procreative energy of changes in social values and beliefs, I would nonetheless agree with Rustow's caution that "not all causal links run from social and economic to political factors," and "not all causal links run from beliefs and attitudes to actions."[7] The point is rather that there is a reciprocal and organic relationship among political, social, and economic factors, so that perturbations in one sphere are apt to have repercussions and reflections and effects in other spheres.

The book's theoretical presuppositions involve five components, to be reviewed in this chapter: (1) a theory as to which factors make for political decay and system collapse (based largely on the writings of Crane Brinton, Ted Robert Gurr, Adam Przeworski, James C. Davies, and Herbert Blumer); (2) a theoretical mapping of the dynamics, pace, and phases of transition from authoritarian/totalitarian rule to pluralism (drawn from work by Guillermo O'Donnell and Philippe Schmitter); (3) formulation of a working definition of *democracy*, followed by a theoretical construct of the necessary preconditions of democracy (which will be set forth against a discussion of the writings of Robert A. Dahl, Barry Holden, Dankwart Rustow, Terry Lynn Karl, Giuseppe Di Palma, Valerie Bunce, and others); (4) an elaboration of the differences between a "strong" society and a "weak" society and an assessment of their importance for considerations of system vulnerability to change (derived directly from the ideas explored under point 1); and (5) a theory about the weakness of new systems and about the relationship between political decay and civil strife (inspired by Crane Brinton and Samuel P. Huntington and based, in part, on previous work of mine).

1. When Do Systems Collapse? (That Is, Why?)

In his classic study of revolutionary processes Crane Brinton outlined seven factors that rendered a system vulnerable to collapse or overthrow.[8] These are (1) economic deterioration; (2) the mobilization of new groups; (3) the defection of the intellectuals; (4) inefficiency and corruption in the system; (5) the loss of credibility by the regime; (6) the loss of self-confidence by the ruling elite and the appearance of fissures and factions within that elite; and (7) the inept use of force. This book was originally launched in early 1988 in the belief that these seven measures could serve as a guide to assessing the prospects for the collapse or overthrow of the communist regimes in the region.

Of the seven factors, three are explicitly *subjective* in character (numbers 5, 6, 7), depending entirely on what either the society or the elite (or both) may think about the given issue. A fourth factor—economic deterioration (number 1)—is also latently subjective, because, as Gurr reminds us, its capacity to frame and shape political choices depends entirely on its perception and construal—what Gurr calls *relative deprivation*.[9] Adam Przeworski has similarly laid stress on collective perception as the mediating variable between objective conditions and system vulnerabilities.[10] The remaining factors on Brinton's list (2, 3, and 4) have a more "objective" character, although the importance that corruption (factor 4) has is also ultimately a matter of collective subjectivity; to put it another way, if nobody cares about corruption, it is not politically important.

The transition from an authoritarian system to a pluralist system does not come about as the result of a sudden snap. Even revolution is an evolutionary process, which unfolds over years through definable phases. In the first phase, there is the organization of underground resistance, the creation of the political *alternative*, which, as Przeworski notes, is the ultimate sine qua non of revolution.[11] This phase necessarily involves years, because the resistance needs time first to build itself, and second, to prove itself. The process involves the establishment of a network of committees at central, district, and town levels, and the establishment of secure underground channels of communication. The process in contemporary authoritarian systems is the same whether one speaks of post-1980 Poland or Iran in the 1970s or certain Latin American countries in the 1970s and early 1980s or the organization of the Resistance in Vichy France.[12]

As long as the regime can break up opposition cells and arrest their members, severely restricting the circulation of opposition publications, the regime remains in this first phase, and it is not in danger of collapse. It is when the regime loses the ability to control its political environment that the system may be said to have entered into its second phase: regime deterioration. As Baloyra points out:

> *Deterioration* is the loss by an incumbent government of its ability to cope with the policy agenda, particularly the two key concerns of political economy—security and prosperity—and other salient issues of high symbolic appeal to the public. Deterioration is the situation in which governments find themselves when they are unable to conjugate minimally acceptable levels of efficacy, effectiveness, and legitimacy.[13]

This phase is likely to stretch over years, although its most telling moments are often compressed in a few months. Finally, the society reaches a threshold, at which real change suddenly seems irreversible. James Davies has underlined the importance of this factor—the expectancy of change—and I have therefore added it as factor 8 among the measures applied in the next chapter.[14] However this expectancy is triggered— whether by internal developments (e.g., the dramatic roundtable talks in Poland in late 1988) or by external events (e.g., the deep impression that changes in the GDR, Poland, and Czechoslovakia had on the Bul-

or less simultaneously."[33] George Schöpflin, for his part, was writing in the early 1980s about the political decay of communist systems—a decay that could have only one conceivable ultimate stage.[34] Or again, J. F. Brown, in a 1984 essay, predicted accurately that "the Polish experience may have begun a gradual shift in power relationships within the communist system."[35] Or again, Ivan Volgyes, in a 1987 essay, accurately assessed that Hungary was on the brink of a political "storm."[36] Or again, Annali Gabanyi, a researcher at Munich's Südost Institut, announced as early as September 1988 that Ceaușescu's days were numbered.[37] Or again, Brigitte Schulz predicted in early 1989 the imminent end of communism in the GDR. Or again, Zbigniew Brzezinski wrote prophetically in early 1989: "It is almost a certainty that at some point in the relatively near future, given some major economic or political upheaval, politics as the expression of authentic social aspiration for multiparty democracy will return to the life of Eastern Europe."[38] And for that matter, there was my own early warning in 1984 of Yugoslavia's gradual drift toward civil war,[39] and my subsequent prediction in February 1991 that civil war in that country was only a matter of weeks away.[40] Or, for that matter, Jaček Kuron, the Solidarity adviser, declared rather significantly in February 1988 (two months before major strikes rocked the country): "The specter of a social explosion is haunting the country."[41] I could continue to add examples, but the point is clear enough; in Niko Toš's words: "with respect to the changes so far, their peaceful course [aside from Yugoslavia] and the moment of their occurrence have been unexpected, but not the changes themselves."[42]

Given this impressive record of rather prophetic analyses, it is surprising to find the usually more sagacious Timothy Garton Ash writing in 1990: "The events of 1989 in Eastern Europe . . . [are] a powerful argument for never again writing about the future. No one predicted them."[43] Against this unwarranted (and even solipsistic) pessimism, I would counter that just because some scholars failed to see the tea leaves at the bottom of their cups—or worse yet, to take them seriously—does not mean that we should not offer prognoses about the likely success or failure of individual East European countries in their efforts to democratize (as I did in 1992 in an article for *Orbis*),[44] or that we should not develop arguments for pessimism about the prospects of the Soviet successor states, and Russia in particular, of avoiding growing chaos and civil strife and ultimate relapse into authoritarian rule (as I did elsewhere in 1992),[45] or that we should not offer prognoses about the most promising strategies of democratization for postcommunist states (as Juan Linz and Alfred Stepan did so well in yet another 1992 publication).[46] The fact that many persons have taken to citing Ash's comment approvingly only shows to what extent many scholars fail to keep up with the writings of other scholars.

3. Democracy—Definitions and Preconditions

As Barry Holden notes, there are two related and persistent tendencies (1) either to dismiss as unnecessary any proposal to set forth a definition of democracy, on the grounds that we all know what democracy is, or (2) to take as constitutive those elements that resemble features found in systems that we take for granted as being democracies. Holden argues that these tendencies are pernicious—and I agree with him—not only because people inevitably differ as to which states belong in the "democratic" set, but more importantly, because in the absence of a clear expostulation of what is meant by the term, articulate observers may have in mind entirely different values when talking about "democracies," and thus they may emphasize entirely different institutions as necessary safeguards for their cherished values.[47]

Of course, almost as many definitions of *democracy* exist as there are democratic theorists. Many of these theorists favor a strongly *structural* definition, that is, they believe that a democracy means that certain structures or institutions exist. An example of what I have in mind is offered by Philippe Schmitter and Terry Lynn Karl: "Modern political democracy is a system of governance in which rulers are held accountable for their actions in the public realm, by citizens, acting indirectly through the competition and cooperation of their elected representatives."[48] Here, *accountability* is the value to be safeguarded, and the structural mechanisms specified are elections and competitive politics. Larry Diamond offers a similar approach:

> Democracy is, by its nature, a system of institutionalized competition for power. Without competition and conflict, there is no democracy. But any society that sanctions political conflict runs the risk of its becoming too intense, producing a society so conflict-ridden that civil peace and political stability are jeopardized. Hence the paradox: Democracy requires conflict—but not too much; competition there must be, but only within carefully defined and universally accepted boundaries. Cleavage must be tempered by consensus.[49]

No explicit statement is made here as to the value or values to be safeguarded, but the structural dimension is clear enough.

There are also structural definitions with a highly detailed character, such as the following overly elaborate definition by H. V. Wiseman (published in 1966):

> *Political democracy* is the regime of civilian rule through representative institutions and public liberties. Its components are first, a legislative body periodically elected by universal (adult or male) suffrage, empowered to initiate legislation . . . and to exact or repeal legislation initiated by the executive. The latter is subject to review and control. . . . The executive carries out its policies through a hierarchically organized nonpolitical bureaucracy. . . .
>
> Candidates for the legislature are normally members of contending political parties. . . . Executive and legislative action is subject to periodic review through free elections, as well as being continually scrutinized by free organs of public opinion. Within the legislature, opposition and minority rights are guaranteed, and governments can be changed by regularized procedures of election. . . .[50]

For Wiseman, thus, universal *male* suffrage is sufficient to warrant calling a system a democracy, but universal *female* suffrage would not be; incorporating sexism into the very definition or understanding of democracy in this way can only suggest that Wiseman is unable to distinguish between a posteriori and a priori. Aside from the rather obvious resultant idiocy in suggesting that females are definitionally inessential to democracy, Wiseman's definition is flawed by its conflation of supposed necessary conditions with defining characteristics—a conflation to which all overly elaborate definitions are vulnerable.

Interestingly enough, none of the foregoing definitions make any reference to majority rule, whether because the writers consider the principle entailed in the concepts of accountability or competition or elections, or because they consciously choose to place their emphasis elsewhere. On the other hand, Norberto Bobbio, the prominent Italian political theorist, places his stress squarely on majority rule. For him, "it is impossible to ever understand anything about democracy until it is realized that a democratic system nowadays signifies first and foremost a set of procedural rules, among which majority rule is the main, but not the only one."[51]

Although all of these definitions point to facets of democracy that are rather salient, I prefer a more *cultural* definition of democracy, treating its institutionalization and structure as practical (i.e., derivative) rather than definitional questions. I propose the following definition: *A democracy is a system based on the principles of political choice and social tolerance.* Here one has an explicit declaration of values, with their realization being deferred to discussions of preconditions. That this definition is Madisonian in spirit—recall Madison's concerns to protect minorities from "the tyranny of the majority"—should be obvious.

This definition has the advantage of avoiding the all-or-nothing fallacy that may be associated with some structuralist approaches. Thus, it permits one to say, the more political choice *and* the more social tolerance one finds in a given society, the more democratic it is; and conversely, the less political choice *or* the less social tolerance one finds, the less democratic a society is. I replaced "and" with "or" in the negative correlation to emphasize that both values are necessary conditions for the successful functioning of a democracy.

What this means, in practice, is that even the existence of significantly different political alternatives, together with the accountability of elected officials through regular free elections, counts for nothing if the political mainstream is dominated by intolerant attitudes, and by the same virtue, that democracies are literally placed under siege whenever socially intolerant groups (such as antiabortion activists) succeed in imposing their agendas on the entire society—regardless of whether elections and competition continue. Or, to put it in a few words, there is no such thing as a democracy without social tolerance.

Now no *intrinsic* moral judgment attaches itself to this definition of democracy. Whether one considers democracy—defined as I have done, or defined some other way—a good system depends on which values one thinks the given system strives to protect, how well the system does so, and what one thinks of the given protected values in the first place. Hence, if one believes—as I do—that social tolerance is *the* most important value to safeguard, and that political choice is positive only insofar as it safeguards social tolerance, then one may well find some authoritarian systems, governed by benevolent despots, that are more effective in protecting the value of tolerance than some structurally pluralist systems—at least for the life span of the given despot. As Aristotle noted two millennia ago, the best system is rule by a benevolent despot; but the worst system is rule by a malevolent despot. On the face of it, authoritarianism could offer more than democracy, but the risks of malfunctioning and of subversion are far greater in authoritarian than in democratic systems. On this point, Plato and Aristotle agree.

Now to say that tolerance is the *most* important value is not to say it is the *only* important value. As Budziszewski aptly expressed it, "Tolerance is a virtue indeed; but if it is the only virtue, it can hardly be anything more than good conscience in our continuing lack of convictions."[52] Just what, then, is tolerance? When I use the word, I mean three things: first, a respect for difference and an allowance that different people may have legitimate differences of need, custom, belief, and behavior; second, the acceptance that the basis for assessing to what extent needs, customs, beliefs, and behaviors may be worthy of toleration or not is the criterion of harm to human or animal life; and third, acceptance of the principle that there is an important operational difference between universal reason and restricted associational assent in defining what is and is not morality. What I mean by this last point is that we may take it as a given that almost all people can arrive at the conclusion that murder is wrong by pure reason; the exceptions that may be cited are not, I would argue, significant. On the other hand, in practice, one cannot say the same thing about abortion; on the contrary, the belief that abortion is morally reprehensible in all instances is largely restricted to persons associated with specific religious bodies (and often to people living in specific regions, for example, the rural American South). Hence, when a moral minority (such as antiabortion activists) attempts to impose its moral norms on a society as a whole, a tolerant person will oppose that minority. Tolerance, in short, does not mean anything goes; and it certainly does not mean a tolerance of intolerance.

Insofar as I tie toleration to the criterion of harm to human or animal life, I am connecting it with the notion of Natural Law (which itself entails the aforementioned concept of Universal Reason).[53] "True tolerance"—to borrow Budziszewski's elegant term—accords respect to such customs, beliefs, and behaviors as do not harm human or animal life; whatever does harm to life, to any living being—whether physical harm, psychological harm, or harm of any other kind—without just cause, is unworthy of toleration.

But why tolerance in the first place? Why not allow powerful majorities far-reaching capacity to dictate social norms and practices? Historically, two competing democratic traditions arose between the seventeenth and eighteenth centuries: the French tradition (exemplified by Sieyès and Rousseau) and the Anglo-American tradition (exemplified by Hobbes, Locke, and J. S. Mill). The French tradition defined democracy in terms of the successful assertion of the general will and held that individual wills at variance with the general will had no validity, and were therefore unworthy of toleration. Talmon calls this tradition *totalitarian democracy*.[54] The Anglo-American tradition, by contrast, defined democracy in terms of the acceptance of opposition and debate.[55] But if opposition is to have any meaning, it must be premised on the guarantee of the autonomy of individual actors. This is why in seeking to lay the ideological groundwork for democracy, eighteenth-century English liberals were so concerned to protect the autonomy of individuals.[56] But as Joseph Raz has noted, "a commitment to autonomy entails a commitment to moral pluralism," and respect for others' autonomy entails the duty of toleration.[57]

It is sometimes argued that toleration further entails "ethical neutrality" or the abdication of any presumption to know the difference between right and wrong, as if tolerant people should model their behavior on that of sociopaths. Both Budziszewski and Raz deny the validity of this inference, with Raz arguing further that nothing about the principle of toleration binds a government to an "anti-perfectionist" stance.[58]

Democracies may be improved in various ways. Two ways that occur to me are: by incorporating women into the political system on a fully equal basis with men; and by making substantive, rather than procedural, justice a central concern, and in association with this, by resisting the temptation to subordinate the interests of society (e.g., society's need for safety) to the supposed "rights" of individuals (e.g., the "right" of recidivists to parole). On the first of these points, however, no society in recorded history has treated women fully equally, and the history of humankind may quite fairly be understood, in part, as the history of variations in the subordination of women.[59] It is tempting to argue that given this appalling record, there have never been any "democracies" worthy of the name. But if we were to succumb to this temptation, we should just have to devise a term to cover the cases presently called "democratic." It seems wiser to keep the traditional term and merely note the shortcomings of such (and all other) systems.

As for the second point, there is more variation here. It is the United States, as Frank Coleman has argued, that has most completely enshrined the Hobbesian philosophy and, in the process, gone further than other systems in subordinating the interests of society to the interests of individuals.[60] Yet, since the early 1980s, a number of West European and South European states have restructured their systems, in ways that bring them closer to the American model.

A definition of democracy helps us understand what we think a democracy should look like. It does not tell us how we get there. To have a notion about how one gets to a democracy is to have a notion about the ingredients, or as I prefer to call them, the *preconditions* of democracy. Inevitably, opinions on this subject have varied dramatically. The most cynical view is probably that taken by Terry Lynn Karl, who wrote off the quest for democratic preconditions as "futile." In his view, "what the literature has considered in the past to be the preconditions of democracy may be better conceived in the future as the outcomes of democracy."[61] Karl concludes that the only recurrent patterns are to be found in these outcomes, and that there are no patterns in preconditions, indeed, no preconditions at all. And if there are no preconditions for democracy, then it would follow that democracy can be established anywhere, at any time, by any set of leaders, and have equal chances of success— including, for example, in the middle of a genocidal civil war, as the economy plummets, and chauvinistic hate propaganda colors the atmosphere. (I am thinking here of Serbia since 1991.) Few scholars are willing to tread this path. For most, it is taken as a given that there are some preconditions, or prerequisites, for democratization.

Leaving aside Karl's ostentatiously deviant opinion, the recent writings of most American sociologists and political scientists dealing with democratic preconditions fall into one of four broad categories.

First, there are those who emphasize economic and social preconditions, such as widespread literacy, significant urban population, and general prosperity. Seymour Martin Lipset and Philip Cutright are among analysts in this group.[62] Usually, it is assumed that if economic prosperity is a precondition, then it must precede the establishment of a democratic system. Giuseppe Di Palma reverses the order, however, and argues that having chosen democracy—the sense in which that is true being the subject of chapter 16—East European societies will necessarily create free markets, which, presumably, will lay the basis for an economy capable of sustaining democracy.[63]

The second group comprises those who favor an emphasis on the *cultural* preconditions of democracy. The classic work here is Almond and Verba's 1963 study, *The Civic Culture*, which outlined a syndrome of ideal attitudes and dispositions to which the authors assigned the label given in the title.[64] Larry Diamond, another analyst in this tradition, includes these elements among the constituent parts of democratic political culture: "tolerance of opposition and dissent; trust in fellow political actors; a willingness to cooperate, accommodate, and compromise; and hence, a certain flexibility, moderation, civility, and restraint in one's partisanship."[65] Certainly, if these ingredients are essential to democracy, then several postcommunist states in Eastern Europe (most obviously Slovakia and Romania, let alone Croatia and Serbia) are off to a bad start.

Back in 1942, at the end of Eastern Europe's first troubled efforts to institute democracy, Hugh Seton-Watson argued that "the most essential condition . . . for the establishment of democratic Government in Eastern Europe is an improvement and intensification of general Education. This means not only the education of youth, but the raising of the tone of the press, literature, and all forms of expression of public opinion."[66]

In practice, governing authorities have often taken the emphasis on education and democratic political culture very much to heart. After World War II, for example, Allied occupation authorities in Germany, Austria, and Japan undertook systematic efforts to purge persons with a Nazi or fascist past from the media and the schools, to establish detailed guidelines for public radio and to monitor understanding and compliance, to restrict newspaper licenses to "reliable democratic publishers," to reorient the press (in Germany) to give more attention to worldwide and nationwide news and less to local news, to introduce a reportorial style in journalism, and to revise the textbooks and teaching methods in the schools.[67]

The third group comprises those who demand the satisfaction of certain *situational* preconditions. Lipset, already listed under group 1, also fits here, through his argument that widespread political apathy is supportive of democracy and that extensive political interest is in fact harmful.[68] The argument offered by Rabushka and Shepsle in 1972,[69] that ethnic fragmentation is not conducive to democratic politics, is also in this group. A somewhat different emphasis, but still of a "situational" nature, is the widespread understanding that a basic agreement on the rules of the game is essential to the stability of a democratic system— or, I would argue, in fact to the long-term stability of *any* system.[70]

Finally, some theorists prefer to stress *institutional and structural* preconditions. Robert Dahl, for example, has produced a list of "minimal" procedural conditions for modern political democracy to function. His list enumerates seven elements—among them, regular elections, near-universal adult suffrage, the right of citizens to run for office, the existence of alternative sources of information, freedom of political association, and freedom of speech.[71] Valerie Bunce places her emphasis elsewhere, stressing four central ingredients: a representative government chosen in free elections, a depoliticized bureaucracy functioning according to written rules, the rule of law, and legal guarantees of basic rights.[72] And Robert Moss, looking more broadly to the preconditions for *the rule of law*, has suggested the following minimal preconditions (quoted in full):

1. An independent judiciary to which appeal is allowed from administrative decisions, and of universal laws transcending the aims of governments.
2. Freedom from arbitrary arrest, which should mean that even under martial law or a state of emergency (where the authorities would be empowered to exercise special powers of arrest and detention) there should be a legal requirement to present prompt and explicit charges, and a right to appeal, within a specified time, to a superior court.

3. The right to proper legal representation before a court or tribunal.
4. Appearance before a magistrate or tribunal within a specified length of time.
5. The right to a medical examination before any formal hearing.[73]

Holden has wisely cautioned that there is no reason—as some theorists suppose—to believe that the necessary preconditions for democracy must be drawn entirely from one of these sets. On the contrary, there may be a variety of economic, social, cultural, situational, and structural preconditions for the stable functioning of democracy.[74]

For the purposes of this book, democracy, as I have defined it above, will be seen to require the satisfaction of six situational preconditions and six institutional preconditions. The situational preconditions are (1) a modicum of economic prosperity, sufficient to keep people from rioting; (2) general system stability and the absence or nonpoliticization of profound social polarization; (3) some degree of ethnic harmony; (4) the education of the public in the values of toleration and agreement on the rules of the game; (5) the presence of valued and effective institutions capable of maintaining civil order; and (6) the prevalence of a spirit of tolerance. The institutional preconditions are (7) free elections for a popular mandate, with elected officials held responsible to the citizenry; (8) the existence of an effective, independent judiciary; (9) a depoliticized bureaucracy and police functioning according to written rules; (10) legal guarantees (usually of a constitutional nature) of individual autonomy and basic rights; (11) the effective separation of Church and state; and (12) the reliable availability of alternative information, potentially through a free press.[75]

As before, these preconditions should not be seen as all-or-nothing affairs, either individually or collectively. Rather, they permit us to say, for example, that the fewer legal guarantees of basic rights there are, the less democratic the system is apt to be—though how formal such guarantees need to be is another matter. I would argue that a failure or deficiency in even one of these preconditions, whether situational or institutional, already diminishes the prospects for a stable democracy. And the greater the number of preconditions which are not met, the poorer the chances that a democracy can be established, or if already established, maintained.

Now it is sometimes thought that in itemizing preconditions, one is listing elements that must already be present *before* one even starts to construct a democratic order. On this understanding of the intention of compilations of preconditions for democracy, Myron Weiner urged (in 1987), "Perhaps it is time to recognize that democratic theory, with its list of conditions and prerequisites, is a poor guide to action as well."[76] And in the same spirit, Giuseppe Di Palma has insightfully noted: "just as the circumstances surrounding the birth of modern democracy were unique, another unique cluster of circumstances could account for the adoption of that same democracy elsewhere—perhaps precisely by diffusion. . . . Unique circumstances are not the same as requisite circumstances, and fortuitous outcomes are not the same as nonrepeatable outcomes."[77] And Di Palma went on to argue that the only real precondition for democracy is the willingness of the major political actors to agree to create such a system.

As long as one views the notion of "preconditions" in the sense of *preexisting* factors, then these cautions are necessary corrections. But there is another sense in which one may speak of "preconditions for democracy," namely, in the sense of *necessary ingredients* if one wishes to reach the desired result. And *this* is the sense in which I write of such preconditions. To draw an analogy from cooking, it is not necessary that cheese be in the pot before you start to make a French onion soup. But if you intend to produce something recognizable as French onion soup, you will have to add the proper cheese at the right time. And if you intend to produce something recognizable as democracy, you will need to hold free elections, with a choice among candidates. For that matter, Di Palma himself concedes that "no transition from dictatorship has successfully done away with the market without doing away with the prospects for democracy."[78] (No cook has successfully done away with onions without doing away with the prospects for producing French onion soup. And similarly, to the objection that one may not need to hold elections in order to have a "good" political system, I reply, One does not need onions to have a good soup either, but no onions, no onion soup.)

How the postcommunist states of Eastern Europe rank on the scale of these preconditions will be taken up at the end of chapter 16.

4. Strong Society, Weak Society

By "strong society" I mean a society capable of defending itself against tyranny in whatever form it might take. By a "weak society" I mean a society that is not capable of such self-defense. The stronger a society, the less likely it is that tyranny can sustain itself.

It follows that where a government is strong and the society weak, the system remains stable regardless of the level of popular contentment or discontent. This combination is the most conducive to tyranny. The combination of weak government with weak society is typical of traditional societies, where the government lacks infrastructure, extensive financial and coercive resources, sophisticated information networks, and instruments of propaganda and socialization, and where society itself lacks a highly developed structure or alternative information sources. The combination of strong government with strong society is the standard pattern in contemporary Western democracies, and points to the dual bases for the endurance of liberal systems in England and America. Any of the foregoing are apt to remain stable, as long as external pressures are not brought to bear.

But the combination of weak government and strong society is potentially explosive. Given popular contentment and consensus, a system with this combination of features can survive for a while. But in the absence of popular contentment, a weak government is vulnerable to overthrow and can scarcely be expected to withstand the pressures of mass defection (which is essentially the process that overthrew the governments of the GDR and Czechoslovakia in late 1989). The collapse of a weak government under pressure is no guarantee, however, that a strong government can be constructed to take its place; indeed, the historical record is replete with examples of societies which replace weak governments of one type with weak governments of another type, without assuring stability.

I shall take *governmental strength* to mean: (1) the capacity of the government to reach a consensus about appropriate action, and its capacity to carry out such actions and to assure that its decrees and laws are executed and enforced; (2) the ability of the government to obtain accurate information about events and developments in the country; (3) the possession by the government of a developed infrastructure (including advisory bodies), extensive financial and coercive resources, and instruments of propaganda and socialization; (4) the conviction, on the part of the governing elite, that they are entitled to govern, i.e., that their governance is legitimate; and (5) either clear legitimacy of the system in the population's eyes, or the ability of the government to terrorize, intimidate, and crush any hint of criticism or opposition. On the basis of this understanding, it would seem to follow that by the mid-1980s, the communist systems in Eastern Europe were having problems with factors 1, 4, and 5.

I shall take *societal strength* to entail: (1) access to accurate and indicative information about social and political processes; (2) the ability to organize autonomous organizations free from government surveillance; (3) an educated public and an independent stance among intellectuals; (4) access of the public to channels of mass communication not controlled by the government; and (5) the mobilization of the public, by which I mean the public's awareness of issues and engagement in public debate about them. Since these points are developed in extenso in chapter 12, I shall defer further discussion until then.

5. The Weakness of New Systems

Authoritarian systems tend to collapse according to a predictable pattern, in which economic deterioration, the decay of political institutions, challenges posed by religious organizations, a heightened role for the army at certain points in time, and the fragmentation of power all play a role.[79] The very factors which provoke the failure of the authoritarian system, however, set challenges for the incoming elites. In contemporary Eastern Europe, thus, the new elites have had to deal with economic problems, the legacy of partial political decay (and the incremental nature of system rebuilding), a new feeling of confidence and exultation among churches (with political overtones), worries about the possibility of a coup by the army (in Poland[80] and Bulgaria), and the need to legitimate the new order. Legitimation, in turn, requires the acceptance of new values; and the difficulties inherent in this task are most clearly evinced in Germany, where after decades of looking to West Germany with a feeling of kinship, even identity, "easterners" ("*Ossis*") now find that their values have become quite different from those of the "*Wessis.*"[81] As a result, by mid-1993, only 22 percent of West Germans and only 11 percent of East Germans felt that they shared a common identity; a majority of "*Ossis*" (as the easterners have come to be called) "now tell pollsters they consider themselves 'former citizens of East Germany' rather than part of a unified Germany."[82]

After four decades of communist political monopoly, the initial cry was for "freedom." But as old political and cultural barriers collapse, and with new ones not yet in place, diverse social groups press their cases, and others feel threatened. Throughout Eastern Europe there is rekindled national feeling, prompted not so much by "liberation" from communism as by inchoate fears fueled by political uncertainties, economic uncertainties, and (as a result of massive migratory movements) even demographic uncertainties.

In the present context the new state-builders of Eastern Europe have conceptualized their present choice as one between a presidential system (the French model) and a parliamentary system (the German model). But as Ken Jowitt reminds us, there is, in fact, a third liberal alternative, which he calls *liberal authoritarianism*. Such a system, he argues, might be better equipped to withstand and contain the sundry pressures of religious intolerance, militant nationalism, and neofascist racism that have already created some complications in the region.[83]

Concluding Remarks

I have called the transition associated with 1989 a *revolution*—in contra-distinction to the large number of scholars who have hastened to endorse Timothy Garton Ash's neologism, *refolution*. By the latter term, Ash meant to signify that the process of transition combined reformist forms with revolutionary effects. I believe that this construal reflects a misunderstanding of what occurred.

The events of 1989 were not, in themselves, a revolution, but they were *a phase in a longer revolutionary process*. As long as one insists that a revolution must be encompassed within a few months, one will not find any revolutions anywhere, at any point in history. Revolutions are complex, multiphased processes, which unfold over time. The actual "passing of the torch" from the old elite to the new is only the symbolic tip of a much larger political iceberg, only the most climactic and symbolically resonant moment in a process which begins years before and which continues for years after. What is distinctive about this latest revolution, as Claus Offe has pointed out, is the relative paucity of coherent thought given before 1989 itself to the positive content of the postcommunist political order;[84] the dissidents of pre-1989 spent a lot of time elaborating their thoughts about human rights, and about the need for political pluralism, free markets, and national self-determination, and comparatively little time analyzing how such values might be realized and protected.

It was clear in 1980–81 from events in Poland and from their repercussions elsewhere in the region[85] that revolutionary processes were underway. The ultimate goals and aspirations of the opposition were well-known, as was the deep and widely felt discontent of the populations, especially in urban areas. The question was not whether the communist systems would be dismantled, but when.

2. Social Currents and Social Change

The pressure for change in Eastern Europe was building for years. It was unrelenting—as reflected in the perennial crises with which local communist elites had to wrestle in the postwar era. By the late 1980s the combination of economic deterioration, political decay, the growing strength of society, the long-term effects of urbanization, the accession of Mikhail Gorbachev to power in the USSR, and other factors made great change inevitable. An early symptom of the coming Great Trans- formation was the greater confidence shown by dissidents and religious activists throughout much of the 1980s. Finally, it was the flight of more than 225,000 East Germans to the Federal Republic of Germany in a matter of months in 1989 that spelled the final collapse of communism in Eastern Europe, with immediate effects in the German Democratic Republic, reinforcing pluralizing tendencies in Poland and Hungary, and with ripple effects in Bulgaria, Czechoslovakia, Romania, and, in con- junction with everything else, Albania.

Some could see change coming. For example, in late 1987 Mieczysław Rakowski, a member of the Politburo of the Polish United Workers' Party (PUWP), wrote a sixty-page report arguing that the entire region was in political crisis and that the communist party would face serious threats unless it "finds the creative energy, courage, and imagination to free itself of useless ideas and outdated concepts. . . . [If it does not do so,] one can assume that in the future our formation will see up- heavals and revolutionary outbursts initiated by an increasingly better educated populace."[1] Impending social and political change became in- evitable, but when it arrived, it seemed sudden. After seeming, in the age of Brezhnev, to have succeeded in freezing time, the region now seems to be changing all the more quickly.

This book is concerned with the current dynamics of change in Eastern Europe and with the sources and consequences of change. I shall argue that social and political change is the product of social pressure and can best be understood through an examination of social currents—issue-oriented or group-centered patterns of thought and behavior—such as religious currents, ethno-nationalist currents, political currents among independent activists, feminist currents, and cultural currents among young people. I shall also argue that in several cases, the roots of change go back farther than is apparent at first sight and that the pressures for change have been multifaceted, interrelated, and more or less comparable throughout the region. The changes that have occurred are no less than revolutionary. In Yugoslavia, for a variety of reasons having more to do with interethnic antagonisms and societal fragmentation, civil war erupted in June 1991.

In the following pages I shall outline the vulnerabilities of the area to destabilization and revolutionary change, as they emerged in the late 1980s. These vulnerabilities to destabilization and revolution were symptoms of social and political change and of ensuing structural distortions that put pressure on the system to find a new equilibrium.

Cultural Drifts and Social Movements

There has been a growing awareness in the past two decades that political change cannot be isolated from social change, and that changes in the group consciousness and behavior of people may be symptoms of pervasive changes in institutions, customs, and attitudes. A key element in such changes is change in people's values—what Herbert Blumer calls "cultural drifts."[2] Examples of cultural drift in recent decades include the increased value placed on health and exercise, the drive for the equality of women, and a heightened concern for the environment and for animal life. In Eastern Europe, examples of recent cultural drift would include a new openness to nontraditional religion (discussed in chapter 6), a new consciousness among urban women (discussed in chapter 9), a heightened value placed on "alternative culture" (discussed, in different aspects, in chapters 3, 4, 5, and 10), and a new drive for genuine pluralism, epitomized in the drive for independent trade unions and political parties in Poland, Romania, and elsewhere (discussed in chapters 4, 5, 13, 14, and 15). As cultural drifts occur, they give rise to popular self-conceptions which are at variance with social reality or in tension with political reality. This variance and tension provide the context in which new social movements arise.

Blumer defines *social movements* as "collective enterprises to establish a new order of life."[3] Social movements may be amorphous or highly organized, though they tend to lack organization initially and to acquire more organizational features as they evolve, including hierarchical structures and formalized routines. Social movements may be successful or unsuccessful: if successful, their program becomes accepted in society at large and may result in the restructuring of society; if unsuccessful, the movement may adopt a different program, evolve into a "sect," or fall apart. Social movements may be political, religious, or cultural in nature. They may also combine all three aspects like the Hussite movement in fifteenth-century Czechoslovakia and the Solidarity movement in contemporary Poland. Solidarity has spawned a rich art in which the themes and symbols of labor, pacifism, and religion recur.[4]

Angela Aidala notes that the exotic new religions which appeared on the American scene in the later 1960s responded to "the fragmentation of cultural symbol systems" and to a sense of drift among young people who felt they lacked clear standards for sexual, social, and political behavior.[5] They were thus symptoms of social stress associated with a particular phase of development.

Cultural drifts occur in specific social and cultural contexts, and may develop in diverse ways. They may reflect the influence of certain activist groups (such as feminists or human rights activists), or result from the dissemination of new information or understanding. They may reflect generational shifts due to different formative experiences. They may also be triggered by traumatic or energizing events experienced by the society as historical in a grand sense. An example of the latter is provided by the Albanian riots in Kosovo in April 1981, which triggered a Serbian national awakening and drove Serbs to look inward, bemoaning what came to seem like "hundreds of years of Serbian solitude,"[6] and to draw parallels between the Battle of Kosovo in 1389 (fought between Serbs and Turks) and the new battle for Kosovo in the 1980s and 1990s (pitting Serbs against Albanians).[7] Again, cultural drifts may reflect an increase in society's confidence in its ability to determine its own fate (as occurred in Poland between July 1980 and August 1988). *Social currents,* which may be defined as processes of social and cultural replication and development, often serve as the vehicles of cultural drift.

A social current may thus be understood as a milieu in which social and cultural ferment is energized and focused. Social stress may be reflected in diverse social contexts of varying importance. To the extent that a cultural drift affects the perceptions or instrumentalities of basic social values, it may engender a politically relevant social movement that aspires to "revitalize" the system by changing aspects of its cultural and social order.[8] Sometimes in a society in stress, social questioning and the search for new solutions become so widespread that one may speak of the appearance of an "apocalypse culture."[9]

The appearance of revitalizing social movements is organically linked with the potential for revolutionary turmoil, but they are not reducible to each other. Social movements figure as one mode in which society mobilizes itself; social mobilization has revolutionary potential only when existing institutions are unable to channel disposable social energies into politically acceptable arenas.

When the development of political institutions is able to keep pace with the demands placed on the system, and when institutions are adaptable, the result is civic order. But when political institutions are unable to keep pace with social and economic change, political decay is the result. Political decay signifies that existing institutions have lost their capacity to process demands and to maintain order without resorting to force; as a result, in a system in which institutions lag behind rising participation—what Huntington and others have called *praetorian society*—"social forces confront each other nakedly," without the benefit of generally accepted, routinized intermediary bodies.[10] "In all stages of praetorianism social forces interact directly with each other and make little or no effort to relate their private interest to a public good."[11] A praetorian situation is potentially but not necessarily revolutionary: a praetorian society may continue to muddle along in political chaos with the apparatus in a state of partial decay, or it may succumb to a revolutionary upheaval leading to a restructuring of the system.

The Illusion of Stability

In the early 1970s some astute researchers thought that Eastern Europe had achieved a substantial degree of political stability. In a brilliant if wrong-headed article, Zygmunt Bauman argued that the communist systems of Eastern Europe had become "immune" to revolution due to the "ability and readiness of the government to deal with the basic social and economic issues"[12]—a claim that looks very odd today, given the record of the Gierek and Jaruzelski governments in Poland, the Ceauşescu government in Romania, and the eventual overthrow of communism throughout the region. In fact, in the early 1970s there was a tendency for Western observers to forecast continued stability for the foreseeable future, sometimes expecting change to emanate from the top down rather than from the bottom up. This book argues that change has emanated—and will continue to emanate—primarily from the grass roots. Elite changes in course have very often been responses to pressure from below.

Bauman developed an elaborate argument designed to demonstrate that none of the forms of *social dissent*—or *disaffection,* in the sense I define it in the next chapter—can be profoundly destabilizing or translated into revolutionary upheavals. Bauman's analysis thus specifically excluded the possibility that anything like Solidarity could appear.[13] His argument takes the form of an enumeration of seven categories of social dissent. Since his enumeration aspires to comprehensiveness, it will be useful both in furnishing insight into why Eastern Europe was once thought to be "stabilized" and in suggesting zones of social destabilization.

The first type of social disaffection identified by Bauman is simply maladjustment. Newly urbanized peasants experience difficulty in adjusting to their new environment but, Bauman confidently predicted, with the passage of time they acclimatize to city life and develop vested interests in their new status. Bauman's argument was misleading insofar as it suggested that urban life in communist states was largely serene and anxiety free (is it *anywhere?*). It is also incomplete in that it ignored the role of urban centers as the primary generators of "alternative culture." Hence, although in the short run "the susceptibility of a country to revolution may vary inversely with its rate of urbanization,"[14] in the long run social dissent is articulated and developed in urban settings. The recent history of Berlin, Warsaw, Gdańsk, Prague, Budapest, Belgrade, Zagreb, Ljubljana, and other cities amply demonstrates this maxim.

The second type of disaffection noted by Bauman is linked with a specific generation and is therefore by definition ephemeral. The "partisan" generation, whose members fought their way to power and consequently developed skills appropriate to the early utopian phase of the new order, becomes disgruntled when political developments leave them behind. A third type of disaffection is associated with the generation held back by these partisans. Bauman conceded the seriousness of this latter form of disaffection, and noted that the interfactional tension it generates has long-lasting negative consequences for the exercise of power at the center. Both types are resolved by time. Bauman's fourth category[15] is also associated with generational cleavage and involves social expectations stirred by the socialist revolution itself. In Bauman's view, "the critical period [comes] approximately twenty years after the social upheaval."[16] At this stage people become impatient to reap the expected benefits of socialism, and frustration sets in. His only comment as to how elites will deal with this challenge was to observe that they have moved away from ideals of social equity in the direction of a market economy.[17] On the whole, however, "Bauman seems to believe that after carrying out the demographic revolution socialist systems are more and more able to domesticate their working population, while the recent development reveals that the opposite is true."[18]

But this account omits the crucial role played by the late Stalinist terror and the post-Stalinist relaxation in defining generational attitudes and hopes. As Hungarian dissident János Kis has perceptively noted:

> [I]n the early 1950s, mobilized people could not reap the fruits of the reorganization because of the terror and the general misery. . . . The generations that participated in the events following the crushing of the revolution and the concomitant terror were very deeply affected by it. The very deep [difference] between then and now was decisive for these generations. It was really an unexpected gift for them that the same power that had crushed them, later allowed them to re-establish a normal social life. As a result they didn't bother about putting pressure on the government. They simply didn't think in those terms.
>
> But the last parts of these generations are passing away in this decade and new generations have since grown up for whom the Kádárian regime is already a precondition, not something they received as a present.[19]

The result is that generations respond to economic conditions not in absolute terms, as Bauman suggests, but, as Davies, Gurr, and others have noted, in terms relative to their experiences and expectations.[20] Kis's portrayal of generational differences is insightful in another respect: its presumption of generational exhaustion, which may have a cyclical quality.[21]

One final point about generational change should be made here: the generational gap, which sometimes gapes wide, sometimes relatively more narrow, is in part a function of generationally linked "cultural drift." Hence, when members of Eastern Europe's younger generation demand new ways of doing things, the older generation—and particularly members of the partisan generation—feel that their central values have been betrayed and react with fear and hostility.[22] This phenomenon is, of course, not unknown in the West.

Bauman's fifth category of social disaffection is labeled "trade interests." By this he meant that people with specific job-related and career-related interests may at times find those interests to be at variance with the interests of the system as a whole, as defined by the political elite.

This variance is so fragmentary and at such a low level of politics as to be marginal to the calculus of stability, as Bauman was, of course, aware.

His sixth category of disaffection is the yearning for national sovereignty among bloc states, and a consequent anti-Soviet orientation. But Bauman was quick to qualify this factor:

> But to conclude from this that a major *social* revolution becomes more likely in any of the socialist states, judged in its own right, is to push one's imagination too far. . . . As a matter of fact we know [of] no single fact which would support such a conclusion. Whether the relationship of a given socialist country to the Soviets has been warm, lukewarm, or cool, whether the grip of Russian power remained firm, weakened, or disappeared entirely, there were no signs at all of the State retreating from its socialist path.[23]

Not at any rate in 1971 when Bauman wrote his essay. The difficulty is that communism in all the East European states except Yugoslavia and Albania was clearly an import imposed and maintained by Soviet power, and until the advent of Gorbachev resentment of Soviet colonialism was readily compatible with hostility to the system. Beginning in 1985, however, malcontents in East Germany, Czechoslovakia, and Romania applauded Gorbachev's program, hoping it might provide an antidote to the multifarious ills afflicting their respective societies.

Bauman's last type of social disaffection is "the intellectuals' demand for more freedom of expression." But Bauman wrote off the intellectuals as an isolated caste, commenting on "the (at best) apathetic response which the intellectuals' manifestos win in the other strata of the nation" and on the impossibility of an effective alliance between intellectuals and workers.[24] Since Bauman intended his essay as a prediction, it is fair to point out that the record since 1971 has proven him wrong on both counts—for instance, the alliance between the intellectuals of the Polish Committee for the Defense of the Workers (KOR) and the workers of Solidarity in Poland. It is also necessary to keep in mind that ordinary citizens' responses to demands for freedom in conditions of dictatorship are apt to be conditioned by caution, fear, and circumspection rather than by apathy; the difference becomes politically important when power decays, because the hitherto circumspect can be mobilized for radical politics, while the truly apathetic cannot. Conformity is safe, while even so rudimentary a "protest" as removing the mandatory portrait of the leader from the shop window becomes a perilous, perhaps even reckless, act that can result in social ostracism by cautious conformists and reprisals from authorities.[25]

What is striking about Bauman's list is that the first four categories of disaffection are specifically transient (or seen as transient), the fifth is economic but narrowly conceived, the sixth is anticolonial but seen by Bauman as nugatory, and the seventh is limited to the desire for more "freedom of expression." The list excludes both traditional foci of discontent—religious, ethnic, and economic deprivation broadly conceived—which Bauman could have been expected to take into account, and newer foci—pacifism, environmentalism, feminism, and the campaign for free labor unions—which emerged only in the late 1970s.

Potential for Destabilization

When systems are able to handle the demands placed on them, they remain at equilibrium; when they cannot, the result is destabilization. Revolution is a possible outcome of destabilization; hence, in tracing certain ideas about the patterns conducive to revolution, I shall be indicating in the same breath the patterns conducive to destabilization more broadly.

Among the foremost theorists of revolution and destabilization is Crane Brinton. In *Anatomy of Revolution* he identifies certain uniformities in the Puritan, American, French, and Bolshevik revolutions.[26] First, these revolutions took place not in stagnant societies, but in societies with developing economies. Based on a study of Dorr's Rebellion of 1842, the Egyptian Revolution of 1952, the American Revolution, and the Bolshevik Revolution, James C. Davies concludes that revolutions are most likely when a prolonged period of economic growth with associated rising expectations is followed by a sudden economic downturn with associated frustration. In the Russian case, a period of growth in the late nineteenth century was followed by an economic slump (1904–17).[27] Ted Robert Gurr's theory of "relative deprivation" explains how the widening of a gap between expectations and actual benefits mobilizes the discontented and fuels destabilization.[28]

The second uniformity identified by Brinton is a change in the relationships of social classes and groups stimulated, as Charles Tilly argues,[29] by the mobilization of important new strata in the political arena (who may, in the process, acquire a new group identity) and characterized by a widening rift between the rulers and the ruled. The result is increased demands on the system and an intensified pressure for political participation.

Third, the desertion of the regime by the intellectuals is important because their defection signifies a more articulate and more focused political opposition. Fourth, the inability of the government to develop efficient means for channeling public participation and for processing public demands on the system leads directly to political decay and the disintegration of the system. As Huntington has also noted, when this occurs destabilization follows, and its translation into revolution may be the only route out of prolonged political chaos. Symptoms of governmental inefficiency include widespread corruption and the mobilization of nongovernmental groups on the streets.

Fifth, the financial failure of the government undermines its credibility in the eyes of the public and its ability to conduct effective policy. Factors 4 and 5 lead directly to the sixth uniformity, the loss of self-confidence on the part of the ruling class. This is expressed in intraelite polemics and infighting, recurrent purges, and repeated public breast-beating by officeholders. And seventh, the government's capacity to maintain order is seriously crippled if it displays ineptness in the use of force against rebellious elements.

The record of Eastern Europe's governments in these seven areas provides a useful barometer of the region's susceptibility to destabilization and, consequently, of the urgency of change. In the following pages I will discuss the situation in Poland, Czechoslovakia, Hungary, Yugoslavia, Romania, and Bulgaria as it relates to these seven factors. East Germany is discussed in detail in the next chapter, and that discussion will not be anticipated here. The entire scale of the problems has been much smaller in Albania and Albanian society has been generally weaker and more atomized; for that reason, Albania will also be excluded from the following discussion.

Economic Downturn. The chief economic indicators reveal that the East European countries registered uniformly high rates of growth in the 1950s and, with the exception of Czechoslovakia, continued to register modest to high rates of growth into the 1960s and early 1970s. But the Polish and Hungarian economies lost their dynamism in the late 1970s, and the Czechoslovak, Romanian, and Yugoslav economies were clearly in trouble by 1981. In 1985 even the adaptable Bulgarian economy experienced a downturn. These trends are reflected in the data for national income growth (table 1) and in the data for growth of gross industrial output (table 2).

Similarly, in the agricultural sector there were difficulties. The region as a whole registered steady growth into the 1970s, but difficulties subsequently emerged, first in Poland, then in the agricultural sectors of the other countries (table 3).

Table 1. Average Annual Growth Rate of Produced National Income, 1971–88
(in percentages)

Year	Bulgaria	Czechoslovakia	Hungary	Poland	Romania	Yugoslavia
1951–55	11.2	8.2	5.7	8.6	13.1	17.9[a]
1956–60	9.6	6.9	6.0	6.6	6.6	13.9
1961–65	6.7	1.9	4.1	3.4	9.2	8.7
1966–70	8.8	7.0	6.9	4.6	7.5	6.3
1971–75	7.8	5.6	6.2	9.8	11.3	5.9
1976–80	6.1	3.7	3.2	1.6	7.3	6.5[b]
1981	4.5	0.2	1.8	−13.0	2.1–2.2	−0.4[c]
1982	4.2	0.2	2.6	−5.5	2.5–2.7	−0.2[c]
1983	3.0	2.3	0.3	6.0	3.4–3.7	−1.5[c]
1984	4.6	3.5	2.5	5.6	7.7	0.0[c]
1985	1.8	3.0	−1.4	3.4	5.9	−0.5[c]
1986	5.5	3.2	0.5	4.9	7.3	3.5
1987	5.1	2.1	2.0–2.5	1.9	4.8	−1.0
1988	6.2	2.3	−0.1	4.5–5.0	3.2	−2.0

Sources: For statistics, 1951–81 (except Yugoslavia): Jan Vanous, "East European Economic Slowdown," *Problems of Communism* 31, no. 4 (July–Aug. 1982): 2–3. Other statistics: *Yearbook of National Accounts Statistics for 1961–62* (New York: UN, 1962), 309; *Yearbook of National Accounts Statistics for 1976* (New York: UN, 1977), 2:242; *Yearbook of National Accounts Statistics for 1981* (New York: UN, 1983), 2:342; Romanian Situation Report, *RFER*, 22 Jan. 1985, 9; Ljuben Georgiev, "Bilanz und Perspektiven der Wirtschaftsreform in Bulgarien," *Europäische Rundschau* 13, no. 1 (Winter 1985): 134; *Anuarul Statistic al Republicii Socialiste România 1986* (Bucharest: Directia Centrala de Statistica, 1986), 57; *Rocznik Statystyczny 1987* (Warsaw: Glowny Urzad Statystyczny, 1987), 88; calculations from *Statistički Godišnjak Jugoslavije 1987* (Belgrade: Savezni Zavod za Statistiku, 1987), 34:92; *Financial Times*, 18 Feb. 1987, 2, and 10 Mar. 1987, 4; UN Economic Commission for Europe, *Economic Survey of Europe in 1986–1987* (New York: UN, 1987), 116; *Countries of the World and Their Leaders, Yearbook 1988* (Detroit: Gale, 1988), 1:302; Paul G. Hare, "Industrial Development of Hungary since World War II," *Eastern European Politics and Societies* 2, no. 1 (Winter 1988): 143; Romanian Situation Report, *RFER*, 12 Feb. 1988, 5; Czechoslovak Situation Report, *RFER*, 15 Feb. 1988, 29; Bulgarian Situation Report, *RFER*, 8 Mar. 1988, 19; Hungarian Situation Report, *RFER*, 30 Mar. 1988, 25; Warsaw PAP, 26 Jan. 1989, in FBIS, 2 Feb. 1989, 47; BTA (Sofia), 22 Feb. 1989, in FBIS, 23 Feb. 1989, 7; Hungarian Situation Report, *RFER*, 1 Sept. 1989, 29; and *Hungarian Statistical Handbook* (Budapest, 1992), p. 92.
[a]Data for the period 1953–55. [b]Data for the period 1976–79. [c]Per capita data.

The data in these tables suggest a close correlation between economic deterioration and social destabilization. In the Czechoslovak case, the low annual growth rate of 1.9 percent in national income in the early 1960s was one symptom of economic stagnation which contributed to the pressure for reform. More particularly, Poland in the late 1970s recorded minimal growth in national income (1.6 percent annually) despite party secretary Edvard Gierek's program of heavy borrowing from the

Table 2. Average Annual Growth Rate of Gross Industrial Output, 1971–88 (in percentages)

Year	Bulgaria	Czechoslovakia	Hungary	Poland	Romania	Yugoslavia
1971–75	9.2	6.7	6.4	10.4	13.0	8.1
1976–80	6.0	4.7	3.4	4.6	9.4	7.1[a]
1981	5.6	2.0	2.3	−19.0	4.5	4.0
1982	4.7	1.9	1.9	−0.2	1.0	−1.0
1983	4.5	2.8	1.0	5.8	4.8	1.9
1984	4.3	3.7	2.8	5.5	6.4	5.7
1985	4.0	3.6	0.9	4.2	5.1	2.7
1986	4.3	3.1	1.8	4.4	7.7[b]	3.9
1987	4.1	2.3	3.7	3.4	4.6[c]	1.0
1988	2.2	2.0	−2.3	5.4	3.6	−1.0

Sources: For statistics, 1971–81 (except Yugoslavia): Vanous, "East European Economic Slowdown," 3. Other statistics: "Economic Development, 1971–1975," Yugoslav Survey 17, no. 3 (Aug. 1976): 68; Henry Spetter, "The New Economic Reform in Bulgaria," Crossroads, no. 9 (Autumn 1982): 122; Bulgarian Situation Report, RFER, 17 Feb. 1986, 18; Industrial Statistics Yearbook 1985 (New York: UN, 1987), 1:65, 127, 243, 461, 479, and 599; Statistički Godišnjak 1987, 100; Wolfgang Höpken, "Wirtschaftsreform in Bulgarien," Südost-Europa 36, no. 1 (Jan. 1987): 45; UN Economic Commission for Europe, Economic Survey of Europe in 1986–1987 (New York: UN, 1987), 143; Romanian Situation Report, RFER, 12 Feb. 1988, 5; Czechoslovak Situation Report, RFER, 15 Feb. 1988, 29; Hungarian Situation Report, RFER, 30 Mar. 1988, 26; Romanian Situation Report, RFER, 29 Dec. 1988, 3; Warsaw PAP, 26 Jan. 1989, in FBIS, 2 Feb. 1989, 48; Economic Survey of Europe in 1988–1989 (New York, 1989), 137; and Czechoslovak Situation Report, RFER, 16 Feb. 1989, 8.
[a]Data for period 1977–80. [b]Data reflect marketable production. [c]Data reflect net production.

West to finance extensive industrial investment. During the same period Polish agricultural output actually shrank an average of 1.6 percent annually. By 1980 the Polish economy was clearly in crisis.

Of the six countries, Bulgaria experienced the fewest economic shocks prior to 1989. The adoption of the so-called "New Economic Mechanism" in 1979–80 was designed to head off problems through a combination of selective decentralization of decision making, greater emphasis on cost-effectiveness, and enhancement of the autonomy of enterprises.[30] And Bulgaria's specialization in computers, electronics, transport industry, and nuclear energy since the 1960s earned it a reputation as the "Japan of the Balkans."[31] Yet there are some problems. To begin with, growth rates in the major economic sectors sagged in the 1980s and, although overall growth rates in industrial production were impressive, growth rates for "marketable industrial production" were more modest (4.3 percent in 1986, 4.1 percent in 1987).[32] In addition, repeated shortages of consumer goods like tomatoes, clothing, and kitchen utensils eroded confidence in the system.[33] The weakest sector in the 1980s was agriculture, where production plunged a disastrous 9.0 percent in 1985, made a partial re-

Table 3. Average Annual Growth Rate of Gross Agricultural Output, 1971–88
(in percentages)

Year	Bulgaria	Czechoslovakia	Hungary	Poland	Romania	Yugoslavia
1971–75	2.9	2.6	4.6	3.7	6.5	3.2
1976–80	0.9	2.1	2.5	−1.6	3.8	2.2
1981	4.0	−3.4	0.0	4.0	−0.9	1.0
1982	3.0	4.4	7.3	−2.8	7.5	7.0
1983	−7.2	4.2	−2.7	3.3	−1.6	−1.0
1984	7.0	4.4	2.9	5.7	13.3	2.0
1985	−9.0	−1.6	−5.5	0.7	0.1	−7.0
1986	7.0	0.5	1.0	5.0	12.8	11.0
1987	−3.8	2.7	−2.0	−3.0	2.3	−5.0
1988	0.1 [b]	0.9	4.3	0.6	2.9	−5.0

Sources: For statistics, 1971–81 (except Yugoslavia): Vanous, "East European Economic Slowdown," 3. Other statistics: "Economic Development, 1971–1975," 69; Spetter, "The New Economic Reform," 122; *Anuarul Statistic,* 147; Bulgarian Situation Report, *RFER,* 17 Feb. 1986, 18; Romanian Situation Report, *RFER,* 20 Mar. 1986, 14; UN Economic Commission for Europe, *Economic Survey of Europe in 1985–1986* (New York: UN, 1986), 142; UN Economic Commission for Europe, *Economic Survey of Europe in 1986–1987,* 133; *Statistički Godišnjak 1987,* 239; calculations from *OECD Economic Surveys 1986/1987—Yugoslavia* (Paris: OECD, Jan. 1987), 85; Höpken, "Wirtschaftsreform," 45; Romanian Situation Report, *RFER,* 12 Feb. 1988, 5; Polish Situation Report, *RFER,* 25 Feb. 1988, 3; Bulgarian Situation Report, *RFER,* 8 Mar. 1988, 21; Romanian Situation Report, *RFER,* 29 Dec. 1988, 3; Warsaw PAP, 26 Jan. 1989, in FBIS, 2 Feb. 1989, 48; Czechoslovak Situation Report, *RFER,* 16 Feb. 1989, 9; and BTA, 22 Feb. 1989, in FBIS, 23 Feb. 1989, 7, and *Hungarian Statistical Handbook* (Budapest, 1992), p. 106.
bStock-breeding.

covery in 1986, and dropped another 3.8 percent in 1987.[34] On the whole, however, this does not appear to have been a cause for alarm on the part of the Bulgarian authorities. Moreover, Bulgaria's foreign debt ($6 billion in late 1988) was the smallest of the Soviet bloc countries.[35] Eventually, the Bulgarian press reported the outbreak of strikes in certain industries, but the strikes themselves were not enough to produce a destabilizing potential.[36]

Czechoslovakia was a different story. Industrial growth rates fell below 4 percent in the 1980s, sagging to a modest 2.3 percent in 1987. Even *Rudé pravo,* the official party organ, admitted that economic performance in 1987 was "in many respects far from satisfactory."[37] Some 26.8 percent of enterprises failed to meet their assigned production targets in 1986; 31 percent fell short in 1987. But in 1988 industrial growth was even slower—2.0 percent. More serious still were the qualitative shortcomings, with poor quality constricting sales on both foreign and domestic markets. In fact, Czechoslovak economic managers certified only about a third of new products as being of a "high technical standard." There were periodic problems with energy supplies, and supplies of meat and other food products. Servicing the foreign debt absorbed 20 percent of Czechoslovakia's export earnings,[38] and its economic perfor-mance became rather uncertain in recent years.[39] First-quarter economic losses in 1988 were twice as high as comparable figures for 1987.[40] But the main concern for the communist regime was how the Czechoslovak public would react to this economic uncertainty, and this hinged above all on the standard of living. In the early 1970s the standard of living rose steadily,[41] but in the 1980s it came under strain.

Hungary, long the economic success story of the Soviet bloc, also ex-perienced economic stress. Economic growth was sluggish in the 1980s —consistently below 3.0 percent in annual growth rates of national in-come—and a combination of rampant inflation, climbing foreign debts, and trade deficits imposed new hardships.[42] The economy grew by a mar-ginal 1.6 percent in 1987, while the budget deficit that year amounted to an estimated Ft43.5 billion (nearly $1 billion). Meanwhile, the coun-try suffered trade deficits of $401 million and $361 million in 1986 and 1987 respectively, tallying a gross debt of $17 billion as of April 1989, or more than $1,600 per capita—the highest per capita debt in the bloc.[43] The increase in the standard of living in the 1970s stopped in 1984, and in order to keep pace with inflation at least half of the work force took a second job. Some people even worked three jobs. As part of a much broader effort to make the economy more competitive, the regime re-moved many price subsidies in 1988, but the immediate effect was to further damage the standard of living, which sank to the level of 1973.[44] The trend at the lower end of the wage scale was also unfavorable. Ac-cording to official government statistics, 24 percent of Hungarians now had incomes below the "social minimum" of Ft4,010 per month.

Studies by the Social Science Institute found that the number of those living in poverty increased 10 percent between 1982 and 1986.[45] The deterioration in the economy led directly to a decline in public confi-dence in the government, as the government itself openly admitted. In late 1987, for example, Prime Minister Károly Grósz, who became gen-eral secretary of the party in May 1988, said of the public mood: "The political atmosphere and public feeling are noticeably worse than a few years ago, even worse than is justified by the average living standards. The public mood is deteriorating as the living standards of considerable strata of society have stagnated over the last years and even decreased for a not negligible segment of society. Confidence in the leadership has dwindled, and sometimes the viability of socialism is put in doubt."[46] Ivan Volgyes, a noted authority on Hungarian affairs, highlighted the interconnection of political, economic, and social crisis in the country, concluding that the situation in 1987 was more dangerous than at any time since 1956.[47] The Hungarian socialists responded with a program of introducing income tax,[48] allowing unemployment to rise,[49] opening a limited stock exchange,[50] approving an austere state budget for 1988,[51] and drawing up plans for a transition to a market economy[52] in an effort to defuse the situation.

By contrast with Bulgaria and Hungary, Poland was confronted with staggering problems. With a foreign debt of $32 billion to Western countries and $5 billion in transferable rubles to fellow COMECON states, as of late 1987, Poland was compelled to use 67 percent of its export earnings to service its debt.[53] Between 1981 and 1987 food prices rose 500 percent while wages rose only 100–200 percent, and authorities announced in advance their expectation that consumer prices would rise at least 40 percent in 1988.[54] Some 25 to 30 percent of Poles were living in poverty as of 1985.[55] The figure rose for several years. Supplies of food and other staples were uncertain, and Poles responded by hoarding food and other items. The flare-up of workers' strikes in several cities in May and in August 1988 was a reminder that the situation remained volatile.

To prevent the debt from rising even more, the Polish government slashed imports by 40 percent (1978–86), but this has hindered economic development. The general economic crisis was compounded by an energy crisis and by difficulties in the agricultural sector (see table 3).

Along with Poland, Romania and Yugoslavia faced the most serious economic challenges. In Romania the growing economic morass had its source in the leadership's unwise decision in the 1960s and 1970s to try to establish major petrochemical, steel, and machine-building industries despite the absence of sufficient domestic raw materials, and to invest in advanced industries such as data processing, computers, and aerospace. By 1981 Romania's hard-currency debt had climbed to $10 billion (reaching $13 billion in 1982) and debt service payments were becoming difficult.[56] President Nicolae Ceauşescu decided on a radical policy of slashing imports and expanding exports in order to pay back the debt, and by 1989 had succeeded. A series of measures were introduced to reduce power supplies for domestic consumption and public services: the first cut of 20 percent came in 1979, followed by further reductions of 20 percent in 1982, 10–20 percent in 1985, another 20 percent in February 1987, and 30 percent in November 1987.[57] A forty-six-hour work week was introduced, and in 1983 the minimum wage was abolished, with earnings linked to the level and quality of production at the workers' enterprise.[58] Compulsory agricultural deliveries abolished in 1956 were reintroduced in 1983. Quality consumer goods and foodstuffs were marketed abroad, and Romanians were reduced to relying on a cornmeal mush called *mamaliga* as their basic nutrition source.[59] To prevent hoarding the state council issued a decree in 1981 establishing punishments of six months to five years in prison for persons who stockpiled more than a month's supply of food.[60] By 1988 social frustration had hardened into deep hatred of the political leadership, especially Ceauşescu and his family.

Yugoslavia was faced in the 1980s with declining rates of growth in industrial output (see table 2), a foreign debt of $20.5 billion in 1989,[61] a decline in foreign currency reserves from $1.5 billion in December 1986 to $658 million in February 1988,[62] the necessity to devote 36 percent of exports earnings to debt servicing (for 1987, see table 4), unemployment in excess of 16 percent in 1986,[63] and runaway inflation projected at one point to run at a staggering 11,000 percent in 1990.[64] One of the obstacles to economic reform was the absence of a unified Yugoslav market—a legacy of the decentralization of the 1960s and early 1970s—but any movement toward recentralization was firmly resisted by at least two of the six federal republics (Slovenia and Croatia). Indeed, in May 1988 Slovenia and Croatia made the first move to bring down the government of Prime Minister Branko Mikulić by urging a vote of no confidence in the parliament.[65]

Wages did not keep pace with prices, and real wages in 1986 were said to be on a level with 1967 wages. Yugoslavs survived financially through the black market and a barter economy, and by exchanging services. A 1987 poll found that 95 percent of Yugoslavs did not think they could live normally on the basis of their regular income alone, and 50 percent believed that their standard of living had fallen below the "existential minimum."[66]

Yugoslavia experienced a series of workers' strikes in 1987, including a strike by 1,400 miners of the Rasa coal-mining company at Labin in March in support of demands for a doubling of wages, and protests by 3,000–5,000 railway workers in Skopje in November against the government's wage freeze.[67] Further strikes in 1988 idled some 10,000 workers at a vehicle assembly plan in Maribor in June, a thousand textile workers in Paraćin and several hundred workers at a tractor factory in Rijeka in August, and additional numbers other locations during the year. In late June, between 4,000 and 10,000 Yugoslav workers gathered in front of the Federal Assembly in Belgrade to protest the government's ineffective economic policy and to demand the resignation of Branko Mikulić as chair of the Federal Executive Council.[68] Subsequently, in early July some 5,000 workers from Borovo and Vukovar came to Belgrade for similar

Table 4. Percentage of Export Earnings Assigned to Servicing the Foreign
Debt, 1987

Country	%	OECD Rating of Financial Vulnerability[a]
Bulgaria	41	slight vulnerability
Czechoslovakia	20	slight vulnerability
Germany, East	45	invulnerability
Hungary	50	vulnerability
Poland	67	high vulnerability
Romania	28	slight vulnerability
Yugoslavia	36	N/A

Sources: Danas, no. 294 (6 Oct. 1987): 59; Vladimir Sobell, "Eastern Europe's Debts: Heavy
Burden, Little Benefit," *RFER*, 22 Mar. 1988, 2.
[a]Based on an assessment of total hard-currency assets against current claims.

protests.[69] There were several more protests by workers in Belgrade in
July. Meanwhile, in November ironworkers in Bosnia formed their own
"independent trade union."[70]

These developments were naturally unsettling to the authorities. Stipe
Šuvar, the incoming chair of the League of Communists of Yugoslavia
(LCY) Presidium, admitted in mid-July that the emergence of a "parallel
trade union" could be averted only if the official trade union developed
new, more effective methods of work.[71]

A poll taken in 1986 found that 37.83 percent of those surveyed blamed
"the politicians" for the economic crisis.[72] A subsequent poll taken in
1987 revealed who these politicians were: 44 percent blamed republic
and provincial authorities, while only 20 percent blamed the Federal Executive Council and 4 percent blamed the party as a whole or the party's
central committee specifically.[73]

Jim Seroka argued in 1986 that Yugoslavia was most vulnerable to
destabilization in the early 1980s, but that by 1986 the real danger of destabilization had passed.[74] Growth rate figures for produced national income (table 1) provide some support for this hypothesis, but the principal
reasons why Yugoslavia was long able to postpone political breakdown,
I would argue, are that (1) decentralization shifted politics to the federal
units and fragmented the political arena,[75] and (2) social and political
change proceeded "around" the federal government, so that there was no
need to confront the federal government head-on.[76]

For a while the Yugoslav government's chief remedy was to freeze
wages and increase food prices, as in November 1987.[77] The limited private sector did well for itself,[78] and if Yugoslavia's 30,000 millionaires
(1986 estimate)[79] had been allowed to invest in profit-making enter-

prises, the entire economy might have gotten a boost. Instead, the authorities insisted on keeping a tight rein on ownership, and this available capital was spent on luxuries. Yet bureaucratic resistance to reprivatization remained stubborn. In June 1988, for example, a party conference in Slovenia, where support for reprivatization was always strongest, concluded that "neither Slovenia nor Yugoslavia as a whole [is] sufficiently prepared for market orientation."[80] By 1989 economic duress had won new converts to marketization and even high-ranking LCY members talked about the necessity of moving to a market economy.

All of these countries experienced rapid economic growth in the 1950s, 1960s, and in some cases into the 1970s, followed by economic downturns. This is the classic economic pattern preceding a revolution. Of the six countries discussed, Poland was quite obviously the country whose economy was in the most serious shape and which was the most vulnerable to political destabilization. Romania was an easy second. Seroka's optimism notwithstanding, I would list Yugoslavia as having been just behind Romania on this factor, followed by Czechoslovakia, Hungary, and Bulgaria.

The basic problem in all of these societies was the same: the absence of private enterprise, except on a small scale and in marginal areas. This suggests that there were (as of mid-1989) the following alternative futures: (1) social and political destabilization leading to prolonged chaos and praetorianism, with no clear resolution of the difficulties; (2) social and political destabilization leading to revolution and the forcible overthrow of communism; (3) the introduction of private enterprise on a large-scale basis (already begun in Hungary and Poland in the course of 1989 and proposed by some economists and other prominent figures in Yugoslavia), whether from above or below, leading to economic recovery; and (4) continued economic and social decline, leading to the steady disintegration of civilized society. Communist authorities regularly spoke of reforming the system, as if it were a distinct fifth alternative future. In actual fact, such reform could be subsumed under options 1, 3, or 4, depending on its particulars. Which of these four paths would be followed by any country has been, in each case, affected by other variables, and it is to these that we now turn our attention.

The Mobilization of New Groups into the System. When new groups appear on the political stage, or when old groups lose their meaning and group boundaries are redefined, the political game necessarily changes. The communists themselves encouraged the emergence of certain groups—Macedonians and ethnic Muslims in Yugoslavia, for instance—and through the propaganda of workers' democracy gave the working class a sense of political entitlement, a sense which proved to have unforeseen consequences (Solidarity being the most dramatic illustration to date). Social changes produced by urbanization, expanding education, changes in sexual ethics, and a combination of both organic and induced secularization also kindled a new activism among young people, women, religious groups, and malcontents. William E. Griffith suggests that the importance of this "excess of mobilization over institutionalization" is that it is directly at the root of the major crises in postwar Eastern Europe.[81]

Hungary aptly illustrates what this can mean in practice. In 1976 László Szentirmay and a group of other students at the Karl Marx University of Economics in Budapest decided to organize a political discussion club (POLVAX). Its purpose, Szentirmay admits candidly, was to provide a forum for the free exchange of information, in recognition of the fact that "because of the limits and deficiencies of the official information distribution, there was an enormous hunger of the students for information. We considered it extremely important that frank debates should not be relegated to the hallways, messhalls, or even to some nearby saloons, but that an organized forum should supply the framework."[82] By 1984 the club had organized several hundred discussion programs touching on the situation in socialist countries, human rights, pluralism, the international communist camp, and issues in domestic Hungarian politics, and bringing in various luminaries and political dignitaries as speakers. The talks were regularly attended by some five hundred people, mostly students.

Later, in the spring of 1988 thirty-seven law students at Budapest's Eötvös Lóránd University established the Federation of Young Democrats as a rival to the unpopular communist youth organization and quickly signed up a thousand members.[83] About the same time, a group of academic researchers and scientific workers set up an independent union, the Democratic Union of Scientific Workers. The thousand-member union was said to have been formed in response to the government's decision in 1987 to cut funds for science and education. The union members felt they needed an independent advocate to represent their views to the government.[84]

Imre Pozsgay, the reflective head of the Patriotic People's Front, drew attention to the meaning of these symptoms: "The nature of the citizen has changed. The earlier common consent [which] was based on the resignation of citizens rather than on their active participation [is] over. Hungarians need new institutions in which they can exercise their rights as citizens."[85]

Environmental concerns mobilized special public groups into political action in Yugoslavia. In 1986, for instance, an independent ecology group was formed at the philosophical faculty in Zagreb, while a second group devoted to ecological, pacifist, and feminist concerns was established on citizens' initiative within the Zagreb-Trnje district conference of the Socialist Youth League of Croatia.[86] An antinuclear protest movement arose in Yugoslavia in the wake of the Chernobyl nuclear accident,[87] and in November 1986 "several hundred citizens marched through the streets of Kraljevo to express their disgust and indignation at the latest pollution of water in the city waterworks."[88] There arose also citizens' initiative groups concerned with human rights, artistic freedom, and gay rights active in Belgrade, Ljubljana, and Zagreb.[89] The Yugoslav feminist movement, fragmented though it may have been, was the most important feminist current in Eastern Europe prior to the collapse of communism in the region (this current will be examined in chapter 9). In addition, youth in Yugoslavia acquired a new sense of group identity, and molded the leading youth periodicals—*Mladina* (Ljubljana), *Katedra* (Maribor), *Studentski list* (Zagreb), and *Student* (Belgrade)—into important forums for alternative ideas.

In April 1986 the League of Socialist Youth of Slovenia held its twelfth congress in Krško. The atmosphere at the congress was remarkable. The young participants did not bother to dress formally, and some were obviously from the rock subculture. The discussions were lively and often emotional, reflecting the defiant motto of the congress, "Words are no crime." Finally, the meeting adopted a resolution which said, in part:

> Experience has taught us that nobody should have a monopoly over Truth, over revolution, that the true measure of revolution is the actual change in people's social position. We are not interested primarily in "internal" and "external" enemies . . . [but in the] democratic and self-management decision-making process regarding every aspect of future social development.[90]

The resolution also recommended the direct election of officials at higher levels, more independence for the press, acceptance of an alternative civilian service for conscientious objectors, and abolition of the legal obstacles to establishing small private businesses.

Finally, the Albanian and Serbian populations of Yugoslavia were mobilized as interethnic relations in the largely Albanian province of Kosovo deteriorated (see in chapter 8). The violent Albanian riots of April

1981 revived currents among Albanians for full-republic status for Kosovo as well as currents favoring Kosovo's annexation by neighboring coethnic Albania. The Belgrade government has never been able to regain the Albanians' trust. Random and collective violence periodically shake the province, and a stream of Serbian and Montenegrin families fled the province. Delegations of disgruntled Serbs trekked to Belgrade to confront the authorities and demand effective protective measures. On 31 August more than ten thousand Serbs staged a protest in the provincial capital of Priština against intimidation and harassment by local Albanians. The leadership, which once tried to hide behind optimistic phrases, eventually admitted that the situation in Kosovo was "worsening daily."[91] By 1988 people talked openly of the possibility of civil war.

In 1988 and 1989 alternative political parties began to appear in Yugoslavia (these will be discussed in chapters 13 and 15).

Even in Bulgaria there were some signs of mobilization. Specifically, in late 1985 Bulgarian émigrés in Paris obtained copies of a lengthy leaflet drafted by workers at a Sofia locomotive factory that called for passive resistance to the government's new economic policies and to its "exploitation and oppression."[92] In early 1987 a small group of Bulgarian dissidents founded Bulgaria's first known human rights organization, the Independent Association for the Defense of Human Rights. At least five of its supporters were arrested and interrogated after signing a collective appeal for freedom of movement and emigration, free choice of career, and objective information in the media.[93] There were also rumors that environmental groups were being organized in a number of municipalities; whatever their truth, some two thousand people demonstrated in Ruse on 10 February 1988 against environmental pollution[94] (see chapter 12 for further discussion of social mobilization in Bulgaria).

The mobilization of new groups in Poland, Hungary, Czechoslovakia, and Romania will be discussed in chapter 4 and 5. But by way of a preliminary conclusion, we may say that in the half-century since World War II, various associational groups (women, youth, workers) and issue-oriented publics (pacifists, environmentalists) acquired a sense of collective identity and shared interests. This process became farthest advanced in Poland, followed by Hungary, Yugoslavia, and East Germany, probably in that order. The Bulgarian and Albanian publics have been the *least* mobilized even now, in the wake of communism. The reunification of Germany promises to quicken the process in East German society.

The Defection of the Intellectuals. One aspect of the defection of the intellectuals is the appearance of critical dissent, and in this form the subject will be explored further in the next three chapters. Defection may also display a more moderate aspect in the form of critical forums and conferences, the publication in the regime press of interviews and essays critical of the regime, and so forth. This is sometimes viewed as a safety valve for critical opinion, but such safety valves have at times proven unsettling to the authorities, as the Petöfi Circles in 1950s Hungary and the *Praxis* journal in 1970s Yugoslavia illustrate.

An important segment of the Polish intelligentsia was alienated from the regime for decades,[95] and after 1976 clearly joined the political opposition. The "Flying Universities" in Poland, like the "Flying Kindergartens" in Hungary,[96] were a symptom of both the regime's refusal to allow certain ideas to be discussed in state universities and the intellectuals' corresponding determination to discuss those ideas.

In Romania considerable evidence of the defection of the intellectuals ranges from the deep frustration of ethnic German writers in the Banat,[97] to the submission of proposals for reform to the Soviet embassy by engineer Nicolae Stancescu and architect Ion Fiştioc in 1987,[98] to the appearance of a string of essays by engineer Ion C. Brătianu in favor of classical liberalism,[99] to the human rights activism of mathematician Mihai Botez.[100] Esoteric communication was a popular form of protest by alienated intellectuals, since the adoption of Aesopian language seemed to confuse the censors. The weekly magazine of the Writers' Union, *Luceafărul*, served as a periodic vehicle for such critiques. An apt example is Mircea Micu's series of articles "Alone in Mongolia," published by *Luceafărul* in 1986.[101] Nominally about Genghis Khan, the series portrays a ruler cut off from his subjects, ruling in an arbitrary way, and advancing his son as his heir. A string of unmistakably pointed details highlighting similarities between Genghis and Ceauşescu served as clues to the author's principal purpose.

In Yugoslavia academic criticism of the regime became commonplace in the 1980s and was often sharp. In 1986, for instance, the Serbian Academy of Sciences and Art issued a famous memorandum bemoaning the fate of the Serbian people in Yugoslavia and criticizing the federal system for nurturing "egoism" in the constituent republics.[102] Yugoslav academics repeatedly urged a change in the economic system (for example, in 1985 and 1986 at conferences held in Belgrade). In October 1987 Yugoslavia's renowned economist Branko Horvat urged full legalization of private enterprise in the country.[103] In Slovenia intellectuals demanded greater freedom, including greater freedom of speech and publication. Intellectuals in Slovenia and elsewhere in the country advocated the introduction of a multiparty system in Yugoslavia.[104]

Even in Bulgaria there were some signs of alienation among intellectuals. Gorbachev's *perestroika* campaign found receptive ears in these quarters, and some Bulgarian intellectuals showed themselves eager to criticize past and present policies of the Zhivkov regime. By April 1988 Bulgarian party leader Todor Zhivkov decided that things had gone too far: he condemned the "negative attitude" being promoted by writers in certain publications and called for a purge to "get rid of those who lost their qualifications [as party members], the demagogues, and politically decayed people."[105]

Given the number of relevant variables, it is inevitably a subjective business to assess the comparative degree of alienation on the part of intellectuals in the region. Bearing this caveat in mind, I would suggest that the intellectuals became most estranged from the regime in Poland, Romania, Yugoslavia, and Czechoslovakia—possibly in that order, though as of 1988 it was only in Poland and Czechoslovakia that contacts between dissident intellectuals and workers had become routine. Many intellectuals were clearly discontented with the system. But an ongoing dialogue developed between discontented Hungarian intellectuals and reform-minded members of the political establishment. This took some of the edge off their alienation. This was also, to some extent, true of Yugoslavia, except that what Yugoslavia had learned, and what the Hungarian Socialist Workers' Party (HSWP) did not learn until it was too late, was that such dialogue inevitably opens up channels for critique, which in turn feeds the critical attitude and ultimately reinforces estrangement.

Governmental Inefficiency and Corruption. Governmental inefficiency is a prime source of the loss of credibility among the population, and it goes hand in hand with corruption, which figures functionally as an alternative channel for accomplishing basic tasks. The combination of inefficiency and corruption becomes especially dangerous when the government itself admits to problems. Hence, the launching of anticorruption campaigns, like those in the 1980s in Poland, Hungary, Czechoslovakia, and Bulgaria, not to mention the USSR, while offering some prospect of reform, entailed considerable risk, especially if the campaign was not perceived as effective.

In Poland the fall of Edvard Gierek in mid-1980 was followed by a string of revelations of ministerial corruption and judicial indictments. Wojciech Jaruzelski, the Polish general secretary from 1981 to 1989, tried to exploit his military background to inspire confidence that his government would be free of corruption. But corruption remained a massive problem, and the corruption of communist public officials was well known to Poles.

In Romania inefficiency and corruption were married to nepotism,[106] and there was no talk under Ceauşescu of any campaign to eliminate these problems. Romanians blamed Ceauşescu personally for much of their duress.

In Czechoslovakia corruption was a problem throughout the 1980s. As early as August 1980 the communist party weekly *Tribuna* acknowledged: "The facts are irrefutable. Bribery and corruption damage the development of economic and social relations and are contrary to socialist morality—but despite this they exist."[107] Slovak courts dealt with some 300 cases of bribery between January 1980 and June 1981, and on 29 April 1981 the Slovak regional government issued "a set of binding measures aimed at solving the problem of bribery and corruption in the Slovak Socialist Republic."[108] But this and other measures encountered difficulties, and there were further corruption scandals in 1983,[109] 1985,[110] and 1986.[111] Those implicated in 1985 included Finance Minister Leopold Ler and General Director of Customs Ladislav Kusý, along with some 250 party members.

In Hungary several thousand party members and officials were dismissed or otherwise disciplined every year, as András Gyenes, chair of the Central Inspection Committee, openly admitted.[112] In Yugoslavia a financial scandal in 1987 resulted in the expulsion of forty-two party members, the resignation of Vice President Hamdija Pozderac, and serious damage to the reputation of the regional Bosnian party apparatus.[113] The scandal sent a shock throughout the whole society, but the fragmentation of responsibility under the federal system probably helped to limit the most serious damage to the republic of Bosnia-Herzegovina.

Finally, even in Bulgaria the communist press openly admitted abuses of power and privileges. As early as March 1982 former Deputy Foreign Minister Zhivko Popov was sentenced to twenty years' imprisonment for corruption.[114] Under pressure from Gorbachev a campaign against corruption gathered in Bulgaria throughout 1986 and 1987, and an "unprecedented number of middle and senior ranking officials" were fired for corruption, mismanagement, or incompetence.[115] But when the trade union daily *Trud* published a series of four investigative articles in June 1987, alleging massive corruption by three generations of the same family in the town of Etropole, the party, after initially permitting the dismissal of those implicated, later reversed itself. The Central Control and Revision Committee of the Bulgarian communist party claimed that the articles in *Trud* had built up a misleading case on the basis of a "capricious" selection of facts and "tendentious" interpretation, and recommended the reinstatement of the officials. The author of the investigative series was fired from his job and expelled from the party.[116] Clearly, glasnost had its limits in Zhivkov's Bulgaria, where the leadership may have felt—correctly, I have argued—that the revelation of corruption might be more damaging than the corruption itself.

Loss of Credibility. Of the six systems under discussion, the Polish and Romanian regimes have by far the most serious problems of credibility, though Pozsgay conceded in early 1988 that "the [Hungarian] party's authority is very small and is widely mistrusted."[117] Surveys taken in 1983 and 1985 showed that the Polish United Workers Party (PUWP) commanded minimal credibility among the public,[118] while in Ceaușescu's Romania such surveys were not even published because they would have commanded no credibility. The Yugoslav communist authorities did not command much more credibility, but the de facto liberalization that had unfolded there as a by-product of the weakening of the center temporarily helped to alleviate some of this problem. In Bulgaria and Czechoslovakia, by contrast, apathy and resignation served to partially defuse or muffle this issue, while in Hungary the entire issue of credibility seemed to be up in the air in 1989, as the ex-communist party, renamed the Socialist Party, searched for a new formula.

The ruling parties of the Soviet bloc states tried to build credibility by controlling information,[119] but this tactic had its limits. As Daniel Nelson noted in 1981, apropos Romania:

> as the Romanian population becomes more educated, more mobile, and more diverse occupationally, the wider and more rapid dissemination of information may pave the way for a broader range of interpretations by individuals regarding their social, economic, and political circumstances. . . . Notwithstanding propaganda and misinformation employed by the regime, citizens in a public sample evaluated events reported by mass media in ways quite distinct from that observable in an "elite" sample. The party's control over media content, then, does not appear to have assured a uniformity of interpretations in an environment of increasing socioeconomic diversity and complexity.[120]

Factionalization and Loss of Self-Confidence. When leadership elites become polarized and turn upon themselves, their capacity to govern is weakened. Instances of factionalization within East European leaderships are well known.[121] Suffice it to say here that this problem was, by the late 1980s, most serious in the Yugoslav case [122] and, to a lesser degree, present also in the Czechoslovak, Hungarian, and Polish cases.

Loss of confidence is a related but distinct phenomenon that is deadly to a regime once it passes a certain threshold. The Polish communist regime in 1980 had clearly crossed that threshold, and it took a military coup in December 1981 to normalize the situation.

The first step in the direction of loss of confidence is often the admission of past error or mendacity. As Brinton once wrote, heaven help the prince who decides to confess to having made serious mistakes.[123] This is not a move Ceaușescu would make, but there were other reasons for loss of self-confidence among Romanian officials. On the other hand, both the Polish and Yugoslav parties made many telling admissions in the late 1980s. For example, the Polish communists, in tandem with the Soviet regime, finally admitted that it was the Soviets, not the Germans, who shot 15,000 Polish prisoners-of-war in World War II. They admitted that between 1939 and 1941 Soviet authorities not only deported many Poles to the USSR but also arrested, tried, and sentenced several Polish underground leaders for "anti-Soviet" activities.[124] They confessed that the purge of some 9,000 Polish Jews from official capacities in 1967 and 1968 was the result of anti-Semitism.[125] And they acknowledged the serious blunders and transgressions made by the party during the Gierek era (1970–80).

Similarly, the Yugoslav party admitted that many innocent people were imprisoned and tortured in the early years of communism, that Tito made serious mistakes in Kosovo and elsewhere, and that the self-management system had not worked.[126] Understandably, these admissions shook the credibility of the party and the self-confidence of the political leadership.

Inept Use of Force. The communist regimes of Czechoslovakia, Poland, Romania, and Yugoslavia resorted to the obtrusive use of force to maintain order in the 1980s—Yugoslavia in the case of Albanian unrest in Kosovo. Bulgaria resorted to force as part of its campaign to "Bulgarianize" its Turkish population. Of these five instances, only in Poland could the use of force be construed as "partly" inept, though of course force always entails certain costs.

Expectancy of Change. Brinton's list is complete with the seven foregoing factors, but I would add one element to the list: the expectancy of change. When a population *expects* change, it behaves entirely differently from the way in which it behaves when it does not, even if the basic complaints are otherwise the same. This point is related to Davies's emphasis on the importance of public *mood*.[127]

The outbreak of new strikes in Gdańsk and Nowa Huta in May 1988 and in several locations in August 1988 drove home the point that Polish workers still expected change, in fact nothing less than the relegalization of their independent trade union. Lech Wałęsa, the symbolic head of Solidarity, told the striking workers in 1988, "If we do not carry out *perestroika*, if we do not make reforms peacefully together with the nation and with compromises, then we are threatened with a revolution, and a bloody one."[128] A survey conducted by the government's Public Opinion Research Center found that 70 percent of Poles considered the economic situation "bad" or "very bad," and 80 percent considered "the danger of serious social conflicts" as a result of economic failure to be very real.[129]

There was also a high expectancy of change in Yugoslavia. A Slovenian intellectual told me in 1987 that he expected Yugoslavia to experience dramatic and far-reaching changes around 1990, arguing that by then advocates of change would have gained the upper hand. "The result," he told me, "will be a break with Titoism and its aftermath, a break analogous to and as far-reaching as what the Soviet Union has experienced between 1953 and 1985, i.e., from Stalin's death to the rise of Gorbachev." Not everyone wanted to wait even that long. A member of the Alternative Movement in Belgrade told me also in 1987, "Some people are only hoping for change. In the Alternative Movement, we are actively working for change. We hope it will not take another three years before we see fundamental change."

The expectancy of change was arguably only slightly less in Romania, though it was infinitely more difficult to talk about this there than in Poland or Yugoslavia. Typically, articulate malcontents relied on esoteric communication to spread their message. An excellent example of this was an article published on 8 February 1986 in *Luceafărul*, reprinted from the 12 January 1889 issue of a Bucharest daily. The fact that it was addressed to a different era absolved it of the charge of having been *written* to criticize the Ceauşescu regime. At the same time, the parallels between 1889 and 1986 were clear, revealing the deep expectancy of change in *both* periods. In a crucial passage, the article wondered:

> The problem is whether we are indeed on the eve of events that will bear a decisive influence on the position of the country as a civilized and constitutional state based on modern law and current requirements; whether we do still have the power to strengthen and

improve the country's position from within by extensive reforms and other measures related to them . . . or whether the tendencies displayed by adverse groups with outdated aspirations, as well as the glacial egoism of their ambitious policies, will once more raise obstacles on the road to national development. . . . Let us hope that at least in the future and under a new legislation the habit of naming or dismissing officials only on the narrow basis of their political convictions will cease, because all party and personal considerations ought to be dropped in the appointment of state officials, a process that should rest on the interests of impersonal justice.[130]

Likewise, in Hungary there was widespread expectation of change, and just as in Yugoslavia, Hungary became engaged in a wide-ranging debate about reform alternatives.[131] The leading advocate of reform within the establishment was the popular Imre Pozsgay, at one time head of the Patriotic People's Front (PPF) and later a member of the Politburo. Convinced that change was inevitable, Poszgay pushed for an opening up of the system and a partial repluralization of Hungarian society. Pozsgay told a Budapest party meeting in early 1988 that the party would not be able to maintain its "present positions of power and [present] methods." But, he added, "If the party can guide the masses to modernize the country, then it will have the leading role. If not, it won't."[132] The string of workers' strikes in Hungary in summer 1988 and the multiplication of grassroots initiatives (discussed in chapters 5 and 13) were other dimensions of this expectancy.

A subtle shift also occurred in Czechoslovakia, where popular attitudes and behavior perceptibly changed around 1986. In Bulgaria, on the other hand, expectancy of change was minimal to slight, although by early 1990 Bulgaria also felt the effects of region-wide change. For a while, communists hoped to devise a new approach, a new model: "A new model of socialism is rising up before our eyes," said Oleg Bogomolov, director of the USSR Academy of Sciences Institute of the Economics of World Socialist Systems in 1989.[133] But this vision quickly evaporated.

Conclusion

This chapter has attempted to assess certain pressures for change in Eastern Europe and, in the process, to weigh the individual countries' vulnerability to destabilization on the eve of the Great Transformation. The results are shown in table 5, where I have assigned numerical values to the degree of vulnerability with respect to each of the eight factors

Table 5. East European Vulnerability to Destabilization, September 1988/
November 1989

	Bulgaria	Czecho-slovakia	Hungary	Poland	Romania	Yugo-slavia	GDR
Economic deterioration	1/1	3/3	3/3	5/5	5/5	4/5	3/3
Mobilization of new groups	1/2	2/2	4/5	5/5	2/2	5/5	3/3
Defection of intellectuals	1/1	4/4	3/5	4/4	4/4	4/5	3/3
Inefficiency and corruption	1/1	3/3	3/3	5/5	5/5	4/5	2/2
Loss of credibility	1/2	3/3	2/5	5/5	5/5	3/5	4/5
Loss of self-confidence among elite and factionalization	0/1	3/3.5	3/5	4/5	4/4	3/5	2/5
Inept use of force	0/0	0/0	0/0	1/3	0/0	0/1	0/2
Expectancy of change	1/3	2/4	3/5	5/5	2/3	5/5	1/5
Score 1988:	0.8	2.5	2.6	4.3	3.4	3.5	2.3
Score 1989:	1.4	2.8	3.9	4.6	3.5	4.5	3.5

Key: 5 = extremely serious, 4 = serious, 3 = partial, 2 = slight, 1 = minimal,
0 = not detectable

examined. Though these values do not have quantitative significance,
I hope they are useful as qualitative measures of tangible differences,
including differences of degree. The average scores for each country are
thus *indicative* values that summarize the trends across the eight values.
In computing this average, no effort has been made to give greater weight
to one factor over another, even though some factors are clearly more
important than others. I have assigned two values in each case: the first
reflects the situation in September 1988 and the second reflects the situation in November 1989. I have also added estimates for East Germany,
although the discussion of that country is reserved for the next chapter.

The result is a highly differentiated picture. Poland, with a mean score
of 4.3 in 1988, ranked between "serious" and "extremely serious" in
terms of vulnerability to destabilization. The introduction of a coalition government in summer 1989 reflected that vulnerability but as of
November 1989 the Polish system was not yet "in the clear." Yugoslavia
and Hungary were the next most vulnerable, with Yugoslavia's failure to

deal with its internal political problems making it extremely vulnerable. By contrast, while the reform wing of the ruling party in Hungary moved quickly to deal with the situation, because the expectancy of further change was high, the leadership was no longer able to control the process of change. At *that* point, Hungary's overall vulnerability to destabilization was lower than Yugoslavia's. East Germany and Romania ended up with the same average score (3.5), even though the situations in those countries were very different. In Czechoslovakia, vulnerability was "partial" (2.8). History has proven that these levels of vulnerability are quite sufficient. And finally, Bulgaria, with a mean score of 1.4, seemed to show only slight vulnerability to destabilization. Regardless of the precise numbers, in all seven countries, vulnerability to destabilization and the pressure for (further) change increased between 1988 and 1989.

The tempo of change in Eastern Europe was quickened by another factor, what Fred Riggs has called the *diffraction* of social systems.[134] In a word, what it signifies is that the old social equilibrium is breaking down, and social life is fragmenting. In the political arena, this means the multiplication of discussion clubs, samizdat publications, even political clubs and parties. In the religious sphere it means a weakening of some of the traditional churches, typically with neo-Protestant groups as the chief beneficiaries, and the appearance of guru cults, Hare Krishnas, satanists, and other fringe sects. In the social sphere it means a restructuring of both gender and generational relations, with women and youth assuming different orientations toward the community and increasingly willing to organize autonomous groupings. In the musical sphere it means the fragmentation of musical taste and associated cultural suppositions and the fostering of an epidemic of subcultural currents including new wave, punk, heavy metal, and skags. And in high politics it signifies the passing of a generation: gone is the time when the cult of the personality could go unchallenged and from 1985 to late 1990 the Soviets themselves led the way with calls for new political thinking, assailing the fetishization of slogans.[135] The ancien régime was dead.

Part II
Dissent and Parallel Society
in the 1980s

3. Disaffection and Dissent in East Germany

Fools, you search my suitcases!
You won't find anything hidden there!
The contraband I bring with me
Is in my head.
—HEINRICH HEINE, *Deutschland:*
Ein Wintermärchen

Communism traced deviance, disaffection, and dissent alike to alienation and presocialist forms of consciousness. Insofar as the building of communism was expected to bring about an end to exploitation and alienation, deviance, disaffection, and dissent should have disappeared with them. The persistence of disaffection and articulate dissent, as well as crime, delinquency, and social deviance generally, represented a failure of socialization and thus a failure of the system to live up to its own expectations. Communist regimes tended to be anxious, therefore, to deny the existence of crime, to expel dissenters, and to curb social deviance. Dissent and deviance were troubling in yet another respect: insofar as Marxism aspired to eliminate social conflict and traced it to differences in social or class interest, dissent and deviance could be taken to reflect the persistence of differences in perceived interest, whether "objectively" rooted in class differences or not.

Dissent was therefore a central issue for communist systems and was accordingly amply discussed in Western scholarship. Disaffection as an analytical category has been far less amply treated,[1] though, as I shall argue, it is as great a concern to authoritarian regimes as is dissent. We may begin by drawing distinctions among the chief terms at issue.

Technically, *dissatisfaction* may be seen as discontent with the way in which certain parts of the system operate or with certain policies of the regime, without necessarily calling into question the legitimacy or optimality of the system. Hence, for example, when East Germany ran short of basic foodstuffs in late 1982, workers in Dresden went on strike and shouted, "We demand better supplies! We want meat and vegetables!"[2] The workers were clearly dissatisfied and clearly blamed the authorities, but their protest, although of political importance, could scarcely be called "dissent."

By contrast, *disaffection* may be defined as discontent with the system itself without necessarily entailing a belief in one's ability to change the system, but possibly being expressed in social nonconformism or deviance. The pilferage of socialist property in Czechoslovakia was a highly popular form of protest since the establishment of the communist regime there;[3] it reflected more than mere dissatisfaction, for pilferage was intended as a form of revenge against the system itself. Still, such activity would not ordinarily qualify as dissent.

Finally, there is *dissent* itself, which may be defined as discontent with the system, charged by belief in one's ability to effect change, however gradual or slight, and implying an external standard by which the system's performance is evaluated. The external standard is, of course, the heart of the matter and constitutes the core of the threat posed by dissenters to communist regimes. Obviously, all dissenters are disaffected and all disaffected are dissatisfied; but not all those dissatisfied are disaffected and not all those who qualify as disaffected are dissenters.

There are several reasons for broadening our focus to include not merely dissent but also disaffection:

(1) Disaffection is the seedbed from which dissent sprouts;
(2) It is both a broader and a more accurate measure of the problems, tensions, and dilemmas of a society;
(3) Both dissenting disaffection and nondissenting disaffection can have political consequences—the latter insofar as it engenders apathy, antisocial attitudes and behavior, and antiregime sympathies; and
(4) Disaffection is a more useful measure than dissent of the failure or limits of political socialization because it embraces a much larger portion of the population.

Disaffection may be expressed in different ways. Those disaffected may assert their potency to effect change and adopt a posture of dissent. Alternatively, they may conclude that they are unable to effect change in society and may resign themselves in a spirit of studied apathy. Finally, there is a middle ground in which they may tune out the regime and drop out, becoming in some sense deviant. Deviants may retreat into a counterculture such as punk rock, which will in turn sustain their deviance and reinforce their disaffection. Social deviance may thus reflect a fundamental rejection of the dominant values of the society—in this case, the official political culture of Marxism-Leninism—and East Germany's Socialist Unity Party (SED) accordingly viewed social deviance with consternation. It is for this reason that, as Paul Shapiro has noted, communist regimes treated dissenters as deviants;[4] it is equally true that communist regimes tended to treat deviants as potential dissenters.

There were four basic sources of disaffection in the German Democratic Republic (East Germany) in the 1980s:

(1) As resocialization failed, the population became susceptible to alternative cultures (such as Christianity or punk rock) that crystallized doubts about the system and reinforced disaffection by providing independent criteria for assessing the system.
(2) Specific policy shortcomings, insofar as they were viewed as both systemic and endemic to the system, could spark disaffection and dissent. The militarization of East German education, persistent abuses of human rights, environmental problems, neglect of women's rights, and lingering discontent among the small Slavic Sorb population could be grouped in this class.
(3) Marxism itself may have been a stimulus to disaffection and dissent as socialization instilled values that the regime flouted. The political radicalism of Robert Havemann and Rudolf Bahro, for example, stemmed from their acceptance of Marxist premises.
(4) the gradual economic erosion of the "East German economic miracle"[5] obviously resulted in growing discontent with the regime's capacity to "deliver."

These sources are of different character, weight, and importance. Categories 1 (the failure of resocialization) and 3 (the relative success in instilling new values) are attitudinal. The former affects members of society from diverse sectors, the latter becomes articulate only in the hands of intellectuals. The other two sources reflect regime performance, that is, specific policy shortcomings (category 2) and stagnation or erosion in economic performance (category 4). Policy shortcomings may affect only a particular group within East German society (e.g., the Sorbs) or may have a wider impact (though the environmentalist case reminds us that wider impact does not necessarily translate into wider concern). The effects of economic performance, on the other hand, are felt by the entire spectrum of society and thus have the capacity to excite other latent sources of disaffection—as the Polish case clearly demonstrates. Indeed, although any of these sources can play a catalytic role, the economic factor is perhaps the most potent. Hence, by converse logic, the SED regime hoped to "buy" political conformity.

Discussion of these several sources of disaffection invites a further observation. Insofar as we may find it useful to describe a society as passing through sequential or overlapping crises of identity, legitimacy, participation, distribution, and penetration[6] and, under certain conditions, to speak of a reversal of the developmental process and the onset of political decay, we may expect to find that the strength and importance of any given source of disaffection—as a category, and not merely in terms of specific instances—will vary from phase to phase, and that these categories will play different roles in different crises. Certain kinds of disaffection may be more easily contained in certain developmental phases, and more apt to be translated into dissent in others. For the regime this may signify that policy invariability, which communist parties perfervidly claimed to practice until Gorbachev's arrival on the scene, may be worse than an illusion: it may be a positive weakness. The whole point of perestroika was to adapt policies to changing conditions.

I propose to probe each source of disaffection, to come to a preliminary assessment of the pervasiveness, depth, and importance of disaffection in each category, to examine the extent to which disaffection has translated itself into dissent, and to estimate the untapped sources of dissent in each category of disaffection. The last of these four tasks will necessarily involve a degree of speculation. Finally I shall argue that, far from leading to the transcendence of alienation and the extirpation of disaffection, communist socialization and policy in East Germany multiplied the sources of disaffection and deepened the potential for dissent.

The Failure of Socialization

Communist systems may be understood in part as political engines for cultural transformation and resocialization. The dominant themes of East German resocialization were the superiority of socialism, the identification of socialism with peace, the need for unity among "progressive" forces, antinationalism, secularization, and anti-individualism.[7] Connected with the themes of both socialist superiority and antinationalism was the eventually abandoned effort to instill a concept of a "socialist German nationality" distinct from "bourgeois German nationality," linked to the broader policy of *Abgrenzung*.[8]

The steady erosion in the numerical strength of the Christian churches could be counted as a kind of "success" for SED policy, and some Western scholars even concluded that East Germans and West Germans were drifting apart in national consciousness.[9] Even these successes, however, were compromised by the very tangible resilience of the Evangelical church and its active role in both the independent peace movement and environmentalist concerns,[10] by continuing signs of identification among East and West Germans, and by continuing contacts between citizens of the two states—for example, between the antiestablishment Green Party in West Germany and antiestablishment pacifists in East Germany. Moreover, in a survey authorized by the East German regime, young people overwhelmingly indicated that they viewed themselves as Germans first and as citizens of East Germany second.[11]

In other spheres of SED's resocialization program, the limits were even more tangible. The communist regime tried to foster a kind of *Systemstreue*, but failed to win the trust of the population or even, by some accounts, of the bureaucrats themselves, while the political sympathies of the population clearly lay with social-democratic ideas such as those propagated by the West German Christian Democratic and Social Democratic parties, as the eventual elections of 1990 so dramatically demonstrated. The regime also tried to foster a sense of collective responsibility and ethic and to erode the basis for individualism. Yet, ironically, individualism never flourished in East Germany as it did in the late 1980s, whether one looks to the withdrawal and consumerism of the working and middle classes or to the rejectionism and headlong assertive individualism of those youths caught up in the East German rock scene.[12]

The persistent flow of disaffected East Germans to the West (including, in 1984, the request for political asylum in West Germany by five relatives of East German Premier Willi Stoph),[13] the outspoken remonstrations by articulate East German intellectuals such as Wolfgang Harich, Robert Havemann, and Rudolf Bahro, and the continued incarceration of some three thousand political prisoners in East Germany (as of April 1989)[14] were probably the best-known reflections of the limitations of East Germany's resocialization efforts. Equally troubling to the SED was its inability to control crime. In Marxist-Leninist thought, crime reflected social alienation, which was possible only in pluralist societies ("capitalism") or among persons retaining pluralist ideas ("bourgeois vestiges"). Unfortunately for adherents of this theory, crime was most prevalent among precisely that group which had been nurtured entirely under the socialist system, the youth. After the crime rate had risen for the fifth straight year in 1973, the SED stopped publishing crime statistics.[15] Alcoholism remained a persistent problem (linked to 30–32 percent of violent crimes) and arbitrary assaults by young "rowdies" rose dramatically. By the spring of 1980 the crime level was so high that government authorities admitted that East German crime was rising tangibly.[16]

But whereas crime, alcoholism, and rowdyism represent inchoate forms of disaffection reflecting the failures of socialization in its *social* aspect, antiregime activity represents a more focused and more dangerous strain of disaffection reflecting the failures of socialization in its *political* aspect. In mid-1977, for instance, several hundred East German youths burned the blue shirts of the youth league (Free German Youth, FGY) in Pankow. Later that year, in October, a rock concert degenerated into an anti-Soviet demonstration when eight people became trapped in a ventilation shaft. The crowd (some five hundred youths) shouted "Russians get out!" and "Germany awake!" (*Deutschland erwache!*— an old Nazi slogan). Police used water cannons and batons to suppress the youth.[17]

Two decades ago a Western observer could write that East German youth could no longer conceive of any alternative to the system established by the SED.[18] By the early 1980s, however, the generational gap in East Germany acquired acute political overtones, and the party itself eventually admitted that university students were fed up with the steady doses of required ideological training.[19] Three important catalysts of the estrangement of the youth may be mentioned—the rock counterculture, the militarization of society spawned by the SED, and the consequent attraction of the Christian churches as alternative foci of institutional loyalty.

Rock music will be discussed separately in chapter 10, but a few observations may be made in this chapter. First, rock lyrics have displayed a consistent and unmitigated *subjectivity*, refusing to cater to political parties or programs (East Germany's Dean Reed was an uncommon exception to this rule). As a result, rock lyrics have tended to be either egocentric or critical of social policy. Indeed, one of the roots of East German pacifism was the "make love not war" ethic associated with Bob Dylan, Donovan, and Joan Baez in the late 1960s. Even then the SED regime worried about the effects of their protest songs, and dance clubs that played too much protest music were reprimanded. Indigenous groups began to imitate the protest genre, however, and in 1965, at a performance of the Leipzig rock group Butlers, young people clashed with police and several were arrested.[20]

Second, the SED feared that rock music, and especially disco music, reinforced tendencies toward individualism by accentuating private feelings and dramatizing individual perceptions. Rather than concentrating on relations between the sexes, disco music should be programmed to "contribute . . . to the development of socialist personalities by linking entertainment, sociability, topical information, and education."[21]

With Erich Honecker's accession to power and East Germany's eventual garnering of diplomatic recognition from most states in the international community in the early 1970s, East German youth hoped that the authorities would at last try to live up to their high-sounding ideals. In reflection of this hope, rock groups such as the Renft Combo became bolder in their lyrics. Renft, for instance, took up the subject of conscientious objection in its songs. The regime was not disposed to tolerate a proliferation of protest, however, even if "disguised" as musical diversion, and banned the Renft Combo in 1974. The banning of the prominent rock group was widely interpreted to signify that rock groups should eschew "negative" political themes. The subsequent expulsion of singer Wolf Bierman in 1976 seemed to confirm the accuracy of this interpretation.

Faced with the uncomfortable fact that young people were gravitating toward rock music and that regime hostility to rock music would only deepen the disaffection of youth, the SED decided in 1976 to loosen up strictures on dance clubs and to allow the establishment of carefully monitored discotheques. Under the guidance of the Ministry of Culture, "disco moderators" received training in ideology, and district academies conducted disco workshops. The communist regime watched East German rock groups closely, fearing not merely insidious political criticism but also the "moral decay" promoted by subjective individualism and ostentatious vulgarity. Thus, in March 1983 the East German cultural journal *Sonntag* criticized the "vulgar" lyrics of certain East German rock groups, noting that some rock musicians seemed to believe that the more vulgar their lyrics were, the better.[22] Politically provocative lyrics remained more troublesome than mere vulgarity, however, and occasioned the dissolution of the East Berlin rock group Freigang in 1983. The regime's apprehensive posture was balanced by a strategy of trying to channel rock music away from opposition; in an expression of this strategy, the FGY organized a successful rock festival attended by some four thousand young people in October 1983.[23]

In the 1980s punk counterculture also penetrated the country, and by the mid-1980s a thriving punk rock scene had developed with adherents in all the major East German cities. Punk groups included Abwärts (Downwards), Juckreiz, and Chaiselongue in Magdeburg; Tapetenwechsel (Change of Carpets) and Pankow in East Berlin; Keks, Restbestand (State of Rest) and Ausfluss (Outflow) from Weimar; and Maulsperre

(Locked Mouth) from Gera. Maulsperre was banned from giving concerts because of its name.[24] In its more consistent and articulate strains, punk is a species of cultural nihilism, repudiating as a whole all establishment values: the dissident dimension here is obvious. But even in its less articulate strains, punk culture was unmistakenly an antiestablishment pose in which, in the East German context, Marxism-Leninism, the SED, and the entire program of resocialization were rejected as foolish irrelevancies at best. This attitude was aptly captured in the slogan with which East German punks took to adorning public buildings— *"legal, illegal, scheissegal."*[25] The regime was equally clear about its attitude toward the punk counterculture, which it described as "unmitigatedly hostile" to its program.[26] Students who came to school with multicolored hair and punk fashions were punished by having critical entries made in their permanent academic files; that these entries were intended to block future professional advancement is obvious. The East German security police were likewise mobilized against punk adherents; they broke up punk gatherings in Leipzig of more than a hundred people in March 1981 and of four hundred to five hundred punks in July 1982.[27] Ironically, one band scheduled to perform in Leipzig was called Unerwünscht (Unwanted).[28]

Cultural disaffection is the keynote of punk. A nineteen-year-old East German punk put it this way: "Philistinism turns me off. I am against Germanness. The German is, for me, a *petit bourgeois* and a philistine by nature. I am bothered by this whole pretense, by this mask which is there but which no one removes."[29] Disaffection with "this whole pretense" is the substratum underlying punk nihilism and, although it at initially took the form of a dropout mentality, it could at some future time be catalyzed into more active dissent. In either case, this species of disaffection obstructed the resocialization program and hindered regime efforts to fashion a "new communist man and woman."

Pacifism and the Churches

As alternative social institutions with alternative value systems, the churches remained potent stimuli of nonsocialist thinking and ideas, sharpening the cognitive dissonance between normative standards and the socialist reality, and thus stimulating disaffection from the communist system. State Secretary for Religious Affairs Klaus Gysi recognized this and noted in 1981 that "as long as the church remains a church, it must be independent. We are of the opinion that it will, in this fashion, never be fully integrated in our society as a social force."[30] It could not be fully integrated because it was alien to communism and because church and party offered competing value systems. The churches were also recalcitrant when it came to specific desiderata of SED religious policy. Thus, although the regime hoped at one time to reduce the churches to carrying out liturgical functions, neither the Evangelical churches nor the Catholic church was willing to accept this role.[31] Through the mouthpiece of the Christian Democratic Union-East (CDU-East), the regime urged at one time that "we Christian Democrats can . . . only fulfill our social obligation if we penetrate even deeper into Marxism-Leninism and use Christian faith and atheism—as the instrument of our social work."[32] Neither church embraced this approach. Finally, the regime defined the terms of policy so that *by definition* the regime was a peace movement, the only pacifism worthy of the name was that which supported the regime, critical distance was disloyalty, and disaffection was the breeding ground of opposition. Instead of accepting the practice of "policy by definition," the Evangelical church, under the influence of the World Council of Churches, the Lutheran World Federation, and the Conference of European Churches, spoke out on the subject of peace with increasing frequency after 1968 and, although in 1981 the government threatened action unless the Evangelical church toned down its criticism and severed contacts with West German Evangelicals, the church refused to comply and became even more active in its engagement in public discussion of the theme of peace.[33] The Catholic church's approach to the subject of pacifism was far more low-key, but the Catholic bishops did address the subject in a pastoral letter of 2 January 1983 condemning the militarization of East German life.[34]

Both the fledgling independent peace movement and church involvement in it must be traced to the steady militarization of East German society. From the beginning, the SED held that pacifism under socialism was "objectively" antipacifism.[35] Beginning in September 1978, ninth- and tenth-graders participated in formal "premilitary" training, which included a two-week period of intensive training at the end of the school year. Nursery school children were taught to sing songs about army life and to play martial games. In fourth grade, sports instructors introduced marching and military formation. In sixth and seventh grades, students took part in maneuvers organized by the Young Pioneer Organization in cooperation with officers of the National People's Army (NVA): in sports classes, these students were trained in the use of hand grenades and ran obstacle courses similar to those used in military basic training. In eighth grade, students began special military sports exercises that included the firing of hand arms and hand grenades, rope climbing, first aid, and air defense. Since 1 September 1981 premilitary and ambulance training were also obligatory for all eleventh-graders, with special twelve-day summer sessions. Beginning on 1 December 1981, all East German citizens between the ages of eighteen and sixty-five were obliged to participate in civil defense training exercises, which often involved whole sections of a city.[36]

The accompanying sharpening of hostile stereotypes of the West provoked sharp reaction from Evangelical and Catholic clergy alike. In a series of sermons published in early 1982, for instance, Catholic bishop Joachim Wancke of Erfurt criticized the overemphasis on defense and defense readiness and the habituation of students to think in terms of *enemies*. Bishop Wancke also advocated the institution of a civil service alternative to military service—an idea increasingly popular among East Germany's disaffected.[37] Meanwhile, in April 1981 the "Church and Society" committee of the Evangelical church convoked a congress on the theme "Peace Today," and invited all interested persons to attend, in order to bring together for the first time the previously isolated groups and individuals in East Germany concerned with peace. Pacifist consciousness swelled, and between late 1981 and early 1982 small groups of pacifists appeared in many East German cities. In late 1981 young pacifists planned a peace demonstration to be held at the wreckage of the Frauenkirche in Dresden on the anniversary (13 February 1982) of the bombardment of Dresden. News of the demonstration spread by word of mouth (*Buschfunk*), and the church leadership in Saxony, fearing that the event could lead to open confrontation with the authorities, decided to coopt the demonstration and to try to keep it "within limits." Although only one short notice appeared in a local newspaper, *Buschfunk* worked well enough to turn out some five thousand young people from all over the country. Many others were prevented from attending by police, who headed off many young people on their way to Dresden and who ordered some known pacifists to stay at home that day. At Dresden, speakers demanded the introduction of obligatory "peace education" in the schools, and in the months that followed, similar peace forums were held in Potsdam, Eisenach, and Burg (Spreewald), drawing in a total of more than ten thousand young people.[38]

The Reformed (Calvinist) church likewise took up the pacifist theme, and on 9 November 1982 issued a declaration to the effect that peace is a central question for the church, standing at the very center of the Gospel message.[39]

The Evangelical church started to sponsor various lectures, discussions, and seminars on peace throughout the country and beginning in the early 1980s, began holding a ten-day annual peace conference. It called for arms negotiations in good faith, asked the Soviets to destroy some of their ss-20 missiles, and criticized the militarization of East German society. By April 1982 the SED regime decided that the emerging peace movement constituted a political opposition and banned the "swords into ploughshares" shoulder patch that had become the emblem of the movement; far from buckling under, however, the peace movement established contacts with the antiestablishment Green Party of West Germany. By the end of 1983 the regime was bent on isolating and emasculating the pacifist groups. Well over a hundred East German pacifists were arrested during 1983, and many of these were summarily expelled from the country.[40]

The rising tide of pacifism could only be encompassed within the church since unregistered discussion groups were permitted only on church premises. The result was the steady spread of such groups, generally numbering five to eighty members, based in all the larger cities. Taken collectively, between 30 and 50 percent of group members were not Christian.[41] Of the groups themselves, some were genuinely church groups, while others were essentially secular groups which simply wanted to use church facilities. Some members of these groups were even openly hostile to the church.[42]

In spite of the invigorated opposition of these groups, the SED continued with its program of militarizing East German society, overhauling the educational system in the kindergarten in September 1985. Until then, kindergarten classes had stressed themes of friendship and solidarity; now, in common with other grades, kindergartens stressed the heroic role of the East German military and hatred of the "class enemy."[43] The program passed by the regime specifically noted that "the children should know that the Soviet people are our best friends . . . [and] should experience that there are people who are our enemies and against whom we must fight."[44] This program did not apply, of course, to church-run kindergartens, but for those pupils "friend-foe" thinking began only a year later, when they entered first grade in the state school system.

There had long been currents within the church which felt that the church had not been bold enough. In June 1987 these currents burst into the open with the staging of an alternative church congress alongside the official church congress being held in East Berlin. Some 1,200 persons, mostly young people, attended this alternative congress and took for themselves the name "church from below." They criticized the church hierarchy for quiescence vis-à-vis the state, and declared that many people no longer felt that their interests were represented by the church. Ironically, the "church from below" in East Germany could not be entirely independent and had to approach Berlin Bishop Gottfried Forck for permission to use church premises to stage their alternative congress.[45]

Tensions in what had become a rather tranquil relationship between the Evangelical church and the state arose in the wake of the September 1986 church synod in Erfurt. In an unprecedented but unsuccessful gambit, the church demanded that there be a public discussion of nuclear energy in light of the nuclear accident in Chernobyl. The synod also tackled the issues of the militarization of education and aspirations for a substitute peace service. State Secretary Gysi actually promised to take up these issues in serious discussions with church leaders, but was evidently overruled, and nothing was done.[46]

Frustrated by their inability to obtain any compromise on matters of importance, church leaders adopted a steadily more critical stance in synods held from 1986 to 1988. A church synod at Görlitz in early June 1988, for instance, criticized the "glaring injustice of the division of our fatherland," called "democratization" the principal problem for East Germany, and volubly bemoaned the failure of the East German regime to adopt Gorbachev's policies of *glasnost* (openness) and *perestroika* (restructuring).[47] At the Halle synod in late June 1988 there were again calls for *glasnost* and *perestroika* in East Germany.[48] Twenty theses for domestic renewal were presented and discussed at that synod. At a church conference at Erfurt, local provost Heino Falcke, an influential voice in the Evangelical church, urged church and state to move beyond the "ritual of self-affirmation and self-appeasement" and to learn to accept criticism.[49] And at a synod in Dessau in mid-September 1988 Evangelical church spokespersons complained of "rash administrative actions and unreasonable decisions" on the part of state authorities, called for greater tolerance for dissident opinion, and urged that East German children be eligible to travel to the West.[50]

These were dangerous ideas in the regime's eyes, and in 1988 and 1989 it repeatedly banned church newspapers that sought to report on the synods. The authorities even banned an issue of the East Berlin paper *Die Kirche* in which the editor had planned to reprint an article on Soviet religious policy from the official Soviet newspaper *Moscow News*.[51]

This reached the point that in summer 1988 East Berlin theologian Richard Schröder wrote an article for the West Berlin journal *Kirche im Sozialismus* in which he criticized the East German church's formula "church in socialism" on the grounds that it suggested "that the church incorporate the theory of socialism in its self-image."[52]

April 1989 became a turning point for ecclesiastical engagement in social critique when, for the first time in East Germany, religious communities of different denominations assembled for an ecumenical conference in Dresden devoted to political questions. The Catholic church departed from previous practice to attend the conference, which was held on 26–30 April. The conference adopted twelve resolutions and, in the body of the text, provided "an account of how the communist party, during forty years of rule, had succeeded in suppressing all popular initiative and creating a state in which conformity and opportunism were the norm."[53] The authorities were so disturbed by this that even before the conference was over, State Secretary for Church Affairs Kurt Löffler called Bishop Johannes Hempel of Dresden to an urgent meeting at which he told the bishop that he feared that the text would lay the basis for the establishment of an "opposition group." Löffler added that the text would place church-state relations under great strain. But neither the bishop nor the conference was deterred, and the draft text was approved. By September of that year church-state relations were strained as they had not been in years, and *Neues Deutschland* made a rare attack on the Evangelical church, accusing it of playing the role of a Trojan horse in East Germany.[54]

Policy Problems and Disaffection

Earlier in this chapter five specific areas of policy problems were listed: the militarization of East German education and society, persistent abuses of human rights, environmental problems, women's rights, and discontent among the Sorbs. Disaffection with regime policy in these areas spawned groups of anywhere from five to one hundred persons in size, in various medium-sized towns and in all the larger cities. These groups lacked both the formal structure of the Christian churches and the stable behavioral diversions of the disco and punk countercultures. They also lacked, as a rule an all-embracing Weltanschauung, and, in contrast to the disaffected analyzed under category 1 (failure of socialization), they tended to focus on more specific issues. There is, however, a gray area between categories 1 and 2 produced by the merging of some of these groups (specifically the environmental groups and some feminist groups) and the independent peace movement, as well as by the obvious fact that some of the disaffected in this category are active Christians. (The impact of the militarization of East German education has been discussed above.)

Human rights issues ranged from conscientious objection and the desire for alternative social service (beyond the construction brigade)[55] to demands for freedom of conscience, association, speech, and assembly, as spelled out in a pamphlet distributed in East Germany in the summer of 1981. The authors of this pamphlet also called for the release of all political prisoners, a general amnesty, and free elections with free nomination of candidates and secret ballots. Human rights activist Dr. Werner Schädicke, a Leipzig physician, went to prison in 1974 for a six-year term for writing various letters and tracts calling on the regime to honor basic human rights, including the right to emigrate. Günter and Leni Prager and Bernd and Gerdi Sobe similarly received prison terms for transmitting information likely to tarnish the East German image abroad. The Sobes had written to the UN secretary-general and the UN Human Rights Commission about "serious violations of human rights in the GDR." In August 1980 Andreas Koburg received a four-year prison term in Potsdam for having asked the International Committee of the Red Cross to send a delegation to East Germany to inspect prison conditions. In a related case, Dr. Wilhelm Kock, whose concern for human rights in Poland had prompted him to send financial aid to the Polish independent trade union Solidarity, was imprisoned, as were other East Germans who expressed sympathy for Solidarity.[56]

Aside from occasional church sermons and synodal statements, human rights activism in East Germany remained the work essentially of individuals and embryonic groups until 1985. This picture changed slightly in 1985 with the creation of an independent movement called *Menschenrechte DDR* (Human Rights GDR), which sent an open letter to Honecker demanding freedom of speech, assembly, and movement, and freedom from discrimination on the basis of religion or ideology. As of 1986 the group was said to have "well over 100" activists and a larger circle of sympathizers.[57] Much more important—although primarily in terms of raising consciousness and stirring confidence—was the creation of the New Forum in 1989 by a group of intellectuals that included Bärbel Bohley and Sebastian Pflugbeil. With aspirations to promote democracy, the New Forum quickly registered thousands of supporters.[58]

From time to time the East German regime had recourse to expulsion as a way of dealing with human rights dissent. For example, in January and February 1988 the regime expelled a number of activists, including folk balladeer Stephan Krawczyk and his wife, Freya Klier, and several members of the Peace and Human Rights group who produced the samizdat publication *Grenzfall*.[59]

The situation of the Sorbs is a specific human rights issue. Following the model of Soviet nationalities policy, East German policy toward the Sorbs was supportive in some respects and antagonistic in others. A Sorbian cultural movement, the Domowina, was reestablished with the blessing of Soviet occupation authorities in 1945, but in the mid-1950s, under SED pressure, the Domowina endorsed industrialization and collectivization in Sorb-inhabited Lusatia—measures that were very unpopular among the Sorbs. As a result, the membership strength of the Domowina waned thereafter.[60] Despite the Sorbian-language instruction in kindergartens, primary and secondary schools, vocational schools, and business academies—supplemented by the Slavonic Institute of the Academy of Sciences of the GDR in Berlin, and the Sorbian Institute for Teacher Training and the Sorbian Ethnological Institute, both in Bautzen—the younger generations increasingly became detached from their own Slavic heritage and viewed themselves as immersed in a "German sea." The prizewinning Sorbian author Jurij Brězan captured some of the spirit of the dilemma in his book *Views and Insights:*

> "My literary bilingualism . . . it seems to me very difficult to explain it. My mother tongue is Sorbian. I learned to speak it, the way one learns to speak it in the village. In school we learned the Sorbian alphabet and occasionally took dictation in Sorbian, but never were we assigned to write an essay in Sorbian. Throughout my 14 years in school, the German language was a major subject: here I wrote a hundred essays, read a thousand books—Goethe, Schiller, Lessing, Shakespeare, the Song of the Nibelungen, Cervantes, Zola, Tolstoy were all in German. . . . When I told my sisters stories, and soon after my friends as well, I related the stories in Sorbian. When I tried to write my first story, I wrote it in German. With the girl I loved I spoke Sorbian; when I wrote the first poem for her, I wrote it in German. The spoken word found sufficient room in my mother tongue. . . . The written word . . . could only be built on what I had read.[61]

Interestingly enough, the combination of German cultural engulfment with a general toleration of Sorbian culture[62] and heritage produced, at least in one respect, an effect very similar among Sorbs to that produced by the civil rights repression among human rights activists—that is, atomization, a failure to organize, and a tendency to deal with the situation as individuals.

As of late 1989 there were nine Sorbian-language schools and eighty-five schools offering instruction in Sorbian in East Germany. There were also ten periodicals and one daily newspaper in Sorbian, one Sorbian-language radio station, and ninety-eight Sorbian mayors.[63]

But by late 1989, stimulated by the general opening up of East German society, Sorbs too became restless. Complaints were heard that the Domowina had not shown "the necessary commitment" to Sorbian welfare, a circumstance explicitly blamed on "political structures."[64] And in November 1989 the national executive of the Domowina convened in Bautzen and discussed proposals to transform the Domowina into an independent organization not beholden to any political party,[65] an eventuality that was inevitable at that point anyway.

The situation was dramatically different with regard to environmental and feminist concerns—probably in part because these have been traditional concerns of pacifists over the years and have thus drawn strength from the groundswell of pacifist sentiment in East Germany, and in part because environmentalism and feminism were "live" issues in West Germany, whereas human rights and Sorbian culture were not. Thus, contacts with West German Greens and other confrontations with the West German example (e.g., on television) could stimulate the former but not the latter (at least not in a straightforward manner).

The environmental issue was serious enough. Environmental destruction was, by the mid-1980s, well advanced in five densely populated areas of the country, namely, Halle, Leipzig, Dresden, Karl-Marx-Stadt, and Berlin, and air pollution in Halle, Leipzig, and Zwickau was said to be more than twice the level of that in Chicago, Tokyo, or Düsseldorf. Young people started to become concerned about the environment in the late 1970s. As in the case of the peace movement, Evangelical pastors took the lead in acting as spokespersons for environmental concerns. In 1979 a regional synod at Mecklenburg-Schwerin held discussions on the environmental risks of nuclear power, and in some parishes environmental groups were formed. In November 1979 the first large-scale, volunteer tree-planting event was organized in Schwerin. Since then, annual tree planting and cycling events figured in various parish programs.[66]

Organizers of tree-planting ventures, at least initially, tended to view their actions as having symbolic and educational rather than practical importance. Through their demonstrative actions they hoped to raise public awareness of the issue, to change public behavior, and to stimulate a dialogue about large-scale remedies to be undertaken at a higher level.[67]

The environmental movement received a major impetus in April 1983 when it succeeded in organizing a meeting in Wittenberg of more than thirty church-linked environmental groups, coming from Rostock, Potsdam, Berlin, Rotha, Leipzig, Dresden, Jena-Neulobeda, Karl-Marx-Stadt, and Naumburg. Two months later, at a synod meeting in Rostock, the Evangelical church gave vocal expression to these concerns, and on

5 June, the day the regime itself had designated as the "International Day of the Environment," some two hundred residents of Halle donned gas masks and rode bicycles through town to protest the polluting Buna Chemical Works. The demonstrators were soon stopped and fined by security police, and five people, including the popular parson Lothar Rochau of Halle, were arrested.[68] There can be no doubt that in the case of environmental issues, disaffection has been translated into active dissent. Environmentalists demonstrate not merely against pollution but against the government planning that produces it. Moreover, various environmental conferences from 1983 to 1989 took place under the protection of the church and thus, implicitly, in opposition to the regime.

SED policy toward women, like its nationalities policy, followed the Soviet model: in practice this meant that economics rather than politics dictated policy decisions. Hence, although the German communist party had demanded the legalization of abortion as early as 1931, it was not until 1972 that the SED legalized it. Similarly, the encouragement of women to enter the labor force and the consequent establishment of large numbers of daycare centers and kindergartens were designed primarily to build the economy rather than to advance women's equality— and in fact, only 30 percent of the SED and 12 percent of the members of the central committee of the SED were women (in the early 1980s).[69] Female participation in the work force was critical to East German productivity, and the East German constitution of 1968 proclaimed the duty as well as the right to work. Yet, although "East German women [were] not entirely happy with their lot,"[70] they lacked an organization to represent their interests—unless, of course, the regime-controlled Democratic Women's Federation of Germany counted as such. But as David Childs notes, the federation's main tasks were "to encourage more women to seek employment outside the home, to convince women of the correctness of the SED's policies, and to support the SED/Soviet line in international organizations."[71]

For all of the continued gender inequality, especially when it came to housework (a phenomenon scarcely unique to East Germany), it took the extension of military conscription to women to mobilize them into political opposition. An unfavorable status quo was tolerable, but a regime-dictated change for the worse was unacceptable and catalyzed inchoate disaffection into active dissent. A group calling itself GDR Women for Peace, led by Bärbel Bohley and Ulrike Poppe, was founded basically to press for recognition of a right to female conscientious objection to service.[72] Further, in autumn 1982 several hundred East German women signed a petition addressed to SED general secretary Erich

Honecker protesting female conscription and emphasizing that military service would entail "entirely new duties" that would be "irreconcilable with the concept we have of ourselves." The letter added that the new law had nothing to do with equality since the signatories repudiated "the abstractions of 'enemy' and 'adversary'" and systematic training in "the destruction of human beings."[73] Subsequently, on 17 September 1983 a meeting of East German feminists took place at the Church of the Resurrection in the East Berlin district of Lichtenberg. Some five hundred people attended this first display of organized feminist action. An earlier attempt in 1981 to put together something similar had collapsed.

Clearly, disaffection in this second category had the potential of being translated into active dissent. But just as clearly, disaffection in category 2 was a *less* potent source of dissent than disaffection in category 1. Much of this had to do with the sheer dynamics of the situation. In category 1 there was a substratum of counterculture that provided a vantage point for an *active* orientation toward the system. Christians, like punks, defined their roles in the system on the basis of external criteria. In category 2, on the other hand, the genesis was more *reactive:* it was only because the regime carried out a specific policy that individuals became disaffected and contemplated resistance. Because disaffection in this category was more narrowly focused and did not necessarily entail the application of articulated external criteria (such as the Christian moral code), it was both more apt to prove ephemeral and less potent a source of dissent, unless it could become wedded to other sources of disaffection (as in the symbiosis of environmentalism and pacifism) or the regime provided an impetus by tinkering with the status quo in a fashion viewed as unacceptable (as in the case of female conscription). On a final note, it might be supposed that the church's role in support of pacifists and environmentalists ought to be analytically comparable— that is, that these supportive activities ought not be listed in separate categories. But on the contrary, although the church's engagement with the peace issue was an organic dimension of its commitment to seeking alternatives to mass murder and violence, and thus a stance derivable from its core values, its support for the environmentalists seems to have had a very different source, namely, the traditional role of pastors in representing and articulating the interests of their respective parishes.

Marxism as a Stimulus of Dissent

Marxism-Leninism combines Young Hegelian methodology with a system of empirical and normative theories. The normative element is implicit in the revolutionary project and is proudly admitted by the young Marx in *Economic and Philosophic Manuscripts,* but is stubbornly denied both by the later Marx (beginning with *The German Ideology*) and by the Leninists. The gap between the "ought" and the "is" is bridged by asserting that what is inevitable is progressive and that good communists must therefore work hard to make the inevitable even "more inevitable." This identification of the inevitable with the progressive in practice also entailed an identification of *actual* policy with *best* policy, and a portrayal of *desired* results as *achieved* results. A disjunction between practice and theory could not be admitted because this would open the way to considerations of alternative applications and realizations of the theory, thereby undermining the party's political monopoly. So, since "practice is the criterion of truth,"[74] what is true is what is practical, and Marxism-Leninism reverted to the Hegelian identification of the real (under "socialism") with the rational. Until the advent of Gorbachev, Marxist-Leninist systems thus commonly proceeded from positing what *ought* to be the case—no unemployment, classes, ethnic frictions, crime, or religious affiliation except among the elderly—to declaring that this already *was* the case. These strange avowals of utopia engendered widespread disaffection when people perceived the disjunction between what was declared to be and what really was, and also provided a basis for critique (dissent). Glasnost was slow to penetrate East Germany, and the SED was slow to admit problems. But when the critic in fact accepted the theoretical premises and the normative baggage of the system, the result was Marxist dissent, the third category in our typology of disaffection and dissent.

Because Marxism is so concerned with achieving economic equality and abolishing classes, this type of disaffection ordinarily riveted on the persistence of social and economic inequality and the existence of distinct classes under socialism. This form of disaffection was not limited to the intelligentsia—though they are the only ones capable of translating it into articulate theories of dissent—but could affect all those who came to feel betrayed by the revolution. This feeling of betrayal was a clue to the fact that this third strain of disaffection does not appear until after the lapse of a certain period of time—long enough to convince the discontented that the system has failed to live up to its promises. Zygmunt Bauman says approximately twenty years must pass before large numbers of people feel betrayed by the revolution—that is, enough time for the second generation to reach maturity, seek its place in the social structure, and discover that distributional equality does not exist.[75]

Given this analysis it could be expected that Marxist dissent would become more thorough and more encompassing as time passed. This is exactly what happened. To move from Harich to Havemann to Bahro is to move from criticism of the application of Marxism to a reassessment of certain central Marxist premises to a systematic examination of the Marxist concept altogether. Khrushchev's revelations about Stalin at the Twentieth CPSU Congress in March 1956 made a deep impression on Wolfgang Harich, a professor of social science in Berlin, and on philosopher Ernst Bloch. They responded by urging the democratization of the party and suggesting the unification of the SED and the West German Social Democratic Party (SPD) as a prelude to the reestablishment of a united, neutral Germany. Harich did not question Marx's analysis but believed that the Stalinist model of political development was not merely a perversion of Marxism but might actually impede the development of authentic communist relations within a society. Indeed, the Stalinist endeavor to skip the "capitalist" stage of development represented a deviation from Marxism, and hence it was conceivable to Harich that the pluralist West might achieve "communism" before the collectivist East. Harich organized a group to work for the internal reform of the party, taking into account the contributions of Trotsky, Bukharin, Luxemburg, Kautsky, SPD theorist Fritz Steinberg, and the Yugoslavs. He urged the establishment of workers' councils on the Yugoslav model, a restoration of autonomy for the universities, an emphasis on raising living standards, and the complete abolition of the *Stasi* and the secret trials.[76] He also argued that the *Volkskammer* (parliament) should be in reality, and not just in myth, the highest legislative organ in the land. Harich was imprisoned for a ten-year term, and Bloch was expelled from the party.

Physicist Robert Havemann gained notoriety in 1962 when he launched a series of lectures in Leipzig and East Berlin, denouncing the SED's ideology as neither dialectical nor materialist. Surprisingly, he was not dismissed from Humboldt University until 1964, after thousands of East German students had heard his lectures. Though he reproached the SED for deviating from Marxism, his dismissal was justified on the grounds that he had "gone beyond productive discussion to the point of radical divergence from the party line and Marxist-Leninist theory."[77] Subsequently, Havemann was expelled from the party, and in 1966 he was removed from the GDR Academy of Sciences. He spent his later years under virtual house arrest and eventually came to the conclusion that the SED had erred in abolishing parliamentary democracy. Havemann would demand the abolition of censorship, the establishment of independent media, and the release of political prisoners.[78] For Havemann, as for Harich, pluralism was not incompatible with Marxism but was in fact presumed by it; that is to say, where the SED had resolved the inner tension within Marx's thought between humanism and organized revolutionary force and revolutionary transformation, Harich and Havemann clung to the inchoate humanism most amply developed in Marx's early writings. Their critique thus challenged the very heart of the SED system.

Two books smuggled out of East Germany to be published in West Germany in the mid-1970s carried Marxist dissent one step further. In a work published in 1975, Peter Lübbe argued that socialism had become mired in a bureaucratism in which the state dominated and exploited the people, and concluded that a new revolution would be needed to correct the political subversion carried out by the Soviet and East European communist parties.[79] Two years later came the publication of Rudolf Bahro's *The Alternative*.[80] Bahro's critique proceeded at two levels. On the first level Bahro accepted the structure of Marxist analysis and marshaled it to upbraid Soviet-style systems for radical deviation. On the second level he turned a critical eye toward Marxism itself and revised some of its operational principles. Then, having developed a critique on two levels, Bahro moved on to a third level, spelling out his prescription for a Marxist-inspired reform of East European politics.

On the first level Bahro accepted Marx's argument that the transition from "the realm of necessity to the realm of freedom" required the abolition of the division of labor, but argued that this transition was impossible in Soviet-style systems because society under these systems was dominated by an entrenched bureaucratic apparatus. By establishing a political and informational monopoly, this bureaucratic apparatus produced a "false consciousness" that transformed Marxism from a revolutionary methodology into a legitimizing ideology. Indeed, as Hugh Mosely has noted, Bahro's analysis of Soviet-style systems evoked parallels with Marx's so-called Asiatic mode of production, in which the ruling class maintains its rule on the basis of its control of the ideological and administrative apparatus, not on the basis of private property holdings. Communist party rule had not, therefore, brought an end to human alienation, however much it might claim to have done so; it was in fact the chief obstacle to social progress in Eastern Europe. Yet, faithful to Marx, Bahro scorned political pluralism as backward and aspired to eliminate bureaucratic domination by expanding political participation from below in a new "cultural revolution." Since this new cultural revolution would provide a basis for eliminating fundamental social conflict, Bahro accepted the Leninist belief that there would be no need for labor strikes, and preferred to keep strikes illegal.[81]

Bahro looked to the attempted Czechoslovak reforms of 1968 for inspiration and counseled emulation of Yugoslav self-management. For Bahro, the fetishization of the plan did not serve the interests of economic rationality, as was claimed, but rather the political rationality of maintaining hierarchical subordination and party monopoly of the means of production.

On the second level Bahro took a critical look at Marxism itself and identified three fundamental errors. First, Marx and Engels

> profoundly misunderstood the nature of the modern state. It is not epiphenomenal to society; nor will it wither away; nor is it a means for social welfare and political articulation. Rather it is an apparatus with its own hierarchy and set of institutional interests, ruling and dominating the rest of society and in "tendentially antagonistic relationship to the immediate producers."[82]

As a result, the "noncapitalist" path to socialism produced a series of problems not anticipated by Marx, problems different from those he analyzed in nineteenth-century Europe.[83] Second, Marx believed that the elimination of private property and the erection of a system founded on "people's property" would suffice to eliminate alienation: he did not appreciate that even a "people's state" could foster alienation.[84] And third, Marx overestimated the capabilities of the working class, completely failing to perceive its fundamentally conservative and passive character. The working class could *never* dominate a "dictatorship of the proletariat," whereas the revolution is, from the beginning, apt to be administered by a professional elite—the party.[85]

The upshot for Bahro (as he moved to the third level of his analysis) was that the East European political systems were in serious need of restructuring. He proposed the legalization of extraparty opposition in East Germany and elsewhere; the elimination of privileges for governmental and party workers; the greater equalization of wages; the obligatory participation by all functionaries, managers, and intelligentsia in four to six weeks of low-skilled work in their own workplaces annually; the establishment of workers' councils modeled on the Yugoslav experience; and the creation of a multiregime League of Communists to spearhead cultural revolution throughout Eastern Europe. Bahro was thus aware of the tension in Marx between revolutionary force and humanism, but attempted to resolve it at a higher level. This "higher resolution" was of course no less than a challenge to the entire superstructure of Marxism-Leninism, a challenge all the more troubling to the SED because it took Marx as its starting point.[86] Bahro was arrested the day following publication in *Der Spiegel* in August 1977 of one of the chapters of his book. He was tried and convicted of espionage and sentenced to prison for eight years. In late 1979, however, on the occasion of the thirtieth anniversary of the founding of the GDR, he was granted amnesty and deported to the Federal Republic.

What Harich, Havemann, Lübbe, and Bahro have in common is that they had all marshaled Marxism to argue that East Germany had become too Stalinist and that in this way it had betrayed the revolution. A very different tack was taken by East German Stalinists. Although they agreed with the aforementioned Marxist dissidents that the SED had betrayed the revolution (and they routinely denounced the *Verräter am Sozialismus*), they believed that the problem was that East Germany was not Stalinist enough, and looked to the Albania of Enver Hoxha and Ramiz Alia for a contemporary model. The East German Stalinist opposition was active in the late 1970s and early 1980s, and grew to about 500 adherents in 1981, publishing a bulletin called *Der Rote Stachel*. Despite their hard-line attitude, the East German Stalinists were also defiantly anti-Soviet, and thus presented the SED with an additional challenge. In 1981 eight to ten leading members of this opposition group were arrested, including twenty-eight-year-old Andreas Bortfeldt and thirty-year-old Manfred Wilhelm.[87] At the other extreme, there were reports of the emergence of a new fascist party in 1989, whose members wore Nazi uniforms, desecrated Jewish cemeteries, and celebrated Hitler's birthday.[88]

What strikes one immediately when considering this third category is that the translation from disaffection to dissent entails a challenge to the regime's interpretation and application of Marxism—that is, to both its theory and its praxis. This is a dimension of the practical orientation of Marxism as expressed, for instance, in Marx's famous thesis on Feuerbach, in which he insisted that the real point was to change the world, not to theorize about it.

The authorities seemed to be particularly concerned about this form of dissent because it threatened to create splits within party ranks, to divide the ideology—sowing doubts and creating cracks in which a new form of pluralism might take root and diluting the fundamental operational code of political control. Marxist dissenters brought no external criteria to bear; on the contrary, they used the criteria internal to the official ideology to create an alternative to that ideology. Marxist dissent thus struck at the very heart of the Marxist-Leninist system.

Economic Discontent as a Source of Dissent

The fourth and final category of sources of disaffection is economic performance. East Germans' expectations had been raised both in absolute terms, by the economic boom of the 1960s, and in relative terms, by the ideology of equality. Partly as a result of the general world recession and partly as a function of the structural limits to East Germany's developmental capacity and economic reforms, economic growth rates began to sag in the mid-1970s. East German planners adopted the solution of increasing imports of Western technology and goods in the effort to upgrade capital stock and reverse the economic slowdown. Instead, the debts spiraled and added to the pressures on the economy. East Germany's hard-currency debt to noncommunist countries rose steadily from $1.4 billion in 1970 to $4.8 billion in 1975, $11.6 billion in 1980, and $12.8 billion in 1982. By 1982 it had tallied the largest trade deficits in the Eastern bloc, and 40 percent of its hard-currency earnings went to servicing its debts.[89]

Meanwhile, disturbances in world oil and gas markets in 1978 and 1979 triggered a Western recession, which in turn resulted in an across-the-board drop in the demand for all East European exports except fuel. East German growth rates in national income, gross industrial output, and gross agricultural output were slashed by an average of 40 percent within seven years (1975–82), and nervous East German bankers repeatedly tried to reschedule their debts to the West, only to be turned down. Although East Germany recorded increases in growth rates in national income and industrial production in 1983, and even trimmed back energy consumption by 7 percent, East Berlin's planners were faced with rising unemployment and had to impose a drastic reduction in investments and imports in 1984, with a consequent negative impact on living standards.[90] Ordinary East German citizens routinely complained in the late 1980s that their standard of living was seriously deteriorating, and pointed to shortages of staple commodities.

The East German decision makers responded to these pressures by shifting their trade to the USSR (with whom East Germany conducted an estimated 40 percent of its foreign trade in 1985) and by turning to private entrepreneurs (granting some 30,000 licenses to start private businesses between 1976 and 1982). They were not, however, able to make headway against unemployment, and some East German workers came to interpret the dual-tier pricing system, wherein basic necessities were extremely cheap but other items exceedingly expensive, as supportive of a rigid class system in which the modestly paid workers lacked access to luxury goods except through black market dealings.[91] In 1977 this policy led to worker protests and strikes, after Honecker opened up the hard-currency Intershop chain to East Germans. Since the workers had no guaranteed access to Western currency, the move clearly favored the elite. In one district in East Berlin, workers protested vehemently, forcing the closure of one Intershop outlet. Elsewhere, striking workers demanded to be paid in hard currency. In other instances East German workers struck to protest the substitution of an inferior coffee blend for a preferred one, or to object to other irregularities in commodity supplies. Later, in summer 1981, stimulated by developments in Poland, East German workers in at least five cities staged strikes and clashed with police. Seven workers from four industrial enterprises were arrested for discussing ways of democratizing the East German trade union on the model of Solidarity, and, in response, a group of East German malcontents drew up a manifesto calling on East German workers to revolt and establish democratic rights of free speech and free assembly.[92] Traditional anti-Polish sentiment provided some insulation against contagion from Poland, and this was reinforced by some resentment over East German supplies to Poland to tide it through its period of economic chaos,[93] but the striving for democratization has a life of its own, and anti-Polish prejudice could not undermine its attraction in the long run.

By late 1982 supplies of meat, lard, milk, and vegetables were so unreliable that workers went on strike in Dresden, Boehlen, Espenhain, and in Premnitz, where factory managers used police to stop the demonstration.[94] The authorities admitted to being able to correct only 80 percent of the supply shortcomings, but enacted stiffer measures to deal with unofficial public gatherings, especially where young people were concerned.[95] There were credible and confirmed reports in January 1983 of an attempted assassination of Honecker that month. The regime's haste to deny these reports, offering in their place a strange and not very believable account of how a shot happened to be fired, betrayed a curious insecurity suggestive of latent vulnerabilities.[96]

After economic reverses in 1983 the East German economy rebounded in 1984 with a record growth of 5.5 percent in social product, exceeding the plan by 1.1 percent.[97] Economic performance in 1985 and 1986 seemed strong too, but there were some danger signs, and in 1987 economic growth was reportedly 0.9 percent less than planned.[98] In real terms the East German economy registered no growth at all in 1987, and some 80 percent of its industrial trusts failed to meet their output targets. In 1988 the government reported 3.0 percent economic growth, but for the fourth straight year the actual rate of growth was less than the planned target.[99] In order to make payments on its foreign debt East Germany diverted resources from domestic investment and industrial modernization; much of its industrial machinery had become obsolescent and susceptible to frequent breakdowns. By 1988 East Germany had slipped from its earlier position as the world's tenth leading industrial power to twenty-sixth place. Meanwhile, its agricultural sector also ran into trouble, and authorities began to search for ways to stimulate agricultural production.[100]

There are four preconditions for the translation of economic disaffection into widespread dissent: (1) a general perception of the situation as a problem (by comparison with past performance, performance in other countries, or promises held out by the leadership); (2) a widespread belief that the political elite is responsible for the problem and that it must be opposed (or even overthrown); (3) a diffuse hope; and (4) a belief in one's ability to effect change in one's own condition (sometimes called a "sense of political efficacy"). By late 1989 all four conditions existed in East Germany, although some members of the opposition worried that the opening of the Berlin Wall and the liberalization of travel might sufficiently calm the population so that the wind might be taken out of the sails of the movement for democracy.[101]

The Transformation of East German Dissent

In January 1988 East German authorities arrested at least seventy of the country's leading political activists, expelling them to West Germany. Those who remained were demoralized. Some feared that the authorities had broken the back of East German dissent. Almost exactly a year later, East German police were again arresting independent activists (and again in Leipzig). The police searched several apartments and confiscated various books and other materials. But this time the mood was different. Through all the difficulties imposed on them, including the expulsion of some of their most prominent adherents, independent activists had managed to continue their work and were increasingly encouraged first by Gorbachev's perestroika and subsequently by events in Hungary and Poland.

Much of what was occurring in East Germany in 1988 and 1989 remained below the surface—until the dramatic flight of 225,000 East

Germans to the West forced the world and the authorities to take note. But disaffection was increasingly translated into dissent, as new opposition groups were founded. By August 1989 there were more than 500 grass-roots opposition groups in East Germany, including pacifist, environmentalist, democratic, and countercultural groups, and on 13 August representatives of these groups announced that they would establish a nationwide movement.[102]

Out of this initiative was born the New Forum, a group founded by Bärbel Bohley and Sebastian Pflugbeil among others and conceived as a pressure group for dialogue rather than as an embryonic political party. Within little more than a month, New Forum had 4,000 adherents. By mid-October, two weeks later, it had some 25,000 adherents. On 24 September opposition groups throughout East Germany decided that New Forum would be an appropriate vehicle to serve as an umbrella organization for dissent.[103]

Meanwhile, other opposition groups continued to arise, most prominently: the Citizens' Movement for Democracy Now (established in August or September), Democratic Awakening (established in September), and the reborn Social Democratic Party (established in October).[104] The creation of these groups reflected the broad transformation of the political mindset of East Germans in the course of the late 1980s. But that story belongs more properly to chapters 14 and 15, and will be taken up there.

Conclusion

Although disaffection and dissent are organically related, they remain analytically distinct phenomena. In functionalist terms one might say that, although disaffection serves the "negative" functions of creating a critical distance between the disaffected and the regime, and of undermining socialized expectations and behavioral patterns (the repudiation of military service, workers' strikes, and punk rock all reflecting different kinds of erosion of socialized behavior), the functions of dissent may be seen as "positive." These functions are: (1) the articulation and expression of the meaning of disaffection; (2) critical opposition to the regime and the defense of the right to think differently; (3) presentation of an alternative information source (in this regard the Evangelical church's mini-think tanks on disarmament and peace education served "dissenting" functions within East Germany); and (4) the demonstration of an alternative model.

The differing sources of disaffection are translated into dissent in different ways. Disaffection in category 1 (failure of socialization) is associated with countercultural options and has available transitory or stable institutional resources. It is thus likely to give rise to forms of institutional or "countercultural" dissent. Disaffection in category 2 (policy shortcomings) is apt to provoke discussion among affected persons and lead to forms of group dissent through emergent ad hoc groups of varying sizes. Disaffection in category 3 (Marxist revisionism) carries great risks for the person who speaks out publicly. The state ideology was the state's preserve and it did not allow individuals to chart their own courses through the Marxist-Leninist corpus, let alone challenge the SED interpretation in public. Disaffection in this category is therfore likely to be translated into individual dissent. And finally, disaffection in category 4 (economic malaise) showed that it has had the potential of being translated into social dissent, widespread protest, and even (for that matter) social disintegration.

Of course, the translation of disaffection into dissent is not automatic; if it were, the analytical distinction would break down and the two would have to be seen as, at most, two phases in a single phenomenon. The translation of disaffection into dissent requires several factors, however, among which are hope, the emergence of an alternative vision, a sense of political efficacy, and, often, a "trigger," whether a policy reversal on the part of the regime or a situational change.

Dissent as resistance to accepted or imposed social and political norms may arise in any society; the more narrowly those norms are defined, the broader the scope of dissent. Hence, the very approach taken by monocratic-dogmatic systems like that of the SED tends to subsume larger areas of activity under the term "dissent." But even given this point of departure, the SED hoped, in consonance with its Leninist presumptions, to extirpate both alienation and disaffection altogether, and in this way to banish dissent, except as an epiphenomenon of mental derangement. I have argued above that in fact SED policy multiplied the sources of disaffection and deepened the potential for dissent. The militarization of society produced a critical backlash, especially among youth, and consequently the Evangelical church became increasingly involved both in this area and in environmental concerns. Antinationalism has not worked and has only produced estrangement from the system, and after late 1982 the SED completely reversed this policy and belatedly set about to reclaim its past—Friedrich the Great, Martin Luther, Prussia, and so on.[105] In a related area East Germany's obvious subordination to the USSR, its participation in the 1968 invasion of Czechoslovakia,[106] and its fawning endorsement of the Soviet invasion of Afghanistan rankled German pride and excited anti-Russian sentiments that remained close to the surface. The ideology of equality encouraged workers to expect real equality and fostered disaffection in its absence. Marxism itself proved to be a potential seedbed for oppositional thought and opened new vistas for dissent. Add to that the pervasive frustration with travel restrictions, the inferiority of the East German Trabant to the West German BMW (constantly mentioned by East Germans in the 1980s), and the unavailability of quality merchandise (especially stereo equipment). And finally, the generally repressive approach taken by the SED actually stimulated social deviance and dissent, whether one looks at the effect of political impotence in stimulating egocentric individualism both in supportive (acquisitional) and antagonistic (punk) guises, the politicization of counterculture produced by regime intolerance of either Christianity or punk, or the resistance engendered by human rights violations. In short, the effect of the SED's policy responses to disaffection and dissent turned out to be precisely the opposite of what it aspired to achieve.

Disaffection posed a curious and ambiguous threat to the SED and therefore proved in some ways more complex an issue than dissent. In 1989 East Germany was engulfed in a tidal wave of *disaffection*, not dissent. The increase of organized dissent was symptomatic of widening disaffection but, to a large extent, followed in its wake. Disaffection thus fueled popular pressure, which has been the engine of change in Eastern Europe.

4. Underground Solidarity and Parallel Society in Poland

The concept *parallel society*, like its surrogates *independent society* or *alternative society*, presupposes an *official society* to which it is parallel. The terms may be applied to any society, but they will assume different meanings in different political contexts. In the West if one were to speak of parallel society, or alternative society, one might think of gender subcultures (e.g., cross-dressing associations), the rock counterculture (perhaps especially of punk and, at one time, heavy metal), drugs, prostitution, organized crime, and other collective behavior that defies the dominant culture and norms or seeks to evade the authorities. In Eastern Europe during the communist era not only did official channels and institutions exist, but there was also an official culture as well as a strict definition of legitimate collective action. Accordingly, collective behavior that defied official culture and official norms ipso facto had to defy or evade the authorities.

Parallel society in this sense is a living part of any society. Its breadth varies in inverse proportion to the breadth of allowable open activity: where the political authorities let society organize itself, parallel society inhabits the narrow ravines of subculture, deviance, and crime; where the political authorities seek to impede society's self-organization, parallel society encompasses a much wider array of socially organic processes.

The term parallel society has an advantage over its alternatives in that society cannot completely ignore the official structures, the legal codes, and official economy: it cannot be fully "independent" or create a full-blown "alternative," though it self-consciously tends in that direction. As Václav Benda has noted, the term parallel society suggests the possibility of interaction, interference, mutual influence, and exchange with official society. It also leaves open the possibility of an eventual merger of the two, or as advocates of parallel society envisioned, the swallowing up of official society by the freely self-organized structures of parallel society.[1] This is, in effect, what came to pass in Hungary, Poland, Czechoslovakia, and East Germany, as well as in Slovenia and Croatia, by mid-1990.

Parallel society was not an entirely new phenomenon in Poland or Eastern Europe. Important independent currents in Poland had been present through much of the postwar era.[2] But beginning in the early 1980s parallel society in Poland mushroomed. Three important impulses produced the configuration of parallel society prevailing in Poland in the late 1980s. First, in the late 1970s intellectuals and workers grew in confidence and began to organize themselves, at first separately, and later in contact and coordination with each other. Second, the disintegration of the communist political infrastructure and concomitant rise of the legal independent trade union Solidarity from July 1980 to December 1981 was accompanied by the efflorescence of independent associations of various kinds, including Farmers' Solidarity and the Independent Students' Association. Existing political structures such as the fraternal parties (the United Peasant Party and the Democratic Party) and the proregime clerical association PAX also began behaving in new ways during this period.[3] Hence, the seeds sown in the 1970s could now produce shoots. The third impulse came with the imposition of martial law on 13 December 1981 and the suppression of all legal independent structures. This "restorationist" impulse effectively forced independent currents into a *parallel* channel.

Although the evolution of parallel society in Poland thus occurred naturally, opposition activists also viewed the promotion of parallel structures as a conscious strategy. Warsaw Solidarity activist Wiktor Kulerski, for example, sounded the keynote in early 1982: "This movement should create a situation in which the authorities will control empty stores but not the market; the employment of workers but not their livelihood; the official media, but not the circulation of information; printing plants, but not the publishing movement; the mail and telephones, but not communications; and the school system, but not education."[4] This aspiration entailed the creation of independent theater, concerts, newspapers, book publishing, education, and methods of circulating an independent system's products. In the short run, the goal was to force the authorities to allow freedom of association and freedom of speech and thus liberalize the political system.[5] In the long run, the aim was to erode the official structures of power and create a democratic system from below. The opposition largely succeeded in realizing this goal by late 1989.

Parallel society in Poland was closely associated with Solidarity, which from December 1981 until April 1989 was the single most important symbol of resistance and the single most important underground organization, although numerous other underground organizations of various political and cultural stripes existed. Even some underground organizations not linked to Solidarity were created on its initiative. Consequently, parallel society became strongest in those cities where Solidarity was best organized; it was weakest in the countryside where Solidarity was only lightly active even in 1980 and 1981.

Parallel society was expensive. For example, most publishing equipment had to be obtained abroad.[6] Authors whose works were published underground received royalties. Printers had to be paid. These and other expenses were covered by contributions from Solidarity members, by sales of books, stickers, and other items, and by contributions from Western trade unions and foundations. Although some persons in the underground were paid, most were not.

How many people were involved in parallel society? In August 1985 Zbigniew Bujak, then head of the Mazowsze region of underground Solidarity and one of the organization's leading figures, estimated that 50,000–70,000 Poles were involved in writing for and publishing the underground press and in organizing underground groups and protest actions and that another 200,000–250,000 provided "logistical support" for such activities.[7] If one were to add in those participating in independent theatrical performances or artistic exhibits, the self-education movement, independent youth movements, and independent social support organizations, the number was magnified several times.

Martial Law and Its Aftermath

The proclamation of martial law on 13 December 1981 ended thirteen months of legal existence for Solidarity.[8] It culminated a period of active preparation by the authorities to crush the independent trade union movement. As early as 24 August 1980, even before the registration of Solidarity as a legal entity in mid-November, Prime Minister Józef Pińkowski, General Wojciech Jaruzelski, Politburo members Stefan Olszowski and Mirosław Milewski, Central Committee Secretary Kazimierz Barcikowski (a reputed "liberal"), and Vice Premier M. Jagielski met and first discussed a draft plan for the imposition of martial law.[9] Military preparations started on 22 October. But no final decision had yet been taken. On 26 November 1980 East German leader Erich Honecker wrote a letter to Brezhnev, urging a joint Warsaw Pact invasion of Poland.[10] Romania's President Nicolae Ceauşescu telephoned the Kremlin to say that the developments in Poland were dangerous; he urged a meeting of Warsaw Pact leaders to discuss countermeasures.[11] Czechoslovakia's hard-line communists were also nervous.

An emergency meeting of the Warsaw Pact was in fact held in Moscow on 5 December. Brezhnev told the gathering: "The situation in Poland and the danger that is emanating from Poland are not simply Polish matters. They affect all of us."[12] Later that month the Soviet Politburo discussed the possibility of invading Poland. The Politburo was deeply divided and rejected the invasion option by six votes to five, with Brezhnev reportedly casting the tiebreaking vote. The Politburo, as Edmund Jodkowski revealed in the September 1992 issue of *Literaturniye novosti,* anticipated that the Poles, unlike the Czechs in 1968, would put up a fierce resistance, and it calculated that the cost of military intervention would have been beyond Soviet means.[13]

But the Soviets were impatient all the same to see the restoration of the status quo ante, and Soviet military brass, including Marshal Viktor Kulikov, commander-in-chief of the Warsaw Pact, visited Warsaw in January and March 1981 to monitor Polish plans to deal with "the counterrevolution" and to press General Jaruzelski to take steps to deal with the situation.[14]

On 19 July 1981 General Jaruzelski (prime minister since February) delivered a speech at the Ninth Extraordinary Congress of the Polish United Workers' Party, issuing a stern warning: "there are limits which may not be exceeded . . . . Should the situation demand it, when there are overriding reasons, the authorities will be forced to exercise their constitutional duties to save the State from disintegration and the nation from disaster."[15] But the repluralization of Poland, sparked by the establishment of Solidarity, continued unabated, and the Soviets grew ever more nervous. In September 1981 Jaruzelski had a lengthy conversation with Marshal Dimitry F. Ustinov, the Soviet defense minister, during the "Zapad" military exercises. The two men were seated in a helicopter on the ground, talking for several hours, as Ustinov impressed upon Jaruzelski the urgency with which the Politburo viewed the situation.[16]

Solidarity was aware that hard-liners were pressing for military action, and it could scarcely have failed to notice the numerous military maneuvers being noisily staged by the Warsaw Pact along their borders with Poland. But to the extent that Solidarity leaders foresaw the danger of a military option, they had not anticipated its potential form.

On the contrary, Solidarity's top leaders expected that if things came
to a head, the Sejm would vote to give the government extraordinary
powers. Although Solidarity activists had hidden some weapons caches,
they largely assumed that they would be faced with openly promulgated
legislation and thus remain in a position to use legal channels to resist.[17]
The proclamation of martial law closed all such channels.

The newly established Committee for the Defense of the Country
(KOK) imposed a curfew, closed all schools and universities, banned
all public meetings except religious services (but including cultural
and sports events), and suspended for the interim all trade unions,
youth organizations, Catholic organizations, and professional associations. Solidarity, Rural Solidarity, and the Independent Student Union
were among the suspended organizations and were banned outright a
few months later. The United Peasant Party and the Democratic Party
were brought back into line. Communications throughout Poland were
cut, and KOK ordered the militarization of all public transport, postal
services, the oil and construction industries, and even major factories.[18]
Thousands of persons were detained, and at a peak some 5,500 persons
were interned.[19]

Government spokesperson Jerzy Urban would later claim that the imposition of martial law was supported by two-thirds of all Poles, with
the other third being largely indifferent. The existence of the underground gives the lie to this claim. More honest was *Polityka*'s admission
in March 1985 that most of Poland's intellectuals were opposed to the
Jaruzelski regime.[20] Later, a survey conducted by the Public Opinion Research Center in Warsaw in 1987 found that 80 percent of the Polish
public had a negative opinion of the government and that 60 percent
believed there were makings of a "serious explosion" and "open social
conflict."[21] A 1988 opinion poll conducted for the party found that the
Jaruzelski government enjoyed the trust of only 5 percent of Poles.[22]

Arrests hurt the Solidarity infrastructure. In addition, the government
confiscated most of Solidarity's printing presses.[23] As late as mid-January
citizens' militias were still uncovering secret stores of arms and ammunition hidden by Solidarity supporters.[24] Underground Solidarity had to
be reconstructed, first at the factory level, then on an interfactory level,
and subsequently on a regional level. A former Solidarity leader recalls
those difficult days:

> Part of Solidarity's infrastructure had been underground even in the
> period of the union's legality. But for a period, even this broke down.
> So the union had to be revived. My first task was to get in touch

with the activists in my region. It was extremely difficult. I had to do it myself. I traveled by train and then looked for the people I needed to see. I often found people in very mundane places or even by chance. One man whom I needed to see, for example, I found in a cafeteria.[25]

Two abortive attempts took place to set up national coordinating committees for underground Solidarity. The first, the National Strike Committee (KKS), located in the Gdańsk shipyard and led by Eugeniusz Szumiejko and Andrzej Konarski, fell apart when the shipyard strike collapsed on 16 December. A second attempt came when the National Resistance Committee (OKO) was formed in Gdańsk on 13 January 1982. This second organization was again led by Szumejko. Solidarity activists in other regions, however, suspected that OKO had been infiltrated by the security police, a suspicion seemingly confirmed when a large number of OKO activists were arrested a short time later.

Finally, on 22 April 1982 the Interim Coordinating Commission (TKK) Solidarity was formed jointly by activists from Gdańsk, Mazowsze, Lower Silesia, and Małopolska. The founding declaration was signed by Zbigniew Bujak (head of the Mazowsze region), Władysław Frasyniuk (Wrocław), Władysław Hardek, and Bogdan Lis (Gdańsk).[26] Lech Wałesa, who personified the movement, was in detention, where he remained until November. Arrests of the leading figures (Frasyniuk in October 1982, Lis in mid-1984, and Lis's replacement, Bogdan Borusewicz, in January 1986) complicated TKK's operations.

Solidarity activists had little experience with underground work. Faced with the necessity of surviving underground, they contacted members of the older generation, veterans of the struggle against German and Soviet occupation during World War II, and learned the methods of underground work from them.[27] Imprisoned Solidarity activists learned from convicted criminals how to cope with prison life—how to do gymnastics in a tight space, how to get tea and cigarettes (the basic currency of the prison), and how to communicate with the outside as well as within the prison. Sometimes, for example, prisoners would tie a rope to the window bars of two cells, linking them, and then pass messages along the rope. Or on other occasions prisoners would use the pipes between floors, which efficiently carried voices. The guards were aware of this activity but could not control it.[28]

Already by Christmas (less than two weeks after the imposition of martial law) pamphlets were distributed in Warsaw calling for the establishment of grassroots Committees for Social Resistance (KOS) among circles of trusted friends. Underground newspapers appeared immediately, and they developed quickly. By early 1983 more than five hundred underground newspapers were in circulation.[29]

An underground embracing hundreds of Solidarity activists was soon built up in Gdańsk, led by Bogdan Lis and Aleksandar Hall, an activist in the nationalist underground group Young Poland.[30] A strong Solidarity network was rebuilt underground in Wrocław[31] in the southwest and in other cities. In the early months of underground work Solidarity leaders were fearful of being written off as defeated and of losing their following. The key to dealing with this problem lay in demonstrations of strength, resulting in repeated calls for strikes and further demonstrations. A typical expression of this concern was Bujak's comment in August 1982: "If August passes peacefully, it will mean to the authorities that the society and the union are weak and broken."[32] Or again, Jacek Kuroń, a veteran of KOR, advised the underground union to prepare to use force against the government and to infiltrate the police and the army.[33] In July it was reported that underground Solidarity had some 70,000 activists, mostly young people, under arms in southern Poland, and that they were training in military combat.[34]

In July 1982 TKK Solidarity issued a five-point plan for reconciliation with the authorities, including lifting martial law, amnesty for all political internees including Lech Wałęsa, and restoration of all suspended trade unions. The authorities rejected the proposal and instead delegalized Solidarity in October. TKK responded by calling on its members to work for the creation of a "self-managed republic."[35]

General Secretary Jaruzelski's strategy was to recentralize decision-making, to expel many of the regional party first secretaries, and above all to try to undermine and uproot underground Solidarity. On 13 January 1982 the authorities set up the Association of Clubs for Social and Political Knowledge under the leadership of former Politburo member Tadeusz Grabski. The association was supposed to work for "a return to true socialist practices [in public life] and a rejection of the deviations from the system that undermined socialism in Poland."[36]

In addition, a special "study bureau" under the Ministry of Internal Affairs was entrusted with the task of weakening Solidarity. Coordinated by Eligiusz Naszkowski, a young state security official who at one time had headed one of Solidarity's *voivodship* trade union groups, the bureau concentrated on spreading disinformation. Because morale was low even in the ministry at the time the bureau was established, it was necessary to disseminate disinformation not merely in society at large but also specifically within the Ministry of Internal Affairs. The bureau's work included psychological intimidation, character assassination, the dissemination of alarmist rumors, and the editing of tape recordings of Solidarity spokespersons' comments to change their meaning (some of the products of the tape division were broadcast over Polish radio).[37]

The Security Service also broadcast fake Solidarity programs. For example, on 20 July 1983 a fake broadcast in Warsaw urged underground activists to turn themselves in and claimed that an "elite underground unit" was being created that would replace Solidarity's network of couriers and supporters. The real Radio Solidarity broadcast a disclaimer soon after, and the fake broadcast had no evident effect.[38]

Security Service operatives also successfully infiltrated several underground Solidarity units, leading to the destruction of clandestine committees in Warsaw in 1982 and in Gdańsk and Bydgoszcz in February 1983. Security police also on occasion constructed "Solidarity" organizations of their own, drawing genuine activists into their net. The most famous of these was the Interregional Commission for the Defense of Solidarity (MKO), which was formed in thirteen regions in September 1982. Konarski, a veteran of KKS and OKO, headed the MKO and was suspected of being a police informant. MKO published a samizdat paper, *Bez Dyktatu*, in which it criticized TKK Solidarity. TKK in turn accused MKO of trying to split Solidarity. Within a week of the government's amnesty program three of MKO's leaders turned themselves in and proclaimed the dissolution of their organization.[39] Anti-Solidarity groups were also created, which roughed up Solidarity activists in an effort to sow division and distrust.

The "study bureau" located and contracted a Wałęsa lookalike, who was filmed acting in an obnoxious and arrogant way. The bureau even considered arranging to have Wałęsa eliminated. "Lech Wałęsa would have been murdered long ago if he did not have the Nobel Prize," according to the aforementioned Eligiusz Naszkowski, a former bureau operative, who was to defect to the West in 1985.[40]

But where Wałęsa was concerned, the regime had a parallel strategy, that is, to buy him out. They offered him an important-sounding ceremonial post in the Patriotic Movement for National Renewal (PRON). They offered him a post on the advisory council for trade union affairs. Other offers were broached. Gradually, as Wałęsa observed in his autobiography, it became clear "to them that what they considered interesting proposals had no interest for me. I was careful not to be disdainful, however, because I knew that there was only a narrow margin between the game we were playing and a much more savage one. The game being played was nonetheless exhausting: no one ever put all his cards on the table, and the constant bluffing kept us from ever reaching the moment of truth."[41]

In July 1983 martial law was formally lifted, but restrictions associated with it had been passed into law. In particular, "commissions for special order enforcement" were set up throughout the country beginning early in 1983. The commissions were instructed to assure that persons occupying executive posts in administration, state enterprises, schools, universities, and other social structures carried out their prescribed functions in accordance with approved codes. The commissions obtained their powers under a law passed on 18 December 1982 that authorized them to issue warnings and to demote, transfer, or dismiss uncooperative officeholders.[42]

On balance, 1983 was a difficult year for underground Solidarity. On the plus side, Wałęsa was able to elude his guards in April and attend a clandestine meeting with TKK Solidarity. The brief, matter-of-fact, two-sentence communiqué issued after the meeting so angered authorities that pointed reprisals occurred. On May Day, in response to a call from TKK Solidarity, large demonstrations took place in twenty cities and towns throughout Poland, involving some 40,000 people nationwide, according to Polish television, and some 40,000 people in Gdańsk alone, according to Western journalists.[43] But on the other side, Solidarity was weakened by the arrests of Andrzej Konarski in March, Zbigniew Belz (a member of Solidarity's 107-member national commission) in April, and Józef Pinior (one of TKK's principal leaders) also in April. In addition, a limited amnesty persuaded other Solidarity leaders to turn themselves in. In July, Ryszard Bogacz, a former member of Solidarity's national presidium, and two top local union activists, Andrzej Mazur and Jerzy Nowak, surrendered and appeared on state television. The following month Władysław Hardek, another TKK leader, turned himself in. Appearing on Polish television, Hardek said that Solidarity's strategy had produced only hardship and that society needed "normalization and calm." He closed with an appeal to his former TKK colleagues and other underground activists to "think over the purposes of any further activity."[44]

In spite of these setbacks the Solidarity underground continued to function, and parallel society continued to spread. Indeed, by 1984 it was clear to both the state and Solidarity that Jaruzelski's program of "normalization" had failed to achieve its objectives and that a vibrant and resilient parallel society had emerged.

The Jaruzelski regime responded to this situation by trying a new tactic: amnesty. This tactic had the advantage of gratifying both the church and the West, to which the Polish government was deeply in financial debt. The amnesty became effective in late July 1984 and applied to common criminals as well as to political internees. The authorities hoped for three benefits from the amnesty. First of all, acceptance of amnesty technically implied an admission of culpability, which is why imprisoned KOR activist Adam Michnik tried to decline and to insist on a public trial. Second, since the amnesty extended not merely to those already in prison but to those who might surrender to the police, authorities hoped that Solidarity activists in hiding, especially Bujak,[45] might be lured into the open where they could be placed under surveillance. Indeed, by 20 August ninety-three people had turned themselves in, including twenty-four members of Wrocław's underground Solidarity branch.[46] And third, the amnesty law specified that amnestees who were subsequently rearrested for breaking the law in the future could be tried and punished not merely for the new infraction but also for those acts committed before the amnesty. This, according to Polish dissident Jan Lipski, lent the amnesty act the character of a probationary release.[47] Hence, a spokesperson for the Ministry of Internal Affairs expressed optimism that most of those amnestied would desist from returning to their old activities.[48]

By late August some 285,000 persons were said to have "benefited" from the amnesty, with 31,000 persons actually released from prison. Of the 652 political prisoners who were still behind bars on the eve of amnesty (many having been released earlier), 630 were freed by 24 August.[49] Among those released at this time were former Solidarity vice president Andrzej Gwiazda; Antoni Pietkiewicz, chair of the Wielkopolska Poludniowa regional board of Solidarity; Andrzej Slowik, chair of the Łódź Solidarity organization; Jerzy Krupielnicki, the deputy chair in Łódź; highly placed activists Karol Modzelewski, Seweryn Jaworski, and Andrzej Rozpłochowski; Jan Rulewski, a Solidarity leader from Bydgoszcz; KOR leaders Jacek Kuroń, Adam Michnik, and Henryk Wujec; and former TKK leaders Frasyniuk and Pinior. Before the month was out, warnings were issued to Rulewski, Frasyniuk, and Pinior that they were engaging in activities that might result in their rearrest and the withdrawal of amnesty. The latter two were in fact arrested on 31 August and sentenced to two months' imprisonment for disturbing the peace.[50]

Solidarity, on the other hand, clearly felt more confident now (even before amnesty), as was shown on 1 May when Wałęsa and a large group of Solidarity supporters succeeded in infiltrating the official May Day parade in Gdańsk. Wałęsa and his adherents paraded defiantly, passing within ten feet of the stand where party officials were seated. As they passed, Wałęsa turned to the party barons and flashed a V-for-victory sign. "The officials on the stand were stupefied," one witness later said. "They didn't know what to do."[51] Later, in complete disregard of the cautions and conditions that accompanied the amnesty, Solidarity staged demonstrations of five thousand-strong in Warsaw on 31 July (to mark the fortieth anniversary of the Warsaw uprising) and 31 August (to mark the fourth anniversary of Solidarity's birth).[52]

Far from being cowed by the authorities' threats of reimprisonment, the newly amnestied Solidarity leaders hurried to make contact with each other. By the later part of September, there had been meetings between Frasyniuk and Bujak, Michnik and Bujak, and Wałęsa and all the released leaders of Solidarity and KOR individually, except for Marian Jurczyk.[53] Wałęsa now held the first Solidarity "summit meeting" since December 1981. Andrzej Rozpłochowski, Seweryn Jaworski, Jerzy Krupielnicki, Jan Rulewski, Andrzej Gwiazda, Marian Jurczyk, and Andrzej Słowik of Solidarity, along with Henryk Wujec and Zbigniew Romaszewski of KOR, attended the meeting, held in the Jasna Góra monastery in Częstochowa.[54]

A new boldness was apparent among Solidarity leaders. Bujak talked of looking to the future with confidence and encouraged workers to set up independent unions in their factories, creating faits accomplis that the government would be forced to accept.[55] Wałęsa declared his confidence in the utility of stepped-up organizational activity.[56] Frasyniuk called for the Solidarity leadership to switch to open activity, while Michnik highlighted the importance of open opposition activity.[57]

This gravitation in the direction of open opposition received impetus at year's end from an unexpected source—the brutal slaying by security police of Father Jerzy Popiełuszko in October (discussed further in chapter 7). The widespread sense of tragedy and loss was accompanied by a feeling of outrage. In reaction to Popiełuszko's murder, grassroots monitoring groups called Citizens' Committees Against Violence (KOPPS) arose in Wrocław, Kraków, Warsaw, Łódź, Poznań, Lublin, Gdańsk, Wałbrzych, Szczecin, Toruń, Częstochowa, Słupsk, and the village of Ciepłowody (in Wałbrzych province).[58] The authorities banned the new groups, arranged for the dismissal from work of some of their members, arrested others, and advised foreign journalists that they risked imprisonment for up to six months if they took part in press conferences organized by the new human rights groups.[59] Sociologist Jacek Szymanderski, one of KOPP's founders, explained the philosophy inspiring the new committees in an interview with the samizdat periodical *Czas*:

Lawlessness can and should be opposed through open and not clandestine activities. Open demonstrations of opposition to lawlessness are, in fact, the only effective method. Society must overcome its fear of open activity. Open forms of resistance and public activity force the authorities to take a stand, to admit . . . [that] they are governing against the national will. . . . We want to encourage people to form open committees, and not only ones similar in character to ours. Such organizations must arise everywhere—on the shop floor, in places of residence, in schools—[and] they should monitor compliance with the law, not only with the laws the authorities issue, because they can issue any regulation, but also the compatibility of fresh legislation with that already in force and, primarily, with international agreements. Such committees should ensure the observance of human rights everywhere.[60]

The Ideology and Structure of the Political Underground

After the imposition of martial law, Solidarity activists considered three alternative strategies. Kuroń, looking back to the strategy adopted from 1976 to 1980,[61] urged the formation of a unified resistance movement that would prepare for and force a showdown with the government. Bujak favored setting up a decentralized underground network that would confound the regime in the long term. Kulerski argued for a more evolutionary approach that would sap government institutions of their strength. The second and third strategies proved to be compatible and came to form the foundation of underground Solidarity's strategic thinking in the late 1980s.

Underground Solidarity was very much a grassroots movement. Solidarity strategists believed that its network of clandestine union cells in factories constituted a wellspring from which a future system of factory self-management,[62] similar in some ways to the Yugoslav conception, could develop. Unlike Yugoslav practice, however, Solidarity wanted at that time to couple self-management with trade union pluralism. This presumed the dismantlement of the communist system in Poland and the attainment of independence from the USSR—both essentially realized by mid-1990. Symptomatic of Poland's new independence was the fact that by June 1990 the Polish army, like other East European armies, was no longer under the authority of the Soviet general staff but was effectively under *national* command.[63]

Solidarity inspired the creation of various other groups, opened the way for others, and in some cases gave birth to others as a result of ideological and strategic differences of opinion. The result was that the underground political landscape in Poland in the 1980s became richly diverse. This, I would argue, was a strength, not a weakness (although many Western analysts at the time considered it a weakness).

Solidarity: The Underground Structure. When Solidarity first emerged in mid-1980 it had more of the character of a movement than an organization. Its structure was largely amorphous, it had few regularized procedures, and it had no network of offices with clearly delineated jurisdictions. During the roughly seventeen months of its open existence (thirteen as a legally registered organization) it started to institutionalize itself, to establish procedures and jurisdictions. All of this was effectively destroyed in mid-December 1981, and since Solidarity had made no preparations for continuing work underground, the organization essentially had to be rebuilt. Under the circumstances of illegality, new structures were created for which there had been no precedent during the period of legality.

In some areas the new underground structures first appeared at the factory level, and the organization was rebuilt from the bottom up. In other areas regional bodies appeared first and coordinated the creation of union cells at the factory level. Of the thirty-eight regional committees that Solidarity had operated before December 1981, twenty-three were successfully reestablished by mid-1986. As of 1985, there was no organized regional commission in the Koszalin and Słupsk regions.[64] The Gdańsk, Wrocław, and Warsaw organizations were among the strongest in the country. By contrast, the organization in Upper Silesia and Zagłębie was said to be less active, in part because many of the workers were migrants from other parts of the country who had come to the region to make money and enjoyed a higher standard of living than average; as such, they were considerably less interested in politics.[65]

TKK Solidarity operated on the basis of a network of specialized cells. Among the most important was "the bureau," which kept track of the whereabouts of Solidarity leaders and newspaper editors, and coordinated contacts among other cells. The cell for interregional contacts handled materials and correspondence to and from the regional commissions. An information cell maintained a file of information that could be useful to the organization, including, for example, the names and addresses of people willing to let their apartments be used for clandestine meetings. A financial cell kept a budgetary record of the underground's income and expenses. An instructions cell obtained equipment needed for activities and prepared contacts for large-scale operations. A legalization cell forged official seals and stamps and produced fake documents. And a control cell investigated people offering their services and checked on all other vital information. TKK also had a special cell that maintained a communication system independent of the state-owned telephone and telex systems.[66]

Fighting Solidarity. Based in Wrocław, Fighting Solidarity split off from the main Solidarity organization in June 1982 to develop a more militant strategy. As of 1986, the organization claimed to have several hundred active members plus additional supporters and sympathizers, with centers of activity in Wrocław, Poznań, and Katowice.[67] Fighting Solidarity spelled out its fundamental premises in three manifestos published in its biweekly newspaper *Solidarność Walcząca* (which had a print run of 1,200 to 2,000 copies): "Solidarity Manifesto" in December 1982, "Our Visiting Card" in September 1983, and "The Ideological Principles and Program of Fighting Solidarity" in June 1987.

Fighting Solidarity rejected Western pluralism because it allegedly "treats the interests of the whole community as the sum of the interests of individuals." At the same time, it rejected communism because the kind of equality it generated was an equality in poverty and because it "realize[d] the interests of the Party and state at the expense of the individual."[68] In their place Fighting Solidarity preached "solidarism," which was said to care for the individual, emphasizing at the same time the communal bonds which tie individuals together. These ideas were traced in part to the general philosophy of the original Solidarity movement, but also to Christian social doctrine and the traditions of Polish independence. The final goal advocated was a "Polish Republic of Solidarity" founded on principles of self-management, with a market economy but safeguards to prevent the amassing of huge personal fortunes.[69] Such a republic would be characterized by parliamentary government, an independent judiciary, and safeguards for civil and minority rights.

Fighting Solidarity strongly supported independent youth movements and independent peace initiatives. In February 1984, for example, the organization's newspaper printed a short manifesto from the newly formed Peace and Solidarity pacifist group. Fighting Solidarity also issued appeals in Russian and Ukrainian directed at Soviet citizens on Poland's eastern borders. In June 1987 *Solidarność Walcząca* published a Polish translation of a sympathetic letter from Soviet citizens in Moscow and Leningrad.

Despite its reputation for militance, Fighting Solidarity eschewed terrorism or social violence. Moreover, it fostered good relations with other opposition organizations, including mainstream Solidarity, Niepo-dległość, and the Confederation of Independent Poland (under Leszek Moczulski). It also cooperated closely with KOS.

Because of the constant danger of arrest, Fighting Solidarity took the precaution of naming a substitute for everyone holding an important position in the organization. Andrzej Kołodziej, for example, was the designated substitute for Fighting Solidarity leader Kornel Morawiecki.

The organization suffered a serious setback in November 1987 when security forces in Wrocław arrested Morawiecki. Kołodziej, who then assumed the leadership post, was in turn arrested in January 1988. In early May both Morawiecki and Kołodziej were given the option of flying to Rome for needed medical treatment. Although the church had "guaranteed" them the possibility of returning to Poland, Morawiecki's subsequent attempt to do so failed, his passport was confiscated at Warsaw airport, and he was deported to Vienna. Kołodziej's designated successor, Andrzej Lesowski, was expected to take over leadership responsibilities. In September 1988 Morawiecki succeeded in returning to Poland under a false passport, passing himself off as a member of a Canadian human rights delegation.[70] Like other opposition organizations, Fighting Solidarity remained proscribed for a while even after the relegalization of TKK Solidarity.

Niepodległość. In January 1982 a monthly political journal began appearing under the title *Niepodległość (Independence)*. With a circulation of five thousand and a readership probably much wider, the journal quickly became a forum for political debate of a critical nature. It also became the nucleus of a political organization. In October 1983 *Niepodległość* published a draft party program, which was revised and made final in April 1984. On 11 November 1984 the group announced its formation of a political party (the Liberal-Democratic Party "Niepodległość"). The group set up branches in Warsaw, Kraków, and Katowice, and placed representatives in France and Sweden. Standing outside the mainstream of opposition thought, the group nonetheless had a tremendous impact on the opposition.

Niepodległość's program outlined a vision of a pluralistic parliamentary democracy based on a modified version of the Polish constitution of March 1921. More specifically, it advocated a bicameral legislature, a president elected by both houses of the legislature, an independent judiciary, a free-market economy, and constitutional guarantees to minorities. The centrally planned system was to be dismantled and the factories turned over to the workers, leaving them free to sell shares of stock if they chose to. There was to be no state support for factories or other enterprises, and private business and foreign investment were to be encouraged.

Unlike most other groups that emerged in opposition, Niepodległość accepted Poland's present borders unconditionally, thus renouncing any possible claims to the eastern territories annexed by the Soviet Union in 1939. The party spelled out a bold vision for Eastern Europe: the overthrow of communism throughout the region (including the USSR), the reunification of Germany, and the breakup of the USSR, with independence for its component nationalities.[71] Niepodległość ruled out the possibility of fundamental change in Poland except in association with change throughout the area, and therefore it encouraged Poles to help democratic opposition movements in other communist countries.

Tactically, Niepodległość initially called for the creation of a clandestine revolutionary party to overthrow the system by force.[72] Later, it placed its emphasis on encouraging passive resistance, the rejection of appeals to work harder, and the organization of strikes, demonstrations, and other disturbances.

The Committee of Social Resistance (KOS). Formed immediately after the proclamation of martial law, the Committee of Social Resistance (KOS) occupied a unique niche within the Polish opposition. Unlike most other opposition groups, which spelled out in detail their political aspirations and worked out explicit political programs, KOS limited its ideology to a demand for independence and pluralist democracy. KOS focused much more on the tactics of struggle, since that was the task at hand. In this context KOS denounced any form of collaboration with the communist regime, advocated the ostracism of collaborators, and urged the sabotage of economic sectors that did not produce goods and services needed by the community. With its emphasis on the tactics of struggle, KOS came to place an inherent value on struggle per se. "Each initiative," the group's journal wrote in 1982, "each situation in which a group of people takes into its own hands some fraction of responsibility for itself . . . each such act is an act of liberation in the real sense of the word and the realization of the goal of our fight, which is for people to regain their self-determination and dignity."[73]

Given KOS's eschewal of programmatic statements, it is not surprising that it united people of many different political viewpoints. Furthermore, KOS's journal frequently reprinted statements by various other opposition groups, including the Independent Peasant Movement, Peace and Solidarity, and Freedom-Justice-Independence (WSN). It also issued joint statements with Fighting Solidarity and the National Committee of Resistance of Private Farmers.

KOS involved thousands of people in its work. Its principal publication was the fortnightly journal, KOS, which had a print run of 6,000–15,000 copies, although more than thirty KOS periodicals appeared in various parts of Poland, including at least eight in Warsaw and seven in Kraków.[74]

Freedom-Justice-Independence (wsn). Most of the opposition groups active in Poland in the late 1980s were formed in 1982 during the harshest days of martial law. Freedom-Justice-Independence (WSN) was no exception, having been established in August 1982 in Warsaw. WSN's first programmatic statement boldly called for the establishment of an "underground state" based on self-management bodies in the factories and the local communities. The reference to self-management is a clue to WSN's socialist orientation. Indeed, the group traces its genealogy to the old Polish Socialist Party, and in its founding declaration it placed itself in the "tradition of the Polish Left, based on Christian, absolute ethical principles."[75] Like all the opposition groups, it advocated independence from the USSR and the overthrow of the communist power monopoly. Like most of them, it advocated a mixed economy, individual freedom, and the establishment of a parliamentary democracy.

Based in Warsaw, WSN was probably small. It does not seem to have had any organized branches elsewhere in the country. Its monthly journal, *Idee,* started appearing in February 1984. It also launched a second journal, *Nasz Komentarz,* which it published on an irregular basis in the late 1980s.

Polish Socialist Labor Party. Likewise looking back to socialist roots, the Polish Socialist Labor Party was formed in September 1981, with headquarters in Szczecin. Its founding program took as its starting point the thirteen demands of the Szczecin strike committee formulated during shipyard strikes in 1971. Only one of the demands—for an independent trade union—had at that time been granted.[76]

Polish Socialist Party. The Polish Socialist Party was called into being by forty-two activists in Warsaw on 15 November 1987. Its initial meeting was broken up by police, who cut off the electricity and detained several participants, as well as nine Western journalists.[77] The authorities argued that the organization, and hence its meeting, were illegal. The new Socialist Party challenged this assertion by noting that no law in Poland required the registration of political parties. Spokespersons also cited an internal document of the central committee's information department, which, curiously, said that "because of the special role of political parties in the process of shaping the form and contents of the state system, they are not subject to the same formal and legal limitations as other associations."[78] The intent of this provision with respect to the communist party and its "fraternal" parties is easy to surmise, as is the use to which the Polish Socialist Party wanted to put it. The director of Warsaw's Social and Administrative Department rejected the party's appeal, however, on the grounds that it had not observed the procedures prescribed by the *1932* Law on Associations!

The Polish Socialist Party sees itself as a revival of the party of the same name that was absorbed into the PUWP in 1948. Its founders included Jan Józef Lipski, Zuzanna Dabrowska, Andrzej Malanowski, Jan Kostecki, Grzegorz Myszka, Józef Pinior, and Władyław Goldfinger-Kunicki. The party claimed five hundred members at its founding. In spite of the party's name, its founders claimed that their teaching was closer to the social teachings of the Catholic church, above all to that of Pope John Paul II, than to Marxism.[79]

13 Grudnia. "13 Grudnia" (13 December), named for the date on which martial law was imposed and trade union pluralism suppressed, was a journal, not a political movement. It is included here because it provides a sharp contrast to most of the preceding groups. Published in Kraków, *13 Grudnia* expounded the free-market economy and Western-style laissez-faire, and it placed its emphasis squarely on individual liberty. One of its leading contributors was Mirosław Dzielski, who criticized Solidarity for failing to understand the importance and centrality of individual freedom. His argument was that the Polish opposition had been so socialized by the system that it continued to think in socialist/communist terms, to accept socialist/communist concepts as to what the state should deliver, and therefore remained trapped within the premises of a false ideology. Most of the Polish opposition, according to Dzielski, limited their ambition to making the state deliver on the promises held out by Marxist ideology (equality, self-managing democracy, material progress, guarantees against exploitation, and an end to alienation). Dzielski argued that the promises of a false ideology were themselves false, and he challenged the notion that the state should be expected to deliver *anything at all!*[80] Dzielski took as his models Ronald Reagan, Margaret Thatcher, and Helmut Kohl.

Wyzwolenie. Several of the foregoing parties and organizations underlined their determination to function as open, legal parties. Wyzwolenie (Liberation) was different. Founded in Warsaw in early 1984, Wyzwolenie was a clandestine cadre organization whose members took a secret oath of loyalty and discipline. Its organizational structure, membership, and activities were all secret.

In spite of these differences Wyzwolenie had some things in common with other underground groups. Like Niepodległość, it believed that Polish independence was a prerequisite to democratization, and that change throughout the Soviet bloc was a precondition for independence. Like Niepodległość and WSN, it favored the establishment of a parliamentary system. Like mainstream Solidarity and Fighting Solidarity, its vision embraced a role for self-management councils. Like Solidarity, Fighting Solidarity, and WSN, it favored a mixed economy. And like most of these groups, it advocated broad cooperation among the opposition. Its overall political coloration was thus social democratic.

Confederation for an Independent Poland (KPN). KPN was formed in September 1979 under the leadership of journalist-historian Leszek Moczulski. It was thus one of the few active groups in the underground that predated Solidarity. KPN was in fact the first underground organization in post-Gomułka years to call for the overthrow of communism and the establishment of genuine independence. Initially, these aspirations were viewed by many others in the opposition—let alone in Western academic circles—as "radical" and "unrealistic"; eventually, these demands became widespread in Poland.

Already in February 1979 Moczulski had launched the underground newspaper, *Gazeta Polska,* which became the mouthpiece of the KPN. In its first year of activity KPN set up branches in Warsaw, Lublin, Łódź, Kraków, and Wrocław. In late 1981, despite an earlier decision by KPN to suspend its activities, up to 80,000 new members joined the organization; most of these left when martial law was declared.[81] KPN assisted Solidarity by setting up Committees in Defense of Prisoners of Conscience.

In September 1980 Moczulski was arrested on charges of having slandered the Polish People's Republic; specifically, in an interview with the West German magazine *Der Spiegel* he predicted that the authorities would eventually ban Solidarity.[82] He remained in prison until amnestied in 1984. In March 1985 Moczulski was rearrested with four KPN associates. They were eventually tried a year later in March and April 1986. While in prison, Moczulski contracted mycosis and suffered an impairment of his hearing, and the other defendants also developed health problems. The defendants pleaded not guilty to the charge of operating an illegal organization, arguing that the Polish constitution does not bar the formation of political parties. Eventually, the court convicted all five, handing down a four-year prison sentence to Moczulski, and sentences of two years to thirty months to the other four defendants.[83]

KPN was conceived as a self-consciously conservative movement, proud of its ideological bond with traditional Catholic ethics. Every year KPN organized a pilgrimage march from Kraków to Kielce in honor of Marshal Piłsudski's troops, who made that march during World War I.[84] The Polish communist authorities viewed Piłsudski as an "enemy of socialism." Despite its hostility to the system, KPN declared its intention, from the beginning, of employing only legal means to overthrow the system. Throughout the trial in 1986 Moczulski and his associates insisted that their organization had never broken the law. On the other hand, Moczulski charged the Polish government with violating its oath, specifically in not holding the free elections promised at Yalta; these, he suggested, could be held now.

KPN held its third congress in Warsaw on 4 February 1989 with 150 delegates representing forty districts. Moczulski (freed by then) addressed the gathering, which was broken up by security police before it could complete its work.

Freedom and Peace Movement. On 18 December 1984 Marek Adamkiewicz was sentenced to two-and-a-half years in prison for refusing to take the military oath. Adamkiewicz said he was willing to perform military service but would not take an oath of loyalty to a foreign power. The section of the oath to which Adamkiewicz objected read as follows: "I swear to serve the Fatherland with all my strength, to defend steadfastly the rights of working people, which are guaranteed by the Constitution, to safeguard peace *in fraternal alliance with the Soviet Army and other allied armies.*"[85] In April 1985 a group of outraged young people, led by Jacek Czaputowicz, established the Freedom and Peace Movement to protest Adamkiewicz's imprisonment. The movement adopted a loose federal structure with branches in eleven cities (Warsaw, Kraków, Gdańsk, Wrocław, Szczecin, Gorzów, Katowice, Bydgoszcz, Częstochowa, Kołobrzeg, and Poznań), with six publishing their own bulletins. By 1987 the movement claimed an active cadre of one hundred to two hundred and a following of perhaps 30,000 sympathizers.[86] The movement focused its attention on the military oath, conscientious objection more broadly, peace and environmental issues, and human rights. It had no formal membership or hierarchy, and it relied on friendship and dedication to give it strength. Opposed to violence and force, it shunned the use of these means to further its objectives, preferring more peaceful expressions of will, such as sit-ins and hunger strikes. The emphasis was consistently on nonviolent action.[87] Although Freedom and Peace did not maintain a membership roster, all of its actions were open; hence, the more than 10,000 sympathizers who signed petitions in support of those imprisoned also noted their addresses.[88]

In 1987 Freedom and Peace organized protests against torture in Afghanistan, arrests in Czechoslovakia, Hungary, and Yugoslavia, air and water pollution from the Siechnice steelworks near Wrocław, the construction of a nuclear plant in Żarnowiec, and the use of old Wehrmacht bunkers in southwest Poland for the storage of nuclear waste.[89] The movement also championed the rights of Jehovah's Witnesses to conscientious objection. And in May 1987 it conducted a three-day conference on "International Peace and the Helsinki Agreement," attended by about 215 persons from more than a dozen countries, including Czechoslovakia, Poland, Yugoslavia, the United States, Great Britain, Italy, and West Germany.[90]

The communists seem to have been particularly angered by Freedom and Peace's campaign to honor and popularize Otto Schimek, a Wehrmacht soldier who refused to participate in the liquidation of Poles in World War II, deserted his squad for that reason, and was subsequently executed by his own side. Freedom and Peace saw the Schimek case as a means of overcoming the deep distrust and hatred between Poles and Germans, which it accused the communist regime of actively fostering. As if to prove the accuracy of that charge, authorities cordoned off the roads to Machowa (where Schimek is buried) when Freedom and Peace tried to organize a pilgrimage there in November 1986, beat up several participants, and arrested some.[91]

The steady pressure from Freedom and Peace seemed to have had an effect. In June 1988 *Trybuna Ludu* announced that a bill had been submitted to the Sejm, providing for "substitute service" for conscientious objectors "in specified enterprises for the benefit of the natural environment, social welfare, the communal economy, and the water economy."[92] The bill was subsequently passed into law.

In December 1988 Freedom and Peace endured a split in its ranks when a group around the newspaper *Czas Przyszły* (Future Tense) broke away. The split was described as relatively amicable. In a programmatic statement issued soon after, the splinter group declared its intention to work for a restriction of the military budget, a curtailment in the length of military service, greater rights for Poland's national minorities, better environmental safeguards, and social, economic, and political pluralism. Future Tense also declared itself in favor of a united Europe.[93]

The Orange Alternative.

Question: What does "happening" mean?
Answer: Happening is just what happens to happen.
Question: Do you set up happenings in order to expose the totalitarianism of the system under which we live?
Answer: I do them because I do them.
Question: But one does things because of [some reason], or for something.
Answer: Well, yes. When I was preparing for the gnome happening, I assumed that we would have a good time, with sweets and streamers.[94]

As this dialogue suggests, the Orange Alternative was no ordinary group. The brainchild of Waldemar Frydrych, alias "the Major," the Orange Alternative was an inchoate Dadaist group that took to staging mock celebrations of the system in order to make the communist authorities look foolish. When Solidarity asked Poles to boycott the government's referendum on 27 November 1987, the Orange Alternative issued a manifesto exhorting the citizens of Wrocław (where it was based) to vote *twice*—and make Wrocław "the city of 200 percent turnout."[95] On another occasion the Major drilled his adherents for two weeks, then assembled five thousand students dressed in red by the orangutans at the zoo to sing Stalinist hymns and wave red flags.[96] On another occasion the Major dressed his followers in Santa Claus outfits and led a parade; the Santas carried a banner: "Santa Claus—the hope of the reform."[97]

Banners and slogans are the pabulum of political mobilization, of course, as the Major showed. Among those hoisted by the Orange Alternative:

More People's Councils—fewer hospitals![98]
The Warsaw Pact—an Avant-Garde of Peace![99]
Let's try to make our town outdo Los Angeles—let's dress colorfully![100]
Toilet paper R.I.P.—We can also wipe the government's![101]
Molotov, yes! Ribbentrop, no![102]

In June 1988 a thousand young people gathered with trumpets and horns and, after an appropriate amount of noise, elected Jaruzelski "King of Poland." Pleased with that accomplishment, they staged another election for "Mister Poland," electing a policeman. His election was greeted by the Orange Alternative flock with gleeful shouts of "Down with the opposition!"[103]

The Orange Alternative loved to "celebrate" the police. On Police-man's Day the Orange Alternative brought an eighteen-foot "flower" to police headquarters, serenaded the police with guitars, festooned patrol cars and officers with flowers and decorations, and even danced for them while singing "Happy Birthday!" On another occasion, after the Orange Alternative had celebrated the Bolshevik Revolution and its partici-pants were released from prison, they smiled sweetly at their jailers and shouted, "Thanks for a nice evening" and "All the best."[104]

The Major, who had earned a degree in the history of art, once de-scribed Polish communism as "socialist surrealism." His aim, he said, was "to treat the [communist] political system of Poland as a work of art."[105] Or, as he put it on another occasion: "It is not a question of politi-cal changes, but of psychological change."[106] If people mock the police and laugh at the government, they will lose their fear of the authorities.

This approach may have been contagious, for in October 1988 a group of Warsaw University students not connected with the Orange Alterna-tive attired themselves in red (some down to their socks) and marched to Dzierzhinsky Square bearing portraits of Lenin and procommunist banners. Once there, they proceeded to plaster posters of Lenin on pub-lic buildings. Riot police attacked them and tore down the posters, to which the students responded, "Long live the police!" and "The party's fighting, and it's a winner!"[107] The following month several hundred stu-dents in Warsaw celebrated the seventy-first anniversary of the Bolshevik Revolution by staging a pantomime "storming" of department stores in the city center (redubbing the largest of them "the Winter Palace"). The pantomime revolutionaries came equipped with a cardboard model of the cruiser *Aurora*, which had fired the first shots to signal the start of the revolution in 1917. Rafel Szymczyk, one of the students, became the first Pole since the war to be arrested for carrying a portrait of Lenin in a public demonstration.[108]

Other Groups. Various other active groups were in the Polish politi-cal underground, some more important than others. The number would include the Independent Students' Union, Rural Solidarity (virtually nonexistent by 1987), the Congress of National Solidarity, the Worker Political Group, the Polish Politics Group, the Alternative Society Move-ment in Gdańsk, the Movement for Real Politics, and, allegedly at one time, cells of Young Piłsudskiites.[109] There have also been environmen-tal groups, such as the Polish Ecological Club and the Polish Ecological Party, both based in Kraków with overlapping memberships.[110] In what may have been an abortive attempt to set up a Stalinist-Maoist party in Poland, Kazimierz Mijal, who had escaped to Albania in 1966 to set up a "rival" Communist Party of Poland with a Maoist accent, tried to sneak back into Poland in November 1984 using fake documents. He was apprehended at the border.[111]

Parallel Society as Civil Society

Not all independent associations arose on independent initiative; some were outgrowths of official associations that refused to knuckle under in 1982. With the proclamation of martial law, all unions, associations, and professional organizations were suspended, but some refused to shut down. In early 1982, for example, the suspended Association of Polish Journalists issued guidelines for its members:

> If you can continue your journalistic work in the way you did before martial law, do so without bad feelings; your audience will back you up.
>
> [But] if you praise martial law and try to win for it social acceptance, if you attack those who cannot defend themselves, if you provide false or biased information . . . be sure that you will lose face and your reputation in the eyes of your audience. . . . Besides, don't be surprised if you'll have to face consequences one day.[112]

In March 1982 the regime dissolved the Association of Polish Journalists and replaced it with the Association of Journalists of the People's Republic of Poland. Some 40 percent of the earlier association's members joined the new group, while the suppressed Association of Polish Journalists continued its work underground.

In response to martial law actors and performing artists boycotted officially sponsored shows, and in retaliation the regime banned the Association of Polish Plastic Artists on 20 June 1983. The government replaced it with a series of specialized unions for sculptors, graphic designers, painters, and others, which most potential members refused to join.

When writers produced a code of conduct urging authors who published in official channels to demand that changes made by the censor be marked in the text, the regime dissolved the Polish Writers Union (on 18 August 1983) and created a replacement association with the same name. Writers who refused to join the new PWU were subject to higher income taxes than members; even so, most of the members of the new association were party members and unknown writers.

In early 1982 a group of professors at the University of Warsaw likewise issued a code of conduct, suggesting in particular that scholars refuse to accept official prizes, decline to participate in official events, ostracize newly appointed school administrators, and refuse any research collaboration with the new appointees.

Musicians and composers also issued a code of conduct in the spring of 1982, stating among other things: "We also must immediately start to create an unofficial circulation of music. It is possible and realistic, and it is also realistic and possible to create a financial basis for this activity. . . . Our professional activity does not have to be organized in the offices of the rulers."[113]

In this way the cultural intelligentsia withdrew from the system and set the stage for the development of a lively underground culture paralleling the underground political scene. It is important to stress that the primary impulse for the creation of the underground cultural scene was the desire to preserve the nation's integrity and to defy the moral torpor of the regime.

By 1988 perhaps no part of communal life remained in which parallel society had not penetrated, whether one speaks of education, science, public health, or the arts.

As early as April 1982 the Independent Education Team was formed in Warsaw. With help from KOS, the team organized the publication and distribution of educational materials, established independent networks of lecturers for self-education groups, and began training lecturers for these groups. Later, on 19 July 1982 the National Education Council was formed at Solidarity's suggestion, although the body was not affiliated with Solidarity. Its functions were similar to those of the Independent Education Team. About the same time, the new samizdat magazine, *Tu i Teraz*, devoted exclusively to independent education, began appearing in Warsaw with a circulation of 3,000–6,000.[114] The self-education movement involved hundreds of study circles and attracted people from all sectors of society—workers, peasants, students, even schoolchildren.[115] It was strongest in Warsaw, Lublin, Wrocław, and other towns where Solidarity had been well-entrenched. Underground libraries also developed, by and large set up spontaneously.

Closely linked to the self-education movement was the independent Social Committee of Research, founded in the spring of 1983 with Solidarity's endorsement. The committee encouraged and provided financial support for research on subjects not supported by the regime, including the humanities, ecology, medicine, sociology, and economics.

Where public health was concerned, certain physicians in Kraków published a report on injuries inflicted by the police on participants in the early demonstrations against martial law. Some physicians became involved in efforts on behalf of political prisoners. In February 1984 the Social Commission on Health emerged as an independent representative of medical personnel. The commission established a quarterly journal, *Zeszyty Niezależnej Myśli Lekarskiej*, with contributions from some of the leading medical specialists in Poland. The journal also published some classified documents about public health.[116] The Social Commission on Health and the Social Committee of Research jointly established the Working Group for Environmental Protection, which devoted the first issue of its samizdat bulletin, *Zagrożenie* (5 May 1986), to the Chernobyl disaster.

But in some ways it was in the arts where independence and experimentation went the furthest. The internationally renowned composer Krysztof Penderecki had already provided a model by composing a choral work, *Lacrimosa*, on commission for Solidarity in 1980. But independent culture did not operate only on this level. There were independent art exhibits in private apartments (illegal in view of the law prohibiting unregistered gatherings of more than six people). Other artists resorted to "suitcase art," painting suitcase-size pictures and packing them for impromptu exhibition at the next social gathering.[117] Similarly, home theater filled a vacuum: as a precaution, the prospective audience arranged to arrive at a staggered pace in groups of twos and threes. Independent repertory groups were also established on a legal basis in Warsaw, Kraków, Lublin, and Poznań. Other theatrical performances were presented in churches.

An underground music scene also developed. One underground music ensemble, the Traugott Philharmonia, was named for one of the leaders of the 1863 Polish Uprising who had been hanged by the Russians.

Videocassette recorders gave life to an underground film market. Some underground films were originally made with official sanction, only to be banned by the authorities when they saw the final product. In May 1985 the underground publisher NOWA created a video division, and between 1985 and 1986 it released five movies made officially but subsequently banned, including Ryszard Bugajski's *The Interrogation*, which deals with repression and torture in a Stalinist prison.[118]

Most of the independent culture scene was a spontaneous, grassroots affair. But the Committee for Independent Culture, formed in the winter of 1982–83, tried to stimulate and encourage independent culture with financial support. This support included subsidies to independent publishers.[119]

Finally, some mention should be made of the efforts by students to obtain legalization of the Independent Students' Association. Such an association was registered in 1981, and as of April 1981 it claimed that 25 percent of Polish university students were members. During its period of legality the union pushed for expansion of the autonomy of universities. It was banned on 5 January 1982. After that, it remained dormant until January 1987, when activists from nineteen Polish institutions of higher learning met in Warsaw to revive the association. The resurrected Independent Students' Association staged demonstrations in February 1987 and February 1988 in Kraków, in March 1988 in Warsaw and Kraków, and, with university permission, in October 1988 in Warsaw, Kraków, and Wrocław.[120]

On occasion, the Jaruzelski government was willing to register public associations established on independent initiative. In July 1987, for instance, government spokesperson Jerzy Urban announced that registration would be granted to an economic association in Warsaw and to an industrial association in Kraków; both associations proposed to act as consultants for private entrepreneurs. In October 1988 an independent political club called Dziekania, led by former Sejm deputy Stanisław Stomma, was registered.[121] All the same, however, when registration was sought for a Polish-U.S. Friendship Society in early 1988, permission was denied.

Underground Publishing

The importance of underground publishing for the maintenance of parallel society should not be underestimated. Underground publications were the vehicles for self-education, the arenas for strategic and tactical debate, and the conduits for news and useful information for everyday life. One can safely say that without underground publishing, no parallel society could have existed.

An estimated 1,100–1,300 different underground periodicals appeared in Poland from 1981 to 1986, with some surviving only briefly, and others continuing for as many as four hundred or more issues.[122] Most underground periodicals were sponsored by Solidarity or one of its subsidiary bodies. The underground press also included about forty newspapers published by secondary school students and a women's newspaper, *Amazonka*, which appeared in Bydgoszcz. About 20 percent of underground papers were weeklies, another 20 percent biweeklies, perhaps 35 percent monthlies, and most of the remaining 25 percent bimonthlies and quarterlies.[123] Their average circulation was between 500 and 2,000, although *Tygodnik Mazowsze*, which during the era of Solidarity's illegality was widely treated as the official Solidarity organ, reached a peak of 80,000 copies a week in 1985.

In 1981 and 1982 many in the opposition hoped that the underground press would in time *replace* the official media as a source of information for Poles. But a Solidarity poll taken in 1985 found that some 80 percent of Poles relied on the state media for most information—leaving the underground press the tasks of supplementing and correcting the official media.[124] Initially, the underground press devoted almost all of its attention to internal affairs, above all union affairs, news about the opposition, and the presentation of political viewpoints. In time, however, the underground press devoted a greater portion of its pages to discussing more general national affairs and even to reporting on international developments. "It's amazing," reflected one of *Tygodnik Mazowsze*'s senior editors in 1987, "in that we've been writing far more about developments in the Soviet Union than [is written] in the official media. People are reading *Tygodnik Mazowsze* to learn about Gorbachev's reforms."[125]

The communists fought back in various ways. Arrests and confiscations were one method.[126] Another was to fabricate underground periodicals, inserting one or two forged texts with disinformation.[127] Still another method was to offer concessions. A signal concession came in 1987 when the regime authorized publication of the first independent secular journal in communist Poland, *Res Publica*. Though critical of the government, *Res Publica* advocated cooperation with the Soviet Union and was, in any case, subject to censorship.[128]

Underground book publishing was also important, bringing some seven to ten titles to the public each week, or about 400–450 titles annually in the late 1980s.[129] The average print run was 800–2,000 copies, but some books were published in editions of 5,000–7,000 copies, with a few editions running up to 10,000 copies. In addition to publishing original works of documentation, political and economic analysis, history, poetry, prose, and instruction booklets, underground publishers issued reprints of books and essays by Polish writers in exile and translations of works by Russian, Ukrainian, Czech, and Yugoslav dissidents. These books often enjoyed a wide circulation. In addition, the existence of the underground press prompted state publishing houses to publish books that otherwise would not have been published, such as Maurycy Mochnacki's *History of the Polish Insurrection, 1830–1831* and George Orwell's *1984*.

Ted Kamiński estimated that between 10,000 and 30,000 people were involved in underground publishing in the late 1980s.[130] Since Polish law required that all citizens hold (legal) jobs, work in this sector was strictly after-hours, and those involved said that sheer fatigue was a greater problem than actual police intervention. Still, precautions were necessary. Some publishers frequently changed their names to confuse the police, or they published books without the date of publication. Members of the editorial staff of *Tygodnik Mazowsze* "never, but never, use[d] telephones."[131] For those underground publishers who were unfortunate enough to be discovered, there existed the Insurance Fund for Independent Publications, founded in early 1986, which helped insurees to get reestablished on release from prison or in the event of the confiscation of equipment or issues.[132]

Underground publishing is expensive. Some financing came from Solidarity, thus from union dues; probably the bulk came from abroad: Polish émigré communities and associations such as the Polish-American Congress, the Brussels Solidarity Committee, Western trade unions, and Western foundations.[133]

Underground Solidarity's Continued Struggle, 1985–1988

The amnesty act of 1984 did not reflect a change of strategy on the regime's part but a new tactic in a war of nerves. This was clearly shown by the fact that security forces continued to arrest and interrogate Solidarity leaders in 1985. Early in the year seven Solidarity activists were arrested after a meeting with Wałęsa and charged with undertaking activities aimed at public unrest. Three of them (Bogdan Lis, Adam Michnik, and Władysław Frasyniuk) were subsequently tried[134] and sent to prison for two-and-a-half to three-and-a-half years. Lis had been released from prison only the previous December under the amnesty.[135] Jacek Kuroń and Henryk Wujec both received three-month jail sentences for participation in a May Day counterdemonstration. Kuroń's sentence was subsequently overturned, but in October he was arrested on new charges, along with Zbigniew Romaszewski (head of Radio Solidarity) and Janusz Onyszkiewicz (a former Solidarity press spokesperson).[136] In June a member of Solidarity's underground leadership, Tadeusz Jedynak, was apprehended. Wałęsa himself was threatened with a three-year prison term if he continued his activities.[137]

In late April Solidarity leaders across Poland were taken in for questioning, presumably in an effort to prevent a mass demonstration by Solidarity on 1 May. If that was the intent, the effort failed. Some 10,000 Solidarity supporters marched in Warsaw on 1 May, with a similar demonstration in Gdańsk. The May Day parade sparked three days of demonstrations in which nearly six hundred people were arrested.[138]

With the decline in the Polish standard of living, the economy remained high on the agenda for both Solidarity and the regime. In August 1985 Solidarity released a 500-page analysis of the state of the nation, detailing Solidarity's views on law, repression, economic policy, education, and cultural policy. Wałęsa contacted the authorities and proposed a meeting to discuss it. The reaction from the authorities was "scornful." By year's end, Wałęsa was despondent: "The effectiveness of our work is not very great," he mused. "Until now, we were fighting with the authorities. Now we are looking for different methods, but we don't have any. If we find some, they must be better orchestrated and better understood. . . . I am faithful to my ideals, but for others, if they think other methods are more effective, I don't have any more arguments for stopping them."[139]

Although the boycott of the Sejm elections in 1985 represented a successful show of strength for underground Solidarity, the opposition increasingly felt stunted and in need of a new strategy. The underground journal kos, for instance, wrote in August that Polish public opinion was dominated by two views that produced deep pessimism: "nothing can be done, and things cannot go on this way. The first view is very widespread and concisely expresses the belief that the opposition is powerless. The second, no less widespread, derives from an appraisal of the present state of the nation and its prospects."[140] The samizdat monthly *Replika*, published by Fighting Solidarity, echoed this appraisal, arguing that underground Solidarity had to adapt to a changed situation and, in particular, to encourage more individual initiative in the opposition and less reliance on directives or suggestions from the Solidarity leadership.[141]

Wałęsa concluded that "a new situation" had emerged in Poland and that it demanded a new strategy on Solidarity's part. The new situation was a product of several factors: first, the feeling in the opposition that mere survival was not enough and that it was necessary to find ways of pressing for the legalization of pluralism; second, the increased international stature of underground Solidarity through its affiliation with the International Confederation of Free Trade Unions and the World Confederation of Labor, and the bestowal of the Robert F. Kennedy Memorial Prize on Bujak and Michnik, both events transpiring in 1986; third, the release of the remaining 225 political prisoners in September 1986, including Bujak (who had been arrested only on 31 May) and Michnik;[142] and fourth, the unfolding of a new political context in Gorbachev's USSR.[143]

Underground Solidarity settled on a new strategy by the end of September with the decision to establish the Provisional Council for open operations. The council consisted of Borusewicz and Lis from Gdańsk;

Bujak from Warsaw; Frasyniuk and Pinior from Wrocław; Jedynak from Katowice; and Janusz Pałubicki from Poznań. By coming into the open without dismantling any underground structures, Solidarity hoped to force the government into a new position.[144] The underground journal KOS explained the strategy:

> The recent about-face in the East bloc leaders' strategy has given us an opportunity that can only be exploited one way: by embarking on a policy of faits accomplis. We must create social facts that the authorities will be forced to accept in the name of the peaceful strategy that they now advocate, or they will be forced to counter with violence, which would automatically reveal their true intentions. We must exploit the present cease-fire to create overt opposition centers and legal groups that would exert pressure on the authorities; we ought to implement our human and civil rights with all the means at our disposal. The creation of the Provisional Council of Solidarity is the first step along this path.[145]

Predictably, the authorities reacted by declaring the new council illegal and by summoning its members for questioning.

Within Solidarity, however, there was criticism of the new council. One high-ranking Solidarity activist called the move "premature" and fretted that it would create a dualism in leadership with the TKK.[146] Some lower-level activists drew the same conclusion and complained that the underground union no longer had a "coordinated leadership"; this weakness, in turn, was causing the leadership to lose touch with its grass roots.[147] Solidarity's advisers drew the obvious conclusions and told the leadership that unless it changed its modus operandi, it risked losing its influence.[148] By October 1987 these doubts had reached the point of provoking an organizational crisis, which was resolved by disbanding the two governing bodies of Solidarity (the underground TKK and the public Provisional Council) and replacing them with the National Executive Council. Named to the council were Wałęsa (chair), Bujak, Jerzy Diuzniewski, Frasyniuk, Stefan Jurczyk, Lis, Andrzej Milczanowski, Pałubicki, and Stanisław Węglarz.[149]

Under Polish law a newly formed association was required to file an application for registration. If this was turned down by the regional court, the decision could be appealed to the Supreme Court. During this entire period the association was legally entitled to operate. Even if the application were ultimately rejected by the Supreme Court, however, the association could resume the process from scratch and reapply for registration, thus giving itself a new breathing spell of provisional legality.

This legal loophole inspired a new Solidarity strategy, and when strikes broke out at the Gdańsk shipyards in May 1988 Solidarity militants were able to circulate freely in the shipyards to discuss the situation with the disaffected workers.[150]

Solidarity leaders were also looking for other methods of struggle. Beginning in 1984 the government mixed an increasing dose of liberalism into its political recipe: select private initiatives were allowed; certain private associations were registered; long-suppressed books were published by state publishing houses; and even the regime press started printing articles highly critical of aspects of the regime's policies. A journalist from *Tygodnik Mazowsze* explained the dilemma: "It was simple to fight repression. Now the direct goal has somehow disappeared. It's difficult psychologically. The heroism isn't called for."[151]

Indeed, the official press was becoming increasingly critical and open about the country's problems. The liberal press law of 1981 was, of course, revised. But the revised version was, all the same, more liberal than the press law of the Gierek era. And in the political realm Jaruzelski proposed in 1986 the creation of a new Social Consultative Council in which the opposition could talk directly with the country's top leaders, and he actively sought out prominent figures in the opposition to take seats on the council.[152] Despite vocal criticism by many in the opposition, the council began its work in December 1986. That same year the government belatedly approved an earlier Solidarity proposal to create an office of ombudsman, and in November 1987, Ewa Łętowska, a professor of law, was appointed to this position.

The policy, which could be called "controlled liberalism," emphasized concessions without power-sharing. And the concessions grew. By 1988 even Adam Michnik, a leading oppositionist, was allowed to publish in the official press, signing his own name.[153] But these concessions sowed doubts in the ranks of Solidarity, whose leaders now openly wondered if they had been finessed by the flexible Jaruzelski.

Perhaps the best way to explain the country's mood vis-à-vis Solidarity at the close of 1987 is to say that while Solidarity continued to enjoy broad support and popularity, that support was often passive and tempered by doubts, despondency, and a sense of futility. The strikes of April and May 1988 changed this picture—first, by demonstrating that passivity was not tantamount to the evanescence of support; and second, by reinvigorating the underground union.

There were hints of trouble early in 1988. In January, after the government raised food prices 40 percent (the sharpest price hike since 1982), some three thousand Poles demonstrated in Gdańsk.[154] Five weeks later,

Kraków was the scene of confrontation between students and police as the students rallied to commemorate the twentieth anniversary of the 1968 campus disturbances; similar rallies were held in at least three other Polish cities.[155] But the strikes that were to shake several larger cities in early May were triggered, ironically, by Poland's *official* trade union, which in its first strike action ever shut down bus and tram service in Bydgoszcz for twelve hours on 25 April in an effort to obtain higher wages. That strike ended when the authorities granted the strikers a 63 percent pay increase.[156]

But that action ignited the strike that broke out the following day at Nowa Huta's Lenin steelworks, which was in turn followed by others.[157] Those strikes erupted spontaneously, and even Solidarity's leaders were caught by surprise. Strike organizers reported that between 12,000 to 18,000 of the Nowa Huta plant's 32,000 workers supported the strike.[158] The strikers demanded a 50 percent pay increase as well as a 6,000 złoty increase in monthly checks for all pensioners and health workers in Poland. In the following days further strikes broke out at the Dolmel electronics plant in Wrocław, the small Bochnia steel mill east of Kraków, and the Lenin shipyard in Gdańsk, while an effort to organize a strike at the Ursus tractor factory in Warsaw petered out.[159] In addition, workers at a steel and armaments plant in Stalowa Wola went on strike on 29 April but accepted a government pay offer the following day and resumed work.[160]

The authorities tried to settle with strikers in Nowa Huta and Gdańsk with offers of pay increases, but strikers at both plants refused because the authorities failed to grant other demands, in particular, the release of four detained Solidarity activists and the relegalization of Solidarity.[161] At one point the government seemed to accept the Catholic church's offer to send mediators to work for a solution. But even while seeming to concede to a degree, government spokesperson Jerzy Urban accused the strikers of "terrorist activities" and said that Wałęsa was threatening the nation with "bloody revolution."[162] And as the church-appointed mediators began their difficult task, security forces attacked the steel mill in Nowa Huta and crushed the ten-day strike there by force. In Gdańsk the authorities withdrew their offer of a pay increase, ringed the shipyard with security forces, and threatened reprisals unless the strike was terminated. The number of strikers at the shipyard had declined in the interim, and on 10 May the remaining thousand Gdańsk strikers left the plant peaceably.[163] Meanwhile, the government passed a new law forbidding the official trade unions from calling strikes without permission from their central leadership in Warsaw.[164]

Yet the strikes of April and May transformed the national mood. Shortly after they ended, the underground weekly *Przeglad Wiadomości Agencyjnych* commented: "What took place at the end of April and the beginning of May is only the rumbling of thunder as the storm approaches."[165] The warning was explicit; yet even at that late date many Western observers dismissed this and other references to the approaching political earthquake as "wishful thinking," seeing in the situation "nothing new."[166]

The strikes were accompanied by a new Solidarity membership drive in Nowa Huta, where a large number of membership cards were handed out. Thus, the strikes that had been spearheaded by young workers brought both new blood into the union and gave it a renewed sense of drive.[167]

This new sense of motivation and the country's plummeting standards of living contributed to the outbreak of more serious strikes in August. These began when coal miners at the July Manifesto mine near Jastrzębie went out on 16 August, inflamed by the sudden and unilateral withdrawal of a pay raise granted after the May strikes.[168] The miners now demanded not only the restoration of their bonuses but the relegalization of Solidarity. Strikes quickly spread to four other Silesian coal mines, Szczecin's port and public transport systems, and, on 22 August, to the Lenin shipyard in Gdańsk and three smaller shipyards nearby. By 23 August strikes had spread to twenty locations, idling 75,000 to 89,000 workers. In the first nine days the strikes were estimated to have slashed Polish coal exports for 1988 by 148,000 tons, costing the government some $7.4 million.[169] Additional losses were entailed by the strikes at the ports and other enterprises, and authorities fretted about the possibility of a permanent diversion of cargo traffic from Polish ports to "more reliable" transit points.[170]

At first the government struck a tough pose. "The phantom of self-rule and anarchy is being born again,"[171] General Czesław Kiszczak, minister of the interior, said in a televised address, as he imposed special security measures on three regions and sent large convoys of police vehicles toward the main trouble spots. Police broke down the barricades at the Mieszko coal mine and ended the strike by force. In Szczecin, police occupied a striking bus depot and forced its occupiers to surrender. Riot police also used force to end strikes at the Moszczenica mine at Jastrzębie, the Morcinek mine at Kaczyce, and the Mysłowice mine near Katowice.[172] At the Lenin shipyard in Gdańsk, masses of police ringed the works in a dramatic show of force. But even as a number of strikes ended (some peaceably), new ones broke out, and the central demand was always the same—the relegalization of Solidarity, a demand the regime branded "totally unrealistic."[173] As in April and May, the August 1988 strikes were spearheaded by workers who had been too young to participate in the 1980 strikes. The older generation seemed burned by the experiences of December 1981 and its aftermath, and in many cases they offered passive approval rather than energetic support.[174] But this point should not be overdrawn; all generations in Poland agreed that "things cannot go on like this."

On 18 August Jaruzelski declared himself willing to meet with strikers at the port of Szczecin. On 22 August the Council of Ministers met to review the situation. On 28 August the central committee approved a resolution to initiate roundtable talks with the opposition, which led directly to two rounds of talks between Wałęsa and Minister of Interior Kiszczak. At the same time, the official magazine *Konfrontacje,* which aired views that were not likely to be found elsewhere in the official press, published an interview with Wałęsa. Using this forum, Wałęsa suggested that Solidarity might accept a compromise formula, agreeing to changes in Solidarity's organizational form in exchange for legalization.[175] In a simultaneous demonstration of his good faith Wałęsa summoned his authority and charisma to defuse the few remaining strikes in the first week of September. In the course of their preliminary talks Kiszczak and Wałęsa agreed to hold more elaborate roundtable discussions. The agenda and organization of these talks were worked out in January and early February 1989, and they took place 6 February–5 April.[176] These meetings eventually bore fruit in April 1989 with the relegalization of Solidarity. Other hitherto underground groups were also granted registration. Gradually, parallel society achieved legality, official society withered away, and hitherto parallel society became coterminous with society itself. And in the wake of these changes, the fundamental laws of property rights and laws concerning the role of religion in society were also rewritten. These processes, in combination, were *revolutionary,* in the sense given to the term by Theda Skocpol.[177]

Conclusion

Strikes, demonstrations, and other protest actions have a dramatic quality and therefore tend to seize headlines. But they are only the tip of the iceberg. Specific grievances would frequently be registered— for the withdrawal of price increases, for pay hikes, for the release of specific persons from prison. But the limited nature of some of these demands should not diminish the central point, which is that such actions, increasingly, were either organized by or came to involve underground organizations, especially Solidarity. Protest actions proved one method of struggle on the part of a self-aware parallel society that had been consciously and deliberately encouraged by leading figures in the underground. And, just as the underground hoped, that parallel society provided the nucleus of an emergent noncommunist society in Poland. Kulerski put it this way in 1986:

> We have achieved something unprecedented in the history of communist systems: we have created a civil underground that is campaigning without violence and that has now been in existence for many years, and we must not give it up.
>
> It ought to have the broadest scope and be as varied as possible. A uniform, hierarchical structure is much less able to resist police operations; it is far less mobile and active; and, above all, it corresponds far less to the needs of society. Poland needs independent labor unions and a variety of different social centers that would be concerned with the observance of law, cultural matters, education, and health. Political groups are necessary as well as organizations such as Freedom and Peace, [bodies representing] ethnic minorities, and youth associations. Such variety is normal in a democratic society; and if we are to build such a democratic society for a future independent Poland, then we must start to lay the foundations now—in the form of an underground society.[178]

5. Independent Activism in Czechoslovakia, Hungary, and Romania

Independent activism in Eastern Europe has taken different forms over the years. In the immediate postwar period, when noncommunist parties continued to exist in most of these countries, legal activism concentrated on trying to maintain a parliamentary form of government. The experiences of Poland, Czechoslovakia, Hungary, and Yugoslavia provide examples of this.[1] Others tried to resist communist rule through armed insurgency (for example, in Poland), while Kosovo's Albanians resisted reincorporation into Yugoslavia for ethnic rather than political reasons.[2] The "old dissent" was thus anticommunist or irredentist. As a result of the terror of the Stalinist era, independent activism largely disappeared in the 1950s and 1960s, leading Zygmunt Bauman to conclude that the possibility of dissent was largely evaporating in Eastern Europe, that dissenting intellectuals could not expect to evoke anything but apathy among the general public, and that the communist systems in the region had developed an "immunity" to revolutionary upheavals.[3]

When independent activism revived in the 1970s it had a new content. Activists no longer aspired to overthrow the communist systems: the lessons of 1956 and 1968 were very clear. What they sought, thus, was more limited, in two senses. First, as Vladimir Kusin notes, most East European dissent in the 1970s and early 1980s was defensive in character, seeking to safeguard basic human rights and equality of treatment.[4] Second, it tended to be issue-oriented, as seen in the efforts to obtain alternative service for conscientious objectors (in East Germany),[5] pressure the authorities to take effective measures to halt environmental damage (in East Germany, Czechoslovakia, and Hungary), and obtain price hikes and social benefits (for workers in Poland and Romania).

When Polish workers went on strike in late July 1980 it was clear that something dramatic was taking place. The demand that Solidarity be registered as an independent trade union was, to be sure, issue-specific, but it augured far-reaching changes throughout the system. As a direct result of Solidarity's emergence and under the impact of its influence, independent activism in Eastern Europe began to change—drawing encouragement in Czechoslovakia and Romania from the Gorbachev tide to the East. It changed in three chief respects. First, activists were increasingly inclined to zero in on what they saw as the fundamental issue—the democratization of political and social life in their countries. Second, activists across issue spheres increasingly maintained contact with each other, resulting in an alliance among environmentalists, pacifists, feminists, and human rights activists, and, to a certain degree, a fusing of their energies.[6] And third, beginning in 1978 there were periodic contacts between and repeated instances of cooperation among dissident activists in East Germany, Poland, Czechoslovakia, and Hungary.

The situation in Czechoslovakia (until late 1988) and Romania under Ceauşescu was significantly different from that in Poland: independent activists in these countries could not mobilize large numbers of people, as Solidarity demonstrably could. The same was true of Hungary until late 1988; hence the opposition there, as in the other countries, concentrated on pointing the way to alternative thinking. János Kis, a founding editor of the Hungarian samizdat journal *Beszélő*, conceded as much in a 1986 interview.

I do not think that the role of the opposition in Hungary is to marshal social forces. . . . The main thing to understand about the Hungarian opposition is that its conceivable role in the near future is not parallel to that of the Polish one in smaller dimensions. When the Polish opposition organized in the middle of the 1970s, there was a clear polarization of power and society and clear decomposition of the power structure. In that situation the opposition could really marshal the majority of the politically attentive and active public behind it. In Hungary, the general mood, although rather pessimistic about the capacities of the government to overcome the crisis and to put serious and important reforms into effect, is that of a strong attachment to stability due to Hungary's special situation. . . . This means that social movements begin to form in Hungary not behind the opposition, but between the opposition and the government. So the aim of the opposition is rather more to try to elucidate the situation, to show alternatives, to stimulate discussion and political thinking. It is rather more like an effective independent press in the West than a social movement or an organization.[7]

This analysis also aptly describes the situation in Czechoslovakia and Yugoslavia in the closing years of the 1980s, and to some extent that in Romania at that time, where independent activism was much less developed. In Czechoslovakia, for instance, Charter 77 activists talked about organizing informal discussion meetings in which citizens could talk about political and social issues in a frank manner; this was seen by advocates as laying the groundwork for a free-thinking "civil society" that could push for broader changes at a societal level.[8] In Bulgaria, by contrast, dissident activity was much weaker (and much newer, insofar as it was not until 1988 or later that most of the present independent organizations came into existence).

Thus, what we witnessed in the late 1970s and the 1980s was the repluralization of East European society from below. Distinct social interests began asserting themselves more volubly—sometimes legally, sometimes illegally, most often in the grey zone of extralegality. The communist regimes recognized this repluralization for what it was, and they fashioned diverse strategies ranging from repression (Czechoslovakia) to toleration (Yugoslavia). And in Hungary in November 1987 the reform-minded secretary of the Patriotic People's Front, Imre Pozsgay, called for recognition of the right of citizens to establish autonomous associations while Hungarian legal experts endorsed this position and declared that their founders were entitled to register them without political preconditions.[9] Ultimately, the dissident movements in Czechoslovakia and Hungary provided the nuclei of emergent political parties, thus graphically demonstrating the importance of dissent.

This chapter will explore the rise of the "new dissent" in three East European countries and will outline the growing international cooperation among independent activists in the region.[10]

Czechoslovakia: Being Normal in a "Normalized" Society

On 3 August 1976 Ludvík Vaculík, a Czechoslovak writer banned from publishing in his own country, recorded a curious conversation which he had in a Prague cafe. He and two friends had fallen into brief conversation with a man from Baghdad, who had previously spent time in Greece. Vaculík asked the visitor which he preferred—Czechoslovakia or Greece—and to his astonishment, the Arab visitor declared for Czechoslovakia, explaining, "There's more freedom here." After a somewhat stunned silence, one of Vaculík's associates blurted, "Oh no, this isn't real!" But later, Vaculík reflected on the fact that free thinking and free action may exist under any regime, and may indeed have greater weight in more closed systems.[11] Or, to put it another way, being *normal* in a pluralist society is not a particular accomplishment, while in *normalized* Czechoslovakia, one may speak of the endeavor to be *normal* as a politically charged project.[12]

One of the earliest dissident actions in post-Dubček Czechoslovakia was the samizdat issuance on 21 August 1969 of the Ten-Point Manifesto signed by several reformers. The fourth point of the manifesto remonstrated against the banning of the Society for Human Rights, which had been active during the Prague Spring of 1968. In the early 1970s small dissident groups appeared, often led by expelled party members, and tried to press for political reform. The best known of these groups was the Socialist Movement of Czechoslovak Citizens, which included several prominent would-be political reformers. This movement published its Short Action Program in early 1971; the group collapsed in summer 1972 with the arrest and subsequent trial of several of its leaders.[13] Other reformist groups in the 1970s included the Student-Worker Coordinating Committees, the Movement of Revolutionary Youth, Communists in Opposition, the Czechoslovak Movement for Democratic Socialism, and the Civil Resistance Movement. None of these survived the decade.

In the 1980s the most important currents of independent activism in Czechoslovakia were the human rights group known as Charter 77, the Committee for the Defense of the Unjustly Persecuted, the Jazz Section, and religious activists (mainly Catholic). Other groups included the Preparatory Committee for the Foundation of Free Labor Unions, the Revolutionary Action Group, the Legal Defense Committee of the Hungarian Nationality, and the Democratic Initiative.

Charter 77. The oldest and (up to the collapse of communism) the most important activist group in Czechoslovakia was Charter 77.[14] In September 1976 the Prague authorities decided to try the members of a rock band, Plastic People of the Universe, for musical nonconformism and social subversion. The band contacted playwright Václav Havel, already renowned for his 1975 "Open Letter to Husák" pleading for more tolerance in political and cultural life, and asked for his help. Havel and others sympathetic to the accused became involved in the controversial trial, and out of this milieu Charter 77 emerged. The original document was drafted in December 1976, and was made public on 6 January

1977. It bore 243 signatures, including those of Havel, Pavel Landovský, and writer Ludvík Vaculík, who wanted to deliver a copy to the federal assembly but were arrested while en route to that body. This first document defined Charter 77 as "a free, informal, and open community of people of different convictions, different faiths, and different professions, united by the will to strive, individually and collectively, for the respect of civic and human rights."[15] Charter 77 was never a formal organization, having scrupulously avoided such things as rules, statutes, or membership lists. It was represented to Czechoslovak society by three spokespersons selected annually.[16]

The initial signatories of Charter 77 included writers, academics, journalists, former party functionaries, technicians, students, and even some blue-collar workers. Over the years additional persons signed the charter, and by 1987 there were some 1,300 signatories.[17] Despite intense regime pressure, as of 1985 only fifteen persons had withdrawn their signatures.[18]

The chartists decided to spurn clandestine work and to function openly, disclosing the names of all signatories. They also declared themselves open to "constructive dialogue" with the government and committed themselves to act within the framework of the law. They disavowed any specific agenda or political ambitions, and began issuing a series of expository essays. From the beginning, Charter 77 focused on human and civil rights, and stressed its interest in promoting legality. Some of the earliest Charter 77 documents were analyses, covering discrimination in the educational system documented by instructions from the Ministry of Education regarding the political criteria to be applied for admissions (January 1977); economic and social rights in Czechoslovakia (March 1977); freedom of belief (April 1977); and discrimination against writers, documented by a list of 130 Czechoslovak writers who were wholly or partially banned from publishing in the country.[19] Many of the early Charter 77 documents were concerned with violations of legal procedure by the authorities, for example during the November 1977 trial of four of the founding members.

But it proved impossible for Charter 77 to maintain this focus, and from its origins as a human rights lobby group it developed in the 1980s into a body concerned with a wide array of political, economic, social, and cultural issues. Its documents trace its evolution. In January 1978, for example, Charter 77 protested the government's violations of its own labor legislation. In July 1978 it addressed internal Soviet affairs for the first time, requesting the immediate release of human rights activists Aleksandr Ginzburg, Anatoly Shcharansky, and Viktoras Piatkus. The following month it sent a letter of solidarity to human rights activists throughout Eastern Europe and the Soviet Union. Later that same year it issued communiqués addressing the safety of nuclear power stations and the status of Gypsies in Czechoslovakia. Charter 77 supported East German critic Rudolf Bahro, Soviet dissident Andrei Sakharov, and the Polish independent trade union Solidarity.

Charter 77 devoted relatively little attention in its first five years to freedom of religion. Indeed, of the 181 Charter 77 documents compiled by Vilém Precan for the years 1977 to 1981, only one dealt with freedom of religious belief. But in 1982 Charter 77 addressed this subject on three occasions, broadening its concerns simultaneously with statements concerning price increases of basic foodstuffs, solidarity with the East German independent peace movement, and the state of academic research in Czechoslovakia.

By 1984, with the release of "The Right to History," Charter 77 had even taken up the defense of historical memory from the depredations of the regime, thus embracing a dimension of nationalism. This important document charges the regime with severely restricting access to historical archives, especially those relating to the years since 1918, and with smothering research into entire epochs, such as medieval times. The document continues:

> It is typical of the totalitarian manipulation of history that it eventually must lead to history's gradual eradication, because the eradication of politics, public opinion, morals, and other social values cannot be consistently undertaken without the elimination of the historical dimension. We are witness to a great leap backward, before the earliest origins of our culture, a renunciation of all culture, which cannot exist without a memory and a meaning. We believe that this "process of forgetting," which the state authorities find so desirable, must be actively opposed. None of us ought to allow the death within himself or herself of the memory of justice and injustice, truth and falsehood, good and evil, the memory of reality altogether.[20]

Charter 77 also made a contribution to sustaining independent culture in Czechoslovakia by promoting private concerts, exhibitions, theatrical performances, and independent lectures in private apartments (usually by academics barred from teaching), and by creating an educational program for young people barred from the university. This has come to be called Patočka University, after philosopher Jan Patočka, a Charter 77 signatory who died in 1977 after intense and grueling interrogation by the police. To no one's surprise, some of these classes were disrupted by the police. Participant Julius Tomin, a philosopher, was assaulted by "unknown" thugs, and other leading figures in the educational initiative were likewise harassed.[21]

At first there was considerable controversy within Charter 77 along lines similar to those that would divide Polish Solidarity during 1981. At the time of its formation there were five groupings within the organization: *reform communists,* who tended to believe the system was reformable and who did not want Charter 77 to develop into a political organization; *democratic socialists and independent liberals,* such as Rudolf Battek, some of whom criticized the reform communists for excessive moderation or wanted to develop a political organization; *self-styled revolutionary Marxists* led by Petr Uhl, who wanted a revolutionary program of action; *religious activists,* whose influence has increased over the years; and an assortment of *unaffiliated intellectuals,* including Havel and young people from the cultural-musical underground.[22] With time these early differences lost their importance and the prevailing approach—eschewing any effort to build a mass movement in favor of concentrating on educating the public and on stirring the public conscience—gained in credibility.

The authorities were unequivocally hostile toward Charter 77 from the very beginning. On 7 January 1977 the government began a big press campaign against Charter 77, thereby giving it far more publicity and visibility than it otherwise would have had. The government also pressured workers to sign anti-Charter resolutions, but typically the workers asked first to see what they were asked to condemn. When the authorities refused to make the text available, the workers refused to sign. The police were assigned to harass and threaten coworkers, associates, and neighbors of Charter 77 signatories in an effort to ostracize all signatories. These tactics were relatively successful in the small towns and villages, and signatories in those places usually moved to larger urban centers.[23] The authorities repeatedly arrested Charter 77 spokespersons, and in 1981 pessimistic Czech émigré sources concluded that the human rights group had been "broken."[24]

Czechoslovakia's independent activists lived in nervous anticipation and fear that the secret police were going to search their apartments and confiscate their manuscripts. Vaculík playfully alludes to this fear in a feuilleton written in 1975: "Someone rings my doorbell, so I quickly remove the paper from my typewriter and hide it before going to open the door. It was the rent collector. What a pleasant surprise!"[25] Similarly,

Havel was long afflicted by fears that his manuscripts would be seized before he could finish them and smuggle them out of Czechoslovakia. His solution was to hide multiple copies in the apartments of friends and, of course, to hide pages in progress whenever the doorbell rang.[26]

In 1988, under the impact of the faint breeze of hope inspired by Gorbachev, Charter 77 boldly proposed the erection of a monument to the victims of Stalinism.[27] In a separate action, two signatories of Charter 77, Rudolf Bereza and Tomáš Hradílek, brought a legal suit against central committee secretary Vasil Bilak for "high treason" because of his role during the 1968 Soviet invasion of the country. Gorbachev would subsequently force Bilak's retirement from politics, as Bilak continued to show himself antagonistic to reform.[28]

Charter 77 aspired to be the social conscience of Czechoslovak society, not its leader. Even so, not everyone in Czechoslovakia, even leaving aside the political and coercive apparatus, supported Charter 77's efforts. Some viewed Charter 77 as counterproductive, threatening to evoke broad repression. Some were suspicious of any movement that included former communist officials. Others simply preferred the safety of political passivity and were troubled by Charter 77's activism. And still others either had not heard of Charter 77 or had no clear idea as to what it was.

Having said that, it seems obvious to me that Charter 77 was an important political phenomenon in at least two respects. First, it addressed issues which were of wide interest to the population, from environmental deterioration to discrimination in education and hiring to religious freedom; and it contributed to the sustenance of a lively underground publishing scene and an equally lively underground culture. Second, it signaled the defection of at least part of the intelligentsia, and this, as was noted already in chapter 1, is one of the central ingredients not only in political decay but in any emergent revolutionary situation, regardless of its final outcome.

The Committee for the Unjustly Persecuted. Usually known by its Czech initials (VONS), the Committee for the Unjustly Persecuted was created on 24 April 1978, on the inspiration of Charter 77. In December 1978 VONS became affiliated with the International Federation for Human Rights based in Paris, which is in turn associated with the UN. Between 1978 and mid-1986 VONS prepared and issued more than five hundred communiques and other materials on state repression in Czechoslovakia.[29] Authorities arrested and tried ten VONS leaders in May 1979 and sentenced six of them to prison terms in October of that year.

Repression proved ineffective, however, as new members assumed the roles played by those imprisoned.

The Jazz Section. Unlike most of the groups discussed here, the Jazz Section began quite legally. It was born in 1971 when a group of jazz enthusiasts obtained permission to form a special interest section within the Czechoslovak Musicians' Union, on the model of the Music Critics' Section. Under guidelines issued by the Ministry of the Interior, the Jazz Section was limited to a membership of 3,000.[30] The Section started the members-only bulletin *Jazzbulletin* that ran for twenty-eight issues, held jam sessions, and sponsored annual jazz festivals in Prague. It organized trips to jazz festivals and concerts in East Germany, Poland, and Hungary, and launched the *Jazzpetit* book series which included titles on Czech art, John Lennon, and living theater, an anthology of rock poetry, a history of rock music in Czechoslovakia by Vladimír Kouřil, a two-volume dictionary of American rock musicians, and the 1984 Nobel Prize acceptance speech by Czech poet Jaroslav Seifert.[31] Passed from hand to hand, the 3,000 copies of *Jazzbulletin* reached at least 100,000 readers. As Josef Škvorecký notes, "It was not exceptional for one especially appealing title to be read by the entire student body of a high school (as well as most of the teachers) even if only one of its students was a Section member."[32]

In 1980 the Jazz Section's annual "Prague Jazz Days" were banned on the pretext that the event, for which some 15,000 fans had purchased tickets, might become the occasion for "public disturbances." The ban came on the eve of the event and a large crowd of musicians and fans gathered in Prague unaware that the festival had been canceled. The Jazz Section calmly informed the fans of the cancelation, refunded their money, and paid the musicians. But in seeking redress, the Jazz Section disregarded the possibility of appeals through channels and instead mobilized its many supporters. To the control-minded Czechoslovak bureaucracy, this signaled that the Jazz Section had become a "dissident" organization. Shortly thereafter, the Jazz Section applied for membership in the International Jazz Federation (an affiliate of UNESCO) and was admitted.

In early 1983 the regime decided on a headlong assault on popular music, taking in everything from punk rock to jazz. The authorities initially pressured the Czech Musicians' Union to dissolve its Jazz Section, and when these efforts proved unavailing, the authorities simply dissolved the entire union in fall 1984.[33] By that point, the Jazz Section numbered some 7,000 members—4,000 more than permitted by the ministry.

At that point Karel Srp and Vladimír Kouřil, the chair and deputy chair of the Jazz Section, had a choice. They could simply accept the orders from above as a fait accompli and disband. Or they could seek some way of resisting the decree, an alternative that would convince the regime that the Jazz Section was literally *out of control.* Srp and Kouřil chose the latter option, and with the assistance of attorney Josef Průša, appealed the decree in the courts. But despite 130 letters, Srp and Kouřil were unable to obtain any answer, let alone an explanation. Later, at his trial in March 1987 Srp would ask, "Why did the Liquidation Committee not answer the letters we were sending?" The ministry official offered this Orwellian reply: "We could not answer letters from an organization that did not exist."[34]

Finally, in September 1986 the authorities arrested and jailed five leaders of the Jazz Section—Srp, Kouřil, Josef Skalník, Čestmir Hunat, and Tomáš Křivánek. Průša continued as defense counsel, only to find his car badly damaged by "unknown hooligans."[35] They were ultimately convicted in March 1987 of engaging in an "unauthorized business venture." Srp received a sixteen-month prison term which he completed in January 1988, and Kouřil a ten-month term, while the other three defendants received suspended prison sentences and were put on probation.

Ironically, the Jazz Section's greatest "crime" may have been that it had established great credibility[36] with its constituency. For a specialized branch of a totally illegitimate bureaucratic apparatus to achieve credibility suggests a fundamental difference of orientation between the branch and the central apparatus, and that difference was most certainly apparent to all concerned.

Religious Activists. The Catholic church, which accounted for about two-thirds of all believers in Czechoslovakia, was always singled out for special persecution in communist Czechoslovakia.[37] Not surprisingly, religious activism has been strongest among Catholics. Such activism took two forms. The first, with a history going back at least to the mid-1970s, was the underground church—called the "catacomb church" by its apologists and the "secret church" by its communist foes. The underground church was no more than that part of the regular church network of priests, nuns, and even bishops driven underground by police repression and the withdrawal of state licenses. The religious samizdat that developed was simply the church press driven underground.[38]

This form was defensive and sought only to continue the spiritual life of the community. The second form, which was slow to develop, was the mass petition, and sought overtly to change the regime's policy vis-à-vis religion. The new confidence among Catholics in Czechoslovakia probably had roots in the election of the Polish pope in 1978, and no doubt the more resilient stand taken by the once-docile Cardinal Tomášek of Prague encouraged believers. After the Vatican's March 1982 declaration condemning priests' associations which supported specific ideologies,[39] a declaration generally seen as aimed specifically at Czechoslovakia's Pacem in terris association, Cardinal Tomášek, who celebrated his ninetieth birthday on 30 June 1989, condemned Pacem in terris explicitly and denied that the regime-controlled newspaper *Katolické noviny* spoke for the church. Tomášek gave further encouragement to believers concerned about the government's policy when he told the Prague World Peace Assembly in a brief address in summer 1983 that true peace presumed a respect for truth and a respect for religious liberty. Subsequently, Czech and Slovak Catholics circulated a petition asking the authorities to approve a papal visit to Czechoslovakia; the petition gathered some 28,000 signatures.[40]

Believers were also encouraged by the mass gathering (100,000–200,000 strong) at Velehrad, Moravia, in July 1985 to celebrate the 1,100th anniversary of the death of St. Methodius, bishop of Moravia. And in July 1987 100,000 Catholic believers assembled at Levoča for a pilgrimage, and members of the Franciscan and other orders donned their habits in defiance of a government ban. Fortified by the reawakening sense of religious community and encouraged by the changes being pushed by Gorbachev in the USSR, a group of Catholics in Moravia drew up and circulated a thirty-one-point petition in November 1987.[41] Cardinal Tomášek gave the petition his blessing, and by late February 1988, in addition to the 300,000 Czech and Slovak Catholic signatures, it was starting to attract Protestant and Jewish signatories.[42] By May there were half a million signatures. Among other things, the petition called for an end to state interference in church organization, the nomination of bishops, the appointment of parish priests, and the selection of students and instructors at theological faculties; the reopening of the theological faculty at Olomouc; permission to establish independent lay associations and to reestablish religious orders; unlimited access to religious publications; and an end to discrimination against Christians in schooling and on the job.[43]

By the mid-1980s there was a new determination among Catholics in Czechoslovakia, a new spirit of defiance. In March 1988, for instance,

2,000 Catholics gathered in front of Bratislava's National Theater for a candlelight rally that had been proscribed by the authorities. Jan Carnogurský, a rally organizer, told an Austrian radio interviewer, "It was a new form of civil protest in this country after forty years," and added that a demonstration of citizens that had been announced beforehand "has practically never taken place here before."[44]

Other Groups. Organized dissent was slower to develop in Slovakia than in the Czech regions. Almost all the organized dissident groups were, in fact, essentially *Czech* groups. In the early 1980s the creation of a new dissident organization was a relatively unique event; in the late 1980s the pace quickened, with at least five new groups emerging in the course of 1988.

Among the earlier groups one should mention the Preparatory Committee for the Foundation of Free Labor Unions, which was established in June 1981 under the influence of Polish developments. It issued two statements in support of Polish Solidarity, but declared that for the immediate future it intended to concentrate on trying to democratize the existing communist labor unions. The group remained clandestine but claimed members in Prague, Pilsen, and Kladno in Bohemia, and in Ostrava and Brno in Moravia.[45]

A more militant organization calling itself the Revolutionary Action Group was likewise created in 1981, taking shape within two weeks of the imposition of martial law in Poland. In January and February 1982 police detained several individuals suspected of being associated with this clandestine group. A trial followed in December 1982, with four persons, including Václav Soukup and Jan Wunsch, being accused of printing and distributing subversive materials.

The Legal Defense Committee of the Hungarian Nationality is a self-defense group in Slovakia, where ethnic Hungarians constituted 11 percent of the population in 1984. As its name implies, it has been primarily concerned with the civil and cultural rights of the Hungarian minority in Slovakia. In March 1987 it reported several incidents reflecting what they believed to be officially condoned animosity toward ethnic Hungarians in Slovakia.[46]

At least at one time there was an embryonic independent environmentalist group. But a Western report in 1985 said that Czechoslovak police had used a combination of threats and interrogations to demolish the group.[47] Subsequently, the independent Ecological Initiative was revived in Prague.

One of the most important activist groups was an organization called the Democratic Initiative, which sought the overhaul of the system. In a petition to General Secretary Miloš Jakeš, the Democratic Initiative spelled out four key proposals: the overhaul of the economic system to take into account consumer interests; the abandonment of the party system of appointments and promotions (nomenklatura); the establishment of a free press; and political and religious tolerance. This last point was taken to mean amnesty for all political prisoners, the freedom to establish independent organizations and cultural societies, and an end to state supervision of churches.[48] On 5 March 1988 the police detained twelve members of the group, but released them shortly thereafter.

Steady police pressure forced the Democratic Initiative to suspend its activities in mid-November 1988 (at which time it had an estimated 200 members). The organization resumed its work the following year, however, convening a constituent congress in Prague on 16 September. In a programmatic statement adopted on that occasion, the group called for the creation of a pluralist democracy based on the market economy and a new constitution that would abrogate the leading role of the communist party.

The Independent Peace Association (IPA), established by five Czech citizens on 16 April 1988 is a different story, since the Jakeš regime would eventually decide to engage in dialogue with its leadership. The IPA initially called on the authorities to "demilitarize society, promote overall *glasnost*, and make efforts to strengthen peace and confidence among nations."[49] Among other things, the association supports the right of conscientious objection to military service. In June 1988 the association collaborated with Charter 77 in attempting to hold an international peace seminar in Prague. The police prevented the event from taking place.[50]

Finally, among the several new groups established in 1988 and 1989 one is worthy of special mention: Obroda, A Club for Socialist Restructuring. Inspired by Gorbachev's reforms in the USSR, Obroda is the creation of several former senior party officials who had been purged from the party after the Soviet invasion of their country in 1968. Founded on 16 February 1989, Obroda called for a pluralist social democracy based on a market economy and an end to the communist party's power monopoly.

Publishing Activity. Aside from these specific groups, there should be some mention of independent publishing activity in Czechoslovakia. The best-known underground publisher is Edice Petlice (Padlock Editions) created by Ludvík Vaculík in 1972, which issued more than 250 titles before it was shut down in 1983. Edice Kvart (Quarto Editions), started by Jan Vladislav, put out some 120 books. Other underground publishers have included Edice Expedice (Expedition Editions) created by Václav Havel, the short-lived Edice Popelnice (Ashcan Editions), and religious editions such as Život (Life), Přátelé (Friends), and Cesty myšlení (Paths of Thought).[51] All told, independent publishers were probably producing more books as of 1985 than the official publishing houses, according to Jiří Pelikán.[52]

There were reportedly between forty and sixty samizdat journals as of 1987, dealing with such spheres as literary criticism, music, philosophy, theology, history, culture, sociology, and politics. Two of the more recent were the Slovak literary journal *MAR.3-1 K 1987* (the meaning of the title is anyone's guess) and the sociological journal *Sociologické Obzory*, both launched in 1987.[53] The independent newspaper *Lidové Noviny* (*People's News*) was launched in January 1988 with uncensored material about such topics as East-West disarmament talks and the Soviet role in Afghanistan. Edited by Václav Havel, Jiří Roml, Jiří Dienstbier, and Josef Zverina, *Lidové Noviny* published original interviews with Michael Dukakis, George Bush, Alexander Dubček, and Milovan Djilas, and was probably the most prominent samizdat periodical in Czechoslovakia as of March 1989.[54] Other samizdat periodicals include *Revolver Review*, which published its ninth issue (248 pages) in summer 1988 and became extremely popular among young people; *New Junk*, a magazine likewise aimed at young people; *Jazz Stop*; *Ecological Bulletin*, published by the Ecological Initiative; and *Bulletin of Czechoslovak-Polish Solidarity*.[55]

Summary. Until the blossoming of democracy in the closing weeks of 1989, independent activism in Czechoslovakia was the preserve of a small minority. To what extent did this activity reflect broader social malaise? In an essay which appeared in the West in 1988, Václav Havel suggested that there is a fundamental point of agreement between independent activists and the general public: "the belief that the only meaningful cure for the economy is real pluralism of economic enterprise and that the only meaningful alternative to the present political system is political pluralism (without which, in the last instance, economic pluralism is unthinkable)."[56]

A clandestine poll taken among 342 Czechoslovak citizens in 1986 found that 37.7 percent of respondents took part (occasionally or regularly) in unofficial concerts and theater performances, 35.3 percent took part in unofficial lectures and seminars, 30.6 percent watched private film shows, 18.4 percent took part in religious gatherings, and the "overwhelming majority" preferred a pluralist democracy and foreign policy neutrality.[57] Participation in unofficial events was a form of "positive" dissent. There was also "negative" dissent or protest which amounted to a kind of collective sabotage. As Ladislav Hejdanek, a former Charter 77 spokesperson, explained in 1985, a person engaging in this form of protest

> undermine[d] measures from above, so that it look[ed] after only two or three weeks as if these measures had never existed. In a factory a hundred people regularly show[ed] up late, but some fellow workers work[ed] the time clock for them. Management [found] out about it and set up a special check at the gate. For a couple weeks perhaps, the loafing [would] stop. Then suddenly other "difficulties" crop[ped] up somewhere else in the factory. The checkers [were] transferred there, and the old cycle start[ed] over.[58]

The widespread and evident disaffection among Czechs and Slovaks proved, I would argue, to be a measure of the resonance that independent activism had with the general public.

Hungary: The New "Greek Agoras"

The dividing line between officialdom and opposition in Hungary became increasingly blurred in the 1980s. For instance, communist authorities permitted the establishment, by twenty-two elderly persons in April 1986, of a self-help organization called the Retired Persons' Cultural and Self-Assisting Association.[59] Authorities also permitted émigré George Soros to set up a private cultural foundation in Budapest in 1984, which in 1987 disbursed some $4 million to support private educational and research projects, musical groups, museums, and amateur theaters.[60] In the early 1980s the government let independent environmentalists publish their views in the official environmental journal and invited them to give lectures. Again, in 1987, the regime daily *Magyar Nemzet*, organ of the Patriotic People's Front (PPF), published in full the founding declaration of a nascent dissident organization. Indeed, the PPF's general secretary, Imre Pozsgay, sounded as critical as any of the opposition when he told an interviewer, "People need greater freedom, civic autonomy, and participation in [making] decisions, that is, a situation in which government for the people is replaced by government by and through the consent of the people."[61] On the other side, the independent Peace Group for Dialogue, though critical of the regime's concept of peace, hoped to cooperate with the regime and engage in constructive dialogue with the authorities. The Peace Group found itself unwelcome.

The political atmosphere in Hungary was relaxed all along—especially when compared to Czechoslovakia or Romania—and between summer 1987 and autumn 1988 a string of independent noncommunist associations ranging from student groups to a forum of intellectuals appeared, many of them seeking legal recognition.[62] Still, for all that, most of the authorities were, at first, not entirely serene about these developments, as a "strictly confidential" Politburo document of July 1986 amply reveals. Leaked in early 1987 the report had been intended for distribution to about forty high-ranking officials, and fretted that cooperative links both among Hungarian independent activists and between them and other activists abroad had grown "significantly" since 1982.[63] But by early 1989 the atmosphere was significantly more open, and according to one estimate there were already several hundred independent associations and political groups.[64] The pressure for change came from *mass* strength, and was typically manifested in the proliferation of mass rallies and demonstrations. When some 75,000 people marched in Budapest on 15 March 1989, the 141st anniversary of the Revolution of 1848, it was clear that society had become politically aware.

Until the late 1980s the major currents of independent activism in Hungary were the Budapest School, the Peace Group for Dialogue, the Blue Danube Circle (an environmentalist group), and miscellaneous intellectual circles and initiatives. Between 1988 and 1989, however, a number of political groups and embryonic parties were established, including the Hungarian Democratic Forum, the Association of Young Democrats, the Smallholders' Party, the Szárszó Front, the Christian Democratic Party, the Liberal Party, and the Social Democratic Party.

Early Independent Activist Groups.

The Budapest School. One of the earliest initiatives was the Budapest School, a group of nonparty philosophers and sociologists gathered around András Hegedűs (the former premier), Mihály Vajda, János Kis, and György Markus, who wanted to return to the "original" ideas of socialism. Their influence in Hungarian society was always somewhat marginal at best, and at their peak they probably enjoyed a greater following in the West than in Hungary itself. Now, in the heady atmosphere of the 1990s, the Budapest School is completely irrelevant. The School's idea of a pluralized Marxism was important in its day, to be sure, in roughly the same manner as the Yugoslav Praxis group, but by the late 1980s the Budapest School was completely overtaken by events. Almost no one in Hungary was very interested in Marxism anymore, even a "pluralized" Marxism, except for some of the people in what used to be the communist party, the Left-Wing Alternative Association, the Ferenc Munnich Society, and the János Kádár Society, all of which were established in or after October 1988.[65]

The Peace Group for Dialogue. Apart from the Budapest School, the early independent initiatives in Hungary tended to be issue-specific. For example, pacifism provided an early impulse to independent activism. Thus, in November 1981 the student parliament of the arts faculty of the University of Budapest set up a ten-member peace group with the idea of spawning a network of such groups throughout the university's student community. When other faculties failed to follow the lead of the arts faculty students, the plan proved stillborn.[66] But pacifism assumed a more organizational form the following year when a group of Budapest students and artists formed the Peace Group for Dialogue in July. The Group sought dialogue with the authorities and even spoke of wanting to cooperate with the official Hungarian Peace Council. Adopting a posture that might seem to have been gratifying to the authorities, the Peace Group, led by Ferenc Kőszegi, argued that peace and political freedom were distinct and *separable* issues. In January 1983 the Peace Group actually held talks with the official Peace Council. But the Group insisted that East and West bore equal responsibility for the arms race, and was therefore unacceptable to the regime.

In November 1982 the Peace Group numbered 200 to 300 adherents; by spring 1983 it may have claimed the loyalty of some 3,000 members. In May 1983 the Peace Group mobilized a bloc of 500 members to take part in an official peace demonstration in Budapest.[67] In July the Peace Group had planned to conduct an international "peace camp" in Debrecen, but authorities outlawed the event and sent the police to put pressure on the Peace Group. The following month, in the face of police pressure, the Peace Group dissolved itself, while pledging to continue to work "informally."[68]

The Blue Danube Circle. Another issue-oriented group begun in the early 1980s was the Blue Danube Circle, whose concerns centered on protection of the environment. By contrast with most other independent activist groups in Hungary (but very much like Charter 77), the Blue Danube Circle owed its birth to a specific development, in this case, the decision on the part of the government to pursue plans for a hydroelectric plant and dam on the River Danube, the Gabčikovo-Nagymaros project. Initially there was an effort to establish an "Association for the Protection of the Danube Region" along legal guidelines, but the authorities disallowed it. Then, in 1981 fifteen young scientists and intellectuals, disquieted by the severe environmental damage they expected the dam to cause, organized the Blue Danube Group and began writing articles about the environmental issue, many of them published in the regime press. They also circulated a protest petition signed by some 10,000 Hungarians, and launched a samizdat journal, *Vízjel* (*Watermark*). *Vízjel*'s editor, Ferenc Langmár, later ran unsuccessfully for National Assembly on an environmentalist platform.[69]

Subsequently, the Blue Danube Circle was awarded the Nobel Prize for peace, which the embarrassed authorities tried to persuade János Vargha, on behalf of the group, to turn down. Vargha refused, so the authorities did their best to make the award seem like an award to Vargha as an individual rather than to the group per se.[70]

In early 1986 some 2,655 citizens signed a request for a referendum on the project, noting that the Hungarian constitution permitted the citizenry to request referenda on policy issues. The authorities replied that there was no need for a referendum since the issue had already been decided by experts. But the authorities could not ignore the pressure and halted construction of the dam until an official commission could assess potential environmental damage and make recommendations. In May 1986 the commission finished its work and proposed the expenditure of some $75 million in environmental safeguards. Blue Danube continued to protest, however, claiming that the safeguards were inadequate. Meanwhile, Blue Danube broadened its critique to nuclear power. In 1987 Vargha warned that "by promoting nuclear power, we are substituting one danger for another. We don't even have the proper devices to measure radioactive emissions."[71] Only a year earlier another Blue Danube Circle leader, Iván Baba, had thought, "Nuclear power is a taboo. It is built with the help of the Soviets. That makes challenging it like asking the Soviets to take their troops out of this country."[72] In early 1989 the Blue Danube Circle collected more than 100,000 signatures in protest of the Gabčikovo-Nagymaros dam and forced the Hungarian government to finally withdraw from the project.

Other Political Groups. As civil society reemerged in Hungary, diverse cultural and political currents have also come into focus. Western press accounts sometimes made it appear that there were only two alternatives in Hungary: old-style communism and Western-style parliamentary democracy. In reality, Hungarians even now see many possibilities, and today there are not only liberal tendencies in the Western meaning, but also radical-democratic tendencies (looking to workers' self-management as a model), tendencies associated with concern for social justice and support for some kind of welfare state, humanists concerned about the erosion of morality and high culture, Marxist loyalists, antireform currents associated with concern for law and order and economic efficiency, and populist-nationalist tendencies.[73] Populist-nationalist thinking is heavily oriented toward questions of "national destiny," including the decline of the population, the fate of Hungarians abroad, the growth of the Gypsy population, alcoholism and suicide, and the threat posed by Western consumerism.

There is thus a fundamental tension between populist-nationalist thinking, which abhors consumerism and worries about moral decline, and liberal-democratic thinking, which welcomes consumerism and sees no threat in the Westernization of values. These two tendencies are embodied in two of the leading organizations in the opposition: the Hungarian Democratic Forum (HDF) and the Association of Free Democrats. The latter, which was founded on 13 November 1988 and which had some 3,800 members in thirty-five chapters as of July 1989,[74] takes constitutional freedoms as the starting point. The HDF (17,350 members in August 1989) placed its emphasis elsewhere. István Csurka, at that time one of its leaders, made this clear when he noted that in the organization's name, "Hungarian" is the more important adjective.[75] Predictably, friction developed between the two groups.

The Hungarian Democratic Forum. The roots of the HDF can probably be traced to a mid-June 1985 meeting of forty-five writers, actors, sociologists, historians, and economists at a campsite near the village of Monor (thirty miles southeast of Budapest). Drawing on at least four different currents of thought—populism, nationalism, economic reformism, and political radicalism—the meeting focused on discussion of the nation's future, and heard nationalist writer István Csurka lament, inter alia, that "the culture of today's Hungarian society is the culture of a defeatist, agonizing, . . . self-exploiting, and neurotic society, a kind of quasi-culture if you will."[76] Another activist, philosopher János Kis, sketched out a program for radical political change, including more enforceable legal guarantees of civil rights.

Csurka and Kis were among the 150 to 160 Hungarian intellectuals who convened in the small town of Lakitelek in southeastern Hungary in September 1987. They met in the backyard of the populist writer Sándor Lezsák for a meeting that lasted from 10:30 A.M. to about 7 P.M. Among those present were Miklós Vásárhelyi, the former press secretary of the executed prime minister Imre Nagy, writer György Konrád, and PPF secretary Pozsgay. The meeting produced an agreement to create a body (the Democratic Forum) dedicated to helping solve the nation's problems. Those present also adopted a formal statement, which said, in part:

The Hungarian nation has drifted into a serious crisis in its history. Its national strength has been broken, its self-confidence and bearing have been shaken, the bonds of its cohesion have been tragically loosened, its self-knowledge is startlingly insufficient. It is anticipating possible economic collapse. . . . In the course of the discussions, mention was made of the socioeconomic crisis shaking the country, the lack of democracy, the inadequacies of the institutional political system, the worsening problems of public morality, the alarming symptoms in cultural life and public education, and the worries about our survival. . . .

Filled with a feeling of responsibility for the fate of the country and of the Hungarian nation, those assembled felt it necessary and timely to establish a framework that would permit the members of society to participate as true partners in the creation of a social consensus. . . . The present system of political and social organization does not provide any guarantee for the expression of autonomous and independent views. This is why [we] propose the establishment of a Hungarian democratic forum as an arena for sustained public discussion.[77]

Discussion was lively and critical. Political scientist Mihály Bihari called the communist system a "self-complacent dictatorship." Writer Gábor Czákó claimed that Hungarians had been used as human guinea pigs in unwarranted medical experiments, and compared the practice to the Nazi experiments under Josef Mengele.[78] Author Béla Horgas agreed that change was desirable but despaired of achieving it as long as those responsible for the current failed policies remained in office. Pozsgay, who was cultivating a reputation as a liberal reformer, seemed to encourage the discussion, urging the formulation of an explicit alternative program and advising that the government was prepared to consider it.

Three months later the new organization held its first meeting in Budapest's Jurta Theater, with five hundred people in attendance. Among other things they discussed parliamentary democracy, the role and prospects of the National Assembly, constitutional revision, and creation of a constitutional court. György Konrád sang the praises of parliamentary democracy, and the HDF eventually adopted a resolution which concluded that the only path out of political crisis and rising social tension was to establish a functioning democracy in Hungary, including guarantees of individual liberty and an independent, effective parliament responsible only to the electorate. The National Assembly, the resolution said, should be in permanent session instead of eight days annually, should permit the formation of parliamentary "factions" (parties), and should permit a secret vote of confidence in the government on the initiative of any deputy.[79]

The formal establishment of the HDF and the adoption of statutes followed in September 1988. Pledging to abide by the existing constitution, the HDF also promised to work for the introduction of a multiparty system in Hungary and to nominate candidates to contest parliamentary seats in future elections. In addition, the HDF established an organ, *Hitel*, with official permission from the authorities, electing two of its inner leadership, Zoltán Bíró and Sándor Csoori, to serve as editor-in-chief and chair of the editorial board respectively.[80]

It should come as no surprise that the communist regime press hastened to repudiate the self-assigned watchdog role of the HDF. *Magyar Hírlap* fancied that "the age of the Greek *agoras* was over."[81] But the appearance of these new "Greek agoras" was itself a revealing symptom of the sociopolitical impasse and general mood of crisis in Hungary.

Other Groups. A number of the new organizations underlined the importance of Hungarian sovereignty and advocated neutrality. The Social Democratic Party, for example, urged the dismantlement of both military blocs followed by a declaration of Hungarian neutrality. Somewhat more boldly, the Republican Circle established on 23 April 1988 urged Hungary's unilateral withdrawal from the Warsaw Pact.

Most of the new groups advocated a multiparty parliamentary system. The Association of Free Democrats, for example, saw itself very much in the Western liberal tradition. It also urged the "democratization" of Warsaw Pact structures. The Federation of Young Democrats, founded in spring 1988 and claiming some 5,000 members by the end of 1989, combined advocacy of parliamentary democracy with a deep concern for human rights and a conviction that only a strong society can guarantee democracy. The group stated this concisely in a programmatic statement issued in November 1988:

> We do not believe that any new organization attaining power would by itself bring about human and civil rights. This is because the ultimate guarantee and repository of democracy is a democratic, politically aware society, not the State. [The] existence of political parties vying for power is an essential, but not sufficient, condition [for democracy]. Our task is not to grasp the power to govern; rather to promote grass roots organization in the hope that the reborn society, building on its own communities, will be able to choose its own government.[82]

Resurrected on 18 November 1988 after forty years and with an esti-mated 6,000–7,000 members by June 1989,[83] the Independent Small-holders' Party likewise aspired to free elections and political neutrality. As a peasant party, the organization emphasizes the revitalization of agriculture.

Pacifism, one of the earliest impulses to lead to organized dissident activity in the 1980s, was also an important component inspiring the Republican Circle. In a document on military service and disarmament issued on 23 June 1988, for example, the Republican Circle urged:

> Except while in pursuit of armed criminals, the police should not carry weapons.
>
> Children should be taught not to use force. Therefore, all text-books and other educational materials should be reviewed with re-gard to this issue; also, the Pioneers' Union should be dissolved.
>
> Paramilitary groups, such as the Young Guards, Workers' Guards, and the Hungarian National Defense League should be abolished.[84]

There were at least three independent youth groups active by the end of 1989 (the other two being the Szárszó Front and New Generation), as well as the revived Christian Democratic Party, the revived People's Party, the Party of Hungarian Gypsies,[85] and two fiercely anticommunist parties, the Hungarian October Party and the Hungarian Radical Party, both established in mid-1989.

Three more groups worthy of mention appeared in 1988. First, sev-eral hundred Hungarian intellectuals established the Openness Club in July to promote freedom in publishing. Interestingly enough, the ini-tiative seemed to enjoy the support of the PPF. September brought the creation of an independent grouping of intellectuals similar to the Club of Rome that called itself the New March Front in order to suggest a spiritual unity with the prewar March Front that had sought to pro-mote democracy in Hungary.[86] Among its founding members were Rezső Nyers, then a member of the Politburo and later chairman of the ex-communist party, Sándor Fekete, editor-in-chief of *Új Tőkőr*, and Szilárd Ujhalyi, one of the founders of the original March Front. The New March Front described itself as a "spiritual" movement rather than a political party. Yet its purposes were clearly political. Nyers himself noted that the founders were motivated by a "sense of danger and [a] sense of re-sponsibility, along with the idea that the party must renew itself. In my opinion, at the same time we also thought that it is not sufficient to try to advance or to resolve social renewal merely with party politics and via party politics."[87]

And finally, 1988 brought the creation of the Network of Free Initiatives, formed in Budapest's Hági restaurant on 1 May as an umbrella organization for sundry independent activist groups.[88]

Historical Consciousness. Europeans are, in general, far more conscious of their history than Americans are of theirs. But even by European standards, Hungarians seem particularly history-conscious. Anniversaries of the Hungarian revolutions of 1848 and 1956[89] had the potential to ignite social unrest, at least in the nation's capital. On 15 March 1986—the 138th anniversary of the outbreak of the revolt against Austrian rule—Hungarians marched through Budapest, only to be dispersed by police wielding truncheons and tear gas. The following year some 2,000 Hungarians marched arm-in-arm through Budapest on the 139th anniversary, singing, chanting, and applauding calls for democracy and freedom of the press. The crowd formed at noon at the monument to Sándor Petőfi, the nineteenth-century poet whose name is identified with the 1848 Revolution and with Hungarian resistance to foreign rule. The marchers later converged on a shrine erected in memory of Lajos Batthány, a Hungarian leader executed during that same revolution. Dissident György Gadó delivered an oration there, drawing comparisons between Batthány and Imre Nagy, executed by the Soviets in 1958. Another dissident, Tíbor Pak, called for the withdrawal of Soviet troops from Hungary.[90] The nationalist component was unmistakable, as was its close link with the pressure for democracy.

On 15 March 1988 an even larger crowd commemorated the suppression of the 1848 Revolution. Some 10,000 Hungarians marched through Budapest chanting "Democracy" and carrying banners reading "Real Reform," "Freedom of Assembly," "Freedom of the Press," and "Free Elections." The crowd stopped to lay wreaths and hear speeches at monuments to the heroes of 1848—Petőfi, Batthány, President Lajos Kossuth, and Polish general József Bem (who fought with the Hungarians). As before, the procession was nationalist and liberal in orientation. And as Western news agencies noted, the mood of the demonstrators was "festive and confident."[91]

Romania: The Breakdown of Civil Order

Social Unrest. Partly because of the ruthlessness of the Romanian *Securitate* and partly, perhaps, because of the country's lower level of development, independent activism in Romania has been more important in its anomic forms than in the form of formal dissident bodies.

In the early years of the Ceauşescu dictatorship there was a tendency for Romanians to "forgive" the regime for its Stalinism, taking a certain pride in Ceauşescu's ability to chart a course somewhat independent of the Soviet Union. But in the course of the 1970s there were increasing symptoms of discontent among workers, intellectuals, ethnic minorities, and religious groups. In response to the Polish workers' riots of December 1970, which toppled the government of Władysław Gomułka, Ceauşescu called for a program to improve the work of the trade unions and encouraged the workers to participate in discussions in this regard. Vasile Paraschiv, a worker at a petrochemical plant in Ploieşti, responded to this by sending a letter to the central committee in which he proposed the creation of trade unions independent of party control and run by the workers themselves. The regime's reply to Paraschiv's letter took the form of his forcible incarceration in a psychiatric clinic. In 1977 he was allowed to leave Romania.[92]

The regime of Nicolae Ceauşescu (1965–89) was confronted by periodic social unrest for more than a decade. The first chapter in this story was written in August 1977, when coal miners in the Jiu Valley went on strike and demanded to see Ceauşescu personally. The immediate cause of the strike was the announcement of a string of changes in social legislation that would adversely affect the miners and their families: the miners' workday was to be increased from six to eight hours, the retirement age was raised from fifty to fifty-five, various categories of sickness benefits and disability pensions were curtailed or abolished, and workers were informed that there would be new financial penalties for failures to meet production targets.[93]

Even before strikes broke out on 1 August there were rumors throughout the valley that preparations for a strike at the Lupeni mine were under way. Shortly after the strike was proclaimed at Lupeni, it spread throughout the valley, with miners from other mines converging on Lupeni in a show of solidarity.

Three strike leaders took charge: a mining engineer from the Lupeni mine, named Jurcă; the pit brigade chief from the Paroşeni mine, named Dobre; and a woman who may have been a local party or youth activist.

The miners issued demands for the restoration of the status quo ante in social legislation, the guarantee of adequate food supplies and medical care, the establishment of workers' commissions at the enterprise level empowered to dismiss incompetent or corrupt managers, and a pledge that there would be no reprisals against the strikers.

Ilie Verdeţ, a Politburo member, was sent to the Jiu Valley as the head of a delegation of high-ranking party and state officials. But when Verdeţ arrived the morning of 2 August he and the other high-ranking officials were imprisoned by the strikers. Verdeţ was compelled to telephone the vacationing Ceauşescu and summon him to Lupeni; Ceauşescu arrived the following day.

After an initial, hopeless attempt to order the strikers back to work, Ceauşescu promised to grant all of the miners' demands. The miners thereupon released Verdeţ, agreed to return to work the next day, and even offered to make up the time lost during the strike. The concessions held long enough for the authorities to break the organizational backbone of the resistance. The three strike leaders disappeared permanently in September.[94] Other miners who had been outspoken during the strike were rounded up piecemeal over the following months and dispersed to other parts of the country. Eventually most of the concessions were withdrawn and the eight-hour workday imposed, although this was not made official until 1983.

While the authorities thus contained unrest in the Jiu Valley, a symbolically important precedent was set in early 1979 when a group of fifteen workers and several intellectuals from the industrial center of Turnu Severin in southwestern Romania set up the Free Trade Union of Romanian Workers. The union made a number of bold demands, including the legalization of independent trade unions, the abolition of privileges for high party officials, changes in the retirement system, the abolition of censorship, and an end to compulsory "patriotic labor" on weekends. The authorities moved quickly before most Romanians were aware of the union's existence, and most of the known founding members soon "disappeared."[95]

There was further unrest in October 1981 among mine and quarry workers in the Motru basin, in September 1983 among miners in Baia Borşa, Gura Baia, and Toroioaga, in November 1983 among one thousand workers at the Braşov Steagul Roşu truck factory, in February 1985 among workers in Timişoara, in August 1986 among transport workers in Arad in western Romania, and in November 1986 among factory workers in Cluj and Turda in Transylvania. In both of the latter two instances, as in September 1983, pay cuts and poor food supplies triggered the stoppages.[96] The unrest in November 1986 was sparked by the official announcement that the bread ration in Transylvania would be reduced to 300 grams a day and pay at several major factories would be cut dramatically for nonfulfillment of the plan. On 1 November graffiti and leaflets in Romanian and Hungarian appeared, demanding meat, bread and "milk for our children," and condemning the "Ceauşescu dictatorship."[97] Strikes broke out at the heavy equipment and refrigeration machinery plants in Cluj, and at the glass factory in Turda. The strikers demanded improvement in the food supply and a retraction of the pay cuts. Authorities replayed the tactics used in 1977—granting concessions at first, then questioning the workers, dismissing the suspected organizers, and gradually withdrawing the initial concessions. Along the way, some twenty-five organizers of the strike disappeared without a trace, leaving even their families uncertain of their fate.[98]

After permitting the Romanian national debt to climb to $13 billion in 1982, Ceauşescu decided on radical belt-tightening to bring down the debt. Residential consumption of gas and electricity was forcibly cut by 90 percent between 1979 and 1987.[99] Food was rigidly rationed. Imports were sliced, while anything exportable was sold abroad. Noncompetitive industrial products were sold at prices below production costs.[100] These radical measures bled the country but succeeded in halving the debt. In the midst of all this privation, Ceauşescu indulged in an architectural megalomaniacal fantasy, bulldozing a large section of historic Bucharest in order to create a permanent "monument" to himself, half a mile wide and ten miles long. The main plaza is spacious, framed by rigid rows of neoclassical buildings in the grand style, complete with Roman columns, fake arches, and gargantuan balconies.[101] All of this only deepened the general hatred for Ceauşescu.

February 1987 saw renewed unrest in Iaşi, Moldavia, among workers and students, with the latter ostentatiously burning textbooks on "scientific socialism." But this unrest was completely overshadowed by the dramatic demonstrations in Braşov in November 1987. Angered by new wage cuts and persistent food shortages, several thousand workers from Braşov's Red Flag truck factory staged a protest march to party headquarters on 15 November. During the one-hour march they sang a revolutionary song ("Awake, Romania") from the Revolution of 1848 and chanted "We want bread" and "Down with dictatorship." Other townspeople joined them and soon there were up to 20,000 people protesting. Upon reaching party headquarters some demonstrators forced their way inside and hurled furniture, files, and portraits of the *Conducator* out the window. Other demonstrators found the exclusive party shop storing special food provisions for party officials, and, amid great indignation, brought the foodstuffs to the public square.[102]

Romanian police arrested some 400 persons,[103] and troops were sent in to patrol the streets.[104] But there was no mention of the riots in the Romanian press, although *Scînteia* somewhat elliptically reproved local officials, urging the importance of "fruitful cooperation between citizens and elected officials."[105]

Crane Brinton, it will be recalled, identified several uniformities in the emergence of revolution, including the financial failure of the government, governmental inefficiency, class antagonism and the alienation of the people from the government, the abandonment of the regime by the intellectuals, and the loss of self-confidence on the part of the governing class.[106] All these elements were present in Romania at the close of the 1980s, including the loss of self-confidence within the elite itself.

There were various signs of this, including a purge at the upper rungs of the Defense Ministry in the wake of rumors of army resistance to Ceauşescu's policies.[107] Later, in the wake of the Braşov riots, Romania's former ambassador to the United States, Silviu Brucan, publicly compared the situation in Romania to that in Poland in 1980, adding that "a period of crisis has opened between the communist party and the working class." To make matters worse, he called on the leadership to make "a sincere effort to come to terms with [the public's] legitimate grievances" and declared that the "overwhelming majority" of the party itself agreed with his assessment of the situation.[108] Brucan was later forced to retract his statements, but meanwhile Ceauşescu was compelled to postpone the party's national conference for a week, evidently to make sure his internal opposition was muzzled.[109] Criticism of Ceauşescu even came from the eighty-five-year-old former Romanian prime minister, Ion Gheorghe Maurer.[110]

Independent Activist Groups. It is the depth of social malaise and the recurrence and deepening of anomic unrest that suggested that Romania was the most vulnerable to revolutionary upheaval of the three countries surveyed in this chapter. Because of the relative lack of organized dissent, however, it was the last of the three to begin the transition to "post-communism." But there were *some* forces for social change, which fit more properly under the rubric of "independent activism."

Democratic Action. In late 1985 thirteen pseudonymous signatories signed a manifesto announcing the creation of an opposition movement dedicated to the establishment of democratic pluralism in Romania and inspired by Christian ideals. Calling their movement Democratic Action, the signatories swore "to undermine and destroy the communist regime in the course of time and to uphold the idea of democracy."[111] During 1987 the group distributed three manifestos emphasizing the importance of private property and individual initiative as prerequisites for economic prosperity, and calling for the establishment of a parliamentary system on the West European model, with guarantees for ethnic minorities.[112] In 1988 Democratic Action drew up a twenty-two-page "Green Report" on the environmental situation, criticizing the Ceauşescu regime for irresponsible mismanagement and complaining of the general secrecy in which information about the Romanian ecology was shrouded.[113]

Free Romania. Most of the members of Free Romania were white- and blue-collar Romanians concentrated in the Banat region. A small number of Romanians linked with this group moved to Budapest, and maintained contact with members inside Romania.[114] The movement was implacably hostile to Ceauşescu and called for his overthrow; it was necessarily clandestine. At the same time, however, unlike the anti-communist Democratic Action, Free Romania advertised its fidelity to the bloc, praised the Gorbachev line, and called for the introduction of *glasnost* and *perestroika* in Romania. The group even made contact with the Soviets at a Soviet embassy (presumably the embassy in Budapest, since access to the Soviet embassy in Bucharest was well guarded and monitored). But the Soviets told the Romanian malcontents that Romanians must resolve their crisis by themselves.[115]

In April 1988 the Budapest wing of the organization launched a Romanian-language samizdat periodical, *România Liberă*, with the intention of distributing it in Romania. The Free Romanian group was able to use the printing facilities of the Hungarian democratic opposition.[116] Meanwhile, in Romania itself, Ceauşescu's sweeping plans to physically destroy seven to eight thousand villages in Romania impelled Romanian and minority malcontents to form a "coalition" and to draw up a protest.[117]

In November 1988 *România Liberă* published an appeal to Romanians calling for the release of political prisoners, freedom of religion, an end to censorship, cancellation of Ceauşescu's rural resettlement program, equality for all nationalities, trade union pluralism, and freedom of movement.[118]

National Peasant Party. Outlawed in 1947 after winning nearly 70 percent of the vote in the 1946 elections, the National Peasant Party once championed the interests of the peasantry. After the communist takeover, party leader Iuliu Maniu and tens of thousands of other party members were imprisoned, many until 1964. The party seemed to have disappeared, but small groups of survivors, including once prominent leaders, began meeting in private, and some of them issued political statements in the name of the National Peasant Party in 1983, 1984, and 1985. In the last instance, the party issued a comprehensive political platform drafted by sixty-seven-year-old Ion Puiu, once a party youth leader. The platform called for respect for constitutional guarantees of individual rights, the abolition of party privileges, the dismantling of the *Securitate*, the separation of the labor unions from communist party control, the depoliticization of education, the restoration of the former (precommunist) role of the Grand National Assembly, and complete freedom of religion.[119] Subsequently, the National Peasant Party's former leaders attracted a following among young people and established a human rights organization (1986) with branches in Bucharest and Transylvania.[120]

An Expanding International Network?

One of the earliest efforts on the part of independent activists to establish cooperation across borders came in 1978, when signatories of Czechoslovakia's Charter 77 and members of the Polish KOR held two meetings somewhere along the Polish-Czechoslovak border. Cross-border contacts could be useful for sharing experiences, exchanging ideas, and possibly coordinating common strategies and joint actions. The issuance of joint manifestos could also serve to underscore the weight of the protest.

Gorbachev's drive to export reform to Eastern Europe made such coordination among independent activists more attractive than ever.[121] "With Gorbachev's reforms," János Kis said in October 1987, "you have a region ready for great change, even ferment. It only makes sense to develop a common strategy."[122] Technological advances also helped, as Janusz Onyszkiewicz, the former spokesperson of Polish Solidarity noted in January 1987: "There has definitely been a change. Psychologically, there was always the will to cooperate across borders but the technical capabilities lagged behind."[123] Direct-dial telephoning was pivotal in this regard, even with bugged lines.

Pacifists and human rights activists were in the forefront of efforts to build an activist network. In 1984 activists from Czechoslovakia's Charter 77 and the East German independent peace movement issued a joint declaration showing their agreement on two key issues: the deployment of new Soviet nuclear missiles in their two countries which endangered peace, and the inseparability of peace from respect for human rights.[124] The declaration was signed by seventeen East Germans and sixteen Czechoslovaks. Later, on 23 October 1986, dissidents from four Soviet-bloc countries—Czechoslovakia, East Germany, Hungary, and Poland—

issued a joint statement to which three Romanian dissidents later sub-
scribed. The statement commemorated the thirtieth anniversary of the
Hungarian Revolution, noting, in part:

> [T]he essential demands of the revolutionaries have not been satis-
> fied. On this anniversary, we call on all our friends in the world to
> join us to commemorate the 1956 Hungarian Revolution. We pro-
> claim our common determination to struggle for political democ-
> racy in our countries, for their independence, for pluralism founded
> on the principles of self-government, for the peaceful unification of
> a divided Europe and for its democratic integration, as well as for
> the rights of all national minorities.[125]

The coordination was unprecedented, and the text itself suggested a new
confidence in the possibility of change.

Recent years also saw a joint protest by Polish and Czech environmentalists (1987), a joint appeal for the right of conscientious objection
to military service signed by more than 400 activists from throughout
Eastern Europe (1988), and a joint memorandum signed by hundreds
of pacifists and environmentalists in both Western and Eastern Europe
(1987), which called for freedom of travel, legalization of independent
publishers in Eastern Europe, and an end to restrictions on the import
of books, journals, and tapes intended for the use of the traveler.[126]

From mid-1986 through early 1988, sundry groupings of independent
activists in Eastern Europe began establishing regular contacts and organizing clandestine strategy sessions, joint declarations, and independent
conferences.[127] Such conferences were held in Warsaw and Budapest.[128]
Inevitably such cooperative contacts assumed an organizational dimension. For instance, in May 1986 four "special interest sections" associated
with underground Solidarity contacted Charter 77 with offers of cooperation in specific areas: the sections concerned were the Social Commission for Health, the Social Committee for Science and Scholarship, the
Group for Independent Public Education, and the Helsinki Committee in
Poland.[129] Again, in July 1987 thirty-four Polish and Czechoslovak activists announced the creation of a joint committee, the Circle of Friends
of Polish-Czechoslovak Solidarity, for the exchange of information and
coordination of activities.[130] Shortly thereafter, the organization met and
issued a statement. In a key passage, the twenty-one signatories noted:

> All our endeavors so far have been based on the conviction that
> the widening of civil liberties, and a better life for the societies of

the Soviet bloc, depends above all on these societies themselves, namely, on what they themselves attain through active work. This conviction of theirs has not been changed by the onset of the Gorbachev era. Today, too, we want to rely first of all on our own strength. We are aware, at the same time, that the policy of the Gorbachev leadership is creating more favorable conditions for the self-emancipating efforts pursued in the countries of the Soviet bloc. . . . Those attending the meeting have once again acknowledged and affirmed that, no matter how different the situation is in the various European countries of the Soviet bloc and no matter how diverse their own approaches are to the resolution of the problems of their societies, the fundamental ideals of all those who take independent public action in these countries are essentially identical.[131]

In addition, the steadily deteriorating economic conditions of Romanians provided a special focal point for intergroup cooperation. In Romania the excesses of the Ceauşescu regime prompted Hungarian dissidents in Transylvania and Romanian dissidents to support each other's struggles.[132] And in January 1988 Charter 77 called on all Europeans to demonstrate against Ceauşescu on 1 February.[133] The result was a series of solidarity protests in Czechoslovakia, Hungary, Poland, and the Soviet Union, as well as demonstrations by East European émigré groups in London, Paris, Bonn, Munich, and other West European cities. Although police broke up the demonstrations in Warsaw and Prague, the Czech police even arresting some of the demonstrators, the police in Budapest restricted themselves to removing banners displaying slogans like "Human and Civil Rights for All Romanians" and asking the crowd to disperse.[134]

By spring 1988 Polish-Czechoslovak Solidarity operated more or less openly, publishing a monthly newsletter and organizing conferences and demonstrations.[135] It also issued a joint protest against reprisals in East Germany as part of a coalition of Poles, Czechoslovaks, Hungarians, Yugoslavs, and Russians.[136]

Polish-Czechoslovak Solidarity provided a model for a similar cooperative committee involving Czechoslovak and Hungarian activists. The HDF and Czechoslovakia's Democratic Initiative took the lead in this regard and on 26 August 1989 established the Committee for Czechoslovak-Hungarian Democratic Cooperation.

The growing mutual support among independent activists signified, on one level, a growth in "genuine internationalism of the peoples in the region," as the Hungarian samizdat journal *Beszélő* put it in December 1987.[137] It also signified a new confidence among activists and a growing sense that real change could be effected. The Czechoslovak playwright Václav Havel put it this way in early 1988:

> I am convinced that this chasm between ideology and the basic power-political principles on the one hand and the authentic beliefs of society on the other will continue to deepen for a long time but not indefinitely. The growth of the chasm is acquiring the dimensions of an ever more important political fact that sooner or later must translate into political change.[138]

Part III
Religious and Ethnic Currents

6. Religious Change and
New Cults in Eastern Europe

Religious change has its sources in *secularization*, which changes the relationship between religious institutions and society, and *cultural drift*, which is associated with changes in religious needs, cultural distortion, and general social stress. As traditional religious institutions cease to be seen as repositories of answers to emerging questions, the receptivity of society to new religious movements increases, both in specific subcultures and in general. The result is that both religious innovation and the importation of religious creeds from foreign lands are more successful. And as new cults and religious movements find fertile soil and sprout, social and cultural fragmentation is reinforced and the traditional sense of *Volksgemeinschaft* is further undermined.

Secularization has been variously defined. One useful definition equates it with "a societal process in which an overarching and transcendent religious system is . . . reduced to a subsystem of society alongside other subsystems, and the overarching claims of which have a shrinking audience."[1] In its early stages secularization involves the decline of religious content in art, literature, music, and philosophy. Later secularization takes the form of the creation of a political sphere autonomous from the religious, and the gradual demystification of the community's understanding of the universe.[2] The expansion of scientific knowledge steadily reduced social reliance on religion for explanations of natural phenomena. In later stages secularization is associated with a shift in the focus of communal life, which ceases to revolve around the church. Insofar as no other institution is capable of assuming the church's traditional role, the life of the community becomes fragmented as different sectors look to different institutions and different activities to satisfy primary associational needs. In this connection, Thomas Luckmann's comment linking secularization with the "dissolution of the traditional, coherent sacred cosmos"[3] is apt. Secularization necessarily fosters social stress, which in turn fuels religious revival and religious innovation.

The starting point for this chapter, then, is that secularization is part of a broader syndrome organically associated with religious revival in traditional religion, confessional change where mainline churches fail to adapt, and the appearance of new religious cults. One may even say that the latter phenomena are *manifestations* of secularization.[4] These aspects will be examined in sequence.

Secularization

Secularization in Western Europe has been a spontaneous process that has unfolded despite the protective attitude of some governments (e.g., Spain and West Germany). Secularization in Eastern Europe was a conscious goal of the communist authorities from the beginning. Prior to the communist takeover, religion was included in the school curriculum in each of these countries. The communists removed religious instruction from state schools, nationalized most religious schools, and set in motion antireligious campaigns, and, in Czechoslovakia and Yugoslavia, attempted to link Catholic clergy with the wartime fascist puppet states. Atheist Circles were established among schoolchildren in Czechoslovakia. Among their activities were the viewing of antireligious films and field trips to museums and exhibitions of revolutionary traditions. Communist youth organizations became vehicles for "atheization," and a youth initiation ceremony (*Jugendweihe*) was introduced in 1954 in East Germany as an atheist substitute for Christian confirmation. Young people often grew up without any knowledge of religious doctrine, teachings, or history.

Secularization was also implemented by making social advancement dependent on party membership and party membership dependent on the rejection of religious belief, although by the late 1980s there were known to be crypto-Christians in several of the ruling parties in the region, including the Czechoslovak,[5] East German, Polish,[6] Romanian,[7] and Yugoslav.[8] (In 1989 the Hungarian party passed a decree allowing believers to join the party.)

Finally, churches were financially undermined by the confiscation of landholdings, hospitals, old-age homes, and so forth. This policy was not applied in East Germany, where churches always owned a large number of such institutions, but elsewhere these confiscations deprived churches of independent income and forced them to accept state salaries for clergy. The regimes thus found themselves in the position of being able to withhold or lower salaries to obtain ecclesiastical cooperation and to reward cooperative clergy with larger salaries.

The combined result of these policies was that church attendance dropped off in most of the countries, reaching the lowest levels among East Germans, Czechs, Serbs, and Bulgarians. In Albania the government simply closed all churches and mosques in 1967 and declared religion "abolished." Gradually the number of registered adherents dropped.

Secularization proceeded fastest among the Bulgarians and the Czechs. As early as 1962 nearly 65 percent of the Bulgarians declared themselves nonreligious[9] according to one report, while another source reported that about 45 percent of the population were believers in 1978.[10] In Czechoslovakia the historical legacy of anticlericalism in Bohemia and Moravia[11] facilitated the process, and official statistics recorded a sharp fall in the number of believers. In 1946, for instance, 64 percent of the population believed in God and only 12 percent did not; as of 1963, only 34 percent said they believed in God, while 38 percent said they did not. Church attendance also declined, with only 13 percent attending regularly in 1963 (versus 20 percent in 1946), and 51 percent never attending (versus 24 percent in 1946). The differences in the experiences of the component nationalities were reflected in the fact that while 31 percent of the Czechs were said to be atheists in 1963, only 13 percent of the Slovaks were so described.[12] Surprisingly, official statistics from 1984 show little change among those over the age of fifteen: 36 percent remained religious believers (51 percent in Slovakia and 30 percent in the Czech lands).[13] Since the church has traditionally been weak among Bulgarians and Czechs, state authorities found less resistance to atheization programs.

The church seemed much stronger in East Germany, but by 1983 membership in the Evangelical-Lutheran church had been reduced from 15 million in 1946 to 7.7 million, and, counting in the other religious organizations, only 56 percent of the population were believers in 1983 (as opposed to 99 percent in 1946).[14]

Elsewhere, secularization proceeded more slowly. In Yugoslavia 70.3 percent of the population were believers as of 1964.[15] But a comparison of survey data from Belgrade from 1986 with earlier surveys reveals an interesting trend: the numbers of both believers and atheists were at that time declining, with increasing numbers declaring themselves agnostics.[16]

In Hungary between 76 and 81 percent of the population are nominal believers, and at least two-thirds of adults avail themselves of some religious ceremonies. But less than 20 percent of Hungarian adults attend Sunday services regularly. To some extent, religious adherence in Hungary has become hollow and superficial.[17] Religious affiliation is also negatively correlated with television ownership and urbanization; accordingly, those most active in religion are often the least involved in the sociopolitical life of the nation.

In Romania fully 81 percent of the population were recorded as believers in 1984,[18] and party theorists expressed their frustration with their relative lack of success in this area, attributing it in part—and with justification—to the ability of certain Christian organizations to adapt to social changes and to thus "revitalize" themselves.[19] There have been interconfessional shifts, to be sure, but actual atheization seems to be less tangible, judging from other figures, than in most of the countries of the region.

Finally, in Poland 93 percent of the population are baptized Roman Catholics and 83 percent of the population are believers.[20] The long association of the Catholic church with Polish nationalism is part of the explanation of this intense religiosity.[21] But the relatively greater anthropocentrism of Polish religiosity, focused on the Virgin Mary and the saints and placing a greater premium on communal relations rather than on the individual's relationship to God, also helps to explain the evident immunity of Polish society to secularization. As Barbara Strassberg explains,

> Since [Polish] religious culture is not really based on a knowledge of the doctrine and the church's teaching, it is not threatened by the dissemination of the scientific approach towards the natural and social world. Not caring very much for dogmas, people do not apply scientific criteria to them. . . . [Furthermore,] if secularization can be understood as a process of detheocentrization and of anthropocentrization of culture, then it becomes obvious that in a sociocultural context in which religion itself is anthropocentric, the change leads to a deeper "penetration" of religion into the entire national culture rather than to its "functional separation," "individualization," or "privatization."[22]

Secularization is not merely a question of a decline in formal adherence and actual participation in rituals; other processes are involved. In the first place, secularization tends to introduce doubts about specific church doctrines and teachings. Depending on the nature of the teaching thrown into question, the believer may even decide to retain some teachings while rejecting others, or may leave the church, possibly gravitating to another religious body. About 30 percent of Polish Catholics, for instance, evince selective religiosity in this sense, while only 13 percent of Hungarian believers say they are "religious according to the teaching of the church."[23] This latter option is in turn reinforced by a second, parallel process—the relativization of affiliation. Traditionally, believers were taught that their church was uniquely holy and that all other churches were debasements of God's will. Confessional pluralization contributes to the erosion of this confidence, and believers tend to have a lower threshold of resistance to other denominations. Since the Second Vatican Council, this applies also to the Roman Catholic church. The result is that "the former rigid barriers between the denominations have become and are becoming permeable."[24] Third, secularization brings with it pressures for the laicization of the church as laypeople demand more active roles in church life. The basis communities of the Catholic church are a graphic illustration of this process, and will be discussed below.

Changes in Traditional Religion

That ferment has occurred in certain traditional churches, above all the Catholic church, has been clear for some time.[25] It is characteristic of religious revival that its principal impetus comes from the grass roots—this is its source of strength. Revival operates by the selective scuttling of old traditions, creative innovation of new traditions, and the harnessing of existing traditions in new ways; thus, religious revival is transformative. The challenge that this poses to communist party cadres was noted, for instance, in a decree issued by the Georgian party central committee on 18 September 1979, which warned that "in training atheistic cadres we must keep in mind that religious worldviews [and] cults are undergoing modernization, and are becoming more flexible, trying to adjust to present circumstances. Under such conditions, the tasks of atheistic indoctrination are becoming more complex and impose new requirements on atheistic cadres."[26]

Religious revival has been strongest in Hungary and Yugoslavia, though neighboring Ukraine shares in the syndrome. In Poland and (perhaps) eastern Germany it may be more accurate to speak of religious adaptation, since neither religiosity nor respect for the institutional church was ever seriously in danger. Impulses toward religious revival in the traditional (Orthodox, Catholic, Lutheran, Calvinist) churches in other countries of the region are weaker.

The Evangelical Church's support for pacifist and environmentalist activism in East Germany has been discussed in chapter 3. Since the transition of 1989–90, the Evangelical Church has faced allegations that an undetermined number of its pastors, including even Friedrich-Wilhelm Krummacher, onetime Bishop of Greifswald, and Church Superintendent Manfred Stolpe, had maintained unwarranted contacts with the East German secret police; the church has responded by conducting extensive checks of all its personnel.[27] At the same time, German Protestants and Catholics formally left their churches in record numbers in 1991–93, driving East Germany's Catholic bishop to hire professional admen to try to "sell" the church. Meanwhile, likewise feeling the pressure, the Evangelical Church consecrated its first female bishop (in Hamburg in 1994), embraced aspects of feminist theology, and in other ways tried to present itself as a voice for the twenty-first century.[28]

In the Polish case the traditional nationalism of the lower clergy and the anthropocentrism of Polish folk piety gave the Catholic faith an uncommon resilience. The church also displayed adaptive capacity in establishing new rituals on the national level, which in turn heightened the consciousness of the Poles as a Catholic nation.[29] In addition, the Oasis and neocatechumenate movements, which developed their own religious rituals, reinforced Polish religiosity. Independent religious youth organizations were technically illegal in Poland until early 1989, but Oasis, which emerged in stages in the latter 1950s as a renewal movement for Polish youth, thrived from the 1960s through the 1980s. Attracting more than 45,000 young people for its summer retreats, the movement sees itself "as an evangelistic movement, dedicated to leading people to accept Christ as Savior and Lord."[30] It also preserved the Marian cult. The election of Kraków's Karol Cardinal Wojtyła as pope in 1978 only reinforced an already resilient religious feeling among Poles.

In Hungary transformative processes are perhaps as far advanced as anywhere in the region. Hungarian sociologist of religion Miklós Tomka says flatly that traditional religiosity in Hungary is finished.[31] Its replacement is a heavily laicized religiosity in which believers experience their faith as a personal quest for understanding rather than as subordination to clerical authority. To some extent both the Catholic and the Protestant churches have already accommodated themselves to this current, but grassroots pressures sometimes go farther than the respective hierarchies are wont to allow.

The Catholic basis communities are a case in point. The movement can be traced to the creation of the Regnum Marianum in 1903. In the late 1950s there were already many small basis communities operating in Hungary, albeit illegally. In 1976, however, two important changes occurred that affected the church-state relationship. The first was the conclusion of a church-state accord following László Lékai's succession as archbishop of Esztergom and primate of Hungary. The second was the passage of a statute pursuant to Hungary's ratification of the Helsinki Accords, which allowed private citizens to meet in private homes for religious purposes. The result was a "boom" in the founding of basis communities, and by 1987 there may have been as many as four or five thousand.[32]

The basis communities revive the sense of communal bonding which gave early Christianity its great strength, and permit members to talk to each other about questions that concern them. At least five major currents can be discerned among Hungarian basis communities (not to mention various smaller currents): the Charismatic, Focolari, Taisei, Regnum Marianum, and Bush networks. All but the last enjoyed untroubled relations with both hierarchy and the communist state. Bush, led by the inspiring Father György Bulányi, differs from the others in seeking "radical change in the structure of the church, which would involve a redefinition of the roles of the laity, the priesthood, and the bishops,"[33] and in opposing obligatory military service. The Hungarian bishops refused to support Bulányi's advocacy of conscientious objection, and have even suggested that it is contrary to the teachings of the church.[34] State authorities were likewise discomfited by the pacifism of Bush, with Imre Miklós, chair of the State Office for Religious Affairs, reportedly telling Vatican officials that "the way will be made green" for the Bush, provided only that it abandon its pacifism.[35] But what concerns us here is not the controversy between Bulányi and both secular and ecclesiastical authorities, but the general striving of the entire basis community movement to "restore" what its adherents see as "authentic" Christianity, and the specific aspiration of Bush to restructure the church.

The Lutheran church in Hungary was also touched by the winds of change. Long tied to a "Diakonia theology" which preached unambiguous church support for the political system,[36] the Lutheran church now saw the emergence of internal criticism. In April 1986 nineteen pastors and laymen sent a letter to Bishop Gyula Nagy and all of the country's Lutheran parishes urging "radical inner renewal," including the election of church leaders not subservient to the communist regime. In January 1987 members of the unofficial reform group met with the church leadership and produced a joint statement calling for extensive discussion of the church policy of cooperation with the state and for more open discussion of church problems. The bishops balked, however, at the reform group's call for decentralization of the church's judicial structure.[37] Before the end of the year Bishop Nagy promised that his church was on the threshold of a "new era" and that the issues raised by the reform group, including its challenge to Diakonia theology and its demand for the restoration of a Lutheran grammar school, would be discussed in an open way. He gave symbolic expression to this resolve by partly rehabilitating the reputation of the deceased Bishop Lajos Ordass, who had been imprisoned by the state. Not surprisingly, Imre Miklós used a ceremonial occasion to warn the Lutheran church not to stray "from the path hitherto followed."[38] With the opening up of Hungarian politics, by 1989 Diakonia theology was dead.

In Yugoslavia and Ukraine impetus to religious revival came from a very different source—reports of miraculous apparitions of the Madonna that produced a wave of pilgrimages and a marked rise in expressive religiosity among Catholics. In fact there was a rash of such apparitions in Eastern Europe since 1981: first in Bosnia-Herzegovina, then in Dalmatia (in Gala in 1983,[39] and in Split in 1987),[40] in Poland and Czechoslovakia (where the reported apparitions evoked little response), and in western Ukraine in 1987.[41]

The best known is the apparition of the Madonna seen by six youths in the village of Medjugorje in Herzegovina on 24 June 1981. The youths continued to experience apparitions on almost a daily basis for several years, and four were still reporting apparitions in 1988.[42] Meanwhile, pilgrims started to arrive by the thousands, and Franciscan fathers came to say mass and hear confessions. By mid-1987 there had been 290 reported miracle healings. More than 50,000 pilgrims would arrive on some holy days, mostly Croats or other Yugoslavs, but also increasing numbers of foreigners. Yugoslav Airlines added several flights to cater to Medjugorje pilgrims, expecting some 25,000 foreign tourists to come to Medjugorje in 1987. Local officials belatedly gave permission for Yugoslav tourist agencies to build a big tourist complex in Medjugorje. The swarm of pilgrims contributed to a feeling of deepened piety among many in Herzegovina and visibly strengthened the position of the Franciscan order in that region. When war came to Bosnia-Herzegovina in March–April 1992, the religious tourism slowed down, but visitors note that Medjugorje, alone among municipalities in the region, has been unscathed by war.[43]

In a separate development, in April 1987 a young Ukrainian girl named Maria Kizyn reported that she had seen "a light in a long-closed church, looked inside, and saw a shining female figure surrounded by radiant light and carrying a child."[44] After that, as many as 45,000 pilgrims per day traveled to the village of Grushevo, where Kizyn reported the apparition.[45] Unlike Medjugorje, where the vision was restricted to the six young people, many people at Grushevo reported seeing the Madonna.

The Madonna's "message" at Medjugorje was a clue to the meaning of these apparitions: pray, repent, and think of God. The message was absolute simplicity with no adornment whatsoever. The receptivity of Yugoslav Croats and west Ukrainians to the apparitions signified the desire of many in these countries to find a simple piety with simple answers that would cut through the complex challenges posed by contemporary life. These expressions of folk piety necessarily risk serious distortion of the church's rather more complex teachings; thus, the Vatican reacted very slowly and cautiously, and held back from pronouncing final judgment on either of these alleged miracles.

Finally, the Serbian Orthodox church has experienced a kind of revival, albeit a secularizing one fueled by Serbian nationalism. The outbreak of Albanian nationalist riots in the Serbian province of Kosovo in April 1981 and subsequent incidents set thousands of Serbs and Montenegrins to flight and provoked a Serbian nationalist backlash. Serbian Orthodox church clergy spoke out about Kosovo, and the church newspaper *Pravoslavlje* began running articles on national themes, celebrated the anniversary of Serbian orthographer Vuk Karadžić, and even published poetry about Kosovo. All of this found resonance among Serbs, and even nonreligious Serbs started to take an interest in "their" church. A poll was taken among the citizens of Belgrade in 1987, revealing that one out of every five respondents "agreed with the statement that the Serbian Orthodox church was the *most* lasting and the *most* dependable Serbian institution."[46]

Confessional Change

Religious revival changes the character of religious organizations. Confessional change affects the balance between religious organizations. People leave churches for different reasons. Some, of course, leave because they cease to credit the supernatural claims of religion. Others transfer their loyalty from one denomination to another. The transferral process, or *confessional change,* has taken two forms in Eastern Europe: movement between traditional churches (typically as a result of confessional intermarriage or the unavailability of the services of one's original church in a particular community); and conversion from a traditional church to a "neo-Protestant" church (chiefly Baptists, Pentecostals, Plymouth Brethren, Congregationalists, Mormons, Seventh-Day Adventists, Nazarenes, and Jehovah's Witnesses).

Leaving aside Albania (for which no data are available), these dual processes have been occurring in *all* the countries of the region. They are
weakest in Poland, although even there neo-Protestants are winning converts. Neo-Protestant conversions are most numerous in Romania and
Hungary, as young people especially abandon the Romanian Orthodox
church and the Hungarian Reformed church.

In fact, most traditional Protestant churches in the region, as well as
the Bulgarian and Romanian Orthodox churches, declined in the 1980s,
due largely to the subservience of their bishops to communist state authorities.[47] The major exception was the Evangelical-Lutheran church in
East Germany, which experienced a revival, but that church's association
with pacifist dissent was also exceptional.

The Bulgarian and Romanian Orthodox churches, like some Protestant churches, came to agreement with the communists soon after World
War II. Typically they agreed to support the internal and foreign policies of the regimes, endorse Soviet bloc peace propaganda, and remain
silent about internal injustices. In exchange, the churches would be
granted state salaries for clergy, and the opportunity to operate seminaries and theological institutes, and to publish church periodicals. In
Romania, in fact, the accommodation of Patriarch Justinian (1948–77) to
the regime provoked open mutiny among some bishops and believers in
the early part of his reign.[48] By the 1970s disgusted Orthodox believers
were switching to the Baptist and Pentecostal churches. Beginning in
1973 the former grew at a rate of about 13 percent per year.[49]

In Hungary, as in Latvia, the ratio of Protestants to Catholics steadily
declined as dissatisfied Protestants left their quiescent churches for the
more outspoken Catholic church or, at least in Hungary, for smaller
sects. The Reformed (Calvinist) church is by far the weaker of the
two mainline Protestant churches in Hungary. Presided over by Bishop
Károly Toth, the Reformed church signed a major capitulary agreement
with the state in 1948, by which it abided until the collapse of communism; the agreement set the limits within which the church could
operate. In 1987 the Reformed church signed another agreement that
regulated religious education on church premises. Keston College reported that the agreement was "designed to guarantee that the church's
Christian education program develops in harmony with the interests of
the state."[50] But during 1987 Christian reformers within the church repeatedly criticized the 1948 agreement and called for a new legal basis.
Bishop Toth addressed this question in his report to the synodal council in December 1987, but rather than embracing the idea of reform, he
called instead for the strengthening of his church's "alliance" with the

state.[51] In the same report, however, Toth conceded that church numbers were declining and that church funerals outnumbered baptisms two-to-one in 1987. The church was also *qualitatively* weak, with only about 5 percent of its young people participating in religious instruction.

In most countries in the region the Baptists constitute a nominal presence: 22,000 in Eastern Germany,[52] 7,000 in Poland,[53] 4,000 in Czechoslovakia,[54] 2,000 in Yugoslavia,[55] 1,000 in Bulgaria,[56] and 20,000 in Hungary.[57] In Romania, by contrast, the Baptists have been able to establish a more perceptible presence. As recently as 1980 there were only 120,000 Baptists in Romania,[58] a number far ahead of the other Baptist communities; but by 1986 the Romanian Baptist church numbered 200,000 members with an additional constituency of 100,000 and was the fastest-growing Baptist church in Europe.[59] Fired with enthusiasm, Romania's Baptists attracted the attention of the regime. Various Baptist pastors were imprisoned and harassed, and some Baptist churches were bulldozed. Whereas Orthodoxy and Catholicism are priest-centered churches, the Baptist movement is more believer-centered and prides itself on its democratic structure and lay participation. The fact that this movement is experiencing high growth in Romania is a clue to undercurrents of political attitudes.

Pentecostals are present in the Balkans, with about 300,000 in Romania[60] and up to 9,500 in Bulgaria.[61] Like the Baptists, the Pentecostals have had constant problems in Romania. In a well-publicized case in 1974, for instance, Pentecostal activist Vasile Rascol was given a two-year prison sentence for the illegal distribution of Romanian-language religious literature printed abroad, specifically, 150 Bibles and books, including Romanian translations of Billy Graham's *The Secret of Happiness,* John Bunyan's *Pilgrim's Progress,* and C. H. M.'s *Thoughts on Leviticus.*[62] Despite various forms of harassment, the Pentecostal church in Romania continued to grow, and it opened a seminary in 1976. The combined number of converts to the Baptist, Pentecostal, and Plymouth Brethren churches in Romania comes to about 15,000 to 20,000 per year—a statistically significant figure that points to cultural stress in Romanian society.

Despite its small size the Bulgarian Pentecostal church is the largest Protestant denomination in that country (with perhaps as many as 160 churches in 1989). From 1944 to 1976 this church experienced little growth, but in the latter 1970s its ranks were augmented, chiefly by young people. Alongside the registered Pentecostal communities, there are also unregistered Pentecostal communities like the "Tinchevists," which add roughly 4,000 believers to the total.[63] Pentecostal pastors by and large prudently avoided politics in their sermons, but the intensity of their religious feeling attracted the state's hostility.[64]

Among fundamentalist Christians the best represented in Eastern Europe and the fastest growing are the Seventh-Day Adventists and the Jehovah's Witnesses. Both groups are present throughout the region. The largest Adventist congregation is again the Romanian, with an official membership of 75,000, and a constituency of between 80,000 and 100,000 "affiliated" sympathizers.[65] There are also 11,300 Seventh-Day Adventists in eastern Germany,[66] 10,000 in Poland,[67] 7,000 in the Czech and Slovak republics,[68] roughly 11,000 in Yugoslavia (in 1983),[69] 3,000 in Bulgaria,[70] and a small number in Hungary.[71] Adventists believe that the Second Coming of Christ is close at hand and that their primary task is to prepare for that event. As such, their orientation is distinctly otherworldly.

Relations between the Adventist church and the Catholic church in Poland are distinctly hostile. Stanisław Dąbrowski, president of the Polish Seventh-Day Adventists, told a Polish journalist in 1985, "The Roman Catholic Church has not rid itself of its hegemonist tendencies and practices vis-à-vis adherents of other faiths, and . . . its clergymen, contrary to spectacular assurances, often can't resist temptations leading to discrimination against a religious background."[72] In October 1987 the trans-European division of the Seventh-Day Adventist church organized a mission in Gdańsk. More than 1,500 people attended the nightly meetings, with some 6,000 turning out for the New Life program conducted over a two-week period. Dąbrowski concluded that "people, especially the young, are looking for alternatives to their present day lifestyle and aspirations."[73]

The outspokenness of the Adventists earned them difficulties in several countries, though probably nowhere as great as in Romania, where they are strongest. In 1984 Romania's Adventists had 526 congregations served by 143 priests. At one time there were nine churches in Bucharest alone. But by late summer 1986 only five of those churches remained,[74] the others becoming victims of Ceaușescu's urban planning program. Still, until Ceaușescu started demolishing churches, the Romanian Adventists had little difficulty with the regime.

I shall omit separate discussions of the Plymouth Brethren (45,000 in Romania), the Mormons (4,700 in East Germany, less than 250 in Hungary as late as 1988),[75] and the Congregationalists (1,000–2,000 in Bulgaria) and pass immediately to the discussion of the Nazarenes and the Jehovah's Witnesses. Unlike the other groups discussed here, the Nazarenes and the Jehovah's Witnesses had some difficulty obtaining legal status. The Nazarenes were legalized early on in Hungary and Yugoslavia, but were banned in Ceauşescu's Romania.[76] They are convinced pacifists and refuse to bear arms; in Hungary they obtained official dispensation as conscientious objectors, but in communist Yugoslavia[77] and Romania their refusal to perform military service brought them only trouble. The Nazarenes were also vocally critical of the communist social and political order, refused to let their children attend state schools, and take a millennial view of the Second Coming of Christ, which they believe is close at hand.

But as Earl Pope notes, "the most feared group, with their vehement criticism of ecclesiastical, social, and political institutions" has been the Jehovah's Witnesses movement.[78] The Jehovah's Witnesses enjoyed legal status in Yugoslavia for many years, and were relegalized in Poland in 1989 and in East Germany in 1990. The largest concentration of Jehovah's Witnesses may be in Poland, where there may be as many as 100,000 adherents.[79] There were reportedly between 25,000 and 30,000 active Jehovah's Witnesses in East Germany in 1987[80] and up to 10,000 in Yugoslavia in 1983[81] with additional adherents in Czechoslovakia, Hungary, and Romania. Their refusal to bear arms landed many Jehovah's Witnesses in jail in Hungary,[82] Poland,[83] and Yugoslavia.[84] In spite of that, Yugoslavia's community was able to publish *Kula stražara* (*Watchtower*) in more than 32,000 copies in four linguistic variants.[85] In July 1987 Poland's community organized a three-day assembly in Lublin attended by 12,000 people,[86] an indication that the regime was turning a blind eye toward this "illegal" organization. Moreover, in summer 1988 Poland introduced alternative social service for conscientious objectors,[87] and granted the Jehovah's Witnesses legal registration on 12 May 1989. They subsequently hosted the massive World Congress of Jehovah's Witnesses in Warsaw on 11–13 August, attended by 60,000 people from thirty-seven countries.[88] In Yugoslavia in 1987 authorities released one Jehovah's Witness from prison after serving less than two months of a five-year sentence, with no official explanation, and acquitted another later that year on the grounds that his pacifism made him "mentally unfit" for military duty.[89] The Jehovah's Witnesses' radical millennarianism and their energetic efforts to proselytize made them particularly unwelcome to the communist states.

Finally, something should be said about Dragan Marjanović, the so-called "messiah from Veliki Mokri Lug." His early life was unexceptional, but in 1973, the thirty-seven-year-old Marjanović left his wife and children and began to change his life. By 1987 he was holding open-air meetings before hundreds of Yugoslavs, dispensing miraculous cures and inspiring rumors that he was Christ incarnate.[90] A year later he had disappeared from sight; I was told that the authorities had pressed him to curtail his activities.

The high-growth sects discussed above have been recruiting mainly from adherents of the Orthodox church in Romania, Bulgaria, and Serbia; the Reformed church and, to a lesser extent, the Lutheran church in Hungary; and from among vulnerable agnostics. To a lesser extent, the Catholic church has been vulnerable, especially in Poland and Hungary, while the Evangelical-Lutheran church in eastern Germany probably holds the largest pool of potential recruits for the neo-Protestant sects in that country. Interconfessional conversions have become much more common since the 1960s; thus, interconfessional boundaries have become somewhat fluid.

The mainline churches have started to become concerned about losses to these newer organizations, especially the Jehovah's Witnesses. For example, Hungarian bishop József Cserháti of Pécs issued a pastoral letter in January 1987 warning about the growth of that sect in the previous three years. Similarly, the East German Protestant weekly *Glaube und Heimat* called on church members and clergy to be on guard against Jehovah's Witnesses. The Vatican even commissioned a study of sects and new religious movements from its Secretariat for Promoting Christian Unity, in collaboration with the Secretariat for Non-Believers and the Pontifical Council for Culture.[91]

The Appearance of New Cults

In contemporary Eastern Europe, as in the United States of the 1960s, the explosion of new cults has been chronologically associated with a flourishing of social and political protest as symptoms of a single syndrome. Underlying both religious innovation and social protest is the deepening of social stress and the breakdown of traditional associational channels for coping with stress. Cult recruits are typically people who have had difficulty in adjusting to society or to changes in society.[92] Edward Tiryakian has highlighted the transformative impact of social change on the "normative structure" of society, which suggests a connection between social change and the rise of new religious movements.[93] Individual stress may arise from any of a number of sources, including the diminution of the status and presence of traditional churches (Stark and Bainbridge suggest a direct negative correlation between the strength of traditional churches and the growth of cults),[94] change in gender roles,[95] and alienation from materialism and the work ethic.[96] Cults may, of

Table 6. Cult and Sect Membership in the Countries of Eastern Europe, 1993

	Poland	Romania	Hungary	Czech. and Slovakia	Former Yugo-slavia	Bulgaria	Albania
Jehovah's Witnesses	107,876	50,000	27,800	25,435	7,186	265	150
Hare Krishna	150,000		1,500			300	
Mormons	900	200	1,100	900		400	80
Scientology			5,000				
Baha'i	85	601	55	59	438	112	81
Children of God (the Family)						2,000	
Unification Church		400	200			300	
Totals	258,861	50,801	35,655	26,394	7,624	3,377	311

Source: East-West Church & Ministry Report 1, no. 4 (Fall 1993), 5. Repr. by permission.

course, develop in different ways and may satisfy sundry needs on the part of individuals.[97]

Eastern Europe has suddenly become fertile ground for cults. Some related symptoms are readily visible, such as the recent boom for psycho-analysis in Hungary[98] and the astrology and faith healing fads in Russia.[99] Other signs of cultural fragmentation and symbolic innovation remain below the surface. See the membership figures for East European cults and sects in table 6.

One may differentiate among four types of cults in Eastern Europe today: Oriental and neo-Oriental (Buddhism, transcendental meditation, yoga, and Hare Krishna); occult (spiritualism and Satanism); pseudo-Christian (the Unification church of Sun Myung Moon); and atavistic/mystic (theosophy, Bogomilism, and Danovism). While highly diverse, these cults are all *oppositional movements* reflecting the total rejection of the dominant culture of the given society.[100] The Unification church ("Moonies") aims at no less than the total transformation of the world and its unification in subordination to the personal authority of Reverend Moon, who is viewed as the new redeemer.[101]

Transcendental meditation (TM) and yoga probably enjoy the greatest exposure in Eastern Europe, with bookstores openly displaying books on these subjects. There have been yoga circles in Poland at least since 1985, and in Belgrade, Yugoslavia, since 1987.[102] By 1989 there were some 30 TM centers with an estimated 26,000 adherents in Yugoslavia. TM gathered steam in Romania in 1982, winning adherents among university faculty and students, when a Romanian émigré teaching at the Bucharest Education and Psychology Research Institute began to propagate it. In winter 1982 he was fired, the institute was closed, and several prominent officials lost their jobs.

There is also a yoga commune in Hungary in the town of Vagot Puszta, in the Mecsek Mountains just north of Pécs. The commune conducts meditation sessions twice a day and urban dwellers typically drive there for the weekend, using it like a retreat house. The commune has incorporated elements of Hinduism into its practices and prayers are recited in Sanskrit. Although that is the only such commune in Hungary, Joshi Bharat (a Hungarian married to an Indian woman) teaches yoga in Gödöllő, a far suburb of Budapest. Hungarians have also become interested in mental telepathy.[103]

In Bulgaria, by contrast, TM and yoga benefited from the active support of the one-time minister of culture, Lyudmila Zhivkova (1942–81), the daughter of party leader Todor Zhivkov. Zhivkova, who traveled widely and read voraciously, seems to have been familiar with the writings of early twentieth-century Russian mystics Georgi Ivanovich Gurdjieff and P. D. Ouspensky. In the process of reading their and other works, she developed her own synthesis of Marxism-Leninism and Eastern mystic traditions. As minister of culture, she became involved in the National Program for the Harmonious Development of Humanity, presenting periodic celebrations of outstanding "Titans of the Spirit." In 1978, celebrating the work of Russian artist Nikolay Roerich (1874–1947), whose work shows a blend of neomedieval romanticism and Buddhist mysticism, she gave an address, citing, in passing, "the Fiery Sign and the Fiery Sword, the Temple of Light, the Himalayas [which] pulsate and vibrate in the Heart of our Universe, [and] the beauty of psychic energy radiating from the heart."[104] The following year a central course in yoga was established in Bulgaria by the Committee on Culture, under Zhivkova's personal supervision. An Indian guru also came to Zhivkova's home for an unspecified duration to initiate her into yoga. Since her time, the practice of TM and yoga have spread in Bulgaria, with textbooks circulating in photocopies.

Bulgaria has also seen the recent revival of two domestic movements. The Danovist Cult, or White Brotherhood, founded between the wars by Bulgarian philosopher Petar Danov, has reemerged. The Danovists blend Hinduism and Orthodox Christianity. In 1980 they were reported to have established a central society in Sofia, with branches in twelve

provincial towns. Highly secretive about their organization, the Danovists have conducted open-air rituals at sunrise and at sunset, often on
Mount Vitosha or at Danov's grave near the Soviet embassy in Sofia.[105]

The Bogomil movement, which can be traced back to the ninth century and which owes its theological origins to Mesopotamian Mani-
chaeanism, also experienced a revival. On 25 June 1985 the provincial
newspaper *Haskovska Tribuna* reported that Bogomil groups were winning converts in the towns of Dimitrovgrad, Lyubimets, and Merichleri,
and in the villages of Dobrich, Krum, Stalevo, Garvanovo, and Levka.[106]

Buddhism has also won converts in Bulgaria, Czechoslovakia, Poland,
and Estonia (where there were about one hundred Buddhists as of early
1988),[107] and secret Oriental devotional societies were set up in Bulgaria and Yugoslavia. Interest and belief in reincarnation has also mushroomed.[108]

Buddhism came to Poland in 1972 when a Korean monk called Sung
San Son Sa (literally, the Zen Master of Sung Mountain), visited Warsaw
and Kraków at the invitation of Antoni Szoska and converted sixteen
persons. In 1979 two Poles spent time in Korea studying Zen Buddhism,
returning to their native country at the end of the study program. By
1981 Polish Buddhists had established the Zen Culture Society and registered it with the state. Temples were established in Kraków (1978),
Warsaw (1979), Gdańsk (1979), Łódź (1980), and Lublin (1981), and study
groups in nine other cities. As of 1988 there were 1,000 Korean-style Zen
Buddhists in Poland.[109]

Eastern religions and extrasensory perception groups have gained
popularity in Lithuania at the expense of its traditional religion, Catholicism. The two leading figures in this trend have been Abay and Mirza,
two self-proclaimed gurus from the Karakalpak ASSR in Uzbekistan.
In 1985 the journal *Svyturys* published an article by Juozas Jurevičius
about Lithuanians making pilgrimages to the Karakalpak ASSR to visit
Mirza. According to Jurevičius, Mirza and his translator extracted sex
and money in exchange for training in the ways of attaining spiritual
contentment.[110] Initiates then returned to Lithuania and set up "personal
liberation" camps.

A large number of Oriental and pseudo-Oriental cults have also won
adherents in Yugoslavia, including the conspiratorial group Ananda
Marga, founded in India in 1955, which seeks the revolutionary transformation of the world.[111] The Ananda Marga cult was introduced into
Yugoslavia in 1972 when one of its gurus made a visit to Zagreb. He won
a number of sympathizers and a branch of the cult was subsequently set
up in that city. Within a few years Belgrade had its own thirty-member

branch, while Ljubljana claimed an even larger number.[112] Ananda Marga sends missionaries to Yugoslavia on a regular basis, including a missionary visit in 1983 and a visit by guru Judasil in 1987. The cult seeks to promote world government, envisages the development of a single world language based on English, and portrays feminine energy as negative, masculine energy as positive, signifying the cult's desire to move women into a more subordinate position.

With the newfound interest in Oriental religion comes a receptivity to the Hare Krishna consciousness movement. Indeed, by early 1982 the Hare Krishna cult numbered 3,000 adherents in the USSR and additional numbers in several East European countries, including Yugoslavia. The Krishna cult, which originated in India but floundered in that hostile domestic terrain,[113] came to the USSR in 1971 when spiritual leader Bhaktivedanta Swami Prabhupada visited Moscow and initiated a young Russian into Krishna teachings. One Russian who joined the cult later recalled: "We would meet in the homes of members of the group, prepare vegetarian dishes in accordance with the Vedas and invite people in—just people off the street—some would always accept.'. . . We would view films and slides about India, about the Hare Krishna movement, illustrations to the sacred texts, chant mantras. So the circle of devotees gradually expanded until the repressions began."[114]

The cult repeatedly filed for registration as a legally recognized community (for example, in Riga in mid-1987), but for a long time it was turned down. As one Soviet official put it, the Council for Religious Affairs considered the cult "ideologically deviant." As of early 1986 fifty members of the Krishna cult were in Soviet prisons or psychiatric institutions; yet the cult showed defiance by holding a *kirtans* (spiritual chanting) in Moscow's Arbat shopping center on 16 August 1987.[115] By the mid-1980s there were also relatively large Krishna groups in Bulgaria and Poland.[116] Finally, in May 1988 the Hare Krishna community in the USSR was informed that it would be permitted to register as a legal religious organization, to build a temple, and to import religious literature.[117] As of late 1989, however, the sect was still experiencing problems.

In Yugoslavia the Hare Krishna cult dates its presence from 1980, when Vladimir Radek returned from London and organized the first Krishna group in Split with fifteen members. Additional branches were established in Zagreb, Pula, and Belgrade. The Krishna cult began issuing books and brochures, mostly authored by Swami Prabhupada. By 1984 the Krishnas had established a firm foothold in Yugoslavia and the cult grew more tangibly over the next three years, expanding into Slovenia under the name Society of Hindu Assemblies (with about fifty members and several hundred sympathizers as of early 1987).[118] Like the Ananda Marga cult, the Krishna cult advocates the "superiority" of males over females. The Yugoslav weekly magazine *Danas* described the Hare Krishnas as the most male-chauvinistic of all guru cults.[119]

The Polish religious scene has also become quite diverse. Aside from the Hare Krishna groups, yoga circles, and Buddhists, Poland has recently seen the emergence of Zen and Hindu communities, Rastafarians, and faith healers of various stripes.[120] In Hungary, a Federation of Hungarian Witches was registered in 1993.

Religious change came more slowly to East Germany, but even here there was an awakened interest in the new religions, as reflected in the 1984 publication of an important sociological treatment of the subject by Helmut Obst.[121]

Even Scientology has made its entry into the region, building a base of five thousand converts in Hungary and, as of spring 1994, making preparations for extensive proselytization in the Balkans, including Albania.[122]

The Theosophist Society, which holds that religious heterogeneity derives from semantic confusion and which claims to have tapped the essential truth of all religions, has adherents in Yugoslavia too. Founded in 1875, the society spread to Yugoslavia in 1924, after establishing chapters in Germany and Austria (Vienna). The first chapter in Yugoslavia was set up in Zagreb with Valerije Mayerhoffer as secretary, but the society soon established chapters in Belgrade and Ljubljana, and later in other cities. Some of its early members were also Masons. By 1927 the Yugoslav Theosophist Society was publishing the journal *Teozofija*, which continued on a regular basis until World War II. Of Yugoslavia's sixteen prewar Theosophist chapters, fourteen survived the war. At the end of the 1970s a young and energetic Emilio Trampuz set about "modernizing" the society and attracting new members. Two new journals were launched: *Teozof* and *Mladi teozof*. At the outset of the 1980s the society experienced a crisis when Franjo Miličević's efforts to establish an internal guru cult following polarized the society. The crisis was finally resolved when Miličević was expelled from the society in March 1981.[123]

Finally, the occult has started to attract a following in Eastern Europe, Russia, and Ukraine. The "Eastern" occult revival was, as is well known, presaged by a similar revival in the West in the late 1960s and early 1970s, and takes in everything from astrology to spiritualism to satanism. The lure of the occult is the lure of the arcane and the bizarre, the ambivalent fascination of the alien and potentially threatening. For those desperate to escape their mundane world, the occult offers a possible path.

Of the different strains of occult revival, the most innocent is astrology. As Marcello Truzzi noted some years ago, among the factors which reinforce the fascination with astrological prediction and advice are: the fact that they cater to the ego and provide ego-gratifying attention; the element of the esoteric, which also gives it a quality of entertainment; the ambiguity of astrological forecasts, which imparts an air of mystery and permits multiple interpretations; and the self-fulfilling nature of some astrological prophecies.[124] Astrology probably has adherents throughout the region.

Spiritualism is a far more serious affair. Founded in the United States in 1848 and introduced into Great Britain in 1852, the spiritualist movement believes that the survival of the human personality after the death of the physical body is a provable fact, and attempts to make contact with the deceased; thus, its primary activity is not worship but the séance.[125] Spiritualism came to Eastern Europe in the early years of the century but spiritualist groups have recently grown and spread in Bohemia, Hungary, Serbia and Croatia (chiefly in Belgrade and Zagreb).[126]

Satanism exists in various strains from a largely fashion-oriented fad to the glorification of evil and positive worship of its incarnation in Satan. Among the former one might mention the satanic theatrics of the Polish rock group Kat. But in 1987 and 1988 various reports emerged of the existence of violence-prone satanists in Leningrad,[127] Czechoslovakia, Hungary, Poland, and Yugoslavia. In 1988 there were also satanists in the East German city of Leipzig, while the Serbian city of Niš has become a more recent haven for self-proclaimed satanists.[128] From these reports it is clear that theatrical satanism and satanist fashions have stimulated the engagement in satanic rituals and even violence. What is not clear is how many people actually believe in Satan, let alone worship him.

The Polish case is probably a clue to regional trends. There was, for instance, a satanist fad among the Polish elite classes in the interwar period, complete with a functioning Church of Satan, books about satanism, and elements of satanism reflected in the poetry of the period. None of this survived World War II and it was not until the 1980s that satanism once more entered Poland, this time on the coattails of the heavy metal rock scene.[129] In 1986 a large group of rock fans showed up for the annual rock festival at Jarocin attired in black outfits emblazoned with the number "666" and the devil's pentagram, wearing studs and chains and an upside-down cross. One night during the festival they celebrated a "black mass" by engaging in the ritual slaughter of a dog and the desecration of a grave.[130] "Sacrificing animals, desecrating graves, violence, and even forcing persons into prostitution are all part of satanism in Poland," according to Ewa Smolinska-Borecka.[131] How many young people are involved in the satanist scene? Reverend Czesław Cekiera, an assistant professor at the Catholic University in Lublin, estimates that they may number as many as 10,000 in Poland as a whole.[132]

In 1987 the Czech samizdat periodical *Informacé o cirkvi* cited evidence of satanic practices in Czechoslovakia:

> Reports from Bohemia, Moravia, and Slovakia are now multiplying about the presence of this dark reality. It is mainly students who are becoming addicted to satanism. They wear upside-down crosses, invoke the name of Satan in prayer, conduct perverse rites and hold "black masses," and vow to perform an evil deed every day. They fanatically avow all power to Satan over this world, which must be destroyed.
>
> Members of this movement vary. Some join out of curiosity, others due to a mistaken romanticism, others out of defiance or the feeling of frustration, some from unbelief, and, finally, there are those who join due to a genuinely dark, demonic wrath.[133]

In Yugoslavia the suicides of a twenty-two-year-old girl in 1986 and of a thirteen-year-old girl in 1988 were tied to satanism, and satanic graffiti (including the number "666") were painted on a wall in Split in March 1988. A satanic movement called Dark is alleged to have existed in that country for several years and to promote "mystic death" as a means to "rebirth." It received relatively little mention in the press, although a brief flurry of press attention in March 1988 linked the group to a string of suicides in Zagreb over the course of the 1980s.[134] As in Poland, satanism in Yugoslavia has been linked to the rock scene, with adherents allegedly listening to Bauhaus and Joy Division.[135] In 1989 a small publishing house in Šabac published a thin book entitled *The Solution of the Mystery 666*, which, among other things, predicts that the apocalypse will come in the year 2333.[136] Likewise in Hungary, there have been reports of a satanist movement. As in the other countries, it is, at this point, restricted to young people.[137]

Astrology, spiritualism, and satanism do not qualify as religious in any usual understanding of the word. But they clearly may substitute for and displace conventional religion (at least in the case of spiritualism and satanism). Truzzi has suggested an alternative conceptualization: that is, to view them as *pop religions*. What is distinct to pop religion is that it preserves and in some ways even exaggerates some of the externals of religiosity, especially when it comes to ritual behavior, but scuttles concern with the moral and theological content. Pop religion thus demystifies religion and is a symptom of secularization. But as Truzzi points out,

> It is precisely because we no longer believe in the fearsome aspects of the occult that we are willing to experiment with them. Most of those who would willingly draw a proper pentagram on the floor to invoke a demon would do so precisely because they do not really believe that some Devil's emissary who might just pluck their souls down to Hell would possibly ever visit them. If we fully believed in demons, we certainly would not want to call them up.[138]

Closing Thoughts

In communist aspirations secularization was supposed to eliminate popular belief in the supernatural and to cut the institutional umbilical chord with Tradition, that obstacle to orthodox communist resocialization as it was conceived in the decades prior to Gorbachev. But as Peter Berger noted more than two decades ago, the principal effect of secularization is to bring about "a demonopolization of religious traditions [which] thus, *ipso facto*, leads to a pluralistic situation."[139] Hitherto unchallenged spiritual and normative explanations are challenged in the course of secularization; this, combined with social change and culture contact, increases the likelihood that alternative explanations may find receptive audiences.

While the situation differs to some extent from country to country, religious institutions in several of these societies, most obviously in Poland, Croatia, Slovenia, Serbia, and Slovakia, have tried to take advantage of political changes to obtain the passage of laws serving religious agendas. In the Czech Republic, Prime Minister Václav Klaus declared at one point (July 1993) that the Catholic Church was assuming a role "which does not suit its position in this country."[140] And in Poland, "fears that church and government were creating a church-dominated society have led to street demonstrations."[141] The coalition government (of peasantists and former communists), which was sworn into office in October 1993, seemed prepared for a collision course with the Catholic church.

The religious phenomena examined in this chapter are highly diverse, but they have some things in common. First, they are *symptoms* of change, whether it be change in the strength of traditional religion, in the expectations and needs of people, or in the relations between generations and their distinct orientations toward popular culture. Second, they figure as *reactions* to social and confessional change and to social and confessional stress. And finally, they are, at least potentially, *forces for further change*, whether in the sense that one or more of these phenomena may produce or evolve into a major new religious organization, or in the sense that both separately and collectively these phenomena may have diverse effects on a society by compelling the response of other organizations or by stimulating debates and discussions which might otherwise not have arisen.

7. Church and Dissent in Praetorian Poland

After a decade of communist rule the Polish review *Przegląd kulturalny* published an article by Jan Szczepański warning that the formal political institutions were "comparatively inefficient and only superficially established."[1] The warning was not heeded, however, and Poland's communists failed to develop valued political institutions. The result was weakness of the party, perennial problems with corruption, and inconsistencies in the application and execution of the laws. In this political setting social groups came to face each other without widely accepted channels for mediation and political power itself became fragmented. In this context organized institutions such as the military, students,[2] labor unions, and churches behaved in a more politicized way. Samuel P. Huntington has called this syndrome *praetorianism*.[3]

The church is a logical player in the praetorian syndrome: it is hierarchically organized, commands an independently recruited cadre, lays claim to the loyalty of all or much of the population, and has financial, psychological, and political ("the power of the pulpit") resources at its disposal. In the early phases of the slide into praetorianism the church also has the advantage that society is in some ways still simple, insofar as the incipient stages of praetorianism may coincide with a break with traditional politics (in some sense of the word). But, as Huntington notes:

As the praetorian society becomes more complex and differentiated, the number of social groups and forces multiplies and the problems of coordination and interest aggregation become increasingly complex. In the absence of effective central political institutions for the resolution of social conflicts, the military [like the church too] become[s] simply one of several relatively insulated and autonomous social forces. Their capacity to elicit and to induce cooperation declines.[4]

From a functionalist perspective one might say that certain functions need to be carried out in a society, and that when the "normal" channels are unavailable for certain purposes, other institutions (in this case, the church) take up the slack. The church's recurrent role as mediator between striking workers and the government during the May 1988 strikes in Gdańsk and Nowa Huta illustrates this point. But as society becomes more complex, its functional needs become more complex. In this context the church finds itself confronted with tasks which are not only more complex, but may even be at odds with each other.

It has become fashionable in recent years to think of the Polish church as the unfailing and constant ally of dissent and underground labor. This portrayal is misleading in two respects. First, the church's attitude toward dissent has not been constant over the years, and has been affected by a number of factors, including the appearance of opportunities for cooperation with the government. The church, after all, has its own institutional needs in mind: this is certainly true where the decisions and policies of the hierarchy are concerned. This in turn suggests my second point: it is to some extent inaccurate to generalize about "the church" and dissent, insofar as different members of both hierarchy and lower clergy have taken rather different attitudes toward dissent. Bearing these two caveats in mind, I propose to argue in this chapter that the traditional social role of the clergy as nurturer of culture, community, and sometimes civil liberties[5] has been transformed by the political mobilization of the Polish public, with the result that long-standing ambivalences within the church are reflected in new ways. Whereas the nineteenth-century hierarchy worried about offending the royal monarchies and upsetting the delicate forms of *modus vivendi* established in partitioned Poland, and felt ambivalent about nationalism insofar as Poles were clearly a "Catholic nation," Polish primates Stefan Wyszyński (1948–81) and Jósef Glemp (since 1981) have cautiously built up and safeguarded various prerogatives for the church, including Catholic deputies in the *Sejm*, Catholic intelligentsia clubs, and, beginning in the early 1970s, generous allowances for the construction of new churches. They have therefore been loathe to see these threatened by reckless advocacy or by the headlong destabilization of society. Far better, then, that people "keep calm. Do not drive our country to still greater disaster. Only self-control and the maintenance of calm can save the country and the Church which fulfills her mission in it."[6]

Primate Glemp has at times seemed to shy away from a political role. Part of the reason may well be his evident belief that the politicization of the church might sap its moral authority.[7] But in conditions of praetorianism, the Polish church ultimately found it impossible to skirt politics, both because the church is *already* political in the articulation of its core values, and because those discontented with the system look to the church for succor.

As of 1988 the Catholic church in Poland had 98 bishops, 23,432 priests, 23,711 nuns, and 9,038 seminarians; it operated 10,719 churches, 1,835 chapels, 2,506 convents, 447 monasteries, 12 high schools, and the Catholic University at Lublin with faculties of theology, philosophy, law, the humanities (including modern languages), and social sciences.[8] According to the episcopate's figures, the church was publishing at the time 35 mass periodicals (out of a total of 2,943 Polish periodicals total).[9] And in April 1987 the church established an agricultural committee, with more than $10 million in funding from abroad, in order to fund water and sewage projects in the 2,200 Polish villages which still lack modern water and sewage systems, provide private farmers with the opportunity to buy machinery normally unavailable in Poland, and conduct limited programs in farm education.[10] These resources gave the church real strength in both the city and the countryside.

Despite the formidable strength and the legendary fervor of the Poles for their church, communist regime spokespersons regularly referred to religion as a "private affair," suggesting that the church steer clear of social questions. Alternatively, the daily newspaper *Trybuna Ludu* argued in 1986 that part of the clergy based its attitude toward pluralism on its misconstrual of pluralism "as a system of relations that guarantees Catholicism exclusiveness in every field."[11] Such a characterization may be appropriate to a discussion of Polish Catholicism in the 1920s and 1930s, but it represents an oversimplification of contemporary church thinking.

The church in fact nurtured pluralism in several areas—and under communism, pluralism was often tantamount to dissent. First, after the 1981 suppression of Solidarity, the church dramatically expanded its role in education. Church schools throughout the country began offering classes across a wide range of subjects from European history to pig breeding. One of the most formidable schools was the Institute of Christian Culture in Lubochnia headed by Reverend Mirosław Mikulski, which offered classes at all age levels from preschool to age nineteen, with extensive adult education in subjects like Christian ethics and the Bible. During the 1987–88 academic year, the adult education curriculum at Lubochnia included lectures on "Noncommunist Resistance in World War II" and "Citizens' Protection under the Law." St. Maximilian's Church in Konin organized a meeting of opposition journalists, who discussed their views of the Iran-Iraq war and the 1988 American presidential election, and criticized the Polish government's economic policies.[12]

Second, the church actively backed "alternative culture" in communist Poland by sponsoring art exhibitions, poetry readings, theater groups, and film festivals. In 1975 the Warsaw Campus Ministry launched its annual Week of Christian Culture, embracing lectures, concerts, poetry, discussion groups, and meetings with noted scholars, writers, and artists. A related event, the Sacro-Song Festival, has attracted both Polish and foreign performers since its inception in 1968 and has drawn tens of thousands of listeners, mostly young people.[13] Ernest Bryll's play *The Circle,* which deals with the feelings of despair experienced by Christ's apostles in the period between the Crucifixion and the Resurrection, was banned by the authorities, but was staged by Andrzej Wajda at Easter 1985 in the ruined church on Żytnia Street in Warsaw.[14] On another occasion, in late 1984, the Week of Christian Culture brought together forty-four Polish novelists, including Marek Nowakowski, A. Braun, and Wiktor Woroszylski, and staged a number of plays, including one by Halina Mikołajska, known for her sympathies for KOR. On 10 December 1987 a Warsaw church played host to a human rights seminar attended by Jacek Kuroń, Leszek Moczulski, Czesław Bielecki, Bronisław Geremek, Janusz Onyszkiewicz, Zbigniew Romaszewski, and other well-known dissidents.[15] "Our churches no longer are just churches in the religious sense," Catholic journalist Krzysztof Śliwiński commented in 1987. "They are full-fledged community centers."[16]

Third, the independent Catholic newspaper *Tygodnik Powszechny,* edited for more than forty years by Jerzy Turowicz, offered an outlet for dissenting opinion. During the anti-Semitic campaign of 1968 Turowicz resolutely continued to publish Jewish writers, and when the Polish-Jewish poet Antoni Słonimski was blacklisted for criticizing official anti-Semitism, Turowicz invited him to join the staff of *Tygodnik Powszechny* as a contributing editor. On another occasion Turowicz devoted an entire issue of the weekly paper to a short story written by a Protestant whose work might otherwise have gone unnoticed. In the 1960s and 1970s *Tygodnik Powszechny* published the works of various dissidents, most of them agnostics, and after the suppression of Solidarity in mid-December 1981 the journal published poems by a jailed member of Solidarity and regular columns by jailed dissidents.[17]

Fourth, the church developed a network of services, including child day-care centers, pharmacies, and summer camps. Through the Rural Pastoral Communities established in early 1983, the church organizes religious retreats and pilgrimages in the countryside, finds legal counsel for private forums, and organizes self-help among the peasants (for example, care of the sick and the elderly). The Pastoral Service to Workers, reorganized in April 1982, is a parallel organization which caters to the needs of factory workers. The Primate's Relief Committee for People Deprived of Liberty and for Their Families was established in 1981 to organize aid such as food and medical supplies for political prisoners. In the cultural field, the Organization for the Pastoral Care of Artists is worth mentioning. Closely affiliated with the Week of Christian Culture, the organization is under the supervision of Monsignor Jan Oblak of Olsztyn. And finally, the church has maintained active student centers in Kraków, Warsaw, Poznań, and elsewhere, organizing student pilgrimages to Częstochowa and holding philosophical symposia and public discussions.[18]

The Wyszyński Years

The church in Poland was divided from the beginning. In the early postwar period, two lay Catholic currents emerged: a loyalist current centered in Kraków that aspired to reflect the views of the church authorities loyally; and an opportunist current centered in Warsaw and associated with Bolesław Piasecki's PAX group, which was prepared to make greater accommodations with the regime and which in time came to see itself as a kind of mediator between church and state.[19] For its part, the hierarchy supported both the land reform bill of 1944, even though the large estates expropriated under that measure included some of the church's landholdings, and the communist nationalization of industry.[20] There were tensions between church and state in those years, but in April 1950 the Polish episcopate signed an agreement with the government in which it pledged to teach Catholics to respect state authority and to seek Vatican recognition of the Oder-Neisse line as the western border of Poland in exchange for a guarantee of religious education in schools, the continued operation of the Catholic University of Lublin, and state recognition of the ecclesiastical supremacy of the pope.[21] A year later in Rome Archbishop Stefan Wyszyński explained Polish views on the western territories to the pope and obtained his acquiescence to the naming of Polish bishops on a permanent basis in those territories.

Despite this agreement, various priests were arrested and imprisoned in the years 1951–53, often on charges of collaboration with subversive organizations. On 9 February 1953 the Council of State issued a decree unilaterally reviving selected sections of the previously abrogated[22] Concordat of 1925—specifically the provisions that only Polish citizens could be appointed in the church hierarchy, that church leaders were required to take an oath of loyalty to the Polish government, and that prior approval of the government was mandatory for all appointments, removals, or transfers in the hierarchy.[23] After this the government frequently interfered in church appointments, and in a number of dioceses the office of vicar-general was assigned to a "peace priest." On 8 May 1953 the episcopate addressed a lengthy letter to the Polish government, protesting the authorities' failure to live up to the 1950 agreement. The government replied by putting Bishop Czesław Kaczmarek of Kielce on trial and arresting Wyszyński. The latter remained in prison until 1956.

These harsh measures were designed to weaken and tame the church. Instead, they ensured that the church would be seen as the innocent victim of an illegitimate, Soviet-imposed regime. Indeed, in the late Stalinist period Wyszyński came to be called *Interrex*, a reference to the tradition in prepartition Poland wherein the supreme power of state would be temporarily vested in the Polish primate between the death of the monarch and the election of his successor. Wyszyński also came to view himself as the spiritual father of the nation.[24]

Although Wyszyński's release from internment in October 1956 was followed by some improvement in church-state relations, the waxing association of the church and dissent belongs more properly to the Gierek years (1970–80). During the first secretaryship of Władysław Gomułka (1956–70), there was little in the way of organized opposition in Poland and the church itself still felt very much on the defensive. Where the communists were concerned, moreover, this era began with a flourish of optimism in that Gomułka's limited opposition to Soviet *diktat* made him immensely popular. Even in the early Gierek years it was still possible for the communist party to hope for an eventual, partial legitimation in the eyes of the people.

Wyszyński quite properly viewed the situation as potentially perilous for the church: between communist efforts to foment division and discord within the church and steady efforts to whittle the church down directly, there was room for uncertainty as to the outcome. Wyszyński's solution was to assert his personal authority as primate—sometimes implicitly bypassing both the Vatican and his fellow bishops.

It is generally acknowledged that Cardinal Wyszyński's strong and fearless exercise of authority played a crucial role in the church's survival and successful resistance to communist efforts to destroy it. On more than one occasion, this meant bypassing normal canonical procedures to remove from office duly elected leaders of religious congregations, summarily silencing or transferring outspoken clerical critics, unilateral rendering of decisions, and other markedly authoritarian actions. But in the final analysis, it is widely believed that it was this strong hand of authority that saved the Polish church.[25]

Wyszyński drew two complementary lessons from this experience: the chaos produced by intrainstitutional freedom can produce weakness and uncertainty, leaving the institution vulnerable to assault; and the vigorous assertion of authority builds power and institutional strength. These lessons were not lost on Wyszyński's understudy, Karol Wojtyła.

Both Wyszyński and Wojtyła outspokenly criticized the anti-Semitic campaign of 1968, and the episcopate lent strong support to the groundswell of opposition to the proposed changes in the constitution in 1975. The subtle transformation in the church's social presence in the mid-1970s mirrored the broader systemic changes occurring at that time: in particular, the 1976 riots in the Ursus tractor factory and in the city of Radom were followed by the creation of KOR and the mobilization of intellectuals in a critical role. From its very inception, the intellectuals involved in KOR maintained contacts with the church hierarchy, and the two began to coordinate their criticisms of the regime. The hierarchy commented favorably on KOR's work for human rights on several occasions.[26]

The tensions that developed between church and state in the later Gierek years were a symptom of the church's new strength and the greater recognition it had won from the state. Meanwhile, Polish society was changing, the economy was slipping, the workers were becoming impatient,[27] and the dissident sector was becoming organized. The church was no longer thrust on the defensive; on the contrary, it was able to speak out on issues confronting Polish society. Taken collectively, these phenomena were symptoms of Poland's slide into praetorianism. Poland's church was becoming a "praetorian church." It follows that this ecclesiastical praetorianism was not a factor of Wyszyński's personality or a matter of the hierarchy's choice; on the contrary, the phenomenon had systemic, structural roots.

Praetorianism in Full Bloom

What happened in summer 1980 is that the political superstructure crumbled and society sprouted a vast array of independent organizations, from the independent trade union Solidarity, to the farmers' union Rural Solidarity, to the new Independent Students' Association created in early 1981. Existing structures began acting in new ways: the normally docile Democratic Party (SD) and the United Peasant Party (ZSL) suddenly started to convene meetings independently, to adopt resolutions without coordinating them with the PUWP, and to respond to their natural constituencies.[28] PAX, by then led by Ryszard Reiff, took a position strongly supportive of Solidarity, and shortly after the Catholic intelligentsia clubs set up a committee to advise the workers in fall 1980, PAX did likewise.[29]

The leaders of Solidarity looked to the church for consultation and mediation from the beginning, and the church easily assumed its new role as mediator between the newly organized Solidarity and the badly shaken and increasingly disorganized secular authorities. In autumn 1980 Wałęsa sought Wyszyński's advice as to whom to nominate as editor-in-chief of the trade union's weekly, *Tygodnik Solidarność*; on the primate's advice, he named Tadeusz Mazowiecki, the former editor of the Catholic monthly *Więź*.[30]

Popular participation had been suppressed for so long that the opening achieved in August 1980 inevitably fueled general excitement and stimulated new and more ambitious aspirations. Archbishop Józef Glemp, who succeeded Wyszyński as primate of Poland upon the latter's death on 28 May 1981, was clearly fearful that Polish society might dissolve into social chaos and conflict and hence urged restraint.[31]

The suppression of Solidarity on 13 December 1981 and the concomitant proclamation of martial law put the church under great stress. Glemp's initial reaction, like that of Wyszyński to the nationwide strikes of summer 1980, was to urge moderation and the avoidance of violence. In a message auspiciously carried on Radio Warsaw on 13 December, Primate Glemp told his flock:

> It does not matter if someone accuses the church of cowardice. The church wants to defend each human life; and therefore, in this state of martial law, it will call for peace wherever possible; it will call for an end to violence and for the prevention of fratricidal struggle. There is nothing of greater value than human life. That is why I myself will call for reason, even if it means that I become the target

of insults. I shall plead, even if I have to plead on my knees: do not start a fight of Pole against Pole.[32]

Glemp's sermon did not refer explicitly to Solidarity and did not condemn Jaruzelski's coup. The Vatican's reaction was likewise restrained, and both Agostino Cardinal Casaroli and the pope evidently feared the eruption of a major conflict in Poland; yet within a few days the Episcopal Main Council issued a somewhat tougher statement, condemning the curtailment of rights and demanding the release of all political prisoners and a revival of Solidarity's legal activities.

The primate was not content, however, to give the regime a blank check. When the regime started to require loyalty oaths of all state employees, Archbishop Glemp sent an open letter to Jaruzelski condemning the oaths as incompatible with constitutionally guaranteed rights. At the same time, Glemp seemed to want to distance himself from those in the political underground who had been radicalized by the suppression of Solidarity.

> The consequences of standing up for the truth are enormous. Firstly, one must not, in the fervor of conflict and struggle, slander either the rulers or the ruled, utter falsehoods about them, exaggerate flaws, pass over merits, make them look ridiculous. Secondly, one must demand honest information from the mass media, both domestic and foreign. Thirdly, there must be demands that people deprived of freedom or dismissed from their place of work should know why they are being given such a punishment.[33]

Glemp went further, and declared that Solidarity shared culpability with the state for the ultimate course of events—an assessment that alienated many Poles. Subsequently, on 13 April 1982 the primate's Social Council, an advisory body of twenty-eight lay Catholics, issued a report urging Solidarity to critically reexamine its own culpability in the attendant crisis.

There were violent clashes in several Polish cities in the first week of May 1982, but, perhaps surprisingly, in his sermon on the feast of St. Stanisław a few days later, Glemp seemed to endorse the regime's line that underground Solidarity had planned the clashes in advance. Glemp later appealed for calm on the second anniversary of Solidarity; his appeals were ignored, and more than 4,000 demonstrators in dozens of towns were arrested. Glemp was increasingly criticized, often in the context of unfavorable comparisons with his predecessor. Typical of such criticisms is a letter written on 24 April 1982 by Anka Kowalska, a writer, poet, and former member of KOR. In this letter she protested that the report issued by the primate's Social Council on 13 April in effect endorsed martial law and justified the state's criminality.

> We all turn our eyes and hearts towards the church. Why does she not raise her voice against those traders peddling human souls? How can the church suggest instead that this tortured and betrayed society admit to being naughty and behaving improperly and show understanding for its hangmen who lost their temper?[34]

Meanwhile, the traditional gulf between the hierarchy and the lower clergy was becoming once again evident as priests like Jerzy Popiełuszko, Mieczysław Nowak, and Kazimierz Szklarczy began delivering fiery sermons in defense of Solidarity. Popiełuszko and Reverend Teofil Bogucki (Popiełuszko's spiritual mentor), both assigned to the parish of St. Stanisław Kostka, began celebrating "masses for the fatherland" in 1981; from April 1982 on, Popiełuszko recited special prayers for the victims of martial law, including the imprisoned Wałęsa. Popiełuszko's criticisms of the government were direct and unflinching, as he hammered away at the positive contributions of Solidarity.[35] Similarly, in a June 1982 sermon Szklarczy denounced martial law as "evil," praised Solidarity as "immortal because it represents justice," and told his listeners that Christianity's confrontation with communism is a war of good against evil, love against hate, truth against lies.[36]

Against these bold words, Glemp sought more modest concessions. Soon after the proclamation of martial law, the regime made a small concession to the church, issuing a decree which permitted hospitalized children to obtain weekly religious instruction if requested by the parents. Later, in August 1982 he registered three requests: that Wałęsa be released from prison, that the remaining internees be released and trade union work recommenced "at least in stages," and that a date be established for the pope's second visit to Poland.[37] On 8 October the authorities formally banned the suspended trade union. Exactly a month later Archbishop Glemp met with Jaruzelski and confirmed the second papal visit for June 1983, prompting some to say that Glemp had concluded that the prospects for Solidarity's relegalization were nil and that it was pointless to continue to defend the now-banned organization. At any rate, when the coordinating committee of underground Solidarity called for antiregime demonstrations on 10 November, Glemp sharply criticized the planned demonstrations.[38]

The following month, two hundred priests, angered by Glemp's soft approach to the regime, paid a three-hour visit to the archbishop. In reply to criticism, Glemp charged that too many priests were behaving like "journalists and politicians."[39]

In early 1983 Polish police reportedly gave Glemp a list of sixty-nine "extremist priests" who needed to be reined in. Aside from Popiełuszko, Nowak, and Szklarczy, the list probably included Bogucki, Henryk Jankowski (an adviser to Wałęsa), Stanisław Małkowski, Rufin Abramek (a Pauline monk), Tadeusz Zaleski-Isakowicz (well known for his pro-Solidarity sympathies), and Zenon Ziomek. All were either beaten, tortured, or harassed, some were vilified in the press, and the homes of Popiełuszko and Małkowski were ransacked on orders from above.[40] Glemp tried to accommodate the authorities by transferring Nowak from his parish in the Warsaw working-class suburb of Ursus to a remote parish, provoking vociferous protests,[41] and rebuked the outspoken Popiełuszko for displaying Solidarity emblems at his fatherland masses, for his contacts with Solidarity activists, and for allegedly neglecting his official duties to devote his time and energy to his fatherland masses.[42] Later, after Popiełuszko was murdered by Polish secret police, Glemp suspended Małkowski from preaching in Warsaw—perhaps to protect him, but perhaps to pacify the authorities, who had been assailing Małkowski in the press.[43]

Glemp sometimes appeared to be the most timid of all of Poland's prelates. Whereas Glemp now argued that Solidarity had lost its meaning after it went underground, and that "the Solidarity now in existence has moved a great deal away from its principles,"[44] bishops Tadeusz Gocłowski of Gdańsk, Kazimierz Majdański of Szczecin, and Andrzej Śliwiński of Gdynia, and Henryk Cardinal Gulbinowicz of Wrocław all struck more radical poses. Gocłowski, for instance, commemorated the fifteenth anniversary of the riots of December 1970 by reminding his listeners of the shooting of the defenseless citizens by security forces.[45] Majdański and Śliwiński both conducted solemn masses on the fifth anniversary of the imposition of martial law, the former raising pointed questions about the Szczecin agreement of 1980 on another occasion.[46] Bishop Damian Zimon of Katowice seemed even more radical, reassuring tens of thousands of Polish workers gathered at Częstochowa in September 1987 of their right to their own "independent and self-governing trade unions."[47] And Cardinal Gulbinowicz, who became Poland's third cardinal in 1985, openly encouraged pro-Solidarity sentiment at an open-air mass at the shrine of the Black Madonna in September of that year and sent a joint telegram with Wałęsa to the pope in the name of the Polish workers.[48]

In addition, Jan Sikorski, a Warsaw parish priest at St. Joseph's Church, played a highly visible role. In September 1984 he said a special mass to honor the critics of the regime, particularly Jacek Kuroń and Adam Michnik; thousands attended. In December 1985 he described the period of Solidarity's legality as "a time of joy when we won back our freedom and dignity." And in December 1986, on the fifth anniversary of the imposition of martial law, he led a solemn procession of thousands to St. Joseph's Church for a special memorial mass. On that occasion he said of his congregation, "These are the people who did not give up the struggle for the ideals that are alive in Poland. And to defend them, to allow them to meet, is the permanent role of the church."[49]

But Cardinal Glemp (by now "Comrade Glemp" to his critics)[50] was basing his strategy on his desire to obtain government approval for a church-sponsored fund to help private farmers (achieved in 1987) and enactment of a bill guaranteeing the church's legal status in clear and unambiguous terms (achieved in May 1989). In addition, according to Tadeusz Kamiński, a professor at the University of Hamburg, Glemp may well have felt that during the Jaruzelski years (1981–89) Poland was threatened primarily by the West which, in its desire to weaken Soviet communism, might be willing to "sacrifice" Poland by inciting a sanguinary anti-Russian revolt.[51]

Opposition Views of the Church

The imposition of martial law led directly to the fragmentation of Solidarity, as rival factions split apart and formed autonomous underground organizations. Predictably, the diverse para-Solidarity groups developed rather diverse attitudes toward the church.

Głos, a more or less formal organization which traces its roots to the National Democratic Party of Roman Dmowski in the early twentieth century but which actually emerged in 1977 from the ranks of KOR, is firmly pro-church, and has defended Glemp from criticism.[52] (Dmowski, incidentally, was well known for his belief that the primary danger to Poland came from the West, not from Russia.) Polityka Polska, which viewed itself less as a formal organization than as an arena for political expression, published an analytical journal beginning in autumn 1983. It too viewed itself as an ally of the church. By contrast, the Committee of Social Resistance (KOS) was more critical. KOS's attitude toward the church is basically positive, but when Glemp transferred the popular parish priest Mieczysław Nowak to a remote parish in early 1984, KOS warned that "the policy of conciliation with the regime, which has been forced through by the primate apparently with support from the episcopate, has brought the church perilously close to the point where it must lose social support. The church's successive concessions to the demands of the authorities have not brought the fulfillment of any of society's more significant demands, or even of the church's own, purely religious, demands."[53]

Much less sympathetic to the church was Fighting Solidarity, a radical underground spin-off from the original Solidarity. Created in June 1982 in Wrocław by Kornel Morawiecki and others, the organization sought the violent overthrow of the communist system and the establishment of an independent republic. Fighting Solidarity was not sympathetic to Glemp's Occidentophobia but more generally believed that the church did not have a role to play in politics, not even in defending human rights.[54]

Of all the underground organizations—and there were far more than I can enumerate here—Niepodległość (Independence) was among the least sympathetic to the church. Functioning underground since at least early 1982, it advocated militant underground organization as a preliminary to the overthrow of the communist regime. Niepodległość viewed the church with skepticism, believing that its institutional interests must necessarily compel the church to seek forms of modus vivendi with the government, entailing elements of cooperation rejected by Niepodległość.[55] On the whole, there was an important current of thought in the underground which held that the church could not help the resistance. As one Solidarity spokesperson put it in 1984, "The church will drift away from us and it should. Let Cardinal Glemp and the pope concern themselves with the souls of Europe and let Bujak lead the revolution in Poland."[56]

The Second and Third Papal Visits

The Polish pope played an ambivalent but effective role in the triangular relationship of church, regime, and opposition. On the one hand, the pope repeatedly signalled his support of the cautious Glemp, most symbolically by elevating him to the College of Cardinals in January 1983. On the other hand, the pope's own comments were defiant and, for the opposition, often exhilirating. Pope John Paul II's first papal visit to Poland in 1979 is now widely credited with having contributed to the social revolution of 1980. His second visit in June 1983 came at a time of widespread despondency, and the pope used his visit to lift Polish spirits.

The keynote of the pope's second visit was his emphasis on Poland's right to political sovereignty and self-determination, and his calls for dialogue were always placed within the context of the need for self-determination. He called for amnesty for all political prisoners, and endorsed Polish aspirations to establish authentic, self-governing trade unions.[57]

There were rumors on the eve of John Paul II's third trip to Poland in June 1987 that the tone of the visit would be more subdued and that the visit itself would be more purely pastoral. On the contrary, the pope, now able to travel to Gdańsk, Szczecin, and Lublin (unlike in 1983), used the visit to express church support for the relegalization of Solidarity and Rural Solidarity, and for the principles of the ill-fated Popiełuszko. At Tarnów on 10 June the pope quoted from the memoirs of Wincenty Witos, one-time leader of the prewar Peasant Party and prime minister of the prewar Polish Republic, calling on the government to respect its 1981 agreements at Rzeszów and Ustrzyki and relegalize Rural Solidarity.[58] At Kraków later that same day, he told the hundreds of thousands of Poles present to resist disillusionment and to continue their "patient fight" for freedom; he repeatedly praised the goals and ideals of Solidarity.[59] At Gdańsk on 12 June the pope told a crowd estimated at one million persons that workers have the right to organize "independent and autonomous trade unions." There, and elsewhere, he frequently repeated the word "solidarity," always with great emotional impact.[60] And in Warsaw on 14 June, the final day of his trip to Poland, the pope paid a visit to the Church of St. Stanisław Kostka and prayed at the grave of Popiełuszko. Throughout the trip he spoke of the nation's right to determine its own fate, of the importance of religious freedom, and of the right of the workers to independent trade unions.[61] Understandably, underground Solidarity expressed considerable satisfaction with the papal visit.[62]

From time to time the Polish communist press attacked the pope.[63] In so doing, the press betrayed the regime's fear of the Polish pope and his command of the hearts of Poles. For in his sermons in Poland, the pope eloquently endorsed every major demand of the democratic opposition in Poland.

The Great Transformation

The Catholic church was unremitting in its support for the relegalization of Solidarity. In September 1987, for example, Bishop Damian Zimon of Katowice told a crowd of tens of thousands at Częstochowa that the church supported the people's "right to their own independent and self-governing trade unions."[64] In August 1988 Dominican friars in Gdańsk organized a pro-Solidarity rally involving some 3,000 persons.[65] And on 20 October 1988 representatives of Catholic intelligentsia clubs from across Poland issued a nine-point statement calling, among other things, for the relegalization of Solidarity and the establishment of a parliamentary democracy.[66] In the most concrete way, the church helped Solidarity by making facilities at St. Brygida's Church in Gdańsk available to the trade union for use as its headquarters while it remained illegal. And the Vatican insisted on the relegalization of Solidarity as a precondition for the restoration of diplomatic ties—something Warsaw wanted.

Poland's bishops collectively issued a programmatic pastoral message on 26 August 1988 that spelled out their support for trade union pluralism and described the wildcat strikes as a symptom of a lingering disease afflicting the sociopolitical system.[67]

Toward the end of 1988, at the same time that preparations began for roundtable talks between Solidarity and the government, there were also signs of an impending "great transformation" in church-state relations. Talks were continuing between the Vatican and the Polish government, and in late October Warsaw made a serious bid for the restoration of diplomatic ties. Meanwhile, Polish authorities legalized the Catholic opposition group Dziekania, whose 100 members had been pressing for political and economic pluralism since the group's founding in 1984. They also agreed to register Catholic student unions in Częstochowa, Lublin, Warsaw, Gdańsk, and other cities.

Subsequently, on 17 May 1989, after the relegalization of Solidarity, the Sejm passed three laws which, for the first time since the war, guaranteed the church's legal status, guaranteed religious freedom, and extended state health coverage and pensions to Catholic clergy. Under the new law, the state recognized the legal status of the Catholic University of Lublin and the various theological academies and seminaries. These bills granted the church the right to organize radio and television programs, guaranteed freedom for the church press, and allowed the church to resume control over the Caritas charity, which it had lost in the 1950s. The new legislation also allowed the church to establish and administer hospitals, old people's homes, schools, and orphanages, and, in an especially surprising provision, the government agreed to return church property seized in the 1950s or, in the event that the church no longer wished to regain certain property, to pay appropriate compensation. In addition, the formation of new dioceses, construction of new church buildings, establishment of new convents and monasteries, and staffing of personnel posts in the church would no longer require regime approval. The legislation abolished military obligation for seminarians and novices. It also provided for the restoration of religious instruction in the school curriculum (with registration at the discretion of the parents). And finally, it confirmed 1 January, All Souls' Day, Christmas Day, Easter Monday, and Corpus Christi as nonworking holidays, and added an additional one: 15 August, the Feast of the Assumption of Mary.[68] Exactly two months later the Vatican announced that it had established full diplomatic relations with Poland and that it would be appointing a papal nuncio to take up residence in Warsaw. Subsequently, in October 1989 the government submitted amendments which would abolish the state Office for Religious Affairs. Taken collectively, these developments signified a dramatic change in the situation of the church in Poland, promising more security for church personnel and church life generally.

On the other hand, some mention should be made of the fact that three pro-Solidarity priests were brutally murdered in the course of 1989: Stefan Niedzielak of Warsaw, known for his intense devotion to his congregation, whose badly battered body was found on 21 January;[69] Stanisław Suchowolec of Białystok, whose asphyxiated body was found on 30 January;[70] and Sylwester Zych of Krynica Morska, who had served four years in prison (1982–86) for having allegedly sheltered two men convicted in the murder of a policeman and whose body was found on 11 July.[71] If one assumes that state security police were behind these murders—and there is no other reasonable explanation—then one is led to the conclusion that some elements in the political establishment were militantly hostile to any normalization of relations with the church.

The relegalization of Solidarity in April 1989, the passage of new religious legislation in May, and the appointment of a Solidarity prime minister (Tadeusz Mazowiecki) in August resulted in a dramatic change in conditions for society broadly and for the church specifically. These developments spelled the end of Poland's praetorian era and laid the basis for Poland's emergence from praetorianism, though there were still some hurdles remaining as of mid-1994.

Within a matter of months of Mazowiecki's appointment, the Polish Catholic church switched to the offensive and began pushing hard for the reintroduction of religious education in the schools—despite voluble protests from Protestants, Old Catholics, Orthodox, agnostics, and nonbelievers.[72] At the same time, the Catholic church applied heavy pressure on the Polish legislature to ban abortion, even though public opinion polls showed that most Poles opposed such legislation.[73]

Conclusion

Ecclesiastical articulation of institutional and social interests is not unique to praetorian systems. The Catholic church in the United States, for instance, has taken part in the public debate about the Strategic Defense Initiative.[74] The distinguishing feature of praetorian systems is the failure to build or sustain legitimate and effective political institutions capable of channeling rising public awareness of political issues. As a result, instead of functioning as an interest group as in effective pluralist systems, the church in conditions of praetorianism becomes more politicized.

Scot Paltrow has argued that the church could not have acted more timorously or more timidly in the 1980–81 period without undue risk to its fundamental interests,[75] and the argument might be extended to the entire period since 1980. Certainly the advocacy of church-state dialogue is a matter of necessity in many minds. But the very concept of dialogue is telling: one would not dream of talking about church-state dialogue in pluralist systems, because church and state do not confront each other there as antagonists. The concept of dialogue is appropriate to a meeting of erstwhile foes, rivals who view each other with distrust, but who may nonetheless have some common interests in pursuing cooperation. In such circumstances, as *Sejm* delegate Zbigniew Zielinski put it in 1985: "An attempt at mutual trust and good will is necessary."[76]

At the same time, the church has often been bold in the defense of its own institutional interests. In September 1986, for instance, Poland's bishops issued a statement advising the necessity of "establish[ing] the constitutional possibility for people to organize themselves without conditions based upon party membership. The lack of such possibilities impoverishes public life."[77] That this possibility would extend to Catholic social organizations was understood. Two months later, Reverend Alojzy Orszulik, director of the church press office in Warsaw, wrote an article for the weekly newspaper *Tygodnik Powszechny*. Orszulik contended that there was nothing in Polish law which prohibited workers, farmers, women, young people, and lay Catholics from forming associations outside communist control.[78] The article deplored the fact that Polish Catholics had been "pushed onto the sidelines of public life" and that many Catholic lay organizations had been suppressed, and suggested that this was partly to blame for the political apathy of the Polish public.[79] The article was banned by the censors.

But only a month later—in December 1986—another church newspaper, *Niedziela*, published a more moderate but no less explicit defense of the church's right to establish lay associations. Their purpose, *Niedziela* said, was to "imbu[e] the secular order with Christian spirit."[80] More to the point, *Niedziela* declared,

> The laymen's right to set up, lead, or join apostolic associations has its source in natural law; all the people have the right to set up associations corresponding to their genuine well-being. This is among the fundamental rights of a human being. Therefore, such right may not be denied to laymen by any human authority, whether secular or ecclesiastic, as long as the aims and activities of such associations comply with the canon law and the constitutional order.[81]

Earlier, in 1984, Solidarity cofounder Kazimierz Świtoń went on a three-week hunger strike in an effort to obtain authorization to set up Catholic trade unions like those that existed prior to World War II. He finally ended his hunger strike at the urging of Monsignor Bronisław Dąbrowski on behalf of the Polish episcopate.[82]

Huntington once wrote that "the primary problem of politics is the lag in the development of political institutions behind social and economic change."[83] Throughout the 1980s Poland was confronted with this problem, and this fact was, in itself, a powerful determinant of the political behavior of the church. But praetorianism—which is the result of that lag—is inherently unstable, and this generates pressure for a new equilibrium. When that new equilibrium is reached, the role of the church will inevitably change as well. Indeed, it has already changed.

8. Serb-Albanian Tensions in Kosovo

The province of Kosovo was one of eight federal units in the federated republic of Yugoslavia. It was by far the poorest of the eight units, had the second smallest population (ahead of Montenegro), and, as one of two autonomous provinces lying within the republic of Serbia, had more constraints on its autonomy than the six full-fledged republics. Yet since the turbulent days of early April 1981 when the province was shaken by widespread rioting, Kosovo had increasingly preoccupied party leaders in Belgrade and aroused fears that the country might be sliding toward civil war.[1] In the resulting uncertainty, the authorities abandoned their once-conciliatory posture vis-à-vis the dissatisfied Albanian residents of Kosovo and adopted a hard line, even while the situation slipped ever further out of control.

Whether the largely Albanian population wanted merely to obtain the fuller prerogatives associated with republic status, as some observers speculated,[2] or whether the majority viewed any continued association with Yugoslavia with distaste, as others believed,[3] was a complex question until 1989, when the suppression of Kosovo's autonomy (by the Serbian government) convinced many local Albanians that secession had become imperative. With the collapse of the Yugoslav federation in June 1991 and the outbreak of ethnic war, those Albanians who had earlier hoped to find a solution *within* a unified Yugoslavia began to see separation as the only viable option—the questions were when and how.

After the Albanian riots of 1981 and continuing violence, Yugoslavia bore witness to a Serbian nationalist backlash, which undermined communal stability in both Kosovo and Macedonia, provoked the exodus of some 45,000 Serbs and Montenegrins from the province between April 1981 and January 1990,[4] and seriously strained interrepublican relations, most especially between Slovenia and Serbia, but also between Croatia and Serbia.[5] Moreover, Serbian maneuvers to reduce the prerogatives of the autonomous provinces inevitably produced repercussions in Vojvodina. The Vojvodinan connection to the Kosovo crisis was graphically demonstrated on 9 July 1988 when some Serbs and Montenegrins from Kosovo went to Novi Sad (the Vojvodinan capital) to demand that the Serbian government's proposals to reduce the power and jurisdiction of the provinces (Kosovo and Vojvodina) be accepted and to protest Vojvodina's resistance to these proposals.

It is clear that the eruption of violence in Kosovo in spring 1981 and the continued underground antiregime activity there exploded the Yugoslav authorities' bold claim of the 1970s to have "solved" the national question and shook the foundations of Yugoslav nationalities policy in general. What is more—and here I agree with Branka Magaš—the Kosovo riots of 1981 marked a watershed in postwar Yugoslav history.[6]

The Nature of the Problem

In one respect at least, the Kosovo problem could be aptly compared to the Palestine problem: two ethnic communities with distinct languages and religious traditions lay claim to the same territory with competing historical arguments as evidence. The Albanians claim to be descended from an Illyrian tribe named "Albanians" that inhabited the eastern coast of the Adriatic in the second century and to have maintained a presence in Kosovo preceding the advent of the Serbs; they also cite the role of Albanian patriots such as Isa Boletino, Hasan Prishtina, and Bajram Curri in the history of Kosovo. The Serbs, by contrast, claim to have migrated into the region as early as the sixth and seventh centuries, maintain that the Albanian presence in Kosovo cannot be documented further back than the 1070s, describe twelfth- and thirteenth-century Kosovo as "purely Serbian," and view the province as the ancient heartland of the Serbian kingdom.[7] The fact that it was in Kosovo in 1389 on the Field of the Blackbirds that the Serbian kingdom made its last great stand against the Ottomans has contributed to the view, widely held by Serbs, that Kosovo is "sacred ground." Kosovo is, in a sense, the Serbian Jerusalem.

Kosovo was initially part of the independent Albania that first emerged in 1912, until the Great Powers intervened and, under Russian pressure, turned Kosovo over to Serbia. Hence, when the Kingdom of Serbs, Croats, and Slovenes (Yugoslavia) was created at the end of World War I, Kosovo lay within its jurisdiction. This fate was, however, fiercely resisted.

In 1919 Kosovar Albanians formed a political organization, Dzemijet, which held annual congresses and published the newspaper, *Moudjaeda (Struggle)*. Albanian uprisings against the Serbian monarchy between 1918 and 1919 were ruthlessly crushed by the Serbian army, and the local population was disarmed. Forced expulsions helped to cut the Albanian population in Kosovo in half between 1918 and 1921, from between 800,000 and 1,000,000 to 439,657.[8] According to one participant, however, the alleged "Albanian uprising" of 1920 was no longer an Albanian initiative, but, on the contrary, a regime provocation, enabling it to liquidate untold numbers of unwanted Albanians.[9]

The authorities shut down all Albanian-language schools in 1918 in order to "Serbianize" the Kosovar population. Later the authorities decided that the Albanians would only use their education to fight the regime, and adopted a policy of discouraging any public education for Albanians in order to keep the Kosovar Albanians ignorant and illiterate.[10] The Albanians, a Serbian official wrote in 1921, "will all remain backward, unenlightened, and stupid; nor will they know the state idiom [Serbian], which would help them to fight against us. It is in our interest that they remain at the present level of their culture for another twenty years, the time we need to carry out the necessary national assimilation in these areas."[11] This "assimilation" was to be accomplished through Serbian colonization of Kosovo. Indeed, between 1918 and 1940 the Belgrade regime seized 154,287 acres of land in Kosovo, turning 57,704 acres over to new settlers, mostly Serbs, and keeping other land for the army, the police, state schools, and other state agencies.[12]

Not surprisingly, when Kosovo was appended to Italian-occupied Albania in 1941, many Kosovar Albanians greeted the occupation as a "liberation."[13] The Italian occupation was generally supportive of Albanian culture, and ejected some of the Serbian settlers brought in by Belgrade. One source estimates that between 70,000 and 100,000 Serbs were forced out of Kosovo during the war.[14]

As of November 1944, as German troops were being driven out of Kosovo, an Albanian nationalist organization called Balli Kombetar resisted reincorporation of the province into Yugoslavia and even succeeded in infiltrating the new government being set up in Kosovo-Metohija. In Metohija a Ballist resistance assumed the proportions of an uprising, centered in Drenica. Armed operations against the uprising were launched in December 1944, with two brigades from the Albanian National Liberation Struggle participating on the side of the Yugoslav communists. Fierce battles took place in January and February 1945 between the Ballists and the Yugoslav communist army, and the state of war continued in Kosovo until July 1945.[15] Even after the suppression of open resistance, however, Yugoslav authorities remained suspicious of the Kosovar Albanians, and later, between the beginning of 1955 and the middle of 1957, the state security service conducted house-to-house searches throughout the province, confiscating all the weapons it found. At the height of this process, state security organs arrested a group of Albanians said to have been dispatched by Albania to incite rebellion in Kosovo. They were tried and convicted in the famous Prizren Trial of 1956.[16]

Incorporation into Yugoslavia had a retarding effect on both the cultural and economic development of Kosovo. On the one hand, "the teaching of Albanian cultural traditions, literature, folklore, and history was severely constrained, and emphasis on the past unity of the Albanian nation was strictly prohibited."[17] On the other hand, although Kosovo was economically the most backward region in the country, it was excluded from any special treatment as an underdeveloped region until 1955, and even after that it received less investment, which in any case was targeted mainly into the region's extractive industry. During the 1945–56 period, gross investments in Kosovo were 36.0 percent of the Yugoslav average, rising to 59.1 percent from 1957 until 1965. As a result, despite certain tangible economic achievements,[18] per capita income in Kosovo shrank from 42.0 percent of the average of the four richer federal units of Yugoslavia in 1953 to 28.0 percent in 1971.[19]

Belgrade's policy toward Kosovo remained restrictive until July 1966, when Aleksandar Ranković, head of the state security service, was stripped of his posts. In the wake of that development, federal policy became more accommodating toward Albanian interests, and after violent demonstrations in Kosovo and Albanian-populated parts of Macedonia in late 1968, the federal government introduced constitutional changes that greatly expanded the prerogatives enjoyed by the regional party barons in the autonomous provinces, and made a number of concessions designed to appease Albanian national sentiment, including the establishment of an independent university in Priština. Although the Albanians were better represented in provincial political echelons after that, renewed unrest broke out repeatedly in Priština throughout the 1970s.

While at least some Kosovar Albanians certainly desired separation from Yugoslavia, it was obviously impossible to use official forums (such as the legal press or party meetings) to vent this idea. But even full-republic status, which at times could be broached in public, was foreclosed. *Borba*, for instance, in its 10 April 1968 issue, reported former minister Mehmed Hodža's pained question as to why 1.2 million Yugo-

slav Albanians could not have full autonomy when 370,000 Montenegrins had their own republic.[20] Shortly thereafter, Rezak Šalja, a former
member of the provincial committee of the League of Communists (LC)
of Kosovo, declared himself "categorically and unambiguously" in favor
of establishing a republic for Albanians in Yugoslavia, which would also
enjoy the formal right of secession.[21] Similarly, Mahmut Bakalli, who
became provincial party chief in Kosovo in June 1971, warned federal
authorities that the situation in Kosovo could blow up if the province
were not granted wider autonomy. Serbian republic leaders resisted this
idea, and Bakalli developed the tactic of going over their heads to resolve
provincial issues at the federal level. This tactic contributed to an incremental slackening of ties between the autonomous province of Kosovo
and the Serbian Republic, of which it was juridically a part; yet even in
1977 the provincial leaderships of Kosovo and Vojvodina would join in
complaining that they did not have enough autonomy.[22]

Federal authorities proved willing to turn a blind eye, in the late
1970s, to the extraconstitutional augmentation of Kosovo's autonomous
powers, but remained unwilling to grant the province republic status.
The authorities feared that allowing jurisdictional changes partially
based on demographic shifts would open up discussion of the possible
allocation to a Kosovo republic of Albanian-populated districts in Montenegro, Macedonia, and Serbia proper.[23]

The Economic Quagmire

Economic development in Kosovo can be assessed from different perspectives yielding somewhat different conclusions. From the perspective of gross development, infrastructure, and the provision of medical
care and educational facilities, there have been major strides since the
war. The provincial capital of Priština in particular shows the benefits of ongoing urban improvement. From the more political perspective that assesses Kosovo's relative standing vis-à-vis the other federal
units across a string of economic measures over time, however, the picture proved disappointing for Kosovars: Kosovo slipped steadily further
and further behind the other federal units. Bakalli himself complained
(somewhat euphemistically) in 1980 that "the resources set aside in the
last medium-term plan [for 1976–80] obviously were not sufficient to
ensure . . . developing Kosovo as rapidly as possible."[24] Clearly, as the developmental gap separating Kosovo and the rest of Yugoslavia widened,
Kosovar Albanian bitterness and frustration could only deepen. Finally,
from the perspective of actual economic conditions in Kosovo there

were a number of serious, unresolved problems, the most important of which has been unemployment. Already in 1971 provincial unemployment stood at 18.6 percent. By 1981, on the eve of province-wide rioting, this had risen to 27.5 percent. As of 1987 the figure stood at 55.8 percent in the province, compared with 15.8 percent for the country as a whole.[25] Despite efforts to create new jobs in Kosovo, the birthrate continued to outpace growth in the economic sector. Hence, as *Borba* observed in 1985, the Kosovar economy would be unable to absorb the annual influx of new entrants into the available labor force even by the year 2000. And by then, Kosovo was projected to become the fourth most populous federal unit in Yugoslavia, with 2.5 million inhabitants (from 1.6 million in 1981).[26]

Part of the reason for Kosovo's economic backwardness must be traced to the inadequacy of labor-intensive investments and of economic assistance generally. But part of the reason lay also in the misuse of funds that *were* allocated. Unproductive investments accounted for part of the problem. In addition, in a flagrant abuse of the assistance program, Kosovar authorities allegedly used some federal developmental funds to buy land from Serbs and turn it over to Albanians.[27] Alex Dragnich and Slavko Todorovich note, further, that "the Kosovo Albanian authorities were also anxious to break up the compactness of Serbian areas. To do this they would, for example, build a factory in a solidly Serbian settlement. Under the population key of the Yugoslav government, 80 percent of the workers in that factory had to be Albanians, who then would be brought in, and thus break up the compactness of the Serbian settlement."[28] Given such politically motivated policies, it became all the harder to show tangible economic results.

The 1981 Demonstrations and Aftermath

With the long history of Kosovar-Albanian aspirations for union with Albania, Serbian suppression of Albanian culture from 1918 to 1966, provincial economic stagnation, and armed uprisings against Belgrade in 1918–20, 1945, and 1968, it is difficult to understand why Belgrade failed to see signs of the gathering storm in the late 1970s. It is true that by the 1970s the Albanian-dominated provincial committee was withholding much of its intelligence about underground organizations from authorities in Belgrade. Moreover, much internal information in Kosovo was published only in Albanian, rendering it virtually useless for most non-Albanians, whether in Kosovo or in Belgrade. But there was enough material in open, Serbo-Croatian sources as of spring 1980 to suggest that trouble was brewing; for that matter, Edvard Kardelj, Tito's right-hand man, warned in 1977 that in the absence of resolute action, Kosovo would eventually see large-scale violence.[29] His warning was ignored at the time.

In April and May 1981 the province was convulsed by antiregime demonstrations involving tens of thousands of persons. The regime boosted the local security forces from 1,200 to 1,500, declared a state of emergency, and sent in the army. Eventually, about a third of the Yugoslav army was stationed in Kosovo.[30] Instead of offering new concessions, as it had after the 1968 riots, the regime relied on a combination of armed force and the promise of economic stimulus to regain control of the situation. In the initial phase after the riots, however, the developed republics actually scaled back plans for joint investments in Kosovo and insisted on a credit relationship in economic transactions with the province; investments in Kosovo declined 40 percent between 1981 and 1982. But the authorities were unable to reverse the negative economic trends in Kosovo. That left coercion (and "differentiation of cadres") as the alternative means of stabilization.

Between spring 1981 and September 1987, according to official figures, criminal charges were brought against some 5,200 Kosovars of Albanian extraction, with 990 being sentenced for "political crimes" between 1981 and 1984.[31] According to the London *Sunday Times*, however, some 35,000 Albanians had been tried for "counterrevolutionary" activities by mid-1985, with more awaiting trial.[32] These trials proved controversial and some provincial judges evidently refused to be a party to the proceedings: between March 1981 and June 1983, 124 judges in Kosovo left the judiciary, 110 at their own request.[33]

Some 1,800 members of the Kosovo LC were expelled from the party. Among the 1,600 Albanians was provincial party chief Bakalli, who was given a twelve-year prison term. Some Albanian members of the Tetovo party organization in Macedonia were also expelled from the party.[34] More than 200 faculty members of the University of Priština were fired, along with the editors of the radio and television stations in the provincial capital. Between 1981 and 1984 the enrollment at the university was reduced from 37,000 to 20,000.[35]

Month after month there were fresh reports of the surfacing and suppression of new underground groups, many of which were described in the official Yugoslav press as Stalinist in orientation and almost all of which were said to be succored by the Albanian regime in Tiranë. Between April 1981 and March 1986 ninety-six irredentist organizations were discovered and broken up.[36] Their membership typically fell between 20 and 120.

Among these groups were the National Movement for the Liberation of Kosovo and other Albanian Districts in Yugoslavia, which had proclaimed itself in favor of union with Albania (suppressed in 1982);[37] the Communist-Marxist-Leninist Party of Albanians in Yugoslavia, whose goal was the union of all Albanian-inhabited regions into an enlarged Kosovo republic within the Yugoslav federation (suppressed in 1982);[38] the Call for Freedom organization based in Tetovo, which maintained contacts with Albanian exiles in Western Europe (suppressed in 1983);[39] the Front of National Liberation and the Kosovo Party of Struggle, both of which advocated creation of a Kosovo republic within the framework of the Yugoslav federal system (both suppressed in 1984);[40] the secret Movement for Liberation, which included a number of ethnic Albanian military officers in the Yugoslav national army among its members and had informants in the provincial security apparatus (suppressed in December 1985);[41] and the Marxist-Leninists of Kosovo, whose members were sentenced in spring 1986.[42] The Movement for Liberation was among the best organized and equipped and was said to have amassed considerable quantities of arms and ammunition, had obtained communications and printing equipment from Albanian exile communities in the West, and operated the six medium-sized illegal radio stations captured at the time.[43]

Albanian irredentist organizations also appeared in the Albanian-inhabited districts of western Macedonia, in particular Vinica, Kičevo, Tetovo, and Gostivar. The irredentist organizations in both Kosovo and Macedonia were said to be engaged in weapons smuggling and illegal dealings in gold and drugs.[44] In addition to these irredentist organizations, 216 subversive cells were discovered within the Yugoslav national army between 1981 and 1987. According to Fleet Admiral Branko Mamula, minister of defense, their program included "killing officers and soldiers, poisoning food and water, sabotage, breaking into weapons arsenals and stealing arms and ammunition, desertion, and causing frequent nationalist incidents in army units."[45]

Despite this patent evidence of dissatisfaction with the status quo, the central committee of the League of Communists of Yugoslavia (LCY), meeting in December 1983, reaffirmed its policy of "no negotiations with the Kosovars and no concessions to them."[46] This remains Belgrade's policy today. Since advocacy of constitutional reform is treated as tantamount to treason, Kosovar Albanians are left with two choices: submit or resist. Similarly (and in a typical copycat syndrome), certain elements in Vojvodina began to talk of republic status for that province—to be dubbed "the republic of Hungarians, Croats, Serbs, and other nationalities." *Politika* was quick to denounce the idea as "reactionary" and "extreme."[47]

Stirrings Among the Serbs

The 1981 riots and their aftermath completely polarized Kosovo. In an open expression of this polarization, Serbs and Albanians took to walking on opposite sides of the main promenade (corso) in Priština.[48] Albanians had allegedly attacked and destroyed part of the ancient patriarchal building at Peć, prompting the Serbian Orthodox church newspaper *Pravoslavlje* to publish an "Appeal for the Protection of the Serbian Inhabitants and Their Holy Places in Kosovo." Signed by twenty-one priests, the "appeal" assailed regime policy in Kosovo, which was portrayed as the Serbian "Jerusalem."[49] In the church's view, the Serbian nation itself was vitally threatened. Meanwhile, Serbian and Montenegrin families were pouring out of Kosovo, raising the specter that the Serbian Jerusalem might become totally Albanian in composition.

Serbs began to talk of these developments as a "national" issue. Some Serbs countered the slogan "Kosovo—republic" with the wry "Serbia—republic," an expression which implied that Serbia was being milked and exploited by ungrateful autonomous provinces. In October 1983 a survey of 1,000 Belgrade residents found that 50 percent favored reducing economic assistance to Kosovo and other less developed regions.[50] Typical of the Serbian backlash were the comments made by delegate Dragan Gligorić at a joint session of the Serbian assembly's three chambers.

"Serbia proper"—this clumsy, ridiculous, and humiliating term that has come into official use—unfortunately and to our political shame reflects the true state of affairs and Serbia's real status as a republic. On the other hand, everything has been done to make Kosovo a de facto republic. Irredentists are asking for what they already have, but are doing it so that tomorrow they can demand that Kosovo secede from the SFRY.[51]

With rising Albanian consciousness and occasional disorders also in Macedonia and Montenegro, there have been reports of nationalist backlashes among Macedonians and Montenegrins, and of the appearance of separatist currents among the Montenegrins.[52]

In both Kosovo and Macedonia there were reports of Albanian pressure on the local population and of Albanians buying up land from non-Albanians. Reports of violent assaults on Serbs, the killing of cattle owned by Serbs, and attacks on Serbian property contributed to a sense of urgency. In 1984, moreover, two Albanian judges were accused of causing an unwarranted delay in the prosecution of Albanians charged with crimes against Serbs.[53]

As early as 1982[54] local Serbs from Kosovo drew up a petition asking federal authorities to adopt more effective measures to restore order
in the province; seventy-nine Serbs signed the petition.[55] But little was
done, and the out-migration of Slavs continued. Between April 1981 and
December 1987, 24,209 Serbs and Montenegrins left Kosovo, often to live
in Serbia proper, reducing the Slavic component in Kosovo's population
from 14.9 percent to less than 13.5 percent.[56] With official encouragement, 3,000 Serbs and Montenegrins returned to Kosovo between September 1982 and June 1987, but of this number only a small portion
found work upon their return. When an organized group of Yugoslav journalists came to Kosovo in December 1985, however, they were told that
"over a longer period of time the characteristic trend is one of permanent
improvement."[57] The provincial authorities were anxious to minimize
the involvement of republic and federal officials and therefore tried to
present the situation as under control.

But it was not merely a question of the activity of illegal organizations. Kosovo's administrative infrastructure itself remained unreliable,
despite repeated shuffling of personnel. Four and a half years after the
April riots, the editorial board of the Albanian-language Priština daily
Rilindja was still said to be wayward, and the Association of Journalists
of Macedonia complained that *Rilindja* was issuing "tendentious disinformation." Several persons were subsequently weeded out of *Rilindja*
and Radio-Television Priština for "hostile" points of view.[58] And while
in February 1986 Sinan Hasani, a prominent Kosovar politician and
then vice-president of the SFRY Presidency (later president), continued
to insist that the organizational center of Albanian irredentist activity
was *outside* Yugoslavia, he noted, in an interesting phrase, that it was
"wrong and unacceptable to look for the enemy *exclusively* within the
LC ranks."[59]

A second citizens' petition submitted at the end of 1985 was signed by
2,011 Kosovar Serbs and Montenegrins. In this petition they vented their
frustration at the continued deterioration of the political situation in the
province. Provincial authorities in Priština denounced the petition as
"subversive, unacceptable, [and] extremely nationalistic." The signatories had anticipated this kind of reception in Priština, and had addressed
their petition to the organs of the Socialist Republic of Serbia—a fact
that, according to Sadri Godanci, a provincial party Presidium member,
demonstrated that "the signatories did not have faith in the political
structure of Priština and Kosovo."[60]

In January 1986 a group of 212 Serbian academics, writers, artists,
physicians, and engineers addressed a petition to the Federal Assembly,

complaining that the Albanians of Kosovo were pursuing a policy of "genocide" against non-Albanians.[61] This petition declared, in part:

> Under the guise of the struggle against "greater Serbian hegemonism," the Serb nation and its history have been subjected for decades to a show trial. . . . All those in our country who are not indifferent have long since realized that the genocide in Kosovo cannot be halted without deep social and political changes in the whole country. Such changes are impossible without a change in relations between the Socialist Autonomous Provinces and the Socialist Republic of Serbia, or indeed [in] the whole of Yugoslavia. No genocide can be stopped by means of [the] policy which had made it possible in the first place, i.e., [the] policy of a gradual handover of Kosovo to Albania, capitulation with no capitulation being signed, [a] policy of national betrayal.[62]

Subsequently, in March 1986, ninety-five Kosovar Serbs turned up in Belgrade and asked to be received by the Federal Assembly. There they complained that Albanians were buying up property in Kosovo, and that Serbian communities were being encircled by Albanian ones. They alleged that sex crimes against non-Albanian women had been ignored by provincial police, that the police had undertaken illegal actions where non-Albanians were concerned, and that provincial bodies had ignored the complaints of Serbs and Montenegrins. One citizen openly charged that the political situation in Kosovo was actually worse then than five years earlier.[63] The group demanded greater protection by the authorities from attacks by their Albanian neighbors. As if to confirm the truth of the Serbs' allegations, the provincial authorities arrested the organizer of the petition, Kosta Bulatović, upon his return to Kosovo, and charged him with having engaged in "hostile propaganda."[64]

When the thirteenth party congress convened in Belgrade's Sava Center in late June 1986, several hundred Serbian villagers from Batusae and other communities near Priština decided to march to Belgrade to bring their plight to the attention of the congress. Kosovo authorities dispatched the provincial police, however, who blocked the road and prevented the marchers from crossing the Kosovo-Serbia frontier.[65]

In such circumstances it comes as no surprise that a Belgrade meeting of ex-partisans from Kosovo raised questions as to whether leading functionaries of the Kosovar apparatus had been in secret contact with the Albanian communist party.[66] The veterans claimed that former federal information minister Ismail Bajra had engaged in talks in Tiranë at least three times a year prior to 1981 without ever reporting his presence at the local Yugoslav embassy, and demanded that both he and former state president Fadilj Hodža be brought to account for pro-Albania sympathies.

In early 1986 Miodrag Trifunović, president of the federal chamber of the Yugoslav Assembly, described the Slavic emigration from Kosovo and the deteriorating atmosphere in the province as the most serious political problem currently facing Yugoslavia. Irate Serbs in Kosovo demanded, *inter alia*, that the Socialist Autonomous Province of Kosovo be eliminated as a juridical unit and that the use of the Albanian language and Albanian national symbols in Kosovo be suppressed.[67]

The Limits of Yugoslav Socialist Patriotism

Until 1987 and the rise of Slobodan Milošević in Serbia, Yugoslav officials claimed to base their nationalities policy on "brotherhood and unity"—a vague Titoist formulation that embraced a federal system based on ethnic differences, guarantees for the language and culture of the sundry nationality groups, and a ban on noncommunist political organizations (described as inimical to brotherhood and unity). For much of Yugoslavia's postwar history it also involved the significant decentralization of political powers to the eight federal units and a "population key" mandating fixed quotas for specific ethnic groups in federal and republic appointments and in other spheres.

Closely related to this broad concept was the notion of "Yugoslav socialist patriotism," described in one publication as "the consciousness of, feeling, and love for the socialist self-managing community."[68] Since there is no Yugoslav nationality per se, Yugoslav socialist patriotism is not, according to its advocates, related to nationalism. Indeed, it is described as diametrically opposed to particularism and localism, which allegedly represent forms of collective egoism.[69] On the other hand, Yugoslav spokespersons claimed that far from negating the values, traditions, and interests of the component national groups (such as Serbs, Albanians, and Montenegrins), Yugoslav socialist patriotism presumed them.

Since Yugoslav socialist patriotism was long presented as a norm for public and private behavior, it followed that the actions and policies of the regime must conform to that norm if it was to have any prospect of success. There were various inconsistencies between theory and practice over the years, but the most serious, arguably, were manifested in Kosovo. To begin with, the Albanians viewed Yugoslavia (literally, Land of the South Slavs) as a Slavic country, and hence considered Yugoslav socialist patriotism an attachment to what is, in cultural terms, a predominantly Slavic community. Second, since Albanians now outnumbered both Macedonians and Montenegrins, and would in fact outnumber Slovenes in the next census, excluding them from full-republic status while allowing Macedonians, Montenegrins, and Slovenes that privilege could only be justified on the grounds that they were a minority diaspora from a neighboring state—Albania. But this in turn implied that Albanian national sentiment was not on a par with Serbian, Slovenian, and other Slavic attachments, and that while the latter were "presumed" by Yugoslav socialist patriotism, the former was tantamount to irredentism. Third, while the slogan "brotherhood and unity" suggests a policy supportive of mutually tolerant cohabitation by distinct ethnic groups, in summer 1986 Yugoslav authorities took the unusual step of legally barring any Albanian settlement in the few ethnically homogeneous Serbian villages left in Kosovo—a measure which Viktor Meier called Yugoslavia's "little 'apartheid.' "[70]

Finally, despite the population key, Serbs and Albanians in Kosovo continued to argue over appointments. Each side accused the other of enjoying unfair advantage. In June 1985, for instance, the Belgrade news agency Tanjug released a report of a session of the federal conference of the Socialist Alliance of Working People of Yugoslavia (SAWPY), in which complaints were registered that almost all managerial positions in culture, education, and the media in Kosovo were reserved for Albanians.[71] Radio Priština offered a very different picture, however, citing statistics to the effect that 68.4 percent of those employed in the social sector were Albanians (though they accounted for more than 80 percent of the provincial population by 1986), while Serbs held 22.5 percent of such jobs and Montenegrins 3.3 percent (though together they accounted for less than 9.0 percent of the provincial population in 1986).[72] The national composition of the Kosovar party organization as of June 1985 seemed to bear out Radio Priština's viewpoint: despite the population key, only 67.0 percent of the Kosovo LC was Albanian, versus 22.4 percent Serb, 5.3 percent Montenegrin, 2.8 percent Muslim, 0.88 percent Turk, 0.61 percent Gypsy, and 0.95 percent other.[73]

The Party's Analysis

Despite underground actions, sabotage, pamphleteering, trials, riots, polemics with Albania, expulsions of party members, and controversies between the Serbian and Kosovar party organizations, the authorities wavered until early 1987 between portrayals of the situation as stabi-

lized and improving and frank admissions that interethnic relations in
Kosovo were "far from satisfactory."[74] One of the first Tanjug releases
in April 1981 optimistically stated that "the broad masses of citizens,
youth, Albanians, and members of other peoples and nationalities of Kosovo and Yugoslavia, sharply condemned [the antiregime demonstration
in Priština], realizing its hostile background."[75] In 1983 *Borba* claimed
that "during the 21 months since the first demonstrations in Priština,
the enemy [has] lost battle after battle."[76] Later, Tanjug reported that
the "situation in the Yugoslav province of Kosovo is constantly improving, security is strenghening, and political conditions are more stable,"
though that release conceded that "anti-Yugoslav activity is still intensive."[77] And in April 1985, repeating what had by then become part of the
routine formula, Tanjug declared that "the political situation in Kosovo
is improving from day to day."[78] Occasionally, certain Yugoslav politicians protested retention of this formula. At a SAWPY meeting in 1985,
for instance, Ilija Djukić urged abandonment of clichés "that no longer
correspond" to the truth, such as "the situation is good."[79]

Yet the party was distinctly uneasy about any public discussion of
Kosovo, initially tried to circumscribe media reportage of the demonstrations,[80] subsequently imposed an embargo on press coverage of the
Kosovar Serbs' petition to the Federal Assembly in March 1986,[81] and developed a "schematic framework" to which party spokesmen and media
were obliged to adhere. Olivija Rusovac alluded to this in a 1985 report,
commenting that "today's debate on the emigration of Serbs and Montenegrins from Kosovo has in many respects gone beyond the schematic
framework according to which the situation in Kosovo is better but emigration has not been curbed."[82] SAWPY delegate Milan Rakas was even
more explicit:

> What is at stake above all is the standardization of some assess-
> ments and attitudes referring, above all, to the political security
> situation. We have had various views about the situation in Kosovo;
> they range from the situation being fairly poor to the other extreme
> of being very favorable. . . . Now this assessment has been standard-
> ized and is as follows: The political security situation in Kosovo is
> favorable if one proceeds from the grave consequences left by the
> counterrevolutionary events. . . .[83]

What this meant for the media was abundantly clear: "Journalists must
not fall into the trap of daily upsets and disagreements about controversial issues and concrete solutions."[84] On the contrary, "It is the duty
of Communists and other forces in Kosovo to direct the interpretation

of specific provisions of the constitution of the Socialist Republic of Serbia,"[85] not to mention of Albanian demands in Kosovo.

In a word, between 1981 and early 1987 the authorities tried to impose a party line involving the following elements. First, every nationalism was dangerous. Second, the demand for republic status for Kosovo was a smokescreen for efforts to mobilize forces to bring about the secession of the Albanian-inhabited districts of Yugoslavia and engineer their annexation to Albania. Third, because of this, the autonomist aspirations of Albanians were in essence "irredentist" and threatened the territorial integrity and cohesion of the Yugoslav federal state. And fourth, Albanian activists in Kosovo sought an ethnically "pure" Kosovo, free of Slavs.[86]

This is a curious list—curious, first, because each element is an oversimplification or exaggeration that concealed and confused more than it illuminated, and second, because an appreciation of the seriousness of the situation did not require that *any* of these claims be maintained. Were the party to have yielded on these points, however, the result would have been to grant that the Albanian activists had some reasonable demands, an acknowledgment that would suggest a policy of compromise. In short, the party line, was not designed to illuminate the situation, but to block any compromise by uniformly portraying all Albanian discontents as "extremists." The reasons for refusing to consider compromise will be explored later.

By the end of 1986 the party line began to change. In November a third deputation of Kosovar Serbs created a furor in Belgrade by telling authorities that if the police could not defend them, they would defend themselves.[87] During a two-day informational meeting the following January, Azem Vllasi tried to reassure the federation that Kosovar authorities had stabilized the situation, but, as the Zagreb newspaper *Večernji list* commented a few months later, far from improving, interethnic relations in Kosovo had worsened even within the provincial party apparatus.[88] By then the party's assessment had become bleak. Slovenian politician Franc Šetinc called developments in Kosovo "the deepest crisis in new Yugoslavia," and blamed it on "big, fateful errors in the developmental policy of the province,"[89] Marko Orlandić, a member of the presidency of the LCY central committee, admitted that the situation in Kosovo was steadily worsening, and that this threatened the stability of Yugoslavia and stirred discontent among the broader Yugoslav public.[90] And in a speech to the party committee of the Yugoslav national army on 23 September 1987, Defense Minister Mamula warned that "problems in Yugoslavia are rapidly increasing to a level beyond the . . . leadership's ability to control [them]."[91]

In June 1987 the central committee of the LCY held a two-day session devoted to Kosovo in which it passed a resolution calling for measures to halt the emigration of Slavs from the province and to restore law and order. In October, after admitting that organized irredentist activity in Kosovo had increased to the point that public security was seriously undermined, the state presidency placed Kosovo's security under federal control and authorized the dispatch of militia from the Federal Secretariat of Internal Affairs.[92]

In late 1987 Serbian party chief Slobodan Milošević emerged victorious from a power struggle with rival Ivan Stambolić and proceeded to transform the weekly magazine *NIN* and the daily newspaper *Politika* into mouthpieces for his political ideas.[93] Kosovo lay at the core of Miloševićs political program. Milošević, who built up a charismatic following among Serbs, believed that Serbia had to take a hard line in dealing with Kosovo—what Yugoslavs call the *čvrsta ruka* (strong arm).

Despite the tough talk in summer 1987 and Milošević's emergence as the leading political figure in the Serbian republic, when the Serbian assembly convened in late June 1988 it found that no effective measures had been adopted for dealing with the situation in Kosovo, which was therefore deteriorating.[94]

Milošević triumphed over his rival Stambolić in a political contest that centered on policy in Kosovo. Milošević contended that Stambolić's policy amounted to empty rhetoric and that it was necessary to restructure the relationship between Serbia and its provinces. To achieve this end, Milošević established the Committee for the Organization of Protest Meetings of Kosovar Serbs and Montenegrins, under the leadership of his lieutenant, Miroslav Solević.[95] This committee organized mass rallies involving tens of thousands of Milošević supporters in Vojvodina and Montenegro, forcing the resignation of the leaders of those regions in October 1988 and their replacement by Milošević loyalists. In late 1988 it also appealed for the organization of similar protest actions in Bosnia.[96] But the committee concentrated on the organization of large-scale demonstrations in Kosovo and in Serbia proper.

September 1988 saw mass demonstrations involving 10,000 or more Milošević supporters in Zvecan, Leposavić, Zubin Potok, Ranilug, Sremska Mitrovica, Titov Vrbas, and other locations, with smaller rallies (3,000–5,000) in Lebane, Nova Pazova, Koretiste, Rakovica, and elsewhere. Demonstrators typically carried Milošević's portrait and sang patriotic songs such as "Comrade Tito, we swear to you that we will not deviate from your path." They also sang certain lines from a hit song by the rock group White Button (*Bijelo dugme*):

> Yugoslavia, on your feet and sing!
> Whoever doesn't listen to this song,
> Will hear a storm![97]

Protesting Milošević's populist strategy, Slovenia's Franc Šetinc and Vojvodina's Boško Krunić resigned from the party presidium in October 1988. The resignations sent ripples through Yugoslav society but did not deter Milošević.

Milošević forced the adoption of Serbo-Croatian as the official language in Kosovo (making Albanian henceforth unacceptable for official use),[98] forced the resignation of Azem Vllasi and Kolj Široka from the Kosovar leadership, promoted Provincial Interior Secretary Rahman Morina to the presidency of the Kosovar provincial committee, and authorized the preparation of a series of amendments to the republic constitution designed to disembowel the autonomous provinces. Within Kosovo itself, the polarization between local Serbs and Albanians was reflected in the very different treatment given to these amendments in their respective media. *Jedinstvo*, the Serbian-language daily published in Priština, took a basically neutral position on the proposed amendments. By contrast, *Rilindja*, the Albanian-language daily, especially in the second half of November and in December, bitterly attacked the proposed amendments, which, it said, threatened the autonomy of the province.[99]

In February 1989 the amendments were adopted, eliminating the province's authority to pass its own legislation and making the Serbian Supreme Court the highest judicial court of appeal for Kosovo prior to appeal to the federal level. Jubilant Serbs celebrated the "elimination" of borders between Serbia and its autonomous provinces. Albanian workers and students replied with a wave of strikes across the entire province, leading some Serbs to demand that the army send units into Kosovo. Army units in Kosovo were in fact placed on combat alert, and large columns of tanks and other army vehicles were reported on roads entering the province.[100]

To complete his victory, Milošević had Azem Vllasi and fourteen others arrested and tried for treason ("counterrevolution") and ordered extensive revisions to the party statutes of the Kosovar party organization. These measures did not ensure calm, however, and a meeting of the Provincial Committee of the Kosovo LC in November 1989 admitted that the activity of Albanian nationalists was undiminished and that there had been armed attacks on army installations and units and on members of local security organs.[101]

A New Wave of Tensions

By early 1990 discontented ethnic Albanians increasingly looked to political pluralization as a way out of the impasse. Three new alternative movements in particular championed the idea of pluralism as the key to solving the crisis. These were the Democratic League of Kosovo (which urged restraint on both sides), the Popular Movement for the Republic of Kosovo (which also highlighted the importance of full-republic status), and the Social Democratic Party of Kosovo (which was founded in February 1990).

On 18 January 1990, after many years of resisting pressure to negotiate, Kosovo's communist leaders finally sat down with representatives of the Kosovar opposition. Šakir Maksud, a member of the Kosovo party leadership, readily conceded after the first round of talks: "It is evident that the main aim of the alternative groups is the abandonment of the single-party system."[102] And indeed, speaking on behalf of the alternative movements, former journalist Veton Suroi insisted that "political pluralism is the only way to solve the problems of Kosovo."[103]

But the talks broke down, and on 24 January some 40,000 ethnic Albanians took to the streets of Priština, demanding free elections and the immediate resignation of provincial boss Rahman Morina, a Milošević ally. Those disturbances ignited several weeks of violence in which Albanian demonstrators fought with police. On 31 January there was even an open-pitched battle between armed groups of Albanians and Serbs in the village of Srpski Vrševac, near Lipljan.[104] Tens of thousands of Albanians took to the streets in towns across Kosovo. Meanwhile, back in Belgrade, thousands of disconsolate Serbs gathered on the Square of the Republic, shouting insults against the late president Tito and demanding an end to communism. The protestors shouted "Tito—criminal!" and "Tito—Ceauşescu!"[105]

The federal authorities sent in armored vehicle units of the Yugoslav People's Army; the death toll exceeded nineteen.[106] Meanwhile, Yugoslav president Janez Drnovšek proposed a birth control plan to slow the rapid population growth among Kosovo's Albanians.[107]

By this point the Serbian party press had become accustomed to shrillness in its reportage of Kosovo, and routinely blamed troubles in Kosovo on "terrorists" and "separatists." In February 1990 the Belgrade daily *Poli-*

tika ekspres described Fadil Hoxha, the former Yugoslav vice-president, as the mastermind of "terrorist actions" designed to advance his alleged "insane fascistic plan to create a Great Albania."[108] Such rhetoric only helped to alienate other republic leaderships, and the longer the Kosovo crisis continued, the more isolated Serbia became.

The Slovenian and Croatian leaderships both criticized Serbia's policies in Kosovo, and Slovenia called for a lifting of the state of emergency in the province. The Bosnian leadership warned that time was running out for finding a solution in Kosovo. Of the five other republics, only Montenegro stood by Serbia.[109]

Kosovo had thus become a powerful factor for change in Yugoslavia for several reasons: it was the scene of the complete deterioration of interethnic relations, it massively contributed to the breakdown of dialogue among the republics, and its economic dilemmas ultimately created a serious pressure on the entire region. A fourth way in which developments in Kosovo reinforced pressure for change was through the spawning of independent civil and political initiatives such as the Kosovo Committee for the Protection of Human Rights, the Association of Independent Journalists of Kosovo (established in February 1990), and the aforementioned alternative movements. Political pluralization was of course farther advanced in Slovenia, Croatia, and Serbia; but all the same, the pressures for pluralization generated by interethnic tensions in Kosovo had independent importance.

Setting the Stage for Civil War

It is worth remembering that rioters in both the 1968 and 1981 demonstrations were heard to chant "Long live Enver Hoxha!" Nor is there any reason to doubt Yugoslav reports that some underground organizations in Kosovo had contacts with Albanian exile organizations in the West and perhaps also with officials in Albania. Until 1990 or 1991, however, it is doubtful whether many Albanian activists saw the necessity of choosing between an *autonomist* program (republic status within Yugoslavia) and an *irredentist* program (secession followed by annexation by Albania). What mattered was that Kosovar Albanians were fed up with the status quo, increasingly alienated from the Serbs and the Montenegrins, and faced a deteriorating economic situation that could not make the prospect of remaining within Yugoslavia seem by any means easy.

Most Kosovar Albanians simply wanted the situation to improve. Some were basically autonomist, most basically irredentist, and many for autonomism and irredentism at one and the same time. A 1985 report of a "plan to form armed shock brigades headquartered in local communities, regions, and districts" in Kosovo to function as "the first irredentist military organization" suggested that Kosovar Albanians might be giving up on Yugoslavia.[110]

The continued tensions in Kosovo had broad effects within Yugoslavia. First, the continued stream of Serbian and Montenegrin families to Serbia catalyzed an anti-Albanian Serbian nationalist backlash, which in turn contributed to the rise of the charismatic Slobodan Milošević. Second, the inability of provincial authorities to protect the basic human and civil rights of local Serbs and Montenegrins blew wind into the sails of support for the transfer of some of the provinces' jurisdiction back to the Serbian republic, with the result that the Serbian amendments were passed in early 1989. And third, by confronting Yugoslavia with the possibility of localized civil war, the continued political instability in Kosovo contributed to the more general pressure on Yugoslavia to rethink the political and structural premises of the system.

"Kosovo" was the wedge that Serbian nationalists used to force open the doors to massive political change in Serbia. "Kosovo" was their instrument to infuse the Serbian public with a rapture over Serbia itself, in the process suffocating "Yugoslav socialist patriotism." "Kosovo" was a fever that seized the Serbian public and that raised up new elites. "Kosovo" was the test of loyalty for Serbs: to be a good Serb was to believe in a *Serbian* Kosovo, and not in an *Albanian* Kosovo. "Kosovo," by 1989, had been raised from the status of myth to that of passion. As Matija Bečković, president of the Serbian Writers' Association, said in a speech on 4 March 1989: "There is so much Serbian blood [shed in Kosovo] and so many sacred relics that Kosovo will remain Serbian land, even if not a single Serb remains there."[111] The cult of King Lazar's bones, ceremoniously celebrated in 1989, acted out this psychology on the symbolic level.[112] "Kosovo," in short, inspired Serbs with a sense of apartness from the other peoples of Yugoslavia and, in this way, set the stage for civil war.

Part IV
A New Generation

9. Feminism in Yugoslavia

"Now," said I, "take the male and the female sex; if either is found to be better as regards any art or other practice, we shall say that this ought to be assigned to it. But if we find that they differ only in one thing, that the male begets and the female bears the child, we shall not take that difference as having proved any more clearly that a woman differs from a man for what we are speaking of; but we shall still believe that our guardians and their wives should practise the same things."—PLATO, *The Republic, Book V*

Blaženka Despot opens her 1987 book *The Woman Question and Socialist Self-Management* with a challenge: if, as Marx and Engels say, the ruling ideas of any epoch are the ideas serving the ruling *class*, then one may add that they are also the ideas serving the ruling *sex*.[1] It follows that if the radicalization of the working class is only the first step toward the overthrow of the old system of class relations, then the radicalization of women is only a first step toward the overthrow of patriarchal society and its complete replacement with something else.

Despot is one of a small but vocal number of feminists who beginning in the late 1970s were trying to change the way Yugoslav society thought about the sexes and their roles in the family, society, and politics. Yugoslavia's feminists were concentrated in three cities: Belgrade, Zagreb, and Ljubljana. For the most part they were non-Marxists. Most of them were young professionals and academics born since World War II. Like their counterparts in the West, they faced a combination of challenges. On the one hand, they had to live with the scorn and self-righteous anger of people who grew up with patriarchal values and who therefore considered any challenge to those values as impudence at best, sacrilege at worst. Further, they were confronted by suspicion from the party, which considered the implication that the "woman question" was not being resolved an affront to its own authority, and feminist activity an intrusion into its political sphere. And finally, they were challenged by the older generation of women, the partisan generation, many of whom had fought against the occupation forces in World War II and had risen to positions of responsibility in the postwar apparatus. For this generation, the partisan experience and the mobility they personally experienced after the war were proof that socialist society in Yugoslavia had made a decisive move toward restructuring the relations between the sexes on more egalitarian lines.[2]

When the partisans first took power, they proposed to "solve" this question within the framework of a power monopoly.[3] The 1946 Constitution included a clause guaranteeing equality of the sexes both before the law and in social life, and when the Fifth Party Congress passed a new program in July 1948, it underlined the need for work "in educating women in the spirit of socialism, in achieving greater mobilization of women for the building of socialism, for strengthening the equality already attained, by means of a constant solicitousness for their cultural and political advancement . . . and for the more massive inclusion of women in all areas of social and economic life."[4] Further resolutions were passed at each succeeding congress. The Eighth Congress (1964), for instance, urged basic organizations of the LCY to devote more attention to the advancement of women's status and in particular to the promotion of greater numbers of women to positions of responsibility and authority in administration, while the Tenth Congress (1974) entrusted communists with particular responsibility for ensuring the ever greater participation of women in the political life of the country.[5]

Dramatic results were achieved in mobilizing women into the industrial labor force,[6] and, for a time at least, the proportion of women occupying seats in women's councils, on enterprise boards of directors, and in councils of agricultural collectives steadily grew.[7] Moreover, there is little question that, in comparison with women in many other countries, Yugoslav women have been as well or somewhat better represented in the echelons of power.

But the passage of the Economic Reform in 1965 resulted in a reversal of trends toward bringing larger numbers of women into positions of political and managerial authority. For example, the number of women elected as deputies in the federal assembly fell dramatically, from 15.2 percent in 1963 to 6.3 percent in 1969, as did female representation in the republic assemblies (from 16.1 percent to 7.5 percent) and in the district assemblies (from 14.2 percent to 7.9 percent).[8]

The Ninth Congress of the LCY (March 1969) expressed concern at this trend, interpreting it as an indication of a loss of momentum and stagnation in the sphere of women's equality, and admitting positive *regression* in the years immediately prior.

Some momentum was later regained, and by the mid-1970s many indicators showed that women had retrieved the position they had had in elective bodies in the early 1960s.[9] Yet in 1976 there was only one woman among the fifty members of the presidium of the LCY, two women among the fifty members of the presidium of the LCY, two women among the fifty members of the presidium of the SAWPY, thirty-three women among the 144 members of the presidential council of the League of Trade Unions, eight women among the thirty-nine members of the presidium of the League of Socialist Youth, two women among the twenty-two members of the presidential committee of the veterans' organization, and two women among the thirty-two members of the Federal Executive Council.[10] In June 1975 only 41 (5.2 percent) out of the 792 highest ranking federal functionaries were women. In a final irony, the number of party members who are women was proportionately smaller in 1979 (about 20 percent) than in 1945 (about 25 percent).[11]

In 1987 a small controversy erupted over female representation in the Federal Secretariat for Foreign Affairs, when several magazines and newspapers received letters charging that the secretariat had demanded that the executive councils of the federal units remove all women candidates from their lists of names proposed for appointment in the secretariat. A tabulation of positions showed that only 28.8 percent of secretariat officials were women, and that, as of early 1987, only two of Yugoslavia's ambassadors were women—Ana Jovanović in Denmark, and Ljiljana Todorova in Guinea.[12]

But problems ran deep. Illiteracy was three times as great among Yugoslav women as among Yugoslav men (14.7 percent versus 4.1 percent in 1981). Women were, in the mid-1980s, still in a clear minority among recipients of higher degrees (in 1984, 659 females out of 2,138 M.A. recipients, 185 females out of 820 doctorates). As of 1981, Yugoslav women's average wages were 16 percent less than that of men.[13] Unemployment has also been more serious among women, with 19.0 percent of females registered as unemployed in 1986, versus 10.4 percent of males.[14]

In March 1981 *Politika* conducted a survey of Yugoslav women that asked if they felt they had achieved equality. Many women refused to answer, while a large number expressed confusion about the notion of equality itself. Of those who did answer, there were some who answered that socialism had fulfilled its promise. Others, however, denied that they had achieved anything even close to equality either at the workplace or at home. Interestingly enough, when *Politika* approached a sample of men a week later with the same question, there was unanimous agreement that Yugoslav women were definitely *not* equal, with some respondents adding that that was the way it should be.[15] The difference in response reflects a well-known syndrome that women are less inclined to "admit" their subordination than are men.

Nataša Djurić stated the Yugoslav women's case clearly in a 1980 article for *Borba:* "A lot has been accomplished, but we want more. We want women to be more fully included in sociopolitical life," she wrote. "Where cadres policy is concerned, for example, everyone will agree that women are 'second-rate citizens' or a reserve work force."[16]

The LCY openly admitted its failure to achieve the goals it set in this area, and conceded that proportionally few women were involved in self-managing bodies, executive organs, or delegate assemblies, or occupied leadership positions in the society. Worse yet, the party apparatus had failed to heed the resolutions of its own party congresses, and the presidium of the LCY central committee felt obliged to concede in spring 1980 that the basic party organizations had been occupied only in a sporadic and unorganized fashion with advancing the position of women in Yugoslav society.[17]

The Cultural Problem

In the late 1970s various voices challenged the notion that bureaucratic resistance and "liberal" tendencies were entirely to blame for this persistent foot-dragging. Radivoje Iveković, Mirjana Poček-Matić, Gabi Čačinović-Vogrinčić, and others now called for a reassessment of the role played by the familial division of labor and by the persistence of "petit bourgeois" and religious consciousness, admitting that their tenacity and importance had been drastically underestimated. One observer even declared that Yugoslavia had failed to do away with the bourgeois family. Negative traditionalism, it was now argued, had to be attacked head on.[18]

A group of feminist scholars in Zagreb started to meet on a regular basis in the late 1970s to exchange ideas. Their meetings took on the character of seminars in which research findings on the past and present role of Yugoslav women were presented and discussed.[19] Long-standing traditions were identified as only part of the problem, which they saw as aggravated by the commercialization of the female body. They reached the conclusion many Western feminists have reached, that

> the cheap novels and television serials only imitate the television commercials in their depiction of women as stereotypes. In commercials for cars, cosmetics, and a host of other products, every woman is beautiful, sensuous, and full of life, computerized, and programmed for the game of sexual relations with men. Woman's beauty is portrayed exclusively as there for the satisfaction of men. In commercial after commercial, woman's body is glorified, not for itself, but to sell commodities. The mother sells dishwashing detergents, and smiling two-children families sell toothpaste, vacations, cereal. Human relationships become reduced to what they can sell or buy.[20]

The Zagreb circle published essays about feminist concerns in the secular press, and stirred some public awareness. The LCY began to take a second look at primary school readers, television programs, and so forth. In March 1981 *Komunist* even condemned the "women's press" (represented by such magazines as *Praktična Žena* and *Bazar*) as a reservoir of patriarchalism that catered to the "traditional interests of women"—cooking, child-rearing, room decoration, makeup, and fashions.[21] The "woman and family" page, which featured mostly articles on childcare, fashions, cosmetics, cooking, and family relations, with an occasional article on the subject of women's equality in Yugoslav society, disappeared from *Politika* in 1983.

The Feminist Challenge

Feminism first emerged in Yugoslavia in the mid-1960s, when a group in Zagreb tried to capture *Žena*, the journal of the Croatian Conference for Women, and transform it into a forum for feminist ideas.[22] After three years of exertions, the attempt petered out; by 1968 local feminists had given up this idea. For a while they were dispirited, but the early 1970s brought new blood into the feminist movement.

By the mid-1970s groups of professional women in Zagreb, Ljubljana, and Belgrade were becoming politically mobilized. They believed that the Conference for the Social Position of Women (established in 1961) had remained marginal. They felt that SAWPY was unwilling to take up the important question of family relations and was not satisfying the needs of women's equality. They were concerned that women in Yugoslavia were not even taking advantage of their legal rights because of cultural traditionalism, and they saw that women were typically reluctant to assume leadership positions in the party or governmental apparatus.[23] They felt that the most important task was to work toward changes in upbringing and education. After analyzing Yugoslav textbooks, they identified a pattern of systematic stereotyping, with women portrayed as passive by nature and inherently masochistic.

Out of this milieu came Woman and Society, a group formed in Zagreb in 1979 with a membership consisting principally of sociologists and philosophers. They met two to three times a month since then, with a core membership of twenty to thirty. Their focus was academic, with members often presenting the results of historical research. One member, the late Lydia Sklevicky, for instance, was deeply involved in researching the history of the women's movement in Yugoslavia.[24] Although viewed with suspicion by many in the apparatus, they made themselves heard— through guest lectures at universities, public talks, and articles published in *Argumenti, Danas, Delo, Dometi, Duga, NIN, Pitanja, Start, Studentski list,* and other leading periodicals.

About the same time, feminist intellectuals in Belgrade were also beginning to meet and exchange ideas. The challenge, as they saw it, was above all *cultural.* As one of the leading members in the Belgrade circle told me in 1987,

> We have good laws. In fact, under the law we have full emancipation. But in life it is a different situation. We have a very progressive family law, for instance, also for divorce and for other things. But our men are very primitive. It is difficult to find civilized men in Serbia. The men and boys are very irresponsible; this is their style. The boys don't take school seriously, while the Serbian girls tend to do much better than the boys. Wife-beating is very common in Serbia.[25]

The Belgrade circle decided to organize an independent international conference on the subject of women's equality. The resulting conference, held in Belgrade 27 October–2 November 1978, was attended by feminists from Poland, Hungary, France, West Germany, Great Britain, and Yugoslavia, with an especially large contingent from Italy.[26] Perhaps surprisingly, the conference did not catalyze any further organization, but served chiefly to impress upon participants the weight of the difficulties which they were facing.

Later, in 1981, three Belgrade intellectuals—Sophia Trivunac, Lina Vušković, and Sonja Drljević—started to meet on a regular basis for discussions at the Student Cultural Center. Eschewing the formal organizational framework of the Zagreb circle, the Belgrade feminists deliberately kept things informal. The group was built up through friendship channels. The organizers telephoned people to remind them of meeting times. As many as two hundred people would come to their meetings. The group was active for about two years, and when it became dormant, it was succeeded by a new group, created in 1986 by Lepa Mladjenović, a Belgrade psychologist.

In the meantime, a second, less institutionalized and less academic Croatian feminist group was formed in the Trnje district of Zagreb by Katerina Vidović in 1985. This new group attracted younger women in their twenties who were not professionally interested in feminism or in the history of the women's movement. It concentrated on consciousness raising, and established a phone line for battered women. With a core membership of twenty to thirty activists, including some men, the Vidović group issued leaflets on exhibitions and other events considered chauvinist: one example was a photo display of nude and seminude women.[27]

Finally, a feminist organization called Lilith was created in Ljubljana in April 1985 by researchers of the faculty of sociology. Unlike the other groups, Lilith was consciously created to serve two quite different purposes—practical work and recreation. Lilith put out its own magazine on an occasional basis (with four or five issues by summer 1987); the magazine was about twenty-four pages typed and xeroxed, and looked like some kind of samizdat, but it obtained support from the Student Cultural Center and therefore a legal basis. The magazine's circulation was 300–400 copies. "Something happened in the atmosphere when Lilith emerged," a member told me. "Lilith started to be talked about in the media. The various women's magazines had interviews with Lilith members. There was a certain interest generated in Lilith. People took notice."[28] In 1986 and 1987 Lilith members took the initiative in organizing open-air "protest celebrations" in which feminist, pacifist, and environmentalist concerns were brought together. The second of these, which included a peaceful march to the center of town, was timed to coincide with the first anniversary of the nuclear accident at the Soviet nuclear station at Chernobyl.

Hostile to the ideas of hierarchy and subordination, Lilith had no formal leadership, although Mojca Dobnika served as the informal spokesperson of the group.

Besides Lilith, a second group was established in Ljubljana and also became active in this field, the Group for Women's Movements, originally attached to the Republican Conference for Youth. This was an officially sanctioned body, rather than a grassroots organization, but it organized protests against sexism and demanded political quotas, suggesting that 50 percent of the leadership positions in the youth organization at both the federal and republic levels be reserved for females.

Zagreb, Belgrade, and Ljubljana were clearly the centers for feminist activity in Yugoslavia, where feminism was very much an urban phenomenon. But there were also some unassociated feminists in Novi Sad, and a Sarajevo sociologist, Nada Ler Sofronić, was well respected among feminists. The Serbian nationalist backlash which became dominant in Serbia by 1987 was accompanied by a revival of patriarchal chauvinism, however.

Reactions of the Authorities

If taken seriously, feminism is fundamentally revolutionary, because it rejects the existing social order, of which the political order is one dimension. The feminist movement in Yugoslavia did not, of course, speak of overthrowing socialism, but it did speak of the need to overthrow patriarchy and of the failure of socialism to do so.

But for all that, the political establishment always reacted quite diversely. As already mentioned, most if not all of the leading periodicals opened their pages to feminist writings. *Start* magazine, in particular, was warmly supportive of the feminists, and the staff members of *Start* maintained contact with members of the Zagreb circle Woman and Society.[29] One member of the establishment, herself a member of the partisan generation, told me in 1982 that she had told women in Kosovo that they needed a special organization to advance the interests of women—a recommendation which went beyond the usual recommendations of the party. She felt that promoting the organization of women in the villages could be a step in the right direction.[30] In Slovenia the authorities felt vaguely threatened by Lilith at first, but later they became more relaxed and would call up Lilith members to talk to them.

On the other hand, the gulf between the feminists and the communist women's organization was always great. One feminist put it this way: "Our official women's organization is really a joke. They are doing nothing useful but they are very, very afraid of the feminist organizations because we are doing their job for nothing, and they are worried that soon people will see that their organization is unnecessary. . . . They are afraid for their salaries, but they are masking that fear in ideology."[31] And in June 1982 Branka Lazić, representing the Yugoslav Women's Conference, told the Twelfth Party Congress that it was necessary to fight against feminism with all available forces. Five years later, that same women's conference, while still hostile to the feminist movement, organized a conference on feminism in Yugoslavia and invited feminist writer Slavenka Drakulić-Ilić to present a paper. The topic Drakulić-Ilić chose for herself: do we need a conference on women and what purpose does it serve?

Visions of the Future

Jugo-feminizam (and feminism in the Yugoslav successor states) is very much under the shadow of the West. The region's feminists have read the major works of Western feminists, follow social and cultural trends in the West with deep interest, and are conscious of the fact that their small groupings are not at all comparable to the institutionalized feminist organizations of the West. Like Western feminists, those in the Yugoslav successor states reject as both undesirable and impossible the idea of replacing patriarchy with matriarchy; they do not aspire to promote "female civilization"—which, as one astute feminist noted, could only be accomplished through totalitarian measures[32]—but rather a truly "human civilization." The chief problems they identify are gender role stereotypes; social, economic, and political inequality; the myth of female weakness; and the relationship of false history to ideology.

Of these, the most serious may be the first, fueled by social pressure to conform to stereotyped standards of appropriate behavior for one's sex. "Sex roles are one of the means of estrangement not only between the sexes," a Belgrade-based psychotherapist noted, "but also of limiting a person's development. They make a person less free."[33] Sex roles are perpetuated in the family, the school, films, and the media, and persons who reject these stereotyped roles do so at the risk of being ridiculed and branded as deviant.

Feminists responded by organizing study groups to monitor and report on school texts and curricula, films, and television programs. One five-year study found that Yugoslav kindergarten teachers were preventing communication between the sexes by organizing separate study corners for girls and boys. The researcher, herself a trained psychologist, made the teachers conscious of their chauvinism, and as a result of her influence some of Belgrade's schoolteachers began to encourage joint games for girls and boys. The researcher argued that division is the first step toward the subordination of one group to the other, and of both to constricting mythologies of the past. "If we are divided as sexes and cannot form the same language of communication, then we can be easily ruled."[34]

Similarly, Yugoslav studies of school textbooks have found that children

> read school books that encourage boys to fight back, girls to with-
> draw. They teach girls to be neat, to cook, wash, iron, sew, and
> play with dolls, and teach boys to climb trees and not to cry or
> play with dolls or cook. Stories show mothers cooking dinner, iron-
> ing, washing, and caring for their appearance (makeup, dress) to be
> sexually attractive; fathers carry coal, do outside tasks, drive and
> repair automobiles, do home repairs, shave, and read the newspaper.
> Even a study of secondary schools in Croatia, in 1970–71, found
> the school handbook of rules defining gender differences in dress:
> "Students, *and especially the girls,* must dress neatly and in keeping
> with their age."[35]

Yugoslavia's well-known cultural differences have been also reflected in gender relations. Among the Albanian village populations of Kosovo, women are said to be treated as subhumans less important than farm animals. Elsewhere the situation is not as extreme: the status of women in Slovenia and Croatia is on a par with neighboring Austria and Italy. The status of women in the Yugoslav successor states is closely correlated with the level of economic development in the region in question.

The second problem, that of social, political, and economic inequality, has already been discussed in earlier sections. The starting point for any remedy is, of course, good information, and Yugoslavia's feminists have devoted considerable energy to establishing the facts. In an important study published in 1985, Željka Šporer, a researcher at the University of Zagreb, showed that there were statistically significant correlations between the feminization of Yugoslav professions, on the one hand, and their prestige and remuneration on the other.[36] The inescapable conclusion is that underlying cultural prejudices must be eradicated before the opening of specific professions to women can be expected to produce real equality.

Another important work is Vjeran Katunarić's *Female Eros and the Civilization of Death.* Katunarić despairs of the utility of quotas or campaigns to improve the political representation of women, arguing that their efficacy is undermined by the characteristic "authoritarian attitude toward women." He also denies that women have any less interest in politics than men, citing research conducted in Slovenia. Before any progress can be made, he warns, it is necessary to steer clear of the pitfalls of *false universalism,* which denies there is a "woman question" and thereby reduces everything to an oversimplified humanism, and *in-*

strumentalism, which is interested in the status of women only as it relates to other problems and issues.[37]

Instrumentalism is well illustrated by a controversy centering on the problem of rape. The penalty for rape (five years in prison) has long been considered too light by feminists. But after the Albanian nationalist riots in Kosovo in 1981 (see chapter 8), Albanian men allegedly began vindictively raping Serbian women. There was a huge public outcry in Serbia, which spilled over into the television and magazines, but oddly, its focus was on the suffering of Serbian women as *Serbs*, not as women—that is, it was treated as an interethnic issue and not as an intersexual issue. Eventually, in March 1987, the Serbian republic passed a law doubling the penalty for rape when another nationality is involved—meaning, of course, that rape is considered less serious if it is between Serbs! Local feminists were outraged by this implication and protested loudly.[38]

The myth of female weakness underpins and reinforces the previous two problems. According to feminist writer Drakulić-Ilić, this myth is used to buttress a phallocracy that tells women that their subordination is natural and reflective of their allegedly inferior abilities.[39] The celebration of 8 March as International Women's Day has long been seen by the region's feminists as a dimension of this phallocracy: the absence of a corresponding day for men suggests that they do not need it. Or, as a Belgrade feminist put it, "March 8, Women's Day, is a stupid day and a stupid idea, because if you have 364 days a year without respect for women, what good is one day?"[40]

This myth is even carried over into legislation. In Croatia, for instance, women were long compelled to retire five years before men. Finally, in the early 1980s a group of women professors appealed this law to the Supreme Court. Their petition was supported by Croatian feminists. Their pressure paid off when the law was changed in 1984 to give women the option of working the extra five years.

The myth also reflects familial relationships. Sophia Trivunac, who has counseled women and men with marital problems, relates:

Women are unaware that they are persons. They spend their whole lives serving everyone, and sometimes they do not see this as a problem. The pay-off is to be viewed either as a victim or as a "good woman."

Women often have phobias. They are afraid of the outside world. When they cannot use the world for their pleasure, they retreat back into their phobia. They feel guilty if they are virgins. They feel guilty if they are promiscuous. They feel guilty if they have only a few lovers. They feel guilty if they have many lovers. The Yugoslav woman—and, of course, not just the *Yugoslav* woman—typically feels like a sex object. Her body is not for her, but for display. She becomes alienated from her own body.

It often takes a long time before women see the problem. Then it takes a *very* long time to convince the husbands that there is a problem.[41]

And finally, the fourth problem addressed by Yugoslav feminists is the relationship of false history to ideology. This was a central concern of historian Lydia Sklevický, who struggled to keep alive the memory of noncommunist feminist currents in prewar Yugoslavia and to debunk the myth that Yugoslav feminism was somehow a Western export. On the contrary, she emphasized, feminism has a long tradition in Yugoslavia.[42] The key distinction between the "bourgeois" feminists and the left-wing feminists in precommunist Yugoslavia lay in the fact that the former insisted on organizational autonomy, while the latter were prepared to see their activity integrated broadly within the framework of the party.[43]

Another feminist put it even more forcefully: "Leftist culture is basically *macho* culture. Marx and Lenin are very thin on women. Even the New Left doesn't have much to say on the subject. Sexism is built into socialism. In Serbo-Croatian they write 'Žena i čovjek [woman and humanity],' which means that women are excluded from the human race."[44]

In mid-December 1987 about a hundred Yugoslav feminists from Belgrade, Zagreb, Ljubljana, and Sarajevo (two from Sarajevo) gathered in Ljubljana for a conference. That some of them were afflicted by doubts was clear. One current held that feminists had done enough "theorizing" and that it was time for action. Another view held that feminism had remained divided and inconsistent and that the time had come to move toward some form of unity.[45] One opinion registered in the press held that feminism was in crisis, and that Yugoslav society had already moved into a "post-feminist" period.[46] Others were not so gloomy, and forecast a consolidation of the feminist movement in Yugoslavia over the next few years. Optimists could take encouragement, at any rate, from the founding in March 1990 of the Zagreb-based League of Women in Croatia, an independent political party which aims to promote women's rights.[47]

The emergence and persistence of feminist activism in Yugoslavia reflected the passing of a generation and signified a search for new solutions and new approaches. It was symptomatic of the "structural distortion" identified by Blumer, and reflected incipient cultural drift. The feminists aspire to accelerate that cultural drift and realize that the task of changing social attitudes is a long one, which needs to be attacked from below as well as from above.

Why Yugoslavia?

Yugoslavia was the only country in communist Eastern Europe in which a coherent feminist movement developed. At first sight this is surprising, not only because the problems women face in the Yugoslav region appear to a greater or lesser degree in all the countries of the region (and the world), but because there have been a number of articulate feminist intellectuals in several East European countries. In Poland, for example, sociologist Magdalena Sokolowska devoted much of her life to arguing the case for female emancipation,[48] and in 1980 there was even an attempt to set up a feminist group in Poland, which foundered for lack of interest.[49] East German and Hungarian women have also written cogently about the situation of women in their respective countries, but in neither case has a feminist movement developed. Instead, as in Czechoslovakia, socially aware women have become involved in other forms of dissident activity, chiefly pacifist groups or, in the case of Czechoslovakia, Charter 77.

Poland at the dawn of the 1980s looked like propitious terrain for feminism. Women were staging protest marches,[50] women's organizations were becoming more active,[51] and the number of women elected to the central committee in early 1981 rose sharply; a woman was even elected to the party Politburo.[52] Around this same time, a group of women at the University of Warsaw drew up a list of demands, which included the publication of feminist periodicals, a feminist theater, feminist art galleries, independent meetings and seminars devoted to feminist concerns, the establishment of a central pool of information about all feminist movements and about the situation of women in Poland and worldwide, and the establishment of links with feminist movements in other countries. The signatories claimed that they had already established cooperative links with feminists in West Germany, France, and the Soviet Union.[53] But the erosion of the economy and the introduction of martial law quickly reversed these incipient trends, and a 1986 article found that although the number of women obtaining higher education was growing faster than the corresponding number of men, they continued to find it more difficult to obtain responsible professional jobs.[54]

Independent women's organizations were set up in Czechoslovakia, Romania, and Bulgaria in early 1990. In Czechoslovakia an organization called Public for Family—Women's Party emerged in mid-January. Its chief organizer was Viera Pospisilova.[55] In Romania the National Women's League was established in Bucharest on 30 January with Smaranda Ionescu as chair. In Bulgaria the Alternative Women's Union was founded in mid-March; it was advertised as a successor of the original (noncommunist) Bulgarian Women's Union, established at the beginning of the twentieth century.[56] A second independent women's organization in Czechoslovakia—the Confederation of Women and Family Initiatives of Czechoslovakia—came into being at the end of September 1990, and stressed its intention to act as a lobby group representing women's interests before the government.[57] In Poland there were several independent women's organizations by the end of 1990, including the Democratic Union of Women, the Committee for the Defense of Women, and the League of Polish Women. They faced their first major policy struggle in protesting a planned law (backed by the Catholic church) that would ban abortion.[58] To what extent these organizations can function as effective feminist forums remains open to doubt. In the German case, for example, as the two Germanys finalized their move toward reunification, Brunnhilde Fabricius, chairwoman of the West German Women's Council, complained, "Half the population is being shut out of the unification process. In the second state treaty [on social issues] there is no perceptible concept of women or children's issues."[59]

Several factors account for Yugoslavia's uniqueness in this regard. First, the Yugoslav system was long the most open system in the area, with the greatest tolerance for autonomous groups. Elsewhere in the region, only churches were allowed to engage in fully autonomous activity—until the dramatic changes of 1988–89. Second, because of the system's greater openness, the society was more permeable by Western influences, and women intellectuals in Yugoslavia were much better situated to obtain and read Western feminist materials or to travel to the West to attend feminist meetings. Third, Yugoslav women had already developed a feminist movement in the interwar period. This earlier movement had promoted women's interests through strikes and other actions, and spearheaded a grassroots campaign for women's suffrage. As Barbara Jancar has observed, "The demand for women's suffrage mobilized women from every national and social segment of society, and culminated in a mass demonstration for the right to vote in 1939."[60] And fourth, women's participation in the wartime partisan struggle had a potent effect on women's consciousness in Yugoslavia.

But for all of this the mobilization of feminist consciousness and strength in Yugoslavia has been relatively limited and is by no means irreversible. In Serbia the nationalist revival promoted by Slobodan Milošević since 1987 has been associated with a new patriarchalism and retrogressive changes in intergender relations. As a by-product of these changes, Belgrade's feminists became increasingly cut off from other intellectuals, and by 1989 felt that they lived in a kind of ghetto in intellectual isolation. But such changes are not restricted to Serbia. On the contrary, there is a rebirth of neoconservatism throughout the area that comprised socialist Yugoslavia, a rebirth that emerged as a reaction to deep social crisis and that proposes a return to "traditional" values—meaning that women will do all the housework, obey their husbands, and stay out of politics.[61] Significantly, pictures of Serbian peasants demonstrating in support of Milošević from 1987 to 1989 show large crowds consisting exclusively of males, whereas photos of anti-Milošević crowds from that period always include both women and men.

The emergence of feminist groups is one measure of the *strength* of a society. It is one symptom of a broader process of self-organization through which society gains the strength to criticize and challenge the existing order. The more diverse the independent groups, the more diverse and all-encompassing the pressure that society can bring on the system. Feminism is one sign of a transformation of social consciousness and of what Gabriel Almond once called the "sense of political efficacy."

10. Rock Music and Counterculture

Any musical innovation is full of danger to the whole State, and ought to be prohibited; when modes of music change, the fundamental laws of the State always change with them.—PLATO, *The Republic*, Book IV

Rock music is an organic inseparable part of the sociocultural conscious-ness and activity of a society. Rock music, therefore, both reflects *and* contributes to the ideas of the age and the changes taking place in con-sciousness and behavior. In the context of Eastern Europe more specifi-cally, rock music played a role in reinforcing the steady growth in the demand for freedom and in providing outlets through which alterna-tive political ideas could be expressed and nurtured. As Goran Bregović, leader of the Yugoslav rock group White Button, told me in 1989, "We can't have any alternative parties or any alternative organized politics. So there are not too many places where you can gather large groups of people and communicate ideas which are not official. Rock 'n' roll is one of the most important vehicles for helping people in communist countries to think in a different way."[1] By the same token, the passage of communism created a crisis for rock musicians in Russia, Poland, Czechoslovakia, Hungary, and, for as long as it still existed as a separate entity, East Germany.

This chapter will trace the dissenting role played by East European rock in the 1970s and 1980s, and suggest some reasons why the toler-ance level for rock music differed from regime to regime during those years. It will close with some thoughts about the present status of rock music in the region.

Students of political culture are fond of reminding us that the self-perpetuation of systems is contingent upon the successful socialization of the young. Political culture—"the system of empirical beliefs, expressive symbols, and values which defines the [context] in which political action takes place"[2]—is the attitudinal environment in which governments function, and may be either supportive, corrosive, or indifferent to authority. The superstructure of communist regimes is attuned to the task of molding a "new communist man and woman," that is, to the task of transforming political culture and instilling specific values and attitudes in the younger generation.[3]

The task of "building communism" signified that communist regimes saw themselves as the managers of programmatic and purposive social change. While there may be some dispute as to whether there was any purposive social change being pursued at all in Poland, Hungary, and Yugoslavia by the early 1980s, in the abstract the cultural goal pursued under communism would embrace both behavioral and attitudinal patterns; therefore, any alternative culture or set of patterns would be unwelcome. Archie Brown argued in 1977 that changes in culture generally and political culture in particular are likely to be accompanied by changes in social structure, thus confirming Plato's observations in *The Republic*.[4] This says nothing about causality, which presumably would operate in both directions, but it does underline the fact that neither aesthetic nor attitudinal variables are politically innocent. The interest demonstrated by Soviet, Bulgarian, Romanian, and other communist regimes until the end of the 1980s in encouraging the development and spread of a common culture and political culture[5] indicates that at least some communist elites operated on that premise.

Differences in regime levels of toleration of rock music seem to roughly parallel differences in toleration toward religion, ethnic subcultures, dissent, and the scope of autonomy allowed to writers and journalists. These differences may be traced, as Andrzej Korbonski has observed, to the presence and extent of six background conditions:

(a) alienation of intellectuals and youth;
(b) political reforms;
(c) economic difficulties;
(d) divisions within the party;
(e) contacts with the West; and
(f) anticommunist attitudes.[6]

Rock music is clearly relevant to variables (a) and (e), and arguably also to (f)—all variables relevant to political culture and socialization. Rock music may thus express and articulate the alienation of youth, with the danger that articulation of disaffection will serve to sustain and deepen it. Moreover, rock music overtly promotes contacts with the West: directly, when Western rock groups tour Eastern Europe; indirectly, when indigenous groups sing Western songs and imitate Western styles; and vicariously, through the proliferation of Western rock records and associated paraphernalia from Michael Jackson sweatshirts to punk fashions.

Finally, while there was nothing intrinsically anticommunist in rock music, despite occasional charges to the contrary in the bloc press, rock music has, empirically, often served as the vehicle for protest—a feature that has scarcely been unique to the communist world. The evidence for this statement will be provided later, but by way of an explanation of this phenomenon, there are several aspects that in fact make music in general, an *ideal* vehicle for social criticism and political protest. First, music is a kind of esoteric language whose messages, however clear to the target audience, may be excused as "entertainment" where unsympathetic listeners are concerned. Second, music creates a feeling (whether limited or intense) of collective solidarity among concert-listeners: Woodstock serves as an obvious example, or the "Polish Woodstock" at Jarocin as a less well-known one. Third, music has always served as a kind of escape valve (as the blues genre exemplifies), with the possibility always existing that an escape valve may be transformed into a beacon for mobilizing opinion.

Counterculture may be defined broadly or narrowly. Broadly defined, any culture which challenges the party's official culture, which is premised on the concept of a single, legitimate general interest, can be seen as a counterculture. More narrowly defined, counterculture could be seen as a set of ideas, orientations, tastes, and assumptions which differ systematically from those of the dominant culture, recognizing that *dominant* culture and *official* culture are not the same.[7]

Under the broader definition, one can identify four broad categories of counterculture, at least within the context of communist politics: political dissent and opposition, including peace movements, feminists, and ecological groups;[8] religious alternatives, insofar as religious organizations propound alternative explanations of the purposes and meaning of social life;[9] criminality and social deviance, chiefly insofar as these represent and further stimulate the desocialization of their practitioners;[10] and foreign culture importations, usually via youth.[11] This chapter is concerned with a specific aspect of the last of these.

Music will be treated here as symbolic language—that is, as a medium of communication of given meanings. In some ways music is less precise than a spoken language; in other ways it is more precise. The nature of the communication process may in fact differ, but it is communication all the same. As such, music depends on conventions to convey its meanings. These conventions may be specific to a given culture, subculture, or group, and those outside the reference group or lacking familiarity with its conventions will not be able to understand the music except as opaque confusion. To put it another way, those who listen to rock music habitually and those who avoid it necessarily *hear* rock differently.[12]

The Politics of Rock

The political effect of rock music depends on explicit (or perceived) messages in the lyrics and includes reinforcement of political attitudes through reference to the peer group.

Music has always lain within the sphere of the politically relevant for communist regimes. When the Bolsheviks first seized power, they were convinced that it would be necessary to create "a totally new culture, one that would eventually permeate every aspect of life and art."[13] Symptomatic of this orientation were the establishment in 1923 of the Association of Proletarian Musicians for the purpose of spawning ideologically approved music, and the activity of the Blue Blouse movement between 1925 and 1929, which, under director Boris Yuzhanin, took party views on events and issues of the day and set them to dance and song.[14]

Soviet wariness of popular music began with the fox-trot, which, like jazz, was seen as a "capitalist fifth column" aimed at subverting the forces of progress. The Soviets changed their minds, however, when the Nazis condemned the genre. If the Nazis hated it, the Soviets rationalized, perhaps it was not so bad after all; and besides, they were starting to develop a liking for jazz.

The emergence of rock 'n' roll in the 1950s confronted the Soviets and their allied East European regimes with a new challenge. The Soviets feared that the overt rebelliousness of rock 'n' roll would have deleterious effects on the political consciousness of the young, and rock music was banned. "When the Beatles craze hit Russia in the mid-sixties, efforts to reinforce the ban were strengthened."[15] This proved untenable. A constant refrain—repeated by Soviet Politburo member Konstantin Chernenko in June 1983—was that through Western rock, "the enemy is trying to exploit youthful psychology."[16] As recently as 1988 the ultraconservative journal *Rabochaya gazeta* wrote that rock was "the devil's work, morally corrupting, antinational and ideologically subversive."[17] In orthodox communist eyes, Western rock seemed to encourage the withdrawal from social engagement to a focus on personal feelings; the glorification of the West; the infiltration of political skepticism, if not outright dissidence; the introduction of cultural standards, fashions, and behavioral syndromes independent of party control; and a general numbness thought to foster political indifference and passivity.

The focus on personal feelings, encouraged by songs about "feeling good" and "doing your own thing," was clearly unwelcome in the more strident regimes of Czechoslovakia, Romania, Bulgaria, and, until Gorbachev, the Soviet Union. Curtis notes that in the process of obsolescing big bands, rock 'n' roll encouraged "a new sense of the singer as an individual," a sentiment that after 1964 would grow into adulation of specific rock figures. This symbolic individualism also has its psychological counterpart in the stimulation of narcissism noted by Curtis.[18] The Prague newspaper *Tribuna* commented, in this vein, that "individualization of life as a program does not have anything in common with a socialist way of life. It is motivated by old egotism; it is accompanied by petit bourgeois mentality."[19] Similarly, *Sovetskaya Kultura* attacked rock idol Michael Jackson in June 1984 for being "apolitical in the extreme, a vegetarian, sentimental, and a religious believer,"[20] while *Literaturnaya gazeta* blasted Donna Summer for singing songs full of "vulgar sexual shrieks," describing her as a "marionette" of the "ideological masters" of the United States.[21] The Soviets' refusal to issue a visa to Boy George in mid-1984 probably reflected a related concern—that is, that Boy George's transvestism might stimulate transvestism in the Soviet musical scene.

Glorification of Western culture was a latent feature in Western rock when transplanted to the communist world. Even if not consciously, Western rock promotes certain values and behavior which are associated with Western society, and there is a historical tendency for urban youth throughout the world, and perhaps especially in Eastern Europe and the Soviet Union, to be attracted to things Western, and to believe that the West is culturally superior. As an intellectual position, this orientation has a long history in Russia.[22]

East European youth, including members of official youth organizations, commonly wear blue jeans and sometimes stars-and-stripes emblems and crucifixes. The East German government forbade the wearing of blue jeans,[23] viewing the fashion as a potential "Trojan horse." American university sweatshirts became so popular, moreover, that by the late 1970s the Yugoslavs were making their own facsimiles and selling them in the stores. In Romania, however, the popularity of American university sweatshirts and of T-shirts with pictures of American pop singers was seen as evidence of "moral pollution."[24] Similarly, in Czechoslovakia, an official commentator warned that Western paraphernalia in music and fashion converted their buyers into "walking advertising pillars for Western companies" and thereby "shape and nourish illusions about the Western way of life and the superiority of the capitalist social system and impede the shaping of a socialist life-style."[25] In Bulgaria, where only about a third of "pop music" broadcast on Bulgarian television and radio was native (the rest being mostly American or British), young people started making and wearing exact facsimiles of Western military uniforms in the early 1980s, American and British being the most popular.[26]

The infiltration of political dissidence was a more serious problem, however, and East European rock groups repeatedly drifted toward social criticism and political commentary. One of the best-known rock groups in Eastern Europe was a Czech group, Plastic People of the Universe. This outspoken group was put on trial in 1976 after releasing an album titled *Egon Bundy's Happy Hearts Club Banned.*[27] The album came with a sixty-page softcover booklet entitled "The Merry Ghetto," and included a song with the message, "war is hell." The album was banned by the authorities.[28] A similar fate befell the East German Renft Combo (see chapter 3).

Among rock groups of the 1980s, the now-defunct Yugoslav band Pankrti (Bastards), based in Ljubljana, was one of the more daring. In open mockery of the partisan mythology, the group proposed to release an album showing a young man hugging a war monument, and to call the album *The Bastards in Collaboration with the State.* The producer circumspectly disallowed the title and refused to run a picture using any monument from World War II. The Bastards therefore staged the same pose using a monument from World War I, and titled the album *Bastards—Lovers of the State.*[29]

The fourth epiphenomenon associated with rock music is *the propagation of cultural standards, fashions, and behavioral syndromes independent of party control.* To the extent that they persist in spite of party antagonism, they become implicitly antiparty, quite independently of any political messages being propounded. Punk and heavy metal countercultures penetrated the USSR, East Germany, Poland, Czechoslovakia, Hungary, and Yugoslavia, imposing a cultural specificity in fashion with rejectionist and nihilist overtones. In the Yugoslav republic of Slovenia, punk appeared at the same time as cultural "pop totalitarianism," with the famous Slovenian group Laibach donning Nazi-style uniforms for their concerts.[30] The Albanian party paper *Zeri i popullit* put it this way:

To accept the extravagant bourgeois and revisionist mode of dress is to create an appropriate terrain for undermining socialist attitudes, behavior, and convictions. To think that long hair and narrow pants or miniskirts have nothing to do with one's world outlook, one's ideology, is as naive as it is dangerous. Not to fight alien fashions means to give up the fight against the penetration of the degenerate bourgeois and revisionist ideology.[31]

Finally, rock music was seen to produce a *general numbness*, blurring concentration. Party spokesmen sometimes argued that the passivity and retreat into indifference fostered by certain bands was a deliberate ploy by "the bourgeois manipulators of thought, ideologues, and subversive centers" of Western capitalism.[32] Czechoslovak communist newspapers compared the "new wave of rock" to a drug, arguing that the "deafening noise, monotonous tunes, and primitive, often vulgar texts" were well chosen to *inculcate* nihilism and cynicism.[33]

The bottom line for more orthodox elites, as phrased by Albanian communist spokespersons, was that liberal attitudes in arts and fashion (underpinned by an ultraliberal philosophy expressed in songs) lead to liberal attitudes in morals, which in turn lead to liberal attitudes in politics. Political liberalism thus would undermine communist rule, which could lead to the overthrow of the communist power monopoly.[34] It seemed only logical for Vladimir Makarov, writing in the Krasnodar youth newspaper *Komsomolets Kubani*, to link Western rock with a CIA master plan to subvert the communist bloc. Indeed, claimed Makarov, Allen Dulles once "said that if we teach young Soviet people to sing our songs and dance to them, then sooner or later we shall teach them to think in the way we need them to."[35]

The Polish Rock Scene

Rock music and fashions hit every East European country to one extent or another (including even Albania). In the communist era, their most tangible impact was in Poland, Germany, Czechoslovakia, and Yugoslavia.

The three most popular rock countercultures in Poland in the late 1980s were punk, popper, and hippie (possibly in that order). The Polish punk scene was diverse. At least seven types of Polish punks appeared, including punks and skins, skanks, Krasowcy, skinheads, and others. There were probably well over three hundred active rock groups in Poland in 1984, including numerous punk bands, in such cities as Warsaw, Gdańsk, Nowa Huta, and Kraków.[36] Polish Radio broadcast as much as twenty-four hours of *Western* rock per week on channel 3, and ten hours per week on channel 4. And a survey conducted in 1982 by Leszek

Janik found that listening to rock music was the most popular form of recreation for young Poles, and that more than 70 percent of Polish high school students were "well acquainted" with rock music and culture.[37]

Polish rock was infused with politics in the communist era, and many of the leading rock bands took overtly political names, such as Delirium Tremens, The Fifth Column, ss-20 (renamed, under pressure, The Deserter), Pathology of Pregnancy, Verdict, Crisis, Shortage, Paralysis, and Protest. Other well-known groups of the 1980s included TSA, Republika, Perfect, Kombi, Exodus, and Turbo. Where punk is concerned, this trend may have been reinforced, in particular, by the despondency created by the suppression of Solidarity and numerous other independent structures in December 1981. The Jaruzelski regime was especially sensitive to punk, but uncertain how to cope with it.

In August 1984 the fifteenth annual Jarocin rock festival attracted nearly 19,000 youth to listen to sixty Polish groups perform. Three hundred groups had applied for regime permission, but only sixty were approved after submitting their songs for clearance. The uncertainty in such a procedure is illustrated by the case of the approved group, Perfect, which had properly submitted the texts of its songs to the authorities. At the concert, the approved line "we want to be ourselves" was replaced with "we want to beat ZOMO,"[38] and the approved line "don't be afraid of anyone" was replaced by "don't be afraid of Jaruzelski."[39] The group was subsequently disbanded by the authorities, but staged a comeback at the 1987 Jarocin rock festival.

Most new wave bands were unable to obtain official clearance to cut a record, but private tapes of garage performances proliferated. Although Polish punk was a Western import, Polish punks felt they represented a purer, even superior, strain of punk culture. "Those in Britain sing 'no future,'" said a leading Polish punk vocalist. "But I'd like to be on welfare payments there! If you want to know what is 'no future,' come to Poland!"[40]

This bleakness colored the lyrics sung by Polish punk bands in the mid-1980s. The punk band WC, for instance, offered a nihilistic vision in one song:

> Posers, fetishists—destroy them all!
> A generation of conformists—destroy them all!
> Your ideals—destroy them all![41]

And in another song, WC mocked the coercive foundation upon which the post-Solidarity regime was built:

> I am a tank, I am a tank.
> I am strong, I am healthy.
> I can only beat everyone . . .
> I can go only [straight] ahead
> And I do not need to eat.
> I am afraid of nothing,
> You are tight—so what[!][42]

Other bands, with names like Cadaver and Clinically Dead, projected despair that deepened into resignation and apathy. Another band, Manaam, won critical acclaim in 1983 for the release of an album called *Night Patrol.* One of its songs was set against the background of wailing sirens and the sounds of breaking glass, and, in a dispassionate falsetto, described daily life in martial-law Poland in these terms:

> Shadows in the dark city
> Linger through the night.
> Danger lurks by your doorway,
> Don't turn out the light . . .
> Don't go out alone
> Evil is prowling . . .
> Night patrol's alert
> Making sure that you're OK
> That you don't get hurt,
> Anxious to protect you.
> Everything's all right.
> Shadows in the sad city
> Bleed through the night.[43]

Lyrics like these drew charges of "fascism" from the communist party dailies *Żołnierz Wolności* and *Trybuna Ludu.*

Manaam's lead singer, Kora Jackowska, was among the most outspoken, and won prizes from the youth weekly *Sztandar Młodych,* and the magazine *Jazz Forum.* Jackowska also came to the regime's attention, and for good reason, since she did not shy away from searing commentary. In one criticized song, for example, she sang:

> Treason, treason
> Cunning, cold, calculating . . .
> Broken promises, broken light,
> White is black and black is white . . .
> Don't talk back, turn the other cheek . . .
> Talk out of line if you dare.

Don't make me look, I don't want to see.
Is everyone a traitor or is it just me?
Treason sneaks into your bed.[44]

What happened in Poland, as this song reflects, is that the nihilism
and skepticism of much of rock, and of punk especially, became more
focused, more clearly antigovernment. Rock culture in Poland was thus
overtly political.

In the early 1980s Polish rock had an antiregime edge, and tended
to blame the regime for society's pathologies. By the late 1980s rock
groups began to sing a new song: people were responsible for their own
problems and had enslaved themselves.[45]

To deal with the groundswell of "social pathology" (as the regime
called it) among Polish youth, Warsaw issued directives in January 1984,
advising school teachers and administrators to compile lists of punks,
hippies, "fascists," and social "misfits."[46] These lists were turned over
to the police, and those thus identified were placed under surveillance.
In addition, the Ministry of Education drew up a set of "social preven-
tative and resocializing measures" aimed at "eliminating the causes of
poor social adaptation" and "protecting children and young people from
the effects of social pathology."[47]

In the West, punk was already passé by the mid-1980s. Not so in Jaruzelski's Poland, where punk became a favorite vehicle for expressing
youth's complete despair of the system. The punk group Insects, for
instance, boasted that it took the name "because you can't kill off all
the insects." Another group, Göring's Underpants, combined a coquetry
with nazism with outright ribaldry—an odd combination. Their motto:
"the underground must piss against the wind." Another group took the
name Trybuna Brudu (Dirt Tribune), which rhymes with *Trybuna Ludu*
(*People's Tribune*), the communist party paper. General Secretary Jaruzelski confessed on Polish television that he did not understand all this
"screechy youth music."[48] So much the better, as far as punks were
concerned.

Aside from punks, a satanist movement also emerged within the Polish
rock scene. The rock group Kat, which reveled in satanic imagery and
one of whose albums (1987) was titled *666*, is in part responsible for this
trend. Polish satanists would dress in black adorned with satanic emblems (such as 666 or the devil's pentagram, a star within a circle), and
wear chains and an upside-down cross pendant. A group of one hundred
satanists attended the 1986 Jarocin rock festival, where they burned a
large cross and celebrated a black mass.[49]

Straightlaced in Czechoslovakia

The Czechoslovak rock scene presented a striking contrast to that in Poland. In communist Czechoslovakia, the kind of noisy defiance displayed by Polish groups was out of question. Lyrics had to be more subtle if the band planned to stay out of prison, and the singers had to be content with irony or, at most, ridicule and ambiguous sarcasm. An untitled Czech number from the early 1980s illustrates this clearly:

> Women leave me unmoved
> Emotions I scorn
> I'm well liked at work
> My record stays clean.
> I welcome after-hours chores:
> The bosses always get my vote.
> I ask for extra duties free
> And hope they will take note . . .
> I'll miss [my] date
> But not the meeting—
> Union of Youth, you know.
> Sessions and lectures
> All day long.
> Friends of Cremation
> Have asked me to call.[50]

By contrast, the Czechoslovak group Šafrán produced a song entitled "Prison," in the late 1970s:

> As we eat our bread in prison,
> each of us can be certain,
> that he has perpetrated terrible things
> and therefore sits behind bars.
> Leave me in peace with politics,
> I am a criminal:
> I could not keep my mouth shut,
> Now I am a prisoner.[51]

These lyrics clearly went beyond irony and ambiguity, as did the regime's response. Šafrán members Jaroslav Hutka and Vlastimír Třešňák were arrested, abused by the police, brought to trial, and eventually deported to the West, despite thousands of letters of protest from young fans.

Rock music arrived in Czechoslovakia in the early 1960s and quickly took hold. The Comets, a Prague-based group, gave Czechoslovakia's first major rock concert in spring 1962, and in 1963 Czechoslovakia saw the launching of *Melodie,* the country's first rock magazine. By 1964 there were 115 big-beat groups in Prague alone, and by 1985 more than a thousand such groups country-wide. In Bratislava a young man who called himself George L. Every put together the James Bond Club, whose members, generally twenty-year-old university dropouts, wore jeans, let their hair grow, and gathered together to listen to rock music.[52]

During the liberal phase of Dubček's rule in 1968, a Prague psychedelic band called the Primitives graduated from "fire-and-light" shows to generally crazy "animal happenings" in which the musicians had special costumes and everybody pelted everybody else with fish and birds. During the "Fish Fest," band and audience also hurled water at each other, so that the extramusical elements finally became more important than the music itself.[53]

The end of the Dubček era meant the end (until 1989) of liberalism in official policy toward rock, among other things. For twenty years, the Prague regime was to remain suspicious of *all* rock music. Yet certain groups were the beneficiaries of official sanction, such as Olympic, Abraxus, and Catapult, though the last of these was banned in 1983 from performing in central Bohemia, including Prague. Another group, the Yellow Dog Band, changed its name in 1983 to The Musical Entertainment Group of O. Hejma, and adjusted its repertoire in order to stay off the blacklist. The straight-laced Czechoslovak regime thus forced the more daring music underground.

Yet even among those groups that received official support, lyrics could be provocative. If they had not been, it is difficult to see how they could have established any credibility among youth. An example is the rock band Bronz, which performed a rock opera in Prague with official support. One of its songs included the line, "Our master is king; his name is heroin."[54]

The 1976 suppression of Plastic People of the Universe and DG-307, two of the most popular groups in their day, was followed by a general clampdown on the rock scene.[55] From 1976 to 1981 Czechoslovak authorities kept a tight rein on rock music. The bureaucrats decided what was permissible and what was not, though these decisions were not taken on the basis of aesthetic training or expertise. As a rule, authorities were most concerned about lyrics, but two talented musicians, Vladimír Merta and Vladimír Mišík, ran into trouble after authorities decided their music was "too inventive and interesting."[56]

In the late 1970s avant-garde groups like Electrobus, Extempore, Stehlík (Goldfinch), and Žába (Frog) began to strain the prescribed limits in semiofficial concerts. Their performances played havoc with rhythm and melody, interspersed periods of silence between songs (in one case for half an hour), and naturally attracted the attention of the police. It was not until 1981, however, that punk, by then five years old, reached Czechoslovakia.

Czechoslovak punk bands such as Jasná Paka (Patent) and Letadlo (Aeroplane), and the hard rock ensemble Pražský Výběr (Prague Selection) were able to hold a number of concerts in Prague by mid-1982. Their songs dealt with sexual problems and the drab and depressing life in Prague apartment buildings.[57] Various student clubs also began to organize punk concerts about this time. Since every concert had to be cleared by a party official, it appears that some of the supervisors of musical tastes were inclined to ease up.

In March 1983, however, an aggressively abusive article by Jan Kryzl in *Tribuna* signaled a stiffening of resolve on the regime's part. Rock music, charged Kryzl, encouraged

> passivity and a retreat from reality into a dream world. . . . Be indifferent to the life around you, do not go with anyone and be against anything! Nothing has any meaning! This should become the creed of the young generation. The enforcement of this creed was, and is, to be aided by the so-called punk rock, crazy rock, or repugnant [*previt*] rock. . . . The aim is more than obvious—to . . . instill in young people's minds the philosophy of "no future" and attitudes, conduct, and views that are alien to socialism.[58]

Patent and other bands were banned, and many groups were stripped of their managers and sponsors. The official blacklist of "unrecommended" rock groups, which contained thirty-six entries in 1981, was tangibly augmented, and by September 1983 the blacklist for the central Bohemia region alone listed twenty-seven bands.[59] Punk bands came to be considered "public enemies."

Melodie, the officially supported pop music journal which had established a substantial following among devotees of the rock scene, fell into disfavor. The entire, highly qualified editorial staff was ejected, and replaced by people lacking the appropriate professional credentials.

The crackdown stimulated public outcry. *Tribuna* was flooded with letters of protest, and the issue which had carried Kryzl's rather overstated article became a high-demand commodity. The Jazz Section of the Czech Union of Musicians published a reply to Kryzl in May 1983, linking punk with *left-wing* politics and pointing out that the increase in social violence in Czechoslovakia attributed to punk predated its arrival in that country. The dissident movement Charter 77 also spoke out on behalf of Czechoslovak rock groups. *Tribuna* itself, in a series of follow-up articles, mused ambiguously on the "lack of knowledge" of Czechoslovak youth [60] and even seemed to back off: "Leading officials, who are usually people belonging to the older generation, should realize that their notions of music and its 'correct' form are not necessarily always adequate and realistic," hence there should be "greater tolerance of the divergent tastes of different generations. . . . We should support searching, the raising of questions, critical reasoning, and the solution of real problems, even if this entails taking risks." [61]

Public outcry had only the slightest impact, however, on regime policy. The protesting Jazz Section of the Czech Union of Musicians, which had published a history of Czechoslovak rock, was subsequently harassed, and eventually ordered to disband in October 1984. [62] A rock festival planned for June 1983 in the village of Zábčice was cancelled by the authorities at the last minute. The blacklist was enforced, and recalcitrant bands retreated to garage performances. An exceptional relaxation came in spring 1984, when Czechoslovak authorities allowed British rock star Elton John to play in Prague. He had already been booked to perform in Poland, Hungary, and Yugoslavia. [63]

As of late 1986 there were more than fifty popular rock groups in existence in Czechoslovakia, including punk bands enjoying large followings, and an estimated two hundred lesser-known bands, many playing illegally. In June 1986 the government allowed the musicians to hold a rock festival at the Palace of Culture in Prague. Some eighty rock groups took part, including two Prague bands, Bossa Nova and Vitacit, Brno's Z Kopce, Genesis from eastern Bohemia and Yetti from northern Bohemia. [64] Zdenko Pavelka, evidently an advocate of rock music, wrote that the success of the festival showed that "it [was] not necessary for rock music to languish somewhere in dark corners." [65]

But for a rock group in Czechoslovakia to emerge out of the "dark corners" and obtain a professional license, its members had to pass a written test covering topics ranging from musical theory to the doctrines of Marxism-Leninism. [66] Not surprisingly, this test proved an obstacle for many groups.

East Germany: Echoes of Stirner

Philosophical nihilism like that espoused by punk counterculture was not new to East Germany. On the contrary, Berlin is its original home. It was here that Max Stirner (1806–56) penned his famous work, *The Ego and His Own*, in which he denounced socialism, communism, liberalism, philanthropy, altruism, religion, law, government, and morality.[67] Stirner's incantations—"The people is dead—Up with me!,"[68] "Everything sacred is a tie, a fetter,"[69] "My freedom becomes complete only when it is my might,"[70] and "All truth by itself is dead. . . . Of itself it is valueless"[71]—find resonances in contemporary punk. It may be further noted that a nihilist-anarchist movement in Germany in the 1890s was heavily influenced by Stirner's ideas.[72]

Rock music "invaded" East Germany in 1957, when young people at an unprecedented Leipzig concert heard the music of Little Richard, Fats Domino, Bill Haley and the Comets, Peter Kraus, Hazy Osterwald, and Ted Herold.[73] But it was only in the 1963–64 period that East German rock music, as such, got off the ground. In the meantime, authorities had passed a resolution concerning "Appearances of Decadence and Decay." The regime press and media attacked rock music sharply for several years, but the genre was never expressly forbidden. Only in the late 1960s did the authorities' attitude begin to soften;[74] yet, as early as 1960 the regime had given its approval to an initiative from Canadian Perry Friedman to stage a hootenanny in Berlin's Sports Hall. The event proved a success and was repeated the following year. It became an annual event, and in 1966 led to the creation of the national Song Movement within the framework of the Free German Youth (FGY) organization.[75] The new beat could, authorities calculated, add vigor to "progressive" impulses.

With Erich Honecker's accession to the SED leadership in early 1971 came a new approach, embodied in the newly developed concept of "youth dance music" by which authorities now proposed to refer to rock. The ministry of culture explained that young people clearly wanted a new dance genre, but insisted that this genre could be developed without overlays of "Western decadence."[76] The annual Festival of Political Song was launched in 1971, and over the years drew folk, pop, folk rock, and rock groups from all over the world, including the West. At the fifteenth Festival of Political Song in 1985, for example, the Polish rock duo Urszula and Budka Suflera sang a song about Auschwitz taken from a larger rock song cycle, while the eighteenth Festival in 1988 included a song dedicated to Sandinista Nicaragua.[77]

Rock music remained political in East Germany. In 1974, for instance, the Dresden-based Lift put on their "Solidarity Concert" for the people of Chile on the first anniversary of the military coup that overthrew Salvador Allende. That same group produced the symphony-length "Che Guevara Suite" in 1978. There were also a number of rock concerts for peace.[78]

The banning of the Renft Combo in 1974 (see chapter 3) may have sent a chill through the East German rock scene, but it neither stifled musical creativity nor ended the careers of that group's component musicians. Renft members Peter "Caesar" Glaser (vocals, guitar, flute) and Jochen Hohl (keyboards) went on to found the highly successful rock quintet Karussell, which received a variety of state awards and decorations, including the FGY Prize for Art and the Diploma of the Ministry of Culture.[79]

Indeed, despite the close watch of the authorities, East German rock groups occasionally sent out subtle messages, albeit typically with restraint. The mood was one more of resignation, however, than of protest. Take, for example, rock composer Kurt Demmler's lines,

> They deny me any laughter
> They deny me any song
> They deny me land and life
> Which passes me by.[80]

The mood is one of helplessness. Or again, there is the musically innovative group Silly, considered by many to have been one of the best groups in East Germany. On a 1985 album, *Liebeswalzer*, the group sings,

> I look so fondly in the distance
> with my binoculars.
> I look so fondly in the distance,
> that makes me happy.
> The distance is a nicer place
> though when I'm there, it turns its face.
> The distance is, where I am not.
> I walk and walk and do not get there.[81]

For a nation divided in two, with families split by a political boundary and condemned to follow West German events on television, this text was not so innocent.

The best-known East German group was probably the Puhdys. With fifteen albums to their credit by 1988, including one of 1950s American rock favorites sung in English, the Puhdys were one of East Germany's longest lasting groups (established 1965) and one of its most decorated, having won the National Prize for outstanding artists in 1982.[82]

Rather than turning its guns on all rock indiscriminately (like the Czechoslovak communists), East German communists tried to encourage *tame* rock, and to put it to use. A decree on discotheques issued in 1973 required "discothequers" (disc jockeys) to enroll in a course on ideological and political thinking. Once they graduated, discothequers were expected to ensure that at least 60 percent of the music they played originated from the bloc, and to intersperse topical information and "positive" political commentary between hits.[83] The FGY operated 5,000–6,000 discotheques in the early 1980s, and most discothequers were also functionaries of the youth organization. The FGY even organized a major public rock concert in October 1983. For as long as the communists held power in Berlin, it would appear that their policy paid off. In contrast to neighboring Poland and Czechoslovakia, there was a sense that rock music was not bad in and of itself. In fact, by the 1980s East German educators included selected rock "classics" in their lesson plans in order to teach youngsters about an important aspect of social and cultural life.[84] This qualified acceptance of certain kinds of rock— though not of punk—created a "gray zone" in which many East German youth found it possible to function.

The Yugo-Rock Scene

Of the remaining East European countries, it was clearly Yugoslavia that had the liveliest rock scene. It was also politically the most innocent, partly because of the tangibly more liberal disposition of the regime in the cultural sphere. Much of the "Yu-rock" scene was either new wave or a local synthesis of "old wave," new wave, and indigenous innovations. Croatian groups like Dee Dee Mellow (which made use of Peruvian and Indian folk melodies) and Psihomodo-Pop, and the Slovenian group Videosex, served up a lighter fare (until recently)—though Videosex's explicit treatment of lesbianism, sadism, and voyeurism created a sensation. In the mid-1980s break dancing (brejkdens) hit Yugoslavia too.[85] A Belgrade group called In Trouble became one of the most popular rock groups in the country by pointedly shunning social messages and scandals. In Trouble's lead singer, Milan Delčić, disarmingly confessed to Vjesnik, "We wanted to escape the [Balkan shock] style and be just an ordinary rock group."[86]

The degree of acceptance of rock in Yugoslavia was implicit in the wide coverage given to rock music in Yugoslav periodicals. The Zagreb free-lance writer Darko Glavan started a regular column about rock music for Vjesnik in 1972, and Politika began similar coverage a few years later.[87] Borba, Politika ekspres, and the Macedonian newspapers Nova Makedonija and Večer also established regular columns devoted to rock music, with occasional articles appearing in the magazines Start (Zagreb), Danas (Zagreb), and Mlad Borec (Skopje).

There have also been numerous magazines catering to the rock audience. The best known is the now-defunct Pop-Rock (formerly Rock, Belgrade). *Disko Selektor* (Skopje) appears in three languages: Macedonian, Serbo-Croatian, and English. A third magazine, *Ritam,* began publication in February 1989. Teenagers briefly had a special magazine of their own—*Ćao* (which replaced the now-defunct *ITD*).[88] But that is now also defunct, as is *Gram,* a fan magazine which lasted for a few issues in 1991. There were also regular rock columns in *Iskra* (Split), *Val* (Rijeka), *Valter* (Sarajevo), *Naši dani* (Sarajevo), *Polet* (Zagreb), *Studentski list* (Zagreb), *NIN* (Novi Sad), *Mladina* (Ljubljana), *Ekran Revija* (Skopje), and *Una* (Sarajevo). Rock records also became big business, and most major cities (including Sarajevo, Skopje, and Split) could boast local groups before the civil war destroyed much of the country.

As of 1982 there were roughly three thousand professional and amateur rock groups in Yugoslavia. As of 1987 there were thirty to fifty professional rock groups in the country, and perhaps as many as five thousand amateur groups.[89] Among these groups one could find a wide variety of subgenres ranging from rockabilly (Tonny Montano) to punk (Pankrti, now defunct) to industrial rock (Borghesia) to protest rock (Fish Soup) to heavy metal (Wild Strawberries) to folk rock (Plavi orkestar) to various strands of new wave and hard rock, and a specifically Vojvodinan strain called "šogor rock," which blended traditional Hungarian folk music with a soft rock beat.[90]

The most controversial rock group in Yugoslavia in the 1980s was surely Laibach, a Slovenian group with a greater following even today in the United States and Western Europe than in its native country. The members of Laibach wear nazi-style brown shirts, uniforms, and jackboots in their concert appearances, festoon the halls with banners bearing the hammer and sickle, the red star, the swastika, and the iron cross, and distribute maps showing an enlarged Slovenia. Their music is unabashedly fascistic in inspiration, imitating nazi music-making and Wagnerian music drama. Their lyrics are often nonsensical or tautological, as in the nearly endless repetition of the refrain "Life is life" in the song of that title (on the album *Opus Dei,* released in 1988). Their performances are not designed to be entertaining but to appeal more directly to the psychic space where the libido comes into contact with the superego, and accomplish this through evocative cult celebrations of the collective.

In a 1984 "Resolution" Laibach alleged that its purpose was to contribute to the construction of a world totalitarian system:

> Laibach takes over an organizational system of work after the model of industrial production and totalitarianism—which means, not the individual, but the organization speaks. Our work is industrial, our

language political. [Laibach's] organizational activity is an intense
agitation and a constant systematic ideological offensive. Any social
activity affects the mass. Laibach functions as a creative illusion,
with a censored program. Laibach's musical approach is a move to
the area of pure politicization of sounds, a means of manipulating the masses. When, in politically and economically complicated
situations, the antagonisms in society become strained, only force
remains as the ultimate *ratio* of social integration. [This] force must
take the form of systematic physical and psychic terror. For the
totalitarian government, the systematic terror becomes a constitutional instrument of authority.

Through the mystic, erotic, mythological sound, constituted in
an ambivalence between fear and fascination, which rudimentarily
affects the consciousness of people, through stage performances of
ritualized demonstrations of political power, and through other ma-
nipulative means, Laibach practices systematic psycho-physical terror, in order to effectively discipline [the masses], which results in
a state of collective aphasia, which is the principle of social organization. By darkening the consumer's mind, [Laibach's music] drives
him into a state of humble contrition and total obedience. By destroying every trait of individuality, it melts individuals into a mass,
and mass into a humble collective body.[91]

Although the resolution was melodramatically overstated to the point
of suggesting tongue-in-cheek, Laibach's music unmistakably evokes an
interest that is not purely satirical but is best seen as a sublimated form
of "pop fascism" enabling aggressive instincts to be channeled inno-
cently, rather than as the literal instrument of a real fascist movement,
as Laibach pretends. At any rate, the liberal-minded local authorities in
Slovenia took all this in stride. Whether Laibach intends its message as
a critique of communism or as an advocacy of fascism or as thought-
energizing art, the authorities (both communist and postcommunist)
have felt comfortable knowing that Laibach is unlikely to stir up a neofascist movement.

The Serbian group Fish Soup has always had far greater resonance
among the Serbian public and treats political themes in a way that reflects specifically Serbian thinking much more accurately. Led by published poet[92] and "master of verbal terrorism"[93] Bora Djordjević, Fish
Soup does not shy away from politically provocative themes. In its 1987
album *Ujed za Dušu*, the group sings a satirical song equating the communist party with the Mafia.[94] Djordjević has repeatedly hurled himself

headlong into controversy, whether in his songs, his poems, or in regular columns for the magazine *Duga*. In one of the latter he tackled the sensitive problem of Kosovo, offering an independent perspective. His poetry is often scatological, sexual, or political. In one poem he assailed the mythology of the National Liberation Struggle (NOB):

> Some were really in the NOB,
> but by now they are all buried.
> Those who are concerned with the NOB today
> are only concerned with themselves.[95]

Djordjević has also been outspoken in numerous interviews with the press, predicting civil war in Yugoslavia on at least one occasion.[96] In 1987 Djordjević provoked the authorities with a fifteen-minute reading of some of his provocative poems before an audience of four thousand that included the mayor of Belgrade and other party dignitaries. He created a stir, and was later taken to court on charges of three verbal misdemeanors. The judge threw the case out of court, praising Djordjević as a "true poet, who loves his people."[97]

Among male solo vocalists in Yugoslavia, one may mention Oliver Mandić, a Belgrade musician who created a small storm in the mid-1980s by appearing in drag, and Rambo Amadeus, a kind of P.D.Q. Bach of rock music, who once created a concert piece for twelve vacuum cleaners.[98] The best-known female solo vocalist is Snežana Mišković Viktorija, a Belgrade-based musician who was named top female vocalist by *Pop-Rock* readers in a 1988 survey.[99]

Among other groups in the Yugoslav rock scene one should mention Leb i Sol (based in Skopje and generally recognized as the best instrumental ensemble in the country), Bijelo dugme (Sarajevo, the "Beatles" of Yugoslavia), Belgrade groups Bajaga and YU-Group, Indeksi, and the now-defunct bands Azra and Korni group. A transitory sensation in 1988 was YU-Madonna, alias Andrea Makoter of Maribor, who began imitating her Western namesake, copying everything from singing style and mannerisms to makeup and attire.[100]

Increases in the popularity of heavy metal were also noticed,[101] but neither the old LCY nor the postcommunist elites have betrayed any serious concerns, either with this subgenre or with rock music in general. The consensus among the elite seems to be that rock music is merely an innocent diversion, at worst an ineluctable form of escapism. Besides, Yugoslavia was long open to Western cultural penetration to a far greater extent than other countries in Eastern Europe; hence, the specter of a new strain of influence is intrinsically less threatening in the Yugoslav (and ex-Yugoslav) case.

Elsewhere in Eastern Europe

In Romania and Bulgaria, by contrast, a true rock scene was slower to develop. Discotheques have become popular in both countries,[102] and groups like Sphinx in Romania and Crickets in Bulgaria built up enthusiastic domestic audiences. By the mid-1980s even punk rock had penetrated Bulgaria and Romania.[103]

The Bulgarian communists were not friendly to rock music, especially Western rock records. Hence, the Bulgarian Council of Ministers issued a decree on 17 February 1984 aimed at Bulgarian radio and discotheques that popularize Western music,[104] Georgi Dzhagarov, vice president of the State Council and chairman of the Standing Commission on Spiritual Values, went so far as to declare that "the whole country has been disquieted by the muddy stream of musical trends sweeping away all the true values of music."[105] The solution, as the Bulgarian Communist Party saw it at that time, was to revive Bulgarian folk music and dances.

Bulgaria's earliest rock 'n' roll groups—Bandi's Boys (Bandaratsite) and the Silver Bracelets (Srebarnite Grivni)—were inspired by British bands, especially the Beatles and the Searchers. These groups continued to be influential in the Bulgarian rock scene well into the 1970s.

The leading Bulgarian bands in the 1980s were the Crickets (established in 1966), FSB (Formation Studio Balkanton, composed of session musicians who obtained permission to put together a group), Tangra (formed in 1982), LZ, Diane Express, Factor (a hard rock group), and Signal. Dr. Doolittle (a progressive rock group from Varna) and heavy metal groups Lucifer (also from Varna) and Era (from Sofia) were also popular.[106] The Crickets created a commotion at a 1980 concert at Sofia's University Hall with their song "Wedding Day," which lamented the loss of freedom. Exactly what kind of freedom the group *really* had in mind was insidiously suggested by the fact that the lyrics were set to the melody of the old Beatles' song, "Back in the USSR." The audience became wild, the police told the audience to sit down, and when the audience failed to respond, the police turned on all the lights in the hall. In protest, the Crickets abandoned their approved program and played only Rolling Stones and Beatles for the rest of the night, forcing the police to retreat to the sidelines. After that concert, the Crickets were out of sight for some time, possibly as a result of an "administrative" decision. Similarly, Signal fell afoul of the authorities in 1982 by stirring up "excessive excitement" at a concert in the Black Sea port of Burgas.[107]

Perhaps surprisingly, in 1987 *Narodna kultura* (a magazine published by the Committee of Culture) and *Pogled* (the weekly organ of the Journalists' Union) ran articles stating that emergent informal groups of punks, heavy metalists, rockers, neo-hippies, and *discari* (disco fans) should not be seen as pathological, and that party officials and schoolteachers should accept young people on their own terms and not engage in sterile monologues.[108]

One of those associated with this tentative liberal view of rock culture was Vasil Prodanov, a professor of philosophy. In an article for the 24 July 1987 issue of *Otechestven Front*, Prodanov warned that in the absence of tactical liberalization, these informal groupings could develop into centers of opposition to the party.[109] The party daily *Rabotnichesko delo* seconded this suggestion with a prominent article by Dragomir Dakov and Mariana Mihaylova, which cited the opinions of experts on youth policy and rock performers, including members of heavy metal bands Lucifer and Era. As Stephen Ashley notes, *Rabotnichesko delo*

> entirely supported Prodanov's plea for tolerance and concluded with a series of recommendations that would revolutionize party policy toward hard rock music and "informal" youth groups. It called, in short, for official acceptance of heavy metal and punk music and for the relaxation of youth club regulations to abolish membership schemes, drop entrance charges, and permit a more diverse range of nonpolitical and recreational activities. The authors proposed that television and radio allot more time to hard rock music and encourage amateur Bulgarian groups. It advocated the establishment of a national rock concert agency to organize performances throughout Bulgaria on behalf of professional, semiprofessional, and amateur musicians. Lastly, it called for the improvement or construction of facilities for performing rock music in every region of the country.[110]

It is vital to keep in mind that this is a form of tactical liberalization, in which the *instruments* and *methods* of policy are changed in order to ensure the best chance of realizing an unchanged policy *goal*—in this case, the effective socialization of Bulgarian youth. In line with this new thinking, Bulgaria's cultural czars allowed the punk group Kontrol to record an album with the state-owned Balkanton label in 1989,— the first time a nonprofessional rock band in Bulgaria was granted that opportunity.

This tactic notwithstanding, Bulgarian rock performers became more outspoken about social issues after 1986, and sang about such topics as AIDS, drug abuse, ecological problems, the powers of the bureaucracy, adolescents' conflicts with their parents, and young Bulgarians' frustrations over the lack of personal and economic independence.[111]

In keeping with its general neo-medievalism, the situation in Romania was much more difficult for rock groups while Ceauşescu was in power. During Romania's "mini-Cultural Revolution" in the late 1960s and early 1970s, Ceauşescu suppressed the rock scene wholesale.[112] Subsequently the rock scene reemerged, but it was drawn into "patriotic" currents supportive of Ceauşescu's cultural line. Ceauşescu dreamt of witnessing the creation of a specifically Romanian rock genre that would underpin his official policy of national chauvinism, but a 1975 Romanian study found that young people were increasingly drawn to American-style folk music rather than to traditional Romanian music.

The leading Romanian rock bands in the 1980s were Phoenix and Post Scriptum (both symphonic rock ensembles), Sphinx (which evolved from symphonic rock to "sympho-pop"), and Progressive TM (a reference to the once-proscribed practice of transcendental meditation). There have also been heavy metal bands in Romania, specifically Domino, Compact, and Iris.[113]

Ceauşescu's twenty-four-year rule was deadly to Romanian rock music. It was bad enough that high-quality instruments were unavailable except through the black market or overseas, but Ceauşescu's energy conservation plan was especially deadly. As one Westerner observed, "How could you expect rock-and-roll to survive in a country where there is barely enough electricity to power a light bulb, let alone drive an electric guitar?"[114]

With the fall of Ceauşescu in December 1989 Romania opened up somewhat. Between January and March 1990, Hungarian rock groups crossed the border repeatedly to perform for their ethnic kin in Transylvania. Meanwhile, in February 1990 several Yugoslav rock groups staged a mammoth three-day rock festival in Timişoara before 20,000 enthusiastic fans. Among the groups performing were Valentino, Viktorija, Galija, Bajaga and the Instructors, and Fish Soup.[115]

Finally, there is the more relaxed atmosphere in Hungary, which brought in the film version of *Jesus Christ Superstar* in June 1983, staged a mammoth rock concert in the village of Pilisborosjenö in August 1983 (in connection with the filming of a rock horror film, *The Predator*), and premiered the first Hungarian rock opera, *Stephen the King*, on 20 August 1983, St. Stephen's Day.

Disco had already become big business, with some four hundred licensed youth clubs in Budapest by early 1982, and additional dance clubs in almost every town and village.[116] But it was *Stephen the King* that stirred the most discussion. Based on the play by Miklós Boldizsár, the opera relates the story of Stephen's founding of the Hungarian kingdom in 1001 and his conversion to Christianity. It opened to an impressive crowd of 10,000 spectators. The opera is unabashedly nationalistic and "ends with a poignant scene in which the music celebrating the newly crowned king changes almost imperceptibly into the national anthem, and a large Hungarian flag appears over the crest of the hill. A provincial daily reported that the applause that followed [one performance] lasted for 45 minutes."[117] The production drew an emotional response from Hungarian audiences, and the work was quickly contracted for performances for both record and film. And while dramatist Boldizsár denied any interest in using the opera as a vehicle for commentary on the present,[118] opera director Gábor Koltay told an interviewer that part of the opera's popularity is attributable to the continued relevance of its themes: "the question of how a small nation finds its way to survive is always valid."[119]

Only four bands were able to achieve national acclaim in the three decades from 1960 to 1989: Illés, Omega, Metro, and Locomotiv GT. These commercially successful bands eschewed politically delicate or socially critical subjects, and stuck to safe lyrics about love and sex.[120] Groups like Beatrice and Coitus Punk Group filled the void where lyrics were concerned.

New groups emerged in the 1980s, and "teeny-bopper" groups like R-GO, Hungaria, Dolly Roll, Kft, and P. Box drew large crowds of young fans.[121] Heavy metal bands such as Edda Works, P. Mobil, P. Box, Von Band, and Piramis have consciously modeled themselves on West European bands. Also worth mentioning is the art rock group Solaris, which in 1984 issued a rhythmic and strangely fascinating album entitled *The Martian Chronicles*. Composed by Solaris members Róbert Erdész, István Cziglán, and Attila Kollár, *The Martian Chronicles* is arranged in six movements as an instrumental suite.[122]

In the context of Hungary's more relaxed atmosphere the groups that attracted the most criticism from the communists were those playing punk, described by certain Hungarian authorities in 1983 as having a "pernicious effect on the morals of the young."[123] Hungarian punk groups at various times insulted the dignity of Romanian party leader Nicolae Ceauşescu (a favorite Hungarian pastime anyway), expressed the desire to indulge in corporal dismemberment, evoked a phrase calling forth the defecatory bombardment of the planet, and endorsed extermination of the Gypsies. It was the punk group Mosoly that, in an un-advertised appearance at a February 1983 concert, expressed the latter sentiment:

> The flame thrower is the only weapon
>   with which I can win;
> I destroy every Gypsy, adult and child!
> Annihilate them altogether;
> When we have dispatched them,
>   we can put up a sign:
> Gypsy-free zone! [124]

In a country that still retains lively memories of World War II, such lyrics have a positively nightmarish quality. Worse yet, that nightmarish quality is deliberate.

The two most legendary punk groups in Hungary are still Beatrice (which broke up in 1981) and Coitus Punk Group (whose members were given eighteen- to twenty-four-month jail sentences in 1984). Beatrice addressed the everyday concerns of young people and consciously rejected any prefabricated values, including those of the regime. Beatrice sang about waiting for an apartment, relating to one's boss, official peace demonstrations, and the economy. And its audience responded. During concerts Beatrice habitually threw bags of milk at the audience; the practice was utterly devoid of symbolic content, but was a huge success with audiences. The authorities tried to buy out Beatrice with offers of promotion and an album, but its members did not want to be tamed, and when the group folded in 1981, it did so without having released a single album.[125]

Coitus Punk Group (CPG) was a more difficult case from the authorities' point of view since, unlike Beatrice, it wanted, very deliberately, to be provocative. Instead of bags of milk, CPG would tear apart live chickens on stage and throw the bleeding chicken parts at the audience. Instead of merely reflecting on social reality, CPG passed judgment on it. The very titles of their songs—"Rotten Angels," "Our King Is a Puppet," "Pigsty," and "Everyone Is a Louse"—were designed to be provocative. And their lyrics clearly strained against the limits of the allowable. In "Everyone Is a Louse," for example, CPG sang:

> I will be free.
> What I want is this:
> Not to be governed by a stupid beast.[126]

In the same song, the group predicted the coming of anarchism; the political context is quite explicit. Again, in "SS-20," CPG challenged the taboo against anti-Soviet "propaganda":

> The Soviet atom is also an atom,
> I can't stand this totalitarianism.
> The police is always hassling me.
> We have ss-20s in the East,
> They have the neutron bomb in the West.
> ss-20, ss-20, ss-20 in the East.
> In the East and in the West,
> The almighty power is the test.[127]

Those lyrics were obviously unacceptable, as CPG itself clearly knew. It could only be a matter of time before the authorities would move to silence the group.

But CPG did not stop there. In "Standing Youth," the group used the nonsense word *duli* to adorn some explicitly anticommunist lyrics:

> In the meadow a young shock-worker is standing.
> He had just come from a Communist Saturday meeting
> Duli-dul-balalajka, duli-dul-balalajka.
> Statues, pictures—you schematic bandit,
> The workers' hero has to play along with it.
> Duli-dul-balalajka, duli-dul-balalajka.
> Rotten stinking communist gang—
> Why has nobody hanged them yet?[128]

While singing this song, the group's leader tore up the familiar chicken and slashed his own face and arms with a razor blade. This was too much for the authorities and led directly to the group's trial and imprisonment in 1984. Three band members received two-year sentences, while the fourth received an eighteen-month jail sentence.

Yet the case of Coitus Punk Group was exceptional. Although there were punk groups and heavy metal groups and other "outlandish" fashions in communist Hungary, seeking above all to express their rejection of the world as it was, the authorities by and large took a disinterested view. Even where punk was concerned, the Hungarian political establishment was, at most, divided over the best policy response, if any should be needed.

The first attempts to politicize rock music in the mid-1970s ran into trouble. Spions was forced to disband after a 1976 concert which touched on political subjects, while Galloping Morticians was frozen out of the major concert circuits after a similarly sensitive concert in 1978. Attila Grandpierre had signaled the tone of the 1978 concert when he told his audience: "We are not here to entertain you. Don't even think that you'll be having a good time at this concert. If you want to have a good time, get lost. Go home and watch TV. Now you'll have something different."[129] Not good times, but politics. By the 1980s the new "political" music was increasingly prominent in the Hungarian rock scene.

Conclusion

I am very much inclined to agree with László Kürti that there was a direct connection between the growing decay of communism in Eastern Europe and the emergence of politicized rock in the late 1970s and 1980s. The former led directly to the latter, and the latter applauded and reinforced the former. Rock music offered itself as a form of counterculture, an alternative reference point, which shifted the terms of discourse.

Of course, not all rock music is conceived as counterculture per se. New wave, for instance, seems better described as self-assertion; on the other hand, the whole point of punk is to reject everything that civilized society offers. A Polish punk explained punk philosophy in these terms:

> Sometimes I am a pacifist; other times I am a vulgar cad. I provoke through my appearance. I want others to feel that here is still a bit of freedom. [The adults] want to profit from us, to organize us, and I do not want to be a prisoner. I am going to evade them. . . . I joined the punks to protest against constraint.[130]

The spread of rock counterculture in the communist states of Europe was, as in the West, at least temporarily associated with increased drug abuse, outlandish fashions, and a self-conscious striving to be "socially deviant."[131]

The collapse of communism throughout much of Eastern Europe by mid-1990 had consequences for all spheres of social activity, including rock music. In Poland, Hungary, and Yugoslavia, record sales slumped drastically—in Yugoslavia, primarily for economic reasons, in Poland and Hungary for both economic and sociopolitical reasons. With the success of the popular rebellion, there was no need for the music of rebellion; hence, Eastern Europe's musicians, especially those in Poland, Hungary, and Czechoslovakia, groped their way to a new commercialism.

The East Berlin industrial band Pankow, which built its reputation on songs about alienation and pollution, disbanded in 1990. Pankow's lead singer, Andre Herzberg, explained, "We are no longer relevant. I'm not sure what I'm going to do now."[132] But by 1994, "Ost-Rock" was reviving and some East German stars again were playing to jammed halls.[133]

In Poland, the Riviera-Remont Club, which once hosted punk rock concerts, now offers its space to computer fairs and flower markets. Many rock musicians have either left music or Poland itself. Others have taken jobs playing soft-pop at the Marriott Hotel. "Rock is dead in Poland," said Zbigniew Holdys, of Perfect, in sadness. For the time being, he may be right. In Hungary, attendance at rock concerts declined and as a result, rock bands were not able to schedule as many concerts as before.

And in Yugoslavia, or rather the Yugoslav successor states, the civil war that broke out in June 1991 has affected rock music along with everything else. Some groups, such as Falcons (Slovenia), Steamroller (Croatia), and Ekaterina Velika (Serbia), alongside rock solo artists like Rambo Amadeus have performed at peace concerts.[134] Others have opted for the role of mystagogues of nationalism—such as the Croatian group Psihomodo pop whose 1991 album included the hit song, "Croatia Must Win."[135] Some, such as Serbian rock stars Oliver Mandić and Simonida Stanković, have toured the front lines and serenaded the soldiers. Stanković, for example, celebrates Serbian warlord Arkan in song:

> They're protecting Serb glory,
> They're defending Serb lands,
> Arkan's Tigers,
> They're heroes without a flaw.[136]

Rock lost much of its political role in Eastern Europe in a matter of months. But in the annals of rock history the 1980s will go down as a heroic age in both Eastern Europe and the Soviet Union. The spirit of the age is perhaps best captured in the famous "Get Out of Control," first sung by the Leningrad rock group Televizor at a 1986 concert:

> We were watched from the days of kindergarten.
> Some nice men and kind women
> Beat us up. They chose the most painful places
> And treated us like animals on the farm.
> So we grew up like a disciplined herd.
> We sing what they want and live how they want.
> And we look at them downside up, as if we're trapped.
> We just watch how they hit us.
> Get out of control!
> Get out of control!
> And sing what you want
> And not just what is allowed.
> We have a right to yell![137]

11. Young People: The Lost Generation

In the villages,
The sound of the bugle is ringing,
Calling the young men to join the army,
And people do not hurry to meet it.
Nobody believes any longer
In the calling of the bugle.

The new generation . . . listens to the bugle
And does not understand . . .
How shall we call each other to battle?
How shall the alarm be given?
The bugle has become outdated . . .

—ADRIAN PĂUNESCU, *Let's Make Love On Cannons*

"Savka" is a twenty-four-year-old graduate of the philosophy faculty. She has been engaged for four years to a young worker, but they are postponing their marriage until they can find an apartment. Meanwhile, she lives with her parents. Although she obtained her degree in architecture, she was required to take courses on dialectical materialism, atheism, and the history of the communist party. She took the classes in 1988, but usually skipped these lectures, which she found boring, and sometimes even missed the exams. When asked to identify Karl Marx, she thinks he was probably a Russian "philosopher." She joined the communist youth organization at one time, but found the organization so dull and so tediously political that she remained completely inactive. As for politics, she had contempt for the communist political authorities, whom she described as basically corrupt and self-serving, holds the party responsible for most of the country's problems, and until recently saw little hope for the future. Even now, she cannot view the future with confidence. Until recently, she had enough money, thanks to pocket money from her parents and to the government's student stipend, to buy the clothes she likes; her aspirations were (in communist times) limited to the acquisition of consumer items, often on the black market. But recently family finances have become tight as a by-product of privatization. Where social and political issues are concerned, she has long been apathetic because she felt there was nothing she could do. She felt like part of a "lost generation." Even now she still feels somehow "lost."

"Savka" is a composite, not a real person. But the syndrome I have described is broadly typical of young people in Eastern Europe. In the communist era, apathy derived from the combination of deep frustration with a sense of powerlessness. Now the situation is changing totally but this has above all made for uncertainty. But the long experience with stultification and apathy has left a certain feeling of bitterness about the past.

When the communist parties took power in Eastern Europe, they conjured before their minds' eyes a vision of the youth of the future, a youth dedicated to the communist party, socially engaged, atheist, obedient, enthusiastic about socialism, and hard-working. In addition, the elites hoped that young people would imbibe the jargon of Marxism, coming to think in Marxist categories, and trust the political authorities. On every count the party was disappointed.

Pacifism was an early problem for East European elites. The communist party talked of class war, internal enemies, and the threat of world imperialism; the people, however, remembered World War II vividly, their offspring grew up amid ruins and the task of rebuilding, and the younger generations were infected by feelings of pacifism. This was especially true in East Germany, where the introduction of general military service in January 1962 stimulated pacifism and conscientious objection among some young people.[1] By the 1980s pacifist movements had also appeared in Poland, Czechoslovakia, and Hungary.

But pacifism actually engaged only a minority of young people. Pacifism is still a form of activism, of commitment, and, as a general rule, East European youth under communism were inward-looking and politically withdrawn. "Many young people feel convinced that in general they have no influence over what is happening around them," Polish sociologist Grzegorz Nowacki said in 1986, "particularly whenever national or regional issues are concerned. The principal . . . reason why the commitment and eventually activism of youth are deficient is precisely this feeling of lacking influence [over] what is happening."[2]

If today's youth feel less capable of affecting their environment than did previous generations, it is at least in part because their circumstances are different. In the 1980s and early 1990s youth in Eastern Europe live with and remain partially dependent on their parents for longer than did earlier generations. At home their responsibilities are minimal, with parents usually satisfied if their sons and daughters do well at their studies. A Polish writer suggested that "that is why there are so many children in their twenties that do not at all feel like adults. These are grown-up boys [and girls] with infantile personalities and no feeling of responsibility for their behavior. As when they were children, they expect only pleasure from life and no responsibilities or restrictions."[3] Diminished personal independence sows the seeds of frustration. But it is only one source.

In the late 1940s and 1950s, when entire classes were despoiled or incarcerated and vast numbers of Germans were expelled from Poland, Czechoslovakia, and Yugoslavia, there were great opportunities for social mobility. The so-called "partisan generation" grabbed up important posts and, for a while, talented young people (and even untalented young people) could afford to be ambitious. In the 1960s and 1970s the economies of Eastern Europe started to slow down, and the channels for mobility were gradually choked off. One of the reasons that the rock protest of the 1970s found resonance in Eastern Europe was that young people were starting to feel a deepening frustration and the evanescence of hope.[4] Some looked to personal connections to get them established, while still others retreated behind a protective shield of indifference.

Young people became obsessed with the West and yearned to visit or even to move there. For example, when a 1968 poll taken among Czechoslovak youth asked in what country they would ideally live, only 7.4 percent named a "socialist" country (a result possibly inflated by the inclusion of Yugoslavia in this category), while 13.1 percent named a "capitalist" country (typically, the United States, West Germany, Australia, or Great Britain), and 66.8 percent named a "neutral" country (Sweden, Austria, or Switzerland).[5] While the results of similar polls in Poland were less dramatic, the trend was toward declining commitment to reside in Poland: whereas between 82 and 85 percent of young people chose Poland as their first choice for permanent residence in surveys conducted from 1959 to 1978, only 62 percent did so in a 1983 survey, meaning that more than a third of Polish youth would prefer to live abroad—obviously, above all, in the West.[6]

East European youth are sometimes described as "pragmatic" or "rational." What this means, in practice, is that their aspirations center on private pleasures—friends, fashions, and material possessions. This consumerism very naturally became linked with the aforementioned admiration for the West because of the higher quality of Western commodities. And given the region's tight regulation of quality imports, this naturally fed the black market in all countries in the region (though in pre-1991 Yugoslavia to a lesser extent). A seventeen-year-old Romanian high school student gave vivid expression to this syndrome: "I was the first one in my class to have a Walkman. . . . I bought it with a lot of money from a foreign student from Mozambique. When I showed up with the earphones in the morning in the classroom, the whole class crowded around me. . . . It passed from hand to hand. Everybody looked at me with envy and admiration."[7] Similarly a nineteen-year-old Romanian student confessed: "Frankly, girls are crazy about Western clothes; they know that if you have these clothes you are rich and the target of envy. Do you know what it means to give a girl a pair of stockings from Italy, or a bottle of bath oil from West Germany?"[8] Predictably, the party press has attacked such consumerism both for its relationship to social withdrawal and for its association with Western commodities.

Social Pathology

But consumerism cannot serve as a universal escape valve, for one thing because only a few young people are sufficiently well off to be able to satisfy a consumerist mentality. Some young people seek release in rowdyism. A Bulgarian publication described this "solution" in a 1984 article:

> You will see them sitting on the steps of monuments or half lying at the main entrances of universities, public offices, and railroad stations. They smoke, chew [gum], munch and spit noisily, and look down upon the world with bored eyes. They shuffle around in scruffy shoes and torn socks, they are filthy, their clothes untidy, and bags of various kinds with all sorts of emblems and pictorial signs hang from their shoulders. Every now and then they shout out a senseless and vague protest—it does not matter against whom. . . . They loaf about in coffee houses, pastry shops, day bars, and clubs until their hour strikes: the hour of discos, dance halls, video arcades, the hour of an all-encompassing spitting at everything and everyone outside the gang.[9]

Others respond by adopting the language and attire of fascism. Young people sporting fascist insignia and giving vent to racist sentiments were reported in East Germany, Poland, Czechoslovakia, and Hungary, as well

as in Yugoslavia, where this has concerned above all pro-Ustaše sentiments among young Croats.[10] In April 1982 Polish police broke up an
eighteen-member group calling itself the Fascist Organization of Renewal; all but two of its members were between fifteen and seventeen
years of age.[11] On the other hand, Hitler's continued "popularity" in Eastern Europe—if one may call it that—was often a reflection of the fact
that young people saw the expression of pro-Hitler sentiments as the
most potent provocation they could sling at the communist regimes.
The punk movement was appealing for roughly the same reason.

And for those who could not find an appropriate release, there was the
risk of lapsing into mental illness. In Hungary, at any rate, the number
of mentally sick young people already had begun to increase in the early
1980s.[12] Since the collapse of communism a dramatic increase in mental
illness has occurred throughout the region.[13]

Finally, in most of the countries of the region, there have been the
growing problems of alcoholism, drug abuse, juvenile delinquency, and
criminal activity. Skinheads became a social problem in East Germany,
Poland, and Hungary; in the latter, skinheads have terrorized the local
Gypsies, forcing them to arm themselves.[14] In Bulgaria, as of 1988, two-
thirds of all criminal offenders were under thirty years of age and were
responsible for 86.6 percent of all rapes, 87.3 percent of robberies, 85.3
percent of all house break-ins, and 92.9 percent of all car thefts. Bulgarian girls have turned to prostitution at the age of twelve or thirteen.[15]
And in Czechoslovakia the rise in social problems among youth gave
rise to serious discussions within the Socialist Youth Union.

Youth Slang and Jargon

Eastern Europe has not yet experienced a generational conflict parallel
to what existed in the United States in the 1950s and 1960s, but by the
mid-1960s there was a growing rift between young people and officialdom. Nowhere is this more clearly expressed than in the development of
a special language peculiar to young people, or to particular subcultures
among youth, such as punk, the disco crowd, and so forth. In the late
1970s, for example, a specific subcultural argot called "Disco-Deutsch"
appeared among young Germans in both Germanys; it was heavily influenced by the rock and disco milieu.[16] Other jargon expressions favored by
East European youth developed within the criminal subculture. For example, in Poland *Grypsera*, the jargon of the self-designated "good guys,"
was developed originally in juvenile penitentiaries. *Grypsera* gradually
acquired a certain currency and ultimately left traces in the more general

youth slang.[17] In part, thus, youth slang has grown organically, drawing inspiration from sundry milieux. But in part it is also a more or less conscious reaction to the "other jargon"—what East German young people called "party Chinese."

Slang typically multiplies synonyms for oft-needed meanings. For example, one study of Bulgarian youth slang found fifty-one synonyms for *stupid,* twenty-nine for *hit,* eighteen for *beautiful,* eleven for *dissemble,* ten for *steal,* and seven for *money.*[18] Slang is also used to convey judgment, as in the Bulgarian *machilishte* (literally, torture) and Romanian *la Bastille,* both used to refer to school. Similarly, the Polish slang words for adults—*ramole* (weak heads), *mumie* (mummies), *ekshumy* (exhumates), and *nietoperze* (bats)—leave no uncertainty of the user's attitude toward the adult world. Young Poles refer to a demanding teacher as a piranha and to the school faculty collectively as the *inkwizycja* (Inquisition), while Bulgarian students employ twenty-five synonyms for sexual intercourse.[19] More than a decade ago, Polish writer Zbigniew Mentzel commented,

> Linguistic inventiveness most fully reveals itself in certain areas of life, and in the jargon of students this concerns such things as the relationship to teachers, the erotic, and friends. It is similar with the language of adults, where the relationship to employers, promotion or advancement, and money somehow achieve a linguistic double-life. Researchers and publicists have long ago noted that in the language of a given society, most surrogate expressions arise from situations and themes which are especially taboo in this society. . . . Precisely in the case of taboo themes, the language [of the subculture] brings group complexes and frustrations to the light of day.[20]

Many words used specifically or primarily by young people are derived from foreign sources. In Bulgaria, Turkish is a source of many loan words in the youth subculture. English loanwords are, of course, widespread throughout the region. Rock music has been the conduit for some of these, bringing the words *available, background, blue, challenging, competitive, concerned, generous, impressive, loser, mellow, motivated, outspoken, pusher, responsive, self-made, single-minded,* and *trip* into common use among Polish youth. In Romania, the English words *actually, business, eventually, grapefruit, knockdown, knockout, smash, tennis player,* and *updated* have achieved currency. In Serbia and Croatia, the words *biznes, brejkdens, hit, new wave, ritam mašina, rock bend, sendvić, sintisajzer,* and *star* have all come into common use. In addition, Polish young people have also assimilated a few German expressions, such as *Schadenfreude* (gloating) and *Sitzfleisch* (perseverance with desk work), as well as a select set of Russian expressions, such as *molodets* (good going).

As Wolf Oschlies has noted, the flourishing of youth slang and jargon is an important indication that young people do not passively assimilate the values and conventions of the adult world, but in fact actively confront those values and categories with values and categories of their own.[21] Slang and jargon, of course, also serve another purpose, that is, to isolate one group from another.

Attitudes Toward Politics

If young people want to isolate themselves from the adult world, it is in part because they already feel cut off from it. An eighteen-year-old Serbian student, Sladjana Andjelković, stated the case quite simply: "We are neither dumb nor stupid; yet we are silent." Another young Serb, Vigor Majić, elaborated, "The first words one learns are *mommy, daddy,* and *shut up.* We have not been taught to speak. On the contrary, we are systematically taught to be silent—in the family, school, youth organization, [and] League of Communists."[22]

Pushed thus into a passive role, young people were later criticized for their passivity. Having forced young people to study Marxism-Leninism, mouth communist slogans, and take part in communist pageants such as Youth Day, party elders subsequently seemed taken by surprise that the natural rebelliousness of youth should turn against *them.*

In fact, however, the frustration of East European young people with the communist system went far beyond the mere question of "natural rebelliousness." In some cases, elites had to reckon with the partial failure of socialization and the alienation of a generation fed up with the disjunction between theory and practice. In Poland, political training had largely broken down by 1980,[23] and in several countries (most certainly Poland, Hungary, Yugoslavia, and Bulgaria) the youth organizations were either in crisis by the late 1980s, or were evolving new roles which departed radically from traditional patterns.

This phenomenon was late in developing—at least in this form. As recently as the early 1970s young people in Romania and Yugoslavia had largely positive attitudes toward their systems or about the attitude they should adopt toward their systems.[24] And in the case of Poland, of course, the imposition of martial law in 1981 and 1982 had a severe negative impact on young people's orientations toward political authorities.[25]

As of the mid- and late 1980s the political attitudes expressed by young people gave the authorities cause for concern. In Hungary, for instance, a 1987 survey found that a majority of young people had "no confidence" in the communist party and preferred to introduce a Western-style democratic system.[26] An earlier survey in the same country found that less than half of responding students felt it was safe for people to express their opinions on political and economic subjects, roughly 75 percent felt that Hungarian political life was "not more democratic than before," and 40 percent declared that the political system was undemocratic.[27]

A 1982 survey of young Croats found that only 28.6 percent of respondents endorsed the delegate system, while 18.3 percent criticized it as undemocratic, with another 55.1 percent declining to answer. In that same survey, only 39 percent gave unconditional approval to the one-party system, while 6.7 percent said they were opposed to one-party rule under any circumstances, and 39.5 percent said they did not know or had no opinion.[28] A 1989 survey among 5,000 Yugoslav youth found that roughly 65 percent felt they needed to act outside the framework and programs of official political organizations, 42 percent declared themselves in favor of a multiparty system, and 20 percent favored abolishing the communist party altogether. In Slovenia 84 percent of young people favored a multiparty system, while 60 percent considered the communist party obsolete; the corresponding figures for Croatia were 65 and 33 percent, respectively.[29]

Until the mid-1980s, East European youth typically believed that, while some form of socialism would be ideal, their own systems had failed to realize the *potentials* of socialism. An eighteen-year-old East German student put it this way:

> The face of GDR socialism could also have looked different. It is not necessarily this way. But it has a lot to do with us ourselves. The roots of many erroneous developments lie in the history of the Germans. One simply cannot overlook that. One cannot try to trace all the explanations and solutions of the day to the errors of Marxism.[30]

This impressionistic picture is confirmed by survey data from Poland and Yugoslavia. In Poland, for instance, a survey was conducted among 1,082 young people. Asked whether they thought the world should develop in the direction of socialism, 49.8 percent answered in the affirmative, while 28.1 percent answered in the negative; the remainder "did not know" or refused to answer.[31] In Yugoslavia, the previously cited survey of 1,100 Croatian youth found that most respondents rejected social equality—the central value of socialism—as negative.[32] Of the chief values propounded by these regimes—the superiority of one-party rule, social ownership of the means of production, equality for all non-believers, the standardization of thought, the myth of steady progress and "democratization" under communism—the social ownership of the means of production was the most generally accepted (for instance, by nearly 75 percent of young Poles in a 1984 survey). Other values tended to be rejected by the majority of young people, especially the standardization of thought. A 1986 poll showed that young people in Czechoslovakia were overwhelmingly convinced that people should be able to think as they please, while university students in Hungary demanded extensive changes in the curriculum in order to include the teaching of "bourgeois and religious philosophies."[33] In fact, by the mid-1980s Hungarian youth became highly critical of party policy in general and increasingly willing to speak their minds. Hard hit by unemployment and housing shortages, young Hungarians saw substantive change as urgent.[34]

An opinion poll conducted by the central council of the Socialist Union of Polish Students in early 1982 among high school and university students in Warsaw revealed some interesting statistics. For example, only 3.5 percent of university students and 2 percent of high school students said that the introduction of martial law was "completely justified." A somewhat larger number (15 and 17 percent) said the move was "correct in principle." Most respondents described it as either "completely unjustified" (48.5 and 34 percent) or "wrong in principle" (20.5 and 38 percent). Asked about their appraisal of the role played respectively by the party, the church, and Solidarity in 1981, 72.5 percent of university students and 70.5 percent of high school students appraised the party negatively, 67 and 84 percent approved of the church's role, and 67.5 and 64 percent gave Solidarity positive marks.[35]

Young people were thus increasingly disillusioned with the system, and as the 1980s drew to a close, they wanted to see it overhauled at the very least. "The young blame the older generation and want to modernize socialism, make it more open and efficient," said Tomaz Mastnak, an independent Slovenian sociologist.[36]

This disillusionment was reflected in the heroes adopted by young people. Few of these countries published or even conducted such opinion polls in communist times. But in Yugoslavia and Poland, Pope John Paul II placed high, at least among Catholics, far outdistancing local party bosses. In a 1985 Yugoslav poll conducted among 750 high school students in Split, Mother Theresa (the Albanian nun from Yugoslavia) was the most admired of twenty-four persons listed, with the pope in third place, and Lenin in last place, with only thirty-seven votes. In a similar poll taken twenty years earlier, Lenin had rated very highly, while Pope Paul VI had ranked fifth.[37] On the other hand, a 1988 survey in Poland found that Gorbachev was the most widely respected personality among young people, with a 45.7 percent rating. Pope John Paul II claimed another 29.7 percent, leaving only 9.5 percent for the nation's leader, Wojciech Jaruzelski.[38]

The youth organizations were supposed to deal with this challenge. The charter of Yugoslavia's League of Socialist Youth (ssoj) was probably representative of the underlying formal ideology:

> The ssoj is a united and mass-based political organization. As the broadest democratic front of the young generation in Yugoslavia, the various interests, aspirations, and creative energies of the youth are expressed and directed toward socialist self-management in and through this organization.
>
> The ssoj is committed to developing and strengthening the organized ideological-political unity of the young generation; it concretely prepares the youth for their active and direct participation and involvement in our self-managed organizations and its structures, in the delegate system, and in the political organizations and social life in its entirety.[39]

But in fact, by the later 1980s the East European youth organizations were everywhere in crisis. "My comrades are not interested in self-management by the students. They prefer the discotheque, excursions, sports. They come to ssoj meetings only when we put under 'miscellaneous' on the agenda—dance," said Milan Dočić, a Yugoslav eighth grader.[40] In Romania leading officials of the youth organization admitted in 1985 that they had been unable to respond effectively to the aspirations of members.[41] Csába Hámori, first secretary of the Communist Youth League in Hungary, admitted in 1986 that his organization's influence among young people was in decline; in an effort to deal with the problem, extensive administrative changes in the organization were carried out in 1988.[42] In Bulgaria there were calls for "new approaches in the organization and leadership of the movement for fostering creative thinking in young people," "qualitative changes . . . in the style and methods of work," and, in general, "greater perspective, initiative, and tenacity."[43] And in Poland, so serious did the situation become that the regime authorized the creation of a second organization in 1982, the Polish Students Association, hinting that it would enjoy considerable practical independence. But Polish students were not won over, most viewing the new organization as "just another politicized and politicizing party bureaucracy."[44] As a result, young people stayed away.[45]

One clear alternative was for the youth organizations to evolve into something more than mere transmission belts. On this score, the youth organization in Yugoslavia was a pacesetter. After Tito's death in 1980, the Yugoslavs redesigned the annual Youth Day festival. No longer was it to be a drab affair with long columns of athletic youth parading with banners in hand while a military-style band plays patriotic marches. Now the centerpiece of the festival was rock music, and the entire event was redesigned to appeal to the membership. The "House of Youth" (*Dom omladine*) found in many cities became a true meeting place for young people, with provocative books on sale and rock concerts and dances in the evening. In 1987 the slick new magazine *Potkulture* (*Subcultures*) was launched, devoted entirely to alternative lifestyles.

Politically, the youth organization in Yugoslavia also changed. In Slovenia, for instance, the youth organization opened its doors to alternative movements, allowing them to use SSOJ facilities to carry on their more or less opposition activities; in this way, the youth organization in Slovenia came to play a role parallel to that of the Evangelical-Lutheran church in East Germany.

Indicative of the new tone in Slovenia in particular was the twelfth congress of the League of Socialist Youth of Slovenia held in Krsko on 4–6 April 1986. Of those in attendance, only guests from other political organizations came formally attired; the majority were casually attired, some even wearing punk or heavy metal fashions. Many wore badges from the alternative movement in support of peace, ecology, feminism, and free speech. The congress itself opened with a rock concert. At the end of three days of lively discussion, the congress issued a document declaring, "in our opinion, the pressures toward conformity of thought that accompany the polarization of wealth and poverty are one of the weapons for maintaining the polarization of ruling and submission."[46] The congress called for a radical departure in official policy toward alternative thought and for the pluralization of politics and cultural and social life.

Two years later, in the wake of the highly controversial trial of three journalists and an enlisted man in Slovenia for publishing an article accusing the military of plotting a coup, the youth organization took another bold step. It declared its intention to monitor the work of "individuals who in its opinion are not trusted by the public and should leave their functions."[47]

In essence, what started to happen in Yugoslavia and, initially, in Slovenia, is that young people took over the youth organization, making it responsive to their needs and aspirations. Ultimately, the radical young members converted the Slovenian youth organization into a political party (Liberal Democratic) and fielded candidates in the 1990 elections as part of the Demos coalition.

Illegal and Underground Activities

Illegal and underground activity usually involves a minority of young people. The dropout syndrome is much more widespread. As a Czechoslovak publication noted in 1987, "the majority [of young people] are preoccupied with their own private concerns, such as partners and friends, while 'social involvement' . . . is rated at the bottom of their list [of priorities]."[48]

When young people do become politically involved, it is sometimes in organizations of their own creation, organizations toward which the communist authorities take umbrage. One of the earliest illegal youth organizations was a secret political organization called *Ruch* (The Movement) among Polish high school students in the early 1970s. The organization was uncovered in 1971, and its leaders were given seven-year prison sentences.[49]

The tendency toward self-organization is probably strongest among young Poles and weakest among young Romanians and Bulgarians. In the Polish case there were recurrent reports over the years of different underground youth groups. In 1982, for example, three clandestine youth groups were uncovered among secondary school students in the Katowice *voivodship.* They were said to have been involved in hostile pamphleteering and in scribbling antiregime graffiti on public walls.[50] Earlier, in 1981, the Movement of School Youth was formed in the Tri-City region (Gdańsk, Gdynia, Sopot), and there was a renewed attempt to revive a "democratic" youth organization in Kraków.

Polish youth in fact became relatively active in the opposition beginning in 1981. High school students became involved in dissident activity: for example, a group of students in Gorzów Wiełkopolski started a journal, *Sokół* (*Falcon*); nine were subsequently arrested in March 1985. Altogether at least thirty underground publications produced by Polish youth reached the West after 1981. In Warsaw, for instance, the Independent Youth Organization published *Gnom* (*Gnome*), while the Lower Silesian regional council of the Solidarity Youth Resistance Movement in Wrocław published *Wolna Polska.* Kraków was the organizational center for Promieniści (Rays), a group which has published a journal under the same name since September 1982. It claimed a circulation of 3,000 in 1986 and covered a wide array of social and political topics.[51]

One of the best-known underground youth organizations in Poland was the Independent Students' Association, originally registered as a legal association in February 1981, but subsequently suppressed. Despite illegality, the Association continued its activities, albeit on a limited scale, and convoked its "second congress" on 10 January 1987 in Warsaw. The congress drew student representatives from nineteen universities and other institutions of higher education in Warsaw, Wrocław, Kraków, Łódź, Katowice, and Radom. The association was overtly hostile to communism, basing its activity on the Christian ethical tradition and pledging itself to work for an independent and democratic Poland.[52]

But even in Czechoslovakia there were some stirrings among young people. The scouting movement, which was resurrected in 1968 during the evanescent Prague Spring, continued to operate underground.[53] And in 1984 a human rights group based in Slovakia and calling itself the Young People of the CSSR sent a letter to President Gustáv Husák demanding, among other things, the restoration of the Slovak double-barred cross on the state seal of Czechoslovakia.[54]

And in Bulgaria too, alternative youth organizations appeared, by the end of the decade. The best known is the Federation of Independent Students' Unions (FISU), which was founded in the wake of Zhivkov's ouster as general secretary and which claimed a membership of 6,000 at the end of December 1989.[55] Despite its nonparty status, FISU won endorsement from a Bulgarian CP faction called The Bulgarian Road to Europe, which called for Bulgaria's social, political, cultural, and economic integration into mainstream Europe. Another alternative youth organization, Youth for European Socialism, was set up at Sofia University and declared its support for the Bulgarian Road concept.

Attitudes among young people vary considerably, of course, and among those who are criticized as "passive" are many who are simply disinterested in politics. In surveys of Yugoslav youth, generally 60 percent (but sometimes 75 to 80 percent) were broadly supportive of the system or of its principles, at least until the late 1980s. Some 15 to 30 percent (mostly unskilled workers, poor peasants, and the unemployed) were classed as "dogmatic-etatistic" types—which is another way of identifying working class authoritarianism. Only 10 to 15 percent had liberal-democratic values and orientations.[56]

The Values and Hopes of Youth

The chief determinants of the value system of young people, according to a Yugoslav sociologist, are their social and economic position—with low status tending to reinforce antisystem tendencies because those concerned have little hope of bettering their lot *within* the system—and the dominant ideological and cultural currents.[57] The latter may of course include exposure to rock music and Western cultural trends. To these one may add the family, which plays a crucial formative role. On this subject an East German research institute concluded in 1980 that "the vast majority of children and young people base their world view upon that of their parents. An average of 88 percent of pupils in grades 6 to 10 and 75 percent of job apprentices set for themselves, with certain restrictions to be sure, the goal of always following the advice of their parents, 'because it is usually right'. . . . The father and mother rank far above all others on the list of recognized authorities."[58] Television may also play an independent role, judging from the high rate of TV watching among East European youth.[59] But Western shows like *Dynasty* and *Dallas* were long much more popular among youth than the more didactic programs preferred by authorities.

There is a broad consensus among East European youth that the most important ingredients for happiness are a happy marriage and family life, and privacy. Other values frequently cited in polls taken in Romania and Yugoslavia include health, friendship, personal independence, material sufficiency, professional success, leisure, and respect. A mere 0.5 percent of Romanian respondents said that "achieving a high position in the hierarchy" was important for personal happiness, although some 15.8 percent of Yugoslav respondents listed "power" among the ingredients of happiness.[60]

But levels of interest in politics and the specific rankings of values are susceptible to external pressures. As the economic and political systems of Eastern Europe came under greater stress in recent years, the level of interest in politics rose, and data on political interest from one year may be of little indicative value a few years later. Until the dramatic political changes in Hungary and Poland in 1989 and the opening up of borders in the course of that year, young people throughout most of Eastern Europe felt a combination of resentment against the system, frustration with the limits of their travel possibilities and opportunities for social mobility, and, in the case of Poland, Romania, and Yugoslavia, an apprehension linked to the sense that things could not go on as they had in the past. In fact, young Poles were long the most pessimistic in Eastern Europe. One young Pole, for example, commented in 1983, "People don't believe in anything any more. They don't believe in a speedy emergence of Poland out of the crisis. They don't believe there will be any improvement in supplies."[61] Or, as another young Pole put it, "Aside from crises, socialism has given us nothing."[62]

The younger generation in Eastern Europe ultimately played a role in the revolutionary transformation of the region. But from August 1968 (a symbolic date) to the end of the 1980s, young people were gripped with a sense of powerlessness and a consequent apathy. Until the end of 1989, it was a lost generation that looked on the world of politics with frustration and bitterness. The Polish rock group Turbo gave expression to this mood in "Grown-up Children":

> They taught us rules and deadlines,
> Beat it into us what's allowed and what is not,
> Convinced us what is good or bad,
> Absolutely nothing could be forgotten.
> Only that we no longer know
> How we should live.
> Grown up children feel sadness
> With the wretched recipes for this world.
> Grown up children feel sadness
> Because someone has stolen
> So much of their lives.[63]

Part V
Collapse of the Old Order

12. Bulgaria: A Weak Society

Through much of the late 1980s Bulgaria seemed to be uniquely immune to the stresses afflicting other states in the region. Its economy benefited from a series of somewhat unclear prophylactic measures taken by the regime. The Zhivkov regime chalked up an impressive record of political stability. And the winds of glasnost and perestroika were only weakly felt in Bulgaria. In all of these ways Bulgaria offered a sharp contrast to what was developing in Poland, Hungary, Yugoslavia, East Germany, and Czechoslovakia. What accounts for this difference?

Crane Brinton's analysis of revolutionary situations summarizes seven uniformities. Of these, four refer to the weakness of government (the inability of the government to develop efficient means for channeling public participation, the financial failure of the government, the loss of self-confidence on the part of the regime, and the inept use of force), and two refer to the strength of society (the mobilization of important new strata into the political arena and the desertion of the regime by the intellectuals). His argument may be paraphrased thus, that when government is weak and society is strong, and when there is widespread popular discontent (the last remaining factor of the seven he lists), the system is apt to become unstable, a situation possibly leading to revolution. By contrast, when society is weak the system is stable and the government can maintain order on its own terms.

Brinton's list also provides some clues as to the components of a strong society. *Mobilization* of people involves two things: political awareness and the ability to organize. A mobilized public is by definition an *aware* public whose activities are channeled into existing organizations. People may be mobilized into structures that are supportive of the government or into opposition structures; only the latter is *necessarily* a sign of a strong society.

Political awareness in turn requires a certain level of information. A society without information is necessarily weak. It can become strong only by developing reliable sources of information. In addition, opposition structures must either have independent channels for communication or be able to use official channels to communicate their ideas.

And finally, the defection of intellectuals is important because the intellectuals bring various skills—above all communication skills.

All told, Brinton's analysis suggests at least five components of a strong society: a modicum of information, the ability to organize, the defection of skill-bearing intellectuals, access to channels of communication, and mobilization of the public. These factors, I shall argue, either were not present in Bulgaria prior to 1990 or were only faintly present. As a result, for the entire decade of the 1980s Bulgarian society was not merely not radicalized; it was actually, and still is to a large extent, *weak*. This is the key to understanding the political quiet which prevailed up to late 1989 in that country.

Information. The Bulgarian press and other media were long virtually barren and unreadable; this was symptomatic of a regime policy to monopolize information. The result was that information became a prized commodity. There were several associated problems. First, the list of those things which qualified as state secrets in Bulgaria in the 1980s was quite long. In 1980, for example, the list of facts and information which were state secrets was expanded, and the new listing included, inter alia, information on Bulgarian trade protocols with bloc countries, credits to and from other countries, foreign currency credits for imports, the annual and quarterly plans for exports and imports, crude oil imports, and deposits of nonferrous and precious metals.[1] Other facts, such as those relating to the Macedonian minority, were likewise suppressed.

A second problem is that even when statistical information was published, its quality and reliability were often low, and certainly less reliable than comparable data from all other East European countries except Romania and Albania.[2]

Third, there was the system of censorship itself, which regulated what might or might not be published. Books which offended the authorities were simply banned altogether; works by Bulgarian authors were screened and their authors subjected to the "method of persuasion" in order to obtain desired prepublication revisions in the text. Meanwhile, excessive press censorship was so demoralizing to Bulgarian journalists that there were indirect admissions that they suffered from low morale and even, at times, offered "passive resistance."[3] In Bulgaria the publication of information on the incidence of neurosis in Bulgarian society in 1984 was itself a newsworthy event.[4]

Fourth, the state publishing monopoly distorted the selection of titles for publication and ignored market demand. The result, as *Bulgarski Zhurnalist* admitted in 1983, was that funds were often diverted to luxury editions of works for which there was little or no demand, and which therefore sat on bookshelves unsold.[5]

A similar situation prevailed in science. In 1977, for example, Sofia hosted the International Conference on Space-Time Absoluteness, which set itself the task of debunking Einstein's theory of relativity.[6]

In the late 1980s, the Bulgarian regime gave lip service to the need for more openness in the press, and there were some striking reports in the Bulgarian press in the past few years. But the Zhivkov regime, which finally collapsed on 10 November 1989, was clearly unenthusiastic about any major change in media policy. Hence, for example, when the sixth congress of the Bulgarian Writers' Union, meeting in Sofia in March 1989, gave vent to spirited criticism of official policy on the media, press reports were generally unilluminating. The party daily *Rabotnichesko delo* reported that the speeches had been "lively," but said little about their content. The union's own paper, *Literaturen Front*, published a nebulous account that gave no information linking speakers and topics, and admitted that "a number of recommendations" had been made without saying what they were.[7]

One looked in vain in the Bulgarian press for criticism of official policies, for debates, for probing analyses of relevant issues, or, until November 1989, for opinion polls on government performance.[8] And when in June 1987 the trade union daily newspaper *Trud* published an exceptional four-part series exposing the corruption of the influential Mihaylov family in Etropole, the Central Control and Revision Committee ordered the expulsion of journalist Georgi Tambuev from the party, his dismissal as head of the Economic Department of *Rabotnichesko delo*, and a review of the incumbent editor, Damyan Obreshkov.

If it had not been for Radio Free Europe and other foreign broadcasts, citizens of Bulgaria would long have been in danger of being cut off from the realities of their own society.

The Ability to Organize. Until its abolition in early 1990, the Bulgarian control apparatus (including the secret police) was singularly effective in containing would-be opposition organizations. Thus, for example, the first unofficial human rights group, the Society for the Protection of Human Rights in Bulgaria, came into existence only in 1988. Even then, of its two dozen members, only four dared to sign the group's founding document, and shortly thereafter one was placed under house arrest, another was sent to internal exile, and a third was expelled from the country.[9]

As of March 1989 nine independent (dissident) organizations were reportedly active in Bulgaria.[10] The Discussion Club for the Support of Glasnost and Perestroika was formed in November 1988 and unsuccessfully applied for legal papers. In May 1989 eleven members were temporarily arrested after appealing to the National Assembly for democratic reforms. An independent association devoted to the defense of religious freedom and known as the Committee for Religious Rights, Freedom of Conscience, and Spiritual Values was set up under the chairmanship of Father Hristofor Subev on 9 March 1989. It declared its intention to campaign for an end to state interference in religious life and discrimination against believers in public and professional life, the legalization of religious instruction for the young, and freedom of religious information. The Holy Synod of the Bulgarian Orthodox church appealed to the state judiciary not to grant legal registration to the new committee. Meanwhile, the group's foreign representative, Father Blagoy Topuzliev, was immediately expelled from the country, and Subev himself was imprisoned for more than a month, even though no charges had been lodged against him.[11]

There were also small groups of environmentalists. In late 1988 a group announced that it was setting up a "Green" Party. The Greens later established a branch in the town of Burgas.[12] And in December 1989, armed with 4,000 signatures, environmental activists in Plovdiv established the Youth Association for Ecology and Environmental Protection, affiliated with Plovdiv University.[13] An earlier organization called the Ruse Committee had attracted a lot of intellectuals, but was suffocated by the authorities when it became too voluble. Some Ruse members joined the Eco-Glasnost Movement that emerged in March 1989. This new organization sought legal registration but was predictably turned down.

Finally, an independent trade union, Support, was founded in February 1989 under the chairmanship of Konstantin Trenchev. As of August 1989, it claimed sixty members.

These groups were small and weak, and there were in any case very few of them. By comparison with the weakness of the opposition, the regime showed itself strong enough to convoke a mass meeting of ethnic Turks in support of its policy of annihilating Turkish culture in Bulgaria.

Specifically, in September 1989 the regime organized a meeting of some 800 Bulgarian expellees turned back by Turkey under the motto, "Bulgaria: Our Homeland, Fate, and Future." As if to mock those attending the meeting, speakers told them, "It is high time that people in Bulgaria and around the world become aware of Pan-Turkism as a dangerous resurgence which is inconsistent with new political thinking and which poses a threat not only to Bulgaria [but also] to many other countries."[14]

Until the closing months of 1989 discontented Bulgarians displayed very little ability to organize themselves successfully, and such groups as took shape are all recent.

The Intellectuals. Until late 1989 opposition among the intellectuals was an individual affair. One of the most striking instances of opposition on the part of the intellectuals came in July 1989, when the Discussion Club for the Support of Glasnost and Perestroika issued a declaration protesting the regime's treatment of the Turkish minority. The Bulgarian Writers' Union, as already noted, became a particular focus of intellectual ferment, and in May 1989 some members of that union drafted an appeal for democratic reforms in Bulgaria, addressing it to the national assembly. Significantly, several of the points in the appeal dealt with access to information and to communication channels, and the right to organize. In particular, the appeal called for the declassification of all information not directly harmful to national security and of all files older than twenty-five years, the elimination of secret shelves in the state libraries, an end to the banning of works of literature and art, free access of citizens to the media, and the right to organize independent groups and associations, with the permission of the government.[15]

There is evidence thus that Bulgarian intellectuals were becoming politically aware. Yet, at the same time, their opposition was inchoate and it would be too early to claim that a "defection" of the intellectuals has occurred, either before December 1989 or since.

Communication. In a society in which the state asserts a monopoly over all media, printed information, and organizations, independent communication is a formidable challenge. In such a society word-of-mouth communication takes on much greater importance than it would have in an open society, and friendship networks function as de facto conduits of information.

The problem of communication was organically connected with the question of independent organizations. The very modest presence of independent organizations meant that independent communication enjoyed only modest organizational resources. Even the Orthodox church, the largest religious body in the country, was kept under the thumb of the communist regime, and its publications merely supported the regime line. The same was true of the hierarchy of the Islamic community.[16]

Mobilization of the Public. As a result, the public as a whole was not mobilized and the regime was long able to pursue policies calculated to alienate specific sectors of the society.

The entire campaign against the Turks poignantly illustrates both the virtual inability of the Bulgarian public to mobilize itself effectively in opposition to the regime's policy and, more broadly, the general weakness of Bulgarian society.

As early as the late 1940s and early 1950s the Bulgarian government pressured its Turkish minority to emigrate.[17] In the late 1950s all Turkish-language schools in Bulgaria were closed. Later, particularly since the 1970s, Turks, Muslims, Gypsies, and Pomaks (ethnic Bulgarian Muslims) came under strong pressure to assimilate.

In late 1984 the Bulgarian regime launched a new campaign to assimilate the Turks. It closed down Turkish-language media, banned the use of Turkish in public, restricted certain Islamic religious practices (such as circumcision), and forced indigenous Turks to assume Bulgarian names. In late 1984 and 1985 there were armed clashes between Turks and Bulgarian army and police units, in which hundreds of Turks and dozens of soldiers and police lost their lives. But that was only the first phase of the Bulgarianization campaign.

Despite international outcry, especially in Turkey and the Islamic world, there was no effective resistance offered within the country. There were protests and violent outbursts on the part of Bulgaria's Turks in May 1989 in several towns. In the northeastern village of Todor Ikonomovo, twenty to twenty-five ethnic Turks were killed when troops opened fire on a crowd of about two thousand people. Tanks, helicopters, and heavy security surrounded the towns of Razgrad and Šumen, where demonstrations were also taking place. In Razgrad (100 miles east of Sofia), four to five thousand protesters clashed with police, who arrested two hundred people and cut telephone lines to Razgrad.[18] The regime now decided on the expulsion of ethnic Turks who were resisting assimilation and engaging in protest actions. Between 6 May and 7 June, almost three thousand Turks were deported to Turkey. By 22 August Turkey had closed its border pending an emigration agreement, but about 310,000 Bulgarian Muslims (mainly Turks) had already crossed into Turkey, reducing the Turkish population of Bulgaria by as much as a third.[19]

Among those expelled by the government were Ismet Ismailoglu Emur-lah (secretary of the Association for Vienna '89, a human rights group), Avni Veliev (chairman of the same association), Mustafa Yumerov (chairman of the Democratic League), and Ali Ormanliev and Sabri Iskenderov (two secretaries of the same league). Shukri Sherifov, an ethnic Turk who had written an open letter appealing for minority rights, was arrested and sentenced to prison on charges of inciting unrest and spreading falsehood.

In mid-August 1989 fresh disturbances and deaths occurred in several villages near Gotse Delchev. The renewed unrest was sparked by the authorities' decision that many ethnic Turks and Pomaks who had changed their names in 1984 or 1985 would have to change their names a second time because the names were "insufficiently Slavic." Hundreds of villagers filed for passports, but ironically, despite Zhivkov's televised public announcement in which he granted the Muslims the right to leave, local officials declared that Zhivkov's decision did not apply to the Sofia and Plovdiv regions and blocked their emigration.

The mass exodus resulted in an acute labor shortage in several regions in which the emigrants had been concentrated, and this new shortage had a knock-on effect in other parts of the country too. Production dropped in 121 municipalities—particularly, in Razgrad by 10.5 percent, in Haskovo by 8.5 percent, and in Varna by 3.7 percent. A few thousand Turks returned to Bulgaria but they were not necessarily given much of a welcome. In Varna oblast, for example, the labor collective resolved that Turks "who have left of their own free will should not return to their former workplaces. Proof is needed that they are really aware of their mistakes and guilt."[20]

The officially recognized Supreme Religious Council of Muslims remained cowed, and at an enlarged session in late August 1989 the council adopted a declaration stating that Islam enjoyed complete freedom in Bulgaria, and benefited from the respect and assistance shown by the authorities.[21]

With the fall of Todor Zhivkov, stirrings began among the Bulgarian public. On 17 November, for example, about 100,000 Bulgarians gathered in front of the National Assembly building in Sofia to show support for perestroika and to shout slogans against demagogy and corruption.[22] At a rally called by the nine independent associations at Aleksandr Nevsky Square the following day, there were calls for freedom of speech, pluralism, and free elections.[23] The regime started to feel a need to make concessions. It therefore met with members of the democratic coalition (the Union of Democratic Forces in Bulgaria), promised to hold free elections and end censorship of the press, and on 29 December rescinded its earlier decision imposing Bulgarian names on local Turks.

Needless to say, Bulgaria's remaining Turks were jubilant at this decision. But ethnic Bulgarians reacted differently. For them it was not a matter of democracy and rights, but a question of whose country it was. Hence, although the Human Rights Committee of Bulgaria quickly issued a statement to welcome the resolution rescinding the anti-Turkish policy and restoring the right to a free choice of names,[24] thousands of Bulgarians participated in anti-Turkish rallies and demonstrations in towns across the country, including Plovdiv, Tŭrgovishte, Šumen, Ruse, and Smoljan.[25] In Sofia, nationalistic Bulgarians took to the streets by the thousands, shouting, "Bulgaria for the Bulgarians," "Let there be no ground for pan-Turkism," "Do not decide instead of the people," "Who kissed the Turkish hand?," and "The Army is with us."[26]

In the town of Kurdzhali tensions reached a fever pitch, and local communist authorities simply refused to implement the new policy, thus provoking Turks to shout, "Give us our names back! We want our rights!"[27] Local Bulgarians sang anti-Turkish songs dating back to Ottoman times and shouted, "No to Turkish slavery!"

"No one's thinking about the question of democracy or dictatorship," said Deyen Kiuranov, a leading figure in the Eco-Glasnost movement. "The nationalist issue dominates everything."[28] As if in acknowledgment of this, the Bulgarian government decided in early 1990 to change its National Day from 9 September (the date of the communist takeover in 1944) to 3 March (the date of the overthrow of Turkish rule in 1878).[29]

Conclusion

Several conclusions seem in order. On the one hand, the Bulgarian regime remained (until mid-1990) confident of its ability to control and channel political change in the country. Indeed, its decisive victory over the opposition in the 10 June 1990 elections (capturing 48 percent of the vote, versus 34 percent for the chief opposition bloc) seemed to confirm this control. It was also willing to resort to draconian measures to achieve ethnic homogenization. At the same time, the society remained atomized; symptomatically, not only was there little solidarity shown by ethnic Bulgarians for the oppressed Turks, but Bulgarians in fact showed that they did not consider Turks part of the same "civil society." One might say that the whole concept of "civil society" was foreign to Bulgaria. During the aforementioned elections many Bulgarians were said to have voted communist out of fear and weakness. "People think the communists are omniscient," commented Filip Dimitrov, deputy chair of the Bulgarian Green Party. "That is how they are intimidated." Similarly, Tibor Vidos, a Hungarian observer, said there were psychological pressures "not visible to the naked eye—one could smell it."[30] More generally, a member of the Independent Discussion Club argued in October 1989 that "the Stalinist model has met less resistance in Bulgaria [than elsewhere in Eastern Europe]. One gets accustomed to fear. It is now the third generation that is living in these conditions, people who are not active politically and who feel there is no hope."[31]

On the other hand, however true this was during more than forty years of communism, one should not forget the various signs of social awakening in the late 1980s. Gorbachev's policy of *glasnost*, though introduced only slowly and reluctantly in Bulgaria, had some effects. "People have started talking openly about judicial errors, about poor work by the investigators, militia officials, public prosecutors, and judges, and about unjust legal edicts," an article in *Anteni* noted in 1989.[32] Glasnost opened up the possibility of change, and belief in the possibility of change is, after all, a precondition for organization to promote change. Democracy, a vain illusion as late as 1986, started to beckon by 1989. This erupted to the surface on 3 November when 4,000–9,000 Bulgarian citizens took to the streets of Sofia to demand democratic reforms. For forty minutes, they chanted "Democracy!" and "Glasnost!" in what was the first large prodemocracy rally in Bulgaria since World War II.[33]

But if democratization proceeds at a slower pace in Bulgaria, will it reach the same result? The answer to this question is not yet clear.

But Bulgaria is not just a "slow version" of Poland. Its political culture has a content of its own. "It is different here," a Bulgarian educator explained in November 1989. "In other countries, they have political traditions. We don't really."[34] Hence the absence of a concept of civil society. Bulgarian passivity is legendary. "People are not used to having anything to do with party and Government affairs," a member of the Eco-Glasnost movement noted.[35] Accordingly, change has come more slowly to Bulgaria, in part because its society has been weak—and it remains weaker than most other societies in the region—and in part because of its political culture, which is itself a factor in the strength or weakness of a society. But if weakness has retarded political change in the past, the strengthening of society opens up possibilities of change, including those in the direction of democratization. Weak societies are not condemned to remain weak forever.

13. Strong Societies: Hungary, Poland, and Yugoslavia

In 1956, in the wake of Khrushchev's famous "secret speech," Hungary and Poland revolted against Stalinism and demanded the restoration of authentic leaders—Imre Nagy and Władysław Gomułka. Thirty-three years later, these same two countries were again stirring. The Hungarian communist party renamed itself a *socialist* party and pledged itself to introduce a genuine multiparty system. The Polish communist party was forced to legalize Solidarity and to accept a Solidarity member as prime minister. This consistency may be attributed to the *strength* of these societies, as defined in the preceding chapter.

The Yugoslav situation was rather different. Viewed as a whole, Yugoslav society showed many signs of strength. But taken in its regional parts, it is clear that the diverse ethnic publics that made up this multi-ethnic state were quite distinct. The Slovenian, Croatian, and Serbian publics are organized and articulate, and in the course of the 1980s developed independent communication networks that by-passed and made use of official networks. The Albanian population of Kosovo is mobilized, but on a number of measures Kosovar society remains weaker than Slovenian or Croatian society. In Slovenia, Croatia, and Serbia, independent associations for the protection of human rights and artistic freedom, environmental concerns, feminism, gay rights, and peace were set up in the early 1980s, and a number of new fledgling political parties arose by 1989. In Macedonia, Montenegro, and Bosnia alternative politics is of much more recent vintage, and basically dates from about 1988. In Kosovo the only independent initiatives which were undertaken until late 1989 and early 1990 were linked with local Albanians' striving for self-determination. Since then, however, several other associations have been set up, including the local Social Democratic Party. The Kosovo associations are described in chapter 8.

The relative ethnic homogeneity of Hungary and Poland have also been a source of strength, insofar as the sense of crisis has served to bring these nations together. In Yugoslavia, by contrast, the deepening crisis drove the composite nationality groups apart, and increased distrust particularly between Serbs and Croats, Serbs and Albanians, and Serbs and Slovenes.

Across the five measures of societal strength outlined in the preceding chapter, Hungary, Poland, and Yugoslavia rank high. When it comes to *information* (the first measure), the Yugoslav press, in particular, had long been lively and informative, and had often presented opposing sides of controversial questions. But the Polish and Hungarian presses had also been informative, albeit sporadically—the former especially during the crisis of 1980–81 and later, after about 1984 or 1985, when the Jaruzelski government concluded that it needed to compete with the samizdat publications circulating in Poland. By contrast, the East German, Czechoslovak, Romanian, Bulgarian, and Albanian communist presses were always remarkably dry, uninformative, and propagandistic.

In terms of published statistical material, Hungarian data ranked in the communist era as the best in the region, followed closely by Poland and East Germany.[1] Polish sociology is ranked among the best worldwide, and both Hungary and Yugoslavia produced some excellent sociological studies.

The educational revolution of the postwar era is directly relevant to the question of information available to the broad public. In postwar Eastern Europe there was a big push to expand educational opportunities. In Poland alone the number of university graduates increased from 80,000 in 1945 to more than a million in 1980. Among those employed in the state sector, the proportion of those with either secondary school or university education rose from 24.2 percent in 1945 to 75 percent in 1986. The working class is also better educated: in 1958 only 10.5 percent of Polish workers had more than a primary school education; by 1986 almost 50 percent of workers had secondary school diplomas.[2]

In terms of the *ability to organize* (the second measure of a strong society) Polish society has consistently rated high, but especially in the years after 1980 when an underground "independent society" was in essence constructed from the grass roots. In Yugoslavia, by contrast, the growth of independent society in the 1980s was completely in the open and, for the most part, legal. In Slovenia independent associations often obtained legal protection by registering as "activities" of the Socialist Alliance of Working People of Slovenia (SAWP-Slovenia) or of the League of Socialist Youth—a convenient legal fiction which did not compromise their independence in the least. In Croatia the local SAWP organization played a similar role, while in Serbia the Serbian Association of Writers and the Serbian Academy of Sciences and Art took some of these independent associations under their wings.[3] And in Hungary independent society was a sporadic affair until the mid-1980s, but in late 1988 the regime threw the doors open, stimulating the headlong repluralization of Hungarian society.

The role of the intellectuals (measure 3) has been more diverse. Only in Poland and, in a certain way, Yugoslavia can one really speak of the "defection" of a part of the intelligentsia, although the Praxis group in Yugoslavia, along with alienated nationalist and democratic-minded intellectuals in Slovenia, Croatia, and Serbia, certainly provided a source of rival intellectual energy. One need only think of the role played by Serbian novelist Dobrica Ćosić to appreciate how Yugoslav intellectuals challenged the ruling elite to rethink the premises of its policies and even contributed to redefining the premises of political action.

Communication networks (measure 4) were available to alternative ideas, especially in Poland and Yugoslavia. In both countries the secular media were open even before 1989 to alternative ideas: in Yugoslavia, for example, the Zagreb magazine *Start* and the Ljubljana magazine *Mladina* became renowned as forums for alternative and even dissident ideas. Again, in both countries, the press of the Catholic church offered itself as an arena for the articulation of alternative ideas (although this did not apply to Hungary). And in both Poland and Hungary a number of underground publications were in circulation by the mid-1980s.

Finally, in terms of the *mobilization of the public* (measure 5), the growth of independent associations was directly correlated with this phenomenon, to the extent that one may speak of an awakening of civic consciousness in these societies in the 1980s. The development of an independent society and of independent networks linked to Solidarity gave the Polish opposition a unity and an ability to mobilize the public that could not be compared with anything elsewhere in the region. But in each case, mobilization was to some extent spontaneous.

This brief introduction has already suggested that in many ways Polish and Yugoslav society seemed "stronger" than Hungarian society, at least up to 1988. And yet it was Hungary that, between late 1988 and late 1989, underwent the most radical change. The question is: why Hungary?

Hungary: Toward a Multiparty System

In retrospect, it appears that the critical months for the transformation of the Hungarian political landscape were from November 1988 to April

1989. It was during those months that the Hungarian Council of Ministers approved new laws that allowed the establishment of independent political parties and trade unions, that the Soviets sent repeated overt signals that they would not interfere to obstruct Hungary's evolution toward political pluralism, and that the Hungarian party ousted four conservative leaders from the Politburo: chief ideologist János Berecz, senior administrator János Lukács, Minister of Health Judit Csehak, and agricultural specialist István Szábo.

Pressure for transformation came from many sides: from the ultimate failure of the economy; from pent-up aspirations for democracy stimulated by Gorbachev's reforms to the east; from the withering away of the semilegitimacy once enjoyed by János Kádár and the failure of his successor, Károly Grósz, to win the trust of the population; and from a gathering sense that change was in the air, a sense that infected ever greater numbers of people until change became inevitable.

The transformative crisis can be dated to October 1986, when Kádár publicly admitted that living standards were declining and that the reason lay in the party's failure to implement appropriate economic reforms in the 1970s. Aware that the situation was becoming volatile, Kádár tried in March 1988 to regain control of the situation by expelling four of the most popular liberals from the party, including liberal economist László Lengyel, writer Zoltán Biro (a founder of the Democratic Forum), and Zoltán Király, a parliamentary deputy "who became famous for demanding to know, at a session of Parliament, what the forty billion forint expenditure in the budget marked 'miscellaneous' was—the only larger item in the budget was the deficit—and no one could explain it to him."[4] Kádár hoped to undermine the reform wing in the party and put Imre Pozsgay on the defensive. Instead, the move provoked a reaction: at the party conference in May 1988 Kádár and most of his closest associates were removed from the Politburo, while Pozsgay and Rezsö Nyers, a liberal economist closely identified with the economic reform of 1968, were promoted to the Politburo.

Nyers, a founding member of the New March Front, had spelled out his views on democracy in a 1986 article for *Acta Oeconomica*. In his view, the problem of economic inefficiency is organically linked to the curbing of democracy; hence, economic revitalization presumes democratic reform.

I am of the opinion that, in the course of the development of socialism, it is impossible to lastingly curb the development of democracy, since otherwise the necessity of later political reforms would become so urgent that only the elimination of restrictions could bring a solution. . . . It should be obvious that the achievements of bourgeois democracy cannot be refused in their entirety, since certain parts of it are products of the development of humanity and do not merely serve the bourgeois class.[5]

In the course of 1988 two parallel developments created great pressure on the party to accept systemic change. The first was the rapid formation of new independent associations (detailed in chapter 5). The second was the proliferation of mass demonstrations. The first demonstration took place on 5 February, when five hundred people gathered in front of the Romanian embassy to protest Romania's treatment of its Hungarian minority. A month later, on 15 March, a large demonstration commemorated the 1848 uprising. Demonstrators shouted "Democracy!"; it was the only demand. On 17 June there was yet another demonstration, this time in honor of Imre Nagy; unlike the others this demonstration was violently dispersed by police. But just ten days later, 50,000–100,000 people turned out in response to appeals from twelve independent associations to protest President Nicolae Ceauşescu's program of eradicating village life in Romania.

By May the central committee of the Hungarian Socialist Workers' Party (HSWP) was reviewing opposition demands for legal guarantees of freedom of assembly and association. In mid-July the central committee unanimously approved a proposal to authorize the National Assembly to draft appropriate legislation, but Politburo member and CC Secretary János Berecz cautioned that the proposed guarantees would be within the framework of the one-party system and that any modification of the party's monopoly would have to await passage of a new constitution.

Until November it was by no means certain that party liberals would triumph over party conservatives, or that this proposed legislation on freedom of assembly would really move Hungary much closer to political pluralism. Grósz, a middle-of-the-roader, was threatened not merely by liberals like Pozsgay and Nyers, but also by a conservative faction led by Berecz, the chief ideologist. Berecz's strategy was to limit the new legislation, hold fast to the principle of democratic centralism in party life, and infiltrate new groups such as the Hungarian Democratic Forum so that reliable communists could influence them from within.[6]

Ultimately the conservatives proved too weak to hold back the tide, and on 10 November 1988 the Hungarian Council of Ministers adopted revised draft laws on the rights of assembly and association which extended broad guarantees for the formation of political parties, trade unions, mass movements, interest groups, and other organizations. Nyers commented that the legislation provided a basis for the development of "a *natural* political system" in Hungary.[7] Subsequently, on 15 December the HSWP committed itself to the introduction of a multiparty system and promised that independent parties would be able to contest the parliamentary elections in 1990.[8]

It is important to understand that these concessions came as a response to political pressure from below, and that without such pressure, political pluralization would not have been on the agenda in the first place. This is suggested by the party's hesitations and doubts as it contemplated the possibility of being voted out of power and devised stratagems to avoid that result. One such strategem was a proposal by Zoltán Király under which new political parties would have to recognize the leading role of the HSWP within the framework of a parliamentary system, accept Hungary's membership in the Warsaw Pact, and agree to the retention of some form of socialism as preconditions for legalization.[9] This formula for a "limited multiparty system" seemed in part reminiscent of the Mexican system, and was based on the assumption that the new parties would enter into a coalition with the HSWP. The entire formula was a case of too little too late.

About this time, Mátyás Szuros, a central committee secretary of the HSWP, commented that the question of political pluralism would be decided by society itself, not by the party.[10] This was already clear enough, and events continued to bear this out. To begin with, independent political parties continued to grow. By January 1989 the Hungarian Democratic Forum numbered 10,000 members; the Federation of Young Democrats (FIDESZ) could claim 2,500 members; the relatively young Ferenc Munnich Society, which advocated communist orthodoxy, almost 6,000 members; the Social Democratic Youth Circle, then barely six weeks old, had a hundred members; and the Independent Smallholders Party, which resumed activity on 18 November 1988, had three thousand members (22,000 by November 1989). The Federation of Free Democrats founded in November 1988 did not report membership figures, but had succeeded in organizing five rural branches and two urban branches by January 1989.[11] Meanwhile, a series of independent trade unions and professional organizations were set up, including the Democratic Trade Union of Teachers, the Democratic Trade Union of Scientific Workers, and the Federation of Young Professionals. And in January 1989 Inform Studio Ltd., a private company launched on 2 January with a starting capital stock of F7.2 million, announced that it would publish the independent political weekly *Jelenlet* (*Presence*) from Debrecen beginning

in March. Later, in February, in a telling move, the Union of Metallurgi-
cal Workers, Hungary's largest union, set up a strike fund estimated at
about F4 million ($72,000).[12]

Subsequently, several more independent parties were established, including the Social Democratic Party (which claimed 10,000 members at
the time of its founding in February 1989, and 12,000 just two months
later), the Christian Democratic People's Party (suppressed in 1947 and
revived in April 1989 with more than 28,000 members), and the Hungarian Independence Party (which quickly launched the newspaper *El-
lenzek* (*Opposition*) to convey its views).[13]

According to some observers, the strongest of these opposition parties
seemed to be the Social Democratic Party (SDP); certainly its membership was the largest. Yet Mihály Bihari, the executive secretary-general
of the SDP, cautioned that much organizational work still needed to
be done. An interview he gave to the "168 hours" radio show is worth
quoting:

> In my opinion, today in Hungary there is not one party which can
> be taken really seriously. The developing parties are not yet parties.
> They are just in the process of adopting their election programs,
> their members are just getting organized, and their organizational
> frameworks are [still] being formed. However, within a year, of these
> developing parties, four or five can grow into being a very serious
> and strong political factor.

Where the HSWP (Hungarian initials, MSZMP) was concerned, Bihari saw
the seeds of internal crisis sown into the very fabric of party life:

> Of course, what is more mysterious is whether the MSZMP is a party.
> To my mind the MSZMP is an etatist public power, a static public
> power which does not carry out a party-type function. Its activity
> does not have a party character, and it does not politicize in a party-
> like manner, because, for example, it does not consult even with
> its own members about extraordinarily important political ques-
> tions like the transition to a multiparty system, the problems and
> questions of constitutional processes, or how it relates to the other
> developing alternative organizations. The fact is that it does not
> politicize with its own membership.[14]

István Csurka, a leading member of the Hungarian Democratic Forum,
spelled out the implications of this political crisis for the opposition in
an interview with *Magyar Nemzet*. The present task, he argued, was to

convince the HSWP that it had to compromise with the opposition and at the same time to prepare society to demand compromise.[15]

In mid-February 1989 the party daily *Nepszabadsag* published a lengthy "draft position" of the central committee regarding the political system. Significantly, the draft conceded that a crisis had emerged in Hungary over the previous fifteen years, admitted shortcomings in the prevailing system, and promised to cooperate in the transition to a multiparty system on the condition that the HSWP continue to play a decisive role during the transition period.[16]

Throughout this period the HSWP was nervously watching for signs of disapproval from the Kremlin. Hence, when Gorbachev declared in a public speech in mid-February that the introduction of a multiparty system in the Soviet Union would be "politically and theoretically unsound," Hungarian liberals jumped.[17] But the remark was not aimed at the Hungarians. On the contrary, at about the same time Soviet academician Oleg Bogomolov reassured Hungarian politicians that a putative Hungarian evolution along the lines of an Austrian or a Swedish model would not threaten Soviet security interests. In his words, "It is up to the Hungarian people to decide what version of internal and external politics they consider suitable. And the possibilities do not have to be worked out by us in Moscow either, but by you, in Hungary."[18] Two weeks later, when Hungarian Prime Minister Miklós Németh visited Moscow, Soviet Premier N. I. Ryzhkov confirmed this, telling Németh that the Soviet leadership accepted the principle that "each people has its own specific characteristics, and each one determines its own path of socialist construction and its forms and methods."[19] Later that month, when General Secretary Grósz traveled to Moscow, he met with Gorbachev and was assured that the USSR had no intention of interfering in Hungarian political decisions.[20]

By February all the major political organizations in Hungary were confronting internal chaos. In the HSWP, some local party organizations defiantly rejected the fresh winds from Budapest and instead clung rigidly to the old organizational rules, while other party organizations disregarded the rules altogether, as if democratic centralism had already been abandoned. Meanwhile, the SDP suffered from so much internal discord that its secretary-general Mihály Bihari, announced that he was leaving the party because of differences with the party chairman, András Revesz. The Independent Smallholders Party was troubled by disagreements between the old guard who had been in the original Smallholders Party and newer, younger recruits. This generational conflict had become inevitable as soon as eighty-six-year-old Tíbor Partay, party chairman, named his six-member politburo—the average age was eighty-four! Even the Democratic Forum seemed to have some difficulties, centering chiefly on a personality conflict between two prominent leaders—Zoltán Biro and Sándor Csoori—and on signs that the party's membership was far more radical than its leadership.

The problem was particularly acute within the HSWP: by April liberal reformer Pozsgay was threatening to split the party in two, setting up a rival, more liberal communist party to challenge the older, more ortho-dox one.[21] The liberals captured the day, however, causing the inevitable split in the other direction when a group of hard-line communists led by forty-three-year-old filmmaker Roland Antoniewicz set up a rival organization which they chose to call the János Kádár Society. In October 1989 Antoniewicz demanded the resignation of the government, the establishment of a true "revolutionary worker and peasant government," and the surrender of all party property to the János Kádár Society. Maria Kádár, widow of János Kádár, issued a statement to the effect that she was "appalled" that her husband's name was being used by a group with goals so much at variance with those of her late husband.[22]

Until April 1989 the ruling party continued to lay great stress on the preservation of socialism, and any endorsement of multiparty democ-racy was always within the context of the maintenance of a socialist order. In April, however, Foreign Minister Gyula Horn said that the party recognized no difference between "bourgeois and socialist crite-ria for democracy and human rights" and that the leadership wanted to adopt a system of government in the West European tradition.[23]

One of the cardinal principles of any communist party was a ban on the formation of factions. That ban notwithstanding, liberal reformers within the party put together a factional grouping in April 1989, call-ing it the Eger Reform Circle of the HSWP. Imre Pozsgay took part in its founding session.[24] The following month, in an unusual departure from customary practice, the party daily *Nepszabadsag* gave space to Grósz's liberal critics, who accused him of presenting his personal views in an interview as those of the party.[25]

A public opinion poll conducted in April 1989 showed a dramatic de-cline in confidence in the party since 1985. In 1985, 66 percent of the re-spondents believed the HSWP was concerned about and represented their interests; in 1989 the figure was 24 percent. In 1985, 70 percent of respon-dents expressed confidence in the National Assembly; in 1989 the figure was 44 percent. And if free elections had been held then and there, respondents in April 1989 indicated the following party preferences: HSWP, 36.0 percent; SDP, 13.0 percent; Democratic Forum, 11.4 percent; Association of Free Democrats, 5.6 percent; Independent Smallholders Party, 5.4 percent; and Christian Democratic Party, 4.4 percent.[26]

Democratization could not, of course, be achieved without free access to the media or without openness about the past. Both of these areas were confronted in spring 1989. A party plenum on 29 March proved the occasion for an intense discussion of new legislation to govern the media, since all concerned recognized that a genuine multiparty system was impossible as long as one party monopolized the media. Under the "blueprint" adopted by the party on that occasion, any Hungarian citizen was entitled to establish a newspaper or commercial radio or TV station, to own or use printing equipment, and to distribute the material printed. In addition, increased amounts of foreign capital were to be allowed to fund joint ventures in the media. Some examples of joint media ventures include the successful newspaper *Reform*, and the prominent daily *Magyar Hírlap*, long the official organ of the Hungarian government, which was purchased by a group of private British investors (including Robert Maxwell) in February 1990. Three weeks earlier, Maxwell's rival, Robert Murdoch, invested $4 million to buy half-shares in two new Hungarian tabloids.[27]

Openness about the past meant, above all, openness about the Hungarian Revolution of 1956 and the rehabilitation of Prime Minister Imre Nagy, whom the Soviets had executed in 1958. Hungarian society had never accepted the official propaganda that Nagy was a counterrevolutionary or that the United States was heavily involved in the events of 1956, and on 6 October 1988 some three hundred demonstrators gathered in downtown Budapest to demand the political rehabilitation of Nagy.[28] In September a member of the Hungarian Politburo had proposed that a monument be erected to Nagy.[29] Meanwhile, Pozsgay started referring to the events of 1956 as a "popular uprising," rather than a "counterrevolution" as prescribed by official parlance.[30] In early February 1989 the central committee convened a special session to review differences betwen Grósz and Pozsgay, and agreed on a compromise formula on 1956, declaring that it was both a popular uprising and a counterrevolution, and conceding for the first time that it had had positive aspects.[31]

In early May 1989 Radio Budapest rebroadcast Imre Nagy's speech of 4 November 1956, in which the prime minister announced the Soviet invasion of Hungary. The broadcast broke a taboo of more than three decades.[32] Before the month was out, the party had decided on the full rehabilitation of Nagy and had conceded that his execution had been illegal. Finally, on 16 June, thirty-one years after his execution by the Soviets, Imre Nagy was given a state funeral with full honors.

The new openness also affected relations with the church. The old State Office for Church Affairs, long headed by Imre Miklós, was closed down and replaced on 1 July by the new Secretariat for Church Policy headed by Barna Sarkadi Nagy. The secretariat's task was the "coordination" of relations between church and state.[33] The 1950 ban on religious orders was subsequently lifted, and two independent religious associations were set up: an independent Catholic priests' association called Cultores Pacis, and an independent ecumenical association of Christian academics and intellectuals known as the Christian Ecumenical Fraternity. The judgment against Cardinal Mindszenty was revoked and, in a significant move, the party decided in July 1989 that henceforth it would not discriminate against believers, who would in fact be allowed to join the party.[34]

Meanwhile, the party began to restructure itself, eliminating the Central Control Committee and replacing it with coordinative bodies.[35] The party also created a new four-member presidium to head the party provisionally until the party congress scheduled for 7 October: the presidium consisted of Grósz, Nyers, Pozsgay, and Prime Minister Miklós Németh. Unexpectedly, Nyers was named president of the presidium; Pozsgay was nominated for the state presidency.

Two more parties were established in June: the Organization for a Democratic Hungary (with Pozsgay attending its inaugural meeting), and the Hungarian People's Party, which viewed itself as a reincarnation of the National Peasant Party of the 1940s and which immediately pledged itself to work for wide-ranging autonomy for villages. In August 1989 it was announced that a Hungarian Health Party had been formed with the aims of promoting good health and mood, and protecting the family. The Health Party also vowed to work for Hungary's independence and for the "settlement" of the status of Transylvania, possibly in the framework of a federal union with Hungary.[36] Initially, the HSWP hoped that the fragmentation of the opposition would work in its favor; but in three of four special local elections held in late July 1989, opposition forces outpolled communist candidates. In Gödöllő, twenty miles northeast of Budapest, the HSWP candidate obtained only 29.9 percent of the vote, losing to an alliance led by the Hungarian Democratic Forum, whose candidate secured 69.2 percent. In Szeged the Forum's candidate won 59.4 percent of the vote, against a 39 percent vote for the Patriotic People's Front. And in Kecskemét the Forum polled 47.3 percent, against 22.2 percent for the communist candidate.[37] The opposition won additional parliamentary seats in by-elections held in August.

By July the HSWP had legalized strikes, adopted a program to encourage private agriculture, allowed Radio Free Europe to open an office in Budapest, and significantly increased political and economic contacts with the United States. The old Communist Youth Union was renamed the Democratic Youth Federation, although this stirred hard-line communists into creating their own youth organization under the old name.[38] In mid-August the HSWP published a draft program pledging to work for Hungary's transformation into a democratic socialist system and its own transformation into a Western-style socialist party; the program also accepted the principle of the market economy.[39]

On 7 October 1989, in a highly symbolic and portentous move, the HSWP renamed itself the Hungarian Socialist Party and adopted structural changes corresponding to the name change; Nyers was elected chairman of the party, and Grósz went into retirement. The party's 720,000 members were informed that they would have to apply if they wished to join the redesignated organization. A month later, only 30,000 people had bothered to do so, making the "Socialist" Party only slightly larger than the second largest party, the Christian Democrats, who claimed 28,000 members.[40] At first the party resisted pressure to disband its cells in the workplace and in the paramilitary Workers' Militia. The party gave way within a matter of days, however, when the parliament passed the new Law on Association, formally legalizing the opposition political parties and requiring the now-renamed Socialist Party to disband its cells in workplaces and offices by at least ninety days prior to the 1990 elections, and cells in the armed forces by the end of 1991. The Hungarian People's Republic was now renamed the Republic of Hungary, which, according to the amended constitution, is said to be based on "the values of both bourgeois democracy and democratic socialism."[41]

The proclamation of the new republic was timed for 23 October to coincide with the thirty-third anniversary of the 1956 uprising against Soviet domination. Some 100,000 Hungarians flooded the square around the parliament to listen to emotional speeches from veterans of 1956, waving flags and lighting candles as evening set.

Poland: Solidarity Inherits Power

In late 1988 Lech Wałęsa, leader of the still illegal Solidarity trade union, dreamed of wresting power from the communists "in ten years." Six months later he was asked to name a prime minister for Poland from the ranks of Solidarity. History, Wałęsa discovered, has an energy and momentum of its own, independent even of its prime movers.

Poland's communists ultimately agreed to negotiate with Solidarity about the nation's future. They did so because they had no other choice; the political situation had so seriously deteriorated by late 1988 that it could be characterized as "revolutionary."

The strategy of the opposition from the 1970s on had been to work for the creation of an open, democratic society, rather than trying first to democratize the state; democratization would be created from the grass roots, rather than from the top down (as had been attempted, for example, in Czechoslovakia in 1968). By 1988 the creation of an independent civil society was a reality. In the area of environmental protection alone, there were more than 2,000 independent voluntary associations. In Warsaw, Kraków, Gdańsk, and Wrocław, citizens tried to establish private, officially recognized schools. In the course of 1988 alone, two hundred private associations were registered.[42] Many more functioned in legal limbo. Solidarity itself, whose local networks had atrophied, began to rebuild its local committees. Solidarity activists began to revive union activities in many enterprises—for example, at the Wisla shipyard in Gdańsk and the automotive factory in Lublin, where workers established founding committees and petitioned the courts for official registration.[43] And in December 1988 Wałęsa convened a meeting of 128 prominent intellectuals, artists, and union activists to create the Solidarity Civic Committee, which established a series of subcommissions to collect information on, among other things, political reforms, union pluralism, law and justice, agriculture, housing, health, culture and the media, the environment, and youth affairs.[44]

There were also repeated instances of spontaneous demonstrations and strikes (and it is worth recalling that neither the April nor the August strikes had been called by Solidarity). On 11 November, for example, independent demonstrations took place in Warsaw, Kraków, Gdańsk, Wrocław, Poznań, Katowice, Tarnów, Lublin, Łódź, Puławy, Rzeszów, Białystok, Bydgoszcz, and Gorzów Wielkopolski; 15,000 people demonstrated in Warsaw alone. At the same time, instances of police brutality were "rapidly multiplying." The Solidarity Commission for Intervention and Legality, headed by Zbigniew Romaszewski, issued a bulletin on 11 November in which it was noted:

In the period from 13 August until 7 November, 49 persons fell victim to brutal mistreatment. It affected primarily young people: out of 49 detained students, 18 were beaten; out of 40 high schoolers—

14. It must be emphasized that their mistreatment had nothing to do with police activities designed to keep order during demonstrations or open festivities, but constituted deliberate acts of cruelty to detained persons.

Such incidents as humiliation, punching of faces, hitting with truncheons, kicking or even refined beating of the heels, [the] kidneys, or the genitals, were taking place in vehicles and on the premises of the ministry of internal affairs. In numerous cases, the perpetrators were drunk members of the riot police. As in the cases of . . . Andrzej Gusztyla and Robert Krzywulicz from Gdańsk, so in many other ones, mistreatment resulted in long hospitalization periods. Four victims still remain hospitalized.

The celebrations of the National Independence Day on 11 November produced new victims. In Katowice, 63 persons suffered bodily harm. In Poznań, where 9 persons were mistreated, it was the city councilman Michal Downarowicz who, while trying to mediate the conflict, fell victim to particularly vicious brutality being beaten for over an hour inside a police vehicle. He suffered [a] concussion and a broken nose and jaw.[45]

Among the public broadly, there was growing impatience with the government. Moreover, public opinion polls conducted by the official Center for the Study of Public Opinion found that the overwhelming majority of citizens wanted freedom of association and speech, an end to the party's monopoly of power, and drastic changes to the nomenklatura system under which the party had controlled appointments to responsible positions in every sector of public life.[46] "Our situation is like just before the French Revolution," dissident intellectual Adam Michnik warned in November 1988. "I am against the guillotine and the death penalty, but this government will also be driven out of power by an explosion."[47] Bogdan Lis, a major Solidarity leader, expressed the same sentiments in July 1988: "I can't predict when the explosion will come, but all the ingredients are present."[48]

The Polish and Soviet authorities discussed the situation in bilateral talks, and in September 1988 the Soviets declared publicly that they had no objection to a relegalization of Solidarity.[49] Soviet concurrence was surely a precondition for Polish authorities to proceed, although it cannot be said that Polish authorities nurtured particularly tender feelings for the Solidarity activists whom they had persecuted for seven years.

The idea for talks between the government and Solidarity first emerged in an unusual way. General Czesław Kiszczak, minister of the interior, summoned Wałęsa to a meeting in a small government villa in Magdalenka, a Warsaw suburb, on 31 August. The general told Wałęsa that if he could persuade striking workers to go back to work, the government would agree to discuss the relegalization of Solidarity. If Wałęsa succeeded, the government would obtain some breathing space on the economic front; if he failed, his credibility would be permanently impaired. "Minutes after the meeting ended, Kiszczak confided to a Polish magazine editor that he had tendered the offer because he was convinced Wałęsa would not be able to sway the strikers."[50] Instead, Wałęsa was able to persuade, cajole, harangue, and convince the striking workers to return to work. This paved the way for talks.

But the government now raised repeated objections. First, the authorities demanded of Solidarity a declaration of loyalty to the political system. Then they demanded that the union sever all links with trade unions and other institutions abroad. And finally, they objected to the inclusion of human rights activists Michnik and Jacek Kuroń among Solidarity's negotiating team. Solidarity refused to concede anything on these points.[51] In October a document surfaced, which was alleged to be a secret directive to local party cells; the document described Solidarity as a "major threat" to the party's rule and said that Solidarity had to be combatted by all means available, and that any agreements signed with Solidarity should be considered invalid in advance. Wałęsa chose to dismiss the document as a spurious provocation—though not without warning the authorities lest it be authentic—and the party immediately distanced itself from the document.[52]

Finally, after a series of preliminary meetings, the two sides agreed to start formal roundtable talks on 6 February 1989 and organized separate working groups to discuss economic reform, political reform, and trade union pluralism. Solidarity spokespersons were open about their goal to democratize Poland and understood that the realization of such an objective required that key levers of control be restructured. Solidarity adviser Bronisław Geremek outlined the union's strategy in an interview with an Italian newspaper. To set in motion what he called the "locomotives of change," it was necessary to guarantee the independence of the judiciary, freedom of association, the right to establish independent media, and the autonomy of local authorities.[53]

When the government and Solidarity finally reached an agreement on 5 April, much of Solidarity's program was in fact realized. Specifically, the agreement relegalized Solidarity and Rural Solidarity, liberalized provisions for establishing independent associations and political clubs, granted Solidarity permission to publish a daily newspaper with a circulation of 500,000 (the party weekly *Polityka* only had a circulation of 400,000) and pledged that local government would enjoy greater autonomy than in the past. The agreement restored the upper house (senate) of parliament, with 100 members to be elected in free and open elections, and granted Solidarity 35 percent of the 460 seats in the lower house (Sejm). The agreement also established the new office of president of the republic. On the other hand, a government offer to end all censorship was firmly rejected as premature by Solidarity's negotiating team. "We realized that we needed preventive censorship to protect ourselves," explained Krzysztof Kozlowski, a Solidarity negotiator. "We don't have an independent judiciary like you in the West. Our authorities could just decide they don't like what we write, indict us for liberalism [or apply charges under the vague provision of violating state security], confiscate our newspaper, and destroy us financially."[54]

Elections to the parliament were scheduled for 4 June, and a noisy campaign was soon got under way. The party daily *Trybuna Ludu* ran a series of attacks on Solidarity, accusing it of trying to overthrow communism. Simultaneously, the government intervened at one point to cancel Solidarity's weekly television campaign program. The courts also refused to legalize the union's student movement, which Solidarity spokespersons claimed was inconsistent with the accords. Solidarity also alleged that the communists were playing "dirty tricks" in the campaign. When election day arrived, voters were handed at least four separate ballots, but not a single candidate was identified by political affiliation. Despite all these difficulties, Solidarity won a resounding victory, capturing 92 of the 100 Senate seats outright, along with 160 of the 161 seats it was allowed to contest in the Sejm. On the average, its candidates won with comfortable margins of 70–80 percent. By contrast, the communist party did not win a single seat, even where its candidates ran unopposed; to win their seats, they needed to obtain at least 50 percent of the vote, and many received only 10 percent or less. Two weeks later, in runoff elections, Solidarity captured seven more seats in the Senate, winning 99 of the 100 seats in that chamber; the one exception was an independent self-made millionaire named Henryk Stoklosa, who spent Zl.20 million (or 200 times what the average Pole earns in a month) to finance his campaign. Shortly thereafter, Wojciech Jaruzelski won confirmation as president of the republic, with the parliamentary vote at 270 in favor, 233 against, and 34 abstentions—the bare minimum he needed. Jaruzelski resigned as party general secretary, a position now taken by Mieczysław Rakowski, one-time editor of *Polityka* and heretofore prime minister.

Although Solidarity won a clear mandate in the elections, Jaruzelski initially declined to offer the prime ministership to Solidarity, arguing that the USSR, East Germany, and Czechoslovakia "would look at this askance."[55] Instead, he asked General Kiszczak to form a government. For his own part, Wałęsa repeatedly underlined Solidarity's preference to remain in opposition, even when Kiszczak proposed a "grand coalition" in which Solidarity would participate.

But Kiszczak, Wałęsa's jailer and the man who had once guided the suppression of Solidarity, was an unacceptable choice for prime minister as far as the opposition was concerned. By early August Solidarity was engaged in an effort to lure the United Peasant Party and the Democratic Party away from their traditional alliance with the communist party. By the end of the first week in August, the ice was beginning to crack; first the Peasant Party (76 deputies) and then the Democratic Party (27 deputies) defected. Together with Solidarity's 161 deputies, they now constituted a majority (against the communists' 173 deputies). Moscow issued a statement underlining that it would not tolerate any change in Poland's status in the Warsaw Pact.[56] But when Wałęsa issued a statement promising to respect Poland's alliance commitments and assuring that the communist party could retain control of the ministries of defense and internal affairs, Moscow praised Wałęsa and declared that it was up to the Polish people to solve their own problems.

In mid-August Kiszczak resigned as prime minister, having failed to put together a working coalition. Solidarity was asked to form the government, and submitted three names to Jaruzelski as candidates for the prime ministership. From among those names, Jaruzelski selected sixty-two-year-old Tadeusz Mazowiecki, editor of the Solidarity weekly, to serve as prime minister. Lech Wałęsa declared that the Solidarity-led government would attempt to take Poland "from a communist system of ownership to capitalism. Nobody has previously taken the road that leads from socialism to capitalism. And we are setting out to do just that, to return to the prewar situation, when Poland was a capitalist country."[57] Mazowiecki said of himself, "I'm a Christian, a Catholic, who follows the social teachings of the Catholic church, which emanate from the instructions of Pope John Paul II."[58] The Soviet Council of Ministers promptly sent a note of congratulations to Mazowiecki, promising that "the traditional relations of friendship and all-around cooperation" would continue with the new government.[59] But Mazowiecki called for a new tone in foreign policy: "We want our relations to be dominated by ties between people and between states, rather than offices, enterprises, parties, and so on."[60]

Confirmed by 378 votes (with 41 abstentions and only 4 negative votes), Mazowiecki set up a coalition government in which Solidarity took six portfolios (finance, industry, housing, labor, education, and culture), the United Peasant Party received four portfolios (agriculture, justice, health, and ecology), the Democratic Party received three portfolios (internal trade, technology, and communications), and the communist party received four (internal affairs, defense, transport, and foreign trade).

Throughout this period there were strikes, demonstrations, and other outbreaks of public disorder. For example, there were strikes and demonstrations by students in several cities demanding registration of an independent students' union.[61] Demonstrations occurred in December 1988 on the anniversary of martial law, spontaneous antigovernment demonstrations by young people in Gdańsk in March 1989, sporadic strikes at various enterprises throughout much of 1989, and anti-Soviet demonstrations in Kraków in May and in Poznań in June. Even as the new government of Mazowiecki began its work, the Confederation for an Independent Poland, Fighting Solidarity, and other independent groups staged a big demonstration in Katowice in September, chanting "Soviets go home!"[62] Throughout all of this, Wałęsa appealed for calm and patience.[63]

Yet these disorders probably contributed to the final outcome because they exerted a constant pressure on the communist party, reminding it that society had grown strong and had a mind of its own.

In fact, the political landscape of Poland continued to change at the grassroots level too, as new independent institutions took shape and, in some cases, obtained official registration. In April, for example, an independent Democratic Youth Union was registered in Lublin, while officials granted permission in September for the publication of an independent weekly in Poznań, called *Wielkopolska Gazeta Handlowa.* It was described as "the first private regional weekly published by independent publishers and journalists since the war."[64] In February 1989 the Polish Labor Party, a center-right, Christian democratic organization, was established by a mixed group of former members and new adherents. And in August the National Party revived activity, even as the Green Party convened its first regional meeting in Szklarska Poreba. The communist party's control of the youth movement also came under challenge, as independent scoutmasters became emboldened and set up a Scouts' Union of the Republic based on the original principles of Baden Powell, rather than on communist party principles.

As for the United Peasant Party, it showed its new courage in other ways, passing a motion for the full rehabilitation of Stanisław Mikolajczyk, its early postwar leader and briefly deputy prime minister. The

UPP also raised the issue of reclaiming its earlier name, the Polish Peasant Party.

Meanwhile, as independent society continued to grow, official society atrophied. Most obviously, *Rzeczywistość*, a doctrinaire party weekly set up in May 1981 to attack all manifestations of liberalism both in society and in the party, was shut down on 30 April.

The new government quickly adopted constitutional amendments designed to strengthen rights to own and inherit property, and it outlined a two-phase plan for effecting a transition to a market economy. In the first phase, to be completed by the end of 1989, the government would begin the process of dissolving state ownership of property, breaking up state monopolies, reforming the budget and banking system, setting up a system of unemployment benefits to cushion the inevitable side effects, and increasing the efficiency of state enterprises.[65] In the second phase, to be launched in 1990, the government would reform the tax system, curb inflation, convert many state-owned enterprises into private enterprises, and create a stock and bond market. The Polish government also started to consult with Jeffrey Sachs, a young Harvard economist who urged Warsaw to clamp down on the money supply, eliminate all price and wage controls, free imports and exports, and make the zloty convertible against Western currencies.[66] By late October 1989 the communist party was becoming chagrined at Solidarity's evident rush to dismantle the communist system and issued a statement alleging that the government lacked a popular mandate to carry out such radical measures.[67]

Yugoslavia: A House Divided

The repluralization of Yugoslavia got off to a more promising start in the early 1970s but was stifled by two factors: the Titoist (and post-Titoist) system of institutionalized deadlock and the very considerable regional differences. By one estimate there were some one hundred independent grassroots organizations and ten independent political associations in Slovenia alone in February 1989.[68] But no other republic could duplicate that, and in some republics (in particular, Bosnia-Herzegovina and Macedonia) almost no independent activism occurred until early 1990.

From the beginning of the 1980s a large number of independent activist groups were created in Yugoslavia, mostly in Ljubljana, Belgrade, and Zagreb. By summer 1989, for example, there were independent pacifist and environmentalist groups in Ljubljana, Belgrade, and Zagreb; independent feminist groups in Ljubljana, Belgrade, and Zagreb; independent human rights groups in Ljubljana, Belgrade, and Titograd; the Association for the Advancement of Democratic Processes in Nikšić; the Association of Unemployed in Bijelo Polje; the Committee for the Protection of Artistic Freedom in Belgrade; the Committee for the Defense of Freedom of Thought and Expression in Belgrade; a gay rights movement in Ljubljana; and independent multimedia artistic groups in Ljubljana (*Neue Slowenische Kunst*), Osijek (*Metropolie Trans*), Skopje (*Aporea*), Zagreb (*Novi Evropski Poredak*), and Ruma (*Autopsia*).[69]

Existing institutions also changed and, in the years since Tito's death they increasingly acted in an independent fashion. Most important in this regard were the Serbian and Slovenian Writers' Associations, various media, most especially the youth press (*Mladina* in Ljubljana, *Katedra* in Maribor, *Polet* in Zagreb, *Student* in Belgrade, and *Valter* in Sarajevo), and certain other periodicals, such as the fortnightly magazine *Start*. Radio Student in Ljubljana was, of course, established by the students as their own, independent radio station.

From mid-1988 social pluralization expressed itself also in the formation of embryonic political parties, first in Slovenia, and subsequently in Croatia. The process was ignited by the controversial army trial of Janez Janša, Ivan Borstner, David Tasić, and Franci Zavrl for having published military plans to suppress the movement for democratization in Slovenia. In particular, the article they printed in *Mladina* revealed that General Svetozar Visnjić, a Serb and chief of the Slovenian army district, had met with Slovenia's minister of police, Tomas Ertl, in March 1988 to inform him that the army would soon start arresting people in Slovenia and that they had drawn up a list of two hundred persons to be incarcerated. *Mladina* published these plans in April 1988 and the four were arrested soon after. The trial inflamed the Slovenian public, who turned out in the tens of thousands for big protest meetings in downtown Ljubljana. On 3 June 1988 the Committee for the Protection of Human Rights was created, which circulated petitions on behalf of Janša and his codefendants, gathering more than 100,000 signatures.[70]

If the trial galvanized the Slovenian public, the formation of the Committee for the Protection of Human Rights set off a chain reaction that soon resulted in the creation of the Slovenian Peasant Alliance, the Slovenian Democratic Union, the Social Democratic Alliance, the Transnational Radical Party, the Green Party, the Slovenian Christian Socialist movement, and the laissez-faire oriented Republican Alliance. By summer 1989 there was even a small anarchist club that mysteriously called itself AAAA and talked with outsiders on the basis of complete anonymity.

By December 1987, to be sure, France Tomšić, one of the organizers of the workers' strike at the Litostroj metalworks, had proposed the founding of a social democratic party to a meeting of 1,500 workers.[71] About six months later, Tomšić, Dimitrij Rupel (a professor of sociology at the University of Ljubljana), psychologist Hubert Požarnik, writer Rudi Seligo (president of the Slovenian Writers' Association), and other Ljubljana intellectuals began talking about taking practical action. The original idea was that they form a *single* social democratic party, but a combination of political and personality differences led to a split and the creation of two parties: Tomšić's Social Democratic Alliance, which was the more labor-oriented of the two (2,500–2,600 members as of September 1989), and Rupel's Slovenian Democratic Union, which espoused laissez-faire economics and politics (3,000 members as of September 1989).[72]

The Slovenian Democratic Alliance spelled out its aims in a preliminary program released to the press in January 1989. The alliance pledged to work for a new constitution based on human rights and on Slovenian national sovereignty, and emphasized the necessity of introducing a parliamentary system and an independent judiciary, and of joining the European Economic Community.[73] The linkage of the demands for democratization and for Slovenian sovereignty was not coincidental, but rather reflected the belief that the concept of democracy implies and includes the idea of self-determination of compact nations. This belief became increasingly widespread in Slovenia during 1988 and 1989, and led to the September 1989 passage by the Slovenian Assembly of constitutional amendments that declared that Slovenia had the right to secede from the Yugoslav federation, that only the *Slovenian* Assembly (hence, not the Federal Assembly) had the right to declare a state of emergency in Slovenia, and that the army could not be deployed in Slovenia in peacetime without the consent of the Slovenian Assembly.[74]

The Slovenian Peasant Alliance established in February 1988 grew rapidly, and by September 1989 it had registered 25,000 members in a hundred branches throughout the republic—making it numerically the strongest independent party in Yugoslavia. Encouraged by its example, the Independent Peasant Union was set up in Subotica, Vojvodina, in August 1989.[75] In particular, the Slovenian Peasant Alliance sought to raise the ceiling for the size of private farms from 10 hectares to 30 hectares (and this latter figure was written into the proposed constitutional amendments).

Parallel with this, but entirely independently, members of the Slovenian League of Socialist Youth began to talk about reorganizing themselves as a political party and fielding candidates in the May 1990 parliamentary elections. In the place of a political youth organization, they proposed the creation of a ministry for youth affairs. The youth organization started to meet with the new alternative parties and to be counted as an alternative party itself. Public opinion polls in summer 1989 indicated that the youth organization was potentially the most popular political organization in Slovenia, with especial strength in the urban centers.

The proliferation of alternative parties created pressure on SAWP-Slovenia to adapt. The leadership of SAWP-Slovenia understood that if the process of democratization continued, their old function as a transmission belt of communist party directives would become irrelevant. They had to find a new formula, or face the possibility of organizational extinction. The choice was obvious, and by summer 1989 the leadership of SAWP-Slovenia talked about severing its connection with the communist party and fielding candidates as an independent party. "SAWP-Slovenia does not want to be a transmission belt any longer," one of its leading figures told me in September 1989. "We want to have our own candidates in the upcoming elections, and to run them against the communist party's candidates."[76] The SAWP-Slovenia leadership removed the reference to the vanguard role of the LCY in SAWP from its statute, thus taking a first step in the direction of loosening its relations with the other regional branches of SAWPY.

Similar processes were taking place in Croatia, where in 1989 the Yugoslav Democratic Initiative, the Croatian Social Liberal Alliance, and the Croatian Democratic Community took shape. All of these organizations, like the independent parties in Slovenia aside from the Peasant Alliance, were the creations of intellectuals—in this case, mostly academics associated with the University of Zagreb. Among all of them, only the Yugoslav Democratic Initiative truly looked to the Yugoslav arena; the others aspired to appeal to the Slovenian or Croatian publics only.

The Yugoslav Democratic Initiative was created on 2 February 1989. Unlike some of the other parties, the Initiative refused to register as an "activity" of SAWPY, and this immediately created problems for its registration. Initiative members applied initially for registration in Croatia, Bosnia, Serbia, and Slovenia, claiming a modest 600–700 members in all of Yugoslavia in September 1989.[77] By November the first three republics had turned down the Initiative's application, and it was awaiting a decision only in Slovenia (which was affirmative). Like other independent parties, the Initiative wanted a democratically elected parliament and the creation of a multiparty system.

Although the Initiative clearly looked to Western models for inspiration, the other two Croatian parties were even more firmly grounded in the liberal tradition. The Croatian Social Liberal Alliance was established in May 1989 as a coalition of Croatia-oriented confederalists and more traditional laissez-faire liberals. With about a thousand members in August 1989 (almost all in Croatia), the Croatian Social Liberal Alliance insisted on the necessity of working for the dismantlement of the bureaucratic party apparatus. Operating in a grey zone of semi-illegality, the party leadership described its activities as "semisecret" and its connections in Belgrade and Vojvodina as "private" and "clandestine."[78] In a programmatic declaration issued immediately after its founding, the Social Liberal Alliance described the individual as the "highest value," underlining the need to protect individual rights and liberties from state encroachment. The Social Liberals declared their support for freedom of association, social equality of the sexes, a multiparty parliamentary system, reprivatization and the establishment of a free market economy, and freedom of trade union activity.[79]

Within a month of the founding of the Social Liberal Alliance, the Croatian Democratic Community was set up under the presidency of General Franjo Tudjman, a retired partisan who had been jailed in the early 1980s. The Democratic Community was the most Croatia-oriented of the three and the most enthusiastic in its endorsement of confederalization. Its programmatic declaration emphasized many of the same points stressed by other parties, including guarantees of civil rights without regard to national or religious affiliation or political conviction, the right of association, the sovereignty of the Croatian people including their right of secession, and the necessity of debureaucratization. Among its specific goals, the Democratic Community demanded the revival of Matica hrvatska, the Croatian Literary Society shut down by Tito in December 1971.[80]

The echo in Serbia was fainter, at least partly because the rise of Slobodan Milošević to power in that republic in late 1987 on the basis of a fusion of populism and Serbian nationalism produced an atmosphere not conducive to the establishment of explicitly political independent associations. The outspoken Serbian Writers' Association, however, increasingly functioned as a surrogate alternative party. Its Thursday night seminars became the forum for lively discussions of controversial subjects. Its publication, *Književne novine*, was in the forefront of the movement for democratization but also loudly championed Serbia's rights in Kosovo. In May 1989 the association issued a seven-point appeal for radical changes in Yugoslavia, including the introduction of a multi-party system. In a key passage, the appeal demanded "that people be allowed to exercise their rights in free political associations and to defend their programs through general, secret, and direct elections; in other words, the introduction of a multiparty system with an opposition, without which there can be no true democracy and also no modern socialism."[81] The appeal also drew an unfavorable comparison with Hungary and Poland, claiming that Yugoslavia, "which was the first socialist country to criticize Stalinism and to have liberalized itself, has been passed on that road and is now watching passively while other countries, such as Poland and Hungary, overtake it in political freedom."[82]

The alternative political scene in Yugoslavia was very much a product of three cities—Ljubljana, Zagreb, and Belgrade. What makes this politically significant was the national question, insofar as the parties created in these cities could appeal only to the Slovenian, Croatian, and Serbian publics. Meanwhile, the echoes of alternative politics have been much weaker in the other republics of Yugoslavia. Pressure from below is thus geographically and ethnically defined in Yugoslavia.

Even so, the power of contagion assured that the question of a multiparty system was taken up also within the League of Communists itself, and by the end of 1989 high-ranking members of the Slovenian, Croatian, and Macedonian parties had, on different occasions, suggested that the adoption of a multiparty parliamentary system had become inevitable.[83]

Similarities and Differences

In all three countries similarities are evident. Pressure from below forced the question of a multiparty system onto the political agenda. Problems of political legitimacy forced the ruling party to enter into dialogue with the opposition, while in Poland and Yugoslavia, the partial defection of the intelligentsia fueled alternative politics. Issue-oriented associations were set up independently in recent years, thereby demonstrating the ability of these societies to organize themselves. A consensus gathered that the economic future lay with a free enterprise economy and that some form of reprivatization was essential. Finally, there was a general debunking of the past; this was particularly clear in Hungary, where the failures of the late Kádár era were highlighted, but much less clear in Yugoslavia, where in the late 1980s, for example, Tito was attacked and criticized in Serbia, defended and praised in Croatia, and ignored as irrelevant in Slovenia.

Yet some obvious differences are also apparent among these societies. To begin with, while Hungary and Poland were members of the Warsaw Pact and therefore had to be concerned about Soviet reactions to political changes in their countries, Yugoslavia was never a pact member and therefore did not have to worry in this regard. In Hungary, where there has been no central organizational focus in the opposition, the party seemed for a while to maintain a semblance of control of the process of pluralization by identifying itself with that process. In Poland, Solidarity became the focal point of the opposition, while the party, far less successful than its Hungarian counterpart, reached the point in mid-1989 of having to share power with the opposition. In divided Yugoslavia, Slovenia came the closest to the Hungarian model, Croatia and Serbia were politically mobilized (although not along the lines of either the Hungarian or the Polish model), and Macedonia showed much weaker signs of change in early 1990 and came closer, if anything, to the Bulgarian model. Montenegro was largely dominated by adherents of Serbian party chief Slobodan Milošević, while Bosnia remained so internally divided between Serbs, Croats, and Muslims that serious alternative politics remained, at least for the time being, impossible.

14. Dominoes: East Germany, Czechoslovakia, and the Future of Europe

When I visited East Germany in the summer of 1988, I was struck by how persistent and consistent the complaints were. One after another, people complained about wanting to travel to the West, about the deteriorating standard of living (hidden behind triumphant-looking but ultimately misleading statistics), and about the low quality of production under socialism ("in West Germany they have the BMW; what do we make—the Trabant!"). The discontent, even disaffection, among East Germans was well known. Their *Sehnsucht* for the West was well known. The fact that East Germans continued to risk their lives to flee to the West was well known. The fact that on 14 March 1989 the Hungarians had signed a UN protocol promising not to force refugees to return home and that they had dismantled the barbed-wire fence along the Austrian border in May 1989 was well known. The fact that East Germans could still travel to Hungary was well known. Less well known was the fact that by 1988 East Germans not only compared their economic system unfavorably with West Germany, but were also starting to look at the Hungarian standard of living with jealousy.[1] The calculus was straightforward: they wanted to leave, they could leave, they *would* leave.

Yet, when tens of thousands of East Germans started to pour into Hungary and from there into Austria and West Germany, and subsequently to scale the West German embassy compounds in East Berlin, Warsaw, and Prague, Western observers were surprised. Not so the Soviets. More than two months before the first East German refugees slipped across the Hungarian-Austrian border in August, the Soviet foreign ministry had reached the conclusion that a serious political crisis in East Germany was inevitable, and the Soviet government let it be known that it had no intention of interfering.[2]

In November, when East German authorities opened the Berlin Wall and even dismantled portions of it, it seemed as if an era had ended. What the future held in store was not, despite endless speculation and plans, fully clear.

The Illusion of Reform and the Reality of Pressure

The dismantlement of the Wall and the attendant changes ushered in quickly in East Germany under the pressure of spontaneous rallies of up to half a million people in Berlin, Leipzig, and other cities amounted to rebellion. But the rallies also signalled the failure of earlier efforts at reform—efforts which had always been premised on the maintenance of the party power monopoly and the preservation of political control of the economy.

Each of the seven communist regimes in the region, all, that is, except Romania, had at one time or another developed major reform packages. In many cases these regimes had subsequently retreated from their earlier reforms—as happened in East Germany in the late 1960s, in Czechoslovakia abruptly since 1969, in Yugoslavia in the cultural and political spheres in the mid and late 1970s, in Hungary (to a degree) in the early 1980s, and in Bulgaria in early 1988. But retreat from reform always faltered on inescapable dilemmas which forced the respective party to confront anew the challenge of "reform." Typically, reform in Eastern Europe encountered several problems. To begin with, "reform" as often as not was designed to deal with the symptoms rather than with the affliction itself. If the problem in the economy is the evanescence of individual initiative, the solution is to take the appropriate measures to restore individual initiative, beginning with the restoration of the free enterprise system. Making prices realistic, calling for belt-tightening, and allowing unprofitable "political factories" to collapse are all measures that deal with the symptoms of economic insolvency and not with its roots. Similarly, to the extent that East European political dissatisfaction centered on the desire for political involvement and responsive local organs, and on deep-seated resentment (everywhere except Yugoslavia and, arguably, Romania) against Soviet domination, maintenance of the party monopoly presented a clear obstacle. Establishing quota systems for the representation of Slovaks, women, workers, and young people did not address these issues, nor did the most prevalent forms of decentralization (with the important exception of the ethnic sphere, where allowing the respective nationalities to run their own republics gave Yugoslavia roughly a decade of peace in interethnic relations [1972–

81]).[3] To the extent that the most pressing problems on the agenda arose out of the nature of the party monopoly, it is evident that "reform" was always designed to ameliorate the problems *within the context of preserving that monopoly*. What was called "reform" could often have been more aptly termed *readjustment*.

Second, reform was usually advocated by one faction of the central leadership in the face of opposition from another faction. This applied to the Khrushchev-Malenkov New Course in the mid-1950s, to the Yugoslav reform debates from 1961 to 1991, to the Czechoslovak experience in the late 1960s and again more recently in the form of Ljubomir Strougal's failed efforts to push for reform in his country, and to Poland in the years 1980–81.

Third, even when advocates of reform were able to obtain official sanction for a comprehensive reform package, it was quite another matter to obtain compliance from middle-level functionaries, who often controlled important levers of power. In Yugoslavia the party leaderships of Serbia, Montenegro, and Kosovo, supported by Vice-President Aleksandar Ranković, sabotaged the implementation of major facets of the reforms of the early 1960s; in the Soviet Union Gorbachev had to deal with serious bureaucratic obstruction, especially in the first two years of his leadership.

These problems were more or less stable features in earlier reform efforts. But the impetus to reform which blossomed in the late 1980s was qualitatively different. First, unlike earlier reform efforts, this one was being coordinated from Moscow and Moscow's sundry allies were nudged into line in a manner for which the only precedent was Khrushchev's deStalinization in the late 1950s. Second, the pressures on the systems of Eastern Europe were now arguably greater and more complex than at earlier reform junctures. And third, the dividing line between reform and revolution became fuzzier in the conditions of 1989: in some ways the two appeared symbiotic. By 1988 it had become common to hear comments such as those made by Czechoslovak economist Valtr Komárek in a 1987 interview: "Socialism, in my view, is on the threshold of crisis. If there is not a total reform, the crisis is inevitable."[4]

Crisis may be produced when change in certain sectors of society outstrips the system's capacity or willingness to adapt. When this occurs, malfunction and inefficiency are inevitable, and in later stages, corruption, chaos, the growth of parallel society, and even collective violence may figure as symptoms of system stress.

In the foregoing chapters, I have traced some of the strands of social change in the East European area. Chapter 1 set forth a theory about democracy and about the process of building democracy after the collapse of an authoritarian system. Chapters 2 and 3 outlined the economic difficulties that fueled social discontent, and assessed the pressures for change and the degree of instability in the individual countries. I argued, among other things, that long-term economic deterioration played an important role in mobilizing mass discontent. Chapters 3 through 5 traced tendencies to organize independent structures, whether for purposes of defending the civil rights of particular groups or individuals or in order to support cultural and educational initiatives independent of party control and censorship. These tendencies developed fastest in Poland, Hungary, and Slovenia, where one may speak of the emergence of "civil society." Chapter 6 outlined the penetration of new religious groups and cults in the region, a phenomenon associated with cultural drift in the population and possessing the potential to influence social attitudes and behavior in many areas.

Chapter 7 challenged the standard interpretation of the role of the Catholic church in Poland, which holds that the church was and is above all a traditional institution, defending traditional values against an imported communist system. I would not dispute the traditionalism of the church, but I would shift the emphasis elsewhere, and therefore argue that the political role assumed by the church in Poland in the late 1970s and 1980s was primarily a symptom of the emergence of "praetorian society" in that country. Samuel P. Huntington saw praetorianism as a prelude to and symptom of social chaos.

Ethnic frictions have long played an important role in Eastern Europe, but the weight carried by any particular ethnic conflict has not necessarily stayed even over the years. Through much of the 1980s, the most explosive ethnic problem in the region was the Serb-Albanian friction in Kosovo, which fueled Yugoslavia's slide to civil war. As a result, Chapter 8 argued, Kosovo became a factor in the larger political debate, and generated impulses for system change.

Chapter 9 through 11 traced the emergence of a new generation in Eastern Europe, a generation which is more Western, more disillusioned, and more materialistic than earlier generations. This generation has also seen the rise of small feminist groups in Yugoslavia and the growth of female activism in East Germany and elsewhere.

Finally, in Chapters 12 and 13 I developed a theory of societal strength and weakness on the basis of Crane Brinton's broader theory about revolution, and argued that while Hungary and Poland have been strong societies, Bulgaria has been a weak society, while the picture in Yugoslavia was mixed and complex. The strength of a society may change over time. Indeed, this book has charted the processes by which all of the societies of the region—including Romania—have become stronger in the 1980s.

Taken together, these strands reflect different aspects of both modernization and decay—a dangerous combination. Adriano Guerra, the Italian communist party's leading expert on Eastern Europe, put it very well:

> What we have here is not a crisis due to circumstances but the simultaneous emergence in all countries, with varying intensity but not in different forms, of a fundamental and completely new contradiction: that which has developed between the economic, social, and cultural development reached through such radical processes of transformation and growth, on the one hand . . . and, on the other hand, the persistence of the old centralizing structures of bureaucracy and authoritarianism.[5]

It must be emphasized that important differences exist among the countries of the region. Differences in economic solvency, the role of the church, and ethnic relations are among the most important. But in all these countries, the "contradiction" to which Guerra alluded had emerged by the end of the 1980s, and the illness to be "cured" (Poland, Yugoslavia, Romania, and arguably Czechoslovakia) or avoided (East Germany,[6] Hungary, and Bulgaria) was political decay. It was precisely this danger to which Gorbachev addressed himself.

The Gorbachev Effect

If there was already a reform agenda in several countries in Eastern Europe, the entire agenda was made to appear more urgent and indeed was made more urgent by the example set by Gorbachev in the USSR. Soviet glasnost (openness), perestroika (restructuring), and *novoye myshleniye* (new thinking) quickly exerted a fascination throughout the region among all sectors of the population, adding internal pressure to the external pressure being exerted by the Kremlin.

In his first three years in office Gorbachev succeeded in opening up discussion of practically every policy sphere in the USSR and in engineering several symbolic changes. The centerpiece of his program of reform was the drive to reinvigorate the economy. At first this largely took the form of giving local enterprises greater latitude and encouraging a small degree of private enterprise and workers' cooperatives.[7] In addition, in August 1988 Soviet authorities approved new legislation to remove the barriers to private farming and make farm land available on fifty-year leases. Some of Gorbachev's advisers were urging more radical measures. Tat'yana Zaslavskaya, a sociologist who enjoyed access to the general secretary, proposed a restructuring of GOSPLAN so that the agency would give up its traditional role in microeconomic planning and restrict itself to broad "strategic" planning, such as the Yugoslavs had been doing for years.[8] In March 1990 the Soviet press reported that President Gorbachev was preparing a package of legislation that would reduce government subsidies of food and other essentials, sell shares in state enterprises to private individuals (including foreigners) as a first step toward making the ruble a convertible currency, and prepare for the establishment of a stock market and commodity exchanges.[9]

Corruption and circumvention of the law by its administrators were targets in both the economic and administrative spheres. This was linked with a greater emphasis on strict observance of the law *by governmental and party organs*, and calls for the USSR to become a nomocracy. The June 1988 party conference stimulated an array of interesting proposals that inevitably aroused interest in Eastern Europe, including popular election of the Soviet president, an expansion of the duties and prerogatives of the Supreme Soviet, a role for nonparty members as departmental ministers, and a change in the party statute to allow party members to criticize draft proposals in public. Subsequently, in October 1988 the Soviet government presented detailed constitutional amendments which transferred some of the powers of the communist party to a new, popularly elected body called the Congress of People's Deputies and set a ten-year limit on any official's stay in office.[10] Earlier, in September, Gorbachev effectively abolished the party secretariat, once the center of executive power in the USSR. In addition, the policy of glasnost made it possible to criticize aspects of past and present Soviet reality, which had long enjoyed immunity from criticism.

Gorbachev also indicated that he favored breathing life into local soviets at the expense of local party organs, and fixed terms for party officials. A noncommunist "popular front" that would function as a kind of loyal opposition, was also proposed,[11] legitimizing similar proposals in Eastern Europe. The proposal was radical, but compatible with Gorbachev's concept of fostering a "socialist pluralism" of views.[12] The notion recalled Yugoslav ideologue Edvard Kardelj's advocacy a decade earlier of a "pluralism of self-managing interests."[13]

Then, in February 1990, came a dramatic speech by Gorbachev to the Central Committee, in which he suggested that the USSR would eventually adopt a multiparty framework.

The party in a renewing society can exist and play its role as vanguard only as a democratically recognized force. This means that its status should not be imposed through constitutional endorsement. The Soviet Communist Party, it goes without saying, intends to struggle for the status of the ruling party. But it will do so strictly within the framework of the democratic process by giving up any legal and political advantages, offering its program and defending it in discussions, cooperating with other social and political forces, always working among the masses, living by their interests and their needs.

The extensive democratization under way in our society is being accompanied by mounting political pluralism. Various social and political organizations and movements emerge. This process may lead at a certain stage to the establishment of parties.[14]

Some of the more startling changes came in the realm of history. Bukharin, Rykov, Pyatakov, Zinoviev, and Kamenev—executed in the late 1930s on charges of anti-Soviet conspiracies—were exonerated and posthumously rehabilitated, along with Radek, who was imprisoned in 1938 and died in prison.[15] Trotsky's role in the early years of Bolshevik rule was now admitted, and in June 1988 Professor Yuri Afanas'ev told a press conference that Trotsky should be cleared of charges and his works republished in the Soviet Union. Meanwhile, Stalin and Brezhnev were exposed to sharp criticism. In an October 1988 article *Moscow News* described how 100,000 Soviet citizens in southwestern Ukraine were murdered on Stalin's orders in 1941.[16] Forced collectivization was also criticized.[17] And after much hesitation, Soviet historians and officials finally admitted that Stalin, and not Hitler, was responsible for the mass execution of some 15,000 Polish POWs in spring 1940. In February 1989 the weekly tabloid *Argumenty i fakty* published the most detailed account of Stalin's victims up to then, estimating that some 20 million died as a result of terror, forced famine, or harsh treatment in labor camps. *Literaturnaia gazeta* even discussed the question of erecting a monument to the victims of Stalin.[18] For a while it seemed that Lenin would remain exempt from criticism. But in May 1988 this taboo was broken when the monthly magazine *Novyi mir* published an article by Vasily Selyunin that credited Lenin with having laid the groundwork for the forced labor camps and the mechanisms of forced collectivization which Stalin put to use. Selyunin argued further that Lenin's destruction of the free market was premeditated and deliberate, and not a mere response to the chaos produced by the civil war.[19] Along similar lines, the monthly journal of the RSFSR Writers' Union, *Oktyabr'*, announced in July 1988, its intention to serialize Vasili Grossman's *Vse techet (All is Flux)*, an even more damning indictment of Lenin.[20] Even the KGB joined the general chorus of exomologesis and in mid-February 1990 published a report in which it conceded that it had executed 750,000 people as enemies of the state between 1930 and 1953.

Meanwhile, scores of hitherto forbidden materials have now become available. In 1988, for example, 6,000 book titles hitherto locked away in special collections were made available to the general public, including works by Lenin, Kamenev, Preobrazhensky, Kropotkin, Trotsky, Savinkov, Milyukov, Bukharin, Rykov, Rozenglots, and Chernov, as well as the memoirs of Kerensky, Krasnov, and Denikin, and Tsar Nicholas II's abdication.[21]

Works of Trotsky were also published belatedly in the USSR, as was Khrushchev's famous "secret speech" of 1956.[22] The Soviets also undertook to publish Robert Conquest's *Harvest of Sorrow* (which deals with the forced famine of 1930–31) in translation, and Alexander Solzhenitsyn's *Gulag Archipelago*. In August 1989 the Soviets even acknowledged—after years of denials—the secret protocols concluded between Molotov and Ribentrop exactly fifty years earlier, which had divided Poland between them.[23]

As if that were not enough, in February 1988 Gorbachev told members of the central committee personally that some of the fundamental teachings of Marx and Engels were outdated and no longer relevant. In Gorbachev's words, "It is necessary to remove the rust of bureaucratism from the values and ideas of socialism . . . The party has to literally fight for perestroika . . . in the spiritual sphere."[24]

Soviet historians also began to break out of the isolation imposed by their own system, and in 1986 and 1987 began to publish works by American and other Western scholars in their journals, and to allow long-banned Westerners such as Robert Conquest and Reverend Michael Bourdeaux to return as honored guests. In April 1990 the Soviets took the dramatic step of inviting fifty leading Western Kremlinologists and historians to participate in a conference sponsored by the Soviet Academy of Sciences.[25]

In social and cultural policy Gorbachev's impact was tangible. Among the early signs of change in the literary scene was the publication of Valentin Rasputin's novella *The Fire*, which described the damaging impact of breakneck industrialization. One of the targets of Rasputin's criticism in the novella was the economic planning system, which he suggested should be scuttled. In October 1986 came the decision to permit publication of Anatoly Rybakov's searing indictment of Stalin, *Children of the Arbat*. The decision to permit publication was allegedly taken at the "highest levels of the Kremlin."[26] Rybakov himself explained his philosophy in this way: "A society that wants to build the future must know its past, its real past, as it was. A society that wants truth and openness must be truthful and open about its past, however it was. Only then will it be insured against the errors of the past."[27] Boris Pasternak's long proscribed *Dr. Zhivago* was also now published in the USSR.[28] In addition, many Soviet writers who had been expelled from the Writers' Union for unorthodoxy were readmitted to the union and allowed to return to the cultural mainstream. Soviet theater became sharply critical and satirized both past and present political figures. One of the most daring was Mikhail Shatrov's play, *Dal'she . . . dal'she . . . dal'she (Onwards, Onwards, Onwards)*, which depicted Stalin constructing a society based on antisocialist principles. While this clearly pushed the limits of the permissible, the play was published in the literary journal *Znamya* in its January 1988 issue.[29] Nudity also hit the Soviet stage. In rock music the old distinction between official and unofficial groups was scuttled, and groups that once had difficulty reaching the public were now tolerated and in some cases obtained recording contracts from Melodiya.[30] The Soviet fashion industry developed a new, chic, occasionally risqué quality.[31] Reflecting on the sudden liberalization, the Soviet rock group Time for Love composed a song in which they worried about the permanency of liberalization:

> And now that we are not afraid of anything,
> they have given us freedom.
> Have they given it forever?

The Gorbachev government also drafted new legislation across a number of areas, including religious affairs, where religious organizations were finally authorized to buy and own property. In the religious sphere, the Russian Orthodox church was at first the chief beneficiary of the "new thinking." Beginning with Gorbachev's accession to power, that church was able to register hundreds of new parishes. Several monasteries confiscated under earlier leaders have been returned to the church, and authorities began to treat registered religious groups with greater tolerance.[32]

Unsanctioned "informal groups" were likewise shown a new toleration spawning a welter of politically oriented groups across a broad spectrum, including the Russian nationalist *Pamiat'* with neo-Stalinist and anti-Semitic features;[33] the Western-oriented Democratic Union, which tried to promote better relations between the USSR and the United States;[34] and the Perestroika Club, a "new left" grouping which supported Gorbachev's program.[35] In Estonia the Green Party, which is concerned about protecting the environment and expanding Estonia's administrative autonomy, was tolerated.[36] For a while, Soviet authorities even tolerated the daring, independent magazine *Glasnost*, which published a detailed discussion of the KGB in one of its early issues.[37]

The new openness in the Soviet Union had reverberations in the non-Russian republics, where resentment of linguistic and cultural Russification had long been simmering. In Armenia and Azerbaijan demonstrations and riots occurred, with Armenians demanding the return to Armenia of the Nagorno-Karabakh Autonomous Oblast and the Nakhichevan ASSR, and Azerbaijanis opposed. In March 1984 Soviet authorities had to use military force to quell rioting in the Azerbaijani city of Sumgait. And in June of that year the Armenian legislature actually endorsed the demonstrators' demand—a move that did not, however, produce the desired effect.

There were also nationalist disturbances in Estonia, Latvia, and Lithuania in 1987 and 1988, involving thousands of people. In August 1988, for example, 100,000 Lithuanians gathered in the squares of downtown Vilnius to mark the thirty-ninth anniversary of the armed annexation of Lithuania; some of the demonstrators demanded independence. Complaints about Russification in neighboring Estonia had grown markedly more voluble since the proclamation of *glasnost*. In August 1988 an Estonian newspaper became the first official Soviet publication to admit and describe the secret Nazi-Soviet protocol of 1939 which ceded the independent Baltic republics to the Soviet "sphere of interest."[38] At first, nationalists in the Baltic republics felt constrained to underline that independence was not a realistic possibility. But in the course of 1989 ever greater numbers of Balts expressed support for secession and independence. And in May 1989 the Lithuanian Supreme Soviet unanimously passed a resolution that declared that the republic wanted its independence from the USSR.[39] Farther south, young people in western Ukraine organized clandestine nationalist groups, possibly of a secessionist nature. In the ostensibly dormant republic of Belorussia, a political demonstration in Minsk on 1 November 1987 drew two hundred people; among other things, participants condemned the "genocide" of Belorussians in the 1930s.[40] And in Moldavia, where the Soviets had long insisted that the Moldavian language (written since World War II in Cyrillic) was distinct from the Romanian language (written in the Latin alphabet), the local communist party admitted in early 1989 that Moldavian is the same as Romanian and began the costly process of reversion back to the Latin alphabet.

Even the old mechanisms of control were subjected to "restructuring." The Soviets admitted to abusing psychiatry,[41] rigging elections and routinely falsifying election returns,[42] and maintaining undue secrecy about information which could have been useful to Soviet citizens.[43] In a particularly striking development, the September 1988 issue of *Kommunist* published an article by a leading KGB official that argued that the maintenance of tight secrecy about basic facts had been used "irresponsibly and uncontrollably in the narrow interests of small groups of people."[44] In the same month, Viktor Chebrikov, then head of the KGB, told *Pravda* that a new law was being drafted which would make the KGB more accountable to the public.[45] The party began to trim the sails of the KGB: Chebrikov was replaced by Vladimir A. Kryuchkov, a new decree stated that no one would be subject to criminal proceedings merely for criticizing the state,[46] and in November 1989 KGB chief Kryuchkov publicly acknowledged the Stalinist KGB's brutality and arbitrary cruelty and pledged on national TV that this would never happen again.[47]

When Gorbachev first came to power, Czech wits used to joke: "What's the difference between Dubček and Gorbachev?" "None. Only Gorbachev doesn't know it yet." That pessimism notwithstanding, the joke suggested not merely a commonality of program but also a kinship of spirit. At an early stage, Dubček publicly endorsed Gorbachev's reforms. In turn, the Soviets rehabilitated him in late 1989, and in token of that he was interviewed on Leningrad TV in early November 1989.[48] The Soviets meanwhile repeatedly affirmed that they would never again send armed forces against their European neighbors.

Contagion in Eastern Europe

Taken in sum, Gorbachev's "new thinking" sent a surge of hope throughout Eastern Europe. The respective governments reacted very differently, however. The communist governments in Poland and Hungary backed Gorbachev's reform package, the latter realizing that in many respects Gorbachev was merely adapting solutions already tried by János Kádár. The Bulgarian government initially dragged its feet, then made bold promises of a Bulgarian perestroika, and later backed off again, dropping Chudomir Alexandrov, the strongest advocate of Gorbachev's ideas, from the Politburo.[49]

The authorities in East Germany, Czechoslovakia, and Romania tried to impede the penetration of *novoye myshleniye*. Gorbachev's speeches were censored in these countries, and reportage of Soviet developments was generally restrained. While the Soviets released Tengiz Abuladze's stirring film *Repentance*, which pokes fun at Stalin's autocracy, the East German paper *Junge Welt* criticized it for "defam[ing] the reputation of Marxist-Leninist historiography."[50] *Neues Deutschland* showed itself willing to admit that mistakes were made in the Soviet Union in the 1970s,[51] but not to admit that any mistakes had been made in East Germany. It is true that East German newspapers gave fairly extensive coverage to the Soviet party conference in June 1988 (though no front-page reportage); yet a subsequent report in *Neues Deutschland* highlighting the Soviet population's discontent with perestroika (quoting *Izvestiia*) suggested that the East German authorities remained cool toward Gorbachev's program.[52] In Czechoslovakia, in a similar spirit, delegates to a 1987 meeting of the Czechoslovak-Soviet Friendship Society were cautioned to be "on guard against the populace's excessive and unwholesome interest in Soviet developments."[53]

Finally, in Yugoslavia there was at first a broad consensus that that country had progressed far beyond the Soviet Union and could not look to Gorbachev for a model, and later a growing sense that the USSR was at least taking steps to solve its problems and that the Yugoslavs could not be smug about the Russians' continued deadlock and deepening crisis. But whether one talks about Gorbachev's repudiation of earlier Soviet claims to be the "leading center" of the socialist community, his advocacy of limited private enterprise and private farming, his tolerance of informal groups, his policy of openness in the press, his stress on legality and toleration in the religious sphere, his endorsement of greater economic autonomy for the constituent republics of the USSR,[54] his condemnation of Stalin, or, most obviously, his early endorsement of workers' self-management, Gorbachev seemed, in so many ways, to be merely adopting the old Titoist policies.[55] Only later did Gorbachev move beyond this.

Gorbachev's dual policies of glasnost and perestroika clearly contributed to the political transformation of the region. Gorbachev's original objective with respect to Eastern Europe was to effect a reinvigoration of the bloc.[56] Along these lines he initially promoted an intensification of intra-COMECON cooperation, although this was done within the context of greater integration and cooperation with Western Europe. By 1989 there was a shift in the wind, and the ever-flexible Gorbachev readjusted his sights and began to think in terms of endorsing the self-determination of the East European states—in effect, dismantling the Soviet empire.[57]

Alternative Regime Strategies in Eastern Europe

The communists were never able to solve the question of political legitimacy. But in the late 1980s the question was posed in new ways by newly mobilized groups with new resources at their disposal, within a new political context created in part by economic crisis and in part by Gorbachev's *novoye myshleniye.* The legitimacy question had four levels. First and foremost, legitimacy is very much tied to economic performance. A society enjoying prosperity is apt to forgive many transgressions or errors on the part of its government. But all the countries of the region, including even East Germany, experienced declines in the standard of living in the 1980s, with three of them (Poland, Yugoslavia, and Romania) functioning like Third World economies. As a result, legitimacy was very much in question on this first level.

Second, communist rule throughout the region was not introduced democratically and had never been made the subject of an honest referendum. Underground and public polls repeatedly confirmed that if free elections were held, the communist party would be swept out of power. A 1981 poll in Czechoslovakia, Hungary, and Poland, for example, found that only 3 to 7 percent of the adult population in these countries would have voted communist if free elections had been held.[58] Most people said they preferred to vote for a social democratic or christian democratic party. (For data on the popularity of the communist and other parties in Hungary, Poland, and Yugoslavia, see the appendixes.)

Third, Soviet domination remained deeply resented in the five countries concerned and further eroded any possibility of legitimation. This factor was irrelevant to Romania and Yugoslavia. As of early 1991, the Soviets had lost their former means of control in the region and could only hope to rebuild relations based on mutual interest, emphasizing mutually profitable trade.

And fourth, in certain countries there were or are ethnic minorities which reject the government in question. Chapter 8 outlined in detail the problems confronting the Yugoslav government in the now largely Albanian-inhabited province of Kosovo. There are at least three other instances in which nationalities issues complicated the legitimacy issue: Czechoslovakia, Romania and Bulgaria.[59]

The sundry changes traced here have variously contributed to the long unresolved crisis of legitimacy (as in the case of economic deterioration and the deterioration of ethnic relations in Kosovo), affected the context in which the illegitimacy of the regimes bore on party-populace relations (as in the case of the development of parallel society in Poland, the emergence of socially engaged churches in East Germany and Poland, and the rise of independent activism in Czechoslovakia, Hungary, Romania, and, for that matter, Yugoslavia), or reshaped social dynamics in such a way as to make irrelevant earlier party strategies (in the case of the appearance of new religious movements, the development of feminism, and the spread of rock counterculture and Western styles among young people). The relationship of this third phenomenon to the larger political context has too often been either ignored or downplayed. But the breakdown of the women's and youth organizations and their increasing self-doubts in the late 1970s and into the 1980s were measures of the impact of changing social identities on the political mechanisms for mobilization and socialization.

The Dam Breaks

There was a shift in the wind in East Germany around 1986 or 1987. This was the time when Evangelical-Lutheran church leaders started to demand Gorbachev-style reforms and East German citizens began to turn to the church in large numbers for help with emigration. Berlin's Bishop Gottfried Forck was even accused in 1988 of operating a de facto emigration office out of his chancery. The pressure for emigration was constant. In March 1989, for example, several hundred East German citizens demonstrated in Leipzig for exit visas to go to the West.[60]

Until early 1989 East German, Czechoslovak, and Bulgarian authorities were able to resist the tide because their people believed that resistance was pointless. As the winds of change penetrated first the USSR and then Hungary, East German authorities banned the Soviet magazine *Sputnik* and the lively Hungarian newspaper *Budapester Rundschau* in November 1988. Subsequently, East German authorities also banned a March 1989 issue of the Soviet magazine *Novoye vremya* because it contained an interview with Lech Wałęsa. The SED stated that it had no need to copy the Soviets, but at party meetings, members spoke out against the banning of *Sputnik*.[61] There were, to be sure, some critical articles published in East Germany.[62] But until May 1989 the pressure for change—leaving aside the periodic synods of the Evangelical-Lutheran church—remained muted. Then on 7 May local elections were held, and large numbers of people took the trouble to vote "no" on the single-candidate slate. When the official press reported that only 1.1 percent of the voters had voted "no," the reaction was outrage. From then until September there were repeated protests against the election fraud, and arrests of protesters.[63]

In September the picture changed virtually overnight. On 10 September Hungary opened its border with Austria. Within forty-eight hours, some 12,000 East Germans vacationing in Hungary crossed over into Austria. The East German government protested, briefly considered clamping down on travel to Hungary, and finally watched helplessly as 225,000 East Germans fled by the end of October. The average age of the East German refugees was twenty-seven, and an economist at the University of Halle estimated that the GDR would lose 0.12 percent of its national income for every 10,000 East Germans who left. The massive exodus was a powerful signal in and of itself, but it also served to catalyze massive demonstrations in East Berlin, Leipzig, and Dresden, where week after week, tens of thousands of people took to the streets in peaceful demonstration of their discontent. Among the larger demonstrations were those in Leipzig on 16 October (100,000 participants), 23 October (300,000), and 30 October (about 300,000), and in East Berlin on 4 November (up to 500,000). The protesters chanted "Ecology instead of economy!," "We are the people!," "Legalize New Forum!," "Gorby! Gorby!," "We want new leaders!," and "Stop the blah-blah-blah!"

The Evangelical-Lutheran church synod at Eisenach in September 1989 drew up a resolution demanding fundamental reforms, including freedom to travel and the introduction of a multiparty system, and sent a note to Honecker demanding democratization and proposing church-state talks on political and social reform. The SED rejected the church's proposal with the comment that it had "taken note of" the church's suggestion.[64] East Germany's usually silent Catholic bishops also took up the refrain, urging serious dialogue and a change in political structures.[65] By mid-September members of the CDU-East also began to demand serious reforms.[66] Professional organizations such as the Union of Writers and the national association of lawyers also issued strong statements in favor of change. The East German newspapers *Junge Welt* (organ of the youth organization), *Der Morgen* (organ of the Liberal-Democratic Party), and *Berliner Zeitung* published letters demanding self-criticism and reform on the part of the regime.

In mid-October the seventy-seven-year-old Honecker, in poor health after a gallstone operation, was removed from power and replaced by fifty-two-year-old Egon Krenz, Honecker's handpicked successor. On his first day, Krenz met with Bishop Werner Leich, chair of the Evangelical Church Federation, and pledged to conduct "a sincere dialogue with society, which will not exclude anyone."[67] Most of the old Politburo was forced to resign, and the size of the Politburo was reduced from twenty-one members to eleven.[68] The regime also promised to release all political prisoners,[69] and agreed to form a coalition government, assigning at least eleven of the twenty-seven ministries to noncommunists. The regime also lifted all travel restrictions and, in a highly symbolic move, opened the Berlin Wall. New Forum was promised registration. And the regime talked of holding free elections.

The East German changes sent shock waves throughout the region, exciting mass protests in Czechoslovakia and Bulgaria. Of course, in Czechoslovakia matters had been coming to a head in any case. Thirty new independent associations were created there in the course of 1989 alone, and preexisting structures also started to behave in a new way. Within the Union of Czech Writers, for example, calls were heard in late 1988 for the rehabilitation of some banned Czechoslovak writers and for greater creative freedom. Within the Czechoslovak People's Party there were signs of revived political consciousness in spring 1989, taking the form of the circulation of petitions. In June sixteen members of the party wrote a letter that criticized their long-slumbering party and called for a renewal of its Christian character.[70] Similarly, Jan Skoda, general secretary of the Czechoslovak Socialist Party, called for a stronger role for his party and the other "fraternal" noncommunist parties in Czechoslovakia, linking the demand to a stress on the need for democratization.[71] Meanwhile, the communist party was showing signs of depressed morale, pessimism, and nihilism, partly as a result of members' lack of confidence in their leaders to lead the country out of crisis.

On 10 September 1988 the Independent Peace Association (IPA) issued a nine-point petition, calling for:

(1) the withdrawal of Soviet troops from Czechoslovakia;
(2) the condemnation of the 1968 invasion of Czechoslovakia by those countries which had participated in it (the USSR, East Germany, Poland, and Hungary);
(3) a truthful reevaluation of the Prague Spring of 1968 and its aftermath;
(4) free elections with the possibility of independent candidates;
(5) freedom of the press and the abolition of censorship;
(6) the observance of basic human rights;
(7) the release of political prisoners;
(8) the right of independent associations to engage in public activities without government interference; and

(9) the right to publish this statement complete and verbatim in the public press.[72]

Four months later, three representatives of the official Czechoslovak Peace Committee met with five members of the Independent Peace Association for an hour-long discussion about issues ranging from the imprisonment of IPA members to problems of military service. Significantly, the two sides agreed to hold further meetings and to exchange materials.[73] Meanwhile, public opinion polls found increasing impatience among working people with the slow pace of perestroika in Czechoslovakia.[74] As *Rudé pravo* put it, "More and more people are getting the impression that everything is somehow taking far too long—restructuring is proceeding too slowly."[75]

Meanwhile, there were ever more frequent and bigger demonstrations in Czechoslovakia. In August 1988, for example, 10,000 people marched in protest through the streets of Prague to mark the twentieth anniversary of the invasion. Just two months later, about 5,000 people assembled at Wenceslas Square on the seventieth anniversary of Czechoslovak independence and demanded political change and more freedom. In December 1988 there was another demonstration to mark International Human Rights Day, and 5,000–6,000 protesters took part. "The courage to criticize is expanding," said Václav Maly, a dissident priest and Charter 77 member, at that time. "Fear no longer rules. Instead of just talking behind the closed walls of apartments, people now are criticizing in the trams, the buses, and the public squares."[76]

No wonder that the party was looking nervously over its shoulders at events in Poland and Hungary. As Miloš Jakeš, the party general secretary, euphemistically put it, "A certain role is also played by anxiety over the developments in Poland and Hungary, where serious changes are taking place. This naturally arouses concern."[77] By summer 1989 Czechoslovakia was already ripe for change and vulnerable to any "trigger."

That trigger came with the East German exodus; some of the East Germans even escaped via the West German embassy in Prague under the very noses of the already disaffected Czechs. On 28 October 1989 some 10,000 protesters took to the streets; the police dispersed the demonstrators, detaining 355 of them. Prague subsequently announced that it would ease travel restrictions and that Czechoslovaks would no longer require formal exit visas to travel to Yugoslavia and the West. They hoped that this would defuse some of the discontent. The Soviets were skeptical, however, and sent a high-level message to the Prague regime in early November, warning against further delay in introducing political reform. (The Soviets sent a similar message to Bulgaria's Todor Zhivkov at this time, which is credited with having persuaded Zhivkov to resign.)

But society had crossed an important threshold and there were repeated mass demonstrations in November, culminating in a march by 200,000 protesters through the streets of Prague on 20 November. There were similar marches the same day in at least three other cities—Bratislava, Brno, and Ostrava. The following day Czechoslovakia's communist leaders held talks for the first time with representatives of the opposition, while more than 200,000 people continued to demonstrate in the fifth straight day of protests. People shouted for an end to communist rule and for democratic freedom. Eighty thousand students also went on strike throughout the country, and three small provincial teachers' colleges were the only institutions of higher learning to remain open. By 23 November the crowd on Prague's streets had grown to an estimated 250,000. Václav Havel, the distinguished Czech playwright, addressed the crowd, saying, "We want to live in a free, democratic, and prospering Czechoslovakia, returned to Europe, and we will never give up this ideal."[78] Alexander Dubček, increasingly the subject of speculations centering on a possible return to politics, called for the resignation of the government and, on 23 November in a short address to about 70,000 demonstrators in Bratislava, gave his support to the resistance. The enthusiatic crowds chanted "President Dubček!"

Even Bulgaria felt the ripples from the East German exodus. After some 5,000 people took to the streets, seventy-eight-year-old Zhivkov resigned and fifty-three-year-old Petar Mladenov took the reins as the new general secretary. Promising democratic change, Mladenov organized a street rally to smash pictures of Zhivkov and muster support for his promises of reform. Some 10,000 people took part, but when the official program was over, 150 went to communist party headquarters and shouted "Democracy!" and "Freedom!" In taciturn, passive Bulgaria, that was itself an unusual occurrence. Bulgaria's Mladenov seemed to have in mind largely cosmetic changes, but it is noteworthy that immediately after his accession, a government prosecutor told the Supreme Court that a lower-court ban on the independent environmentalist group Eco-Glasnost was politically motivated and legally unjustifiable.[79] Registration of Eco-Glasnost would be a first step in the direction of the pluralization of Bulgaria. Meanwhile, changes in the structure and organization of the leading bodies of the Bulgarian CP were in preparation.[80]

Only Romania's Ceauşescu held back, seemingly oblivious of the turmoil unfolding on all sides. Romania predictably condemned the exodus of East Germans to the West, calling Hungary's abrogation of its earlier agreement to return refugees to East Germany "an instance of open interference in the internal affairs of the GDR."[81] The party daily *Scînteia* published a lengthy article defending Romania's separate path and arguing for the superiority of Romania's "worker democracy" over Western-style multiparty systems.[82] But Ceauşescu did not stop at that. On the contrary, in a speech to a plenary session of the central committee of the Romanian CP on 28 June 1989 the Romanian president revived the Brezhnev Doctrine, restating that the fate of socialism anywhere is the concern of the entire bloc:

> We feel seriously concerned about certain issues arising in various countries, because we want all socialist countries, all our neighbors, to make sure that they proceed firmly on the path of socialism. We therefore take the view that it would be of great importance for the countries of the Warsaw Pact, and for the socialist countries generally, to analyze jointly the current issues of socialist construction and to devise more effective means for joint action in order to overcome the difficulties and to ensure that the socioeconomic development of each people proceeds on the path of socialism.[83]

In keeping with this doctrine, Ceauşescu tried to mobilize the Warsaw Pact in August to prevent the transfer of power to the Solidarity-led coalition government in Poland.[84] High-level Romanian officials also made vague threats against Hungary, announcing that Romania now had nuclear capability, while the Romanian army chief of staff intimated that the 1920 Treaty of Trianon, which had stripped Hungary of Transylvania, was "unjust" because there were still regions in Hungary which included ethnic Romanians.[85] The chief of staff did not mention that with the constant flight of Romanians out of Romania, the Romanian contingent in Hungary had recently been augmented. Romanian discontent was already legendary, but the population was frightened, cowed, and careful. " 'We watch Bulgarian television, we listen to short-wave radio, we know about the developments [in other parts of Eastern Europe],' a young Romanian said, phrasing words that, even if overheard, would at most sound ambiguous. 'It is all very interesting.' "[86]

The Future of Europe

"The political situation is not stable. A new balance is emerging. . . . The real challenge is to change people's mind set."[87] So said Mieczysław Rakowski, the Polish communist party chief in October 1989. In the immediate aftermath of 1989, there were major changes in many spheres, including the following four.

The Restoration of Private Enterprise. Reprivatization suddenly became a high priority item in Czechoslovakia, East Germany, Hungary, Poland, and Yugoslavia, albeit, for the interim, a lesser one in Romania and Bulgaria. Popular pressure combined with economic constraint forced all these countries to confront the question of reprivatization. Even in once-proud East Germany there was a different tune. For example, Hans Modrow, who served briefly as premier from November 1989 to May 1990, said, "The GDR is open to suggestions by our capitalist partners that earlier were handled gingerly or fell on deaf ears. Joint ventures, direct investment, profit transfers, pilot projects to preserve the environment are no longer foreign words to us."[88] In Hungary, national bank officials foresaw that within a matter of a few years, the private sector could account for up to one-third of the social product.[89] In Poland a new law made possible the conversion of public-sector enterprises into private concerns—a process to be accomplished in part by distributing shares to the workers themselves. Joint ventures are a key ingredient in the new rush to free enterprise economy. As of late 1989 Yugoslavia had about four hundred joint ventures, Hungary had more than three hundred, and Poland about a hundred. Salgótarján Glass Wool, a Japanese-Hungarian joint venture, started operations in October 1989. The Hungarians also pursued talks with Japan's Suzuki Motor Company and with the Ford Motor Company.[90] In addition, in November 1989 General Electric took advantage of new laws in Hungary to buy out the Tungsram light-bulb company for $150 million. Where East Germany is concerned, West Germany's Deutsche Bank AG, Volkswagen, the AEG AG technology group, and the Schering AG chemical group undertook to enter the new market.[91] As of early 1989, there had been only 562 joint ventures between Western companies and companies in Eastern Europe, excluding East Germany. By the end of June 1990, the number of joint ventures in the region had risen to 5,070.[92] Within ten years the economies of Poland, Hungary, the Czech Republic, and Slovenia may not look very different from the economies of Sweden or Austria (the examples usually cited by East Europeans).

The Integration of Europe. The process of reprivatization may in turn encourage the reemergence of Europe—what Gorbachev took to calling "our common house." Hungary, Poland, the Czech Republic, and Slovakia gained admission in the Council of Europe, and the word is out that both Hungary and the Czech Republic are interested in joining the European Economic Community (EEC), if given the chance.[93] There are other forces at work too, such as the Višegrad Group, which brings together several East European states in regional economic and infrastructure cooperation. Moreover, Italy, Austria, Hungary, and Yugoslavia met in Budapest in mid-November 1989 to discuss a special arrangement for regional economic cooperation.[94] The result was the creation of the Danube-Adriatic Community. The new organization held its second conference in Bratislava in May 1990, at which time Czechoslovakia adhered to the grouping. At the organization's third conference in Venice in August 1990, problems of ethnic minorities and human rights were discussed—an indication that the organization would not restrict its interests to narrow economic and ecological questions.[95]

The integration of Europe necessarily means more regional groupings that transcend the old East-West division, more political, economic, and cultural cooperation, and a shift in trade. Hungary, for example, quickly moved to put its trade with Russia on a hard-currency accounting basis and to shift more of its trade to the West, and in May 1990 it announced that talks would be opened with the EEC about the question of Hungary's entry.[96] Leaders of Czechoslovakia, Poland, and Yugoslavia have also been concerned about integrating their economies into the rest of Europe. Czechoslovakia has pursued ties with Austria with particular vigor.[97] Poland was even pressing NATO to fix a date for Poland's admission to the Western alliance.[98]

The End of COMECON and the Warsaw Pact. The emerging integration of Europe had an immediate impact on perspectives on COMECON and the Warsaw Pact. By June 1990 the Warsaw Pact had returned the armies of the East European states to national command and its members had agreed to study ways to transform the pact into a "democratic alliance." The Czechoslovak government seemed to want to retain the Warsaw Pact, arguing that its preservation would prevent the isolation of the USSR from Europe and provide a balance to U.S. and/or German influence. The Hungarian government, by contrast, demanded the dissolution of the pact and announced its intention to withdraw from the pact by the end of 1990. The Polish government likewise let it be known that it had no use for the Warsaw Pact. In February 1991, the Warsaw Pact was officially dissolved, and, in that same month, ministers from Poland, Czechoslovakia, and Hungary signed a political club, citing the need to counter the continuing Soviet threat.[99]

As for COMECON, a two-day meeting of COMECON representatives in January 1990 produced an agreement to appoint a working group to study ways of restructuring and redesigning the trade group. The official head-quarters of COMECON was to be closed down, and the December 1990 meeting in Budapest was said to be the organization's "last." Although there was talk of a successor organization, to be based on strictly volun-tary membership, in February 1991, COMECON was likewise dissolved.[100] Meanwhile, bilateral trade agreements between ex-bloc countries or be-tween them and a reunited Germany continued to increase in number and importance.

Finally, the various multilateral coordinative meetings through which the Soviets long monitored policies in the economic sphere, youth af-fairs, church-state relations, and so on, rapidly withered away. They could not but do so.

Germany. Then there was the German question, a question that had two faces: German reunification (suddenly discussed in late 1989 after years of repression), and West Germany's role in the new Eastern Europe. The complete collapse of the facade of East German legitimacy, carefully cultivated in the 1970s and 1980s, inevitably reopened the question of reunification. Germans on both sides of the border had always resented the division of their country and looked with longing toward the idea of eventual reunification. In surveys taken in October 1989, 79 percent of West Germans and 71 percent of East Germans said they favored reuni-fication.[101] Almost overnight, German reunification moved from being impossible to being absolutely certain. By July 1990 currency union was achieved as a first step toward unity. Perhaps surprisingly, the Great Powers went along with the idea.

The Soviets at first tried to suggest that German reunification be put to a world referendum. This rather unprecedented proposal failed to ob-tain any Western support and by February 1990 the Soviets signalled their acceptance of the principle of reunification. The question remained as to the status of the two Germanys in the rival military pacts. At first the Soviets categorically rejected the idea that a reunited Germany could be a member of NATO, as West German Chancellor Helmut Kohl wanted. Later Gorbachev proposed that Germany be a member of *both* pacts. When this was rejected by Kohl and U.S. President George Bush, Gorbachev returned with a new compromise, suggesting that "West" German troops could remain in NATO without "East" German troops playing a corresponding role in either the Warsaw Pact or NATO. Reunited Germany would enjoy full membership in NATO and associate member-

ship in the Warsaw Pact, and, according to Gorbachev's vision, honor all
obligations deriving from both alliances. This idea was likewise immediately rejected by Kohl as "unacceptable because it completely misunder-
stands the purpose and foundations of NATO."[102] A NATO spokesperson
added, "A united Germany must have the right, recognized in the Helsinki Final Act, to choose to be a party to a treaty of alliance, without
the establishment of constraints on its sovereignty."[103]

By June German reunification appeared unstoppable. There was, to
begin with, huge pressure for reunification from the population itself,
especially in the east. Second, all the Great Powers had sanctioned reunification, at least in principle. Third, East Germany was by then governed
by Christian Democratic Premier Lothar de Maizière, who owed his
election to his image as a loyal ally of Kohl's and a firm advocate of reunification. And fourth, the two Germanys were moving with dispatch
to achieve currency union, and by February Bonn had already earmarked
$4.1 billion in economic aid to shore up East Germany's sagging econ-
omy.

On 16 July the USSR agreed that united Germany could be a full member of NATO, and that the 860,000 Soviet troops stationed in what was
then East Germany would be withdrawn over a period of three to four
years. The following day, Poland declared itself satisfied with German
guarantees of its western borders. These agreements removed the last obstacles to German reunification. Later, in September, the West German
and Soviet governments signed a twenty-year friendship treaty, under
which the Germans extended a DM3 billion interest-free loan to Moscow to cover the costs of maintaining Soviet troops in the eastern part
of the country and of withdrawing them to the USSR.[104] On 3 October
1990 the two Germanys were united as one.

Even before the reopening of the reunification issue, West Germany
was playing a greater role in Eastern Europe by 1989, and prospects
looked good for growth in Germany's role. On the one hand, the West
German government extended generous credits to Hungary, Poland, and
East Germany in that year. On the other hand, West German businessmen quickly made contacts in Hungary and East Germany, and the 1990s
are likely to see the continued spread of German industrial capital
throughout much of Eastern Europe.

Conclusion

When I started writing this book in the fall of 1987, it was already clear
that Eastern Europe was in a phase of transition. The gerontocrats were

approaching their biological limits. Gorbachev was sending out loud signals that the East European elites had to reform and that reform was urgent. And among the societies of the region, multifaceted changes in cultural outlook and social behavior were transforming the political consciousness of people. The sundry associations of independent activists contributed to this process by providing independent sources of information and critical analysis.

In 1987 it was also clear that the old political formulae had exhausted their practicability everywhere, except perhaps in Albania and Bulgaria (and Bulgaria did not look quite so clear even in 1989). As early as 1984 the signs of erosion in East Germany were clear. As I wrote at that time:

> There are four preconditions for the translation of economic disaffection into widespread dissent: (1) a general perception of the situation as a problem (by comparison with past performance, performance in other countries, or promises held out by the leadership); (2) a widespread belief that the political elite is responsible for the problem and that it must be opposed (or even overthrown); (3) a diffuse hope; and (4) a belief in one's ability to effect change in one's own condition. . . . The first condition exists in East Germany, and perhaps also the third. Moreover, there is ample material suggesting that many East Germans hold the regime responsible for some of the economic problems (and of course for the militarization of society and the tight political controls). [At this point] it is far from clear, however, that there is anything like a general consensus that the regime "must be opposed"—and actually some evidence to the contrary. . . . [But] economic malaise has the potential of being translated into social dissent, widespread protest, and even—in theory—social disintegration.[105]

The signs of pressure for change were even clearer in Hungary, Poland, and Yugoslavia, although the ethnic factor in Yugoslavia imposed some constraints on system adaptability.

What was not clear in 1987 was that the winds of change would come not in a matter of years, but months, and that Czechoslovakia and even Bulgaria would feel them. Still, by late 1988 Czechoslovak officials were treating the subject seriously. Josef Kempný, a member of the Czechoslovak party central committee, hinted at the gravity of the challenge in a September 1988 article for *Rudé pravo:* "Restructuring [*perestroika*] requires that we fundamentally change many things in politics, the economy, the social and cultural spheres, ideology, education, in ethics, and attitudes to[ward] society—simply everywhere."[106]

Gorbachev's genius lay in his having understood both that all-embracing change had become inevitable and that it need not work to Soviet disadvantage. On the contrary, by staking out a position in the forefront of change, Gorbachev became a symbol of hope in Eastern Europe and thus minimized the risk that pressures for democratization would be associated with anti-Soviet feeling. Moreover, as the United States and Germany stepped in with credits and trade offers, some of the economic pressure would be taken off Moscow, and to the extent that the transformation of Eastern Europe will include its economic recovery, that recovery will likewise redound to Russian advantage. And finally, by pushing the East German, Czechoslovak, and Bulgarian parties to adapt, and allowing the communist parties to transform themselves, Gorbachev at least opened up the possibility of finding stable paths to pluralization, and of finding a more satisfactory basis for mutually beneficial relations between Russia and the East European states.

15. The Great Transformation

The LDPD is, if I can put it this way, in favor of a socialism that is fun. That means that it does not merely proclaim joy in life, but makes it possible.—MANFRED GERLACH, *chairman of the Liberal Democratic Party of Germany (31 October 1989)*

In the space of little more than a year, the one-party monopolies of Eastern Europe crumbled, and instead of dissolving into fratricidal chaos (aside from Yugoslavia) as some pessimists had feared, these societies quickly gave rise to a welter of new political formations. By early 1990 there were 17 political parties operating in East Germany, 80 in Poland, 35 in Czechoslovakia (22 appearing on the June 1990 ballots), 22 in Hungary, 78 in Romania, 35 in Bulgaria, and more than 86 in Yugoslavia (3 in Bosnia, 31 in Croatia, 6 in Kosovo, 2 in Macedonia, 13 in Montenegro, 6 in Serbia, 19 in Slovenia, and 6 in Vojvodina). Many of these were embryonic parties with little power and few prospects. Some were little more than special interest associations, such as the Liberal Sexual Party in Hungary, the Friends of Beer Party and the Union of Rabbit-Raisers in Czechoslovakia, and the Hungarian Health Party.[1]

The rapid disintegration of communism—poignantly evinced in the rapid closure of party organizations in enterprises and communities—raised a new set of elites to prominence. Suddenly, politics was dominated by a number of literary and artistic figures: nine of the thirteen members of the Hungarian cabinet were historians, including the prime minister (a specialist in the history of medicine) and the foreign minister (a specialist in Hungarian-British relations); the prime minister of East Germany was a former orchestral musician (a viola player); the prime minister of Poland was a Catholic intellectual and journalist; the president of Czechoslovakia was a playwright; the president of Lithuania was a music professor; the leader of East Germany's new Social Democratic Party (Ibrahim Böhme) was a historian; the incumbent director of the New York Philharmonic (Kurt Masur) was a guiding spirit in the New Forum opposition movement; Kiril Marichkov, leader of the Shturtsi (Crickets—Bulgaria's no. 1 rock 'n' roll band) was elected to parliament; the Czechoslovak head of protocol (Pavel Kantor) was a rock singer; Michal Kočab, once a "heartthrob," was an MP in Czechoslovakia; and in fact, the entire Czechoslovak administration in particular was filled with rock musicians, DJs, rock writers, and journalists. Other slots were taken by other intellectuals, including priests and ex-dissidents. It appeared unlikely that these literary and artistic figures could play more than a transitional role before professional politicians and lawyers would take the reins. But their rise to power, even if transitory, showed where legitimacy was vested after four decades of communism.

The Great Transformation also excited hopes among advocates of restorationist politics, and a string of monarchs reappeared and offered to return to the throne—including Crown Prince Alexander of Serbia/Yugoslavia, King Michael of Romania, Tsar Simeon of Bulgaria, and a collective Union of the Nobility of Russia organized by Prince Golitsyn.[2] In Bulgaria local monarchists were registering 30,000 signatures a day (as of June 1990) in support of monarchical restoration, while in Hungary, in a striking contrast, seventy-seven-year old Otto von Habsburg, scion of the dynastic house that once ruled Austria and Hungary, declined the nomination of the Independent Smallholders Party for the post of president of the republic.[3]

In Romania the fascist Iron Guard was revived in early 1990. In February the organization issued a short proclamation:

> The armed anticommunist organization, the Iron Guards, the Legion of the Archangel Michael, is being set up again after 45 years. The Iron Guards will fight against all those who advocate any leftist ideology. We will not stop until we have eliminated all communists, socialists, and other leftist monsters. Force is our creed. . . . Our time has come at last. The country will be ours again. Heil Hitler! We will prevail![4]

No one had a clue as to the membership of the Iron Guards, but it seemed to be headquartered in the city of Bacău in eastern Romania.

Overnight, Eastern Europe was transformed and the old political-economic order passed from the scene. In taking stock of this transformation, one may say that at least four preconditions exist for the stabilization of a political-economic order: (1) some level of efficacy of formal institutions; (2) a modicum of correspondence between the actual behavior of administrative and legal institutions, and the normative rules that govern their behavior; (3) the satisfaction of the basic economic and adjudicative needs of the population; and (4) a basic acceptance of the legitimacy of the "rules of the political game" by the populace. The greater the shortcomings with respect to these four criteria, the greater the decay of formal institutions and the greater the tendency for informal, underground, countercultural, and dissident-type organizations to arise.

There are many questions that an informed observer must ask herself or himself, including: Why now? Why not earlier? Why everywhere at once? And how important was Gorbachev in unleashing the furies of headlong change?

Why now? Societies, like individuals, have psychological states, and are psychological beings, which accordingly pass through stages. The quickening rhythm of crisis in the region (1956, 1968, 1976, in several Polish cities in 1980–81, and finally 1989) was a sign that the equilibrium was unstable, and that the pressures for change were becoming steadily less containable. The development of dissident networks and samizdat information channels were vital in preparing the way for revolution, as was the example set by Solidarity in 1980–81.

Why not earlier? In actual fact the people of Eastern Europe had attempted to resist many times in the past. In Poland, in particular, anti-communist guerrillas fought the new communist regime for a few years, but without success. In East Germany in 1953 and Hungary in 1956, popular uprisings proclaimed the overthrow of communism. But in each of these cases resistance was smashed by overwhelming military force. Gorbachev signaled very clearly that he considered the use of force unacceptable; in this way he changed the rules of the game and, ultimately, the game itself.

At first sight it may seem that my answers to these first two questions are diametrically opposed. The synthesis which I see is that the use of military force became unacceptable in large part because of changes in society, and not simply because Gorbachev had a different outlook. The change had been evolutionary, and Gorbachev simply recognized what Brezhnev had refused to allow.

Why everywhere at once? Despite initial imperviousness, ultimately even Albania has followed the pack. Why? Because once populations see that change is possible, unstable equilibria become completely untenable, and illegitimate elites are simply washed away in a tidal wave. It is not that Romania or Serbia, for example, should be expected to achieve stable democratic multiparty parliamentary systems along Czech and Hungarian lines, but that these countries have also experienced change.

This points to a fact sometimes denied by ultra-liberals: In political and economic terms Eastern Europe was very much a "set." These countries had similar systems, similar policies, similar elites, and, as a result, similar problems and similar fates. The one case that was always hugely divergent—Yugoslavia—is even now divergent, having remained mired in ethnic war since June 1991.

How important was the Gorbachev factor? In a word, it was *catalytic.* I have tried to show how the pressures for change built up steadily in sundry social sectors, but Gorbachev clearly quickened the process, as I explained in the preceding chapter.

In the remainder of this chapter I will discuss the most salient developments in the eight countries of the region during the initial months of transition, basically from November 1989 to October 1990. They will be taken in alphabetical order for the sake of convenience.

Albania

The first on my list, it was the last to feel the winds of change. One of the earliest hints of change came in May 1989 at a plenary session of the Union of Writers and Artists. In what was a surprisingly daring speech (by Albanian standards), author Kico Blushi, editor-in-chief of the literary monthly *Nentori,* told his listeners that "civilized debate" and public criticism of policies were essential to Albania, and urged the state to show tolerance of criticism. Only a few months later, the state publishing house in Tiranë published Neshat Tozaj's *Knives,* a novel that contained harsh and explicit criticism of the *Sigurimi,* the state security police. Soon thereafter, Ismail Kadare, considered Albania's most successful author, gave an interview to the magazine *Zeri i Rinise,* in which he echoed Tozaj's criticism of the *Sigurimi,* asserting that the *Sigurimi* had fostered "a criminal psychosis . . . that [drove the] country toward crime."[5]

Meanwhile, it was proving impossible to insulate Albanian society from at least some awareness of the processes of change sweeping the rest of Eastern Europe. Albanians were tuning in to Yugoslav and Italian radio stations, and were hearing reports about the Great Transformation. Inevitably, the Albanian media had to address the subject. *Zeri i Popullit* did so in October 1989, with a page 4 story headlined "Fruit of the Ideology of Counterrevolutionary Reformism." Although the article heaped abuse on reform-minded politicians in Hungary, it also admitted that Hungarian politics was repluralizing, that the Hungarian Democratic Forum had won three times as many votes in the regional parliamentary elections as the Hungarian Socialist Workers Party, and that the HSWP had committed itself to the restoration of economic free enterprise.[6] The considerable Albanian interest in these events was conceded by party leader Ramiz Alia at a meeting of the Trade Unions Council in December 1989, although he categorically ruled out the possibility that anything similar could happen in Albania because the country's political evolution was historically different.

Yet in January 1990 there were Greek and Yugoslav reports of unrest in northern Albania, and of the imposition of harsh security measures in Shkodër, Albania's second largest city. Although Albanian officials denied the truth of these rumors, the government passed a series of liberalizing measures in early May 1990 that among other things, restored freedom of religion and freedom to travel abroad.[7] Alia also called for further reforms, including an easing of price controls, to encourage collective farm workers to sell more fresh produce in the towns.[8] Albania announced as well that it now wanted a role in the Conference on Security and Cooperation in Europe, and that it was prepared to resume diplomatic relations with both the United States and the Soviet Union.

These changes were important, but they were, all the same, slight and late in coming. Albanian society has been much weaker than the other societies of Europe, and as of the spring of 1990 most informed observers still predicted only modest reforms within the context of the preservation of a one-party system.

Throughout 1990 large protests took place in various Albanian cities, including Tiranë, Shkodër, and Kavajë, and at least one person was shot dead by police in a July demonstration (in Kavajë). During July more than six thousand Albanian citizens took refuge in foreign embassies accredited to Tiranë and succeeded in obtaining asylum in Australia, the United States, and a number of West European countries. Under the impact of this pressure the Albanian government sacked a number of reputed hardliners, including Interior Minister Simon Stefani, Defense Minister Prokop Mura, and Politburo members Rita Marko, Manush Myftiu, and Lenka Cuko.[9] The government also took the first step toward the reprivatization of agriculture by allowing farmers to have private plots, and it passed a new law allowing foreign investment in Albania.[10] In the sphere of foreign relations Albania resumed diplomatic ties with the USSR in late July, and by October it was actively exploring the possibility of opening diplomatic and other cooperative ties with Israel.[11]

Bulgaria

Bulgaria was unique in another way—by giving the communists their first electoral victory in free elections in Eastern Europe in June 1990.

The drama of Bulgaria's transformation can be dated to November 1989. An important meeting of the central committee had been scheduled for 11 November, but on 10 November Petar Mladenov, long-time foreign minister, was in Moscow as the guest of the Soviet government. The Soviets evidently urged the dismissal of party secretary Todor Zhivkov, for upon returning to Bulgaria the next day Mladenov quickly engineered Zhivkov's removal—a move sanctioned at the scheduled meeting.[12] Even before the month was out the trade unions would declare their independence.[13] Later, the Bulgarian Communist Party would rename itself the Socialist Party, repudiate the disciplinary principle of democratic centralism,[14] and promise the end of press censorship. Other changes quickly followed.

In the wake of Zhivkov's ouster, the Bulgarian Writers' Union posthumously readmitted Bulgarian émigré writer Georgi Markov to its ranks. Markov had been excoriated by the regime and then assassinated with a poison-tipped umbrella in London in 1978. Now he was being granted a full rehabilitation: his memoirs were serialized in the trade union daily *Trud* and in the monthly journal *Otechestvo*, and Markov's widow, Annabel, was received in January 1990 by Politburo member Aleksander Lilov (later party secretary), who promised her that there would be a judicial investigation into Markov's murder.[15] At the same time, various writers involved in opposition activities, such as Blaga Dimitrova, Markov Ganchev, Georgi Mishev, and Stefan Prodev, suddenly found it possible to publish their works in Bulgaria.

Nor was Markov the only figure to be posthumously rehabilitated. Traicho Kostov, a prominent Politburo member executed in 1949 on fabricated charges of antiparty activity, was fully rehabilitated in mid-December 1989, when the party central committee adopted a resolution declaring that all the charges against Kostov had been "slanderous and untrue."[16] Various other party figures persecuted under Zhivkov were rehabilitated in early January 1990. Bulgaria also published figures of the number of people executed without trial, imprisoned, and otherwise repressed after 1944, and in December 1989 the government issued a formal apology for having taken part in the Warsaw Pact invasion of Czechoslovakia in 1968.

By this point the party was suffering an internal crisis of confidence. Symptomatic of this crisis of confidence was its admission that socialist property relations were just as alienating as capitalist property relations.

In particular, the army newspaper *Narodna armiya* noted, "State property in Bulgaria has never been managed by the people. Its management was a privilege of the government departments that control this property in the name of the state."[17]

There started to be some response from the public, who participated in public rallies throughout the country, demanding democracy and an end to one-party rule. In late February 1990, for example, 200,000 people packed Sofia's central square to demonstrate against the communist party. People started to talk about a return to monarchy. Tsar Simeon II, who lived in exile in Madrid, was interviewed on Bulgarian television, but despite his evident popularity, a poll of 3,128 Bulgarians showed that only 6 percent favored a restoration of the monarchy.[18] Despite the poll, the issue came to occupy a niche on the public agenda, and the Christian Republican Party, although committed to a republic, considered it appropriate to call for a public referendum on the question, monarchy or republic.[19]

In a matter of months sundry independent social and political associations came into being, including a Gypsy union, an independent Jewish organization, the Independent Committee for the Defense of Religious Rights, an independent union, and several social democratic parties. The Agrarian Union, freed of communist dominance and reorganized as an independent centrist party, claimed 136,000 members by February 1990.[20] And an opposition press gradually emerged, with such publications as *Svoboden Narod* (organ of the Social Democratic Party), *Narodno Zemedelsko* (organ of the Agrarian Party), *Ekopolitika* (organ of the Green Party), and *Dano*, an unaffilliated magazine devoted to power, business, and sex.[21]

Bulgarian society was awakening—but only belatedly and slowly. A *Der Spiegel* interview probed this issue with opposition figure Petko Simeonov:

> *Der Spiegel:* Why has the Bulgarian opposition woken up only now and has not moved for 40 years?
> Simeonov: Our opposition was and is weak. In addition, it consists almost exclusively of intellectuals, and we lack the responsibility of the intellectuals toward society. . . . [Now] according to a recent poll by the newspaper *Trud*, about half of [the] population are in favor of implementing *perestroika* and *glasnost*.
> *Der Spiegel:* Why not more?
> Simeonov: Because the people are still afraid and because they are busy the whole day long trying to ensure their very existence. The

Bulgarians spend more time standing in line than educating their children. In rural areas, the shelves are empty: no bread, no eggs, no sausage. This does not leave any time for political philosophies.[22]

By January 1990 the communist party was sitting down for talks with leading figures of the opposition, following a pattern already set in Czechoslovakia, Hungary, and Poland. That same month parliament abolished the communist party's political monopoly and declared Bulgaria a *democratic* rather than a socialist republic. In the universities Marxism-Leninism ceased to be a required subject. The Office for Church Affairs, long entrusted with the task of controlling the legal religious establishments, was dismantled. The censorship office was closed. And Department Six, the police unit hitherto entrusted with the surveillance of dissidents, was dissolved.

Finally, in mid-June, after two rounds of elections that some observers said were tainted by fear, the ex-communist party (renamed the Bulgarian Socialist Party) won an absolute majority in the 400-seat unicameral parliament (211 deputies), with 144 deputies elected by the Union of Democratic Forces (a 16-party coalition), 23 by the Turkish Movement for Rights and Freedom, 16 by the Agrarian Party, and 6 by independents. The communists claimed to have won 48 percent of the vote,[23] but the opposition soon charged fraud and manipulation.[24]

Postelection polls found that young people had preferred the opposition Union of Democratic Forces (UDF) to the Bulgarian Socialist Party by a margin of 49.5 percent to 33.8 percent (with the rest of the vote splintered among smaller parties), and that the popularity of the socialists was sinking steadily, even as that of the UDF continued to rise.[25]

The socialists quickly developed problems. In early July Petar Mladenov was forced to resign as president of Bulgaria after a videotape showed him discussing the use of tanks to suppress an antigovernment protest. The parliament chose Zhelyu Zhelev, the fifty-nine-year-old head of the UDF, to replace him as president. Meanwhile, the socialists fell into disarray, amid squabbling between the liberal and conservative wings of the party. Prime Minister Andrei Lukanov (a socialist) was reconfirmed by Zhelev, and attempted to put together a coalition government with the UDF. When the UDF refused to consider a coalition, Lukanov eventually proposed an all-socialist cabinet in September, extending an invitation to the opposition to engage in talks about economic reform and land reform.[26]

Gradually, signs of change emerged. The embalmed body of Georgi Dimitrov, the founder of Bulgarian communism, was removed from its mausoleum in July and cremated. In August thousands of anticommunist protesters stormed Socialist Party headquarters, ransacked it, and set it on fire; thousands more demonstrated in protest of this action. In September Bulgaria's first privately owned bank—appropriately named the First Private Bank—started operations. And in October 1990 the government outlined a comprehensive economic reform that would include the reprivatization of the economy and the marketization of prices, and the parliament began to consider a bill to depoliticize the army, police, law courts, prosecuting magistracy, and ministry of foreign affairs, removing these agencies from socialist party control.[27]

Meanwhile, Bulgaria confronted the results of a decline in production, and braced for food shortages, price hikes, and electricity shortfalls.[28] In these conditions the crime rate soared, stirring expressions of concern in the media.[29]

Czechoslovakia

Change in Czechoslovakia was adumbrated in the cultural sphere, especially in the theater and in the film industry, but also in literature. In January 1989 the Czech ministry of culture ordered the return to library shelves of the works of more than a hundred banned authors. At the same time, the Union of Czech Writers convened a meeting at which speakers criticized literary policy and upbraided the censorship applied in the cultural sphere. In the spring of 1989 two Czech writers, Petr Prouza and Ondrej Neff, held talks in West Germany with Czech émigré writers, and in September 1989 the Czech and Slovak writers' unions participated in a conference in Franken, West Germany, with their émigré cohorts. Writers and critics talked of undoing what exiled writer Milan Kundera called the "massacre of Czech culture" in the post-1968 era of "normalization."

In early 1989 several new films tackled subjects that had previously been taboo. Films made in the liberal era of the late 1960s, and not seen since then, were cleared for release; these included *The Joke* (based on Kundera's novel), *All My Good Countrymen*, and *A Coach to Vienna*. Also cleared was Karel Vachek's *Related through Choice*, a documentary dealing with behind-the-scenes political activities of Dubček and other politicians in 1968. In May there was even a Kafka festival in Prague. Since Kafka had always been the bête noire of the communists, this was in itself an important barometer of change. And in October communist authorities agreed to a new law, changing the way in which theaters would be managed and essentially dismantling the censorship apparatus in the theater.

By the summer of 1989 tension in Czechoslovakia was rising, and there was a sense that things were coming to a head. František Cardinal Tomášek of Prague, then ninety years old, addressed just this question in a letter to government officials dated 4 August, in which he warned of a "dangerous tension [between the authorities and] a growing number of citizens demanding a say in how society is run."[30]

The political infrastructure was also starting to crumble, and usually docile politicians started to speak out without fear. The Czechoslovak People's Party (CPP) issued repeated calls for internal renewal. In June 1989, for example, CPP deputy Chairman Bohumil Svoboda told a session of the municipal committee,

> They try to make us believe that criticism of the party's leadership amounts to antiparty activity. In such a case we have to ask our-selves who the party is: those in the upper echelons, about whom the people laugh or cry, or the regular members? And then they tell us that the party is not in a critical state. . . . Events of the recent weeks have, unfortunately, illustrated that the People's Party leadership is apparently not able to handle the critical situation in which the party finds itself. Thousands of letters from members and a number of documents prove that. It is, moreover, questionable whether the current leadership is able to face our present problems. Not one member of the Central Committee even considers stepping down for the sake of the party. Instead, they seek police protection at the party's regional meetings "to ensure order." Or do they need protection for themselves?[31]

On 14 October seventy-three CPP members and officials met in Prague and formed an internal reform movement called the Stream of Rebirth, dedicated to re-Christianizing the party. Within the CPP there were also signs of internal fissure.

Meanwhile, Soviet President Gorbachev was losing patience with Prague's old-style communism. As early as late 1988 General Alois Lorenc, head of the Czechoslovak secret police, met secretly with certain prominent party officials to work out a plot to remove party secretary Miloš Jakeš. The plan, code-named Operation Wedge, was worked out in cooperation with the Soviet KGB and called for replacing Jakeš with Zdenek Mlynar, a member of Dubček's reform government of 1968, who was living in exile in Vienna (though Mlynar reportedly was not willing to cooperate). The plan called for the organization of mass unrest and the simulation of the death of a student to turn people against Jakeš.[32]

Secret police officer Ludek Živčak infiltrated the student leadership and helped to radicalize it. On 17 November Živčak led crowds of demonstrators to Wenceslas Square for what proved to be the first of several days of protest. Some 20,000 people demanded that Jakeš be fired, chanting "Into the rubbish bin with Jakeš!," "Long live Havel!," and "Down with the monopoly of the Czechoslovak Communist Party!"[33] From the tone of the slogans it was clear that the secret police could not control the demonstrators. The authorities called in the riot police, who used tear gas and clubs to disperse the demonstrators and arrested scores of participants, including Alexander Dubček.[34]

The police brutality proved counterproductive. It failed to deter people, who took part in demonstrations across Czechoslovakia in the succeeding weeks in numbers up to 200,000. The CPP issued a sharp protest against the police repression, thus signalling the party's clear decision to break ranks with the communist regime.[35] Charter 77 likewise condemned the suppression of the 17 November demonstration and called for the party and state leaderships to resign. The Czechoslovak Democratic Initiative, which had declared itself a political party on 11 November, also demanded that the government resign. The Movement for Civil Liberties called for the immediate resignation of the minister of internal affairs and all those involved in the decision to use the police. The suppression of the 17 November demonstration proved to be a catalytic event for Czechoslovakia, just as the August 1988 strikes had been for Poland or the opening of Hungary's borders had been for East Germany. Overnight it changed the way people viewed the balance of political forces.

On 26 November communist Prime Minister Ladislav Adamec entered into negotiations with the Civic Forum, an opposition group formed only a week earlier but associated with Václav Havel. On 3 December Adamec tried to assuage the opposition with what were largely cosmetic changes; he proposed a new twenty-one-member cabinet, in which communists retained sixteen seats, including the defense and interior ministries. The Civic Forum immediately rejected this proposal and demanded a true coalition government. Four days later, Adamec resigned, to be succeeded by his erstwhile deputy, Marian Čalfa. On 9 December the two sides finally came to an agreement, swearing in a new coalition government of "national understanding" the following day. Husák resigned as president, and the hugely popular Václav Havel was elected president. Alexander Dubček, the hero of 1968, became chairman of parliament.

Within a matter of weeks, several dozen political parties announced themselves, though some amounted to little more than lobby groups or political circles. Among the new parties were the Green Party, the Social Democratic Party, the Free Bloc (adhering to conservative economic liberalism), the Alliance of Farmers and the Countryside, the Czechoslovak Democratic Forum (a left-wing group), the Christian and Democratic Union (uniting the old People's Party and a new Christian Democratic Party), the Movement for Autonomous Democracy in Moravia and Silesia, the Friends of Beer Party (in the Czech republic only), the Public Against Violence (the Slovak sister organization of the Civic Forum), the Slovak Nationalist Party, the Slovak Democratic Party (also nationalist), the Freedom Party (yet another Slovak nationalist party), the Czechoslovak Party for Social Justice, the Liberal Democratic Party in Slovakia, the Republican Party (which modeled itself on American parties and focused on program rather than on recruiting members), a Gypsy party, the Party of Czechoslovak Neutrality (aiming for permanent neutrality on the Swedish and Swiss models), and the Transnational Radical Party (which declared itself the champion of "all minorities"—national, religious, cultural, and sexual).[36] The Slovak Independence Movement, a hitherto émigré organization based in Munich, announced in March 1990 that it would relocate its headquarters to Bratislava and register with the ministry of the interior; the party advocated Slovak independence.[37] The communists also split. First, a group of expelled communists convened in Bratislava in November 1989 and formed a new Democratic Socialist Party. Subsequently, in February 1990 a group of reform-minded communists met in Brno and established a new Czechoslovak Democratic Forum. Even the anarchists revived and in March 1990 announced the formation of the Czechoslovak Anarchist Association, dedicated to "searching [for] and asserting various forms of autonomy and direct democracy."[38] But perhaps the most innovative of all was the Party of Constructive Destruction established in Hradec Králové in March 1990. *Smena* reported that "its main program is permanent opposition to all other political parties that might grow to form a system similar to the former totalitarian power. Constructive destroyers do not seek political power, have no apparatus, do not own any assets, and, for the time being, do not publish anything of their own."[39]

As for the communist party, it hastily convened an extraordinary congress on 21 December in an effort to take stock and devise a new strategy. In a wide-ranging resolution the congress annulled the existing party statutes and called for the drafting of new statutes; disbanded the People's Militia; appealed to former members expelled after 1968 to rejoin the party; and charged the central committee with the task of objectively assessing the 1968–69 period and subsequent "normalization," and to assess the political responsibility for the crisis.[40]

Change rapidly swept the Czechoslovak political landscape. By the end of November the Prague government announced that it would dismantle its fortifications along the Austrian border. The secret police were abolished in January, and in February new laws were passed guaranteeing citizens the rights of assembly, association, and petition. A report in the Bratislava daily *Pravda* noted in particular, "No one can be forced to become a member of any association. No one must suffer prejudice because she or he is a member of a certain organization, because she or he participates in its activity, because she or he supports it, or because she or he remains outside of it."[41] Independent newspapers popped up like mushrooms after a rainstorm, beginning with the transformation of the monthly samizdat publication *Lidové Noviny* into a legal daily newspaper. In Prague, Václav Havel's *Audience* was given its Prague premier sixteen years after the play was written. The Catholic church benefited by being allowed to fill the various empty episcopal seats, including the seat of the Prešov Eparchy of the Greek Catholic church, vacant for more than forty years.[42] And the Prague periodical *Prače* published statistics on Stalinist victims in Czechoslovakia, conceding that more than 100,000 persons had been imprisoned and 178 persons had been executed for political crimes between 1948 and 1953. In addition, *Prače* noted, some 8,000 persons were beaten to death during interrogations, were shot at the border, or lost their lives in jails or uranium mines.[43]

The government also closed down the Marxism-Leninism Institute of Charles University, thus ending decades of official indoctrination of that political ideology. And in April 1990 Czech and Slovak jurists and constitutional scholars hosted a conference attended by two dozen of their counterparts from America and Europe. Their objective: to learn from Westerners how to frame a new constitution for Czechoslovakia.

Meanwhile, Prague moved rapidly on the economic front to reintroduce a market economy, stimulate private enterprise, and attract Western capital. One token of this was an agreement signed by Continental AG of West Germany in June 1990 with Czechoslovakia's largest tire company, the Barum Group.[44]

The new government's program of repluralization received an overwhelming endorsement from Czechoslovak voters in June elections, with the Civic Forum (associated with President Havel) capturing some 50 percent of the votes in a crowded field. By contrast, the communists drew only 13 percent. In late June 1990 President Havel named a new noncommunist coalition government led by the Civic Forum. Headed by Prime Minister Marian Čalfa (who had in the meantime resigned from the communist party), the new government also included Civic Forum's Slovak sister organization, Public Against Violence, and the Slovak-based Christian Democratic Movement.[45]

This new government began immediately to dismantle the state structure organized by the communists. The secret service was depoliticized and stripped of any repressive functions.[46] A new law on joint ventures allowed foreigners to hold *more* than 49 percent of the capital stock in an enterprise.[47] In late October the parliament approved a law to auction off some 100,000 small shops and enterprises that the communists had nationalized, with the ultimate objective of achieving the remarketization of the economy by 1992.[48] A potent symptom of the new atmosphere was the fact that Radio Free Europe, the American anticommunist radio station, was allowed to open an office in Prague in August 1990.[49] Havel himself was confirmed as president by Czechoslovakia's freely elected parliament in July 1990, amid reports that the Civic Forum was splitting into left and right wings.[50]

By September 1990 rumors were heard that members of the dissolved secret police were plotting a putsch,[51] and the communist party excited widespread fears the following month, when party general secretary Vasil Mohorita said that the government's reprivatization program "signal[led] an end to national understanding and the beginning of a hard and uncompromising struggle."[52] A few days later, tens of thousands of anticommunist demonstrators crowded into the Old Town Square in a show of solidarity against the discredited communists.

East Germany

Political transformation in East Germany was propelled by the exodus of several hundred thousand East Germans during the summer and early autumn of 1989, by huge protests and demonstrations involving as many as 200,000–500,000 people in Berlin and Leipzig, and by the strengthening of opposition confidence through such methods as the circulation of various petitions (like the appeal by the New Forum signed by 200,000 people within the first twelve days of its legalization.)[53] Unable to cope with these new challenges, two high-ranking SED officials committed suicide: fifty-seven-year-old Helmut Mieth, the party chief of Bautzen; and Gerhard Uhe, the party chief of the city of Perleburg, near Schwerin.[54]

Meanwhile, East Germany introduced freedom of travel and opened its borders on 9 November. Within the first eleven days of the new policy the East German police issued 10,299,107 visas for private trips, and 17,738 permits for permanent emigration.[55]

With labor shortages created by the sudden exodus of large numbers of East Germans, members of the police and the army were deployed to help staff the state railway, the ministry of health and social services, the Red Cross, and various economic enterprises.[56]

By the beginning of December there was open talk of bringing ex-president Honecker to trial for his responsibility for ruining the country. Arrest warrants were issued for 12 prominent party officials including Erich Mielke (former minister of state security), Günter Mittag (former economic secretary of the SED), Harry Tisch (former trade union chair), and Gerhard Müller (former first secretary of the Erfurt party organization).[57] Fearing further repercussions, police officials started burning their files. Seeing clouds of smoke rising from the windows, citizens occupied police offices in various East German cities to prevent the police from destroying any more files.

Before the end of December 1989 the state security police had been disbanded,[58] with nearly half of its estimated 22,000 employees suddenly thrown out of work. The other half were given jobs in two smaller offices: an intelligence agency and an antisubversion office.

On 3 December, after just forty-nine days in power, Egon Krenz resigned as party chief and chair of the Council of State. Hans Modrow, one of the few communists who still enjoyed some credibility because he had been criticized for reformism by Honecker, remained prime minister, and Liberal Party leader Manfred Gerlach became president. Meanwhile, the SED renamed itself the Party of Democratic Socialism and elected Gregor Gysi, a forty-one-year-old Jewish lawyer who had defended East German dissidents in court, as the new party leader. On 7 December the communists came to an agreement with the democratic opposition to hold free elections on 6 May 1990.

East Germany now experienced the same kind of repluralization that had manifested itself earlier in Hungary and Poland, and would later be seen in Czechoslovakia. Among the new parties and associations that emerged in early 1990 were the Christian Social Party, the German Youth Party, the Potentialist People's Party, the Independent Social Democratic Party, the Ecological-Democratic Party, the Carnations Party (uniting reform Marxists dedicated to a market economy and to preserving a sovereign and separate East Germany),[59] the Entrepreneurs' Association, and an independent police trade union. Many leading communists switched political parties, like Wolfgang Berghofer, the reformist mayor of Dresden who resigned from the communist party to join the Social Democratic Party.[60] Overnight membership in the SED/PDS became stigmatized. *Neues Deutschland* reported in December 1989 that factories were posting signs: "Job vacancies. . . . No SED members need apply."[61]

As in other countries of Eastern Europe, independent newspapers and magazines began publication in early 1990. In the East German context one may mention the *Leipziger Andrea Zeitung* and *Die Andere*, both launched in January 1990, and the *Thüringer Anzeiger*, which started in February.

Small signs of change also were noticeable, such as the restoration of text in the national anthem,[62] the disclosure for the first time of the number of East German suicides (5,005 in 1987; 4,768 in 1988),[63] the revelation that the SED had seriously considered building extensive additional internment camps in the 1970s in order to lock up thousands of political dissidents and other opponents,[64] and the political rehabilitation of exiled dissident Rudolf Bahro in June.[65]

In late January the government and the opposition agreed to advance the elections to 18 March. The results came as a surprise to most observers. The Social Democrats, expected by many to take first place, garnered only 22 percent of the vote, while the conservative Alliance for Germany, led by the CDU, took 48 percent. The New Forum, which had emerged during the demonstrations of October and November 1989, collected only 3 percent of the vote. The CDU's strong commitment to early reunification and West German Chancellor Helmut Kohl's strong backing were said to have accounted for the CDU's strong showing (it took 41 percent of the 48 percent for the Alliance as a whole). Lothar de Maizière, viola player and new chair of the CDU-East, became prime minister. The church's strong contribution to the opposition was reflected in three of its pastors being named to the new cabinet: Markus Meckel, leader of the Social Democratic Party, became foreign minister; Rainer Eppelmann, leader of the Democratic Awakening Party, became minister of defense and disarmament; and Hans-Wilhelm Ebeling, leader of the conservative German Social Union became minister of development aid.

As early as 9 November 1989 the East German government (still controlled, at that point, by the SED) dismantled sections of the Berlin Wall and allowed free movement between East and West Berlin. Germans danced on the Wall, and, hungry for souvenirs and mementos, people knocked out pieces of the Wall to take home. In a matter of a few months, the Wall had been largely chipped away.

Popular support for reunification gained strength rapidly, and the movement toward reunification quickly gathered momentum. On 19 May the two Germanys signed a state treaty agreeing to establish economic and monetary union, effective only seven weeks later, on 2 July. The treaty established that West Germany's central bank, the Bundesbank, would control monetary affairs, promised massive West German assistance ($85 billion) to East Germany's flagging economy (with forecasts that it would take at least a decade to bring real per capita income in the east close to what it is in the west), and established a basic conversion rate of two ostmarks (OM) for one deutsche mark (DM). East Germans would be able to convert OM4,000 at the rate of 1-to-1, and beyond that at a rate of 2-to-1. East Germans aged sixty and up would be allowed to exchange up to OM6,000 at the rate of 1-to-1, and children fourteen or younger would be allowed to exchange a maximum of OM2,000 at the special rate.[66] On 1 July the deutsche mark became the national currency of East Germany and the intra-German border was dismantled. On 3 July the East German government agreed to hold all-German parliamentary elections on 2 December 1990.[67] At the same time plans were announced to reorganize East Germany's seventeen provinces into five federal states, in effect restoring the traditional jurisdictional borders which had existed before communism.

The superpowers gave German reunification their blessing, and as of July 1990 it appeared that a reunited Germany would be able to retain membership in the NATO alliance by agreeing to limit its armed forces. West Germany and the United States proposed a nine-point plan to the Soviets, which, inter alia, would guarantee that a united Germany would not develop nuclear, chemical, or biological weapons; would entail German renunciation not merely of Polish territories but also of territories lost to the USSR in World War II; would guarantee that no NATO troops would be stationed in the territory of what was East Germany; and would allow Soviet troops to remain in the area of East Germany for a transition period at German expense. To sweeten the deal, the West German government unilaterally extended a $2.9 billion credit to the Soviet Union to help Gorbachev's economic reform program—the largest Western credit ever made available to the USSR.[68] Ironically, the loan was approved on 22 June, the forty-ninth anniversary of the Nazi invasion of the Soviet Union.

One of the cultural side effects of German reunification was the sudden infusion of Anglicisms, long current in West Germany, into German speech in the eastern territories. Among the loan words currently fashionable in West Germany and now infiltrating East Germany: *dress shirt, city shirt, trend colors, jeans dressing, cash management, after-sales*

service, skin scent, cleansing scrub, razor burn relief, and *disco hip-hop.*
Also noted on the signs of a sock shop: *on wings of fantasy.*[69]

Oddly, after years of claiming that Bonn was not a "real" capital and
that the only city conceivable as a permanent German capital was Berlin,
in the summer of 1990 many West Germans started to express a preference for keeping the capital in Bonn.[70] For their part, the East Germans
were counting on the capital moving to Berlin, since they banked on that
to fuel the economic revival of eastern Germany. The controversy lasted
until early August, when agreement was finally reached that Berlin was
to be the capital. But uncertainty remained because it was stipulated in
the unification treaty that the all-German legislature to be elected in
December 1990 would determine where to locate the various ministries.
The implication was that most ministries could well remain in Bonn.[71]

On 23 August the East German parliament agreed to 3 October as the
date for German reunification, and the new Germany's united parliament held its first session on 4 October 1990—symbolically in the old
Reichstag building.

Hungary

After the removal of János Kádár from power in May 1988 Hungary was
unambiguously in transition. The HSWP took the lead in advocating reform, and at first seemed able to control the process of democratization.
But that process itself reinforced the strength of the HSWP's competition, eventually forcing the HSWP to lose control of the process and,
ultimately, the reins of power. It was thus in November 1988 that the parliament passed a democratization package designed to broaden "socialist
pluralism," and approved the introduction of a multiparty system by
1990 at the latest.[72]

A more decisive step toward repluralization was taken on 18 October
1989 when the Hungarian National Assembly adopted a series of amendments that prepared the way for multiparty elections. Among other
things, the amendments abolished the principle of the leading role of the
communist party, abolished the 21-member presidential council that had
served as the collective head of state, created a strong presidency (with
the incumbent to be elected to a four-year term by the National Assembly), created the Constitutional Court to review the constitutionality of
disputed laws, and provided guarantees for human and civil rights. The
amendment package also gave political parties the right to organize and
operate provided they observed the constitution. Two days later the assembly voted to disband the Workers' Guard, a paramilitary organization

of the HSWP whose members were seen as largely hostile to democratization, as well as the party organizations in the army. By November 1989 some party leaders were becoming fed up with this headlong retreat, however, and in November 1989 they began to talk about a possible coup. Ironically, they counted on military assistance from the hard-line governments of Czechoslovakia and Romania—governments within weeks of falling. Hungarian Premier Miklós Németh received a tip about the plans and alerted the ministry of the interior. The conspirators knew that the ministry was on their tracks, became frightened, and called a halt to their plans.[73]

With the new legal guarantees, political parties registered themselves in rapid succession. By mid-December 1989 thirteen parties had been registered, with applications submitted by another fifteen parties.[74] Among the newly emerging parties were the Independent Social Democratic Party, the Christian Democratic People's Party, the Hungarian Democratic Forum, the Hungarian Social Democratic Party, the Social Democratic Party, the Social Democratic Party of Hungarian Gypsies, the Homeland Party, the Free Democratic Party, and the Green Party. At the end of December the Independent Smallholders' Peasant Party split in two, giving rise to the National Bourgeois Smallholders' Party.[75] The Pan-Magyar Body, an organization operating underground since 1953, came out into the open, expressing concern about the fate of Hungarian culture both within and outside Hungary (that is, among Hungarians living in Romania and other neighboring states).[76] And, finally, there were rather confused reports that the old fascistic Arrowcross Party was being revived.[77]

As Hungary's first free elections in forty years drew closer, it became obvious that anticommunist sentiment was in high fever. All the bitterness and resentment accumulated below the surface for four decades was openly expressed.[78] Miklós Haraszti, the leader of the Free Democrats, drew the logical conclusion: "The communists are finished. They can never win a free election [in Hungary]."[79]

Finally, in March 1990 Hungarians went to the polls to elect all 386 members of the National Assembly. Some 70 percent of eligible voters cast ballots. The result was a resounding victory for the center-right and a decisive end to communist fantasies about retaining the reins. The Democratic Forum, which supports Hungarian neutrality and the achievement of a market economy in gradual, measured steps, won 24.7 percent of the vote. The Free Democrats, who want a faster transition to a market economy and are active supporters of Hungarian membership in the European Common Market, came in second with 21.4 percent of the vote. The Independent Smallholders' Party, which emphasizes the need to return farmland to families who owned it before collectivization, came in third with 11.8 percent. The ex-communists (Hungarian Socialist Party) took fourth place with 10.9 percent.[80] Democratic Forum leader József Antall, a former librarian and scholar of medical history, became prime minister and began to put together a coalition with several other parties—specifically, the Smallholders, the Christian Democrats, and the Young Democrats, thus bypassing the second-place Free Democrats and the fourth-place ex-communists.[81] Arpad Göncz, a founding member of the Free Democrats, was elected president. On 26 June the new parliament voted unanimously (with four abstentions) to negotiate Hungary's withdrawal from the Warsaw Pact.[82]

Westerners quickly identified Hungary as one of the more promising investment opportunities in the new Eastern Europe, and, as already noted in chapter 13, independent newspapers made an appearance, buoyed up by foreign capital. A private, English-language radio station also began operation in March 1990. Meanwhile, General Electric, Suzuki Motors, General Motors, US West Communications, and other Western companies signed major deals, involving automobiles, the modernization of the Hungarian telephone system, commercial and residential development in Budapest, and major transportation and manufacturing opportunities. On the lighter, more sybaritic side, a sex club opened in Budapest, publishing six sex magazines, and with two pornographic films to its credit by July 1990. The club announced plans to set up two "sex cruises" on Lake Balaton, to open brothels across Hungary, to establish a fleet of "sex taxis" to provide transport for call girls, and to market sex tours to Thailand, Greece, and other countries.[83]

In July 1990 Hungary reprivatized agriculture, returning nationalized farmlands to the original owners or their heirs.[84] Where shops, restaurants, and small businesses were concerned, however, the Hungarian parliament decided against returning them to the original owners, and opted instead to sell, in this case, some 10,000 such outlets to the highest bidders, starting in the spring of 1991. The privatization law, adopted on 18 September 1990, allowed that major chains, large department stores, hard-currency shops, pharmacies, and pawn shops would remain in state hands for the interim.[85]

Meanwhile, as of October 1990 there were warnings that Hungary was in for a difficult transition. Inflation had reached 30 percent by then, energy supplies were expected to dry up by December (because of the

USSR's failure to meet agreed oil deliveries), and Hungary's streets became home to thousands of the homeless, many of them new immigrants from Romania, Bulgaria, and various Third World countries.[86]

Poland

As of mid-1990 Poland was a noncommunist country with a communist president (Jaruzelski), ruled by a group of politicians associated with a trade union, rather than a party, who, in turn, governed an emergent free enterprise system in which more than half of Poland's 7,600 state enterprises were expected to still be in state hands even in 1993.[87] There were other paradoxes too. For example, the communist party (renamed Social Democracy), which long fulminated against private enterprise, had now lost its state subsidies and had therefore gone into business: the party converted a members-only guest house into a hotel, opened trade companies, rented office space, turned the Gdańsk party canteen into a public restaurant, opened a laundry and a shoe store, and even began offering driving lessons for an appropriate fee. As of January 1990 the party also hoped to open its own banks (in a joint venture with a Western bank), break into the tourist industry, and—with Swiss and German help—get into pharmaceuticals.[88]

In this land of paradoxes some eighty political parties contested in local elections in May 1990.[89] Yet none of these parties had accumulated any real power. With the communist party shattered and in disarray, the ad hoc political arm of Solidarity functioned as "the only real political institution in Poland."[90] Power was dispersed between two rival groups, both tied to Solidarity: one associated with Prime Minister Tadeusz Mazowiecki, who had been essentially picked by Lech Wałęsa to assume that office, but who had alienated Wałęsa by not consulting the latter as he assembled his cabinet; another associated with Solidarity chair Wałęsa, who accused Mazowiecki of being too slow in carrying out necessary economic changes. The conflict between Mazowiecki and Wałęsa became sharp enough to inspire the Warsaw daily *Trybuna* to suggest that Solidarity divide itself, and spawn two political parties: a center-left and a center-right party.[91]

Economic reconstruction has been more urgent than in Bulgaria, Czechoslovakia, or Hungary (or, for that matter, Albania). The Mazowiecki government concentrated on converting to a free enterprise system, curbing inflation, and making the zloty a convertible currency. To advance reprivatization Mazowiecki established the Agency for Ownership Changes, which was charged with drafting a privatization plan and identifying enterprises in good fiscal health for sale to private investors.

With the government removing price subsidies and hiking prices, at least part of the inflationary spiral was a direct result of government policy: in December 1989, for example, the Ministry of Finance announced that the retail prices of electricity, central heating, warm water, and gas would go up an average of 400 percent effective 1 January 1990.[92] Inflation in 1989 was estimated at 700–900 percent, but started to come down in 1990—70 percent in January, 24 percent in February, and 5 percent in March.

The government also approved twelve devaluations of the złoty in its first hundred days in power, and by January 1990 the official rate was close to the unofficial rate, and it was conceivable that the złoty would eventually become a hard currency.

But this economic medicine has been hard on Poles; industrial sales slumped 27 percent. Farmers complained that rising prices of machinery and fertilizer exceeded their capacity to cope. And by the end of May 1990 some 443,000 people registered as unemployed, in a country which had long been committed to the principle of full employment.[93]

On the political front the Mazowiecki government also confronted the complicated task of creating a legal framework for a pluralist democracy. Censorship was abolished in January 1990, the police force was depoliticized in February, and public control over the Ministry of Internal Affairs (as opposed to communist party control) was also instituted in February. Later, in July, Mazowiecki fired three of the four communist ministers who had been included in the government as the price for Solidarity's assumption of power: Czesław Kiszczak was ousted from the Ministry of Internal Affairs, Florian Siwicki from the Ministry of Defense, and Franciszek Wieladek from the Ministry of Transport.[94] The government also passed a law providing that any group could declare itself a political party and obtain full legal status, and that the authorities could not be empowered to make any decision affecting this process. The law also established that no political party could obtain any financial aid or subsidization from the government, and that no party could establish cells in workplaces, government offices, the police, or the military. The media were likewise depoliticized, with the result that coverage of the affairs of the Polish United Workers' Party (or, as renamed, Social Democracy) plunged.

As it became patently obvious that the old regime had passed, police and security offices started destroying files and official records. Bonfires of police and communist party records were reported in cities throughout the country before the government finally took steps to halt the destruction.[95]

As for the PUWP, its self-confidence was essentially shattered. By December 1988, for example, 38 percent of party members polled said they were ashamed to admit that they were members of the communist party.[96] In late January 1990 the party voted to dissolve itself, reconstituting itself as the "new" Social Democracy Party. Some hundred delegates immediately broke away and formed a rival organization, the Union for Social Democracy, led by reformist communist Tadeusz Fiszbach.

Between January and September 1990 the government returned some 12,000 enterprises to private hands. And as of September Polish authorities expressed their intention of literally giving away a major part of the state-owned economy to Polish citizens by distributing share vouchers to employees and selling additional shares (with discounts for employees).[97] Wałęsa, however, insisted that change could, and should, be faster, having demanded earlier that the government be granted special temporary powers to speed up reprivatization.[98] Wałęsa also criticized the Mazowiecki government for retaining functionaries—from factory foremen to school principals to government bureaucrats—who owed their positions to the communists. All such people, he demanded, should be fired. "Privatization is revolution," said economist Adam Glapinski, a Wałęsa-supporter. "It means 400,000 people will lose their jobs."[99]

In June Wałęsa formed a new political organization, the Center Alliance, to serve as his political machine, and in August he announced his candidacy for the Polish presidency. In July Mazowiecki's supporters, including Zbigniew Bujak and Władysław Frasyniuk, set up an organization known as Democratic Action, to advance the incumbent prime minister's political fortunes. Mazowiecki also declared his candidacy for the presidency. In these circumstances Poland's appointed president, Jaruzelski, announced that he would step down before the constitutional expiration of his term (which would have been in 1995).

In late September, after lengthy debate, the Polish parliament passed a constitutional amendment providing for the direct popular election of the president—a formula preferred by most Poles.[100] Elections were set for 25 November. Wałęsa's victory in those elections set the stage for a power struggle between the executive and legislative branches.

Meanwhile, democratization seemed to have unleashed a new wave of chauvinism, as reports surfaced of waxing anti-Semitism,[101] a rise of Belorussian nationalism,[102] the taunting of Protestant and agnostic children for not enrolling in "voluntary" Catholic religious instruction,[103] and voluble Polish outcry against a Soviet decision to allow German families forcibly exiled by Stalin to Central Asia to return to the family homesteads in the former East Prussian district.[104]

Romania

"No matter how one arrives in Romania," Celestine Bohlen recounted in the *New York Times* in May 1990, "the country looks as if it is falling apart. Bucharest's airport would be a disgrace anywhere. Water drips from the ceiling, floor tiles are cracked, plants are dead or dying in their pots and the first word of greeting for a visitor, passing an armed sentry at a makeshift checkpoint, is a whispered, 'Cigarettes.' "[105] The scene reflects the legacy of nearly twenty-five years of rule by Ceauşescu—a rule characterized by megalomania, self-glorification, corruption, nepotism, persecution, terror, and an economic policy that combined fallacy with exploitation.

Even as communism was collapsing in the rest of Eastern Europe, Ceauşescu refused to believe that change would come to Romania. On the eve of his overthrow, the party daily *Scînteia* published a lengthy article rejecting political pluralism.[106] In late November the Romanian CP held its fourteenth congress in Bucharest, and continued to sing the party secretary's praises as if nothing were wrong; and yet the atmosphere in Romania had been tense and there was a sense that people were stretched to the breaking point.

In summer 1989 a group of high-ranking communist party members hostile to the Ceauşescu regime formed an opposition group called the Council of National Salvation. The French embassy in Bucharest, and probably also the Soviet embassy, were informed at that time.[107] But the Council was shrouded in so much secrecy that as late as 14 December a Radio Free Europe report expressed uncertainty as to whether the organization really amounted to anything more than wishful thinking.[108]

On 15 December demonstrations broke out in Timişoara when local citizens rallied to prevent security forces from arresting a Reformed clergyman, László Tökés, who had been active in promoting the rights of Hungarians in Romania. Demonstrations and clashes between citizens and security forces, who charged the crowds with fixed bayonets, continued for days, and fighting spread to Arad, Braşov, Sibiu (Hermannstadt), and Bucharest. Romania closed its borders with Hungary and Yugoslavia on 18 December, and its borders with Bulgaria and Moldavia on 19 December. By then demonstrators were shouting, "Wake up Romanians!," "Down with the communists!," and "Death to the dictator!"

Ceauşescu then summoned Defense Minister General Vasie Milea, and ordered him to send troops to fire on the demonstrators. Milea refused, and shot himself in the heart in protest. His suicide helped to turn the army against Ceauşescu, and for several days, army troops did battle with security forces loyal to Ceauşescu. Nicolae and Elena Ceauşescu tried to flee, but were captured on 23 December, and executed on 25 December. Estimates of the number of dead ranged from 5,000 (Red Cross estimate) to 12,000 (Tanjug estimate) to 60,000 (official figure).

The National Salvation Front (NSF) quickly assumed control of the situation. The NSF leader was Ion Iliescu, a longtime communist who had been close to Ceauşescu in the 1970s. The NSF soon published its program, which called for the establishment of a multiparty system, free elections by April 1990, restructuring the economy on a free enterprise basis, halting the destruction of villages in Transylvania, and the establishment of freedom of religion.[109]

The new government immediately put Ceauşescu's closest accomplices on trial, including Emil Bobu (a former party secretary), Tudor Postelnicu (the former minister of the interior), Marin Meagoe (chief of security), Dumitru Popescu (former director of the Sociopolitical Academy), Ceauşescu's sons Nicu and Valentin, and various members of the old Securitate forces. The communist party was disbanded and banned. And a decree issued on 6 February 1990 permitted the establishment of private profitmaking businesses with up to twenty employees. The new government also authorized the registration of alternative political parties. By mid-January thirteen new parties had registered, and by the end of the first week of February the number had reached thirty-two. Fresh antigovernment demonstrations in late January forced the NSF to agree to form a new transitional government in which the major opposition parties would be represented. And in the midst of this mêlée, the former King Michael, who had abdicated under pressure in 1947, issued a statement, "If Romanians ask me to return, I am always ready to resume my constitutional responsibilities."[110]

Hungarian-Romanian relations were an obvious policy area of centrality. And the new regime wisely announced that the educational system would be reformed to provide more Hungarian-language instruction in all grades. An early move was the restoration of Hungarian-language instruction at the Tirgu Mureş Medical-Pharmaceutical Institute.[111] The regime also promoted discussion of the possibility of providing "cultural" autonomy for Transylvania's Hungarian population.[112]

Several political parties catering to ethnic Hungarian interests were also founded, including the Magyar Independent Party headquartered in Tirgu Mureş, the Democratic Union of Magyars in Romania (under General Secretary Geza Szocs), the Union of Hungarian Democratic Youth, and a movement dedicated to easing interethnic tensions, the Hungarian-Romanian Democratic Association, created on the joint initiative of members of both national groups.

But on 15 March 1990, when the Democratic Union of Magyars staged some commemorative events, such as laying a wreath at a monument to Hungary's national poet, Sándor Petőfi, the Romanian nationalist organization Vatra Romaneasca (Romanian Hearth) replied with counter-demonstrations, leading to three days of bloodshed in Transylvania and the declaration of a state of emergency in Tirgu Mureş. Tanks cordoned off access roads and observers spoke of the danger of imminent civil war.

In these conditions—a bankrupt economy, a disintegrated political infrastructure, the dangers of civil war, and squabbling among aspiring politicians—the provisional government made preparations for the democratic elections, which had been postponed to 20 May to give the new parties more time.

By the time the elections were held, there were seventy-eight parties competing,[113] including the National Peasant Party (under Ion Ratiu), the Liberal Party (under Radu Campeanu), the Social Democratic Party, the Democratic Agrarian Union, the Free Democratic Youth Party (aiming at recruiting young people), the Humanist Ecological Party, the Democratic Unity Party of Moldavia, the Free for the Change Party (emphasizing safeguards for freedom of speech), and the Romanian Ecologist Movement. During the campaign there were frequent complaints by "opposition" parties that the NSF was using violence to harass and intimidate them. The National Peasant Party claimed that sixty local offices had been attacked or damaged, and both leading opposition parties (Ratiu's Peasants, and Campeanu's Liberals) said that organized squads had disrupted some of their rallies.[114]

When the results were tallied, the NSF claimed that its presidential candidate, Ion Iliescu, had won with 86.5 percent of the vote, with only 9.8 percent going to Campeanu, and 3.7 percent to Ratiu. In parliamentary voting the official tally was National Salvation Front, 69.0 percent; Democratic Union of Magyars, 6.9 percent; National Liberal Party, 6.0 percent; Green Party, 2.5 percent; National Peasant Party, 2.0 percent; and Vatra Romaneasca, 2.0 percent.[115] This gave the NSF 354 seats in the 506-member parliament; the Democratic Union of Magyars had the second largest bloc of deputies, with 41 seats.[116]

But amid charges of fraud and accusations that the NSF was dominated by communists, rioting erupted in Bucharest in mid-June. When the army refused to respond to President Iliescu's call for help, he appealed to the country's miners, a reliable bloc of NSF support. Within a matter of hours thousands of miners from northern Romania, wearing dirty work-clothes and brandishing shovels, pick-axes, and rubber hoses, descended on the capital and seized control of downtown Bucharest. By evening the miners had beaten up large numbers of citizens, cleared the university square where the antigovernment demonstration had taken place, and restored a kind of order.[117] A grateful Iliescu praised the miners as "a strong force with much civic discipline."[118] But in relying on vigilantes rather than institutionalized forces to restore order, Iliescu unwittingly betrayed the fact that Romania was still in a revolutionary state.

Yugoslavia

In Yugoslavia, despite an early start on the road to repluralization, the entire process was made more complex by the national question, and more specifically, by the decentralization of power to rival wings of the party, representing discrete nationality groups and sometimes advocating diametrically opposed political platforms. Thus, at the close of the 1980s, while the Slovenian communist party advocated a further loosening of the federation, full republic status for Kosovo, the introduction of a multiparty system in the country as a whole (or minimally in Slovenia), and the reduction of Slovenia's economic obligations to the federation, the Serbian communist party (captured in summer 1987 by the Serbian nationalist demagogue Slobodan Milošević) advocated a recentralized federation with reduced powers for the federal units,[119] the scaling back of Kosovo's autonomy, the retention of political monopoly by the communist party, and the maintenance of existing interregional economic obligations. In pursuit of the second of these objectives, the Serbian party held a referendum on 1 July 1990 asking Serbs to approve a program that essentially eliminated what little autonomy Kosovo still retained at that point.[120]

In the course of 1989 polemics intensified between Slovenia and Serbia over Kosovo, the constitution, and the country's federal arrangement. There were also renewed polemics between Croats and Serbs over the status of Croatia's Serbian minority, which has, at times, sought to establish a Serbian autonomous province within Croatia. Within Bosnia, ethnic frictions—especially between Serbs and non-Serbs—became serious enough that Bosnian party officials gingerly conceded the existence of problems. And then there was Kosovo. As a result, the national question dramatically overshadowed, and, for a while, even preempted, the issue of democratization.

But the various independent groups and associations that had emerged in Yugoslavia in the course of the 1980s continued to press for repluralization. A decisive turn (noted in chapter 13) came with the trial of Janša, Borstner, Tasić, and Zavrl for their magazine article revealing a military conspiracy to arrest various liberal politicians in Slovenia and restore "socialist order" in that republic.[121] The repluralization of Slovenia was powerfully reinforced and quickened by the fallout from the trial.[122]

As alternative political associations announced their formation in one republic after another, the communist authorities eventually had to adjust, and by June 1990 the communist party organizations of all six republics had endorsed the establishment of a multiparty system. Indeed, two of the parties had been voted out of power (the Slovenian and the Croatian), and had changed their names and foresworn Marxism.[123]

The Slovenian party also walked out of the fourteenth extraordinary congress of the LCY in January 1990, causing it to adjourn, and declared that it no longer recognized any organizational links with, or material obligations to, the LCY.[124] The LCY lacked the will or the ability to do anything about this action. Some Slovenian politicians announced their commitment to seeing Slovenia have its own currency, its own army, and its own foreign ministry[125]—whether as a fully independent state or as a sovereign member of a Yugoslav confederation.

Meanwhile, the infrastructure of party control disintegrated as party members turned in their membership cards, party organizations in economic enterprises and government offices closed up, newspapers severed their connections with party organizations, and pressure was exerted for the disbandment of party organizations in the army as well as the people's general defense and social self-protection committees, also under party control. Symptomatic of this disintegration was the decision, taken in the Serbian republic in June 1990, to remove Marxism from the high school curriculum and to replace it with courses on religion.[126]

The army, long a bulwark of the one-party system, belatedly gave the green light to a multiparty system through an interview with Assistant Defense Secretary Colonel-General Simeon Bunčić. Interviewed by the Sarajevo daily *Oslobodjenje* in February 1990, Bunčić said that Yugoslav society had reached a "consensus" that the country needed a multiparty system, and indicated that the army would not seek to prevent this.

In spring 1990 free elections were held in two of Yugoslavia's six republics, Slovenia and Croatia. The result was a resounding victory for noncommunist political forces that left Yugoslavia a political anomaly, with communists temporarily still in control in four republics and center-right groups in control in two republics. In Slovenia the election was taken by Demos, an opposition alliance of Social Democrats, Christian Democrats, Liberals (the former youth organization), and others, while in Croatia, the Croatian Democratic Community, headed by retired General Franjo Tudjman, handily won control of the Croatian Assembly with 205 of the 356 seats, and elected Tudjman—whom the communists had for years denounced as a "fascist" and had even imprisoned at one point—president of Croatia. One of the new Croatian government's first acts was to remove the word "socialist" from the name of the republic, and to remove the red star from the flag and coat of arms of the republic.[127]

Both Demos and the Croatian Democratic Community shared a common vision of a confederal Yugoslavia, in which the constituent republics would cooperate as sovereign, self-governing states. To this end, the new governments of these two republics jointly coordinated a strategy to press for the earliest possible inception of negotiations on the confederalization of Yugoslavia.[128] Support for this program was strong, with some 51.9 percent of Slovenes favoring confederation in a March 1990 poll, 28 percent preferring secession, and no one expressing support for a unitary Yugoslavia.[129] The drive for confederalization received a further boost on 2 July, when the provincial government of Kosovo declared its independence from Serbia.[130]

In July Slovenia and Croatia proclaimed their sovereignty, followed on 1 August by Bosnia. In October Slovenia and Croatia presented a joint proposal for the restructuring of Yugoslavia as a confederation, as the Slovenes opened liaison offices in Brussels, Vienna, Luxemburg, Washington, D.C., and Moscow.[131] The proposal called for confederation member states to raise their own armed forces, but to coordinate their foreign policy and participate in a joint "advisory" parliament.[132] Slovenia was allegedly planning to raise a peacetime army of 16,000–17,000, an air force of 2,500, and a navy of 1,000, with 40,000–60,000 troops in reserves.[133]

Within Croatia itself, an illegal referendum conducted among local Serbs from 19 August–2 September resulted in an overwhelming vote in favor of a Serbian autonomous district in Croatia. In the wake of this vote, the Serbs declared their autonomy and armed themselves, raiding at least one police station and burglarizing local gun shops.[134] Federal troops were rushed to the Knin region, where most of this was taking place,[135] but as September wore on, there were clashes between local Serbs and Croatian riot police in several Croatian cities.[136] In early October there were reports that Serbs had shot and wounded two Croatian police. The Croatian government belatedly tried to assuage Serbian temper by offering Serbs "cultural" autonomy.[137] But Serbs had earlier indicated that in the event of confederalization, they wanted full political autonomy, if not actual secession from Croatia.

Elsewhere around the country civil order continued to disintegrate. The otherwise promising news that there were some 30,000 private businesses in operation in Yugoslavia by mid-September[138] seemed almost irrelevant as ethnic tensions flared throughout the country, generally pitting Serbs against non-Serbs. In Bosnia, Muslims organized a political party, while Serbs and Croats began to talk of taking parts of Bosnia for themselves. In Vojvodina there were calls for a republic. In Serbia itself, Muslims in the region of Novi Pazar began demanding separation from Serbia and an administrative link with Bosnia. And in Kosovo the Serbian government dissolved the provincial assembly and closed down the Albanian-language daily, *Rilindja*. When the now-dissolved provincial assembly defiantly met in a secret session on 7 September and adopted a constitution proclaiming Kosovo a "republic" within a Yugoslav "confederation,"[139] Serbian authorities ordered the arrest of the members of the dissolved assembly and eliminated most of the few remaining vestiges of Kosovar autonomy.[140] By October 1990 Yugoslavia was on the brink of civil war, and it appeared increasingly unlikely that Yugoslav politicians would find a way to pull back from the brink. Much of the problem stemmed from the demagogic mass manipulation by Serbia's nationalist leadership.

Between December 1990 and January 1991 Serb-Croat relations continued to disintegrate. Serbia's Slobodan Milošević worked in coordination with the army to set up a revived Communist Party (placing his wife, Mirjana, in the leadership of this new party). In mid-January, the army, 70 percent of whose officers were Serbs, put pressure on Slovenia and Croatia to disarm their newly created paramilitary forces, threatening invasion if the two republics did not comply. Slovenia and Croatia refused, placed their military forces on high alert status and signed a bilateral agreement to coordinate security and defense matters.[141] Late January produced a kind of truce in the gathering crisis, and an agreement among the republics to enter into a series of summit talks to search for an exit from the impasse. Slovenia served notice that she was proceeding with the establishment of infrastructure necessary to independent existence, and promised that if there should be no confederal pact by June, she would secede unilaterally from the Yugoslav federation and apply for membership in the UN and other international bodies.[142]

Croatia indicated that if Slovenia seceded, she would follow suit.[143] And Bosnia made it clear that under no circumstances would she remain part of a truncated Yugoslavia, and that she might even join a prospective Slovenian-Croatian confederation, as a third member. The fifth round of interrepublic talks were held in Sarajevo on 22 February but failed to reach any agreement. Serbia and Montenegro continued to press for a tight federation. Slovenia and Croatia held fast to their position that the only basis for a "Yugoslav" solution was confederation. Bosnia suggested a compromise, with Serbia and Montenegro regulated tightly by a central government and Slovenia and Croatia enjoying confederal status, with Bosnia and Macedonia enjoying some undefined intermediate status.[144] This compromise was designed to serve Bosnia's economic interests and to prevent the delicate political balance in that republic (amid gathering frictions between Serbs and non-Serbs) from coming unglued. This compromise was, however, completely unsatisfactory to the Macedonians, who restated their long-standing insistence [145] on the absolute equality of the republics as a prerequisite for any overall solution. The sixth round of summit talks was held in Belgrade on 1 March, but, as before, Croatia refused to attend any talks held in Belgrade. By the beginning of March it was difficult to imagine how Yugoslavia could avoid civil war, and the dispatch of federal army troops to the village of Pakrac in Croatia on 2 March was an ominous symptom of the escalation of localized violence.[146]

Part VI
Building New Systems

16. Core Tasks for a Pluralist Order

The community is a fictitious body, composed of the individual persons who are considered as constituting as it were its members. The interest of the community then is, what?—the sum of the interests of the several members who compose it.—JEREMY BENTHAM, *An Introduction to the Principles of Morals and Legislation (1780; rev. 1789)*

The people is dead.—Up with me!—MAX STIRNER, *The Ego and His Own (1845)*

In many ways the states of Eastern Europe find themselves in a situation reminiscent of and similar to the early years after World War I. Then, as now, the region had a number of newly independent states that needed to construct their political systems virtually from scratch. Then, as now, the task of economic reconstruction occupied a high priority (in the 1920s, as a result of the economic costs of four years of warfare; in the 1990s, as a result of the economic costs of forty years of communism). Then, as now, the new era opened with a period of prolonged chaos and conflict in which borders shifted. In the years after 1918, Czechoslovakia, Yugoslavia, and Romania sent troops into Hungary to annex Hungarian land, Poland invaded Russia in search of additional territory, and the Yugoslav army faced armed revolts against its newly imposed rule in Montenegro, Kosovo, and elsewhere. Now, in the wake of communism's demise in the region, Serbia has gone to war first against Croatia, then against Bosnia, and it may expand the war to the province of Kosovo as well, while Romania has struggled to keep out of the ethnic war brewing in neighboring Moldova. Then, as now, national borders were redefined—in the years after World War I sometimes several times within a short span. And then, as now, the process of adjusting to new realities was accompanied by increased activity by political extremists: in the early 1920s by bolsheviks; by the early 1930s by fascists; and in the early 1990s by various stripes of national chauvinists and skinheads, together with a mixed collection of atavistic monarchists.

In some ways, thus, the present scenario in Eastern Europe looks all too familiar. But differences are present, and some of them may prove crucial. To begin with, the elites of the 1990s are constructing their political infrastructure in a manner unlike their earlier counterparts. Rather than adapting existing institutional structures to new realities (the Yugoslav model in the interwar period) or creating them in a vacuum, today's leaders have made heavy use of foreign, and especially American, expertise in writing their laws and developing new political institutions. This is a critical difference between the earlier era and today.

The East European elites speak of constructing a pluralist political and social order, of creating democracies on the debris of failed communist systems. Parallel undertakings have been pursued earlier in Latin America and elsewhere, and a growing theoretical literature exists about transitions from authoritarianism to democracy.[1] A growing body of theoretical literature also deals alternatively with the debilities of communist regimes,[2] or with the processes of democratization, in Eastern Europe itself.[3] This chapter is built, in part, on insights found in that literature, as explained and developed in chapter 1. I propose to analyze the tasks confronted by the governments of Eastern Europe today and to assess these states' advantages and disadvantages in tackling these tasks. I shall also suggest some alternative variations that may emerge. Bearing in mind the unique features of the German case as well as those of the former Yugoslav republics currently at war, I shall limit myself to an assessment of six countries: Poland, Czechoslovakia (and its successors), Hungary, Bulgaria, Romania, and Slovenia.

In the opening chapter I suggested that the creation of a stable pluralist order—which is certainly the goal sought by the political mainstream in Poland, the Czech Republic, Hungary, Slovenia, Bulgaria, and arguably in Romania and Slovakia—requires the satisfaction of twelve preconditions. To analyze them more succinctly, these may, in turn, be clustered around five core tasks: (1) the revival and privatization of the economy (precondition 1); (2) the establishment of a constitutional order including the rule of law and guarantees for multiparty competition (embracing preconditions 6, 7, 8, 9, 10, and 11); (3) the demonopolization of the media (precondition 12); (4) the moderation of ethnic and regional conflict, including dealing with right-wing chauvinism of diverse stripes (encompassing preconditions 2 and 3); and (5) the legitimation of the new order (preconditions 4 and 5). Other domestic tasks, such as the depoliticization of the army and the effort to come to terms with the past, derive from these core groupings.

Reviving the Economy

Of these five tasks the economy is perhaps the most basic. Without progress on the economic front, social tensions could be expected to escalate, which would fuel extremist politics, especially the extremism of the right.

The years 1990–91 saw economic deterioration throughout the region, with the gross domestic product shrinking in 1990 by as much as 11 percent in Poland and Bulgaria and by about 8 percent in Yugoslavia and Romania. Economic decline turned into economic collapse in 1991, with the rates of shrinkage ranging from 9 percent in Poland to 17 percent in Bulgaria. And in 1992, only Poland managed to even halt the decline; the remaining East European states experienced further drop-offs of 5–25 percent (see table 7). Set against regionwide declines in industrial production and in agriculture,[4] the proliferation of runaway inflation has hampered efforts to revive the economy, in some countries more than elsewhere (see table 8).

On other measures, however, the balance sheet is more mixed. Several countries were able, for example, to net positive foreign trade balances in 1992, and the unemployment rates in June 1992 were as small as 5.5 percent in Czechoslovakia and 6.7 percent in Romania (see table 9). Unemployment in the Czech Republic stood at 3 percent in late 1992, as compared with a rate of nearly 12 percent in Slovakia.[5]

Contributing to the region's economic difficulties has been the collapse of the Soviet-sponsored Council for Mutual Economic Assistance (CMEA), which had serious repercussions for several national economies. As a result of the loss of CMEA-sheltered trade, the Hungarian precision engineering industry has shrunk 50 percent in two years, while the Hungarian metallurgy industry sank 60–70 percent in the same period.[6] Poland was similarly hard-hit by the collapse of trade with the USSR and the loss of protected Eastern markets. Poland has essentially compensated for these losses, however, even if not always to the benefit of the same enterprises.[7] Czechoslovakia and Bulgaria were hurt the most by the collapse of CMEA trade, since intra-CMEA trade had accounted for more than 60 percent of their total foreign trade.[8]

Surveying the region as a whole, the countries can be divided into

Table 7. The Decline of Gross Domestic Product in East European Countries, 1990–1993 (in %)

	1990	1991	1992	1993[**]
Bulgaria	−11.8	−16.7	−15.0	−5 to 0
Croatia	−9.3	−28.7	−25.0	N/A
Czech Republic	−2.0	−14.0	−7.0	−4 to −3
Hungary	−3.3	−11.9	−5.0	−2 to 2
Poland	−11.6	−9	0	3.8[***]
Romania	−7.4	−13.7	−15.0	−5
Slovakia	0.0	−16.4	−9.0	−8 to −5
Slovenia	−3.4	−9.3	−6.0	−1.0
Yugoslavia	−8.5	−20	N/A	N/A

[**] = expected   [***] = actual

Sources: Neue Zürcher Zeitung, 29/30 Mar. 1992, 14; *Neue Zürcher Zeitung,* 21 Oct. 1992, 11; *Neue Zürcher Zeitung,* 3 Mar. 1993, 18; *Neue Zürcher Zeitung,* 4/5 Apr. 1993, 9; and Ben Slay, "The East European Economies," *RFE/RL Research Report* 2, no. 1 (1 January 1993): 114. The Bulgarian figure for 1991 is taken from *Vjesnik* (Zagreb), 28 Apr. 1993, 13, reporting official figures released by the National Bank of Bulgaria. The Polish figure for 1993 is taken from *RFE/RL News Briefs* (17 June 1994), 18.

Table 8. Inflation Rates in East European Countries, 1991–1992 (in %)

	1991	1992
Bulgaria	480	81
Czechoslovakia	58	11
Hungary	35	25.9
Poland	70.3	46.0
Romania	165	210.4
Slovenia	115	207

Sources: Neue Zürcher Zeitung, 21 Oct. 1992, 11; the 1992 inflation figure for Romania is taken from *Neue Zürcher Zeitung,* 24 Feb. 1993, 16; the 1992 inflation figure for Bulgaria is taken from BTA (Sofia), 7 Jan. 1993, in FBIS, *Daily Report* (Eastern Europe), 8 Jan. 1993, 6; the 1992 inflation figure for Poland is taken from *Neue Zürcher Zeitung,* 10 Dec. 1992, 17; the 1992 inflation figure for Hungary is taken from MTI (Budapest), 15 Apr. 1993, in FBIS, *Daily Report* (Eastern Europe), 21 Apr. 1993, 17; the 1992 inflation figure for Czechoslovakia is taken from William Echikson, "Where Eastern Europe is Booming," *Fortune,* 12 July 1993, 22. The Slovenian data (for cost of living) are taken from Egon Žižmond, "Slovenia— One Year of Independence", in *Europe-Asia Studies,* 45, no. 5 (1993), 893.

Table 9. Economic Indices in East European Countries, 1992

	Foreign trade balance in millions of $	Percentage unemployed (June 1992)
Bulgaria	435	12.5
Czechoslovakia	366	5.5
Hungary	−40	11.4 *
Poland	946	12.6
Romania	−877	6.7
Slovenia	250	12.0

* = in September 1992

Sources: *Neue Zürcher Zeitung,* 21 Oct. 1992, 11; and *Magyar Hirlap* (Budapest), 24 Nov. 1992, 10, trans. in FBIS, *Daily Report* (Eastern Europe), 2 Dec. 1992, 18.

three broad groups. The first group consists of eastern Germany, Poland, the Czech Republic, and Hungary—those countries that have begun to turn the corner on economic revival.

Poland. In Poland, for example, despite a harsh drought in 1992 (necessitating heavy wheat imports),[9] and despite higher rates of unemployment in the countryside,[10] industrial production began to rally in March 1992, the decline in construction activity was halted, unemployment was stabilized, and inflation was sharply sliced—from a dramatic 585 percent in 1990 to 46 percent in 1992.[11] Experts argue that Poland's recovery was better secured in 1992 than the incipient recovery of most other states in the region, in part because Poland's private sector was much larger by then than it had been in 1990. Already in 1990 the private sector accounted for 27 percent of total industrial output and 35 percent of the GDP. The private sector embraced more than 80 percent of total retail trade, and by 1991 it contributed 19.8 percent of total exports, recording at the same time 46.1 percent of total imports.[12] By early 1993 the private sector accounted for 57 percent of the labor force and produced about one-third of all industrial products.[13] With foreign investment by Coca-Cola, Amoco, Levi Strauss, McCormick Energy, and others, Polish officials forecast that the country's economy would grow an average of 5 percent per year through 1997.[14]

Czechoslovakia and Its Successors. In Czechoslovakia the economic picture was complicated by the agreement to divide the country in two— thus, splitting the banking and monetary system and creating jurisdictional obstacles to economic cooperation across the border. The Czech Republic has always been the more prosperous region; in 1991, for example, the Czech GDP per capita was 24 percent higher than that in Slovakia.[15] Many Czechs told pollsters that they expected the Czech economy to benefit from the secession of Slovakia. But in July 1992 economic experts of the Czech and Slovak Confederation of Trade Unions offered a more sobering appraisal. In their view "the CSFR's partition [will] have a negative impact on the economy of both sides. Although the impact on Slovakia [will] be more severe, the idea that the Czech Republic [will] shed some sort of burden by means of the state's partition is nonetheless illusory."[16] The trade union experts forecast that as a result of the partition, unemployment would rise 20–25 percent in Slovakia and 10 percent in the Czech Republic (see table 10).

At the same time, Czech authorities expressed confidence that their republic would register an economic recovery in 1993, hoping for a real economic growth of 1 to 3 percent for that year.[17] In Slovakia the mood was less confident, and in the spring of 1992 some Slovak citizens began transferring their savings to banks in the Czech Republic in expectation that the eventual Czech currency would be stronger than the Slovak.[18] The Czech and Slovak economies have been evolving in different directions. Slovak Prime Minister Vladimir Mečiar was troubled by the damage done to Slovak arms industries by Prague's renunciation of arms trade, and he expressed concern that the accelerated privatization favored by Czech ministers would further hurt Slovak industry, fueling unemployment. The result was Slovak foot-dragging in 1991–92, and as of October 1992 some 95.8 percent of Slovak industry was still in state hands, as contrasted with 69.8 percent of Czech industry.[19] Many observers expected Mečiar to seek to maintain the state monopoly in the economy, at least in the larger enterprises. Overall production declined 14.1 percent in Slovakia in 1992, and as foreign currency reserves plummeted, the Bratislava government launched a drive in February 1993 asking citizens to donate jewelry, pendants, foreign cash, even gold fillings to the depleted Slovak treasury.[20] Although most indicators pointed to trouble for their fledgling economy, Slovaks nonetheless could take solace in a foreign trade surplus in the first two months of 1993 and a slowing decline in industrial production.[21]

Between December 1989 and July 1993 foreign investors pumped some $1.7 billion into the Czech and Slovak republics, most of it going to the Czech Republic. But by mid-1993 reports circulated that Czechoslovakia's breakup had made the region composed by its successor states less attractive to foreign investors.[22] Already in May 1993, then–Prime Minister Mečiar confessed that "Slovakia is like a train with 5.3 million passengers, going down a hill with no brakes."[23] With exports sinking

Table 10. Economic Indices of the Czech and Slovak Republics, 1993

	Czech Republic	Slovakia
Unemployment in % *	2.88	12.01
Inflation rate **	11.1	19.3 ***
% of industrial output of former CSFR	71.8	28.2
% of retail trade of former CSFR	67.4	32.6

* = in March 1993
** = January–December 1992
*** = February 1992–February 1993
Sources: Slovak unemployment rate from CTK (Prague), 8 Apr. 1993, in FBIS, *Daily Report* (Eastern Europe), 15 Apr. 1993, 17; Czech unemployment rate from CTK, 9 Mar. 1993, in FBIS, *Daily Report* (Eastern Europe), 15 Apr. 1993, 13; Slovak inflation rate from *Republika* (Bratislava), 9 Apr. 1993, 8, 9, trans. in FBIS, *Daily Report* (Eastern Europe), 19 Apr. 1993, p. 13; Czech inflation figure from CTK, (28 Jan. 1993, in FBIS, *Daily Report* (Eastern Europe), 2 Feb. 1993, 13; other figures from *Financial Times* (London), 24 Mar. 1993, sec. 4, 1.

precipitously after the breakup and hard currency reserves dwindling to a mere $200 million, the Slovak government was forced to order the devaluation of its currency by 10.4 percent on 11 July.[24] Gross domestic product in Slovakia declined 4.1 percent in 1993, but was expected to stagnate in 1994. Bratislava authorities hoped that the gross domestic product would begin to rise once again in 1995, perhaps by as much as 2 percent.[25] After the replacement of the Mečiar government in March 1994 by one headed by Premier Jozef Moravcik, the new authorities undertook sweeping changes to the taxation and budgetary systems, designed to slash government expenditures. As Bratislava achieved some success with these reforms, the IMF moved closer to approving a standby loan for Slovakia—an approval widely interpreted as signaling to potential foreign investors that the government's policies are sound.[26]

Hungary. Hungary has likewise recorded signs of economic recovery. Industrial exports revived and increased in the first six months of 1992, stagnating in July and August, while the decline in industrial production slowed steadily throughout the year, eventually rising by 5 percent in September.[27] Hungary also managed to reduce its foreign debt from a peak of $21.5 billion in 1990 to $19.9 billion in July 1991.[28] Budapest's policies of imposing stiff tariffs to protect key sectors and of emphasizing currency convertibility may be paying off. Hungary attracted some $4.7 billion in foreign investments in 1992, amounting to nearly 25 percent of all Western investments in the former eastern bloc, and succeeded in cutting the inflation rate to 17 percent by early 1993. By 1994 Hungarian authorities hoped that GDP growth would reach 4 percent.[29] By July 1993

Budapest had even built up foreign currency reserves of $5 billion. In May 1994, the government completed the second-stage of a three-stage recapitalization program designed to bolster the capital assets of Hungary's eight largest banks.[30]

Bulgaria, Slovenia, and Romania compose a second group, distinct from the first, in that their economies, while not suffering direct or indirect war damage (as is the case in Serbia, Croatia, and Bosnia), are nonetheless not expected to turn the corner on economic recovery until 1994 or later. The Bulgarian and Slovenian economies also show some positive signs, although difficulties have been mounting steadily for Slovenia since the spring of 1992. One of the problems affecting both Bulgaria and Romania is that unlike Czechoslovakia, Hungary, and Poland, which abolished central planning in a controlled way, in these two countries "central planning . . . appears simply to have collapsed."[31] Formulation and implementation of comprehensive reform and transformation packages have therefore lagged.

Slovenia. Slovenia's economy is simultaneously both the smallest and, potentially at least, the most vibrant in this (second) set of countries. Indeed, before the outbreak of war in Bosnia in April 1992 and the consequent arrival of tens of thousands of Bosnian refugees, Slovenia's overall economic picture would have placed it firmly in the first category.[32] Slovenia's first good news on the economic front came in February 1992 when the first (albeit modest at 1.072 percent) increase in industrial production was reported. Since then, however, Slovenia has had to struggle to cope with refugees in numbers far exceeding what it could realistically accommodate, even as the effects of the disruption of the Yugoslav economic market started to be felt. By late 1993 industrial production in Slovenia was rebounding.[33]

Bulgaria. In contrast, the Bulgarian economy continued to slide throughout 1992. Production and sales declined steadily, while living costs have risen. Bulgaria's economic transition has been rendered more complicated by the large portion of the budget tied up in servicing existing debts (25 percent in 1992),[34] by losses associated with observation of the UN embargo against Serbia (amounting to $60 million per month, for a total of $1.2 billion in losses as of January 1993),[35] by the presence of a number of unrecoverable loans on the ledgers of Bulgarian banks,[36] and by strange errors in the agricultural sector.[37] The budget was so tight that even the army had to pull in its belt. A frustrated Bulgarian general put it this way in November 1992:

> We have not imported almost anything essential in the last two to three years. Some 47 per cent of our military budget is spent on wages, and 38 per cent for food and clothing. This means that we have only 15 per cent left for everything else—the purchase of weapons and equipment, spare parts, and so forth. The weapons of the Navy and the Air Force, and the vehicles of the Ground Troops have become obsolete.[38]

And yet in October 1992 the OECD released a report commending Bulgaria for its progress toward a stable market economy. The OECD was impressed, inter alia, by Sofia's restrictive fiscal and loan policies, by its legislation on privatization, and by its smothering of inflation to an annual rate of less than 2 percent by August 1992 (though the year ended up with a higher overall figure, because of the high rates in early 1992).[39] Moreover, even though the economy overall continued to decline during 1991–92, broken down by sectors it becomes clear that while the state sector has continued to erode, the private sector is steadily expanding, with private sales recording impressive gains (e.g., a 10 percent increase in just one month, July–August 1992). As of September 1992 private distributive trade already accounted for 46 percent of total turnover.[40] Further, after declaring a unilateral moratorium (in 1990) on payments against its $9.2 billion foreign debt, Sofia resumed payments in September/October 1992. Taking stock of these and other factors, the IMF concluded in late 1992 that Bulgaria was "positioned well to begin the second stage of its transition to a market economy, putting state enterprises into private hands."[41]

In January 1993 Prime Minister Ljuben Berov projected a modest economic recovery in the year's second half, and he spoke of holding year-end inflation to 56 percent—which, if possible, would represent a tangible turning point in Bulgaria's economic recovery.[42]

Romania. Surveys conducted shortly after Ceauşescu's fall from power showed strong support for programs of economic restructuring. In a poll conducted 29 September–1 October 1990 among 2,190 persons some 67 percent of respondents expressed support for privatization, with only 17 percent opposed. As for the mode of privatization, only 28 percent favored an equal division of state properties, with 63 percent preferring differential criteria.[43]

But Romania's road to a market economy has been rocky. Industrial production declined by 17 percent in 1990–91 and by another 14 percent in 1991–92. In early 1993 industrial production was still declining—and at a still faster rate.[44] Prices climbed 220 percent between October 1990 and October 1991. Meanwhile, unemployment has risen steadily, resulting in 949,842 unemployed by February 1993 (8.5 percent of the work force).[45] Inevitably, living standards have sunk, spurred in part by a *monthly* inflation rate of 10.3 percent in 1991 and 9.6 percent in 1992.[46] The Iliescu regime has moved slowly to address economic difficulties. In March 1991 a two-tiered banking system was created, setting up commercial banks of the Western type, raising prices on basic foodstuffs and pharmaceuticals, canceling price subsidies, and eventually freeing almost all prices, allowing them to rise to market levels.[47]

By comparison with the record of the other countries discussed above, however, Romania's struggle for economic recovery has been tortured. Numerous reasons can be given for this condition, including the legacy of decades of bad investments and structural distortion under the Ceauşescus, the social turmoil in Bucharest in the summer of 1990, a de facto temporary diplomatic isolation of the Iliescu regime, and an ill-considered erection of formidable barriers to foreign investment—barriers that were lifted, finally, only in March 1993.[48] For these and perhaps other reasons, Romania was the only East European country, aside from embargo-ridden Serbia and war-torn Bosnia, whose GDP declined at a faster rate in 1992 than in 1991. In fact, the Romanian economic situation worsened by all measures except exports, which miraculously rose 7.1 percent in 1992. Even the agricultural sector had an unusually bad year, recording a 9.2 percent decline in gross agricultural production in 1992.[49] There were shortages of many food staples, including bread, sugar, cooking oil, butter, and potatoes during the winter of 1991–92. In a macabre twist even a shortage of cadavers occurred for medical students at Romanian universities.[50] By September 1992, 18 percent of Romanian families lived below the poverty line, and another 21 percent were living in "marginal" circumstances.[51]

But in the spring of 1992 the Romanian government unveiled a new economic strategy that it had drawn up with IMF assistance; at the same time, the IMF granted Romania a standby credit of $500 million, while the World Bank agreed to extend a $400 million loan to Bucharest. Even as these agreements were being hammered out, Romania gradually emerged from its relative isolation, signing bilateral economic agreements with Germany, Greece, and several former Soviet republics.[52]

Later that year, incoming Prime Minister Nicolae Vacaroiu offered a re-finement of the economic strategy, promising to strengthen the role of the state in organizing the economic transition, concerted encourage-ment to would-be foreign investors, a gradual decrease of interest rates, and the creation of new jobs.[53] A high-ranking minister expressed opti-mism in January 1993 that the Romanian government had at last turned the corner on economic stabilization.[54]

If this survey of Eastern Europe continued, a third category would em-brace the remaining Yugoslav successor states and Albania, that is, societies directly or indirectly affected by Serbia's campaigns of aggres-sion or—in the case of Albania—plagued during 1990–92 by widespread chaos, rioting, and mass exodus.[55] For all their problems, Serbia and Albania have at least the advantage of a solid agricultural base, although unemployment is about 50 percent in both states. Croatia and Serbia have both hovered at the brink of economic collapse, while much of Bosnia's economy has been devastated by the war. In Albania, unem-ployment stood at 40 percent in August 1993, the chromium and copper mines were paralyzed, the transport system was in disarray, and the Ti-rana government was able to cover only about 20 percent of the national budget (of $300 million) out of real revenues—50–60 percent is financed by foreign aid, and the balance is covered by inflationary printing of needed currency. But by May 1994 the Tirana government seemed to have turned the economy around. Unemployment had been reduced to about 25 percent (and still declining), inflation had been rolled back to 30 percent annually, and output was increasing at an annual rate of 10 percent. In recognition of these accomplishments, the IMF commended the Albanian government for its sound fiscal and monetary policies.[56]

Privatization

Closely associated with the task of restoring economic stability is the task of privatization. Indeed, for this chapter's purposes I consider these to be two aspects of a single, complex core task. Privatization is a pivotal component in the economic recovery plans of the East European states. It is also highly controversial.

Controversy has centered on the method used to privatize, for ex-ample, whether by distributing shares to all citizens, or to just the workers at the enterprise, or by selling shares to appropriate bidders. There have also been concerns that unregulated privatization could allow foreigners to buy up much of the local economy. In the case of enterprises that existed before 1945 controversies also have arisen as to whether the appropriate course of action might be to return such properties to the original owners or their offspring, regardless of their current country of residence or citizenship.

Ultimately, most of the states in the region have adopted a mixed scheme under which previous owners have been able to obtain at least partial restoration of their property or an appropriate compensation, while enterprises and properties whose owners or families fail to make any claims are transferred to new ownership. Thus, in the Czech Republic more than 100,000 properties nationalized after 1948 were returned to their original owners by January 1993.[57] But the return of property to the original owners has been controversial everywhere. In Poland, for example, the Law on the Privatization of State Enterprises was passed on 13 July 1990, and by the end of 1991 more than 70,000 claims for recovery or indemnification concerning various types of assets had been presented. Officials agreed that under the circumstances "reprivatization cannot be based on the payment of full damages [to aggrieved parties]."[58] Or again, in Bulgaria, as the National Assembly debated the provisions of a proposed Land Law in the spring of 1992, rallies both for and against restitution were staged in front of the assembly building.[59] Eventually, the government passed a compromise measure restoring property expropriated between 1948 and 1990 but providing for the possibility that current residents might purchase land from the original owners at prices set by the government.[60]

The first East European country to embark on a program of privatization was Hungary, whose communist elites passed legislation as early as 1988 authorizing the conversion of state enterprises into joint stock companies. What ensued was a species of "spontaneous privatization," in which the incumbent, communist-appointed managers of state enterprises arranged the sale of these firms. Some managers granted themselves favorable terms by which to purchase the firms; others arranged for their sale—at discount prices—to foreign investors in exchange for guaranteed jobs at higher salaries. After some two hundred firms had been privatized in this way, the Hungarian parliament in 1989 passed a second law that established rigorous procedures for any further privatization. In March 1990 Budapest authorities established the State Property Agency to oversee the process—a move replicated throughout the region.[61] Hungarian authorities, with the assistance of British financial experts, worked out a revised privatization plan in early 1993. The plan called for transferring up to $3.4 billion worth of stock to Hungarian citizens, with every adult being eligible to buy shares on payment of a one-time fee of 1,000 forints (about U.S. $11).[62]

Up to now, however, there have been some important differences in the speed and scope of privatization.[63] The differences between the Czech and Polish approaches are illustrative. Both countries use a voucher system in which citizens are able to buy shares in the enterprises, and in both cases a certain number of enterprises are put up for sale in a series of "rounds." But beyond that similarity, differences have been significant. The Poles have been cautious and have preferred to move more slowly (despite their touted program of "shock therapy"). Under the Polish privatization law, branches of the Ministry of Ownership Changes determine which enterprises to put up for sale, which ones to close down as insolvent, and which to retain under state management for the time being. Polish authorities proposed to make credit available to citizens for the purchase of these assets.[64] The Poles themselves concede that both the processes of closing down unprofitable enterprises and privatizing solvent enterprises have been sluggish, with fewer than 10 percent of all classified enterprises either closed or completely privatized by the end of 1991.[65] In May 1993 the Polish parliament approved a government plan to transfer some six hundred state-owned factories to private owners.[66] By that point more than half of Poland's labor force was employed in the private sector. As of September 1993 the Polish government had succeeded in privatizing 2,265 of the 8,441 state-owned companies in existence in 1990. At the same time, some 1.5 million small businesses were set up in the four years since 1989, so that by 1993 all shops, restaurants, and warehouses were in private hands. But privatization has not been carried out without controversy; indeed, recriminations over alleged corruption and neglect of working people's interests placed privatization at the center of debate during the September 1993 parliamentary elections.[67]

The Czechs have criticized the Polish approach for excessive caution. Prague's authorities (inspired by current Czech Prime Minister Václav Klaus) decided instead to distribute vouchers to all adult citizens at a processing fee of U.S. $35. About half of all eligible citizens took advantage of this arrangement, and by the end of 1991 some 16.4 percent of the Czechoslovak economy had been turned over to private hands.[68] Other differences from the Polish model include the distribution of vouchers essentially free of charge and the speedier rate with which authorities have made enterprises available for investment.

Two critical issues connected with privatization in both countries are the need to create a management/ownership structure that will prove conducive to efficiency and will maximize profits and the need to avoid serious financial losses or revenue problems.[69] Speed, of course, has its risks, but so does a more gradual approach. As economists Borensztein and Kumar note:

> [one] consequence of the gradualist and piecemeal approach would be that the least efficient enterprises would remain in the public sector domain the longest, and indeed might not be sold off at all. Given the potential number and large size of these enterprises, they could constitute a significant drain on the public sector finances and could easily jeopardize the whole reform process.[70]

Slovenia and Bulgaria hesitated between these two models, but ultimately they chose models closer to the Polish example. Slovenian authorities debated three rival schemes between the summer of 1991 and the spring of 1992, finally agreeing on a plan combining sales of 40 percent of stock with free distribution of 20 percent and the retention of 10 percent in a state pension fund.[71] Similarly, in Bulgaria authorities hoped to pass a privatization bill in early 1991, but a year later they were still ironing out wrinkles. Not until June 1992 did the government make the first practical moves toward privatization. Sofia decided to proceed cautiously and put up only ninety-two enterprises for sale in 1992; bidders were required to pay at time of purchase a deposit of 10 percent of the auction price, and Sofia followed other countries in allowing foreign interests to participate.[72]

In Hungary the government rejected a proposal that the employees of any given firm be granted priority in acquiring shares of the firm's stock. Rejecting the example set by Poland, the Czech Republic, Slovenia, and Bulgaria, Hungarian authorities argued strenuously for restricting the purchase of shares to citizens, and—in this respect following the Polish example—they agreed to finance sales of enterprises.[73]

In Hungary, as elsewhere, seemingly endless controversies delayed agreement on a mechanism for privatization of the banking system. Only in February 1993 did the government finally announce that it was contracting the Credit Suisse–First Boston Investment Bank to advise the government on a privatization strategy for the banking sector.[74] Privatization proceeded more smoothly in other sectors, however, and from 1989 until April 1993 the number of private enterprises increased from 200,000 to 500,000 and the number of joint ventures from 500 to 7,000. At the same time, various insolvent companies—2,000 by March 1992—declared bankruptcy and dissolved.[75]

In Romania a land law passed in February 1991 set up the mechanisms for the transfer of farmland to private owners. Some five months later, a law on privatization was then adopted that provided for the distribution of vouchers free of charge (as with the Czech model) to all Romanian citizens to the value of 30 percent of stock, while the remaining 70 percent was placed under the administration of the State Ownership Fund. This agency has moved cautiously, weighing not only questions of profitability, but of the social impact that closing down insolvent plants would have (which has more in common with the Polish model).[76] But for all its caution, Romania's private sector has experienced rapid growth, with some 400,000 private companies registering from December 1989 until February 1993. In 1992 the private sector already accounted for 25 percent of Romania's gross domestic product.[77]

Finally, Slovakia, in contrast to the other states, has applied the brakes to privatization, fearing that any determined move in that direction could lead to additional unemployment and layoffs.

Privatization inevitably opens up sundry claims, but despite these controversies, privatization is clearly contributing to economic recovery in all of those societies where it has been adopted as policy, and it is likely to remain the policy everywhere—even probably in Slovakia—for the foreseeable future.

Political Demonopolization

The guiding goal of the East European elites surveyed is the demonopolization of power. In the economic sphere demonopolization means privatization. In the political sphere it means dismantling the political structures that underpinned the communist party monopoly and the introducing of institutions and procedures that will support constitutionalism, rule of law, and multiparty pluralism. This core task, then, is the second one confronting Eastern Europe's leaders.

Constitutionalism, in this sense, presumes a state that operates according to its own laws and that is capable of enforcing the law and maintaining public order. It also presumes free elections, legal guarantees of civil rights, the existence of an independent judiciary, a depoliticized bureaucracy and army, and conscious efforts in the educational system and in the media to foster notions of tolerance and respect for differences among people. It presumes, in short, some concept of fair play, protected and buttressed, however imperfectly, by institutional safeguards.

In erecting such safeguards the postcommunist politicians of Eastern Europe have traced a path through controversy and bitter debate. But they have not done so unassisted. On the contrary, they have invited sundry scholars from the United States and Western Europe, delegates and specialists from the American Bar Association, and other experts to consult with them, and they have also appointed commissions to study and compare Western constitutional and legal documents.[79] So far the countries under review have had the most success in conducting free elections and in establishing the independence of the judiciary, mixed success in guaranteeing civil rights (with women[80] and ethnic minorities the chief losers), and varying degrees of difficulty in vouchsafing some minimal degree of parliamentary stability and in depoliticizing the bureaucracy and army. The last problem has, in turn, fueled occasional rumors of military coups in the making.[81] These countries have fared abominably in fostering a spirit of tolerance either in the educational system or in the media because they have been absorbed either with encouraging nationalist pride and/or religious values through the schools, or with enjoying the new freedom of the press, regardless of the consequences of its abuse; indeed, the very idea of trying to foster tolerance through the schools and the media might well be rejected by these elites as a kind of legacy from communism—a misconstrual of the real relation of processes.

Taking stock of the constitutional-political landscape broadly, one may divide the countries under review into two categories. In the first are those states that have laid a sturdy basis for a functioning pluralist system and that have not only provided constitutional safeguards for democratic procedure, but been able to build a degree of trust in public institutions, thus providing some assurance of stability and procedural regularity. I place the Czech Republic, Hungary, and Slovenia in this first category. In the second are those states in which political personalities have loomed larger than political institutions, in which public trust in the institutions of state is as yet lacking, in which the dangers of destabilization or manipulation in an authoritarian direction have not yet been transcended. In this category I place Poland, Bulgaria, Romania, and Slovakia.[82]

One of the most elementary choices that confronted the framers of these new systems at the start was whether to adopt the parliamentary model (the German) or the presidential model (the French). In the region as a whole, only Croatia and Serbia adopted the French model, and, as is evident to any observer, this model has lent itself to the abuse of presidential power in both states. Poland adopted a mixed model. Elsewhere in Eastern Europe the German model was adopted, although with some significant variations (the differences between the Hungarian and Romanian adaptations, for example).

The specific difficulty that has bedeviled Poland is that although the country's constitution established a parliamentary system, it failed to assure the prerequisites for successful operation of the model. Clearly, for a parliamentary system to function effectively, the parliament must be set up so as to provide a basis for strong coalitions. In short, a strong parliamentary system requires a strong parliament. Weak and fragmented parliaments can only push the system toward chaos and parliamentary crisis—an experience to which Poland is no stranger.

Much hinged on the specific provisions of the election law, the drafting of which was entrusted (in June 1990) to a subcommission of the Sejm (chaired by Aleksander Luczak of the Polish Peasant Party). This subcommission worked at the pleasure of a transitional parliament, the members of whose lower house owed their seats not to free elections but to the communist system of reserved apportionment. Hence, the members of the Democratic and Peasant parties, together with the former communists, wanted to assure that parliamentary seats would go to even those parties drawing less than 2 percent of the national vote.[83]

Polish President Lech Wałęsa took strong exception to the resultant draft, which he warned would lead to the election of politically fragmented parliaments with weak parties and vulnerable coalitions. Arguing that Poland needed a strong legislature, Wałęsa produced his own draft. Ironically, the advocates of a weak parliament portrayed Wałęsa as the foe of parliamentary rule. Leading figures of the orphaned parties of the old system joined forces in pushing through an election law that guaranteed seats for their electorally weak parties. The resulting electoral system opened the way to political fragmentation and the destruction of parliamentary strength. As early as August 1991 a Radio Free Europe researcher predicted that the election law adopted by the Sejm would contribute to "the continuing marginalization of parties in Polish political life, with potentially dire consequences for voter turnout and party strength in the forthcoming elections."[84] When elections were finally held on 27 October, eighteen parties and eleven groupings elected deputies, with no party garnering more than 12 percent of the vote—thus demonstrating the validity of Wałęsa's warnings.[85]

Wałęsa, who championed a strong parliament and who also has lent his support to efforts by the Council of Ministers to obtain enhanced powers,[86] has ended up concentrating his energy on strengthening the power of the presidency, even threatening to establish a presidential party if necessary (a threat carried out in July 1993). The issue, to Wałęsa's mind, is how to construct a government strong enough to steer clear of the "anarchy and chaos" that he sees threatening the country.[87] Sometimes Wałęsa, who keeps a bust of Marshal Piłsudski in his office, has been compared to his predecessor. Such a comparison is valid. Piłsudski was motivated by concern over political instability, not by personal ambition; the same may be said of Wałęsa.

Similarly, the issue of presidential authority has been the focus of controversy in Hungary and Bulgaria.[88] But the issue has acquired the greatest urgency in Poland, where in April 1992 the public was treated to the spectacle of a general strike by tens of thousands of Solidarity unionists—a strike inspired by the demand for strong government![89] Wałęsa finally achieved a partial victory in the long battle over presidential power in August 1992 when the parliament approved constitutional amendments confirming the powers extended in 1989 to the president and the prime minister. Under these provisions the president remains commander-in-chief of the armed forces, with the right to declare martial law or to order military mobilization. He also can veto legislation (to override which the Sejm must assemble a two-thirds majority).[90]

Then, in the spring of 1993 a parliamentary crisis provided Wałęsa with a further opening. When Prime Minister Hanna Suchocka's government lost a no-confidence vote in parliament (by one vote, on 28 May), Wałęsa dissolved the parliament, called for new elections, and used the interim to sign a new law that would require the parties to obtain 5 percent of the total vote to obtain seats in the parliament; the new law predictably reduced the number of parties represented in the parliament from twenty-nine to about a dozen.[91]

The Czech Republic, Slovenia, and Hungary all decided on a strict parliamentary system. Indeed, with its weak presidency and strong parliament, Hungary impressed Bruszt and Stark as "a political science textbook recipe for democratic governance."[92] In Romania a mixed system has given rise to repeated conflict between the executive and the legislature,[93] while in Slovakia the ultimate resolution of this rivalry is still in doubt.

Of the other policy threads connected to constructing a constitutional order, the two commanding most attention have been the establishment of judicial independence and the depoliticization of the army. *All* states in the region have guaranteed judicial independence, but they have experienced diverse difficulties in making this principle work. In Poland, for instance, efforts have been made to give the parliament the right to override decisions by the Constitutional Court,[94] while in Bulgaria there have been allegations that the new government was undermining judicial independence.[95]

All states in the region established constitutional courts to serve as the ultimate arbiters of legislation's constitutionality. But the power of this institution differs from country to country. In Bulgaria, for example, the Constitutional Court may rescind legislation it deems unconstitutional; it may also resolve disputes regarding the conduct of elections and conflicts regarding the division of powers among the president, the cabinet, and the parliament.[96] In neighboring Romania, on the other hand, the Constitutional Court is empowered to pass judgment on laws *before* they are promulgated, to assess the constitutionality of the rules of the two legislative chambers (on the request of either the chamber's chairman or a specified number of parliamentarians), to adjudge the constitutionality of an already adopted law when it has first been challenged in a lower court, and to hear cases involving charges of unconstitutional conduct against a political party. In the first type of case (laws prior to promulgation) the court's decision may be overridden by a two-thirds majority in both chambers, while in the fourth type of case (the conduct of political parties), such allegations must be brought by one of the chairmen of the two legislative chambers, provided that his chamber has voted to bring charges. In Romania, then, the legislative branch clearly plays a crucial role in the judicial process, effectively supervising the highest court in a way radically different from the Bulgarian case.[97]

Again, it is Hungary and Slovenia that have been the most successful in establishing judicial independence, although Poland, amid controversy, has gradually been able to retire judges hired in the communist era and to replace them with respected academicians and defense attorneys. As early as 1989 Budapest adopted constitutional amendments that laid the groundwork for depoliticizing the judiciary and authorized the courts to review the legality of state decisions. By 1991 the new Constitutional Court (established by the constitutional amendments of October 1989) was playing a major role in reviewing the constitutionality of laws and regulations and in shaping the Hungarian legal system.[98]

As for the military, Slovenia, Hungary, Romania, and the Czech Republic have been the most successful in depoliticizing the army. In Poland and Bulgaria, by contrast, the issue remained unresolved in mid-1994. In Bulgaria one of the two draft defense bills presented to the parliament in November 1992 was said to "concentrate the leadership of the armed forces into the hands of a civilian ministry, . . . [thus] placing the troops under the uncontrollable supervision of a political figure."[99] Again, in Poland, ministers were still talking in 1992 about the need to

"decommunize" the army.[100] Wałęsa warned in that year: "We are building a new system. The changes should not leave the Army untouched. . . .
It is urgent to incorporate the Army into the new political model and
adapt it to the new reality."[101]

And in Slovakia, which has had to establish a new army as a result of
its separation from the Czech Republic, reports hold that a nationalist-
inspired army with offensive capabilities is being formed. The Budapest
daily *Magyar Hirlap* voiced the fears of many Hungarians in fretting that
Slovakia's military preparations are directed against Hungary.[102]

A Free Press?

I have identified the demonopolization of the media and the establishment of safeguards for freedom of the press as a distinct core task. The
reasons for this emphasis should be evident. Throughout the communist era the press was controlled, and in several East European countries
it was all but useless as a source of factual information. The purpose of
the communist media was to manipulate the public's understanding of
events and institutions and thus to control the population. The result
was that the political information necessary for a society to participate
intelligently and cogently in political activity was often unobtainable except through recourse to underground publications and word of mouth.

When the postcommunist elites first took power it seemed clear that
the media had to be freed of state control, that this objective was a prerequisite for what is conventionally (albeit somewhat euphemistically)
called a "free society." Yet in several states the decision was taken to
operate, for the interim, under modified versions of press laws adopted
under the communists. Thus, in Czechoslovakia the "velvet revolutionaries" decided to postpone discussion of a new press law and retained the
existing 1966 law (passed under Novotný), only restoring amendments
attached to the law in 1968 as well as adding some of their own. Similarly, in Hungary, Prime Minister József Antall upheld the continued
relevance of a 1974 decree on the press issued by the Kádár-era Council of Ministers. And in late 1992, Poland was still operating under a
press law passed eight years earlier. But here, too, some changes were
effected, most notably the abolition of censorship (effective 6 June 1990)
and the dissolution of RSW Prasa, the communist party's publishing
house (legally effective 6 July 1990, but delayed, ironically, because of
the publishing house's financial problems).[103]

Despite such delays, however, it was generally understood that new
legislation affecting the media needed to be drafted and that the lines

of government control and influence over the media, both formal and informal, needed to be revamped. Throughout the region the ensuing struggle for the media has been turbulent and rambunctious, with some consistent themes.

The central issue in media policy relates to the potential of information agencies to serve either as the nightingale of the government or as its gadfly. Polish President Wałęsa voiced a widespread attitude in ruling circles when he told journalists: "Take care all of you about the most important things. It is important that parliament, government, and the president should not be defamed by everybody, or all of us will have to suffer for this."[104] Wałęsa has spoken of the need for Polish journalists to respect moral values and professional ethics, and at one point proposed the establishment of a presidential council for mass media and information to be attached to his office.[105]

The communist fall from power was so sudden that the postcommunist elites have inherited institutional structures foreign to their ideologies—and yet have found themselves troubled by a variant of the dilemma that troubled Lenin in 1918, namely, whether to allow complete freedom (of elections and political organization in 1918, of the press in the East European case today) or whether to impose controls to make sure that people behave responsibly (in this case, that the media behave "responsibly"). The general pattern throughout the region has been for the government to authorize the speedy privatization of print media, while holding on, for an unspecified time, to a state monopoly in broadcast media. This pattern has been played out in Slovenia where the postcommunist Demos coalition found it difficult to resist the temptation to exploit its control over certain media appointments to its own benefit, or to restrain itself from offering friendly suggestions to broadcasters and even to print journalists as to what might be judicious or injudicious to report. A key controversy during 1992 and 1993 had to do with the retention by the government television station (RTV Slovenia) of a monopoly control of broadcast frequencies, thus placing its sole competitor, the privately owned Kanal A, at a distinct disadvantage. As long as Kanal A failed to be granted permission for a large transmitter, its broadcasts could be received only in the Ljubljana area.[106] In the same spirit the postcommunist ruling coalition took advantage of prerogatives asserted by its communist predecessors to impose a supervisory board of its own choosing on RTV Slovenia, and it tried to push through a new law on information that would have brought the principal news media under state ownership and control—including even a renationalizing of the influential daily newspaper *Delo*.[107] But strong opposition from journalists blocked this move. Even so, Slovenia's noncommunist politicians (first the Demos coalition, more recently the LDP coalition government) have exerted subtle pressure on the media in order to influence programming.

The same battle has been fought, with some variations, in Hungary. There, the government passed a law on Hungarian radio and television in early April 1992 guaranteeing their independence but entrusting their management to two public foundations to be set up by the parliament. As if to suggest that depoliticization might ultimately be reduced to equal representation of conflicting political interests, the bill called for an eleven-member management board, three of whose members would be selected by the government coalition, three by the opposition, and the remaining five by the previous six.[108] The law also provided for the political independence of regional and local broadcasting stations.

But already in July 1991, in spite of general agreement that the media should be "free," controversy had erupted when Prime Minister Antall (of the Hungarian Democratic Forum) had proposed firing the directors of the Hungarian radio and television (Csaba Gombar and Elemér Hankiss, respectively). Under Hungarian law, President Arpad Göncz's signature was required before the decision could become effective. A member of the opposition Free Democratic Alliance, Göncz, however, refused to sign, voicing a sharp protest against Antall's effort to fill the positions with people tied to the HDF and thus politicizing the media.[109] The controversy dragged on for months with the HDF stirring up polemics against the president. Göncz drew support from an interesting source— the ex-communists. But the controversy continued, provoking public demonstrations in September 1992.

Göncz hoped that passage of a long-delayed media bill would resolve the dispute in his favor, but at the end of 1992, despite two years of wrangling, there was still no media bill. Meanwhile, Prime Minister Antall's office assumed direct control of the two networks' budgets, initiated an investigation into two of Hankiss's deputies, and in other ways harassed the independent-minded directors. Antall and HDF chair Imre Konya openly conceded their distaste for the media's criticism of government policies and admitted that they felt entitled to the media's endorsement.[110] "Like it or not," said Konya, "we are rowing the same boat. Assistance from the press is vital . . . ."[111] Finally, in early January 1993, in the face of intensifying government pressure, Hankiss and Gombar resigned, prompting several opposition parties to issue a statement that, in the context of the politically motivated pressure that had led to this result, they considered the broadcast media's independence to be seriously threatened.[112]

In the Czech and Slovak Republics a schizophrenic situation developed in which the centrifugal political energy was similarly reflected in the media. In March 1990 the Federal Assembly passed a bill abolishing censorship, and in October 1991 it adopted a law enabling private citizens to obtain broadcasting licenses. But differences between the Czech and Slovak republics became evident soon after communism's collapse. In fact, the Czech media have enjoyed a signal degree of freedom, although some experiences of the print media and broadcast media have differed. In the print media, a veritable explosion of new publications has occurred, with at least eight hundred new periodicals appearing in Czechoslovakia in the first half of 1990 alone. Inevitably, financial pressures have driven many aspiring publications out of business. In the broadcasting domain, privatization has been slowed by the dynamics of the state's political division.

In Slovakia efforts to create a free and responsible press have been hampered by Prime Minister Vladimir Mečiar's vaunting ambitions and intolerance of criticism as well as by the maelstrom of nationalism that he and others have encouraged. Since 1990 the Slovak press has produced a steady stream of anti-Semitic, anti-Czech, and anti-Hungarian articles. Czechoslovak President Havel was routinely attacked in 1991 and 1992 as a "fascist" or as a "conspirator" against Slovakia. *Zmena*, a weekly newspaper produced at the journalism and law faculties of Bratislava's Comenius University, declared at one point that Havel enjoyed the backing of the Freemasons and a vaguely sketched Jewish "conspiracy."[113] Another Slovak newspaper, *Nový Slovak*, whose name derives from a fascist-era paper of the wartime Slovak state, has repeatedly returned to the theme of the "Jewish problem." As the whole federal question was heating up, this paper also published an article in early 1992 urging that pro-federalist activities should be illegal in the Republic of Slovakia.[114] During the spring 1992 election campaign Mečiar repeatedly promised that if reelected he would silence all journalists who had criticized him. If they offered resistance, he vowed, he would drive them out of Slovakia, "kicking them in the arse."[115] Shortly after the election he announced to Slovak Television that he intended to have weekly broadcasts of his speeches. Jan Fule, the news director, pointed out that such a practice was contrary to Slovak law and that the government could only dictate such access to airwaves in times of national emergency. Soon after, rumors began to circulate that Fule's days in his job were numbered.[116] In the ensuing controversy the Slovak Television supervisory board became deadlocked, and its chairman was forced to resign, whereupon the Slovak National Council, dominated by Mečiar's party, announced that it would temporarily assume responsibility for Slovak Television's supervision.[117] Further, no sooner did Slovakia separate from the Czech Republic than the editor-in-chief and the director of the bitingly independent daily *Smena* were forced to resign; the Christian Democrats and the Hungarian Civic Party joined Slovak journalists in protesting the move.[118]

In Bulgaria, in contrast, the same issues have been resolved quietly, efficiently, and with minimal controversy. In early 1992, Sofia laid the foundation for the disestablishment of the government's monopoly in radio and television, and a few months later the foundation took the first step toward purging all former agents of the State Security Service from the media.[119] A series of press laws were drafted but failed to obtain sufficient support in the legislature. Meanwhile, a vocal group of journalists lobbied against the passage of *any* press law, claiming that it was not needed.

In Romania during 1990 and 1991 the government tried to pass a press law whose aim was to bring the media under the government's "influence." The government's first draft law would have obliged journalists to exercise their freedoms in "good faith" and would have proscribed publication of anything that might encourage citizens to break the law, that provoked violence, that constituted an affront to people's national or religious beliefs, or that could "alarm" the public. Various enforcement penalties were specified. The ensuing uproar forced the government to withdraw this draft in October 1990.[120] A second draft was prepared in much the same spirit and suffered the same fate, being withdrawn on 19 March 1991.[121] Finally, the government abandoned efforts to pass a press law and adopted a different approach, setting up an Information Department (on 11 June 1991) directly subordinate to the prime minister. Journalists protested the office's creation, complaining that it was intended to function as a censorship and surveillance bureau.[122] The handling of media access to the parliament has conformed to the spirit of these measures. Hence, "members of the Chamber of Deputies still vote in secret. And any journalist whose reports are deemed 'incorrect' may lose the right to attend Parliament and may also be required to publish a retraction written by the chamber's president."[123] As for broadcast journalism, that—as of 1994—is still the Bucharest government's monopoly.

That brings us back to Poland where, after a lengthy process of negotiation and discussion, the parliament in November 1992 finalized a bill that abolished the state monopoly in radio and television but (in the version passed by the Senate) amended the legislation to require both public and private broadcasters to respect Christian values.[124] This effort had clear implications for media reporting of the abortion controversy, and it suggested an attenuation of the principle of the separation of Church and state. In Poland, as in Slovenia, no question exists of the government asserting control over all print media; the stakes have largely been broadcast media. The reason is simple. As Lech Wałęsa put it, "television is the main newspaper of Poles, the only one for many."[125] Perhaps surprisingly, Wałęsa, the man who led a ten-year struggle against political monopoly, now seems tempted to narrow the space for opposition in the interest of strong government. Punctuating a lengthy appeal to television to "present the state's point of view," he concluded that journalists should not undermine the parliament or the government and that "the direction of the state must be carried forward."[126]

All of the states in Eastern Europe are torn between the allurements of power and the advantages of demonopolization and decontrol. All of them have experienced some difficulties and controversies along the way. But all in all, press freedom seems best assured in the Czech Republic, Hungary, Slovenia, and Bulgaria, and it can be described as partially achieved in Poland, given the important qualification that broadcast media not conflict with "Christian," that is, Catholic, values. Journalistic freedom in Slovakia and Romania, on the other hand, seems to rest on shaky foundations.

Regulating Ethnic Conflict

The regulation of ethnic conflict is the fourth task confronting the region's elites. Fueled by economic hardships and grievances and legitimated by the release from subordination to the USSR, state-sponsored nationalism could have been expected to wax only as these states undertook their transition to pluralist systems. But state-sponsored nationalism (as in Slovakia or Serbia or Croatia) ineluctably stokes resentment or fear among minority nationalities; hence, the sudden explosion of demands for Hungarian rights in Slovakia, Albanian and Hungarian rights in Serbia, and Serbian rights in Croatia. That the clash of these two nationalisms can lead to war is clear from the Yugoslav case.

The appearance of neo-Nazis and skinheads in the region is only the most obvious symptom of ethnic tensions. Right-wing chauvinist and racist groups have appeared in most of these countries, although the greatest number of reports of such activity comes from eastern Germany, Poland, and Hungary (leaving aside the question of how to interpret the state-sponsored genocide against the Muslims of Bosnia). (Right-wing extremists, including neo-Nazis and skinheads, are discussed in some details in chapter 18.) It will suffice at this point to note that they figure as exaggerated reflections of more prevalent tendencies and tensions in the broader society and as symptoms of deeper, unresolved problems.

Among these problems are the status of Hungarians in southern Slovakia and Serbian Vojvodina, of Albanians in Serbian Kosovo, of ethnic Turks in Bulgaria, as well as the sundry resentments and difficulties connected with the war in former Yugoslavia.

Authorities in several of these countries are taking the ethnic problem seriously. But up to mid-1994 their concern has been chiefly manifested for their coethnics. Thus, the Hungarian leadership has shown considerable concern over the fate of the Hungarian diaspora in Slovakia and Vojvodina, and in September 1992 the Hungarian foreign minister paid a visit to Bratislava to propose a bilateral treaty and obtain some reassurances about the rights of Slovakia's Hungarians. Two months later, Hungary played host to a two-day international conference (in Tatabanya) devoted to national minorities and self-determination in Eastern Europe. But such moves are the exception.

Far more typical are assertions of exclusive sovereignty by the dominant nationality in the state constitution, expressions of alarm about the intentions of neighbors, policies of repression of local minority languages (especially in Hungarian-inhabited sections of Slovakia and Vojvodina and in Albanian-inhabited Kosovo,[127] but also in Romanian Transylvania),[128] and sudden demands from hitherto quiescent minorities for special rights and guarantees (for example, from Ruthenes in Slovakia, Serbs in Hungary[129] and Macedonia, and Germans and Hungarians in Romanian Transylvania).[130] As has so often been the case in history, increased ethnic chauvinism tends to be associated with anti-Semitism and with attacks on the dignity and equality of women. It is no accident that the rise in anti-Semitism in Poland[131] has been accompanied by ministerial affirmations that "it is essential to bring children up in a Christian spirit"[132] and by a strong drive to push women out of the public sphere, spearheaded by the church's successful drive to revoke abortion rights.[133] Secular Poles have started to talk of a "Khomeinization" of Poland at the hands of the Catholic church and its right-wing allies.[134] The formation of a Catholic voters' alliance under the name "Fatherland" in July 1993—established with the help of Archbishop Tadeusz Goclowski of Gdańsk—is evidence of this trend; the alliance's stated purpose was to influence the outcome of the 19 September parliamentary elections to assure the best result for the church and for advocates of "traditional values."[135] The signing of a new Concordat between the Warsaw government of Hanna Suchocka and the Holy See in late July 1993 added to the rising controversy about the church's role in Polish politics.[136] The alienation of much of the Polish electorate by the

Catholic church's new stridency was a contributing factor to the first-place showing of the ex-communists in the parliamentary elections of September 1993.

Hungarian Prime Minister József Antall warned a group of German businessmen in June 1992 that the West cannot afford to ignore the danger of rising nationalism in Eastern Europe. "Destabilization implies the greatest danger in the Central and Eastern European region," he told them. "It is also in the interest of the industrialized Western world that this not come about. The region's political, military, economic and social destabilization would so seriously affect the West that they would long for the return of the Iron Curtain."[137] There is, of course, a danger that an escalation of nationalist frenzy could provoke further conflicts on the Yugoslav example, but the greater danger is that the rising volubility of nationalist-chauvinists and right-wing elements will so pervert the national agenda that civil rights will be curtailed, discrimination against various out-groups intensified (whether women, ethnic minorities, Jews, gays and lesbians, or refugees), and democratic principles made hostage to a nationalist agenda. This process has already reached an advanced stage in Serbia and Croatia. A danger of this occurring is also apparent in Poland, Slovakia, and conceivably, depending on intraparty and interparty struggles, in Hungary.

One possible solution is to extend wide-ranging autonomy to regionally compact ethnic minorities. This, in fact, is what the Hungarians in Transylvania,[138] the Hungarians in Vojvodina, the Albanians in Kosovo, and the Serbs in Croatia have been demanding (although the Albanians and Serbs have passed beyond to demanding full independence). But in each case the given authorities have turned down such requests, provoking protests by Transylvanian Hungarians[139] and the radicalization of the Albanian opposition in Kosovo,[140] and providing grist for Serbian leaders to throttle Serbs and Croats into ethnic war. Territorial autonomy is best viewed as a specific way of making the principle of toleration work. As such, it is fully compatible with and supportive of democratic systems. On the other hand, assurances to *individuals* of minority nationalities, while at the same time denying them any guarantees of *group* rights—as with the Iliescu regime's policy in Romania[141]—appear unlikely to resolve the dilemma.

Legitimation

The successful accomplishment of the fifth and final core task, that of legitimation, derives from and depends on the successful resolution of the preceding core tasks as well as on at least two other factors. These are (1) the state's ability to come to terms with its past and to resolve the question of holdovers in high posts from the communist era; and (2) its ability to build popular confidence in the new and still emerging political institutions. The postcommunist elites have sought legitimation, in part, by putting the former communist leaders on trial (Honecker, Ceauşescu, Zhivkov) or by passing laws to exclude communists from high-level posts (the Czech Republic, Bulgaria). They have also sought legitimation in two opposing principles—constitutional democracy and nationalism. The difficulty they confront is that in seeking legitimation from opposing principles neither principle may be honored and that the society may be left with a failed program, recrudescent authoritarianism, and incipient social and political chaos.

One of the challenges bearing on legitimation relates to holdovers from the former communist system. Obviously, by retaining bureaucrats from the former system, a government exposes itself to criticism that it has not made a true break with the past. But by making a clean sweep, a government may find itself struggling just to learn the ropes.[142]

Inevitably, though, the easiest weapon that any opposition may wield against any postcommunist regime is to charge it with having failed to break with communism. Romania's Iliescu has been accused of being a crypto-communist who has worked to reconstitute "the backbone of totalitarianism."[143] Bulgarian President Zhelev and Prime Minister Ljuben Berov have both been accused (by UDF leader Filip Dimitrov) of gravitating back to a communist path.[144] Similar charges have been bandied about in Poland.[145] Even Slovenian President Kučan was accused, in an open letter signed by six prominent Slovenian politicians in June 1993, of being an unreformed communist and—in a preposterous flight of imagination—of wanting to take Slovenia back into union with "Yugoslavia."[146]

But aside from appeals to democracy and nationalism, elites commonly use a third route to obtain legitimation for their rule—manipulating memories of the past. What is specific to transitions from authoritarianism is that such legitimating symbols must be chosen either from the roster of martyred opponents of the overthrown authoritarian system (such as Imre Nagy of Hungary, executed in June 1958) or from the previous regime—that is, from the precommunist past. The widespread revival of reverence for interwar and even wartime political figures such as Admiral Miklós Horthy (in Hungary),[147] Marshal Józef Piłsudski (in Poland), Poglavnik Ante Pavelić (in Croatia), and Monseigneur Josef Tiso (in Slovakia)[148] is symptomatic of this desire to anchor the present in the past, and for new states, such as Croatia and Slovakia, it plays an especially critical function. The process of reclaiming the dead is some-times acted out literally. In Hungary anti-Soviet Premier Imre Nagy was disinterred in order to be ceremoniously reinterred; his reburial was a national event. Or again, in Poland it was announced in September 1993 that the body of Władysław Sikorski, prime minister of the Polish government-in-exile during World War II, would finally be returned to his native land, fifty years after his death, in accordance with his express wish to be buried in a "free Poland."[149] And finally, in looking to the past for legitimating symbols, leaders may manipulate the phrases, slogans, and images of the past to serve present objectives. The best example is Polish President Lech Wałęsa's establishment in July 1993 of a new party to serve as his organizational medium. Wałęsa called it "The Non-Party Bloc for Support of Reform"—BBWR. These were the same initials for Marshal Piłsudski's "Non-Party Bloc for the Support of the Govern-ment," which dominated Polish politics during the 1930s.[150] (Such ploys, of course, do not always work—Wałęsa's BBWR captured only 5.5 percent of the vote in the 19 September elections.)[151]

Conclusions

To achieve the first task (economic revival and privatization), Poland, the Czech Republic, and Hungary are the best situated, Slovenia and Bulgaria follow, with Romania and Slovakia probably being the weaker members of this set. Where the second task (building a constitutional-legal order) is concerned, the Czech Republic, Hungary, Slovenia, and Bulgaria all rank favorably, and Poland, Romania, and Slovakia rank somewhat less so. On demonopolizing the media (task 3), problems abound everywhere, but on the whole the situation seems best in the Czech Republic and Bulgaria, more mixed in Poland, Hungary, and Slovenia, and inauspi-cious in Romania and Slovakia. The fourth task entails the regulation of ethnic conflict and the restraint of nationalist-chauvinist impulses. Here, only the Czech Republic and Slovenia get top marks, although Bulgaria, despite the conflicted relationship between the dominant Bul-garian majority and the local Turkish minority, is making clear progress. Chauvinism in Poland is directed principally against women and Jews, although the small neo-Nazi contingent there casts its net much more broadly. Hungarian nationalism must be characterized as "defensive," but Slovak nationalism clearly has an "offensive" cast, as manifested in recent Slovak moves to remove Hungarian street signs from exclu-sively ethnic Hungarian towns and villages. In both Hungary and Slo-vakia, however, nationalism has the potential to contort and subvert national politics, and it represents a clear challenge. In Romania persistent charges of harassment and discrimination against Hungarians reflect unresolved problems from the past. Tallying up the score card on these four tasks, it is clear that the Czech Republic has, by far, the best prospects among the states surveyed. Hungary, Slovenia, and Bulgaria rank just behind, probably in that order. Poland's prospects are mixed, despite a strong economic showing, because of problems in other areas, while Romania and Slovakia rank low on every count and seem to have the worst prospects among these states for achieving something recognizable as democratic politics.

Some striking facts are that the postcommunist elites, having railed for years against communist control of the press, now seem to take it for granted that the media exist to serve as government cheerleaders; that Romanian ministries continued to receive requests for prices or output targets from enterprises on a daily basis long after the decision had been reached to abandon that mode of economic management;[152] that calls have sounded in Bulgaria for establishing a special "privatization police force" with powers to oversee and facilitate that goal;[153] and by occasional admissions throughout the region that the processes of political and economic change are not entirely under control.

Clearly, history is moving at breakneck speed in Eastern Europe, and just as clearly this gives rise to chaos and uncertainty. In an insightful article, Valerie Bunce and Mária Csanádi described Eastern Europe's current uncertainty

> in roles, rules, norms, functions, classes, perceptions, and interests, and, therefore, in the combined configurations of these we think of as systems, cultures, and institutions. In such circumstances, strategic behavior is quite difficult; decision-making tends to be frenzied and irrational; most feel defenseless in the face of a bombarding environment; idiosyncratic variables are powerful and thereby enhance misperceptions and serve to concentrate power; yet the impact of idiosyncratic factors is [itself] uneven, given the poverty of institutionally-based resources. Thus, the basic structure of postcommunism is the absence of much structure. Instead, the central characteristic is uncertainty.[154]

17. Yugoslav Breakup and Ethnic War

The central fact of our life is that there are Serbs and Croats and they don't understand each other. They will finish with war. It will be 1941 all over again. We are heading in the same direction. You can see this even in music.—GORAN BREGOVIĆ, *leader of the Sarajevo rock group White Button, in an interview with SPR (Sarajevo, 14 September 1989)*

The roots of the present war between Serbs, Croats, and Muslims must be traced back to 1918–21 when the Serbs rode roughshod over the national aspirations of Croats, Montenegrins, Macedonians, and Albanians, and imposed a centralized administration dominated by Serbs. Although Slovenes, Croats, and Montenegrins, at least, entered into union with generally positive feelings about their "brother Serbs," Serbian policy was ill-calculated to preserve such fondness. The Slovenes and Croats were taxed at rates far higher than the other peoples of interwar Yugoslavia, and in 1918 their military officers were systematically demoted on transfer into the new Yugoslav army. The Albanians and Macedonians were denied education in their own languages (or in the Albanian case, in any language at all), and both groups lost extensive landholdings to state confiscations—lands that were then turned over to Serb "colonists." The Cyrillic alphabet was imposed on the Croats, against their will. And the constitution of 1921, designed without the consent of some of the key actors (the Croats, in particular), devised a centralized system very much contrary to the federal system favored by the Croats.[1] After twenty years of Serbian rule Yugoslavia's non-Serbs were disgusted, frustrated, and embittered. The ease with which the country shattered into fragments in April 1941 is the best proof that, quite apart from the circumstances, the non-Serbs were more than ready to part with the Serbs.

The reconstitution of a unified Yugoslav state after four years of mutual genocide and terror, in which Croatian Ustaše, Serbian Chetniks, and communist partisans must all get their share of the blame, itself entailed armed coercion. In fact, the last pitched battle of World War II in Yugoslavia came in July 1945, two months after v-e day, when Tito's partisan army crushed an Albanian army trying to preserve Kosovo's union with Albania. But coercion alone could not solve the problems created by Serbian policy in the interwar period.

Tito tried two successive formulas in his effort to "solve" the national question. The first, which was attempted from 1945 until 1963, relied on a largely centralized approach, initially modeled directly on the Stalinist experience in Russia, but later modified by incorporating workers' councils and other refinements. The second formula, launched in 1963, consolidated in 1966, and surviving Tito's death in 1980 for about seven years, combined massive regional decentralization with strict preservation of the communist monopoly, producing a "quasi-confederal" hybrid that was neither entirely confederal nor entirely anything else. The country did not even seem entirely communist. The policy of regional decentralization followed the precept that if regional elites have trouble coordinating a common policy, it is best to give them maximum autonomy and thus minimize the amount of coordination that the system would require. Tito would have agreed with Dahl's hypothesis: "Beyond some point, the sharper the disagreement over policies within a social organization, and the larger the proportion of individuals involved in the disagreement, the greater the amount of social autonomy required for polyarchy to exist at any given level."[2]

This policy of "regional pluralism," if you will, worked reasonably well until the early 1980s. By an ironic twist of fate, Tito's death in 1980 coincided almost exactly with the incipient economic nosedive (which, for simplicity's sake, we may date from about 1978–79) and with the resurfacing of discontent among the Albanians of Kosovo, sparked by ethnic riots in the province in April 1981 (see chapter 8).

Nothing intrinsic about the Kosovo riots necessitated the deterioration of ethnic relations in the country as a whole during the 1980s. Even the emergent Serbian national backlash, sparked by these riots and by subsequent Serb-Albanian frictions in the province, *might* have remained politically innocuous, or at least might have been defused, but for two developments: the politicization of the Serbian Academy of Sciences and Arts, culminating in its drawing up a rabid, 74-page nationalist memorandum in September 1986, which cast Serbs as the great "victims" of historical injustice;[3] and the seizure of power in Serbia by Slobodan Milošević on a program of restoring Serbia's glory, Serbia's land, Serbia's rights. In the context of a unified Yugoslavia, Milošević's program was a recipe for disaster—as Slovenian and Croatian politicians were quick to point out.

Milošević now created a cult of personality that quickly eclipsed the posthumous cult of Tito. Mass rallies became Milošević's most important means of communication. At a November 1988 rally in Belgrade, ironically dubbed "Brotherhood and Unity," more than a million Serbs assembled to show their support of Milošević. It was the largest rally in postwar Yugoslav history.[4]

What Milošević accomplished in a time of growing economic troubles, environmental dilemmas, and institutional decay was to convince most Serbs that the country's number one problem was unfair treatment of the Serbs. Gradually, through his tight control of most of the Serbian press, he succeeded in obscuring these other issues, stoking the fires first of fear and resentment—and then hatred—of Croats, Muslims, and Albanians most immediately, and of the Vatican, Germany, and even the United States more remotely. By 1987 ordinary people were already talking of the *danger* of civil war. By 1989 ordinary people were talking of the *inevitability* of civil war. By the summer of 1990 ordinary people were arming themselves in preparation for an impending showdown, and on Milošević's orders the army command sent massive shipments of arms, paid for out of federal money, to Serbian civilians in Croatia and Bosnia.[5] By early 1991 it was only a matter of time before civil war broke out;[6] by then, only a miracle could have pulled Yugoslavia back from the brink, and no miracle came.

Five dramatic developments changed the entire Yugoslav political landscape after 1989. The first was a near-total rupture in contacts between Slovenia and Serbia—a result of a Serbian decision to institute an economic, cultural, and, to an extent, political boycott of its fellow republic.[7] The second development was the rapid disintegration of the communist party in Slovenia and Croatia in 1989–90 and the disappearance of the federal League of Communists of Yugoslavia in January 1990. The third, and to outside observers the most obvious, development was the election of noncommunist governments in Slovenia, Croatia, and Bosnia and of a coalition (communist and noncommunist) government in Macedonia in 1990. With communists (albeit renamed "socialists") still in control in Serbia and Montenegro, Yugoslavia was by the end of 1990 clearly coming apart. With six republics the "country" (if one could even call it that any longer) was one-third communist and two-thirds noncommunist. The fourth development—ignored in the West but keenly understood in Yugoslavia—was the rapid evanescence of the Yugoslav federal budget as the governments of the six constituent republics started withholding transfer payments (Slovenia and Croatia doing so in retaliation for the unwarranted confiscation by Belgrade of Slovenian and Croatian enterprises operating on Serbian territory).[8] As a result, the federal government closed up various agencies and fell months behind in paying salaries.[9]

And the fifth development was the rapid change in the mission and organizational command of the armed forces. Throughout 1990 "unreliable" officers, especially Slovenes and Croats, were retired and replaced by Serbian officers. At the same time, military regions were reorganized with an eye to minimizing local republic influence.[10] Immediately after the election of noncommunist governments in Slovenia and Croatia, the army stopped the delivery of weapons to those republics and confiscated weapons held by the local territorial defense units—both illegal moves—thus forcing these republics to purchase replacement weaponry on foreign markets.[11] The army command now not only armed the illegal Chetnik militias being set up in Croatia, but it trained them for combat.[12] In the summer of 1990, in an unabashedly hostile move, the JNA staged military training maneuvers in Bosnia, in which Slovenia and Croatia were the designated "enemy force."[13] In a secret report drafted by the Federal Council of National Defense in January 1991, and quickly leaked to the press, the army command explained that "it is necessary right now to ensure a high level of combat readiness of our units."[14] But for combat *against whom?* The answer had already been given at the training maneuvers in Bosnia the preceding summer. Not surprisingly, the Defense Ministry submitted no annual year-end report and request for budgetary authorization to the Federal Assembly in December 1990, despite a legal requirement that it do so.[15] And if the military establishment could so flagrantly defy legal requirements for budgetary allocations without having to worry about its budget, then clearly new de facto lines of authority were replacing the decaying official channels.

In these circumstances, and given the endless mutual recriminations among the republics over alleged "exploitation," it seemed clear to Slovenian and Croatian leaders that the Yugoslav state system needed to be overhauled and replaced with a full, formal confederal arrangement—if Yugoslavia was to be preserved at all. In the course of 1990 officials from both sides drew up a draft confederal scheme.[16] The Serbian nationalist bloc, dominated by Milošević and in control of both Serbia and Montenegro as well as Serbia's no-longer-autonomous provinces, Kosovo and

Vojvodina, not only rejected the Slovenian-Croatian draft proposals but insisted that the federation be scrapped and a tightly centralized system instituted. With memories of Serbian hegemony in the interwar period to serve as a warning, Slovenia and Croatia set a deadline for agreement to their proposal (26 June 1991). In the meantime, they laid the institutional and legal bases for secession.

A series of summit meetings were held in early 1991, involving the SFRY presidency (six sessions between January and March), the SFRY presidency jointly with the Staff of the High Command of the JNA (once, in March), and eleven bilateral meetings between delegations from various pairs of republics as well as talks involving Bosnian President Alija Izetbegović, Croatian President Franjo Tudjman, Serbian President Slobodan Milošević, and Montenegrin President Momir Bulatović. These talks got nowhere. Croatia insisted on its right to establish its own army.[17] Serbia and Bosnia agreed that there should be a single Yugoslav army.[18] Montenegro characterized the internal borders as "arbitrary" and declared that any loosening of federal ties would entail an opening of discussion about redrawing borders; Croatia denied that the borders were arbitrary (most of them having antecedents going back at least a hundred years, if not much longer), and it also denied that any revision of inter-republican borders should be made, except by free consent of republic authorities on both sides.[19] Bosnia and Macedonia hoped to preserve intact the Yugoslav state;[20] Slovenia and Croatia had served notice that they were prepared to dissolve their connection with the Yugoslav federation.

Even as the first incidents of interethnic violence between Serbs and Croats took place, there were still those who clung to their optimism—advocates of rationality in an irrational time. Thus, Svetozar Stojanović, the eminent Serbian scholar and long-serving member of the Praxis group, told a journalist from the *East European Reporter* in February:

> As for Bosnia-Herzegovina, it exemplifies the impossibility of dividing Yugoslavia, as a result of the ethnic mix in all the republics. . . .
> It is impossible to divide up Serbs, Croats, and Muslims, so that there will have to be a compromise with Bosnia perhaps becoming a model for Yugoslavia. People talk about separation but deep inside they know it is out of the question precisely because the republics are so mixed, and so they use hysterical language because everybody understands that there are certain things which nobody can change.[21]

In late February a session of the SFRY presidency, meeting in Sarajevo, concluded that the body should "propose at the next session a constitutional procedure for seceding from Yugoslavia in a constitutional and agreed manner."[22] But scarcely three weeks later, SFRY President Borisav Jović issued the following statement: "I wish to inform all the citizens of Yugoslavia and the Yugoslav public that the work of the Presidency as the body with the greatest responsibility for the situation in the country is paralyzed to such an extent that, in these dramatic circumstances, it has effectively ceased to perform its constitutional obligations and responsibilities."[23] They were ominous words.

In the absence of an agreement among the six republics[24] Slovenia and Croatia carried out their promise, and on 26 June 1991 they declared their secession from the Yugoslav federation. The following day, the JNA struck at Slovenia, temporarily by-passing Croatia. The Slovenian militia held its own against the JNA and captured a large number of young recruits, who seemed confused about the sudden turn of events. Within three weeks the JNA ceased hostilities and agreed to withdraw all units from Slovenia. Serbian President Milošević followed by declaring that Belgrade had no objection to a Slovenian secession.

But the strike against Slovenia had served its purpose—to demonstrate to the Slovenes the unreliability of their Croatian defense pact ally and thus drive a wedge between the two republics.[25] Slovenia learned the lesson, and when local Serbian militias, backed by the JNA, opened hostilities against Croatia, Croatia found that it stood alone.

The Tides of War

From July 1991 to January 1992 the war in Yugoslavia pitted Croatia against the Serb-Montenegrin rump federation (which, after a delay, adopted the name Federal Republic of Yugoslavia). After nearly four years of officially sponsored hate propaganda, the Serbs felt fully justified in perpetrating utterly ghoulish atrocities, and the war quickly gained worldwide notoriety for its sheer brutality. After being repeatedly told that all Serbs have the right to live in Serbia—a right premised on territorial union, not on freedom of migration[26]—Croatian Serbs felt fully justified in demanding that their territories be annexed to Serbia. That, despite the fact that Serbs constituted only 11.6 percent of the population of Croatia (as of the April 1991 census) and that the areas in which they were concentrated were geographically separate from Serbia and were in fact, in relative terms, distant from their chosen "homeland."

The Serbian irregulars were well-nourished by arms supplies from the JNA and benefited from JNA logistical and combat support, including aerial attacks on Zagreb. By year's end the Serbs had driven native Croats out of more than 30 percent of Croatian territory and had placed the historic Croatian cities of Osijek, Zadar, Dubrovnik, and Vinkovci under siege. Meanwhile, Serbian artillery had destroyed large numbers of historical monuments and artistic objects in Croatia, especially targeting Catholic churches.

International mediation by British Lord Carrington (as official EC mediator) and former U.S. Secretary of State Cyrus Vance (as official UN mediator) eventually brought the two sides to agree to what could only be a temporary reprieve: the Serbian forces held onto what they had conquered, and some 13,000 UN "peacekeepers" were dispatched in the hope of keeping the two sides apart.

This truce on the Croatian front enabled Milošević to carry the war into Bosnia. Well-planned at the highest levels,[27] the eventual Serbian attack on Bosnia had been heralded at least two months in advance by reports of arms shipments to local Serbs and Croatians (the Muslims, however, remaining virtually unarmed) and by a significant escalation in interethnic tensions, boiling over into violent incidents.

Composing nearly one-third of the population of Bosnia, Bosnian Serbs were able to field larger forces than their kin in Croatia, and thus they were less in need of active JNA ground support. Armed to the teeth, thanks again to shipments from JNA coffers, the Bosnian Serbs (led by former psychiatrist Radovan Karadžić) were militarily far better-equipped than either the Bosnian Croats or the Muslims. Thus, once the Bosnian front was opened, Serbian militias, backed by JNA air attacks against Muslim and Croatian positions, made rapid advances, and within less than three months they had overrun some 60 percent of the territory of Bosnia-Herzegovina.

At first, the Croats seemed to take the Bosnian side. Repeated discussions took place between Tudjman and Izetbegović, for instance, about coordinating defense efforts. In May 1992 the two republics even discussed the establishment of a Croatian-Bosnian confederation.[28] But as the Muslims were driven from one town after another, and as Serbian forces razed Muslim villages, local Croatian defense forces, led by Mate Boban, developed other ideas. Increasingly, Croatian forces in Bosnia began fighting for *Croatian* interests, regardless of whether this action pitted them against Serbs or against Muslims. The war had become a three-cornered conflict. In July, having seized a large chunk of southwestern Herzegovina, Boban's forces declared the state of Herzeg-Bosna—a state whose only intended future could be union with Croatia.[29]

By the end of 1992 Serbian forces controlled some 70 percent of

Bosnia-Herzegovina, Croatian forces controlled swathes of territory in the southwest and in the north (about 20 percent of Bosnia's territory), and the Muslim government's control was confined to a handful of cities and towns—among them, Sarajevo (the capital), Srebrenica, Goražde, Tuzla, Žepa, and Bihać—together with some surrounding villages. Sarajevo had been under siege for months, as Serbian snipers picked off unarmed civilians. By the end of 1992 at least 150,000 were dead,[30] between 2 and 2.5 million homeless, and an estimated $60 billion suffered in property damage. A truncated Croatia had been forced to accommodate more than a half-million Croatian and Muslim refugees (in addition to unregistered refugees who simply moved in with relatives in safe parts of the republic). There were also (as of August–October 1992), 60,000 refugees in Slovenia, 300,000 in Serbia, 65,000 in Macedonia, 916,000 in Germany, 60,000 in Austria, 50,000 in Hungary, 40,000 in Sweden, and some 67,000 in other countries.[31]

Ironically, through all of this conflict, the West maintained a policy of enforcing a strict arms embargo against *all* former Yugoslav republics. Given the significant military advantage enjoyed by the Serbian side in terms of equipment and arms, training, strategic experience (most of the JNA's generals had always been Serbs), the retention of the capacity of produce their own M-84A tanks,[32] and the sheer fact that the war was being fought on Croatian and Bosnian territory, the Western embargo actually significantly helped the Serbs. Indeed, by the summer of 1993 some officials in the U.S. Department of State were suggesting that the reason that Britain and France insisted on maintaining the arms embargo against Bosnia was that they secretly hoped for a quick and decisive Serbian victory. On the other hand, the British and French feared that the longer the war dragged on, the greater the chances that it could negatively affect their own welfare.

Throughout the early months of 1993, Lord David Owen (Lord Carrington's successor as EC mediator) and Vance worked hard to bring the sides together; failing to do so, they eventually produced their own plan that called for a division of Bosnia-Herzegovina into ten ethnic cantons. Quickly dubbed the Vance-Owen plan, the proposal produced a patchwork quilt that would be any politician's nightmare. Flora Lewis, a longtime reporter and columnist for the *New York Times*, summed up the view of many observers in writing that "the main trouble with the peace plan is that it doesn't go far enough. It offers no real incentive to stop fighting before the protagonists' irreconcilable goals are met. If it can be implemented, there is no reason to expect it to endure any longer than until one side or another feels it has a better chance for victory."[33] Nevertheless, the plan was immediately endorsed by Mate Boban on behalf of the Bosnian Croats, since the initiative essentially gave the Croats everything they could hope for. Bosnian President Izetbegović held out for a while, hoping for the West to decide to lift the arms embargo against the Muslims or perhaps even to respond, however belatedly, to his pleas for a Western military intervention against Serbia. Eventually, convinced that further delay would only have given the Serbs more time to lay siege to Muslim-held towns and villages, Izetbegović endorsed the plan.

As early as 12 January 1993 the Bosnian Serbs announced their rejection of the Vance-Owen plan.[34] But the West continued to apply diplomatic pressure on Karadžić, and on 17 April the economic sanctions against Serbia were tightened. Coming on top of the earlier ban on trade with Serbia, other than for food and medicines, these additional sanctions included "a worldwide freeze on all Yugoslav financial assets, seizure of all Yugoslav planes, ships, trucks, and other vehicles on foreign territory and a strictly enforced embargo . . . on all road, sea, air and Danube River commerce involving Serbia and . . . Montenegro."[35]

Although Radovan Karadžić, president of the Bosnian Serbs, had by then endorsed the plan, he emphasized that the Bosnian Serb parliament still had to agree, and he announced that a referendum would be held in advance of any decision by the parliament. The U.S. special envoy Reginald Bartholemew tried to apply pressure by warning that a failure to accept the plan would result in American support for arming the Muslims.[36] Meanwhile, U.S. President Bill Clinton held private meetings with various members of Congress on 27 April to sound them out on Bosnia.[37] Unimpressed by these rumblings from the West, the Bosnian Serb parliament soundly rejected the Western cantonization plan on 6 May (65 to 1, with 12 abstentions) after the scheduled referendum showed widespread repudiation of the plan among the Serbian population. In the meantime, the Clinton administration had become convinced that the only appropriate response to such a rejection was a strategy of combining arms supplies to the Muslims with air strikes against Serbian military forces and other strategic targets.[38]

Although two weeks earlier the German Bundestag had endorsed the lifting of the arms embargo against Bosnia and the adoption of "drastic measures" against Serbia and Montenegro and against the Bosnian Serbs,[39] Britain and France refused to support Clinton's proposal. In the absence of a consensus the West found itself without any means to enforce compliance, and in late May foreign ministers from the United States, Russia, Britain, France, and Spain—but not Germany—met in

Washington, D.C., to formulate a joint policy; on 22 May, at the conclusion of the meeting, an agreement was announced to create "safe havens" for Bosnian Muslims.[40] These havens would amount to some guarantee for Muslim safety in six of the major towns still held by the government of Alija Izetbegović. *Vjesnik* commentator Nenad Ivanković called this timid Western response "the final 'capitulation' of the international community before Serbian aggression."[41] But Germany was furious at being excluded from the meeting and objected to the "safe havens" concept.[42] On 26 May a meeting of the defense ministers of the sixteen NATO governments rejected the Washington meeting's recommendations, thanks in large part to the resistance of Turkey and Germany.[43] American intelligence officials now admitted that the "safe havens" plan could, at best, create "six impoverished refugee compounds with little law and order and no economic future." A senior U.S. intelligence official conceded further that "neither the safe-area plan nor the Vance-Owen plan represented a way to stabilize the situation in Bosnia."[44] Meanwhile, Bosnian Serb forces, ignoring Western discussions about safe havens and Western pleas for cooperation, continued to lay siege to Muslim-held towns, and on 4 June they announced that they had overrun two Muslim villages (Medjedja and Ustipraca) near Goražde, thus closing in on one of the proposed havens.[45] In the following days Bosnian Serbs subjected Goražde to intensified artillery bombardment and gave its defenders an ultimatum: abandon the city on the promise of safe passage or be slaughtered.[46]

On 16 June, during EC-sponsored negotiations in Geneva, the presidents of Croatia, Serbia, and Bosnia met privately. Croatian President Tudjman and Serbian President Milošević redrew the map, discarding the Vance-Owen plan, which had been based on ten autonomous districts. Instead, they proposed to divide Bosnia into three only nominally autonomous districts under the formal umbrella of a Bosnian state, which would retain no power. Bosnian President Izetbegović walked out in protest and flew to Bonn for talks with German Chancellor Helmut Kohl.[47] London *Times* reporter Misha Glenny reported that the partition plan bore a "striking resemblance" to the lines of demarcation of the old *Sporazum* of 1939; reportedly, in order to obtain Tudjman's cooperation in Bosnia, Milošević had to agree to give back the *krajina* (the central Serb-held section of Croatia), while Tudjman was said to have assured that local Serbs would obtain wide-ranging autonomy.[48] The *Krajina* Serbs rejected this compromise, however, and quickly organized a referendum on union with Serbia; predictably, they reported overwhelming support for union.[49] In Bonn Kohl told Izetbegović that "Germany will never recognize frontiers changed by force."[50] But Britain and France expressed readiness to accept literally any result in Bosnia as long as they would not be constrained to accept refugees. Meanwhile, Clinton declared on 17 June that the United States was prepared to accept a partition of Bosnia-Herzegovina along whatever lines Serbia and Croatia might jointly determine, provided only that the Muslims agreed.[51]

On 20 June the EC ministers announced that their peace plan was dead and that they had no further intentions to revive or promote it. On the contrary, they asked Lord Owen to begin negotiating a new plan more acceptable to the Serbs. Meanwhile, the Belgian, Danish, and British foreign ministers met with Bosnian President Izetbegović the following day and advised him to be satisfied with the partitioning of Bosnia and the survival of a Muslim ministate wedged between Croatian and Serbian zones. By then, details were emerging about the alleged Serb-Croat deal to partition Bosnia. According to these reports, the partition would leave only a small portion to the Muslims, with the Serbs now pressing a formal claim to the Bosnian capital city of Sarajevo.[52] On 10 July the Bosnian collective presidency voted to reject the partition plan and any concessions on the status of Sarajevo. But the Serbs and Croats continued to work out the details of their joint plan, and on 18 July Tudjman and Milošević met face-to-face in Geneva and finalized their agreement on what they described as a "confederal" solution.[53]

On 30 July the Bosnian government caved in and agreed in principle to the Serb-Croat plan now also being championed by international mediators Lord Owen and Thorvald Stoltenberg of Norway (Stoltenberg being Vance's successor as UN mediator). Muslim leaders admitted that they agreed to the plan in the desperate hope of saving as many Muslims as possible from physical annihilation. The agreement called for Bosnia to be reorganized into three ethnically based republics, with the Serb republic occupying 50 percent of Bosnia's territory, the Muslim republic 30 percent, and the Croat republic 20 percent. Nominally, at least, Bosnian citizens who were driven out of their homes would now be allowed to return to the sites of their villages and rebuild their lives. Serbia's Slobodan Milošević positively gloated as he told Serbian citizens over state television on 30 July: "Every citizen is well aware of the burden borne by Serbia in its assistance and solidarity with our people outside Serbia. It turned out that all that we have had to go through in these past few years was worth it."[54]

But subsequent talks bogged down over details. At one point (on 9 August) the NATO allies actually agreed to make contingency preparations for air strikes against Bosnian Serbs. But despite the preparations, the launching of strikes was made so conditional as to nullify any possible threat.[55] Far from being intimidated, however, the Serbs actually reinforced their troop strength around Sarajevo, the key city, and moved in additional heavy weaponry.[56]

On 20 August Lord Owen and Stoltenberg presented a new plan, offering the Serbs 52 percent of Bosnia–Herzegovina, the Muslims 30 percent, and the Croats 18 percent (largely in the southwest).[57] Izetbegović expressed horror at the plan and reminded the mediators that the Muslims had constituted more than 43 percent of the population in the April 1991 census. The Muslim side pressed for territorial adjustments and for international guarantees for the peace arrangement, including, specifically, direct U.S. participation in guaranteeing the peace.[58] Failing to obtain any territorial concessions, the Muslim delegation left Geneva on 1 September, and the talks once again collapsed. Owen and Stoltenberg called the Muslim departure "unexpected."[59]

Three weeks later, after a number of minor concessions and further adjustments to the peace plan, Bosnian President Izetbegović declared himself "not inclined" to accept the adjusted plan, chiefly because of his dissatisfaction with the arrangements offered to assure the Muslims of access to the sea.[60] But by the end of September the Muslims' allocation had been increased marginally to 31 percent, and they were offered guaranteed access, on a 99-year contract, to the Croatian port of Neum, which Germany offered to build up.[61] The Muslim deputies of the Bosnian assembly met in Sarajevo 28–29 September to discuss their options, and ultimately they rejected the Owen-Stoltenberg plan.[62] In the wake of this vote Izetbegović made a desperate appeal to the UN, telling the General Assembly: "Without minimum adjustments being addressed, please do not threaten us into accepting this inequitable peace plan."[63]

Nor was it clear, anyway, that an agreement signed in Switzerland could bring about an end to hostilities. Since then, as before, much of the fighting has been carried out by local militias on the initiative of local commanders. Meanwhile, by mid-1994 the Croats had ended their limited cooperation with Serbian commanders and had agreed on political union and military cooperation with the Bosnian Muslims. Negotiations followed regarding the precise division of territory within the projected Bosnian-Croatian confederation. Finally, on 12 May 1994, the Bosnian Muslims and Croats announced that they had agreed that they would settle for 58 percent of the territory of Bosnia-Herzegovina, dividing it into eight cantons: four Muslim, two Croats, and two mixed. But the Serbs, in control of 72 percent of Bosnia-Herzegovina, refused to settle for anything less than half of the territory of the former republic.[64] Less than two weeks later, Bosnian Muslim forces—equipped with tanks, backed by intensive artillery fire, and enjoying the military support of local Croat forces—launched a counter-offensive against Bosnian Serbs. News reports suggested that much of the Bosnian Muslims' new weaponry had been provided by Iran, although the Muslims had also come into possession of Brazilian infantry assault weapons and Chilean-made antitank guns.[65] Meanwhile, throughout the period from September 1993 to May 1994, the Bosnian Serbs repeatedly violated UN-designated "safe havens"—first Sarajevo, then Goražde and Tuzla. But every time local NATO forces requested permission to begin aerial bombardment of Bosian Serb forces, Yasushi Akashi, the UN special envoy, denied permission. Disgusted, the United States called for Akashi's dismissal, while the French, exasperated with the labyrinthine civilian authorizations now being required for any NATO response to Serbian provocations, announced their intention, on 24 May, to withdraw their "peacekeepers" from the war zone.[66]

On 8 June the warring sides signed a UN-brokered agreement for a one-month regionwide ceasefire, although there was no reason to expect this ceasefire to last any longer than the several dozen prior attempts. In the meantime, in separate moves, the U.S. Senate and the U.S. House of Representatives voted to require the president to take steps to lift the arms embargo against the Muslims.[67]

As the savagery in Bosnia continued, some observers were already looking to other regions, in particular to Kosovo, Vojvodina, and Macedonia, and wondering whether Serbia's hunger for a "Greater Serbia" would be satisfied after its annexations in Bosnia. A September 1993 radio broadcast was especially troubling. Known to reflect Milošević's thinking, Radio Belgrade mocked Macedonia as "a state without a name," as "a pygmy creation," and as a "servant of foreigners" (because the Macedonian government, in sheer fear of a possible Serbian invasion, had invited a small American "peacekeeping" contingent to monitor its borders). "Macedonia is neither an independent nor a sovereign state," declared Radio Belgrade.[68] And as any student of politics knows, when construals diverge from reality, one common way to reconcile the difference is to change reality.[69]

Economic Consequences of the War

The war has had serious economic impacts on five of the six former republics of Yugoslavia. Only Slovenia has had a lesser burden to shoulder. But the nature of these impacts has varied from republic to republic. All six (including Slovenia) have suffered economic losses from disruption of the former domestic market and of traditional trading patterns, and all six have had to deal with influxes of refugees.

But there are also some obvious differences. While Serbia, Croatia, and Bosnia-Herzegovina have all suffered serious declines in industrial production, this identical result has had different causes. In Bosnia, most of the republic's industrial capacity has been destroyed by Serbian artillery and aerial bombardment. In Croatia, the territories occupied by Serbian forces are chiefly agricultural lands, but they also include some industry, and in this republic, too, there has been damage from Serbian bombardment. But in Serbia, which so far has seen no fighting on its own territory, industrial production dropped by half between June 1992 and June 1993,[70] and here the causes are the economic strains of the war, combined with the effects of the sanctions, and the need to pay above-market prices to obtain less-than-adequate supplies of oil.[71]

The figures for the dramatic decline of the social product, inflation, and unemployment for Serbia, Croatia, and Macedonia are given in Table 11. For obvious reasons no data are available for Bosnia. Croatia's relative advantage over Serbia by these measures is to a large extent illusory. Serbia has the advantage of possessing rich and still-productive agricultural sector, and, as the *Times* of London noted, "it is this cushion . . . that staves off complete collapse and means that Serbia's economy can, on paper, reach 'zero' but the country can still avoid widespread hunger."[72] Macedonia's blind eye to cross-border freight traffic, in violation of the UN embargo, provided another cushion, although Macedonia was finally compelled to close its borders with rump Yugoslavia to freight traffic in September 1993.[73] With the signing of the Croat-Serb "truce" in early 1992, Croatia was granted a breathing spell of sorts, while Serbia became the fuel pump and arms supplier for Bosnian Serb militias seeking to annex most of Bosnia. The upshot is that economic indicators for Serbia reflect a steady deterioration in that republic's economic position (at least until the end of 1993). Inflation, for example, which stood at an annual rate of 19,810 percent at the end of 1992 had accelerated to a *monthly* rate of 225.8 percent in March 1993 alone and reached a *monthly* rate of more than 20,000 percent in December 1993. Again, the dinar, which was exchanged at an official rate of 3,300 to the dollar in December 1992, had sunk to 1.1 million to the U.S. dollar after devaluation on 17 June 1993.[74] Unemployment has also risen steadily, reaching a perilously high figure of about one in two by May 1993. And yet, even in the midst of war, some export-import firms in Belgrade have made a profit from the war economy. Progres Enterprise,

Table 11. Economic Indices in Selected Yugoslav Successor States

	Decline of social product 1991–92	Inflation (in percentages)	Unemployment
Serbia	−35	19,810[a]	50[b]
Croatia	−35.5[c]	122.6[d]	17.6[e]
Macedonia	−15	1,790.7[a]	30[f]

[a]= at end of 1992
[b]= as of May 1993
[c]= rate for January–June 1992
[d]= as of early 1992
[e]= at mid-1992
[f]= as of early 1993
Sources: Vjesnik (Zagreb), 28 Mar. 1992, 2; Neue Zürcher Zeitung, 30 Sept. 1992, 16; Tanjug, 13 Nov. 1992, in FBIS, Daily Report (Eastern Europe), 16 Nov. 1992, 41; Tanjug, 1 Feb. 1993, in FBIS, Daily Report (Eastern Europe), 2 Feb. 1993, 53; Neue Zürcher Zeitung, 14 Apr. 1993, 15; 28 Apr. 1993, 5; and 12 May 1993, 19; and The Times (London), 10 May 1993, 10.

for example, racked up a net of $67 million in the first nine months of 1992 alone, amounting to capital formation of $8 million.[75] And the Munich daily, Süddeutsche Zeitung, reported that a new boutique was opening in Belgrade almost every month.[76]

For the Serbian population at large, however, the war has meant a rapid slide into poverty. More than 4 million Serbs lived below the poverty line as of March 1993, and their numbers continued to swell.[77] Many young women have taken desperate measures to maintain a steady income, the result being an unprecedented boom in the Serbian "sex industry." A news report published in Vjesnik in June 1993 held that "there have never been so many brothels, match-makers, topless bars, massage parlours, or other places of this order in 'Yugoslavia' as now."[78]

Other problems afflicting Serbia include skyrocketing fuel prices, fuel rationing, and shortages of anesthetics and other basic drugs. It is no wonder that the republic has seen a massive flight of scientists, researchers, musicians, singers, and other intellectuals.[79]

Even the agricultural and viticultural sectors are suffering. For example, a report in Glas Srpski in January 1993 noted: "this year there will be great difficulties in pruning the fruit trees, which has begun. In the spring, it will not be possible to use seasonal pruners, who for years have come to the Kožara region from Serbia. More than 130 peasant workers in units of the Army of the Serbian Republic are also missing."[80] Finally, in early September the Belgrade regime introduced a partial rationing of foodstuffs, principally as a measure to prevent hoarding and black-marketeering. The once-profitable commercial fleet of Montenegro has

Table 12. Economic Indices for Croatia, 1990–92 (declines in percentages)

	1990	1991	January–June 1992
Gross social product	−8.5	−30.6	−35.5
Industrial production	−11.3	−28.5	−28.1
Exports	—	−24.7	−19.3
Imports	—	−30.7	−24.2
Unemployment (in %)	9.3	15.4	17.6
Inflation rate	609.9	122.6	384.3

Source: Neue Zürcher Zeitung, 30 Sept. 1992, 16.

been largely idle, contributing to the economic decline of the coast.[81] But in the early months of 1994, thanks in part to a belt-tightening effort to stabilize the dinar, Serbia was reported to be staging an economic recovery—although the damage done by Serbia's reckless economic policies of 1989–93 will not easily be undone.

Croatia, on the other hand, has had to deal with the destruction of 40 percent of its industrial capacity, alongside the partial or total destruction of 210,000 apartments, 50,000 houses, 300 churches, 250 schools, 200 cultural monuments, and 14 large hospitals. All told, war damages have totaled $21 billion.[82] If full-scale war between Serbia and Croatia resumes, this toll will go even higher. Moreover, looking at the economic trends in Croatia from 1990 through 1992, the picture is not bright. As can be seen in table 12, the rate of gross social product continued to decline even after the February truce with Serbia, while industrial production continued to fall at the same rate as in the previous year. Unemployment and inflation also worsened between 1991 and early 1992. As of June 1993 more than 1 million people were unemployed in the Republic of Croatia.[83]

Political Consequences of the War

In political terms the war has turned the world upside down for Serbs and Croats alike. Everything they were told for more than forty years of communism is now declared to be false, and entirely new standards are thrown up for judging what is right and wrong. One of the war's most striking political consequences is the rise to power and prominence of people who would otherwise end up in psychiatric care (such as Serbian Radical leader Vojislav Šešelj) or in criminal circles (such as Željko Raznjatović, who calls himself Arkan) and their ability to define the mainstream terms of discourse. This phenomenon is common to conditions of internal war, albeit the degree to which it occurs varies from case to case.

Šešelj, for example—whom Amnesty International had adopted as a "prisoner of conscience" in 1985, after he was jailed for producing a map showing a "Greater Serbia" with dramatically enlarged borders—has defied all standards of rationality by declaring that "Dubrovnik has always been a Serbian city,"[84] that there are only 100,000 Albanians in Kosovo (rather than the roughly 1.7 million recorded in the most recent census),[85] and that Veljko Kadijević, the Yugoslav minister of defense who actively cooperated with Milošević in organizing the JNA assault on Croatia in July 1991, was "an American spy, who did all he could to ruin his own army."[86] In May 1993 Šešelj even threatened to fire missiles at *civilian* targets in Italy if NATO bases in Italy were used for any air strikes against Serbian targets.[87]

Raznjatović got his start as a hit man and was said to be wanted in Sweden and other European countries for bank robbery, attempted murder, and other crimes going back to the 1970s. An Interpol liaison officer at the ministry of the interior at an unidentified European capital called him "the most qualified bank robber in Europe."[88] What does Raznjatović think should be done to improve the present situation? He wants to take steps to make sure that "Kosovo will no longer be a problem for Yugoslavia,"[89] and he has proposed that Šešelj be made minister of defense. Both Šešelj and Raznjatović are members of the Serbian parliament. Then there is Mirko Jović, the founder of the Serbian National Renewal, described by Misha Glenny as "a peculiar psychopath from Stara Pazova."[90]

In parallel fashion Milošević, both of whose parents committed suicide, has been the subject of provocative analysis. Belgrade psychiatrist Stevan Petrović, for example, says that Milošević is "narcissistic [and] has no capacity to feel guilt."[91] Petrović notes that up to October 1992 Milošević had not once visited any of the Serbian wounded or met with any war invalids or refugees, and he further described the Serbian leader as emotionally cold and inadequately in touch with reality.[92] Milošević's recent contacts with Italian neofascists also provide an interesting commentary on how he himself views his politics.[93]

As the politicians turn reality upside down, inevitably the old heroes—Tito, Kardelj, Bakarić—must be denigrated; the same is true for both Serbia and Croatia. In their place new "heroes" are found—namely, the "demons" of yesteryear. For Serbs the semicollaborationist anticommunist Chetniks of World War II, long denounced by the Titoist government, provide a role model (because of their atrocities against Croats), and inevitably, a monument to Chetnik leader Draža Mihailović was erected on Milošević's orders.[94] A similar process has unfolded in Croatia, where the ruling Croatian Democratic Community badly wants to reinterpret the fascist Ustasha quislings of World War II as a Croatian patriotic force. Hence, the reissue in early 1993 of the collected works of Mile Budak, the second-in-command in the Ustasha regime. Commenting at the time of this reissue, Croatian writer Giancarlo Kravar wrote: "As a literary figure, Dr. Mile Budak is already completely rehabilitated. . . . Ustashism, in its history, was undoubtedly also a positive political movement for the state-building affirmation of Croatianism, just as the NDH [the fascist Independent State of Croatia of 1941–45] was the expression of the centuries-long aspiration of the Croatian people."[95] Calls also have been heard for the political rehabilitation of interwar Croatian politician Vlatko Maček.[96]

In such a world as I have described, chaos prevails. In strife-torn Bosnia, armed gangs motivated essentially by hunger for booty are joining in the fighting, using nationalist ideologies and the suspension of normal ethical standards to justify their depredations.[97] And as in so many wars in the past, "ethnic cleansing" has been accompanied by "linguistic hygiene": thus, after members of the ethnic groups are driven out of an area, the district and its towns are symbolically renamed to give it a new history, a new identity. "By eliminating the term," said Bosnian Serb historian Djordje Mikić of the word "Bosnia" itself, "we are eliminating the memory and consequences that stem from it."[98]

The difficulty is that, in a world turned upside down, the only moral thing to do is to stand on the ceiling—a difficult feat without falling.

Serbia: The Media. Serbia today—or the "Federal Republic of Yugoslavia" as it styles itself—is the last bastion of totalitarianism left in Eastern Europe. This is ironic given the modest liberal tradition on which the Serbs used to pride themselves. Symptomatic of Serbia's totalitarian character is the fact that Milošević, nominally president of only the "Serbian" part of the FRY (hence, not of the Montenegrin), easily engineered the ouster of Dobrica Ćosić as FRY president, after the Ćosić expressed concern to army officers about the "malfunctioning" of the state.[99] Consider also the arrest in early June 1993 of Serbia's leading opposition figure, Vuk Drašković, together with his wife, Danica, and several dozen other opposition leaders, after protesters gathered on 2 June to protest the unconstitutional removal of Ćosić and to denounce Milošević as "totalitarian"—arrests executed by Milošević, os-

tensibly with impunity.[100] Supporters of Drašković said that the Draškovićes had been handcuffed and then beaten with police truncheons and
that their injuries were extremely serious. The Draškovićes were subsequently charged with disturbing public order under Article 114 of the
Serbian criminal code, and Vuk was additionally charged with assault-
ing a policeman. The charges entailed prison sentences of ten to fifteen
years.[101] On 6 July Danielle Mitterrand (the wife of French President
François Mitterrand) went to Belgrade to plead for their release, only to
be rebuffed by Milošević. Only when the Russian government (a key Serbian backer) appealed for the release of the Draškovićes did Milošević
order that charges be dropped and authorized their release.[102]

Milošević began his transformation of Serbian politics back in 1987–
88 by asserting his control over the two most important media outlets
in Serbia: the prestigious daily newspaper *Politika* and Radio-Television
(RTV) Belgrade. At his direction, the staffs of both were thoroughly
purged, resulting in the firing of some of Serbia's ablest journalists; they
were replaced by Milošević loyalists. As a result of these staff discharges
and the ensuing changes of editorial policies, "*Politika* and RTV Belgrade
became hollow vessels which Milošević's bureaucracy filled with seduc-
tive nonsense, designed to manipulate and feed the gullible and disori-
ented Serbian people with a diet of suspicion and intolerance."[103] In spite
of the paranoid atmosphere provoked by these machinations the media
still showed some capacity to think for itself; hence, in 1992 the directors
of both radio and television at RTV Belgrade, along with the chief director
of *Politika*, were all forced to resign, and at one point Milošević was even
pressing for an outright nationalization of *Politika* until he got what he
wanted by other means.[104] Milošević has certainly understood the power
of the media. A Belgrade political scientist reported that according to
a public opinion poll conducted in late 1990, 30 percent of the Serbian
public believes everything it sees on state-controlled television in general, and 33.7 percent reported "absolute confidence" in that station's
7:30 P.M. news program.[105] Vlado Mareš, a former journalist in Serbia,
believes that the low educational level among Serbs is partly to blame
for the media's strong influence. Only about half of adult Serbs have
completed elementary school, and 12 percent have no formal schooling. Only some 6 percent of Serbs have had any higher education, and a
large part of these people live in Belgrade, the center of anti-Milošević
sentiment and pacifism in Serbia.[106]

Journalists' heads continued to roll during 1992 and 1993 as Milošević attempted to tighten his grip. Among those dismissed at Serbian

television were Čedomir Mirković, Mihailo Kovač, Darka Novović, Ivan Bržev, Dragan Nikitović, and Jarmila Celović.[107] The Council of Tanjug Journalists protested and issued the following statement:

Although we are aware that all publishers and broadcasting stations have a certain surplus of people, however, the names that the press has stated to be on the lists for so-called compulsory vacations cause us an alarm.

The people we are talking about are the top professionals [in their fields]. . . . Their definite dismissal can only be understood as a vengeance taken upon professional journalism within the most powerful media in Serbia and Montenegro.[108]

But job dismissals have been only one method the Milošević regime has attempted to assert total control over the media. Blackmail, violence, and withheld paychecks have been wielded. Rade Radovanović, a founding member of the Serbian Independent Union of Journalists, told *Index on Censorship* in 1992:

The situation facing journalists is very complicated and dangerous, with journalists facing blackmail on a daily basis. Some are told that they are on deathlists of one or [an]other organization. Nothing is certain, but the psychological pressure is intense.

There has been a direct attempt by the government to break our union. Our members are singled out for attack and threats against us often mention the fact of our union activities. Meanwhile, the official union is given money by the state to feed its members and is able to give them sugar and meat as an incentive not to join us. They have to submit to strict censorship by the state. Our members are suffering because many have not been paid by the state for several months because of their union activities.[109]

Inevitably, Serbia's undereducated public gets confused by Belgrade television's daily reports of the bombardment of Sarajevo, in which the perpetrators are never identified, and in which the "Serbian defensive actions" are praised. A public opinion poll in July 1992 found that only 20 percent of the Serbs queried could correctly answer the question, "Who shelled Sarajevo in May and June from the heights overlooking the city?"[110]

Serbia: Politics. The character of the transition from the Socialist Federated Republic of Yugoslavia to the FRY, which claims to be the legitimate successor of the SFRY, is elucidated by events in October 1992. In what amounted to an administrative coup Serbian special police loyal to Milošević forcibly seized the FRY Ministry of the Interior, confiscating its files.[111] This incident provides a clue as to how Milošević has maintained and tightened his grasp on power. The opposition—and in particular, Vuk Drašković's Serbian Renaissance Party and Dragoljub Mičunović's Democratic Party—have repeatedly voiced their demands for Milošević's resignation, for the deconstruction of the strong executive, for the transfer of power to a broadly representative transition government, and for truly free elections in which the opposition would enjoy equal access to the media.[112] But its support is heavily concentrated in Belgrade, and therefore it has been unable to mobilize a mass movement to confront Milošević. The harsh repression of opposition-oriented street protests in downtown Belgrade on 9 March 1991 temporarily shook the ground beneath Milošević's feet. He was forced to make a number of concessions, which included dismissing the head of RTV Belgrade Dušan Mitević, and Interior Minister Radmilo Bogdanović,[113] but he deflected criticism from himself, and by the next day he had organized a counterrally at Ušće, where speakers talked about the importance of "unity."[114] Milošević was confident that the rapid escalation to war would contract the space in which the opposition could articulate its views.

Since then, Milošević has used the war to whip up Serbian nationalism, to present himself as the saviour of Serbia, and in this way to crucify his opponents. The December 1992 election is a case in point. Milan Panić, the American pharmaceutical millionaire turned Serbian politician, was challenging Milošević for the presidency, drawing bigger crowds, and scoring tangibly higher than Milošević in every public opinion poll. But Milošević applied a strategy that combined the tactics of holding up approval of Panić's candidacy until halfway through the race, using the media to subject Panić to scathing attacks while limiting his opponent's television ads to mere matter-of-fact biographical statements, infiltrating the Panić campaign, invalidating the registration of many young people (those most strongly pro-Panić) as well as that of all voters who boycotted the spring elections (a boycott that had been called by the opposition), requiring students to register for classes precisely on election day, interfering with border crossings of ethnic minorities (again, likely to be anti-Milošević), and bribing voters with preelection bonus pay.[115] "With so many irregularities," said an international observer at the elections (a Dr. Hodjera), "any court would have declared these elections invalid." In addition, Hodjera cited the fact that at the end of the voting "the total number of ballot papers for these elections, both used and unused, was greater than the number delivered to the board and recorded before the polling started."[116]

Milošević's control seemed absolute. But with the Serbian economy in ruins and the war dragging on, there were signs of division within the Serbian camp. Vojislav Šešelj, leader of the Serbian Radical Party and an ally of Milošević's, sounded a new note in early September 1993 when he admitted to having formed a shadow government in Serbia. Šešelj, whose rhetoric has always been more belligerent than that of Milošević, now boasted that his party had the strength to overthrow the Milošević regime.[117] An even more ominous sign had occurred about a week earlier when Milošević carried out a massive purge of higher officers, dismissing, among others, the chief of the general staff and the commanders of the navy, air force, secret police, and territorial defense forces.[118]

Serbia: The Province of Kosovo.

"These goddamn Albanians. They are Muslims, you understand?"
"Yes."
"And there are Muslims in Bosnia. So you see, the Green Axis!"
"Excuse me?"
"The Green Axis! Islam! It's aiming at the heart of Europe. Why doesn't Europe care about this?"
"What would you propose?"
"Well. You should know, I am a nationalist." He smiled at the word, seeming both apologetic and serene. "Maybe you will laugh."
"Somehow I don't think so."
"The Albanians don't belong here. This is Yugoslavia. Yugoslavs belong here. Albanians belong in Albania!"[119]

Such a conversation could not have taken place in Tito's day. That it could take place in 1993 is symptomatic of how much has changed in a land whose ideologists once boasted about the degree of "brotherhood and unity" prevailing among its diverse peoples. It also reflects the symbiotic relationship between racism and totalitarianism noted by Hannah Arendt more than thirty years ago.[120]

In Tito's day the Albanians of Kosovo (who at the time numbered nearly 80 percent of the province's population) enjoyed widespread political autonomy, lively cultural exchanges with neighboring Albania, higher education in the Albanian language at the University of Priština, a wide array of Albanian-language newspapers and broadcast media, and, after 1968, virtually no problems of ethnic discrimination in jobs. By the early 1980s most of the province's officials, including its judges and university rectors, as well as key economic directors, were Albanians.

The picture in the mid-1990s is entirely different. The autonomy of the provinces of Kosovo and Vojvodina was quashed in March 1989. Shortly thereafter, Milošević ordered a widespread economic purge of Kosovo's management. More than 100,000 Albanian workers, many of them in leading positions, were fired; many of these workers were also forced out of their apartments.[121] Staffing at all levels of officialdom today, and especially at the upper levels, is overwhelmingly Serbian—even though more than 85 percent of the province's population is Albanian today (90 percent by many accounts). There no longer are any Albanian judges, university rectors, or ranking political officials in Kosovo. Albanians have been systematically dismissed from their jobs and replaced with Serbs—often "colonists" from outside the province.[122] Between 1991 and 1992 some 1,832 physicians and other medical personnel of Albanian nationality were dismissed from hospitals and clinics in Kosovo and replaced with Serbian personnel.[123] All Albanian-language instruction, from elementary school to university, was terminated in the autumn of 1990 "for an indefinite period" and has not been resumed; in the autumn of 1992, on the first day of the new school year, Albanian schoolchildren and their teachers attempted to approach their schools but were turned back by Serbian police.[124] Belgrade authorities have also used the police to try to prevent Albanian schoolchildren from attending the underground schools in Kosovo.[125] At the University of Priština most of the existing faculty were fired and replaced by Serbian professors, while the Albanian students were expelled and replaced by Serbian students, mostly brought in from outside the province.[126] The Albanians inevitably organized an underground university at people's homes. But Serbian authorities have not viewed this development with favor, and in early April 1993 Ejup Statovci, the rector of this illegal university, was arrested and sentenced to sixty days in prison.[127] As for the media, *Rilindja, Bujku, Zeri,* and *Fjala* have all been suspended, Albanian-language radio service has been terminated, and some Albanian journalists have been arrested.[128]

In the last half of 1992 street names in Priština were Serbianized, with Albanian street signs (in the Latin alphabet) being replaced by Serbian signs (in Cyrillic). Hajdar Dushi Street was renamed Vojvode Stepe, after a Serbian military leader, for example, while Nexhmedin Mustafa Street has become Vase Carapica, named for a hero in the Serbian insurrection against Ottoman (Muslim) rule.[129]

Albanian members of the reserve units of the Yugoslav army were discharged, and their uniforms, weapons, and other equipment were confiscated. This equipment was later distributed to local Serbian civilians.[130] There were various reports of an escalating of incidents of intimidation and harassment of Albanians by Serbs, and in August 1992 the Priština-based underground Kosovo Committee for the Protection of Human Rights and Freedoms claimed that some 103 Albanians had been killed and another 600 wounded as a result of incidents, adding that "violations of the human rights of Albanians are becoming more and more drastic."[131] In addition, Serbian soldiers along the mountainous border between Albania and Kosovo were given shoot-to-kill orders in early 1993, thus ending the cross-border visits that had briefly become possible with the collapse of communism in Albania. In early May, eight Kosovar Albanians and two Albanian citizens were shot dead near the border by Serbian guards; the Serbs justified the killings by claiming that the victims were "arms smugglers"—the standard accusation leveled against dead Albanians in this region.[132]

The underground Kosovar Albanian government of Ibrahim Rugova (elected on 24 May 1992 in proscribed elections) has declared its preference for Kosovo to become an independent, neutral state.[133] But Rugova has insisted that Albanians pursue their goals by peaceful means. Nonetheless, more radical currents exist. For example, the Albanian National Movement for the Liberation of Kosovo, an alternative movement formed in 1993, criticizes Rugova's strategy of avoiding an armed uprising of Albanians against the "Serbian occupation." This movement sees the resort to arms as the only chance of Albanian self-determination in the province. But in June 1994 British Foreign Secretary Douglas Hurd emphatically took the Serbian side in the Serb-Albanian dispute, declaring that Britain was opposed both to Kosovo's secession from Serbia and to any change in Serbia's southern borders.[134] Since the United States, Germany, and France were increasingly deferring to Britain in matters related to the Yugoslav crisis, Hurd was probably speaking for the West as a whole.

Since the summer of 1992 rumors have persisted that Kosovo was "next" in Milošević's military plan and that it was only a matter of time before the war spread to this southern province. Albanian President Sali Berisha has said emphatically that Albania would "resist by any means" any Serbian moves to annihilate Kosovo's Albanian population, and he warned at the end of May 1993 that "an explosion in Kosovo will be the beginning of a real Balkan war."[135] These fears are shared in Bulgaria and Turkey, and above all in Macedonia, which already has a large and restive Albanian minority and which could scarcely cope with a sudden influx of Albanian refugees.

Serbia: Vojvodina and the Sandžak. Aside from Kosovo's Albanians, the two most important ethnic minorities in Serbia are the Hungarians in Vojvodina and the Muslims of the old Sandžak region (the former Sandžak of Novi Pazar). Both were quiescent before the political ascent of Slobodan Milošević; both have been tense in recent years, as rumors have spread and interethnic frictions have mounted.

In Vojvodina, Hungarians make up 16 percent of the population, while Serbs constitute more than 57 percent. The April 1991 census recorded a total population of about 2 million.[136] Since the loss of provincial autonomy in 1989 local Hungarians, despite their minority status, have been in the forefront of efforts to regain autonomous status. The Democratic Community of Vojvodina Hungarians (Andras Agostin, president) has advocated recognition of triune autonomy—personal, territorial, and local, but he denies that the organization seeks annexation to Hungary. The territorial dimension of the proposal would establish a Hungarian autonomous region comprising only those districts in Vojvodina with a majority Hungarian population—Kanjiža, Senta, Ada, Čoka, Bećej, Subotica, Bačka Topola, and Mali Idos. But there is also some support among local Serbs for a restoration of Vojvodinan autonomy, as illustrated by the predominantly Serbian speakers at the "Vojvodina Autonomy Today" roundtable held in Novi Sad in January 1993.[137] The Serbian government, however, has repeatedly rejected all calls for autonomy,[138] and in January 1993, on the same day as a proautonomy convention was held, the Novi Sad headquarters of the League of Communists–Movement for Yugoslavia (a neocommunist party functioning largely within the military) "issued a statement declaring that mediation in favor of Hungarian autonomy is simply a step in the direction of a demand for secession, and that the goal of all of this is to completely dismember Yugoslavia and shatter Serbian unity."[139]

Inevitably, in those districts where Hungarians constitute a decisive majority, local elections have been won by Hungarians. As of April 1993 about 90 percent of the officials in the eight municipalities mentioned above were members of either the Democratic Community of Vojvodinan Hungarians (DCVH) or the Democratic League of Croats of Vojvodina. Viewing this situation, Serbian official Dragan Božinović claimed that these figures showed that the DCVH was carrying out an "occupation" of northern Vojvodina, thus realizing "by perfidious methods its concept of durable autonomy."[140]

In the course of 1992 minatory letters were sent to Hungarian residents of Subotica, threatening them with extermination unless they left the country. Barricades were erected in Serbian villages near Subotica, in a move reminiscent of the early phase in the escalation of Serb-Croat hostilities in the Knin region. Serbian authorities purged the police, customs officials, and the judiciary in 1990–92, and in December 1992 they issued a decree under which all directors of primary and secondary schools in Vojvodina would henceforth be appointed directly by the Republic Ministry of Education in Belgrade. The Belgrade authorities also tightened their supervision over provincial media, and in November 1992 they announced that the Hungarian-language daily *Magyar Szó* would be discontinued.[141] "Hungarians in Vojvodina are in no way endangered," then-Foreign Minister of Serbia Vladislav Jovanović declared in June 1992.[142] But Sándor Hodi, deputy chair of the DCVH, had a different view. According to Hodi, "the social structure of the Vojvodina Hungarians has already suffered irreparable damage because of the tens of thousands of people who fled the country or resettled abroad."[143]

Almost as many Muslims (327,000) as Hungarians (345,000) live and work in Serbia.[144] Most of these Muslims reside in the Sandžak region in the south of Serbia. As early as October 1991 a large majority of Sandžak Muslims registered their demand for autonomy, but Serbian officials refused to consider it. Serb-Muslim tensions in the Sandžak crested in October 1992 when some Muslims in Pljevlja were allegedly attacked by local Serbs. A short time later, local Muslim leaders claimed that some 70,000 Muslims had left the area because of these attacks.[145] The Serbian army claimed at the time that the Sandžak Muslims were arming themselves and forming militia units.[146] But it was not possible to obtain confirmation from an independent source, and such statements are often pretexts used to justify repression.

There were reports that the political situation in the Serbian Sandžak had dramatically deteriorated in early 1993. The Muslim community claimed that Muslims had been killed, wounded, or kidnapped, or, in some cases, forcibly inducted into the Serbian army so that they could be sent to the front lines to fight against Bosnia's Muslims. Sulejman Ugljanin, leader of the Sandžak Muslims, confirmed these claims and appealed to the foreign dignitaries at the "Peace Conference," to the EC, and to the CSCE to take up the issue.[147] On 20 March Muslim intellectuals of the Sandžak, Montenegro, Serbia, and Kosovo adopted a resolution to protest the different forms of the "slaughter of Muslims." In reply, the Committee for Inter-ethnic Relations of the Serbian Republic Assembly began discussions about the political-security situation in Raška oblast and asked the prosecutor's office to establish the signatures' authenticity. The committee concluded that the resolution reflected "the continuation of a long-term subversion of the territorial integrity of Serbia," and it accused the signatories of slandering the Republic of Serbia *and interfering in its internal affairs*—a most remarkable charge considering that all the signatories were FRY citizens.[148]

Croatia. In newly independent Croatia, in a fashion parallel to Serbia, the pressures of fighting a defensive war have encouraged a frame of mind in which greater value is attached to being "a good Croat" than to being "a good person"—as if one were, in the first place, a Croat, and only secondarily and derivatively, under appropriate conditions, also a person. In practice, this has created a tendency to treat any discussion of equality for women, or environmental issues, let alone questions of minority rights, as at best distractions, at worst a kind of "treason." Self-righteousness and narrow-mindedness go hand in hand as the offspring of nationalisms run rampant. But with 30 percent of their territory occupied by well-armed Serbs, how could the Croats *not* surrender to excessive nationalism?

In a study of the first three years in Croatian politics since Franjo Tudjman's election as president of the Republic in May 1990 Dijana Pleština highlights the following complications for a successful democratic transition in Croatia:

> (1) the lack of checks on the near-absolute power of a President who is also head of the party in power . . . [in] the Legislature; (2) the marginalization of the opposition parties; (3) the political interference in the independence of the judiciary; (4) the continuing near-monopoly and resulting censorship of the media; and (5) the creation of an atmosphere in which criticism of the party in power is often equated with disloyalty to the nation-state.[149]

Given these issues, it is not surprising that the political opposition in Croatia has expressed concern that the country was rapidly sliding toward a one-party system.[150]

The question of the declining independence of the media deserves some elaboration. When the Croatian Democratic Community (Tudjman's party) won the elections in May 1990, Croatia had a lively press, with a good ten years of very open investigative reporting and a growing readiness to criticize even the authorities, albeit usually by implication. But in its first three years in power the Tudjman government banned *Start* magazine, suppressed the highly credible weekly *Danas* in August

1992 (creating a new docile magazine of the same name a few months later), nationalized the Split daily, *Slobodna Dalmacija* (which for a few years had come to be revered as Croatia's best daily newspaper), and broke up the "Vjesnik" publishing enterprise. As of March 1993 the only Croatian newspaper of any note to preserve its independence was *Novi List* from Rijeka—a regional paper of marginal significance and with no great influence.[151]

The Croatian media are regulated by a special Act on Information in War, passed in the fall of 1991, which proscribes publication of any information that could harm the security of the country. In the event of an infraction, the police could seize the entire circulation of the issue in question and imprison the responsible parties for up to five years.

Some Croatian newspapers—*Globus*, in particular—have engaged in character assassinations of people whose ideas are not "nationalist" enough (see next chapter). In this way the Croatian press took on the task of hunting down "enemies of the people"—to use a timeworn expression. Toward the end of 1992, as Jasmina Kuzmanović notes: "the Croatian pro-government press, including the privately-owned *Globus*, developed a passion for discovering 'Yugo-nostalgists' or 'spiritual fifth-columnists.' The catchphrase was applied to anybody who publicly voiced any criticism of the government or the ruling party, or expressed dissatisfaction with some aspect of everyday life."[152]

Inevitably, the spirit fostered by such media engenders a social climate in which agreement with the "general opinion" is safer than disagreement and in which considerations of survival inevitably dictate a preference for caution over frankness. Croatian writer Dubravka Ugrešić offered reflections on her experiences in the autumn of 1992:

> I'll survive, I think to myself. I won't go out. I won't see anyone. I have noticed with satisfaction that a crust of indifference is settling round my heart. I don't get upset. If a Serbian house explodes I repeat the responses I've heard: What do they expect when they built on our land? And I see that everyone around me approves. If an innocent Serb is attacked, I don't protest; I say: Let them see what it's like to be beaten up when you've done nothing. And no one frowns, no one comments, everyone nods in unison. It is as though the whole country, my sweet little Croatia, has turned into a school choir, obediently singing in chorus.[153]

Conclusion

In this chapter I have focused largely on the repercussions of the war in Serbia and to a lesser extent in Croatia. I have, thus, passed over the case of Macedonia, which is, in any event, rather different.[154]

From this discussion it should be apparent that the prewar escalation of tensions (1989–91) and the ethnic war itself have been highly destructive of the principle of tolerance, which, I suggested in chapter 1, rests at the very heart of democracy. The destruction done to this principle is, by far, more serious in Serbia, but there are deeply troubling trends in Croatia as well.

Reviewing the preconditions for democracy outlined in chapter 1, it is clear that the war has gutted the economies of both Serbia and Croatia and has produced deep and heavily politicized social polarization (thus undermining preconditions 1 and 2). The destruction done to ethnic harmony in both republics (precondition 3) is likewise clear, as is the evanescence of anything we could call the spirit of tolerance (precondition 6), especially in Serbia. Whether one can speak sensibly of valued and effective institutions (precondition 5) in Serbia after the ejection of Ćosić from the presidency and the subversion of justice in the arrest of the Draškovićes—or even before—is another matter. Hence, on the situational variables, I would rank Croatia's prospects as "poor" and Serbia's as "extremely poor."

On the institutional preconditions, Serbia ranks poorly on numbers 7 (free elections), 8 (an independent judiciary), 9 (a depoliticized bureaucracy and police functioning according to written rules), 10 (legal guarantees of basic rights), 11 (the effective separation of Church and state),[155] and 12 (a free press). Croatia ranks somewhat better on these factors, but this is chiefly because various disputes that will directly affect what becomes of the institutional and legal structure in Croatia are currently unresolved. But even in mid-1994, Croatia ranks poorly on preconditions 10, 11, and 12 (the introduction of Catholic religious instruction in public schools signifying the effective abolition of Church-state separation).

War and democracy do not make good companions, any more than do war and tolerance. Whether because of the use of hate propaganda to mobilize ethnic publics, or because of the subversion of the law in order to quash pacifist oppositions, or because of dramatic deterioration in the economy, war is apt to damage all but the most entrenched and enduring democracies. The ethnic war in what was Yugoslavia is a case in point.

What went wrong in Yugoslavia? Juan Linz and Alfred Stepan have suggested that the problem was one of *sequencing* (as previously elaborated in chapter 1). Linz and Stepan compare Spain's successful transition from fascism to democracy with Yugoslavia's unsuccessful transition and with the USSR's troubled transition from communism to democracy. In their analysis, Spain had three important advantages, two of them explicitly questions of sequencing, and the third having a more subtle but nonetheless important connection with the question. First, in Spain economic prosperity was solidly established on the foundation of an educated middle class *before* any political democratization was undertaken. Second, the system created in Spain after Franco's death blended two principles of legitimacy, thus exploiting the "traditional" symbology of the Bourbon monarchy to protect the embryonic efforts to pluralize the system. Third, despite its sundry regional identities (especially strong among the Basques and the Catalans), Spain tackled democratization *before* moving to devolve power to regional and ethnic constituencies, thus encouraging parties to be formed with programs addressed to the entire nation. Linz and Stepan conclude that "if the first elections in Spain had been regional, rather than nationwide, the incentives for the creation of all-union parties and of an all-union agenda would have been greatly reduced. . . . We also believe that if the first elections had been on the regional level, ethnic issues would have assumed a much more substantial and decisive role in the electoral campaign than they actually did, and that the nationalist parties and their affiliates would have been more extreme."[156] Yugoslavia's path out of communism, by contrast, began with regional elections and the organization of regional, that is, republic-based, parties, some of them adopting highly intolerant, even chauvinistic, platforms and ideologies. Indeed, according to Linz and Stepan, "the actual policies followed in both countries [the Soviet Union and Yugoslavia] were virtually the *optimal* sequence to be followed *if* one wanted to disintegrate the state and heighten ethnic conflict."[157]

18. Civil Society and Uncivil Chauvinism

I do not subscribe to the common notion that the ethnic hatreds and chauvinisms presently visible in Eastern Europe were there all along, but repressed by communist power, and that as soon as that power collapsed, these hatreds percolated to the surface. I consider this interpretation facile, simplistic, and fallacious. At a minimum, one should always want to know *why* a given problem or phenomenon exists, and the "standard" interpretation entirely evades this question by positing ethnic hatred and chauvinism as eternal verities—but not for all humankind, only for Eastern Europe, because in the West we do not need repression to keep our chauvinists in line. So this is a chauvinistic theory about chauvinism.

In this chapter these are the questions in which I am interested: Where and when did the current chauvinisms emerge? Whose interests do they serve? Why do chauvinist parties display a sudden strength? And what is the function of chauvinism in a society? This last question is closely related to the question, who is drawn to chauvinism? Or, more specifically, what is the socioeconomic and psychological profile of the chauvinist?

Before going further, a preliminary and, I think, crucial observation should be made about the nature of chauvinism. Chauvinism and ethnic hatred tend to be diffuse rather than specific in two senses: first, hatred of one ethnic group (for example, Croats) can easily be, and usually is, associated with hatred of other ethnic groups (for example, Bosnian Muslims, Albanians, Hungarians of Vojvodina); and second, ethnic chauvinism per se tends to be associated with chauvinisms of other kinds—above all patriarchal chauvinism (sexism) and religious chauvinism. These points are crucial because they lead us to understand that the "reasons" a chauvinist gives for his hatred of another group are not motivating reasons at all but ex post facto justifications for a chauvinism that is *chosen* for entirely different reasons. Chauvinism, thus, has nothing to do with the rational calculation of wrongs or slights or injuries; on the contrary, it is the wholehearted embrace of the irrational.

So now we may return to our original questions and rephrase them thus: When and why is irrationality chosen? What functions does this form of irrationality perform for the individual and for the collectivity (party, movement, or the whole society)? And whose interests are served by fostering irrational behavior in a society?

Sociologists from Theodor W. Adorno to Rodney Stark who have studied the phenomenon seem to agree on certain functions performed by chauvinism. First, by defining various out-groups, chauvinism also defines an in-group, which thus provides a ready-made basis for interpersonal identification and group solidarity. It follows that people lacking a social framework, especially people whose frames of reference have recently been shattered (for example, by the collapse of the sociopolitical system) may be especially vulnerable to this species of disequilibrium and hence to the chauvinist "remedy" for it. Second, chauvinism is an ego-enhancer. With other groups defined as "inferior," one's own group is ipso facto "superior." From this, it follows that persons with low self-esteem, whether because of low levels of education, low skills, obsolescent skills, loss of job, or loss of some form of stable support system, will be most likely to be attracted to chauvinist movements and chauvinist values.

The data support these propositions. For instance, Adorno and his associates in their monumental study, *The Authoritarian Personality*, found that chauvinistic attitudes reflected low self-esteem, a desire to be subordinated to a powerful authority figure, and a general intolerance of complexity or ambiguity.[1] Stark and William Sims Bainbridge in their pathbreaking study of religious sects and cults found that *sects*, which they define as deviant religious movements emerging from established religious traditions that function at a high level of tension with society,[2] thrive on lower-class recruitment, especially among the powerless and the poor; indeed, one may say that the greater the tension between a sect and the broader society, the greater the sect's appeal to this target audience.[3] In particular, the intolerant belief that only one's own religion is legitimate, an essential element in sect formation, serves "as a compensator for relatively low honor and status in the larger society. As James Coleman has commented, 'Each religious sect is, in a sense, a mutual admiration society.' By defining themselves as especially righteous, members of high tension groups gain a basis for this mutual (and self) admiration."[4] Although they draw a clear distinction between sects and cults, including in patterns of recruitment, Stark and Bainbridge also found parallels in cult compensators. For example, studies of California branches of the Ananda cult found that recruits were overwhelmingly socially withdrawn and socially isolated and discovered in their cult membership a route to social bonding.[5]

Even at a more general level, conditions of privatization plus economic deterioration are already not conducive to socializing people to be oriented to social interests. On the contrary, these are processes conducive to social atomization in which two related processes occur. On the one hand, people are pushed to rely on their own resources and to think in terms of self. The spirit of this process was captured by Max Stirner, a German publicist, in 1845: "Of what concern to me is the common weal? The common weal as such is not *my weal.* . . ."[6] But on the other hand, there is a groping for some *social identity* to help cushion the psychological cascade from the implosion of a system that long provided its subjects with a sense of preordained certainty. Thus, in conditions of social stress, it is not only the "powerless" and the "poor" and those with low self-esteem who gravitate toward the "false consciousness," or "bad faith" (as Sartre called it), of chauvinism; on the contrary, chauvinism offers the otherwise overloaded a release from stress, an escape from the cruel, unrelenting pressure of a world in which economically "rational" processes show no mercy, to a realm of irrational fantasy in which all members of the in-group are decent, hardworking, and deserving, and would flourish, except for the pernicious and unscrupulous activities of certain out-groups. In this way, Jews, Gypsies, women, non-Christians, gays, lesbians, and inevitably, in Eastern Europe today, communists can all be blamed for the troubles of transition.

Under communism, there were two sources for positive social bonding. The first was the village, with its traditions, its religiocentrism, its sense of community; but the village inevitably went into decline as a concomitant of industrialization, and, in some cases (for example, Romanian Transylvania) the communists actually sought for political purposes to accelerate the decline of village life by bulldozing houses, shops, and public places and herding the villagers into high-rise apartments on the edge of megacities. The second source of positive bonding, ironically, was opposition to communism itself; here was an "enemy" that everyone could understand, that certainly affected everyone, and that even claimed responsibility for the basic social processes in society. Now that this "enemy" has been vanquished, the negativity it evoked, which once provided a kind of social glue, has evaporated.

Under communism, there was a third, related process going on, namely

a repression of cultural diversity and choice that habituated people to a
regime of closed borders, secret police surveillance, ideological rituals,
and censored media. As the perspicacious long-time observer of the region Wolf Oschlies has noted, this acculturation did not prepare people
for the frondescence of heterogeneity and choice under pluralism, and,
inevitably, some citizens have wanted to restore the sense of security
and certainty that the old communist order afforded: this psychological frame of mind is simultaneously the source of both antidemocratic
attitudes and tendencies toward radical-right thinking.[7]

Chauvinism feeds on resentments about economic deprivation, economic injustice, alleged advantages enjoyed by "less deserving" groups
(such as ex-communists, Jews, etc.), and self-righteous claims about a
"moral crisis" in the country, as evinced by the widespread corruption
typically associated with processes of rapid social transformation and,
in this particular instance, by the rapid penetration of the area by organized crime, together with the sharp increase of crimes of all kinds. That
crime is a problem in postcommunist Eastern Europe is not disputable.
Whether one talks of organized crime (sharply increasing throughout
much of the region),[8] or of a revival of revenge crimes (in Albania),[9] or
the looting of national treasures from Bulgarian archaeological and art
museums,[10] or the involvement of the state itself in criminal conduct
(in Serbia),[11] or the explosion of drug addiction and drug smuggling in
Macedonia,[12] or the alarming increase in attacks on foreigners—most
dramatically in Germany since 1992—crime rates are up and local authorities are struggling to cope. Various bilateral and multilateral agreements among various East European governments have been made to
coordinate their efforts to combat crime,[13] as have agreements with the
United States to obtain American expertise in crime-fighting. But for the
time being, law authorities are still on the defensive. Typical of the situation is the comment by Gheorghe Ioan Danescu, Romania's minister of
the interior, in an interview with *Romania Libera* in December 1992.
After admitting that the Interior Ministry had to deal with problems of
corruption within its own ranks, the general further conceded that "the
growth of infractions of great social danger—murder, robbery, rape—
is truly alarming," and he cited, as aggravating circumstances, "our in-
adequate equipment and the light sentences stipulated for some penal
infractions" as well as "the pernicious mentality of some people"—the
latter being an issue far from adequately appreciated in the West.[14]

I have dwelled on the problem of increasing crime because the problem is both symptomatic of the weakened enforcement capacity of a
system in transition that creates a vacuum in which extralegal move-

ments can flourish and at the same time partly constitutive of feelings of insecurity, uncertainty, and threat, which can, in turn, contribute to an openness to appeals from the right.

In the rest of this chapter I shall explore the three tentacles of chauvinism: ethnic-national, patriarchal, and religious. I also shall analyze the radical-right opposition that has arisen throughout the region.

Ethnic/National Chauvinism

Ethnic-national chauvinism is increasing across most of Europe, partly because of persistent economic difficulties that afflict the entire continent[15] and partly because of increased numbers of foreigners in many countries, often the combined result of the presence of long-term residents (*Gastarbeiter*) and of the influx of refugees from the collapsed Soviet imperium in the east and from the Yugoslav war.[16] Using a variety of statistical measures of attitudes and behavior, the London-based Institute of Jewish Affairs claimed in a report published in June 1993 that anti-Semitism rose 9 percent across Europe as a whole between 1990 and 1991, with characteristically more frequent efforts to deny that the Holocaust ever took place.[17]

In the past, anti-Semitism has often figured as part of a strategy designed to mobilize group hatred and resentment, to shift attention from economic woes (or shift the blame for such woes from the regime to designated "enemies"), and to create artificial issues that will deflect public attention from whatever *real* issues the elite wants to avoid (in the case of Serbia in the late 1980s, for example, from the issue of genuine democratization). It is thus no accident that both Croatian President Tudjman and Serbian President Milošević have included anti-Semitism in their nationalist ideologies, although in neither case do Jews constitute the principal "enemy." Taking a historical glance back, it should not be forgotten that the Russian tsars deliberately fostered anti-Semitism in Poland as an instrument of control, and that communist authorities throughout Eastern Europe built their systems with the help of sundry anti-Semitic campaigns and purges.

Ethnic-national chauvinism tends to have three stable features: promotion of a myth of *threat to the nation*, perpetuation of notions of a *hostile conspiracy*, and a persistent tendency of *glorification of the national past*, especially of questionable historical episodes. In regard to the third feature, glorifying past literary revivals or achievements in painting is not nearly as useful in mobilizing people to commit mass murder as is the glorification of past episodes of genocide.

The East European elites, perhaps without exception, manipulated ethnic-national chauvinism when it seemed to suit their interests. Hence, the anti-Semitic purges of the 1950s (in Czechoslovakia, Hungary, Romania), the anti-Semitic campaign of 1968 (in Poland), and the campaign to expel the Turks from Bulgaria (in 1984–85). But properly speaking, the first sharp manifestation of right-radicalism in the region came in 1987–89, when the Serbian party (under Milošević) embraced racism as its state ideology. This embrace led directly, as Mirjana Kasapović has noted, to demands for the (re)construction of a Serbian national state and for a "final solution" of the Kosovo question to be achieved by a combination of pressures to drive the indigenous Albanians out of the province and of "colonization" by Serbs from other parts of the country.[18] Central to efforts to mobilize Serbian hatred of non-Serbs (itself a prerequisite for the igniting of interethnic war between Serbs and non-Serbs) was the successful promulgation, among Serbs, of the notion that their nation had been exploited and victimized by sundry peoples of Yugoslavia (and in particular by Slovenes, Croats, and Albanians) and of the conviction that Serbs living in Croatia, Bosnia, and now even Macedonia were threatened by discriminatory, nationalist regimes.[19] This campaign has led directly to Serbian allegations of sundry anti-Serbian conspiracies, whether the Vatican-Comintern-Islamic fundamentalist conspiracy favored by Vladimir Dedijer,[20] or the German-American-Croatian conspiracy, with Kohl's Germany painted as "the Fourth Reich."[21] As for the past, today's Serbian mythologists have chosen two great traumas to serve as the very "soul" of Serbia: the Battle of Kosovo in 1389, in which an Ottoman Turkish army defeated a mixed Serbian-Albanian army, killing Serbian King Lazar and, within a few years, extinguishing the Serbian state; and World War II with its fratricidal bloodshed and the semicollaborationist Chetniks fighting a losing battle against Tito's partisans. But as retold by the new mythologists, the Albanians disappear from the ranks of King Lazar's army and instead of promoting notions of Serbian-Albanian cooperation (the true lesson of the battle), the distorted memory serves essentially to focus Serbian hatred on the Albanians. And in the second instance the Chetniks, who enjoyed cooperative relations with the Nazis and who themselves massacred large numbers of innocent civilians (Croats and Muslims), have come to be seen as great nationalist patriots, their own role in killing innocent people simultaneously being both denied and adulated (in typical nationalist sublation of contradictions), and beginning in 1991, self-styled "Chetniks" have reappeared, singing the old Chetnik songs and recapitulating the atrocities of their forebears.

Similar tactics are being used by other right-oriented politicians. Croatian President Tudjman, for example, dwells at length on the rather
obvious Serbian threat to Croatia, drawing the inevitable conclusion that
all national energies must be harnessed to combat that threat; however,
he adds the questionable corollaries that (a) only one set of policies will
best address this threat, and hence no serious debate is useful (indeed,
it is potentially treasonous), and (b) any efforts to highlight other social
needs, such as legislation to protect gender equality, is covert treason.
Conspiracy theories abound, too, such as Croatian Foreign Minister Zvo-
nimir Separović's belief "that the Serbian-Croatian conflict is largely
due to a 'Jewish-Serbian conspiracy.' "[22] Even the past is exorcised, with
the rehabilitation, as noted, of the Croatian Ustasha. Thus, for example,
Dobroslav Paraga, whose Croatian Defense Force militias wear black
uniforms reminiscent of the Ustasha, says, "The *ustasha* was not a fascist organization. In its fight against the Serbs, it only accepted help
from the only one who provided it. That was Hitler."[23]

But Serbs and Croats are not alone in worrying about conspiracies and
"threats" to the nation. István Csurka, the former vice president of the
Hungarian Democratic Forum, "talks about a vast conspiracy—comprising Washington, Communists, Jerusalem, the World Jewish Congress,
and the Hungarian liberal opposition—that was formed [expressly] to
undermine Hungary's interests."[24] Csurka, in an infamous article published in August 1992, compared the financial elite supported by the
International Monetary Fund (IMF) today with "the communist hench-
men, murderers, and torturers . . . supported by Voroshilov's Allied Control Committee and the occupying Red Army" in the late 1940s.[25] On
other occasions Csurka has expressed contempt for the West and called
for the use of force against "enemies" of the nation. More than thirty
years ago the great political philosopher Hannah Arendt pointed to the
organic, symbiotic relationship between anti-Semitism and totalitarianism.[26] The connection is rather straightforward—it runs through tolerance. For it is tolerance, the very spirit of democracy, that is attacked
and subverted by the anti-Semites and other chauvinists.

It is a direct line from ethnic intolerance, buoyed up by paranoid
visions of threats and conspiracies, to demands for ethnically pure, or, in
the latest language, "ethnically cleansed," states. The oft-repeated Serbian demand, espoused by Milošević himself, that "all Serbs have to
live in one state"[27] is a classic expression of this kind of thinking. But
related phenomena abound all across Eastern Europe, ranging from Slovakia's rush to independence and immediate suppression of Hungarian-
language street signs and obstruction of Hungarian-language higher edu-

cation among its 600,000-strong Hungarian minority,[28] to demands by "Omonia" chairman Theodhori Bezhani that Albanian territories inhabited by the Greek minority be detached from Albania and annexed to Greece and the Greek government's ultimatum to Tirana in July 1993 to extend political autonomy to the local Greek minority or face a prolongation in bilateral tensions,[29] to strangely distorted agonizing in Poland about the fate of ethnic Poles in Lithuania,[30] to persistent Turkophobia in Bulgaria,[31] to complaints by Hungarians in Romania of continued persecution, discrimination, humiliation, and even destruction of important cultural monuments.[32] In what is probably the most bizarre instance of ethnic chauvinism—and in this instance even legitimized and supported by the European Community—Greece succeeded in blocking European recognition of Macedonia for some two years on the argument that the name "Macedonia" did not adhere to any particular area; the name, the Greek government claimed, was the property of the Greek people—even though the region that makes up the Republic of Macedonia has borne that name for more than 3,500 years; Greece went even further in objecting to the Macedonian state coat of arms.[33]

This climate has given rise, on one side, to a series of defensive actions and, on the other, to a swelter of radical-right organizations existing mostly on the fringes of politics. On the defensive side, European Gypsies established a Roma Parliament in Budapest in August 1992, with twenty-two Gypsy organizations from ten European countries participating in the founding meeting. At another level, appealing to the legacy of American black leader Martin Luther King, Jr., Gypsies in northern Bohemia formed a "Black Panther" organization and in January 1993 "declared war" on all racists, fascists, and chauvinists.[34] In a related and interesting move the office of the Jewish Religious Communities Central Union in Bratislava issued a statement in late December 1992 that it "expect[ed] that government structures of the independent Slovak Republic will resolutely dissociate themselves from the practices which might remind [Jews] of the Slovak state of 1939–45."[35]

The Radical Right

By far the most disquieting by-product of Eastern Europe's transition from communism to pluralism is the frondescence of organizations subscribing to radical-right ideologies, advocating violence against foreigners, and, almost without exception, looking back with nostalgia to the Nazi Third Reich. For years, radical-right ideologies appealed essentially to unrehabilitated Nazis and fascists from the World War II era, that is, to an increasingly older generation. Although some young converts to Naziism appeared, they were too few in number and, especially in the East, largely unable to propagate their message. But, to the surprise of politicians, since the late 1980s (beginning even before the collapse of communism in the area) right-radicalism has rapidly gained adherents among young people. And with the reemergence of the radical right has come an explosion of violence against those branded as "foreigners."

In the following pages I shall briefly examine the radical-right scene in the Czech and Slovak republics, Hungary, Slovenia, Poland, and Romania; I have examined the radical-right scene in Germany elsewhere.[36]

The Radical Right in Eastern Europe. In the Czech and Slovak republics skinheads and other right-radicals have formed a number of organizations. The two best-known neofascist groups in the Czech Republic are "New Czech Unity," cofounded in April 1990 by Vladimir Franz and Daniel Landa (Landa being leader of the rock group Orlik), and "National Fascist Society," a Prague-based group. In addition, some other explicitly open Nazis have come forward.[37] Miroslav Sladek's Republican Party, which claims to have some 50,000 members, is the Czech Republic's most successful radical-right organization. Sladek's party drew 7 percent of the vote in 1993, obtaining fourteen deputies in the Czech parliament.[38] Czech skinheads differ from skinheads elsewhere in Europe in being distinctly less concerned with Jews. Their chosen enemies are Gypsies, Vietnamese, and "other colored peoples," and bloody riots have occurred between Czech skinheads and local Vietnamese students. Czech Gypsies have been mugged by skinheads.

Inevitably, skinheads talk about "White Power" and look to the American Ku Klux Klan, as well as Hitler's Nazis, with admiration. Some Prague skinheads have been seen greeting each other with the Nazi salute and shouting "Sieg Heil!"[39] Although there are different strains of skinheads in these republics—above all, nationalists, racists, neo-Nazis, and punks, with the punks being concentrated in Slovakia—they share common emphases on patriotism, comradeship, good physical conditioning, struggle against drugs, a "solution" of the "*Gastarbeiter* question," and the expulsion of Gypsies from the region.[40] As of late 1991 there were said to be about 350 skinheads in Prague.

In nearby Hungary, skinhead anger has become wedded to a misplaced nostalgia for the Lands of the Crown of Saint Stephen, as pre-1920 Hungary was sometimes called (at a time when its territory was three times greater than in the mid-1990s). Hungary's skinheads—who number about four thousand according to a June 1993 estimate[41]—have returned to the traditional Nazi rhetoric. "We must shed as much blood as necessary for the homeland," said István Szoke, a leading figure among Hungarian skinheads. Szoke loudly complains that political power remains in the hands of a "Jewish elite."[42] For many skinheads, the rehabilitation of fascist symbols, such as the turul (a mythological eaglelike bird) is a gripping concern.[43] Leaflets reportedly have been circulated with the imprint of the Arrow Cross movement (the principal Hungarian fascist movement before 1945).[44] The town of Eger, in particular, has become a center of Hungarian neo-Nazi activity.[45] Hungarian authorities have responded to the growing threat by arresting István Gyorkos, leader of the neo-Nazis in Hungary, and by introducing a ban in November 1992 on the display of "Nazi symbols, communist symbols, and other emblems and regalia recalling autocratic systems of government."[46]

In Slovenia, small right-radical paramilitary formations have appeared since the country's first postcommunist elections in 1990; they advocate hostility toward non-Slovenes (basically Bosnian refugees and a handful of Serbs and Albanians), and they speak of the "natural inferiority" of women to men. The Slovenian far right has its own newspaper (*Rudi*) and organization, the National Front of Slovenia (established in April 1990). The Slovenian radical-right groupings have developed international contacts with similar organizations in Austria (especially Graz and Klagenfurt) as well as in Germany and Italy.[47] Like their comrades in Germany, Slovakia, and the Czech Republic, Slovenian skinheads are fascinated by the Third Reich and openly display nostalgic feelings for it. The Slovenian skinhead/right-radical scene is distinctively small and without immediate prospects.

In Poland, perhaps 2,000–3,000 adherents of right-radical organizations are active, according to Jerzy Bogucki, a Polish film director who has made two films about the Polish right-radical scene.[48] Of all the East European right-radicals, those in Poland display the most intensely negative feelings about Jews, although, as of 1993, probably no more than three thousand elderly Jews remained in Poland. The darling of the Polish right is Bolesław Tejkowski (age sixty in 1994), founder of the Polish National Community, who went into hiding in 1992 after being ordered to report for confinement in a mental institution.[49] Tejkowski's party polled 0.5 percent of the vote in 1991. Meanwhile, in Tejkowski's absence, his deputy, Janusz Bober, presides over a party that debunks the standard histories of World War II and claims that 3.5 million Jews still live in Poland. Bober and his coterie enthusiastically supported the legal restriction of abortion in Poland in early 1993, having always construed liberal abortion as "a Jewish scheme to kill millions of Poles."[50] Given its small numbers, Tejkowski's organization has formidable resources, with some of the conservative parties have created subsidiary women's organizations to serve as arms of the parties. These organizations typically focus on propaganda work among women, stressing traditional themes. An example is the Democratic League of Albanian Women, founded in Tirana in July 1991 as a subsidiary of Sali Berisha's Democratic Party.

2. Prohibition of Abortion. The assault on abortion has been one of the most controversial issues in postcommunist eastern Germany, Poland, Hungary, Slovakia, Slovenia, and Croatia, as women have struggled, usually in vain, to hold onto options that they had come to take for granted under communism. Given the complexity of the challenges of political and economic transformation, it is perverse that governments spend such a large amount of time seriously entertaining, and in some cases accepting, the principle that the moral values of a minority might be legally enforced against a society's majority. In Poland, for example, where the debate over abortion rights has been particularly heated, 59 percent of Poles (in a 1988 survey) said that abortion should be an option in cases of poverty, threats to the mother's health, mental illness, an already large number of living children to raise, or AIDS. Some 37 percent of women in the sample said they would choose abortion rather than bear an unwanted child. A subsequent survey (in October 1990) found that 51 percent of Poles were opposed to the restrictive abortion law being considered by the Polish parliament.[86] But for all their opposition, the parliament, under the church's unrelenting pressure, pressed ahead with legislation to ban abortion. A Warsaw Committee for an Abortion Referendum, organized by the long-time Solidarity activist and current MP Zbigniew Bujak, called for televised public discussion of the law and for a referendum on the issue. The committee quickly gathered more than 300,000 signatures in favor of a referendum.[87] But the Catholic church mobilized its strength to block the proposed popular vote. And eventually, in January 1993, the church obtained its abortion law. *Rzeczpospolita*, the Warsaw daily, sounded an early warning:

> We are not prepared for the numerous consequences of this law. There will certainly be "backstreet abortions," with all their consequences. The law will have demographic, economic, and medical consequences. Attention has already been drawn to the medical consequences—an increase in the number of pregnancy complications and of infant mortality. The health service, already on its last legs, will have to cope with all this.[88]

And there will be other, more subtle consequences, including the attenuation of the boundary between church and state (and the consequent encouragement to the church to seek to realize other institutional aims through legislation), and a reinforcement of a cultural milieu in which women are taught to view themselves, *in the first place*, as wives and mothers—or, if single, as potential wives and mothers.

Parallel processes unfolded in eastern Germany where, despite objections by women's organizations, Germany's highest court struck down a compromise law on abortion and asserted in a May 1993 decision that "the right to life begins at conception."[89]

Only in Romania has decommunization actually resulted in the liberalization of abortion legislation. Under Romanian President Nicolae Ceauşescu, a 1966 law stipulated that to be eligible for an abortion, a woman had to have given birth to at least four children and to have them, at the time, under her care. This meant that adopted children or children acquired through second marriages did not count toward an exemption.[90] Moreover, beginning in 1986, women from sixteen to forty-five were placed under close medical surveillance, and some women who were known to have had illegal abortions were confined to a hospital (imprisoned, in effect) to prevent any recurrence.[91] One of the *first* acts of the Iliescu government, announced the day after the execution of the Ceauşescus, was the legalization of abortion once again. Romanian women, both urban and rural, have thus in the most direct sense viewed the fall of the Ceauşescus as liberating.

3. Curtailment of Social Services. Across Eastern and Central Europe the infrastructure of social services that made it possible for women to work is being dismantled, usually on the basis of economic arguments. As Yudit Kiss notes, this has involved "[the] shutting down of the 'economically unprofitable' crèches, day schools, play centers, the cutback of subsidies on restaurants, ready-made food, children's clothes, laundries, cultural services, etc."[92] In reunified Germany the GDR's polyclinic system that combined preventive and care/cure services was scrapped without the matter being given a second thought, while the parliament has moved slowly in taking action to expand the system of refuge centers for abused and battered women (as the incidence of such crimes rises).[93]

The declining employment of women both reflects and reinforces deteriorating trends in social services. "Women are being removed from the labor market in great numbers. With the restriction of employment opportunities also comes the restriction of their educational opportunities."[94]

4. The Active Promotion of Traditional Values. The communist Old Guard and contemporary feminists agreed on at least one thing—that pornography was degrading to women and inappropriate in civilized society. One of the first repercussions in the region of the collapse of communism, of the "new freedom," was the immediate deluge of pornography, which brought a steady growth of sex shops, sex cruises, brothels, topless bars, and other manifestations of the reification of the female body. The growth of the "sex industry" has been accompanied by a rapid increase in crimes of violence against women, especially in the home[95]—a correlation to which American feminists have long pointed. In Serbia, feminist activist Sonja Licht pressed a Belgrade legislator to take up legislation to curb the physical abuse of wives by their husbands. "Don't speak to me about a law against violence in the family," the legislator replied. "It would destroy the essence of the Serbian family."[96]

Insidiously, quietly, without any conscious decision being taken, capitalist societies manipulate and subvert images of love for their own purposes. The resulting dehumanization largely injures women.[97] Yudit Kiss writes:

> There is a hidden sensual dimension beneath every social formation, which is extremely revealing about the inner nature of the system. The way they treat love and sex gives a telling insight about them. . . . Love does not accept social boundaries—Shakespeare's Romeo and Juliet the same way as Orwell's Winston and Julia, break through, almost unconsciously, unacceptable, mutilating social restrictions. That is why repressive systems fear love. They try to oppress it or try to convert it into something more manageable, channel it into religion, sell it in Hollywood, degrade it in sex shops, pervert it into warfare, which is a peculiar expression of impotence: an inability to make contact.[98]

The mainstream media also reflect this tendency. *Playboy* is now appearing in Czech, Hungarian, and Polish editions.[99] Meanwhile, magazines for women, such as the Czech publication, *Betty*, devote their pages to such matters as hair-styling, skin care, and fashions. The upshot is that to men, the revolutions of 1989 appear to have led to "sexual liberation," while to women, they have led to a revival of sexual discrimination and sexual exploitation. Needless to say, lesbians have been stigmatized, if anything, more than they were under communism.

The conservative guardians of the new social order propound values as distant from feminism as they are from socialism. Albanian President Berisha, for example, spoke to a congress of the Democratic League of Albanian Women, about the "sacred" vocation of motherhood.[100] Polish President Lęch Wałesa offered the advice, "I have eight children and I wish the same to everybody."[101]

The linkage between the promotion of women's traditional role, the illegalization of abortion, and the promotion of "births for the nation" is clear enough. An example from Croatia illustrates the connection all too well. Addressing a Croatian audience, Ante Baković, president of the Croatian Population Movement (an agency promoting this triad of values), told a *Vjesnik* interviewer in June 1993:

> CPM is a movement to save the Croatian nation from extinction. . . . Today's average Croatian family operates on a two-child system, with two or with only one child. That practice must come to an end, and it is the fundamental goal of the CPM to create a pro-life disposition among the Croatian population, who will decide on a third child in the city, and on a fourth child in the village.[102]

Once the notion of a threat of national extinction is accepted as an official "truth," then failure to "do one's part" to "save" the nation is automatically defined minimally as moral decrepitude, if not as treason. Baković says as much: "Poverty does not explain why some people have no children. The real reason is an anti-life mentality. By that, I mean moral collapse and decadence. . . . Our Croatian mother is afraid to have children and it is necessary to destroy that fear."[103] It is telling that Baković sees women as *mothers* even *before* they have children. In this context it is apparent that the systematic rape of more than 20,000 Bosnian Muslim women and girls by Serbian forces between 1992 and 1993[104] is only the most savage manifestation of a region-wide problem.

5. Demonization of Feminists and Feminism. There has been a pronounced tendency throughout the region to treat issues of female equality as "details" that can, and should, be postponed until some supposedly more convenient date.[105] Feminists, as the advocates of these "details," must be trivialized in the interests of the agenda of the current elites. But in actual practice the media have done much more than merely "trivialize"—they have *demonized* feminists, painting them as traitors, as extremists, or, as in the Croatian weekly *Globus,* as *witches!*[106] In Hungary, for example, no feminist organizations and no feminist dialogue existed until 1990, but immediately traditionalists lashed out. Judit Sas, a Hungarian defender of patriarchal authority, called feminism "blind" and accused feminists of "not tak[ing] men's problems into consideration at all."[107] And throughout the postcommunist Hungarian media, feminism has been portrayed "as something unnatural and very selfish, certainly not something to which Hungarian women would wish to relate."[108] Symptomatic of women's status in Hungarian society is the formula used in assigning personal identification numbers to citizens, marked on their identity cards. By government decision, every male's identity number begins with the digit "1"; every female's identity number begins with the digit "2."[109] As a result of this media onslaught, the very word "feminism" has indeed become tainted, whether one speaks of Hungary, or Poland, or Croatia, or Serbia, or the Czech and Slovak Republics. In this way, by stigmatizing the very struggle for dignity and equality, patriarchal forces place women under pressure—sometimes intense pressure—to accept their "fate" and accept their politically decreed "inferiority." Two German writers highlighted this problem in 1990: "The most terrible legacy of patriarchy," they write, "is that its structures are present within us, within women. So women are also partly responsible [for the perpetuation of such structures]."[110]

Are feminists trapped in a blind alley? No more than the democratic opposition in Poland was at the height of martial law. And the very same strategy developed by Solidarity, of building alternative structures rather than merely doing battle within existing ones, may well hold the promise of eventual feminist success. At least this is the thinking of some prominent feminists in Germany today. Ina Merkel talks of women creating "their own" publications, newspapers, radio and television stations, cultural centers, even institutes devoted to researching women's history and women's interests.[111] Even more explicitly, Eva Schäfer has called for the organization of women's groups that would operate in great measure autonomously of the patriarchal system and would foster and sustain an alternative culture that would be nonhierarchical and nonconfrontational in content. For this purpose, even such mundane institutions as women's cafés and sisterhood bookstores, not to mention archives and newspapers, all have a part to play.[112] Where will all of this lead? Kate Soper's answer is direct—to "a cultural revolution which delivers us from the very modes of conceptualization within which we have hitherto constructed gender identities."[113]

Religious Chauvinism

From the outset it has been clear that the three strands of this triple chauvinism are symbiotically intertwined, so that it is impossible to speak of one strand without anticipating aspects of the other strands in our discussion. Chauvinism thrives on absolutes, abjures compromise, relativity, or the allowance that different people might have different perspectives. Nothing can give chauvinist absolutism as firm an anchor as can religion. For this reason, religious chauvinism is often the most tenacious and embittered of the three.

In Eastern Europe today, religious chauvinism manifests itself in many ways. Churches in almost all East European countries are again talking about the nation. In Poland, Slovakia, Hungary, and Slovenia, Catholic appeals to the interests of the nation serve as a veil for efforts to ban abortion (as noted). In Serbia and Bulgaria, Orthodox appeals to the interests of the nation serve the purpose of stoking violence against specific out-groups (Catholic Croats and Bosnian Muslims for the Serbian Orthodox church, Muslim Turks for the Bulgarian Orthodox church). In fact, the Serbian Orthodox church as a whole, and especially its news organ *Pravoslavlje*, enthusiastically fanned the flames of Serbia's war against Croatia, singing rhapsodies about the "Orthodox" heritage of overwhelmingly Croatian towns such as Osijek and Dubrovnik, until the spring of 1992 when the Serbian leadership launched a military assault on Bosnia too. At that point a rift within the church came to the surface, as the patriarch and some of his closest aides took a strong antiwar stance, while a number of prominent bishops outside Belgrade, along with the bulk of Serbian lower clergy, continued to endorse the war against Catholics and Muslims alike as a "holy war."[114]

In neighboring Bulgaria, Orthodox believers formed an Orthodox Christian Union under the leadership of Father Stanimir Todorov in the summer of 1990 "to combat false prophecy and its bearers," including Muhammad.[115] Religious chauvinism has also been manifested in more purely religious contexts, as in the success of the Catholic church in Poland and Croatia and its so-far stunted endeavor in Slovenia to place *Catholic* religious instruction on the basic required curriculum for all students enrolled in state schools. In Croatia the introduction in the schools of Catholic religious instruction got off to a rocky start during the 1991–92 academic year because of Croatia's war with Serbia, and many schools were lucky to be functioning at all, without their worrying about religious instruction. But by the autumn of 1992 school curricula were more regularized, and Catholic religious instruction had by then become standard throughout Croatia's public system.[116] In Poland, after a constitutional tribunal struck down a challenge brought by the government-appointed ombudsman, Catholic religious instruction, already introduced in the 1992–93 academic year, was confirmed.[117] And although parents are technically allowed to withdraw their children from the Catholic classes, the children run the risk of harsh ostracism and ridicule by their classmates if they are withdrawn. Inevitably, in both countries this situation has brought complaints from Protestant, Muslim, Old Catholic, atheist, agnostic, and other non-Catholic parents. Already in 1985, Stanisław Dąbrowski, president of the Seventh-Day Adventist church in Poland, expressed deep concern about the behavior of Catholic prelates. "Many instances demonstrate," he said at the time, "that the Roman Catholic Church has not rid itself of its hegemonist tendencies and practices vis-à-vis adherents of other faiths."[118] Viewed in retrospect, the statement sounds rather like a warning, and in any case all too prophetic.

In Germany, Poland, Slovakia, and Slovenia, churches have pressed to remove sex education from school curricula (in Germany in the eastern part). In Poland, Croatia, and Slovenia, the Catholic church endorsed specific candidates and parties during recent multiparty elections and used its weight to assure the victory in Poland and Croatia of proclerical candidates.[119] The church's heightened political presence since the collapse of communism has not always met with broad approval; indeed, it appears ironic that the church has more influence with the *legislatures* of Poland and Croatia than with the respective *peoples* of these countries. In Croatia, at least, some 44 percent of people surveyed in 1992 thought the Catholic church had too much political influence in the country; a somewhat smaller number—38 percent—disagreed.[120]

Christian churches, like the Islamic sects, are founded on the claim to possessing some exclusive and transcendent Truth, a Truth against which no other truth can make any counterclaim. It is this ideological arrogance that underlies the sundry efforts to impose Catholic religious instruction on non-Catholic children, to prevent non-Catholic and nonbeliever parents from having access to abortions, and in the Polish case to require Catholic prayers at the start and finish of *every* class, not just religion class.

Whether one approves or not, it should be clear that this attitude has nothing in common with the principle of toleration, or with the liberal tradition at all (i.e., with the presuppositions of democracy). John Stuart Mill gave articulate expression to the liberal view in his tract, *On Liberty:* "If all mankind minus one were of one opinion, and only one person were of the contrary opinion, mankind would be no more justified in silencing that one person, than he, if he had the power, would be justified in silencing [the rest of] mankind. . . . We can never be sure that the opinion we are endeavouring to stifle is a false opinion; and if we were sure, stifling it would be evil still."[121] Yet clearly when pro-prayer and antiabortion activists demand that the children of nonbelievers pray Christian prayers and that nonbeliever parents not have access to abortion, they are declaring their own opinions about morality to be universally binding, while denying that the moral opinions of those who differ have any force whatsoever, much less an equivalent claim.

Maurice Merleau-Ponty voiced a useful caution in remarking that "true morality is not concerned with what we think or what we want."[122] That is to say, it cannot be about decreeing viewpoints. What, then, can be the guide for behavior, if not "what we think"? Immanuel Kant's answer, some two hundred years ago, that one should always try to act toward others in such a way that if everyone acted according to the same principle, the world would be the better for it,[123] seems like a useful guide today as well. And this, in fact, is not so different from what Helmut Kohl in Germany has recently been telling his countrymen.[124]

Conclusion

I have described the three dimensions of chauvinism in this chapter, and I have suggested that chauvinism—intolerance, to use another word— is incompatible with democracy and that the East Europen societies in transition will find their efforts at shaping and stabilizing democratic institutions challenged, strained, and perhaps even subverted and rail- roaded—as in the cases of Serbia and Croatia—by this three-headed hydra. So what is wrong with intolerance in a democracy, anyway?

In the opening chapter I argued that democracy requires an honoring of the principle of respect for personal autonomy and that this principle in turn entails toleration. It follows further, as Hannah Arendt noted, that doctrines claiming to possess exclusive and transcendent Truth (such as Catholicism and Bolshevism) are intrinsically in tension with demo- cratic culture, just as they are injurious to the principle of pluralism and to the maintenance of a heterogeneity of opinions.[125]

This helps us to understand why an intolerant society is more threat- ening to the preservation of personal autonomy than an intolerant state. For in the intolerant state the individual is unfree in the political sphere, but autonomous, perhaps even in some sense "free," in the social sphere. In an intolerant society, however, probably regardless of the specific in- stitutional forms of government, the individual is unfree in society itself, and without freedom in society no constitutional provisions for the political sphere can make much difference. These considerations point to the most serious challenge confronting the East European political systems in the wake of communism's collapse.

19. Propositions About the Future

This book has been focused, to a considerable extent, on the triad of discontent explained in chapter 3: dissatisfaction, disaffection, and dissent. In that chapter I argued that dissatisfaction is normal (universal, in fact) and without systemic consequences, and that disaffection, rather than dissent, was the prime mover in social change. This is why the endless debate between those who thought that studying dissent in communist systems was important and consequential and those who did not[1] was so frustrating: it missed the main point. Dissent, as potent as it is, becomes consequential for the future of the given system *only* when it can tap into people's dissatisfaction and help to transform it into disaffection.

Authoritarian systems, it is now better understood, are vulnerable systems, more vulnerable than Samuel Huntington realized at the time he was writing *Political Order*. And they are vulnerable insofar as they are unable to solve the central problem of legitimation. Democracies, by contrast, as Anders Åslund has noted, are better equipped in this regard.[2] However, one should add that, contrary to common misperception, democracies are not born fully legitimated; rather, they are born with certain advantages and with the capacity to build legitimation. As they do so, there is a period of transition in which consensus on values, and even on procedures, is not yet deeply rooted (if it is there at all). Hence, the task of a new democracy must also be defensive, to fend off challenges from chauvinistic nationalism, religious bigotry, neofascism, anti-Semitism, and other forms of false consciousness, and to cope with the costs and effects of chaos, corruption, and increases in crime and social violence. With the collapse of the communist systems around them, the societies of Eastern Europe have set out, as Daniel Nelson so aptly phrased it, "on a perilous but utterly unavoidable transit across potentially disastrous waters."[3]

Not all of these societies will stay on a democratic course. Serbia, for one, has veered from the relatively liberal communist system of the mid-1980s to a closed totalitarian system built on chauvinism and militarism; and Croatia, no doubt under the influence of the exigencies of war, had evolved, by mid-1992, into a de facto one-party state with a controlled media. As for the other states in the region, all of them except the Czech Republic and perhaps Hungary and Slovenia could, under appropriate conditions, prove vulnerable to authoritarian appeals. As Moss has noted, five typical justifications can be made for introducing authoritarian rule:

1. The need for "temporary" dictatorship. . . .
2. The appeal to a charismatic leader . . . to "clean up the mess."
3. The appeal to traditional institutions "transcending" democracy. . . .
4. The appeal to an alternative model of "authentic" democracy. For example, the corporationist claims of the Salazarist regime in Portugal (1927–73), the Vargas dictatorship in Brazil (1937–45), or the Perón dictatorship in Argentina (1946–55).
5. The need for a "government of experts. . . ."[4]

It will be a few years before we can have a good sense of what the long-term prospects of the new "postcommunist" systems in Eastern Europe will be.[5] In the meantime, I offer the following propositions as a preliminary guide to assessing the present and future course.

1. Democracy does not come with any built-in legitimation, as people in the United States and Great Britain are often inclined to think. In societies in which democracy is largely untested, it will be judged—by social collectivities—by the criterion as to whether it satisfies certain priority demands (however these may be derived) and protects certain priority values. Therefore, the new systems of Eastern Europe may have to make certain compromises with the democratic model in the interests of stability; failure to do so could jeopardize the experiment in pluralism.

2. In the short run, the greatest threat to the political consensus comes from the right. This is true for Germany, Poland, Slovakia, Hungary, and probably Romania (although in Romania in a rather different way). In Croatia and Serbia the right is already in power, and the center and left are stripped of their support (outside the capital cities) and demoralized.

3. Given the long-term commitment on the part of Britain and France

to value their own comfort over stability and self-determination on the continent (as per their policies during the Spanish Civil War, the Munich crisis of 1938, and the war of Serbian aggression from 1991 to 1994), the West (the EC and CSCE) is effectively blocked from taking any effective measures to control or curb regional violence. The carte blanche enjoyed by the Serbian and Bosnian-Serb forces to take as much land as they can conquer will give a clear signal to other right-wing forces in the region. The West's failure to respond in Bosnia thus increases the risks of destabilization or even war in Kosovo and Macedonia and the escalation of fighting in the Dniester region of Moldova. It also sends a signal to both Bratislava and Budapest that in the event of a Slovak-Hungarian conflict, the West would do nothing except "fret."

4. The demand for social justice, long championed by the communists, has been temporarily eclipsed. But as privatization and recession combine to increase the numbers of poor, and as many of the originally hopeful find that not everyone gets rich under capitalism, discontent will grow. The discontent can be harnessed only by the right in the short term, but in the long term by *either* the left or the right.

5. The religious revival in Eastern Europe is not about a return to the traditional (precommunist) religious order. It is about a shift in religious values, as various religious organizations—some of them brand-new to the region—compete for believers. The religious right (the fundamentalists such as the Assembly of God and the Foursquare Gospel Church, some of them well-funded from American sources) has already won converts in Hungary, Bulgaria, and elsewhere, and it may grow in significance. The emerging religious landscape will result in a redefinition of some of the predominant social values being articulated in these societies. This, in turn, has the potential to fuel new controversies that have not yet reached full bloom (e.g., controversies over the place of women in society, over abortion, over the desirability or undesirability of religious instruction in the schools, over the place of religion itself in society). The religious revival is apt to intensify, rather than to calm, social tensions.

6. The ethnic war in Yugoslavia will have long-term negative effects, both in the Balkans specifically and in Europe as a whole. It has already gutted the industrial sector in both Serbia and Croatia, and it has had a severe effect, albeit indirectly, on the Macedonian economy. The Bosnian economy is utterly destroyed. Bulgaria and Albania have also suffered as a result of the UN sanctions against Serbia. Beyond these, the huge number of refugees—at least 3 million as of October 1993—has had a serious economic impact on Germany, Austria, Slovenia, and Hungary, and a lesser impact on several other societies. In addition, the influx of

refugees—in economic terms, the "worst" kind of immigrant—sharply encourages tendencies to chauvinism and racist violence.

7. Privatization, to the extent that it is carried out, will result in a long-term shift in economic priorities, production strategies, and markets. These shifts will produce ripples of destabilization, as the departure of former customers leaves former sellers looking for new buyers.

8. Democracy's best chances are in the Czech Republic, Poland, Hungary, and Slovenia; each of these societies has certain advantages. Serbia, currently under the region's only remaining totalitarian system, has the region's *worst* prospects for democratization, followed by Slovakia, Romania, and Croatia, probably in that order. Albania falls roughly in the middle, although a Serbian decision to drive the Albanians out of Kosovo would produce highly destabilizing repercussions.

9. The eventual failure of democracy in Russia—which I consider a virtual certainty[6]—will be accompanied by massive unrest, destabilization, and civil strife on a level comparable with the civil war of 1918–21. These developments will have immediate and long-lasting consequences for Poland, and perhaps for other states in the region. Among these impacts, the eventual flood of refugees may well exceed anything seen to date, increasing the proportion of minorities in these states.

10. Culture, presently dormant, will experience a dramatic and inspired revival as things get worse again. Literature, the theater, even rock music will rebound and once more reclaim their mantles as the political prophets of society.

11. The two countries with the best long-term prospects of stability would seem to be the Czech Republic and Slovenia, even taking into account Slovenia's persisting difficulties with war refugees. Both republics have good political management, generally moderate policies, a largely homogeneous population, a work ethic that would put Americans to shame, and long-established economic prowess in both light industry and agriculture. Barring a Serbian attack on Slovenia or ripple effects on the Czech Republic from right-wing extremism in Germany, these two republics have the best prospects in Eastern Europe for developing stable democracy. Hungary's political system is not as solid as it seemed at first, and its economic recovery is still heavily centered in Budapest. Poland, as of mid-1994, had still not solved some essential questions.

I would like, in closing, to make a few further remarks. Social systems reflect and presume specific modal behavior systems, but collective behavior systems themselves reflect and presume consensual clusters of social values, expectations, and assumptions. These values, expectations, and assumptions extend over a wide array of areas, but they are interrelated all the same. As values and assumptions change, behavior changes, and over time changes in behavior produce changes in social systems—whether evolutionary or revolutionary. The creation of Solidarity culminated several years of change in expectations and assumptions and modifications in values, and it proved to be arguably the single most important engine for political change in Eastern Europe. On another level, rock 'n' roll, which began in the 1950s and early 1960s with a focus on sexual liberation, expanded (arguably beginning with *Sgt. Pepper's Lonely Hearts Club Band* in the later 1960s) into a force for broadly conceived personal liberation and projected notions of liberation through music, dance, lyrics, and even dress. Again, feminism ought not to be narrowly conceived; both as a force for independent political thought and action, and more substantively as a force for human equality, feminism is a "modernizing" phenomenon.

At any given point in history, various countervailing social forces support directly opposed value systems. One need only think of the East European religious scene—the conservative Christian neo-Protestants, the liberal Lutheran establishment, "restorationist" Catholicism, male chauvinist cults like the Hare Krishnas, spiritualism, satanism—to appreciate the point. As a result, cultural shifts in society are necessarily mixed (as in the differences between the city and the countryside) and incomplete.

The repluralization of Eastern Europe did not occur merely because the populations of that region became fed up with communism, or even merely because institutional weapons such as Solidarity became available to them. The precondition for this political repluralization was the *broadly conceived repluralization of culture* and with it the creation of stable poles of culture, spiritual, social, and political activity, and value formation. The process of repluralization had multifaceted sources—including economics, high politics, trade unionism, intellectual dissent, human rights issues, youth culture, feminism, and rock counterculture—and will have multifaceted consequences affecting these and other spheres.

Appendixes: Public Opinion Polls

The direction of popular pressure for change can often be gauged from public opinion polls. Such polls have been taken for years in Hungary, Poland, and Yugoslavia, and they have been reported since late 1989 in the other countries in the region. Some results from recent polls are presented in the following appendixes. All results of polling answers, unless otherwise noted, are given in percentages.

Appendix 1. Albania

February 1993
Is the country moving in the right direction?
  Yes   77
  Other answers   23
Do you have confidence in the market economy being introduced in Albania?
  Yes   72
  Other answers   28
Do you think the economic situation will improve in the course of the 12 months ahead?
  Yes   71
  Other answers   29

Source: Gallup poll, carried out among Albanian citizens, as cited in *New York Times*, 3 Aug. 1993, A3.

Appendix 2. Bulgaria

November 1989
Do you approve of the latest National Assembly session?
   Yes   60
   Other responses   40
Do you approve of the election of Petar Mladenov as president of the State Council?
   Yes   48.5
   Other responses   51.5
Do you approve of the merging of three central committee departments into a single ideological department?
   Yes   47.7
   Other responses   52.3

Sources: First two responses reported in *Rabotnichesko delo,* 23 Nov. 1989, summarized in BTA (Sofia), 23 Nov. 1989, in FBIS, *Daily Report* (Eastern Europe), 1 Dec. 1989, 18; third response based on a survey of 405 persons and reported in *Rabotnichesko delo,* 30 Nov. 1989, 3, summarized in FBIS, *Daily Report* (Eastern Europe), 12 Dec. 1989, 18.

15 December 1989
Do you approve of the following political organizations?

	Yes	No
Bulgarian Communist Party	49	31
Bulgarian Agrarian National Union	36	32
Dimitrov Komsomol	30	50
Fatherland Front	27	48
Bulgarian trade unions	26	48

Do you approve of the following independent associations?

	Yes	No
Club for Glasnost and Democracy	55	12
Podkrepa Labor Federation	47	15
Independent Association for the Defense of Human Rights	57	13
Eco-Glasnost	77	6
Progress Committee	24	12
Independent Student Association	52	14
Social Democratic Party	24	19
Nikola Petkov Bulgarian Agrarian National Union	28	20
Union of Democratic Forces	46	16

Source: Survey conducted among 1,512 people (ages 15–60) on 15 Dec. 1989, reported in *Narodna Mladezh*, 20 Dec. 1989, 2, summarized in FBIS, *Daily Report* (Eastern Europe), 18 Jan. 1990, 16.

January 1990
Do you approve of the decision to restore rights to the Muslim and Turkish-speaking population in Bulgaria?
    Yes 89
    No   11

Source: Survey conducted among 182 residents of Sofia, reported in BTA (Sofia), 11 Jan. 1990, in FBIS, *Daily Report* (Eastern Europe), 16 Jan. 1990, 28.

August 1992
What are you most worried about?
    The possibility of losing one's job   57
    Not being able to earn enough to feed one's family   29
    Other answers   14
Will things improve in Bulgaria in the coming years?
    Yes, they will get better soon   35
    No, they will stay about the same   20
    No, they will get worse   32
    Other answers   13
Is the judiciary independent?
    Yes   24
    No   43
    Don't know   33
Are people likely to be arrested on political grounds at present?
    No   34
    Yes   38
    Don't know   28

Source: Survey conducted in August by the National Public Opinion Center and reported by BTA (Sofia), 8 Sept. 1992, in FBIS, *Daily Report* (Eastern Europe), 10 Sept. 1992, 9.

August 1993
How do you feel about the future, in economic terms?
    Pessimistic   49.4
    Desperate   19
    "Prepared to do anything, even crime," to survive   7.5

Is your own personal financial situation better or worse today than in 1989?

Worse   72

Better   5.3

Can you afford to make a major purchase (e.g., apartment, holiday house, car, or furniture)?

Yes   8

No   92

How would you characterize the state of your own personal finances?

Catastrophic   "almost 50"

Very good   3.5

Excellent   1.3

Source: Poll conducted March–May 1993 by the Institute of Sociology in Sofia, reported in *Süddeutsche Zeitung*, 10 Aug. 1993, 6.

Appendix 3. Czechoslovakia

November 1989

Do you consider the people leading the restructuring process (communists) a guarantee of success?

No   58

Other responses   42

Should the restructuring process be continued?

Yes   85

Other responses   15

Which information media do you most trust?

Czechoslovak   25

Western   23

Neither   52

Source: Opinion poll conducted by the Institute for Public Opinion Research, 23–24 Nov. 1989, among 450 people from the whole of Czechoslovakia, and 260 from Prague, reported in CTK (Prague), 25 Nov. 1989, in FBIS, *Daily Report* (Eastern Europe), 1 Dec. 1989, 47.

January 1990

Are you satisfied with the political developments in the past two months (i.e., the overthrow of communism)?

Yes   86

Other responses   14

Are changes in the political system and economic system necessary?
Yes, political   83
Yes, economic   84.3
Will economic reform have any negative consequences?
Yes, short-term deterioration in the living standard   40
Yes, rise in unemployment   25

Source: Opinion poll conducted by the Group for an Independent Social Analysis, 9–19 Jan. 1990 among 2,350 citizens ages 15–69, reported in CTK (Prague), 29 Jan. 1990, in FBIS, *Daily Report* (Eastern Europe), 1 Feb. 1990, 24.

January 1990
What are the country's most urgent problems?
State of the environment   55
Obsolescence of industry and technology   37
State of public morale   30
Liquidation of the [communist party] organization   25
Health care and cost of living   24
Which problems should the government tackle first?
Preparation of free elections and the democratization of society   52
Economic reform   44
Solving environmental problems   42
Social and health issues   30
Supplying the domestic market   26

Source: Opinion poll conducted by the Research Institute of Trade and the London branch of the Gallup Institute, 18–27 Jan. 1990, among 1,500 citizens from the whole of Czechoslovakia, reported in *Rudé pravo*, 13 Feb. 1990, 1, 3, trans. in FBIS, *Daily Report* (Eastern Europe), 16 Feb. 1990, 22.

February 1990
Whom do you trust?
Václav Havel   88 yes, 9 no
Federal government   83 yes, 11 no
National governments   79 yes, 13 no
Federal Assembly   76 yes, 19 no
National committees   31 yes, 58 no
National Security Corps   35 yes˙
Courts   34 yes˙

Trade unions   28 yes˙
˙The figures for the negative responses for the last three institutions
were not reported.

Source: Opinion poll conducted by the Institute for Public Opinion Research, late February 1990, among 1,325 citizens from throughout the
country, reported in *Rudé pravo*, 2 Mar. 1990, trans. in FBIS, *Daily Report*
(Eastern Europe), 29 Mar. 1990, 15–16.

March 1990
Did either Czechs or Slovaks receive preferential treatment in official
policy during the past 20 years?
   Slovaks   4 percent of Czechs
   Not Slovaks   71 percent of Slovaks
   Czechs   68 percent of Slovaks
   Not Czechs   1 percent of Czechs

Source: Opinion poll conducted by the Prague Institute for Public Opinion Research, reported in *Prače*, 16 Mar. 1990, 2, trans. in FBIS, *Daily
Report* (Eastern Europe), 23 Mar. 1990, 26.

Appendix 4. Czech Republic

July 1993
Was it proper to expel the Germans from Sudetenland after World War II?
   Yes, correct   49
   Yes, somewhat correct   27
   No, somewhat wrong   7
   No, wrong   3
Are you in favor of negotiations with the Germans expelled from the
Sudetenland?
   Completely against negotiations   39
   Somewhat against negotiations   23
   Somewhat in favor of negotiations   20
   Decisively in favor of negotiations   6

Source: Poll conducted among 857 Czechs by the Czech Institute for
Public Opinion Research (Prague), reported in *Süddeutsche Zeitung* (Munich), 27 July 1993, 6

Appendix 5. Slovakia

September 1992
How do you feel about the impending partition of Czechoslovakia?
    Concerned   56
    Anxious   40
    Other answers   4
What do you think Slovaks will gain from the partition?
    More freedom   33
    More pride   "Another third"
    Other answers   "Another third"

Source: Lidove noviny (Prague), 22 Oct. 1992, 1, 12, trans. in FBIS, *Daily Report* (Eastern Europe), 29 Oct. 1992, 14.

October 1992
Do you feel confident about political and economic developments in Czechoslovakia?
    Yes, fully   8
    Somewhat   18
    Not very confident   40
    No, not at all   32

Source: Poll of 1,100 residents of the Slovak Republic, reported in CSTK (Prague), 14 Oct. 1992, in FBIS, *Daily Report* (Eastern Europe), 15 Oct. 1992, 13–14.

Appendix 6. Hungary

May 1989
Do you have faith in the following institutions (percentage answering yes)?
    Hungarian Socialist Workers' Party   24
    National Assembly   44
Do you trust the following political figures (percentages answering yes)?
    Imre Pozsgay   69.6
    Miklós Németh   69.0
    Rezsö Nyers   61.7
    Karóly Grósz   50.0
If elections were held today, for which party would you vote?
    Hungarian Socialist Workers' Party   36.5
    Social Democratic Party   13.0

Democratic Forum   11.4
Alliance of Free Democrats   5.6
Smallholders' Party   5.4
Other   28.1

Source: Study carried out by the Social Science Institute and the Socio-logical Institute, reported in Budapest Domestic Service, 6 May 1989, trans. in FBIS, *Daily Report* (Eastern Europe), 8 May 1989, 25.

June 1989
Is it necessary to have other parties, besides the Hungarian Socialist Workers' Party?
Yes   80
No   17
Don't know   3
Will the HSWP preserve or lose its leading role when other parties also function alongside the HSWP?
Will preserve   35
Will lose   47
Don't know   18

Source: Poll conducted by the Hungarian Public Opinion Research Insti-tute among 300 residents of Budapest, reported in *Magyar Hírlap*, 15 June 1989, 6, trans. in FBIS, *Daily Report* (Eastern Europe), 23 June 1989, 51.

Appendix 7. Poland

1980–1988
Are you in favor of strengthening the PUWP's leading role in the exercise of power?

	1980	1981	1984	1988
Yes	32.8	20.4	28.3	25.6
No	55.7	68.4	50.8	45.6
Undecided	11.5	11.2	22.5	28.8

Source: Andrzej Rychard, "Politics and Society after the Breakthrough: The Sources and Threats to Political Legitimacy in Post-Communist Poland," in *Democratization in Poland, 1988–90: Polish Voices*, ed. George Sanford (New York: St. Martin's Press, 1992), 142.

July 1988
Does the activity of the Catholic Church serve the interests of society?
   Yes   74.1
   No   12.9
   No opinion   12.9

Source: Survey conducted by the Public Opinion Polling Center, reported in PAP, 28 July 1988, in FBIS, *Daily Report* (Eastern Europe), 29 July 1988, 38.

August 1988
Is the Church trying to increase its influence over what is happening in Poland?
   Definitely yes   12
   Probably yes   28.7
   Probably no   15.3
   Definitely no   2.5
   No opinion   41

Source: Survey conducted by the Public Opinion Research Center, reported in *Trybuna Ludu* (Warsaw), 2 Aug. 1988, 3, trans. in FBIS, *Daily Report* (Eastern Europe), 5 Aug. 1988, 15.

November 1988–January 1989
Do you think that relegalization of Solidarity will bring benefits or losses?

	November 1988	January 1989
Benefits	28.5	47.6
Losses	21.7	7.2
Don't know	49.8	45.2

Source: George Sanford, "The Polish Road to Democratization: From Political Impasse to the 'Controlled Abdication' of Communist Power," in Sanford, *Democratization in Poland, 1988–90,* 17.

February 1989
How will the standard of living change over the next three years?
   It will improve   29
   It will not change   36
   It will get worse   26
   No opinion   9

Which public institutions do you trust?
  Sejm 61
  Government 51
  Polish United Workers' Party 26
  Armed force 75
Is the economic situation good?
  Yes 4
  No 95
  No opinion 1
How would you describe the supply of foodstuffs?
  Poor 57
  Mediocre 30
  Good 10
  Other responses 3
Should Solidarity be relegalized?
  Yes 78
  No 8
  No opinion 14
What effect would the relegalization of Solidarity have on the economy?
  Economy would improve 57
  Economy would deteriorate 4
  Economy would be unchanged 21
  Other responses 18
What effect would the relegalization of Solidarity have on social frictions and tensions?
  They would decrease 58
  They would increase 10
  They would be unchanged 21
What effect would the relegalization of Solidarity have on Poland's relations with its socialist neighbors?
  Relations would improve 19
  Relations would deteriorate 10
  Relations would be unchanged 52
  Other responses 19

Source: Poll conducted by the Polish Television and Radio's Center for Public Opinion Research, reported in *Trybuna Ludu,* 20 Feb. 1989, 5, trans. in FBIS, *Daily Report* (Eastern Europe), 24 Feb. 1989, 34–35.

July 1989

Who is your preferred candidate for the Polish presidency?

    1st: Wojciech Jaruzelski

    2nd: Lech Wałęsa

    3rd: Bronisław Geremek

    4th: Czesław Kiszczak

    5th: Aleksander Gieysztor and Mieczysław Rakowski (tie)

    [54 percent had no opinion.]

Who is your preferred candidate for the prime ministership?

    1st: Mieczysław Rakowski

    2nd: Bronisław Geremek

    3rd: Witold Trzeciakowski

    4th: Ryszard Bugaj

    5th: Jacek Kuroń

    Others (not rank-ordered): Lech Wałęsa, Ireneusz Sekula, Władysław
Baka, Aleksander Kwasniewski, Czesław Kiszczak, Adam Michnik

    [61 percent had no opinion.]

Source: Poll conducted by *Gazeta Wyborcza* (Solidarity weekly), reported by Warsaw Television Service, 9 July 1989, trans. in FBIS, *Daily Report* (Eastern Europe), 10 July 1989, 44.

September 1989

How significant is the nomination of Tadeusz Mazowiecki for the prime ministership?

    Historic breakthrough 54

    Significant but not a breakthrough 34

    Not of major importance 3

    Insignificant 2

    No opinion 7

Will Mazowiecki be a good prime minister?

    Definitely yes 23

    Probably yes 53

    No 4

    No opinion 20

Will Mazowiecki effect a radical reform of the economy?

    Yes 54

    Other 46

Source: Poll conducted by the Polish Radio and TV Committee, as reported in PAP, 18 Sept. 1989, in FBIS, *Daily Report* (Eastern Europe), 19 Sept. 1989, 53.

September 1989

If elections were held today, for which party would you vote?
 Solidarity   65
 Polish United Workers' Party   3
 Other responses   32

Are you satisfied with Prime Minister Tadeusz Mazowiecki?
 Yes   89
 No   2
 Other responses   9

Source: Opinion poll conducted by the Public Opinion Research Center, reported by Warsaw Television Service, 27 Sept. 1989, trans. in FBIS, *Daily Report* (Eastern Europe), 3 Oct. 1989, 42.

October 1989

Which institutions do you trust?
 The Church   87
 The Sejm   71
 The army   70
 The government   68
 Solidarity   66
 Democratic Party   34
 United Peasants Party   33
 Polish United Workers' Party   11

Sources: Opinion poll conducted by the OBOP Center for Public Opinion Research, reported in PAP, 20 Oct. 1989, in FBIS, *Daily Report* (Eastern Europe), 2 Nov. 1989, 74; and also in PAP, 15 Nov. 1989, in FBIS, *Daily Report* (Eastern Europe), 20 Nov. 1989, 78–79.

March 1990

Should the two German states be allowed to (re)unite?
 Yes   48
 No   39
 Other responses   13

Will German reunification be good for Poland?
 No   67
 Yes   13 (2 percent said *very* good)
 Other responses   20

Will a future united Germany threaten Polish borders?
 Yes   69
 No   31

Source: Opinion poll conducted by the Public Opinion Polling Center of Polish Radio and Television, 5–6 Mar. 1990, reported in PAP, 28 Mar. 1990, in FBIS, *Daily Report* (Eastern Europe), 29 Mar. 1990, 30–31.

March 1990
Should Soviet troops be withdrawn from Poland?
  Yes, as soon as possible, regardless of the situation in Germany   23
  Yes, but the date of their pullout should depend on developments in Germany   47
  No; they should stay in Poland   23
  Other responses   5

Source: Opinion poll conducted by the OBOP TV Center for Public Opinion Research, 4–5 Mar. 1990, reported in PAP, 29 Mar. 1990, in FBIS, *Daily Report* (Eastern Europe), 30 Mar. 1990, 44.

July 1991
In the dispute between the Sejm and President Wałęsa, who is right?
  The Sejm   35
  The president   21
  Both to some extent   25
  Declined to comment   19

Source: Survey conducted by the Public Opinion Research Center, reported in *Rzeczpospolita* (Warsaw), 26 July 1991, 2, trans. in FBIS, *Daily Report* (Eastern Europe), 31 July 1991, 36.

December 1991
What do you wish for Poland in 1992?
  That it "be governed by wise people"   55
  That unemployment be eased   24
  That the economic reforms succeed   16
  Other answers   5

Source: Public opinion poll conducted by the Pentor Research Group in December 1991 and reported by PAP (Warsaw), 27 Dec. 1991, in FBIS, *Daily Report* (Eastern Europe), 30 Dec. 1991, p. 17.

February 1992
Does anyone have any control over developments in Poland?
  No   "Two-thirds" of respondents
  Other responses   About one-third

If you could emigrate to another country, would you go?

    Yes   36 percent of respondents age 24 or under

    Other answers   64 percent of respondents age 24 or under

Would you like to see the country ruled by decree?

    Yes   More than half of respondents (most of these being age 40 or more)

Source: Opinion poll conducted by the Public Opinion Research Center (CBOS), reported in *Wprost* (Poznan), 23 Feb. 1992, 10, trans. in FBIS, *Daily Report* (Eastern Europe), 28 Feb. 1992, 29.

April 1992

Should the influence of the president on the work of the cabinet be increased?

    Yes 52

    No, it should be decreased 16

    No opinion 24

Which of these two should have the greater say in matters related to the armed forces and defense?

    The president 30

    The cabinet 43

Whose influence in the spheres of internal security and foreign policy most needs to be increased?

    The president's 19 (security), 19 (foreign policy)

    The cabinet's 54 (security), 56 (foreign policy)

Source: Poll conducted 22–26 Apr. 1992 by the CBOS Public Opinion Research Center, reported in PAP (Warsaw), 29 Apr. 1992, in FBIS, *Daily Report* (Eastern Europe), 1 May 1992, 20.

August 1992

Is democracy a useful system?

    Only if it produces prosperity 46

    Other answers 54

Does democracy promote economic development?

    Yes 13

    No, it promotes chaos and anarchy 12

    Other answers 75

Have the parliamentary deputies lost touch with reality?

    Yes 87

    No and other answers 13

Source: Public Opinion poll reported in *Nowa Europa* (Warsaw), 1 Sept. 1992, 2, trans. in FBIS, *Daily Report* (Eastern Europe), 9 Sept. 1992, 23.

September 1992
How will the overall situation change over the coming year?
   It will improve   20
   It will deteriorate   35
   It will not change   34
   Don't know and other answers   11
How will the political situation change over the coming year?
   It will improve   22
   It will deteriorate   16
   It will not change   39
   No opinion   23
How will the economic situation change over the coming year?
   It will improve   22
   It will deteriorate   31
   No opinion and other answers   47
How will your own personal living conditions change over the coming year?
   They will improve   13
   They will deteriorate   46
   No opinion and other answers   41

Source: Poll conducted 2–7 Sept. 1992 by the CBOS Public Opinion Research Center, reported in PAP (Warsaw), 14 Sept. 1992, in FBIS, *Daily Report* (Eastern Europe), 17 Sept. 1992, 24.

September 1992
Who has the biggest influence on developments in Poland?
   The president   37
   The government   37
   The Sejm   29
   The Church   10
   No one, the country is out of control   4

Source: Poll conducted by the CBOS Public Opinion Polling Center, reported in PAP (Warsaw), 16 Sept. 1992, in FBIS, *Daily Report* (Eastern Europe), 18 Sept. 1992, 14.

Appendix 8. Romania

May 1992
Is your life better or worse now than under Ceaușescu?
   Worse   41
   Other answers   59

Source: Survey of social attitudes conducted by the Center for Urban and Regional Sociology in Bucharest, cited in Misha Glenny, *The Rebirth of History: Eastern Europe in the Age of Democracy,* new ed. (Harmondsworth, Middlesex: Penguin Books, 1993), 261.

August 1992
How satisfied are you with the current political situation in Romania?
   Very satisfied   0.82
   Quite satisfied   7.92
   Not too satisfied   36.12
   Not at all satisfied   52.51
   Do not know/No response   2.53
Compare your standard of living during the Ceaușescu period with your present standard of living.
   Much higher   2.75
   Somewhat higher   20.84
   About the same   22.87
   Somewhat lower   23.03
   Much lower   29.18
   Do not know/No response   1.32
Are you in favor of using all means to support Bessarabia in the Dniester Region problem?
   Yes   51.57
   Yes, but not militarily   20.07
   No   15.56
   Other noes   0.55
   Do not know/No response   11.71
How do you think your standard of living will change during the coming year?
   Will improve a lot   5.33
   Will improve somewhat   27.93
   Will remain unchanged   23.47
   Will worsen somewhat   19.68
   Will worsen a lot   13.08
   Do not know/No response   10.5

What do you think is the most important problem that Romania is facing?
    Economic problems   38.37
    Unemployment and poverty   13.47
    Inflation   7.04
    Corruption   9.62
    Political problems   15.39
    Other responses   4.45
    Do not know/No response   35.68
Do you think Bessarabia should be united with Romania?
    Yes, immediately   55.47
    Yes, in the next five years   8.08
    Yes, in the next 10–15 years   11.65
    No, it is not a good idea   5.5
    No, this is not the time   2.97
    Other noes   3.08
    Do not know/No response   13.19
How much confidence do you have in President Ion Iliescu?
    Much   8.91
    Some   13.69
    Not too much   12.09
    None at all   57.34
    Do not know/No response   7.97

Source: Public opinion poll conducted at the beginning of August among 1,819 persons both in Bucharest and in the provinces by students from the University of Bucharest, reported in *Tineretul Liber* (Bucharest), 7 Aug. 1992, 4–5, summarized in FBIS, *Daily Report* (Eastern Europe), 26 Aug. 1992, pp. 24–25.

Appendix 9. Yugoslavia

Croatia, December 1988
Are you satisfied with the political situation in the country?
    Satisfied   4
    Somewhat satisfied   51
    Predominantly dissatisfied   35
    Completely dissatisfied   8
    Other responses   2
    By ethnic group, 40.1 per cent of Croats and 63.4 per cent of Serbs said they were "satisfied" or "somewhat satisfied" with the situation.

Who is to blame for the foreign debt?
  Federal officials   33
  Everyone   23
  Republican and provincial authorities   8
  Don't know   25
  Other responses   11
How does the position of Croatia compare with that of other republics?
  Better   7
  Worse   16
  The same   57
  Other responses   20
  By ethnic group, 6 percent of Croats and 15.6 percent of Serbs said that
  Croatia's position was better, while 1.6 percent of Serbs and 18.8 per-
  cent of Croats said it was worse than that of other republics.

Source: Poll conducted by Štefica Bahtijarević and Mladen Zvonarević among 2,000 citizens of Zagreb and surrounding communities, reported in *Borba* (Belgrade), 1 Dec. 1988, 5, trans. in FBIS, *Daily Report* (Eastern Europe), 6 Dec. 1988, 74–75.

February 1989
Which, in your view, is the best political system for Yugoslavia?

	Self-manage-ment	Real socialism	Bourgeois democracy	Dictator-ship	Mon-archy	Don't know
Bosnia	85	5	5	—	—	5
Macedonia	85	10	5	—	—	—
Slovenia	50	10	5	—	5	5
Serbia	70	15	15	—	—	—
Croatia	40	5	20	5	—	30
Montenegro	85	10	5	—	—	—

Source: Poll conducted by and reported in *Borba*, 13 Feb. 1989, 5, summarized in FBIS, *Daily Report* (Eastern Europe), 22 Feb. 1989, 76.

April 1989
When will Yugoslavia emerge from its crisis?
  In 5 years   41.5
  In 10 years   30.0
  "In a long time"   6.0
  In 2 years   5.0
  In 15 years   3.0

When the old leadership has been replaced   3.0
There is no way out (i.e., never)   2.0
By the year 2,000   2.0
In 20 years   2.0
In 30 years   0.5
In 50 years   0.5
After the congress   0.5
Don't know   3.0

Source: Poll conducted among 120 people by *Borba*'s public opinion research center and reported in *Borba*, 10 Apr. 1989, 5, summarized in FBIS, *Daily Report* (Eastern Europe), 24 Apr. 1989, 60.

Slovenia, March 1990
What kind of political future do you favor?
   Confederation   51.9
   Secession of Slovenia   28
   Efficient federation   7.9
   A unitarian Yugoslavia   0
   Don't know   12.2
Which parties do you trust more?
   Slovenian-based parties   79
   Yugoslav parties   6
   Neither   7
   Don't care, don't know   8
What is your political persuasion?
   Democrat   25.4
   Green   10.3
   Liberal   7.3
   Socialist   6.8
   Communist   5.6
   Communist-reformist   5.3
   Undecided   31.4
   Other responses   7.9

Source: Opinion poll conducted by *Delo* among 532 citizens of Slovenia, reported in *Delo* (Ljubljana), 15 Mar. 1990, 1, 3, summarized in FBIS, *Daily Report* (Eastern Europe), 20 Mar. 1990, 73–74.

September 1990
Should Serbs in Croatia have autonomy?

	Yes	No	Other	Do not know
Slovenia	37	50	10	3
Croatia	40	41	14	5
Bosnia-Herzegovina	44	33	6	17
Montenegro	80	3	13	4
Serbia	57	11	9	23
Macedonia	57	19	6	18
SFRY	53	26	10	11

Should Kosovo be a Republic?

	Yes	No	Other	Do not know
Slovenia	29	59	8	4
Croatia	19	73	0	8
Bosnia-Herzegovina	8	79	5	8
Montenegro	4	94	0	2
Serbia	2	96	2	0
Macedonia	0	99	0	1
SFRY	10	83	2	5

Source: Public opinion poll conducted by BORBA's Public Opinion Research Center among 420 persons from 42 cities, involving 70 persons from each of the six republics, reported in *Borba* (Belgrade), 26 Sept. 1990, p. 5, summarized in FBIS, *Daily Report* (Eastern Europe), 16 Oct. 1990, pp. 81–82.

Appendix 10. Croatia

April 1992
Is the political influence of the Catholic Church too great?
    Yes   44
    No   38
    Don't know   18
Should the president of the Republic of Croatia be a Catholic?
    Yes   30
    No   57
    Don't know   13

Source: Danas (Zagreb), 21 Apr. 1993, no. 531, 28.

Late August–early September 1992
Are the objectives of the policy of the Republic of Croatia in Bosnia-Herzegovina clear to you?

  No, they are not clear   51.5
  Yes, they are clear   30.2
  I cannot judge   18.3

What do you personally favor as the future of Bosnia-Herzegovina?

  Partition   6.5
  Cantonization (local autonomy)   11.5
  Status quo ante; intact   63.0
  Do not know   19.0

Source: Survey conducted by Dražen Lalić among 137 persons from all regions of Croatia, in late August–early September, reported in *Slobodna Dalmacija* (Split), 21 Sept. 1992, p. 10, trans. in FBIS, *Daily Report* (Eastern Europe), 15 Oct. 1992, 43.

September 1992
When will Croatian authority be restored in the occupied territories?

  In two to three years   28.7
  By the end of UNPROFOR's one-year mandate   25.1
  In five to ten years   13.2
  By the end of 1992   8.5
  Never   3.8

Source: Poll conducted by *Večernji list* among 470 persons from Croatia, 21–23 Sept., and reported in *Večernji list* (Zagreb), 28 Sept. 1992, p. 4, trans. in FBIS, *Daily Report* (Eastern Europe), 6 Oct. 1992, p. 34.

Appendix 11. Serbia

July 1992
Who has been pounding Sarajevo with artillery from surrounding hills during May and June?

  Muslim-Croatian forces   38.4
  Serbian forces   20.5
  Don't know   22.5
  Not informed   16.8

Source: Public opinion survey conducted by the "Medium" Center of the Political Studies Institute, Belgrade, and reported in *Borba* (Belgrade),

24 July 1992, 13, trans. in FBIS, *Daily Report* (Eastern Europe), 6 August 1992, 40.

July 1992
Do you support Serbian President Slobodan Milošević?
   Yes   20
   No, or other answers   80
[Milošević enjoyed the support of 85.6 percent of Serbs in a 1989 poll, and of 29.2 percent of Serbs in a February 1992 poll.]

Source: Dnevnik (Ljubljana), 31 Aug. 1992, p. 1, trans. in FBIS, *Daily Report* (Eastern Europe), 11 Sept. 1992, 30.

May 1993
Do you support the Vance-Owen plan?
   Yes   "Nearly 70 percent"
   Other answers   More than 30 percent

Source: Opinion poll conducted among residents of Belgrade, as cited in the *Financial Times,* 10 May 1993, 2.

Notes

Abbreviations

ADN	Allgemeiner Deutscher Nachrichtendienst (East Berlin)
AFP	Agence France-Presse (Paris, unless otherwise indicated)
AKSA	*Aktuelnosti Kršćanske Sadašnjosti* (Yugoslavia)
BTA	Bulgarian Telegraph Agency (Sofia)
CDSP	*Current Digest of the Soviet Press*
CTK	Ceskoslovenska Tiskova Kancelar (Prague)
DPA	Deutsche Press Agentur
FBIS	Foreign Broadcast Information Service, *Daily Report* (Eastern Europe, unless otherwise indicated)
ITD	I tako dalje (Yugoslavia)
JPRS	Joint Publications Research Service (*East Europe Report,* unless otherwise indicated)
KOS	*Committee for Social Resistance*
MTI	Magyar Tavirati Iroda (Budapest)
NIN	*Nedjeljne Informativne Novine* (Yugoslavia)
PAP	Polish Associate Press (Warsaw)
RFER	*Radio Free Europe Research*
UPNB	*Uncensored Poland News Bulletin*

1. Aspects of the Transition from Authoritarianism to Pluralism

1   Discussed below.
2   Discussed below.
3   Orally, during a visit to Seattle in early 1987.
4   Discussed below.
5   Orally, during a conversation at the annual convention of the American Association for the Advancement of Slavic Studies, Nov. 1988.
6   For example, Havel, Mečiar, and Milošević obviously do not share a common vision.

7   Dankwart A. Rustow, "Transitions to Democracy: Toward a Dynamic Model," *Comparative Politics* 2, no. 3 (Apr. 1970): 346.

8   Crane Brinton, *The Anatomy of Revolution*, rev. ed. (New York: Vintage, 1965).

9   Ted Robert Gurr, *Why Men Rebel* (Princeton, N.J.: Princeton University Press, 1972).

10 Adam Przeworski, "Some Problems in the Study of the Transition to Democracy," in Guillermo O'Donnell, Philippe C. Schmitter, and Laurence Whitehead (eds.), *Transitions from Authoritarian Rule: Comparative Perspectives* (Baltimore: Johns Hopkins University Press, 1986), 48, 52.

11 Ibid., 52.

12 On Vichy France, see Roy C. Macridis, "France: From Vichy to the Fourth Republic," in *From Dictatorship to Democracy: Coping with the Legacies of Authoritarianism and Totalitarianism*, ed. John H. Herz (Westport, Conn.: Greenwood Press, 1982), esp. 168–69.

13 Enrique A. Baloyra, "Democratic Transition in Comparative Perspective," in *Comparing New Democracies: Transition and Consolidation in Mediterranean Europe and the Southern Cone*, ed. Enrique A. Balorya (Boulder, Colo.: Westview Press, 1987), 10. See also Nancy Bermeo, "Democracy and the Lessons of Dictatorship," *Comparative Politics* 24, no. 3 (April 1992).

14 James C. Davies, "Toward a Theory of Revolution," in *Studies in Social Movements: A Social Psychological Perspective*, ed. Barry McLaughlin (New York: Free Press, 1969).

15 Francis Fukuyama, "The End of History?" *The National Interest*, no. 16 (Summer 1989).

16 Josep M. Colomer, "Transition by Agreement: Modeling the Spanish Way," *American Political Science Review* 85, no. 4 (Dec. 1991): 1283.

17 Guillermo O'Donnell, Philippe C. Schmitter, and Laurence Whitehead, eds., *Transitions from Authoritarian Rule: Southern Europe* (Baltimore: Johns Hopkins University Press, 1986); Guillermo O'Donnell, Philippe C. Schmitter, and Laurence Whitehead, eds., *Transitions from Authoritarian Rule: Latin America* (Baltimore: Johns Hopkins University Press, 1986); Guillermo O'Donnell, Philippe C. Schmitter, and Laurence Whitehead, eds., *Transitions from Authoritarian Rule: Comparative Perspectives* (Baltimore: Johns Hopkins University Press, 1986); and Guillermo O'Donnell and Philippe C. Schmitter, *Transitions from Authoritarian Rule: Tentative Conclusions about Uncertain Democracies* (Baltimore: Johns Hopkins University Press, 1986). The four components were also published in a one-volume edition: Guillermo O'Donnell, Philippe C. Schmitter, and Laurence Whitehead, eds., *Transitions from Authoritarian Rule: Prospects for Democracy* (Baltimore: Johns Hopkins University Press, 1986).

18 O'Donnell and Schmitter, *Transitions from Authoritarian Rule: Tentative Conclusions*, 48–49.

19 Ibid., 49.

20 Ibid., 50.

21 See Ivan Volgyes, ed., *Social Deviance in Eastern Europe* (Boulder, Colo.: Westview Press, 1978), esp. Paul Shapiro ("Social Deviance in Eastern Europe: On Understanding the Problem") and Otto Ulč ("Social Deviance in Czechoslovakia").

22   To borrow an image made famous by Václav Havel in his essay, "The Power of the Powerless," reprinted in *Without Force or Lies: Voices from the Revolution of Central Europe in 1989–90*, ed. William M. Brinton and Alan Rinzler (San Francisco: Mercury House, 1990).

23   Again, an image from Czechoslovak reality, described in a later chapter.

24   O'Donnell and Schmitter, *Transitions from Authoritarian Rule: Tentative Conclusions*, 52.

25   Ibid., 53.

26   Adam Przeworski, "Some Problems in the Study of the Transition to Democracy," in O'Donnell, Schmitter, and Whitehead, *Transitions from Authoritarian Rule: Comparative Perspectives*, 52.

27   For an outline of some alternative trajectories, see Alfred Stepan, "Paths toward Redemocratization: Theoretical and Comparative Considerations," in O'Donnell, Schmitter, and Whitehead, *Transitions from Authoritarian Rule: Comparative Perspectives*, 64–84.

28   I have outlined the elements of this latter syndrome, illustrated by five case studies, in "When Systems Fail: Toward a Theory of the Connection between Political Decay and Civil Strife," in *Adaptation and Transformation in Communist and Post-Communist Systems*, ed. Sabrina Petra Ramet (Boulder, Colo.: Westview Press, 1992).

29   See Hugh Seton-Watson, *Eastern Europe between the Wars, 1918–1941*, 3rd ed. (Hamden, Conn.: Archon Books, 1962), 242–43.

30   O'Donnell and Schmitter, *Transitions from Authoritarian Rule: Tentative Conclusions*, 54.

31   Przeworski, "Some Problems," 56.

32   Adam Bromke, "A New Juncture in Poland," *Problems of Communism* 25, no. 5 (Sept.–Oct. 1976): 15–16.

33   Ernst Kux, "Growing Tensions in Eastern Europe," *Problems of Communism* 29, no. 2 (Mar.–Apr. 1980): 37, also 34.

34   See the following essays by George Schöpflin: "The Political Structure of Eastern Europe as a Factor in Intra-bloc Relations," in *Soviet-East European Dilemmas: Coercion, Competition, and Consent*, ed. Karen Dawisha and Philip Hanson (New York: Holmes and Meier, 1981); "Corruption, Information, Irregularity in Eastern Europe: A Political Analysis," *Südost Europa* 33, nos. 7–8 (July–Aug. 1984); and "Political Decay in One-Party Systems: Yugoslav Patterns," in *Yugoslavia in the 1980s*, ed. Pedro Ramet (Boulder, Colo.: Westview Press, 1985).

35   J. F. Brown, in David Holloway and Jane O. Sharp, eds., *The Warsaw Pact: Alliance in Transition* (London: Macmillan, 1984), as quoted in George Sanford, *Military Rule in Poland: The Rebuilding of Communist Power, 1981–1983* (New York: St. Martin's Press, 1986), 40.

36   Ivan Volgyes, "Hungary: Before the Storm Breaks," *Current History* 86, no. 523 (Nov. 1987).

37   Anneli Ute Gabanyi, "Ceauşescu und kein Ende? Der Kampf um die Nachfolge hat bereits begonnen," *Südost Europa* 37, no. 9 (Sept. 1988).

38   Zbigniew Brzezinski, *The Grand Failure* (New York: Scribner's, 1989), 135–36, quoted in Giuseppe Di Palma, *To Craft Democracies: An Essay on Democratic Transitions* (Berkeley: University of California Press, 1990), 157.

39 Pedro Ramet, "Yugoslavia and the Threat of Internal and External Discontents," *Orbis* 28, no. 1 (Spring 1984): 112–15.

40 Sabrina P. Ramet, "The Breakup of Yugoslavia," *Global Affairs* 6, no. 2 (Spring 1991): 97.

41 In *Tygodnik Mazowsze*, quoted in Sanford J. Ungar, "The Role of a Free Press in Strengthening Democracy," in *Democracy and the Mass Media*, ed. Judith Lichtenberg (Cambridge: Cambridge University Press, 1990), 378.

42 Niko Toš, "Social Change and Shift of Values: Democratization Processes in Slovenia 1980–1990," *Nationalities Papers* 21, no. 1 (Spring 1993): 61.

43 Quoted in Oriol Pi-Sungar, "The Spanish Route to Democracy: A Model for Eastern Europe in Transition?," in *The Curtain Rises: Rethinking Culture, Ideology, and the State in Eastern Europe*, ed. Hermine G. DeSoto and David G. Anderson (Atlantic Heights, N.J.: Humanities Press, 1992), 305.

44 See Sabrina P. Ramet, "Balkan Pluralism and Its Enemies," *Orbis* 36, no. 4 (Fall 1992).

45 See Ramet, "When Systems Collapse."

46 Juan J. Linz and Alfred Stepan, "Political Identities and Electoral Sequences: Spain, the Soviet Union, and Yugoslavia," *Daedalus* 121, no. 2 (Spring 1992).

47 Barry Holden, *The Nature of Democracy* (London: Thomas Nelson and Sons, 1974), 1–8. Re the uses and misuses of definitions and an argument that contemporary people are confused about the meaning of the word "democracy," see Giovanni Sartori, *The Theory of Democracy Revisited* (Chatham, N.J.: Chatham House, 1987), chaps. 1 and 9.

48 Philippe C. Schmitter and Terry Lynn Karl, "What Democracy Is . . . And Is Not," in *The Global Resurgence of Democracy*, ed. Larry Diamond and Marc F. Plattner (Baltimore: Johns Hopkins University Press, 1993), 40.

49 Larry Diamond, "Three Paradoxes of Democracy," in Diamond and Plattner, *Global Resurgence*, 96.

50 H. V. Wiseman, *Political Systems* (London: Routledge and Kegan Paul, 1966), 72, quoted in Holden, *The Nature of Democracy*, 190.

51 Norberto Bobbio, *The Future of Democracy*, trans. from Italian by Roger Griffin (Cambridge: Polity Press, 1987), 63.

52 J. Budziszewski, *True Tolerance: Liberalism and the Necessity of Judgment* (New Brunswick, N.J.: Transaction, 1992), xiii.

53 I have discussed this in some depth in "Democratic Values and the Construction of Democracy: The Case of Eastern Europe," in *Slavic Eurasia in Transition: Multiple Analyses* (Sapporo, Japan: Slavic Research Center, Hokkaido University, 1994).

54 J. L. Talmon, *The Rise of Totalitarian Democracy* (Boston: Beacon Press, 1952).

55 Stephanie Lawson, "Conceptual Issues in the Comparative Study of Regime Change and Democratization," *Comparative Politics* 25, no. 2 (Jan. 1993): 192–93.

56 See John L. Sullivan, James Piereson, and George E. Marcus, *Political Tolerance and American Democracy* (Chicago: University of Chicago Press, 1982).

57 Joseph Raz, "Autonomy, Toleration, and the Harm Principle," in *Justifying Toleration: Conceptual and Historical Perspectives*, ed. Susan Mendus (Cambridge: Cambridge University Press, 1988), 157, 165.

58 Budziszewski, *True Tolerance*, xi; Raz, "Autonomy, Toleration," 155–56.

59 See Bonnie S. Anderson and Judith P. Zinsser, *A History of Their Own*, 2 vols. (New York: Harper and Row, 1988); Vivian Gornick and Barbara Moran, eds., *Woman in Sexist Society* (New York: Basic Books, 1971); Sheila Rowbotham, "Feminism and Democracy," in *New Forms of Democracy*, ed. David Held and Christopher Pollitt (Beverly Hills, Calif.: Sage Publications, 1986), 78–109.

60 See Frank M. Coleman, *Hobbes and America: Exploring the Constitutional Foundations* (Toronto: University of Toronto Press, 1977).

61 Terry Lynn Karl, "Dilemmas of Democratization in Latin America," *Comparative Politics* 23, no. 1 (Oct. 1990): 5.

62 As per summary in Rustow, "Transitions to Democracy," 337.

63 Giuseppe Di Palma, "Why Democracy Can Work in Eastern Europe," in Diamond and Plattner, *Global Resurgence*, 264–65.

64 Gabriel A. Almond and Sidney Verba, *The Civic Culture: Political Attitudes and Democracy in Five Nations* (Boston: Little, Brown, 1965).

65 Diamond, "Three Paradoxes," 103.

66 Seton-Watson, *Eastern Europe between the Wars*, 266.

67 Jutta-B. Lange-Quassowski, "Coming to Terms with the Nazi Past: Schools, Media, and the Formation of Opinion"; Frederick C. Engelmann, "How Austria Has Coped with Two Dictatorial Legacies"; Arthur E. Tiedemann, "Japan Sheds Dictatorship," all in *From Dictatorship to Democracy*, ed. John H. Herz.

68 Seymour Martin Lipset, *Political Man: The Social Bases of Politics*, expanded ed. (Baltimore: Johns Hopkins University Press, 1981). Anthony Arblaster comments: "It is only in the twentieth century that theorists have attempted to produce a version of democracy in which popular participation is treated with suspicion, if not regarded as positively undesirable. This represents a fundamental departure from the traditional understanding of what democracy is, or was." Anthony Arblaster, *Democracy* (Stony Stratford: Open University Press, 1987), 63.

69 Alvin Rabushka and Kenneth Shepsle, *Politics in Plural Societies: A Theory of Democratic Instability* (Columbus, Ohio: Merrill, 1972).

70 For an example of this emphasis, see Schmitter and Karl, "What Democracy Is," 40, 43; also Guglielmo Ferrero, *The Principles of Power* (New York: G. P. Putnam's Sons, 1942).

71 Robert Dahl, *Dilemmas of Pluralist Democracy* (New Haven, Conn.: Yale University Press, 1982), 11, quoted in Schmitter and Karl, "What Democracy Is," 45.

72 See Valerie Bunce, "Rising Above the Past: The Struggle for Liberal Democracy in Eastern Europe," in Ramet, *Adaptation and Transformation*, 243.

73 Robert Moss, *The Collapse of Democracy* (London: Temple Smith, 1975), 265–66.

74 As Holden points out in *The Nature of Democracy*, 184.

75 Precondition 5 comes from Samuel P. Huntington, *Political Order in Changing Societies* (New Haven, Conn.: Yale University Press, 1968). My debt to other scholars for some of the other preconditions listed here should be obvious from the preceding discussion. Re precondition 12 (a free press), see Lichtenberg (ed.), *Democracy and the Mass Media*, esp. Judith Lichtenberg, "Foundations and Limits of Freedom of the Press"; Michael Gurevitch and Jay G. Blumler,

"Political Communication Systems and Democratic Values"; T. M. Scanlon, Jr., "Content Regulation Reconsidered"; Sanford J. Ungar, "The Role of a Free Press in Strengthening Democracy."

76 Myron Weiner, "Empirical Democratic Theory and the Transition from Authoritarianism to Democracy," *PS*, no. 20 (Fall 1987): 863, quoted in Di Palma, *To Craft Democracies*, 5.

77 Di Palma, *To Craft Democracies*, 17.

78 Ibid., 91.

79 For a detailed elaboration of the theory to which I am alluding here, together with five case studies, see Ramet, "When Systems Fail."

80 Re Poland, see TVP Television Network (Warsaw), 6 Apr. 1992, trans. in FBIS, *Daily Report* (Eastern Europe), 7 Apr. 1992, 19; *Glob*, 12 May 1992, 2, trans. in FBIS, *Daily Report* (Eastern Europe), 21 May 1992, 25–27.

81 See Reinhard Bobach, "Mentale Konversion? Kulturelle Aspekte der deutschen Vereinigung," *Deutschland Archiv* (Cologne) 26, no. 1 (Jan. 1993).

82 *International Herald Tribune* (Tokyo ed.), 2 June 1993, 6.

83 Ken Jowitt, "The Leninist Legacy," in *Eastern Europe in Revolution*, ed. Ivo Banac (Ithaca, N.Y.: Cornell University Press, 1992), 222–23.

84 Claus Offe, "Capitalism by Democratic Design? Democratic Theory Facing the Triple Transition in East Central Europe," *Social Research* 58, no. 4 (Winter 1991): 866–67.

85 Re these repercussions, see Pedro Ramet, "Innenpolitische Determinanten der sowjetischen Interventionspolitik. Zu den Auswirkungen der tschechoslowakischen und polnischen Krise auf den Westen der UdSSR," *Osteuropa* 35, no. 3 (March 1985).

2. Social Currents and Social Change

1   Quoted in *Financial Times* (London) 12 Apr. 1988, 3.

2   Herbert Blumer, "Social Movements," in *Studies in Social Movements: A Social Psychological Perspective*, ed. Barry McLaughlin (New York: Free Press, 1969), 9.

3   Ibid., 8.

4   Irena Grudzińska-Gross, "Culture as Opposition in Today's Poland," *Journal of International Affairs* 40, no. 2 (Winter/Spring 1987): 389.

5   Angela A. Aidala, "Social Change, Gender Roles, and New Religious Movements," *Sociological Analysis* 46, no. 3 (Fall 1985): 287.

6   Milan Komnenić, "The Kosovo Cataclysm," *Serbian Literary Quarterly*, nos. 1–3 (1989): 67.

7   See, for example, Tihomir Djordjević, "Kossovo, 1389," *Serbian Literary Quarterly*, nos. 1–3 (1989): 36–37. For a more scholarly discussion of Kosovo, see Miloš Mišović, *Ko je tražio republiku Kosovo, 1945–1985* (Belgrade: Narodna knjiga, 1987).

8   Anthony F. C. Wallace, "Revitalization Movements," in *Studies in Social Movements: A Social Psychological Perspective*, ed. Barry McLaughlin (New York: Free Press, 1969), 31–32.

9   Defined and discussed in Pedro Ramet, "Apocalypse Culture and Social Change

122 See Ramet, *Balkan Babel*, chap. 1 ("Political Debate, 1980–1986").
123 Brinton, *The Anatomy of Revolution*.
124 *New York Times*, 2 Sept. 1987, 5; Polish Situation Report, RFER, 17 Mar. 1988, 25–26.
125 *New York Times*, 6 Feb. 1988, 5; *Corriere della Sera*, 3 Mar. 1988, 4.
126 See Ramet, "Apocalypse Culture"; Wolfgang Höpken, "Jugoslawien: Von der Wirtschaftskrise zur Systemkrise?," *Südost-Europa* 31, nos. 11–12 (Nov.–Dec. 1982).
127 See Davies, "Toward a Theory," 86, 103, 106.
128 Quoted in *New York Times*, 4 May 1988, 1.
129 *Polityka* (Warsaw), 9 Jan. 1988, as cited in Polish Situation Report, RFER, 25 Feb. 1988, 3.
130 *Luceafărul*, 8 Feb. 1986, excerpted in Romanian Situation Report, RFER, 20 Mar. 1986, 20.
131 See Csába Gombar, "Politisches Denken und die Alternativen einer politischen Reform in Ungarn," *Südost-Europa* 36, no. 10 (Oct. 1987).
132 Quoted in *Financial Times*, 11 Mar. 1988, 2.
133 Quoted in *Pravda* (Moscow), 1 Mar. 1989, 4.
134 Fred W. Riggs, *Administration in Developing Countries: The Theory of Prismatic Society* (Boston: Houghton Mifflin, 1964).
135 *New York Times*, 21 May 1988, 1, 4.

3. Disaffection and Dissent in East Germany

This chapter is a revised and updated version of an essay originally published in *World Politics* 37, no. 1 (Oct. 1984). Copyright © 1984 by Princeton University Press. Reprinted with the permission of Princeton University Press.

1 Relevant studies include Zygmunt Bauman, "Social Dissent in the East European Political System," *Archives Européennes de Sociologie* 12, no. 1 (1971): 25–51; Archie Brown and Jack Gray, eds., *Political Culture and Political Change in Communist States* (New York: Holmes & Meier, 1977); Walter D. Connor, "Dissent in Eastern Europe: A New Coalition?," *Problems of Communism* 29, no. 1 (Jan.–Feb. 1980); Walter D. Connor, "Social Change and Stability in Eastern Europe," *Problems of Communism* 26, no. 6 (Nov.–Dec. 1977); Andrzej Korbonski, "Conformity and Dissent in Eastern Europe," in *Politics and Participation under Communist Rule*, ed. Peter J. Potichnyj and Jane Shapiro Zacek (New York: Praeger, 1983); Alfred G. Meyer, "Political Change through Civil Disobedience in the USSR and Eastern Europe," in *Political and Legal Obligation*, ed. J. Roland Pennock and John W. Chapman, Yearbook of the American Society for Political and Legal Philosophy, vol. 12 (New York: Atherton, 1970); and Peter Veres, "Alienation: A Hungarian View," *East Europe* 14 (Mar. 1965). As treated here, disaffection is a specific type of cognitive dissonance. In this connection the general literature on this theory is also relevant, in particular: Elliot Aronson, "The Theory of Cognitive Dissonance: A Current Perspective," in *Advances in Experimental Psychology*, ed. Leonard Berkowitz (New York: Academic Press, 1969), 1–34; Leon Festinger, *A Theory of Cognitive Dissonance* (Evanston, Ill.: Row, Peterson, 1957); and Leon Festinger, ed., *Conflict, Decision, and Dissonance* (Stanford, Calif.: Stanford University Press, 1964).

2 *Bild* (Hamburg), 20 Nov. 1982, in FBIS, 23 Nov. 1982.

3 Otto Ulč, "Social Deviance in Czechoslovakia," in *Social Deviance in Eastern Europe,* ed. Ivan Volgyes (Boulder, Colo.: Westview, 1978), 28.

4 Paul H. Shapiro, "Social Deviance in Eastern Europe: On Understanding the Problem," in *Social Deviance in Eastern Europe,* ed. Ivan Volgyes (Boulder, Colo.: Westview, 1978), 15.

5 *Neue Zürcher Zeitung,* 23–24 (Jan. 1983).

6 See Leonard Binder, "Crises of Political Development," in *Crises and Sequences in Political Development,* Leonard Binder et al. (Princeton, N.J.: Princeton University Press, 1971), 3–72.

7 See Ivan Volgyes, "Political Socialization in Eastern Europe," *Problems of Communism* 23, no. 1 (Jan.–Feb. 1974): 52.

8 See Arthur M. Hanhardt, Jr., "Political Socialization in Divided Germany," *Journal of International Affairs* 27, no. 2 (1973): 188, 192, 196.

9 Otto Luchterhandt, *Die Gegenwartslage der Evangelischen Kirche in der DDR* (Tübingen: J. C. B. Mohr, 1982), 3; Ernst Alfred Jauch, "Katholiken in der DDR," *Kirche in Not* 26 (1978): 66–67; Kurt Sontheimer and Wilhelm Bleek, *The Government and Politics of East Germany,* trans. Ursula Price (London: Hutchinson University Library, 1975), 189.

10 See Reinhard Henkys, "Kirche in der Deutschen Demokratischen Republik," in *Religionsfreiheit und Menschenrechte,* ed. Paul Lendvai (Graz: Verlag Styria, 1983), 165–79; and Pedro Ramet, "Church and Peace in the GDR," *Problems of Communism* 33, no. 4 (July–Aug. 1984), reprinted in revised form in Pedro Ramet, *Cross and Commissar: The Politics of Religion in Eastern Europe and the USSR* (Bloomington: Indiana University Press, 1987), chap. 5.

11 Werner Volkmer, "East Germany: Dissenting Views during the Last Decade," in *Opposition in Eastern Europe,* ed. Rudolf L. Tökes (London: Macmillan, 1979), 114–15. In an interview with a Polish newspaper in 1989, East German dissident Wolfgang Templin sounded a cautionary note on reunification: "There are no political forces at present in the East or the West that would tolerate the unification of Germany. [But] we are demanding the right of GDR society to have its sovereign say on the matter." *Gazeta Wyborcza* (Warsaw), 12 Sept. 1989, 6, in FBIS, 18 Sept. 1989, 38.

12 "Interview with Robert Havemann," trans. Jack Zipes, *New German Critique,* no. 15 (Fall 1978): 41–42, 45; Günter Minnerup, "East Germany's Frozen Revolution," *New Left Review,* no. 132 (Mar.–Apr. 1982): 27–28.

13 *New York Times,* 26 Feb. 1984. See also *Los Angeles Times,* 19 Feb. 1984; *Washington Post,* 21 Jan. 1984, and 28 Jan. 1984.

14 DPA (Hamburg), 18 Apr. 1989, in FBIS, 18 Apr. 1989, 20.

15 Hans-Jürgen Grasemann, "Zwischen Ideologie und Realität: Jugendkriminalität in der DDR," *Deutsche Studien* 14 (Dec. 1976): 368–69.

16 By 9 percent in the 1977–78 period: Ibid., 371; *Frankfurter Allgemeine,* 10 July 1973); *New York Times,* 6 May 1980.

17 *The Times* (London), 10 Oct. 1977.

18 Herbert Prauss, "Jugend in der DDR," *Kirche in Not* 21 (1973): 81.

19 *Die Zeit* (Hamburg), 17 June 1983; *Forum* (East Berlin), Dec. 1982, 3, in JPRS, no. 83252 (13 Apr. 1983).

20 Klaus Ehring and Martin Dallwitz, *Schwerter zu Pflugscharen* (Hamburg: Rowohlt Taschenbuch Verlag, 1982), 90–92.

21 From the East Berlin magazine *Melodie und Rhythmus,* quoted in *Frankfurter Allgemeine,* 15 Sept. 1982, in JPRS, no. 81941 (7 Oct. 1982).

22 *Iwe-Tagesdienst* (Bonn), 26 Mar. 1983, in JPRS, no. 83359 (28 Apr. 1983).

23 *Vjesnik* (Zagreb), 28 Oct. 1983.

24 Norbert Haase, Lothar Reese, and Peter Wensierski, eds., *VEB Nachwuchs. Jugend in der DDR* (Hamburg: Rowohlt Verlag, 1983), 192–93.

25 Euphemistically translated: "legal, illegal, all the same."

26 Quoted in *Der Spiegel,* 3 Jan. 1983, 44.

27 Ibid., 122.

28 See Haase et al., *VEB Nachwuchs,* 243–44.

29 *Der Spiegel,* 3 Jan. 1983, 131.

30 Quoted in Henkys, "Kirche in der Deutschen Demokratischen Republik," 176.

31 Luchterhandt, *Die Gegenwartslage,* 68; Jauch, "Katholiken," 71, 73–74.

32 Quoted in Luchterhandt, *Die Gegenwartslage,* 66. See also Gerald Götting, *Beitrag christlicher Demokraten zu Gegenwart und Zukunft: Reden und Aufsätze, 1981–1986* (East Berlin: Union Verlag, 1987).

33 Luchterhandt, *Die Gegenwartslage,* 71–72; "Notes on Church-State Relations," *Journal of Church and State* 23 (Winter 1981): 166.

34 *Frankfurter Allgemeine,* 4 Jan. 1983, and 7 Jan. 1983.

35 See *Leipziger Volkszeitung,* 1 Feb. 1962, as cited in Ehring and Dallwitz, *Schwerter,* 14–15.

36 *Süddeutsche Zeitung* (Munich), 8 Sept. 1982, in JPRS, no. 81941 (7 Oct. 1982); Ehring and Dallwitz, *Schwerter,* 20–25. See also Timothy Garton Ash, "Swords into Ploughshares: The Unofficial 'Peace Movement' and the Churches in East Germany," *Religion in Communist Lands* 11 (Winter 1983): 245–46.

37 *Wiener Tagebuch* (Vienna), Oct. 1982, in JPRS, no. 82210 (10 Nov. 1982).

38 Ehring and Dallwitz, *Schwerter,* 59, 70; *Die Welt* (Bonn), 21 June 1982.

39 Günter Krusche, *Bekenntnis und Weltverantwortung. Die Ekklesiologiestudie des Lutherischen Weltbundes: Ein Beitrag zur ökumenischen Sozialethik* (Berlin: Evangelische Verlagsanstalt, 1986), 146.

40 *Wall Street Journal,* 22 June 1983; *Facts on File,* 1 July 1983, 490; *Neue Zürcher Zeitung,* 2 Sept. 1983, and 4 Jan. 1984; and *Frankfurter Allgemeine,* 24 Oct. 1983, and 5 Nov. 1983.

41 Interview with clergyman, Berlin, 30 June 1988.

42 Interview with clergyman, Eisenach, 12 July 1988.

43 Ulrike Enders, "Erziehung zu Hass: Zum staatlichen Erziehungsprogramm für kindergarten," *Kirche im Sozialismus* 13, no. 2 (Apr. 1987): 52–53.

44 "Program für die Erziehungsarbeit im Kindergarten," *Kirche im Sozialismus* 13, no. 2 (Apr. 1987): 55, 56.

45 Interview with clergyman, Berlin, 29 June 1988; *Frankfurter Allgemeine,* 26 June 1987, 2, and 29 June 1987, 5; *Die Zeit* (Hamburg), 10 July 1987, 2.

46 Interview with clergyman, Erfurt, 12 July 1988; and interview source cited in note 45.

47 *Die Welt* (Bonn), 7 June 1988, 10, in FBIS, 8 June 1988, 36; *Neue Zürcher Zeitung,* 10 June 1988, 6.

48 *Frankfurter Rundschau,* 27 June 1988, 1, 3.

49 DPA (Hamburg), 12 June 1988, in FBIS, 13 June 1988, 29–30.

50 DPA 16 Sept. 1988, in FBIS, 21 Sept. 1988, 17; *Neue Zürcher Zeitung,* 22 Sept. 1988, 1.

51 *Frankfurter Allgemeine,* 20 June 1988, 1, in FBIS, 21 June 1988, 20; *Die Welt,* 5 July 1988, 1, in FBIS, 6 July 1988, 29; *Frankfurter Allgemeine,* 9 Aug. 1988, 3, and 10 Aug. 1988, 1.

52 Richard Schröder, "Was kann 'Kirche im Sozialismus' sinnvoll heissen?," *Kirche im Sozialismus* 14, no. 4 (Aug. 1988): 135–37.

53 Barbara Donovan, "East German Churches Demand Justice," RFER, 10 May 1989, 2.

54 Cited in *Frankfurter Allgemeine* (22 September 1989), 3. For a survey of all Protestant Churches in East Germany and an in-depth examination of the Evangelical-Lutheran Church in particular, see Sabrina Petra Ramet, "Protestantism in East Germany, 1949–1989: A Summing Up," in *Protestantism and Politics in Eastern Europe and Russia: The Communist and Post-Communist Eras,* ed. Sabrina Petra Ramet (Durham, N.C.: Duke University Press, 1992).

55 East Germany actually allowed a limited number of conscientious objectors to serve in a uniformed construction brigade. But since the brigade worked largely on projects of military importance, some objectors refused even this.

56 Henry W. Degenhardt, *Political Dissent: An International Guide to Dissident, Extra-Parliamentary, Guerrilla, and Illegal Political Movements* (Detroit: Gale, 1983), 16–17.

57 "East Germany's Democratic Movement: 'Human Rights GDR,'" *Across Frontiers* (Spring 1986): 13.

58 *Frankfurter Allgemeine,* 23 Sept. 1989, 1–2.

59 *Neue Zürcher Zeitung,* 26 Jan. 1988, 3; 31 Jan.–1 Feb. 1988, 3; and 6 Feb. 1988, 3. See also *Süddeutsche Zeitung,* 6–7 Feb. 1988, 1–2; *Frankfurter Allgemeine,* 8 Feb. 1988, 1.

60 Zelime Amen Ward, "Minority Politics in the German Democratic Republic: Problematics of Socialist Legitimacy and National Autonomy," in *The Politics of Ethnicity in Eastern Europe,* ed. George Klein and Milan J. Reban (Boulder, Colo.: East European Monographs, 1981), 98, 101–2.

61 Quoted in Peter Jokostra, "Ein Archipel von Sprachinseln: Bericht über die Literatur der sorbischen Minderheit in der DDR," *Deutsche Studien* 15 (Sept. 1977): 279.

62 For details, see Frithjof Heller, "Schön, bemerkenswert und traditionell: Die Sorben zwischen Kruzifix und Thälmannbild," *Kirche im Sozialismus* 13, no. 3 (June 1987): 103–4.

63 ADN, 21 Nov. 1989, in FBIS, 21 Nov. 1989, 37.

64 ADN, 17 Nov. 1989, in FBIS, 21 Nov. 1989, 37.

65 ADN, 20 Nov. 1989, in FBIS, 21 Nov. 1989, 37.

66 *Der Spiegel,* 25 July 1983, in JPRS, no. 84155 (19 Aug. 1983).

67 Wolfgang Buscher and Peter Wensierski, *Null Bock auf DDR. Aussteigerjugend im anderen Deutschland* (Hamburg: Spiegel Verlag, 1984), 39.

68 *Neue Zürcher Zeitung,* 5 July 1983, in JPRS, no. 84084 (10 Aug. 1983); *Süddeutsche Zeitung,* 5 July 1983. See also *Die Welt,* 2 Aug. 1983.

69 Christel Sudau, "Women in the GDR," trans. Biddy Martin, *New German Critique,* no. 13 (Winter 1978): 70–71; David Childs, *The GDR: Moscow's German Ally* (London: George Allen & Unwin, 1983), 251; Sharon L. Wolchik, "Ideology and Equality: The Status of Women in Eastern and Western Europe," *Comparative Political Studies* 13 (Jan. 1981): 459.

70   Childs, *The GDR*, 259.

71   Ibid., 252.

72   *Armeerundschau* (Apr. 1982): 55–56; *Christian Science Monitor*, 5 Jan. 1984. See also *Neue Zürcher Zeitung*, 6 Jan. 1984.

73   Text of letter given in *Der Spiegel*, 6 Dec. 1982, 117, in FBIS, 7 Dec. 1982.

74   Michael Waller, *The Language of Communism* (London: The Bodley Head, 1972), 32.

75   Bauman, "Social Dissent," 46.

76   David Childs, *East Germany* (London: Ernest Benn, 1969), 38; Volkmer, "East Germany: Dissenting Views," 128.

77   Horst Sindermann, at fifth session of the central committee, SED, Feb. 1964, as quoted in Childs, *The GDR*, 74.

78   Bruce Allen, *Germany East: Dissent and Opposition* (Montreal: Black Rose, 1989), 63.

79   Peter Lübbe, *Der staatliche etablierte Sozialismus: Zur Kritik des staatmonopolischen Sozialismus* (Hamburg: Hoffman & Campe, 1975), as cited in Jeffrey Lee Canfield, "Marxist Revisionism in East Germany: The Case of Rudolf Bahro," *The Fletcher Forum* 4 (Winter 1980): 47.

80   Rudolf Bahro, *Die Alternative: Zur Kritik des real existierenden Sozialismus* (Cologne: Europäische Verlagsanstalt, 1977).

81   Michael J. Sodaro, "Limits to Dissent in the GDR: Fragmentation, Cooptation, and Repression," in *Dissent in Eastern Europe*, ed. Jane Leftwich Curry (New York: Praeger, 1983), esp. 97; Hugh Mosely, "The New Communist Opposition: Rudolf Bahro's Critique of the 'Really Existing Socialism,'" *New German Critique*, no. 15 (Fall 1978): 28, 32.

82   David Bathrick, "The Politics of Culture: Rudolf Bahro and Opposition in the GDR," *New German Critique*, no. 15 (Fall 1978): 20.

83   Canfield, "Marxist Revisionism," 32.

84   Ibid.

85   Günter Bartsch, "Mehr als Alternative: Ein Durchbruch und Neubeginn," *Deutschland Archiv* 11, no. 5 (May 1978): 474. See also Fritz Shenk, "Rudolf Bahro und das Dilemma des Marxismus-Leninismus," *Deutschland Archiv* 11, no. 5 (May 1978): 470–71.

86   When Bahro was jailed, Wolf Biermann commented, "What brings them [the SED] to a complete rage and makes them crazy is the inherent criticism that comes from within," *Die Welt*, 3 July 1978, quoted in Canfield, "Marxist Revisionism," 28.

87   *Der Spiegel*, 24 Aug. 1981, 35.

88   *Wall Street Journal*, 17 Nov. 1989, A10.

89   Jan Vanous, "East European Economic Slowdown," *Problems of Communism* 31, no. 4 (July–Aug. 1982): 3; *Business Week*, 24 May 1982, 170, 181; *Neue Zürcher Zeitung*, 23–24 Jan. 1983.

90   Richard Portes, "Effects of the World Economic Crisis on the East European Economies," *World Economy* 3 (June 1980): 26; *Frankfurter Allgemeine*, 2 Jan. 1984; *Neue Zürcher Zeitung*, 12 Jan. 1984.

91   Martin McCauley, "Storm Signals in East German Economy," *Soviet Analyst* 11 (10 Feb. 1982): 5; *Der Spiegel*, 3 Oct. 1983, 126; "Interview with Robert Havemann," 43.

92 Volkmer, "East Germany: Dissenting Views," 119–20; *New York Times*, 3 Aug. 1981; *Christian Science Monitor*, 20 Aug. 1981.

93 Roger Woods, *Opposition in the GDR under Honecker, 1971–85* (London: Macmillan, 1986), 14–15.

94 *Bild*, 20 Nov. 1982, in FBIS, 23 Nov. 1982.

95 *Der Spiegel*, 8 Nov. 1982, 16–17, and 10 Jan. 1983, 16–17.

96 Report in DPA, 11 Jan. 1983, in FBIS, 11 Jan. 1983; *Stern*, 13 Jan. 1983, 17, 126–27. Denied in ADN, 11 Jan. 1983, in FBIS, Jan. 11, 1983.

97 *Neue Zürcher Zeitung*, 11 Jan. 1985, 13.

98 *Financial Times*, 11 Mar. 1988, 2; also *Neues Deutschland*, 12 Jan. 1988, 1.

99 *Financial Times*, 10 Jan. 1989, 2.

100 *Wall Street Journal*, 29 Jan. 1988, 12; *Financial Times*, 11 Mar. 1988, 2; *Frankfurter Allgemeine*, 13 Apr. 1988, 6, and 18 Apr. 1988, 13; Barbara Donovan, "Is the East German Economy Running into Trouble?," *RFER*, 14 Apr. 1988, 1–2.

101 *Wall Street Journal*, 17 Nov. 1989, A1.

102 Barbara Donovan, "Plans for a Coordinated Opposition Movement in the GDR," *RFER*, 18 Aug. 1989.

103 *Frankfurter Allgemeine*, 27 Sept. 1989, 4, and 9 Oct. 1989, 4; *New York Times*, 16 Oct. 1989, A4; DPA, 24 Sept. 1989, in FBIS, 25 Sept. 1989, 22.

104 *Frankfurter Allgemeine*, 18 Sept. 1989, 5; 8 Oct. 1989, 1–2; and 9 Oct. 1989, 4.

105 For the Luther revival, see Robert F. Goeckel, "The Luther Anniversary in East Germany," *World Politics* 37, no. 1 (Oct. 1984); Dan Beck, "The Luther Revival: Aspects of National *Abgrenzung* and Confessional *Gemeinschaft* in the German Democratic Republic," in *Religion and Nationalism in Soviet and East European Politics*, ed. Pedro Ramet, rev. and expanded ed. (Durham, N.C.: Duke University Press, 1989), 223–40.

106 General secretary Walter Ulbricht was eager to suppress the Prague Spring, but East German youth were deeply alienated by East German participation in the Warsaw Pact invasion of Czechoslovakia in 1968, and some offspring of SED elite openly protested against the invasion. See Childs, *The GDR*, 79–80.

4. Underground Solidarity and Parallel Society in Poland

1 "Parallel Polis, or An Independent Society in Central and Eastern Europe: An Inquiry" (Comments by Václav Benda), *Social Research* 55, nos. 1–2 (Spring/Summer 1988): 217.

2 See Jakub Karpiński, "Polish Intellectuals in Opposition," *Problems of Communism* 36, no. 4 (July–Aug. 1987); also interview with Colonel Ryszard Kukliński, in *Kultura* (Paris), no. 4 (Apr. 1987).

3 See Pedro Ramet, "Poland's 'Other' Parties," *The World Today* 37, no. 9 (Sept. 1981): 332–38.

4 Quoted in *Reinventing Civil Society: Poland's Quiet Revolution, 1981–1986* (New York: Helsinki Watch, 1986), 7.

5 "The Strategy is to Keep Pressing: An Interview with Wiktor Kulerski," *Uncaptive Minds* 1, no. 2 (June–Aug. 1988): 16.

6 *Reinventing Civil Society*, 9.

7   Roman Dumas, "Poland's 'Independent Society,' " *Poland Watch*, no. 8 (1986): 65.
8   For an unusual collection of conversations with Lech Wałęsa concerning this period, see Jule Gatter-Klenk, *Vielleicht auf Knien, aber vorwärts: Gespräche mit Lech Wałęsa* (Königstein: Athenäum, 1981).
9   *Profil* (Vienna), 11 May 1987, 53.
10 Revealed in secret documents in the archives of the SED, made public in Jan. 1993, *New York Times*, 12 Jan. 1993, A7 (hereinafter, "Secret Documents").
11 Revealed by Mikhail Gorbachev, interview with *Trybuna* (Warsaw), 9 Nov. 1992, 1, 2, trans. in FBIS, *Daily Report* (Eastern Europe), 17 Nov. 1992, 19.
12 "Secret Documents."
13 As reported in *Nowy Swiat* (Warsaw), 23 Sept. 1992, 4, trans. in FBIS, *Daily Report* (Eastern Europe), 30 Sept. 1992, 17.
14 Jan B. de Weydenthal, "The Story Behind Martial Law in Poland," *RFER*, 14 Apr. 1987, 2; *New York Times*, 17 Apr. 1987, A9; *U.S. News & World Report*, 20 Apr. 1987, 33. For discussion and analysis of Soviet thinking about Poland in 1980 and 1981, see Pedro Ramet, "Innenpolitische Determinanten der Sowjetischen Interventionspolitik. Zu den Auswirkungen der Tschechoslowakischen und Polnischen Krise auf den Westen der UdSSR," *Osteuropa* 35, no. 3 (Mar. 1985).
15 Wojciech Jaruzelski, *Jaruzelski, Prime Minister of Poland: Selected Speeches* (Oxford: Pergamon Press, 1985), 18.
16 Revealed by Jaruzelski in an interview with reporter John Darnton, *New York Times*, 4 Mar. 1993, A7.
17 Lech Wałęsa, *A Way of Hope: An Autobiography*, trans. from Polish by Marete B. Zaleski et al. (New York: Henry Holt, 1987), 211–12.
18 George Sanford, *Military Rule in Poland: The Rebuilding of Communist Power, 1981–1983* (New York: St. Martin's Press, 1986), 119.
19 Ibid., 125.
20 *Tu i Teraz*, 29 Aug. 1984, 3, in FBIS, *East Europe Report*, 7 Sept. 1984, G3–5; AFP, 8 Mar. 1985, in FBIS, *East Europe Report*, 9 Apr. 1985, G1.
21 *Christian Science Monitor*, 8 Jan. 1988, 10.
22 *La Vanguardia* (Barcelona), 29 Aug. 1988, 6, trans. in FBIS, *East Europe Report*, 8 Sept. 1988, 36.
23 Interview with a former Silesian Solidarity leader, Munich, 4 June 1987. See also PAP (Warsaw), 11 Feb. 1982, trans. in FBIS, *East Europe Report*, 12 Feb. 1982, G17.
24 Warsaw Domestic Service, 12 Jan. 1982, trans. in FBIS, *East Europe Report*, 13 Jan. 1982, G10.
25 See n. 23.
26 *Le Monde* (Paris), 30 Apr. 1982, 1, 4, trans. in FBIS, *East Europe Report*, 5 May 1982, G31. See also Sanford, *Military Rule in Poland*, 254–255.
27 Interview with a former Solidarity activist from Toruń, Munich, 1 June 1987.
28 See n. 23.
29 See n. 27.
30 *Los Angeles Times*, 18 Mar. 1982, 4.
31 Ibid., 20 June 1982, 1.
32 Quoted in ibid., 28 Aug. 1982, 4.
33 Ibid., 21 May 1982, 4.
34 *Süddeutsche Zeitung* (Munich), 24–25 July 1982, 7.

35 From the full text of the statement, *Le Monde*, 12 Oct. 1982, trans. in FBIS, *East Europe Report*, 13 Oct. 1982, G8.

36 Quoted in Jan B. de Weydenthal, *The Communists of Poland: An Historical Outline*, rev. ed. (Stanford, Calif.: Hoover Institution Press, 1987), 210.

37 *Die Welt* (Bonn), 25 May 1985, 7, trans. in JPRS, *East Europe Report*, no. EPS-85-097 (23 Sept. 1985): 17–19.

38 Janusz Bugajski, "Polish Security Service Operations Against the Solidarity Underground," RFER, 10 Apr. 1984, 4.

39 Ibid., 6–7; Dumas, "Poland's 'Independent Society,' " 69.

40 Quoted in *Die Welt*, 25 May 1985, 19.

41 Wałęsa, *A Way of Hope*, 237.

42 PAP, 9 Mar. 1983, trans. in FBIS, *East Europe Report*, 10 Mar. 1983, G3.

43 *Los Angeles Times*, 2 May 1983, 1.

44 Quoted in *Christian Science Monitor*, 25 Aug. 1983, 7.

45 At a press conference for foreign journalists, Hipolit Starszak, deputy prosecutor general, said that if Bujak surrendered, the charges of high treason would be dropped and he would be amnestied. See *Rzeczpospolita*, 3 Aug. 1984, 5–6, trans. in FBIS, *East Europe Report*, 8 Aug. 1984, G10–14.

46 *Gazeta Robotnicza*, as cited in AFP, 17 Aug. 1984, in FBIS, *East Europe Report*, 20 Aug. 1984, G10.

47 Jan Józef Lipski, interview with *Der Spiegel*, 30 July 1984, 90–92, trans. in FBIS, *East Europe Report*, 1 Aug. 1984, G5–6.

48 Colonel Zygmunt Rybacki, interview with *Zolnierz Wolności*, 8 Aug. 1984, 4–5, trans. in FBIS, *East Europe Report*, 15 Aug. 1984, G6–10.

49 Warsaw Domestic Service, 24 Aug. 1984, trans. in FBIS, *East Europe Report*, 27 Aug. 1984, G1.

50 AFP, 20 Aug. 1984, trans. in FBIS, *East Europe Report*, 20 Aug. 1984, G11; AFP, 31 Aug. 1984, trans. in FBIS, *East Europe Report*, 4 Sept. 1984, G11; Warsaw Domestic Service, 23 Aug. 1984, trans. in FBIS, *East Europe Report*, 23 Aug. 1984, G5; Warsaw Domestic Service, 31 Aug. 1984, trans. in FBIS, *East Europe Report*, 4 Sept. 1984, G12.

51 Quoted in *Seattle Times*, 1 May 1984, A2.

52 AFP, 31 July 1984, trans. in FBIS, *East Europe Report* 1 Aug. 1984, G2; *Washington Post*, 1 Sept. 1984, A21.

53 AFP, 31 July 1984; AFP (Hong Kong), 29 Aug. 1984; AFP, 3 Sept. 1984; and AFP, 20 Sept. 1984, trans. in FBIS, *East Europe Report*, 1 Aug. 1984, G9–10; 30 Aug. 1984, G10; 4 Sept. 1984, G12–13; and 21 Sept. 1984, G3.

54 AFP, 1 Oct. 1984, trans. in FBIS, *East Europe Report*, 2 Oct. 1984, G1.

55 AFP, 7 Sept. 1984, in FBIS, *East Europe Report*, 10 Sept. 1984, G5; and ZDF Television Network (Mainz), 31 Oct. 1984, trans. in FBIS, *East Europe Report*, 6 Nov. 1984, G2–3.

56 *Expresso* (Lisbon), 3 Nov. 1984, 25–27B, trans. in FBIS, *East Europe Report*, 13 Nov. 1984, G8.

57 AFP, 3 Aug. 1984, in FBIS, *East Europe Report*, 6 Aug. 1984, G8; and Vienna Television Service, 21 Dec. 1984, trans. in FBIS, *East Europe Report*, 24 Dec. 1984, G6–7.

58 ORF Teletext (Vienna), 31 Oct. 1984, trans. in FBIS, *East Europe Report*, 1 Nov. 1984, G1; Vatican City International Service, 11 Nov. 1984, trans. in FBIS, *East*

43   *Keston News Service*, no. 213 (22 Nov. 1984): 5, and no. 214 (6 Dec. 1984): 8; *New York Times*, 2 Dec. 1984, 5.

44   *EFE* (Madrid), 22 Feb. 1984, in JPRS, no. EPS-84-041 (28 Mar. 1984): 93.

45   *UPNB* (London), 30 Jan. 1986, 13.

46   Ibid., 23 Sept. 1986, 25, and 20 Feb. 1987, 18.

47   *New York Times*, 21 Sept. 1987, 4. See also Zimon's sermon on the ecological disaster, in *UPNB*, 14 July 1986, 29.

48   *New York Times*, 16 Sept. 1985, 1.

49   ORF Teletext (Vienna), 17 Sept. 1984, in FBIS, 17 Sept. 1984, G1–2; *New York Times*, 30 Dec. 1985, 5; *Washington Post*, 14 Dec. 1986, A1.

50   *The Economist*, 25 Feb. 1984, 44.

51   Kamiński, "Poland's Catholic Church," 83.

52   Irena Korba, "Five Years Underground: The Opposition and the Church in Poland Since Martial Law," *Religion in Communist Lands* 15, no. 2 (Summer 1987): 172.

53   *KOS*, 27 Feb. 1984, quoted in Korba, "Five Years Underground," 180.

54   Korba, "Five Years Underground," 175–76.

55   Ibid., 176–77.

56   Quoted in *New York Times*, 25 Nov. 1984, sec. 4, 4.

57   Tadeusz Walendowski, "The Pope in Poland," *Poland Watch*, no. 3 (Spring/Summer 1983): 5–8; Karl Hartmann, "Politische Bilanz des zweiten Papstbesuches in Polen," *Osteuropa* 33, nos. 11–12 (Nov.–Dec. 1983): 897, 900.

58   Polish Situation Report, *RFER*, 10 July 1987, 5; *Glas koncila* (Zagreb), 21 June 1987, 3.

59   *Washington Post*, 11 June 1988, A33.

60   *Corriere della Sera* (Milan), 12 June 1987, 15, and 13 June 1987, 12.

61   *Tygodnik Powszechny*, 28 June 1987, trans. into German as "Die dritte Papstreise nach Polen," *Osteuropa* 37, no. 12 (Dec. 1987): A679–80. See also "Papstbesuch in Polen: Was bleibt für die Gastgeber?," *Herder Korrespondenz* 41, no. 7 (July 1987).

62   *Corriere della Sera*, 16 June 1987, 21.

63   See, for example, the report in *Frankfurter Allgemeine* 4 Apr. 1985, 2, and 16 Apr. 1985, 6.

64   Quoted in *Washington Post*, 21 Sept. 1987, A1.

65   AFP, 7 Aug. 1988, in FBIS, 8 Aug. 1988, 16.

66   *UPNB*, 31 Oct. 1988, 5.

67   *Slowo Powszechne*, 29 Aug. 1988, 1, 2, in FBIS, 1 Sept. 1988, 36–37. See also *Süddeutsche Zeitung*, 27–28 Aug. 1988, 1.

68   *Frankfurter Allgemeine*, 6 May 1989, 12, and 18 May 1989, 6; *Keston News Service*, no. 326 (25 May 1989): 2; *Tygodnik Powszechny* (Kraków), 25 June 1989, 1, 3, in FBIS, 12 July 1989, 39–42. See also PAP (Warsaw), 28 June 1989, in FBIS, 29 June 1989, 43.

69   AFP, 22 Jan. 1989, in FBIS, 23 Jan. 1989, 67; *New York Times*, 27 Jan. 1989, A4; Warsaw Domestic Service, 7 Mar. 1989, in FBIS, 8 Mar. 1989, 52.

70   AFP, 31 Jan. 1989, in FBIS, 1 Feb. 1989, 38.

71   *Keston News Service*, no. 330 (20 July 1989): 9; *Glas koncila* (Zagreb), 30 July 1989, 3.

72   Further discussion in Sabrina P. Ramet, "The New Church-State Configuration in Eastern Europe," *East European Politics and Societies* 5, no. 2 (Spring 1991).

73 *New York Times*, 6 Nov. 1990, A1.

74 *New York Times*, 15 Apr. 1988, 15.

75 Scot J. Paltrow, "Poland and the Pope: The Vatican's Relations with Poland, 1978 to the Present," *Millennium* 15, no. 1 (Spring 1986): 10.

76 *Życie Warszawy* (Warsaw), 13–14 July 1985, in JPRS, no. EPS-85-098 (27 Sept. 1985): 133.

77 Quoted in *New York Times*, 9 Sept. 1986, 4.

78 *New York Times*, 13 Nov. 1986, A20.

79 Polish Situation Report, RFER, 2 Dec. 1986, 3.

80 *Niedziela* (Częstochowa), 7 Dec. 1986, 6, in JPRS, no. EER-87-035 (10 Mar. 1987): 99.

81 Ibid., 100.

82 AFP, 31 Aug. 1984, in FBIS, 4 Sept. 1984, G10–11; AFP, 16 Sept. 1984, in FBIS, 17 Sept. 1984, G2; AFP, 22 Sept. 1984, in FBIS, 24 Sept. 1984, G2.

83 Huntington, *Political Order*, 5.

8. Serb-Albanian Tensions in Kosovo

An earlier version of this chapter originally appeared in *Canadian Review of Studies in Nationalism* 16, nos. 1–2 (1989): Reprinted by permission.

1 See, for example, the statement of the League of Communists Municipal Committee of Titova Mitrovka, 31 Jan. 1990, reported by Tanjug, in FBIS, 1 Feb. 1990, 78–79.

2 E.g., Rainer Joha Bender, "Die Krisenprovinz Kosovo: Ein jugoslawischer Peripherraum im Lembruch," *Zeitschrift für Balkanologie* 20, no. 1 (1984): 17; Michael T. Kaufman, *New York Times*, 5 Oct. 1984.

3 E.g., Jens Reuter, *Die Albaner in Jugoslawien* (Munich: R. Oldenbourg Verlag, 1982), 10; Dennison I. Rusinow, "Nationalities Policy and the 'National Question,'" in *Yugoslavia in the 1980s*, ed. Pedro Ramet (Boulder, Colo.: Westview Press, 1985), 145.

4 Tanjug, 12 Jan. 1990, in FBIS, 16 Jan. 1990, 100.

5 Tanjug, 29 Jan. 1990, in FBIS, 30 Jan. 1990, 85.

6 Branka Magaš, *The Destruction of Yugoslavia: Tracking Yugoslavia's Break-up, 1980–92* (London: Verso, 1992), 3.

7 Dimitrije Bogdanović, *Knjiga o Kosovu* (Belgrade: Srpska Akademija Nauka i Umetnosti, 1985), 10–28; Viktor Meier, "Träume von einer albanischen Zukunft?," *Südosteuropa Mitteilungen* 24, no. 4 (1984): 54.

8 Ivo Banac, *The National Question in Yugoslavia: Origins, History, Politics* (Ithaca, N.Y.: Cornell University Press, 1984), 298.

9 Ivan Babić, "U službi Srpske okupacione vojske u Makedoniji i Kosovu," *Hrvatska revija* (Barcelona) 28, no. 3 (Sept. 1978): 476–77.

10 Banac, *The National Question*, 298–99.

11 Quoted in ibid., 299.

12 Ibid., 300.

13 Bender, "Die Krisenprovinz," 6.

14 Alex N. Dragnich and Slavko Todorovich, *The Saga of Kosovo* (Boulder, Colo.: East European Monographs, 1984), 138.

15 Bogdanović, *Knjiga o Kosovu*, 244–46.

16 Miloš Mišović, *Ko je tražio republiku Kosovo, 1945–1985* (Belgrade: Narodna knjiga, 1987), 91–110. Also *Intervju* (Belgrade), 19 June 1987, 10–11.

17 Elez Biberaj, "The Conflict in Kosovo," *Survey* 28, no. 3 (Autumn 1984): 42.

18 See Dušan Bilandžić, *Jugoslavija poslije Tita (1980–1985)* (Zagreb: Globus, 1986), 73–74.

19 For further discussion of the economic fortunes of Kosovo, see Sabrina P. Ramet, *Nationalism and Federalism in Yugoslavia, 1962–1991*, 2nd ed. (Bloomington: Indiana University Press, 1992), 145–48, 150–61.

20 Reuter, *Die Albaner*, 52.

21 Ibid.

22 Biberaj, "The Conflict in Kosovo," 46.

23 Dragoslav Marković, "Ostvarivanje Platforme SKJ o Kosovu," *Socijalizam* 26, no. 12 (Dec. 1983): 1691.

24 Tanjug, 4 Dec. 1980, as quoted in Mark Baskin, "Crisis in Kosovo," *Problems of Communism* 32, no. 2 (Mar.–Apr. 1983): 65.

25 "Rates of Employment and Unemployment, 1980–1987," *Yugoslav Survey* 29, no. 4 (1988): 35.

26 *Borba*, 2–3 Mar. 1985, in JPRS, no. EPS-85-053 (6 June 1985): 133–34.

27 Dragnich and Todorovich, *The Saga of Kosovo*, 161.

28 Ibid., 169.

29 See further discussion and documentation in Ramet, *Nationalism and Federalism*, chap. 9.

30 *Frankfurter Allgemeine*, 4 Apr. 1981; Elez Biberaj, "Albanian-Yugoslav Relations and the Question of Kosovë," *Albanian Catholic Bulletin* 4, nos. 1–2 (1983): 83; *NIN*, 27 June 1982, as cited in Jens Reuter, "Der XII. Kongress des BdKJ," *Südost-Europa* 31, nos. 7–8 (1982): 383.

31 Tanjug, 31 Jan. 1986, in FBIS, 4 Feb. 1986, 16; *Intervju* 29 Mar. 1985, in JPRS, no. EPS-85-066 (11 June 1985): 84; *Danas*, 1 June 1982, 11; Yugoslav Situation Report, RFER, 19 Nov. 1987, 7.

32 *The Times* (London), 9 June 1985, as cited in Peter R. Prifti, "Kosovë Stalemate Deepens: An Updated Report," *Albanian Catholic Bulletin* 6 (1985): 82.

33 Tanjug, 11 June 1985, in FBIS, 13 June 1985, 15.

34 *Borba*, 16 Mar. 1983, in FBIS, 29 Mar. 1983, 110.

35 Peter R. Prifti, "Struggle for Ethnic Rights in Kosovo Continues," *Albanian Catholic Bulletin* 5, nos. 1–2 (1984): 68. See also Ramet, *Nationalism and Federalism*, chap. 9.

36 CMD, 20 Mar. 1986; confirmed in Tanjug, 20 Mar. 1986.

37 *Vjesnik*, (Zagreb), 26 July 1982.

38 Ibid.; Sinan Hasani, *Kosovo: Istine i zablude* (Zagreb: Centar za informacije i publicitet, 1986), 181–91.

39 Tanjug, 12 Jan. 1983, in FBIS, 13 Jan. 1983, 122; and Tanjug, 2 Mar. and 31 Mar. 1983, in FBIS, 4 Mar. 1983, 19, and 4 Apr. 1983, 114.

40 *Yearbook on International Communist Affairs 1985*, ed. Richard F. Staar (Stanford, Calif.: Hoover Institution Press, 1985), 371.

41 *The Times*, 30 Dec. 1985; confirmed in *Christian Science Monitor*, 9 Jan. 1986.

42 *New York Times*, 3 May 1986; *Süddeutsche Zeitung* (Munich), 31 May–1 June 1986.

43 *The Times*, 30 Dec. 1985; South-East European Service, 25 Jan. 1986; *Večernje novosti* (Belgrade), 18 Feb. 1986.

44 Jens Reuter, "Unruheherd Kosovo: Resultat einer erfolglosen Politik," *Südost-Europa* 35, nos. 11–12 (Nov.–Dec. 1986): 637–38.

45 Quoted in *New York Times*, 1 Nov. 1987, 6.

46 Prifti, "Struggle for Ethnic Rights," 67.

47 *Politika*, 25 Dec. 1981.

48 *Christian Science Monitor*, 4 Jan. 1983; confirmed in *New York Times*, 5 Oct. 1984.

49 *Pravoslavlje*, 15 May 1982. For further discussion, see Pedro Ramet, "Religion and Nationalism in Yugoslavia," in *Religion and Nationalism in Soviet and East European Politics*, ed. Pedro Ramet, rev. and expanded ed. (Durham, N.C.: Duke University Press, 1989), 316–17.

50 *Los Angeles Times*, 15 Mar. 1984.

51 Tanjug, 25 June 1985, in fbis, 26 June 1985, 13.

52 Re the Macedonians, see *Borba*, 6 Feb. 1986, in fbis, 14 Feb. 1986, 13–14. Re the Montenegrins, see Marko Špadijer, "Nacionalizam u Crnoj Gori," *Socijalizam* 29, no. 4 (Apr. 1986). See also Hasani, *Kosovo*, 252–53.

53 *Los Angeles Times*, 15 Mar. 1984.

54 Portions of the remainder of this section appeared previously in an earlier article, "Concern About Serbian Nationalism," *rfer*, 27 Mar. 1986.

55 *NIN*, no. 1836 (9 Mar. 1986): 22.

56 Ibid., no. 1904 (28 June 1987): 12, and no. 1941 (13 Mar. 1988): 16.

57 South-East European Service, 25 Jan. 1986.

58 *Nedeljna borba*, 23–24 Nov. 1985, and 28–29 Dec. 1985.

59 Tanjug, 24 Feb. 1986, my emphasis.

60 Ibid., 24 Dec. 1985, in fbis, 9 Jan. 1986, 16–17.

61 *Frankfurter Allgemeine*, 5 Feb. 1986.

62 "The Serbian Kosovo Petition," *South Slav Journal* 9, nos. 1–2 (Spring/Summer 1986): 108.

63 *NIN*, no. 1835 (2 Mar. 1986): 28–29, and no. 1836 (9 Mar. 1986): 22.

64 Priština Domestic Service, 3 Apr. 1986, trans. in fbis, 4 Apr. 1986, 19.

65 *Frankfurter Allgemeine*, 24 June 1986; *The Times*, 29 July 1986.

66 *Die Welt*, 14 Feb. 1986.

67 *Politika*, 16 Mar. 1986.

68 Milan M. Miladinović, "Pojam i suština jugoslovenskog patriotizma danas," *Obeležja* 7, no. 6 (Nov.–Dec. 1977): 1153.

69 Ibid., 1165–66.

70 *Frankfurter Allgemeine*, 11 July 1986.

71 Tanjug, 8 June 1985, in fbis, 10 June 1985, 110.

72 Priština Domestic Service, 2 Nov. 1985, trans. in fbis, 12 Nov. 1985, 16; *Politika*, 3 Jan. 1986.

73 *Politika*, 28 Apr. 1986. For a breakdown of ethnic distribution in Kosovo in successive censuses, including 1981, see Bogdanović, *Knjiga o Kosovu*, 252.

74 Lazar Vujović, chairman of the lc Serbian Commission for the Development of Intranational Relations, in Tanjug, 17 Feb. 1982, in fbis, 18 Feb. 1982, 13.

75 Tanjug, 2 Apr. 1981, in fbis, 3 Apr. 1981, 13.

76 *Borba*, 9 Jan. 1983, trans. in fbis, 18 Jan. 1983, 116.

77 Tanjug, 19 Dec. 1984, in JPRS, no. EPS-85-012 (27 Jan. 1985): 32.

78 Tanjug, 4 Apr. 1985, in FBIS, 9 Apr. 1985, 14.

79 Ibid., 15.

80 See Stevan Nikšić, *Oslobodjenje štampe* (Belgrade: Oslobodjenje, 1982).

81 See *NIN*, no. 1836 (9 Mar. 1986): 9–10, and no. 1838 (23 Mar. 1986): 53.

82 Belgrade Domestic Service, 29 Apr. 1985, trans. in FBIS, 30 Apr. 1985, 120.

83 Tanjug, 4 Apr. 1985, in FBIS, 9 Apr. 1985, 14.

84 7 Oct. 1985 session of the Commission for Information and Propaganda, LC Kosovo, as reported in Tanjug, 7 Oct. 1985, in FBIS, 17 Oct. 1985, 14.

85 Tanjug, 11 Jan. 1986, in FBIS, 15 Jan. 1986, I-11.

86 Most of these can be found in Azem Vlasi, "Neki oblici antisocijalističkog delovanja u SAP Kosovu," *Socijalizam* 29, no. 4 (Apr. 1986).

87 *NIN*, no. 1871 (9 Nov. 1986), 12.

88 *Vjesnik*, 17 Jan. 1987, 3; *Večernji list* (Zagreb), 8 July 1987, 4.

89 Quoted in *NIN*, no. 1904 (28 June 1987): 9.

90 *Politika ekspres* (Belgrade), 27 June 1987, 1.

91 Quoted in Yugoslav Situation Report, *RFER*, 30 Sept. 1987, 3.

92 *Borba* (Zagreb), 26 Oct. 1987, 1.

93 Stambolić later published his collected speeches and writings in Zagreb. See Ivan Stambolić, *Rasprave o SR Srbiji, 1979–1987* (Zagreb: Globus, 1988).

94 Zagreb Domestic Service, 23 June 1988, trans. in FBIS, 28 June 1988, 61.

95 *Eastern Europe Newsletter*, 31 Aug. 1988, 1.

96 *Politika*, 31 Aug. 1988, 10.

97 Interview with Goran Bregović, leader of White Button, Sarajevo, 14 Sept. 1989. The song comes from an album released in 1987.

98 *Politika*, 17 June 1988, 5.

99 Dragana Roter-Crkvenjakov, "Pokrajinska štampa o promenama ustava SR Srbije," *Novinarstvo* 24, nos. 1–2 (1988): 60.

100 Tanjug, 24 Feb. 1989, in FBIS, 27 Feb. 1989, 59; Belgrade Domestic Service, 25 Feb. 1989, in FBIS, 27 Feb. 1989, 65; Tanjug Domestic Service, 4 Mar. 1989, trans. in FBIS, 6 Mar. 1989, 60.

101 *Politika*, 30 Oct. 1989, 6, and 4 Nov. 1989, 5. For further discussion of Milošević's strategies, see Sabrina P. Ramet, "Slobodan Milošević and the Future of Yugoslavia," *Orbis* 35, no. 1 (Winter 1991).

102 Quoted in *New York Times*, 19 Jan. 1990, A5.

103 Quoted in ibid.

104 Belgrade Domestic Service, 31 Jan. 1990, trans. in FBIS, 1 Feb. 1990, 75.

105 AFP, 31 Jan. 1990, in FBIS, 1 Feb. 1990, 76.

106 AFP, 1 Feb. 1990, in FBIS, 2 Feb. 1990, 75.

107 *New York Times*, 8 Feb. 1990, A13.

108 *Politika ekspres*, 1 Feb. 1990, as summarized in Tanjug, 1 Feb. 1990, in FBIS, 2 Feb. 1990, 84.

109 AFP, 1 Feb. 1990, in FBIS, 2 Feb. 1990, 76; and Tanjug, 1 Feb. 1990, in FBIS, 2 Feb. 1990, 80; *Politika*, 18 Feb. 1990, 6.

110 *Intervju*, 29 Mar. 1985, trans. in JPRS, no. EPS-85-066 (11 June 1985): 81.

111 *Kosovo 1389–1989*, special ed., *Serbian Literary Quarterly*, nos. 1–3 (1989): 45.

112 See Renata Salecl, "Nationalism, Anti-Semitism, and Anti-Feminism in Eastern Europe," *New German Critique*, no. 57 (Fall 1992): 55.

524 Notes to Chapter 9

9. Feminism in Yugoslavia

1   Blaženka Despot, *Žensko pitanje i socijalističko samoupravljanje* (Zagreb: Čekada, 1987).

2   Interviews with officials, Belgrade, 14 July 1982; with a high-ranking Slovenian official and former partisan, Ljubljana, 19 July 1982; and with members of the editorial board of *Žena*, Zagreb, 2 July 1982. See also Barbara Jancar, "The New Feminism in Yugoslavia," in *Yugoslavia in the 1980s* ed. Pedro Ramet (Boulder, Colo.: Westview Press, 1985).

3   The remainder of this section draws heavily on my earlier article, "Gleichberechtigung der Geschlechter, Parteipolitik und Feminismus in Jugoslawien," *Osteuropa* 33, no. 7 (July 1983): 539–46.

4   *V. kongres KPJ, stenografske bilješke* (Kultura, 1949), 891, quoted in Nevenka Petrić, "Ravnopravnost žene i muškarca u završnim dokumentima poslijeratnih kongresa KPJ-SKJ," *Žena* 38, no. 1 (Jan.–Feb. 1980): 74.

5   Petrić, "Ravnopravnost žene," 76.

6   For a more detailed survey of this aspect of the question, see Pedro Ramet, "Women, Work, and Self-Management in Yugoslavia," *East European Quarterly* 17, no. 4 (Jan. 1984): 459–68.

7   Olivera Burić, "Položaj žene u sistemu društvene moći u Jugoslaviji," *Sociologija* 14, no. 1 (1972): 68.

8   Ibid., 65–68; Savka Dabčević-Kučar, "Problemi društvenog položaja žene—problemi našeg samoupravnog socijalističkog društva u cjelini," *Žena* 26, no. 2 (1970): 6.

9   Some statistics for this can be found in Olivera Burić, "Izmena strukture društvene moći—uslov za društvenu ravnopravnost žene," *Sociologija* 17, no. 2 (1975).

10 Djura Knezević, "Izbor žena u svjetlu kadrovske politike Saveza komunista," *Žena* 36, no. 55 (1979): 76.

11 Vladimir Bakarić, "Promjene društveno-ekonomskog položaja žene treba vezati uz opći preobražaj našeg društva," *Žena* 36, no. 4 (1979): 2.

12 *Mladost*, no. 38 (30 Mar.–12 Apr. 1987): 20.

13 All statistics from Lydia Sklevický, "Reluctant Feminists: the 'Woman Question'—A New Approach in Yugoslavia," unpublished paper, 1987.

14 *1987 Yearbook of Labour Statistics*, no. 47 (Geneva: International Labour Office, 1987), 578.

15 *Politika*, 15 Mar. 1981 and 22 Mar. 1981.

16 Nataša Djurić, "Emancipacija na pola puta," *Borba*, 1 June 1980.

17 Radivoje Iveković, "Žena u procesu odlučivanja u osnovnoj organizaciji Saveza komunista," *Opredjeljenja* 6, nos. 3–4 (Mar.–Apr. 1978): 87–88; "Zaključci Predsjedništva CK SKJ o zadacima Saveza komunista na daljem unapredjenju društvenog pitanja i uloge žene danas" (25 June 1980), *Žena* 38, nos. 4–5 (1980): 4; *Politika*, 28 June 1980.

18 Iveković, "Žena u procesu," 87–88; Mirjana Poček-Matić, "SK se mora boriti za afirmaciju marksističkih stavova o ulozi žene u društvu," *Žena* 35, no 6 (1977): 6; Gabi Čačinović-Vogrinčić, "Socijalizacija za samoupravne odnose zahtijeva ostvarenje nehijerarhijskih odnosa u obitelji," *Žena* 38, nos. 4–5 (1980): 153.

126   Quoted in Zsolt Krokovay, "Politics and Punk [in Hungary]," *Index on Censorship* 14, no. 2 (Apr. 1985): 20.

127   Quoted in Kürti, "How Can I Be," 84.

128   Quoted in Krokovay, "Politics and Punk," 20.

129   Quoted in Kürti, "How Can I Be," 78.

130   *Sztandar Młodych* (Warsaw), 25 Oct. 1983, 3, trans. in JPRS, no. EPS-84-006 (11 Jan. 1985): 94.

131   S. Frederick Starr, "The Rock Inundation," *Wilson Quarterly* 7, no. 4 (Autumn 1983): 62.

132   Quoted in *Christian Science Monitor*, 31 May 1990, 10.

133   *Stern* (Hamburg), 17 March 1994, 204. Re the current Elvis revival in Hungary, see *The European-élan* (London), 17–23 June 1994, 1–3.

134   Interview with Peter Lovšin, leader of Falcons, Ljubljana, 26 Mar. 1992; *Vreme* (Belgrade), 27 Apr. 1992, 19; Miha Štamcar and Jani Sever, "Mitingaš v Sloveniji" [interview with Rambo Amadeus], *Mladina* (Ljubljana), 17 Mar. 1992, 29; and *NIN* (Belgrade), 5 June 1992, 34. For further discussion of the postures of various indigenous rock artists vis-à-vis the war, see Sabrina Petra Ramet, "Shake, Rattle, and Self-Management: Making the Scene in Yugoslavia," in Ramet, *Rocking the State.*

135   Song "Hrvatska mora pobijediti," on Psihomodo pop, *Maxi Single za Gardiste*, Croatia Records MS-D 2 03553 3 (1991).

136   Quoted in *The European* (London), 4 July 1993.

137   Quoted in Artemy Troitsky, *Back in the USSR: The True Story of Rock in Russia* (Boston: Faber and Faber, 1987), 127.

11. Young People: The Lost Generation

1   See Klaus Ehring and Martin Dallwitz, *Schwerter zu Pflugscharen* (Hamburg: Rowohlt Taschenbuch Verlag, 1982).

2   *Życie Warszawy* (Warsaw), 30 Sept. 1986, 3, trans. in JPRS, no. EER-86-192 (18 Dec. 1986): 97.

3   *Polityka* (Warsaw), 10 Jan. 1987, 5, trans. in JPRS, no. EER-87-057 (9 Apr. 1987): 94.

4   *Magyar Ifjúság* (Budapest), 28 Dec. 1984, 7–9, trans. in JPRS, no. EPS-85-017 (2 Feb. 1985): 19.

5   Wolf Oschlies, *Jugend in der Tschechoslowakei: Kurzer Frühling, lange Winter* (Cologne: Bohlau Verlag, 1985), 209.

6   *Kontakty*, no. 26 (Oct. 1985), trans. in "Extracts from Polish Underground Publications," RFER, 17 Jan. 1986, 13.

7   Quoted in Gabriel Bar-Haim, "The Meaning of Western Commercial Artifacts for Eastern European Youth," *Journal of Contemporary Ethnography* 16, no. 2 (July 1987): 212–13.

8   Quoted in ibid., 214.

9   *Sturshel* (Sofia), 7 Dec. 1984, 1, 2, trans. in JPRS, no. EPS-85-023 (19 Feb. 1985): 8.

10   See, for instance, Tanjug (Belgrade), 3 Feb. 1986, in JPRS, no. EER-86-025 (25 Feb. 1986): 158.

11   PAP, 20 Apr. 1982, in FBIS, 21 Apr. 1982, G20.

12   *Magyar Hirek* (Budapest), 16 June 1984, suppl., 4–5, trans. in JPRS, no. EPS-84-095 (3 Aug. 1984): 39.

13   *Süddeutsche Zeitung* (Munich), 6 Sept. 1993, 5.

14   *Nepszava* (Budapest), 25 July 1988, 5, trans. in JPRS, no. EER-88-075 (9 Sept. 1988): 23.

15   Bulgarian Situation Report, RFER, 7 Aug. 1989, 23; *Rabotnichesko delo* (Sofia), 5 Feb. 1989, 3, in FBIS, 9 Feb. 1989, 3–4.

16   Wolf Oschlies, *Der Jargon osteuropaischer Jugendlicher. Zur sprachsoziologischen, lexikalischen und politischen Einordnung eines Sozialdialekts* (Cologne: Bundesinstitut für ostwissenschaftliche und internationale Studien, report no. 28, 1979), 1.

17   Ibid., 32.

18   Ibid., 34.

19   Ibid., 42, 44.

20   Quoted in ibid., 41.

21   Ibid., 65.

22   *Danas* (Zagreb), 6 Dec. 1983, 21–22, trans. in JPRS, no. EPS-84-016 (3 Feb. 1984): 180.

23   *Sztandar Młodych* (Warsaw), 18–20 Nov. 1983, 3, trans. in JPRS, no. EPS-84-005 (9 Jan. 1984): 117.

24   Wolf Oschlies, *Rumäniens Jugend—Rumäniens Hoffnung* (Cologne: Bohlau, 1983), 153; Wolf Oschlies, *Jugendprobleme in Jugoslawien* (Cologne: Bundesinstitut für ostwissenschaftliche und internationale Studien, report no. 5, 1977), 1.

25   Wolf Oschlies, *"Verlorene Generation." Polens Jugend im "Kriegszustand," 1981–1983* (Cologne: Bundesinstitut für ostwissenschaftliche und internationale Studien, report no. 23, 1983), 11.

26   *Karima* 15, no. 12 (26 Nov. 1987): 14–17, cited in Hungarian Situation Report, RFER, 15 Feb. 1988, 11.

27   *Felsooktatasi Szemle* (Budapest), Nov. 1984, 662–67, trans. in JPRS, no. EPS-85-017 (2 Feb. 1985): 14, 16.

28   Josip Županov, "Radnička omladina i društvena stabilnost," in Vlasta Ilišin, Furio Radin, and Josip Županov, *Kultura radničke omladine* (Zagreb: Centar društvenih djelatnosti saveza socijalističke omladine Hrvatske, 1986), 169, 183.

29   *Borba* (Belgrade), 1 Dec. 1989, 3, trans. in FBIS, 12 Jan. 1990, 76.

30   Quoted in Norbert Haase, Lothar Reese, and Peter Wensierski, eds., *VEB Nachwuchs. Jugend in der DDR* (Hamburg: Rowohlt, 1983), 59.

31   Oschlies, *"Verlorene Generation,"* 12.

32   Furio Radin, "Vrijednosti i vrijednose orijentacije," in Ilišin et al., *Kultura radničke omladine,* 136.

33   *Przegląd Tygodniowy* (Warsaw), 14 Oct. 1984, 5, trans. in JPRS, no. EPS-84-145 (28 Nov. 1984): 131; Czechoslovak Situation Report, RFER, 6 Mar. 1987), 21; Hungarian Situation Report, RFER, 8 Nov. 1985, 23.

34   Hungarian Situation Report, RFER, 3 June 1988, 39.

35   *Krytyka*, no. 16 (1983), trans. in "Polish Samizdat Extracts," RFER, 6 June 1984, 1, 3.

36   Quoted in *Christian Science Monitor*, 2 June 1988, 11.

37   *Danas*, 28 Jan. 1986, 22–25, trans. in JPRS, no. EER-86-061 (18 April 1986): 76–83.

38   *Die Zeit* (Hamburg), 13 May 1988, 3.

39   Quoted in Jim Seroka and Radŏs Smiljković, *Political Organizations in Socialist Yugoslavia* (Durham, N.C.: Duke University Press, 1986), 157.

40 Quoted in *Svijet* (Sarajevo), 24 Aug. 1981, 10–11, trans. in JPRS, no. 79299 (26 Oct. 1981): 31.

41 Romanian Situation Report, *RFER*, 26 June 1985, 35.

42 Hungarian Situation Report, *RFER*, 11 July 1986, 40–41; Hungarian Situation Report, *RFER*, 21 Mar. 1988, 9–10.

43 *Narodna Armiya* (Sofia), 4 Nov. 1986, 3, trans. in JPRS, no. EER-87-006 (12 Jan. 1987): 78–79.

44 *Christian Science Monitor*, 26 Nov. 1984, 16.

45 For Yugoslavia, see the data in Srečko Mihailović, "Društveno-politički aktivizam mladih," in *Položaj, svest i ponašanje mlade generacije Jugoslavije: Preliminarna analiza rezultata istraživanja* (Zagreb: IDIS, 1986), 176.

46 Quoted in Tomaz Mastnak, "Politics and New Social Movements in Yugoslavia," *Across Frontiers* (Spring 1987): 13.

47 Tanjug, 28 July 1988, in FBIS, 4 August 1988, 51.

48 *Život Strany*, no. 1 (3 Jan. 1987): 37–38, quoted in Czechoslovak Situation Report, *RFER*, 6 Mar. 1987, 21.

49 Wolf Oschlies, *Kinder der "Solidarität." Zu Geschichte und Gegenwart der Jugendbewegung in Polen* (Cologne: Bundesinstitut für ostwissenschaftliche und internationale Studien, report no. 24, 1981), 19.

50 *Trybuna Robotnicza* (Katowice), 1 Mar. 1982, 2, summarized in FBIS, 16 Mar. 1982, G20.

51 Roman Dumas, "Poland's 'Independent Society,'" *Poland Watch*, no. 8 (1986): 72.

52 Polish Situation Report, *RFER*, 12 Mar. 1987, 13.

53 *Tribuna*, 21 May 1988, 17, cited in Czechoslovak Situation Report, *RFER*, 28 June 1988, 29.

54 Czechoslovak Situation Report, *RFER*, 20 Dec. 1984, 25.

55 Vera Gavrilov, "The Komsomol and Bulgarian Youth in the Post-Zhivkov Era," *Radio Free Europe: Report on Eastern Europe* 1, no. 11 (16 Mar. 1990): 2, 5.

56 Velimir Tomanović, "O idejnim i vrednosnim opredeljenjima omladine," in *Mlada generacija danas: Društveni položaj, uloga i perspektive mlade generacije Jugoslavije* (Belgrade: Mladost, 1982), 180.

57 Ibid., 176–77.

58 Quoted in Christine Lemke, "Youth and Youth Policy in GDR Society," in *Studies in GDR Culture and Society*, ed. Margy Gerber (New York: University Press of America, 1983), 3:102–3.

59 Oschlies, *Rumäniens Jugend*, 124, 138–39; Oschlies, *Jugend in der Tschechoslowakei*, 313.

60 Oschlies, *Jugend in der Tschechoslowakei*, 220; Oschlies, *Rumäniens Jugend*, 217; Furio Radin, "Vrijednosti jugoslavenske omladine," in *Položaj, svest i ponašanje mlade generacije Jugoslavije: Preliminarna analiza rezultata istraživanja* (Zagreb: IDIS, 1986), 58.

61 Quoted in *Życie Warszawy*, 25 May 1983, 1, as cited in Oschlies, "*Verlorene Generation*," 21.

62 Ibid.

63 Quoted in Oschlies, "*Verlorene Generation*," 23.

12. Bulgaria: A Weak Society

1 Bulgarian Situation Report, *RFER,* 24 Sept. 1980.

2 Paul Marer, "The Economies and Trade of Eastern Europe," in *Central and Eastern Europe: The Opening Curtain?,* ed. William E. Griffith (Boulder, Colo.: Westview Press, 1989), 40.

3 *Index on Censorship* 11, no. 4 (Aug. 1982): 38.

4 In *Zemedelsko Zname,* as reported in Bulgarian Situation Report, *RFER,* 8 June 1984, 11–12.

5 Bulgarski Zhurnalist (Sofia), no. 7 (1983), trans. in *JPRS,* no. 84227 (30 Aug. 1983): 13.

6 *Los Angeles Times,* 1 May 1977, pt. 5, 4.

7 Bulgarian Situation Report, *RFER,* 14 Apr. 1989, 18.

8 Among the first public opinion polls published in the Bulgarian press were a poll on the National Assembly session, published in *Rabotnichesko delo* (Sofia) on 23 Nov. 1989, and a poll on the decisions of the Politburo, published in the same newspaper on 30 Nov. 1989.

9 Robert Sharlet, "Human Rights and Civil Society in Eastern Europe," in Griffith, *Central and Eastern Europe,* 171; Bulgarian Situation Report, *RFER,* 24 Oct. 1988, 15.

10 Bulgarian Situation Report, *RFER,* 9 Mar. 1989, 17.

11 *Keston News Service,* no. 333 (7 Aug. 1989): 3.

12 Sofia Domestic Service, 17 Jan. 1990, trans. in *FBIS,* 18 Jan. 1990, 8.

13 *Rabotnichesko delo,* 1 Dec. 1989, 2, trans. in *FBIS,* 7 Dec. 1989, 21.

14 *BTA* (Sofia), 28 Sept. 1989, trans. in *FBIS,* 2 Oct. 1989, p. 10.

15 Full text in Bulgarian Situation Report, *RFER,* 22 May 1989, 16–18.

16 See the interview with Nedjo Gendzhev, chief mufti of Sofia, in *Trud* (Sofia), 31 Aug. 1989, 1–2.

17 See Horst Dieter Topp, "Die türkische Minderheit in Bulgarien," *Wissenschaftlicher Dienst Südosteuropa,* 27, no. 5 (May 1978): 142–43.

18 *The Guardian of Liberty (Nemzetör)* (Munich), May–June 1989, 10; *New York Times,* 24 May 1989, A8.

19 *Süddeutsche Zeitung* (Munich), 27–28 May 1989, 6; Bulgarian Situation Report, *RFER,* 5 Oct. 1989, 9.

20 *Rabotnichesko delo,* 16 Sept. 1989, 2.

21 *Keston News Service,* no. 333 (7 Aug. 1989): 3.

22 Sofia Domestic Service, 17 Nov. 1989, trans. in *FBIS,* 20 Nov. 1989, 6.

23 *BTA,* 18 Nov. 1989, in *FBIS,* 20 Nov. 1989, 7.

24 *BTA,* 30 Dec. 1989, in *FBIS,* 4 Jan. 1990, 13.

25 *BTA,* 4 Jan. 1990, in *FBIS,* 4 Jan. 1990, 11.

26 *Rabotnichesko delo,* 8 Jan. 1990, 1, 2, trans. in *FBIS,* 12 Jan. 1990, 10.

27 *New York Times,* 1 Jan. 1990, 7, and 3 Jan. 1990, A6.

28 Quoted in *Christian Science Monitor,* 18 Jan. 1990, 3.

29 *Keston News Service,* no. 346 (22 Mar. 1990): 11.

30 Both quoted in *New York Times,* 12 June 1990, A8.

31 Quoted in ibid., 7 Oct. 1989, 5.

32 *Anteni* (Sofia), no. 2 (25 Jan. 1989): 8.

33 *New York Times,* 4 Nov. 1989, 4.

34 Yana Bozhina, an English teacher from Sofia, quoted in *New York Times*, 13 Nov. 1989, A9.
35 Deyan Kiuranov, quoted in ibid.

13. Strong Societies: Hungary, Poland, and Yugoslavia

1 Paul Marer, "The Economies and Trade of Eastern Europe," in *Central and Eastern Europe: The Opening Curtain?*, ed. William E. Griffith (Boulder, Colo.: Westview Press, 1989), 40.
2 Władysław Markiewicz, "Change in Social Structure and the Increased Significance of the Working Class," in *The Polish Dilemma: Views from Within*, ed. Lawrence S. Graham and Maria K. Ciechocinska (Boulder, Colo.: Westview Press, 1987), 77–78.
3 The Committee for the Protection of Artistic Freedom (organized in 1982) and the Committee for the Protection of Humanity and the Environment (organized in 1986) were associated with the Serbian Association of Writers. The Committee for the Defense of Freedom of Thought and Expression (organized in 1984) was associated with the Serbian Academy of Sciences.
4 Interview with Miklós Haraszti, "Hungary in 1989: The Transition to a Post-Communist Society?," *Uncaptive Minds* 2, no. 1 (Jan.–Feb. 1989): 2.
5 R. Nyers, "Efficiency and Socialist Democracy," *Acta Oeconomica* 37, no. 1–2 (1986): 1, 2.
6 "Hungary: Grósz and Company," *Eastern Europe Newsletter* 2, no. 20 (Oct. 1988): 7; "Hungary: Battle Lines Drawn," *Eastern Europe Newsletter* 2, no. 22 (9 Nov. 1988): 4–5.
7 Quoted in Hungarian Situation Report, RFER, 17 Nov. 1988, 4, my emphasis.
8 *Süddeutsche Zeitung* (Munich), 17–18 Dec. 1988, 8.
9 Hungarian Situation Report, RFER, 15 Dec. 1988, 18.
10 MTI (Budapest), 16 Nov. 1988, in FBIS, 17 Nov. 1988, 31.
11 The New March Front describes itself as a movement, not a party, and does not maintain a membership roster. MTI, 11 Jan. 1989, in FBIS, 11 Jan. 1989, 46.
12 The average monthly wage in the industry is about 7,000 forints (U.S. $130).
13 Budapest Domestic Service, 18 Feb. 1989, trans. in FBIS, 21 Feb. 1989, 23; *Süddeutsche Zeitung*, 25–26 Feb. 1989, 11; Budapest Domestic Service, 12 Apr. 1989, trans. in FBIS, 13 Apr. 1989, 19; MTI, 28 Apr. 1989, in FBIS, 1 May 1989, 37; *Keston News Service*, no. 330 (20 July 1989): 9; Budapest Domestic Service, 22 July 1989, trans. in FBIS, 24 July 1989, 19.
14 Budapest Domestic Service, 18 Feb. 1989, trans. in FBIS, 21 Feb. 1989, 24.
15 MTI, 31 Dec. 1988, in FBIS, 9 Jan. 1989, 25.
16 *Népszabadság* (Budapest), 16 Feb. 1989, 3, trans. in FBIS, 22 Feb. 1989, 20, 21.
17 *Financial Times* (London), 17 Feb. 1989, 16.
18 Budapest Television Service, 19 Feb. 1989, trans. in FBIS, 24 Feb. 1989, 19.
19 *Pravda* (Moscow), 4 Mar. 1989, 4.
20 *New York Times*, 2 Apr. 1989, 4.
21 Ibid., 17 Apr. 1989, 7.
22 Ibid., 13 Oct. 1989, A6.
23 Ibid., 25 Apr. 1989, 4.
24 MTI, 17 Apr. 1989, in FBIS, 20 Apr. 1989, 27.

25 *New York Times*, 20 May 1989, 6.

26 Radio Budapest, 6 May 1989, as reported in Hungarian Situation Report, RFER, 17 May 1989, 3.

27 *New York Times*, 14 Feb. 1990, A9.

28 *Frankfurter Allgemeine*, 8 Oct. 1988, 3.

29 *Berlingske Tidende* (Copenhagen), 24 Sept. 1988, 8, trans. in FBIS, 5 Oct. 1988, 27.

30 *New York Times*, 9 Feb. 1989, 5.

31 *Süddeutsche Zeitung*, 11–12 Feb. 1989, 6; *New York Times*, 13 Feb. 1989, 4.

32 *New York Times*, 7 May 1989, 4.

33 *Keston News Service*, no. 330 (20 July 1989): 4.

34 *Süddeutsche Zeitung*, 25–27 Mar. 1989, 6; *Glas koncila* (Zagreb), 13 Aug. 1989, 1.

35 Budapest Domestic Service, 1 June 1989, trans. in FBIS, 6 June 1989, 25.

36 Budapest Domestic Service, 3 Aug. 1989, trans. in FBIS, 7 Aug. 1989, 19.

37 *New York Times*, 24 July 1989, A2.

38 MTI, 22 Apr. 1989, in FBIS, 26 Apr. 1989, 36; MTI, 15 Aug. 1989, in FBIS, 17 Aug. 1989, 23. By coincidence, the first elected chairman of the new Democratic Youth Federation was a thirty-two-year-old mathematician with the name, Imre Nagy.

39 See summaries in Budapest Domestic Service, 18 Aug. 1989, trans. in FBIS, 24 Aug. 1989, 31–32; and MTI, 18 Aug. 1989, in ibid., 32–33.

40 *New York Times*, 7 Nov. 1989, A7.

41 *Frankfurter Allgemeine*, 9 Oct. 1989, 1, 10 Oct. 1989, 1, and 11 Oct. 1989, 1–2; *Christian Science Monitor*, 10 Oct. 1989, 4; *New York Times*, 19 Oct. 1989, A8, 20 Oct. 1989, A10, and 21 Oct. 1989, 3.

42 Warsaw Domestic Service, 31 Dec. 1988, trans. in FBIS, 3 Jan. 1989, 49; *Christian Science Monitor*, 13 Feb. 1989, 19.

43 *News Solidarność* (Brussels), 1–15 Sept. 1988, 4.

44 Ibid., 1–15 Jan. 1989, 1.

45 Ibid., 16–30 Nov. 1988, 2–3.

46 Abraham Brumberg, "Poland: State and/or Society," *Dissent* 36, no. 1 (Winter 1989): 49.

47 Quoted in *Christian Science Monitor*, 22 Nov. 1988, 13.

48 Quoted in ibid., 26 Aug. 1988, 9.

49 David Ost, "The Transformation of Solidarity and the Future of Central Europe," *Telos*, no. 79 (Spring 1989): 94.

50 John Tagliabue, "Lech! Lech! Lech!," *New York Times Magazine*, 23 Oct. 1988, 37.

51 *News Solidarność*, 15–31 Oct. 1988, 1; *Süddeutsche Zeitung*, 29–30 Oct. 1988, 2.

52 *News Solidarność* 1–15 Oct. 1988, 1.

53 *La Repubblica* (Rome), 4 Mar. 1989, 12.

54 Quoted in *Christian Science Monitor*, 13 Apr. 1989, 6.

55 Quoted in *New York Times*, 27 July 1989, A1.

56 *Corriere della Sera* (Milan), 12 Aug. 1989, 1.

57 Quoted in *New York Times*, 24 Aug. 1989, A1.

58 Quoted in ibid., 25 Aug. 1989, A4.

59 Quoted in ibid.

60 Quoted in ibid.

61 Warsaw Television Service (May 25, 1989), trans. in FBIS, 26 May 1989, 30; *Süddeutsche Zeitung*, 27–28 May 1989, 6.

62 Warsaw Television Service, 13 Dec. 1988, trans. in FBIS, 14 Dec. 1988, 53; *Trybuna Ludu* (Warsaw), 13 Feb. 1989, 2; Warsaw Domestic Service, 25 Feb. 1989 and 8 May 1989, trans. in FBIS, 27 Feb. 1989, 32, and 9 May 1989, 39; AFP, 5 Mar. 1989, in FBIS, 6 Mar. 1989, 33; Warsaw Television Service, 17 May 1989, trans. in FBIS, 18 May 1989, 34; Warsaw Domestic Service, 22 June 1989, trans. in FBIS, 23 June 1989, 53; PAP, 15 Sept. 1989, in FBIS, 18 Sept. 1989, 47.

63 *Süddeutsche Zeitung*, 11–12 Feb. 1989, 6, and 25–27 Mar. 1989, 6.

64 Warsaw Domestic Service, 15 Sept. 1989, trans. in FBIS, 18 Sept. 1989, 47.

65 *New York Times*, 7 Oct. 1989, A2.

66 *Christian Science Monitor*, 12 Sept. 1989, 4.

67 *New York Times*, 21 Oct. 1989, 4.

68 Paul Shoup, "Crisis and Reform in Yugoslavia," *Telos*, no. 79 (Spring 1979): 141.

69 Some of these groups are described in Pedro Ramet, "Yugoslavia 1987: Stirrings from Below," *South Slav Journal* 10, no. 3 (Autumn 1987).

70 Interview, Ljubljana, 4 Sept. 1989.

71 *Independent Voices from Slovenia* 5, no. 1 (Jan. 1989): 8.

72 Interviews in Ljubljana with France Tomšić, 4 Sept. 1989; Hubert Požarnik, 6 Sept. 1989; and Dimitrij Rupel, 6 Sept. 1989.

73 *Independent Voices from Slovenia* 5, no. 1 (Jan. 1989): 7.

74 *Svet* (Belgrade), special issue, Sept. 1989: 7.

75 Interview with Marija Markes, secretary of the Slovenian Peasant Alliance, Ljubljana, 1 Sept. 1989.

76 Interview with Dušan Semolić, secretary of the Republican Committee of SAWP-Slovenia, Ljubljana, 5 Sept. 1989.

77 Interview, Zagreb, 13 Sept. 1989.

78 Interview, Zagreb, 29 Aug. 1989.

79 As cited in Slaven Letica, *Četvrta Jugoslavija* (Zagreb: CIP, 1989), manuscript, chap. 3.

80 Ibid., and interview, Zagreb, 11 Sept. 1989. For a full account of the circumstances leading up to the closure of Matica hrvatska, see Sabrina P. Ramet, *Nationalism and Federalism in Yugoslavia, 1962–1991*, 2nd ed. (Bloomington: Indiana University Press, 1992), chapter 7 ("The Croatian Crisis, 1967–72").

81 Quoted in Yugoslav Situation Report, *RFER*, 26 May 1989, 36.

82 Ibid.

83 For details, see Sabrina Petra Ramet, *Balkan Babel: Politics, Culture, and Religion in Yugoslavia* (Boulder, Colo.: Westview Press, 1992), chap. 2 ("The Gathering Storm, 1987–1989").

14. Dominoes: East Germany, Czechoslovakia, and the Future of Europe

1 Conversations, East Germany, summer 1988.

2 *Welt am Sonntag* (Bonn), 4 June 1989, 1, trans. in FBIS, 5 June 1989, 6.

3 Ending with the large-scale Albanian riots in Kosovo in April 1981.

4 Quoted in *New York Times*, 7 Nov. 1987, 4.

5 *Rinascita*, 18 Apr. 1987, quoted in Kevin Devlin, "Italian Communist on Contradictions and Crisis in Eastern Europe," *RFER*, 5 June 1987, 2.

6 I would argue that the onset of political decay in communist East Germany did not actually commence until October or even November 1989.

7   Boris Rumer, "Realities of Gorbachev's Economic Program," *Problems of Communism* 35, no. 3 (May–June 1986): 25; *New York Times*, 1 Aug. 1988; *Financial Times* (London), 3 Aug. 1988, 16.

8   *Christian Science Monitor*, 29 Aug. 1988, 7; Bohdan Nahaylo, "Interview with Tat'yana Zaslavskaya," *Radio Liberty Research*, 15 Sept. 1987, 6.

9   *Chicago Tribune*, 20 Mar. 1990, 9.

10 *Frankfurter Rundschau*, 21 June 1988, 3; *New York Times*, 22 Oct. 1988, 3.

11 *New York Times*, 24 May 1988, 8.

12 *Christian Science Monitor*, 19 Feb. 1988, 32.

13 See Edward Kardelj, *Democracy and Socialism*, trans. Margot and Boško Milosavljević (London: Summerfield, 1978).

14 Quoted in *New York Times*, 6 Feb. 1990, A6.

15 *Financial Times*, 14 June 1988, 2.

16 Cited in *Seattle Times*, 7 Oct. 1988, B2.

17 *Pravda*, cited in *Süddeutsche Zeitung* (Munich), 27–28 Aug. 1988, 6.

18 Reported in *Vjesnik* (Zagreb), 26 Dec. 1987, 3; *New York Times*, 4 Feb. 1989, 1.

19 Vasily Selyunin, "Istoki," *Novyi Mir*, no. 5 (May 1988): 162–89.

20 Julia Wishnevsky, "Grossman's Exposé of Lenin to be Published in USSR," *Radio Liberty Research*, 3 Aug. 1988, 1–2.

21 *Izvestiia*, 3 Apr. 1988, 6, excerpted in Josephine Woll, "Fruits of Glasnost," *Dissent* 36, no. 1 (Winter 1989): 26.

22 *New York Times*, 6 Apr. 1989, 6, and 18 Aug. 1989, A6.

23 *New York Times*, 25 July 1989, A4; *Corriera della Sera* (Milan), 12 Aug. 1989, 4; *New York Times*, 19 Aug. 1989, 1.

24 Quoted in *New York Times*, 19 Feb. 1988, 1, 4.

25 Ibid., 7 Apr. 1990, 5.

26 *Washington Post*, 9 Nov. 1986, H5.

27 Quoted in *New York Times*, 31 Oct. 1986, A11.

28 *Washington Post*, 8 Jan. 1987, A1, and 13 Feb. 1987, A35.

29 Mikhail Shatrov, "Dal'she . . . dal'she . . . dal'she," in *Znamya*, no. 1 (January 1988): 3–53.

30 For further discussion, see Sabrina Petra Ramet, Sergei Zamascikov, and Robert Bird, "The Soviet Rock Scene," in *Rocking the State: Rock Music and Politics in Eastern Europe and Russia*, ed. Sabrina Petra Ramet (Boulder, Colo., Westview Press, 1994).

31 See *Washington Post*, 9 May 1988, B1, B11. For further discussion of Gorbachev's effect on cultural policy, see John B. Dunlop, "Soviet Cultural Politics," *Problems of Communism* 36, no. 6 (Nov.–Dec. 1987).

32 Details in Pedro Ramet, "Gorbachev's Reforms and Religion," in *Candle in the Wind: Religion in the Soviet Union*, ed. Eugene B. Shirley, Jr., and Michael Rowe (Washington, D.C.: Ethics and Public Policy Center, 1989).

33 See Christine Engel, " 'Pamjat.' 'Gedenken und Erinnern' als zentrale Begriffe im kulturellen Leben der heutigen Sowjetunion," *Osteuropa* 37, no. 12 (Dec. 1987): 891–903.

34 *New York Times*, 10 May 1988, 7.

35 Ibid., 9 Oct. 1987, 4, and 19 Oct. 1987, 8.

36 *Frankfurter Rundschau*, 24 June 1988, 3.

37 *New York Times*, 19 May 1988, 6. See also AFP, 12 Dec. 1987, in FBIS, *Daily Report* (Soviet Union), 17 Dec. 1987, 57.

38 *New York Times,* 24 Aug. 1988, 6.
39 Ibid., 19 May 1989, 1.
40 Bohdan Nahaylo, "Political Demonstration in Minsk Attests to Belorussian National Assertiveness," *Radio Liberty Research,* 26 Nov. 1987, 1.
41 *Vjesnik,* 19 July 1988, 3.
42 *Christian Science Monitor,* 17 June 1988, 9.
43 *New York Times,* 8 Sept. 1988, 8.
44 Vladimir A. Rubanov, "Ot 'Kul'ta sekretnosti': K informatsionnoi Kul'ture," *Kommunist,* no. 13 (Sept. 1988): 24–36.
45 *Financial Times,* 3–4 Sept. 1988, 1.
46 *New York Times,* 23 May 1989, A7.
47 Reported in *Chicago Tribune,* 5 Nov. 1989, 12.
48 *New York Times,* 4 Nov. 1989, 5.
49 Ibid., 23 July 1988, 3; *Frankfurter Allgemeine,* 27 July 1988, 2.
50 Quoted in "Weekly Record of Events," RFER, 22–28 Oct. 1987, 6.
51 *Neues Deutschland,* 6 Oct. 1987.
52 Ibid., 6 Sept. 1988, 2.
53 Czechoslovak Situation Report, RFER, 27 Nov. 1987, 11.
54 *New York Times,* 30 July 1988, 4.
55 See Pedro Ramet, "Self-Management, Titoism, and the Apotheosis of Praxis," in *War and Society in East Central Europe,* ed. Wayne S. Vucinich, vol. 10, *At the Brink of War and Peace: The Tito-Stalin Split in a Historic Perspective* (New York: Brooklyn College Press, 1982), 169–94.
56 That is, of course, the purpose behind his export of perestroika to Eastern Europe and his restructuring of COMECON. See Pedro Ramet, "Gorbachev's Dilemmas in Eastern Europe," in *Gorbachev and the Soviet Future,* ed. Lawrence W. Lerner and Donald W. Treadgold (Boulder, Colo.: Westview Press, 1988).
57 Later, at the 28th CPSU Congress in July 1990, Gorbachev had to defend himself against charges that he had "lost" Eastern Europe.
58 *Party Preferences in Hypothetical Free Elections in Czechoslovakia, Hungary, and Poland* (Munich: Radio Free Europe/Radio Liberty, August 1981).
59 Re Romania, see Trond Gilberg, "Ethnic Minorities in Romania under Socialism," *East European Quarterly* 7, no. 4 (Jan. 1974): 435–58; and Hans Hartl, "Nationalitätenpolitik und Nationalismus in Rumänien," in *Nationalitätenprobleme in der Sowjetunion und Osteuropa,* ed. Georg Brunner and Boris Meissner (Cologne: Markus Verlag, 1982), 151–64. Re Bulgaria, see Wolfgang Höpken, "Modernisierung und Nationalismus: Sozialgeschichtliche Aspekte der bulgarischen Minderheitenpolitik gegenüber den Türken," in *Nationalitätenprobleme in Südosteuropa,* ed. Roland Schonfeld (Munich: R. Oldenbourg Verlag, 1987); and Zachary T. Irwin, "The Fate of Islam in the Balkans: A Comparison of Four State Politics," in *Religion and Nationalism in Soviet and East European Politics,* ed. Pedro Ramet, rev. and expanded ed. (Durham, N.C.: Duke University Press, 1989), 378–407.
60 DPA (Hamburg), 13 Mar. 1989, in FBIS, 14 Mar. 1989, 23.
61 *Süddeutsche Zeitung,* 22–23 October 1988, 5; *Die Welt* (Hamburg), 24 Nov. 1988, 4; *Christian Science Monitor,* 23 Jan. 1989, 18, and 24 Feb. 1989, 3; *Der Standard* (Vienna), 15 Mar. 1989, 3, trans. in FBIS, 15 Mar. 1989, 15.
62 For example, Alfred Kosing, "Zur Dialektik der weiteren Gestaltung der entwickelten sozialistischen Gesellschaft," *Deutsche Zeitschrift für Philosophie*

36, no. 7 (1988): Also Johannes Becher's article in *Sinn und Form*, no. 3 (1988), analyzed in Manfred Jäger, "Anti-stalinistisches aus dem Johannes R. Becher-Archiv," *Deutschland Archiv* 21, no. 7 (July 1988): 695–98.

63   For example, Mainz ZDF Television Network, 7 July 1989, and DPA 8 July 1989, both trans. in FBIS, 10 July 1989, 22; *Süddeutsche Zeitung*, 9–10 Sept. 1989, 1.

64   *Die Welt*, 16–17 Sept. 1989, 4; *Frankfurter Allgemeine*, 21 Sept. 1989, 2; *Glas koncila* (Zagreb), 24 Sept. 1989, 1, 4; *Neue Zürcher Zeitung*, 24–25 Sept. 1989, 3.

65   *Frankfurter Allgemeine*, 23 Sept. 1989, 2; 28 Sept. 1989, 5; and 4 Oct. 1989, 3.

66   Ibid., 18 Sept. 1989, 5.

67   *Politika* (Belgrade), 21 Oct. 1989, 1.

68   For the composition of the new Politburo, see *New York Times*, 9 Nov. 1989, A1, A8.

69   *Politika*, 28 Oct. 1989, 2.

70   *Lidova Demokracie* (Prague), 3 May 1989, 1, trans. in FBIS, 9 May 1989, 24; Czechoslovak Situation Report, RFER, 14 July 1989, 3.

71   Czechoslovak Situation Report, RFER, 18 May 1989, 7–10.

72   Ibid., 30 Sept. 1988, 27.

73   Ibid., 16 Feb. 1989, 21.

74   *Rudé pravo* (Prague), 5 May 1989, 5.

75   Ibid., 21 July 1989, 1.

76   Quoted in *Christian Science Monitor*, 13 Dec. 1988, 7.

77   Radio Hvezda, 14 June 1989, quoted in Czechoslovak Situation Report, RFER, 21 June 1989, 3.

78   Quoted in *New York Times*, 24 Nov. 1989, 1.

79   *New York Times*, 14 Nov. 1989, A9.

80   *Politika*, 1 Nov. 1989, 3.

81   AGERPRESS (Bucharest), 14 Sept. 1989, in FBIS, 15 Sept. 1989, C2.

82   *Scinteia* (Bucharest), 1 Sept. 1989, 1, 4, trans. in FBIS, 7 Sept. 1989, 51.

83   Quoted in Romanian Situation Report, RFER, 4 Aug. 1989, 11.

84   *Frankfurter Allgemeine*, 3 Oct. 1989, 6.

85   *New York Times*, 11 July 1989, A3.

86   Ibid., 24 Nov. 1989, A11.

87   *Newsweek*, 16 Oct. 1989, 46.

88   Quoted in *New York Times*, 18 Nov. 1989, 4.

89   *Christian Science Monitor*, 3 Nov. 1988, 1, 8.

90   *The Economist*, 12 Aug. 1989, 7; *Wall Street Journal*, 17 Nov. 1989, A10.

91   *Wall Street Journal*, 8 Nov. 1989, A12.

92   *Handelsblatt*, 25 July 1990, 8.

93   On Hungary, see MTI, 17 Feb. 1989, in FBIS, 23 Feb. 1989, 25–26.

94   *Chicago Tribune*, 3 Nov. 1989, 4; *New York Times*, 10 Nov. 1989, A19. Re the Alpine-Adriatic group, see *Frankfurter Allgemeine*, 6 Dec. 1988, 6.

95   *Süddeutsche Zeitung*, 1 Aug. 1990, 6, and 3 Aug. 1990, 10.

96   *New York Times*, 23 May 1990, A6.

97   *Rudé pravo*, 19 Jan. 1990, 15; *Der Standard* (Vienna), 25 Jan. 1990, 2.

98   *Süddeutsche Zeitung*, 11–12 Sept. 1993, 2.

99   *Die Welt*, 25 July 1990, 5; *Süddeutsche Zeitung*, 27 July 1990, 8, 31 July 1990, 6, and 22–23 July 1990, 9; *Neue Zürcher Zeitung*, 24 Jan. 1991, 3; *Daily Telegraph* (London), 7 Feb. 1991, 9, and 13 Feb. 1991, 10; *The Independent* (London), 25 Feb. 1991, 13.

100 CTK (Prague), 4 Jan. 1990, in FBIS, 5 Jan. 1990, 1; *New York Times*, 11 Jan. 1990, A8; *Rzeczpospolita* (Warsaw), 12 Jan. 1990, 1, trans. in FBIS, 25 Jan. 1990, 1; *Neues Deutschland*, 2 Oct. 1990, 1; *The Times*, 25 Feb. 1991, 12.

101 *Newsweek*, 16 Oct. 1989, 51.

102 Quoted in *New York Times*, 14 June 1990, A6.

103 Quoted in ibid.

104 *Neue Zürcher Zeitung*, 8 Sept. 1990, 13; *Wall Street Journal*, 14 Sept. 1990, A8.

105 Pedro Ramet, "Dissaffection and Dissent in East Germany," *World Politics* 37, no. 1 (Oct. 1984): 109, 110.

106 *Rudé pravo*, 5 Sept. 1988, 3, trans. in FBIS, 13 Sept. 1988, 12.

15. The Great Transformation

1 "Political Parties in Eastern Europe," RFER, 10 Feb. 1990; Tanjug, 16 Mar. 1990, in FBIS, 19 Mar. 1990, 84; ROMPRES, 28 Mar. 1990, in FBIS, 29 Mar. 1990, 47; *New York Times*, 8 June 1990, A5.

2 *Tineretul Liber* (Bucharest), 11 Jan. 1990, 1; BTA (Sofia), 17 Jan. 1990, 6, in FBIS, 25 Jan. 1990, 6; *New York Times*, 31 Jan. 1990, A6, and 11 May 1990, A4.

3 Budapest Domestic Service, 12 Oct. 1989, trans. in FBIS, 13 Oct. 1989, 44.

4 Blending of translations in ROMPRES, 21 Feb. 1990, in FBIS, 22 Feb. 1990, 78; *Adevarul* (Bucharest), 23 Feb. 1990, 1, in FBIS, 5 Mar. 1990, 61.

5 Quoted in *New York Times*, 11 May 1990, A4. Also Louis Zanga, "Significant Albanian Cultural Plenum," RFER, 19 May 1989; Louis Zanga, "Novel Criticizes Albanian Security Services," RFER, 15 Nov. 1989, 1.

6 *Zeri i popullit* (Tiranë), 11 Oct. 1989, 4, trans. in FBIS, 25 Oct. 1989, 2.

7 *New York Times*, 13 Jan. 1990, 5, and 10 May 1990, A1.

8 *The Economist*, 31 Mar. 1990, 49.

9 *Die Welt* (Bonn), 9 July 1990, 1; *Corriere della Sera* (Milan), 9 July 1990, 4.

10 *Die Welt*, 28–29 July 1990, 8; *Süddeutsche Zeitung* (Munich), 2 Aug. 1990, 7, 28.

11 *Frankfurter Allgemeine*, 1 Aug. 1990, 1; *Süddeutsche Zeitung*, 1 Aug. 1990, 2, and 13–14 Oct. 1990, 8.

12 Charles Gati, *The Bloc That Failed: Soviet-East European Relations in Transition* (Bloomington: Indiana University Press, 1990), 182–83, 187.

13 BTA, 27 Nov. 1989, in FBIS, 5 Dec. 1989, 5.

14 Sofia Domestic Service, 1 Feb. 1990, trans. in FBIS, 2 Feb. 1990, 4.

15 Simon Simonov, "New Face of the Bulgarian Writers' Union," *Radio Free Europe: Report on Eastern Europe* 1, no. 9 (2 Mar. 1990): 4–5.

16 BTA, 13 Dec. 1989, in FBIS, 14 Dec. 1989, 9.

17 *Narodna armiya* (Sofia), 5 Dec. 1989, 1, 2, trans. in FBIS, 14 Dec. 1989, 20.

18 *New York Times*, 3 Apr. 1990, A6.

19 BTA, 6 Feb. 1990, in FBIS, 7 Feb. 1990, 20.

20 BTA, 27 Feb. 1990, in FBIS, 7 Mar. 1990, 11.

21 Re *Dano*, see *Trud* (Sofia), 29 Mar. 1990, 3, summarized in FBIS, 2 Apr. 1990, 9.

22 *Der Spiegel*, 4 Dec. 1989, trans. in FBIS, 12 Dec. 1989, 12.

23 *Frankfurter Allgemeine*, 12 June 1990, 1.

24 Petar Mladenov resigned the presidency on 6 July after stirring controversy with remarks about using tanks against an antigovernment rally. His resignation was celebrated by more than 20,000 jubilant Bulgarians in downtown Sofia the following day. See *Frankfurter Allgemeine*, 16 June 1990, 2; *Süddeutsche Zeitung*,

23–24 June 1990, 8; *Los Angeles Times*, 7 July 1990, A1, and 8 July 1990, A6.

25 BTA, 14 Aug. 1990, in FBIS, 15 Aug. 1990, 7; BTA, 18 Aug. 1990, in FBIS, 20 Aug. 1990, 14.

26 Lukanov's proposed cabinet lineup was reported in *Frankfurter Allgemeine*, 22 Sept. 1990, 5. See also *International Herald Tribune*, 8 Aug. 1990, 2; *Welt am Sonntag* (Bonn), 23 Sept. 1990, 6.

27 BTA, 20 Sept. 1990, in FBIS, 24 Sept. 1990, 23; BTA, 5 Oct. 1990, in FBIS, 9 Oct. 1990, 4; BTA, 10 Oct. 1990, in FBIS, 11 Oct. 1990, 1.

28 *Süddeutsche Zeitung*, 24 July 1990, 7; *Die Welt*, 26 July 1990, 6; *Frankfurter Allgemeine*, 20 Sept. 1990, 16; *New York Times*, 21 Sept. 1990, A3.

29 *Mladezh* (Sofia), 10 Oct. 1990, 1–2, in FBIS, 16 Oct. 1990, 5–6.

30 Quoted in Czechoslovak Situation Report, RFER, 24 Aug. 1989, 17.

31 Quoted in ibid., 27 Oct. 1989, 9.

32 *Seattle Post-Intelligencer*, 30 May 1990.

33 AFP, 17 Nov. 1989, in FBIS, 20 Nov. 1989, 19.

34 AFP, 18 Nov. 1989, in FBIS, 20 Nov. 1989, 20.

35 *Lidova demokracie* (Prague), 21 Nov. 1989, 1, trans. in FBIS, 28 Nov. 1989, 25.

36 Re the Transnational Radical Party, see *Večerni Praha* (Prague), 20 Feb. 1990, 5, summarized in FBIS, 7 Mar. 1990, 29–30.

37 *Večernik* (Bratislava), 16 Mar. 1990, 1, trans. in FBIS, 22 Mar. 1990, 25.

38 CTK (Prague), 17 Mar. 1990, in FBIS, 19 Mar. 1990, 34.

39 *Smena* (Bratislava), 8 Mar. 1990, 2, 3, trans. in FBIS, *East Europe Report*, 19 Mar. 1990, 34.

40 *Rudé pravo* (Prague), 22 Dec. 1990, 1989, 2, trans. in FBIS, 13 Mar. 1990, 21.

41 *Pravda* (Bratislava), 27 Feb. 1990, 1, 2.

42 Ibid., 19 Feb. 1990, 2.

43 *Prače* (Prague), 16 Feb. 1990, 1, 2, in trans. FBIS, 23 Feb. 1990, 19.

44 *Wall Street Journal*, 20 June 1990, A16.

45 *Los Angeles Times*, 28 June 1990, A11.

46 CTK (Prague), 14 Sept. 1990, in FBIS, 19 Sept. 1990, 27.

47 *Eurobusiness*, June 1990, 46.

48 *Neue Zürcher Zeitung*, 6 Sept. 1990, 15; *Wall Street Journal*, 26 Oct. 1990, A8.

49 *Süddeutsche Zeitung*, 3 Aug. 1990, 7.

50 *Narodna obroda* (Bratislava), 18 Sept. 1990, 2, trans. in FBIS, 28 Sept. 1990, 14; confirmed in *New York Times*, 16 Oct. 1990, A6.

51 *Welt am Sonntag*, 23 Sept. 1990, 6.

52 Quoted in *New York Times*, 12 Oct. 1990, A3.

53 ADN International Service (Berlin), 20 Nov. 1989, in FBIS, 20 Nov. 1989, 47.

54 *Bild* (Hamburg), 9 Nov. 1989, 3.

55 ADN International Service, 20 Nov. 1989, in FBIS, 20 Nov. 1989, 49.

56 Ibid., 1 Dec. 1989 and 4 Dec. 1989, both in FBIS, 5 Dec. 1989, 41.

57 Ibid., 4 Dec. 1989, in FBIS, 4 Dec. 1989, 40; *New York Times*, 5 Jan. 1990, A5.

58 Doubts about the successful completion of the abolition of the Stasi were expressed in June 1990. See *Süddeutsche Zeitung*, 23–24 June 1990, 5.

59 *Neues Deutschland* (Berlin), 15 Jan. 1990, 2.

60 *New York Times*, 20 Jan. 1990, 5.

61 As reported in ADN International Service, 12 Dec. 1989, in FBIS, 12 Dec. 1989, 32.

62 Ibid., 5 Jan. 1990, in FBIS, 8 Jan. 1990, 57.

63 *Neues Deutschland*, 7 Mar. 1990, 5.

64 *Toronto Star*, 20 May 1990, H2.

65 *Frankfurter Allgemeine*, 5 June 1990, 4.

66 The treaty is published in *Neue Zürcher Zeitung*, 23 May 1990, 7–8. See also *Christian Science Monitor*, 22 Dec. 1989, 8; *New York Times*, 3 May 1990, A6, and 12 June 1990, A6; *Wall Street Journal*, 11 May 1990, A9; *Globe and Mail* (Toronto), 19 May 1990, A2.

67 *Frankfurter Allgemeine*, 13 June 1990, 1; *Corriere della Sera*, 1 July 1990, 1, 4, and 2 July 1990, 2; *Los Angeles Times*, 4 July 1990, A8.

68 *New York Times*, 5 June 1990, A7, 13 June 1990, A1, 23 June 1990, 1, 4; *San Francisco Examiner*, 23 June 1990, A20; *Süddeutsche Zeitung*, 23–24 June 1990, A20.

69 *Der Spiegel*, 7 May 1990, 278, 280.

70 *Frankfurter Allgemeine*, 9 July 1990, 5.

71 *Die Welt*, 26 July 1990, 1; *Süddeutsche Zeitung*, 27 July 1990, 6, and 2 Aug. 1990, 2; *New York Times*, 1 Nov. 1990, A9.

72 Kathrin Sitzler, "Die Anfänge eines politischen Pluarlismus in Ungarn," *Südost-Europa* 38, nos. 11–12 (Nov.–Dec. 1989): 679.

73 Budapest Domestic Service, 3 Mar. 1990, and Budapest Television Service, 3 Mar. 1990, both trans. in FBIS, 5 Mar. 1990, 47–48.

74 *Népszabadság* (Budapest), 14 Dec. 1989, 5, trans. in FBIS, 29 Dec. 1989, 58.

75 Budapest Domestic Service, 7 Jan. 1990, trans. in FBIS, 19 Jan. 1990, 49.

76 Budapest Television Service, 3 Dec. 1989, trans. in FBIS, 7 Dec. 1989, 79.

77 Ibid., 29 Oct. 1989, trans. in FBIS, 1 Nov. 1989, 43–45.

78 *Christian Science Monitor*, 3 Jan. 1990, 6.

79 Quoted in ibid., 12 Feb. 1990, 6.

80 *Chicago Tribune*, 25 Mar. 1990, 6; *The Economist*, 31 Mar. 1990, 47.

81 *New York Times*, 31 May 1990, A7.

82 *Los Angeles Times*, 27 June 1990, A8.

83 Budapest Domestic Service, 15 Mar. 1990, trans. in FBIS, 19 Mar. 1990, 62–63; *Bloc* (Feb.–Mar. 1990): 21–22; *New York Times*, 12 May 1990, 4.

84 *Frankfurter Allgemeine*, 24 July 1990, 11; *Süddeutsche Zeitung*, 24 July 1990, 1, and 25 July 1990, 7.

85 Károly Okolicsanyi, "Privatization: Two Cautious Steps," *RFER*, 19 Oct. 1990, 24.

86 *Neue Zürcher Zeitung*, 17 Oct. 1990, 16; *Daily Telegraph*, 2 Nov. 1990, 11.

87 Louisa Vinton, "Privatization Plan Prepared," *Radio Free Europe: Report on Eastern Europe* 1, no. 14 (6 Apr. 1990): 29.

88 *Christian Science Monitor*, 26 Jan. 1990, 4.

89 *New York Times*, 28 May 1990, 5.

90 Ibid., 19 June 1990, A1.

91 *Trybuna* (Warsaw), 2 Mar. 1990, 1, trans. in FBIS, 7 Mar. 1990, 63.

92 Warsaw Domestic Service, 30 Dec. 1989, trans. in FBIS, 2 Jan. 1990, 45.

93 *The Economist*, 21 Apr. 1990, 51; *Wall Street Journal*, 5 June 1990, A1.

94 *Los Angeles Times*, 7 July 1990, A19.

95 *New York Times*, 1 Feb. 1990, A9.

96 The results were published 7 months later. See Louisa Vinton, "Disintegration of Polish Communist Party Continues Unabated," *RFER*, 28 Nov. 1989, 3–4.

97 *Neue Zürcher Zeitung*, 6 Sept. 1990, 17; *Financial Times*, 7 Sept. 1990, 6.

98 *New York Times*, 14 Aug. 1990, 14.

99   Quoted in *Wall Street Journal,* 31 Aug. 1990, A8.

100   *Süddeutsche Zeitung,* 29–30 Sept. 1990, 7.

101   See Konstanty Gebert, "Anti-Semitism in the 1990 Polish Presidential Election," *Social Research* 58, no. 4 (Winter 1991).

102   *Polityka,* 14 July 1990, 14, trans. in FBIS, 6 Sept. 1990, 36–37.

103   *New York Times,* 14 Aug. 1990, A2.

104   *Welt am Sonntag,* 9 Sept. 1990, 3.

105   *New York Times,* 17 May 1990, A4.

106   *Scînteia,* 1 Nov. 1989, excerpted in AGERPRES, 1 Nov. 1989, in FBIS, 7 Nov. 1989, 65.

107   *New York Times,* 4 Jan. 1990, A8.

108   Romanian Situation Report, RFER, 14 Dec. 1989, 15.

109   Re the overthrow of Ceauşescu and Iliescu's seizure of power, see Anneli Ute Gabanyi, *Die unvollendete Revolution: Rumänien zwischen Diktatur und Demokratie* (Munich: R. Piper, 1990); Anneli Ute Gabanyi, "Rumäniens unvollendete Revolution," *Südost Europa* 39, nos. 3–4 (Mar.–Apr. 1990); Robert Hamerton-Kelly and István Szónyi, "The Nature of the Romanian Regime (1989–1991)," *Österreichische Osthefte* 35, no. 1 (1993); Matei Calinescu and Vladimir Tismaneanu, "The 1989 Revolution and Romania's Future," in *Romania After Tyranny,* ed. Daniel N. Nelson (Boulder, Colo.: Westview Press, 1992).

110   Quoted in AFP, 19 Dec. 1989, in FBIS, 20 Dec. 1989, 66.

111   ROMPRES, 9 Mar. 1990, in FBIS, 12 Mar. 1990, 67; ROMPRES, 23 Mar. 1990, in FBIS, 26 Mar. 1990, 47.

112   ROMPRES, 24 Feb. 1990, in FBIS, 27 Feb. 1990, 67.

113   *Toronto Sunday Star,* 20 May 1990, A1.

114   *Globe and Mail* (Toronto), 18 May 1990, A7.

115   *Neue Zürcher Zeitung,* 24–25 May 1990, 2.

116   *New York Times,* 2 June 1990, 9.

117   Ibid., 15 June 1990, A1, A6, and 16 June 1990, 4.

118   Quoted in ibid., 18 June 1990, A1.

119   See the argument in Radoslav Stojanović, *Jugoslavija nacije i politika* (Belgrade: Nova knjiga, 1988), esp. 171–207.

120   *Los Angeles Times,* 2 July 1990, A10.

121   Interview, Ljubljana, 4 Sept. 1989.

122   Interview, Ljubljana, 1 Sept. 1989.

123   Re the Croatian party, see Tanjug, 10 Mar. 1990, in FBIS, 12 Mar. 1990, 80.

124   Belgrade Domestic Service, 4 Feb. 1990, in FBIS, 7 Feb. 1990, 67.

125   Tanjug, 27 Mar. 1990, in FBIS, 29 Mar. 1990, 52.

126   *Süddeutsche Zeitung,* 23–24 June 1990, 8.

127   Ibid. Re the Croatian elections, see Mirjana Kasapović, "The Structure and Dynamics of the Yugoslav Political Environment and Elections in Croatia," and Ivan Šiber, "The Impact of Nationalism, Values, and Ideological Orientations on Multi-Party Elections in Croatia," both in *The Tragedy of Yugoslavia: The Failure of Democratic Transformation,* ed. Jim Seroka and Vukašin Pavlović (Armonk, N.Y.: M. E. Sharpe, 1992). For reflections on the Slovenian elections by one of its presidential candidates, who puzzles over why he lost, see Ljubo Sirc, "Post Mortem—Elections in Slovenia," *South Slav Journal* 14, no. 1/2 (Spring/Summer 1991).

128   *Frankfurter Allgemeine,* 15 June 1990, 8.

129   Tanjug, 15 Mar. 1990, in FBIS, 22 Mar. 1990, 84.

130 *Los Angeles Times*, 3 July 1990, A6; *Süddeutsche Zeitung*, 23–24 June 1990, 8.

131 Telephone interview with Peter Millonig, official representative of the Republic of Slovenia (in the United States), 2 Mar. 1991.

132 Zagreb Domestic Service, 11 Oct. 1990, in FBIS, 12 Oct. 1990, 51.

133 Tanjug, 11 Oct. 1990, in FBIS, 12 Oct. 1990, 53.

134 More on this in Sabrina P. Ramet, "Serbia's Slobodan Milošević: A Profile," *Orbis* 35, no. 1 (Winter 1991).

135 *Die Zeit* (Hamburg), 31 Aug. 1990, 6.

136 *Welt am Sonntag*, 30 Sept. 1990, 3.

137 *Daily Telegraph*, 4 Oct. 1990, 15; *Politika*, 25 Oct. 1990, 10.

138 *Politika*, 12 Sept. 1990, 14.

139 *Vjesnik*, 14 Sept. 1990, 1.

140 Tanjug, 14 Sept. 1990, in FBIS, 17 Sept. 1990, 51; *Süddeutsche Zeitung*, 29–30 Sept. 1990, 7.

141 *New York Times*, 16 Jan. 1991, A3, 20 Jan. 1991, 7, 21 Jan. 1991, A2, and 22 Jan. 1991, A3.

142 See note 131.

143 *Neue Zürcher Zeitung*, 8 Feb. 1991, 2.

144 *Los Angeles Times*, 24 Feb. 1991, A1, A28; *Richmond Times-Dispatch*, 23 Feb. 1991, A9.

145 See the earlier articulation of the Macedonian position in *Borba*, 8 Nov. 1990, 3.

146 For further discussion of Yugoslavia's descent into chaos, see Sabrina Petra Ramet, "The Breakup of Yugoslavia," in *Global Affairs* 6, no. 2 (Spring 1991); also Sabrina Petra Ramet, *Balkan Babel: Politics, Culture, and Religion in Yugoslavia* (Boulder, Colo.: Westview Press, 1992), chap. 3 ("Brotherhood and Unity, 1989–1991").

16. Core Tasks for a Pluralist Order

1 The most important works here are Guillermo O'Donnell, Philippe Schmitter, and Laurence Whitehead, eds., *Transitions from Authoritarian Rule: Prospects for Democracy* (Baltimore: Johns Hopkins University Press, 1986); Scott Mainwaring, *Transitions to Democracy and Democratic Consolidation: Theoretical and Comparative Issues*, Kellogg Institute for International Studies, Working Paper 130 (Notre Dame, Ind.: University of Notre Dame, 1989); John H. Herz, ed., *From Dictatorship to Democracy: Coping with the Legacies of Authoritarianism and Totalitarianism* (Westport, Conn.: Greenwood Press, 1982); James Malloy and Mitchell Seligson, eds., *Authoritarians and Democrats: Regime Transition in Latin America* (Pittsburgh: University of Pittsburgh Press, 1987); Giuseppe Di Palma, *To Craft Democracies: An Essay on Democratic Transitions* (Berkeley: University of California Press, 1993); Juan J. Linz, "Transitions to Democracy," *Washington Quarterly* 13, no. 3 (Summer 1990). Also useful is Giovanni Sartori, *The Theory of Democracy Revisited* (Chatham, N.J.: Chatham House, 1987).

2 For example, Antoni Z. Kaminski, *An Institutional Theory of Communist Systems: Design, Function, and Breakdown* (San Francisco: Institute for Contemporary Studies, 1992).

3 See, in particular, Valerie Bunce, "Rising Above the Past: The Struggle for Liberal

Democracy in Eastern Europe," in *Adaptation and Transformation in Communist and Post-Communist Systems,* ed. Sabrina Petra Ramet (Boulder, Colo.: Westview Press, 1992); Sabrina Petra Ramet, "Balkan Pluralism and Its Enemies," *Orbis* 36, no. 4 (Fall 1992); Valerie Bunce and Maria Csanadi, "Uncertainty in the Transition: Post-Communism in Hungary," *East European Politics and Societies* 7, no. 2 (Spring 1993).

4   Ironically, with the sole exception of Yugoslavia, which recorded an 8 percent increase in agricultural production in 1990. See *Neue Zürcher Zeitung,* 29/30 Mar. 1992, 14.

5   *Financial Times* (London), 3 Sept. 1992, 4.

6   *Nepszabadsag* (Budapest), 14 Nov. 1992, 5, trans. in Foreign Broadcast Information Service (FBIS), *Daily Report* (Eastern Europe), 18 Nov. 1992, 17.

7   *Handelsblatt* (Düsseldorf), 6 Nov. 1992, 13, trans. in FBIS, *Daily Report* (Eastern Europe), 12 Nov. 1992, 20.

8   *OECD Economic Surveys: Czech and Slovak Federal Republic 1991* (Paris: OECD, 1991), 13.

9   *Financial Times,* 8 Sept. 1992, 28.

10   *Neue Zürcher Zeitung,* 1 Sept. 1992, 4.

11   PAP (Warsaw), 15 Apr. 1992, in FBIS, *Daily Report* (Eastern Europe), 20 Apr. 1992, 20; Radio Free Europe/Radio Liberty (RFE/RL), *Post-Soviet/East European Report,* 15 Sept. 1992, 2; and *Neue Zürcher Zeitung,* 10 Dec. 1992, 17.

12   *OECD Economic Surveys: Poland 1992* (Paris: OECD, 1992), 20. See also *Regional Development Problems and Policies in Poland* (Paris: OECD, 1992).

13   *Der Spiegel* (Hamburg), 26 Apr. 1993, 194.

14   PAP, 23 September 1992, in FBIS, *Daily Report* (Eastern Europe), 25 Sept. 1992, 13; *Handelsblatt* (Düsseldorf), 6 Nov. 1992, 13; *The Economist,* 17 July 1993, 65; and *Financial Times,* 10 June 1994, 3.

15   *Neue Zürcher Zeitung,* 24 July 1992, 12.

16   *Rudé pravo* (Prague), 8 July 1992, 1, 2, trans. in FBIS, *Daily Report* (Eastern Europe), 13 July 1992, 16.

17   *Metropolitni Telegraf* (Prague), 18 Nov. 1992, 1, 6, trans. in FBIS, *Daily Report* (Eastern Europe), 24 Nov. 1992, 16.

18   *Mlada Fronta Dnes* (Prague), 20 May 1992, 2, trans. in FBIS, *Daily Report* (Eastern Europe), 27 May 1992, 14.

19   *Welt am Sonntag* (Bonn), 18 Oct. 1992, 61; also *Die Zeit* (Hamburg), 14 Aug. 1992, 10.

20   CTK (Prague), 8 Apr. 1993, in FBIS, *Daily Report* (Eastern Europe), 14 Apr. 1993, 16; and *The European* (London), 18–21 Feb. 1993, 4.

21   *Republika* (Bratislava), 8 Apr. 1993, 3, trans. in FBIS, *Daily Report* (Eastern Europe), 12 Apr. 1993, 19; and *Republika,* 9 Apr. 1993, 8, 9, trans. in FBIS, *Daily Report* (Eastern Europe), 19 Apr. 1993, 13.

22   William Echikson, "Where Eastern Europe is Booming," *Fortune,* 12 July 1993, 23; and *Süddeutsche Zeitung,* 21 July 1993, 4.

23   Quoted in *The Economist,* 7 Aug. 1993, 46.

24   *Frankfurter Allgemeine,* 12 July 1993, 11.

25   *Neue Zürcher Zeitung,* 4 June 1994, 13.

26   *The European,* 3–9 June 1994, 18.

27   *Magyar Hírlap* (Budapest), 4 Nov. 1992, 10, trans. in FBIS, *Daily Report* (Eastern Europe), 5 Nov. 1992, 23; and *Financial Times*, 25 Nov. 1992, 3.

28   MTI (Budapest), 17 Oct. 1991, trans. in FBIS, *Daily Report* (Eastern Europe), 22 Oct. 1992, 27.

29   MTI, 18 Nov. 1992, in FBIS, *Daily Report* (Eastern Europe), 20 Nov. 1992, 12; and *Neues Deutschland* (Berlin), 29 Mar. 1993, 7.

30   Echikson, "Where Eastern Europe is Booming," 23; and *The European*, 3–9 June 1994, 18. Also *Financial Times*, 9 June 1994, 4.

31   *Reforming the Economies of Central and Eastern Europe* (Paris: OECD, 1992), 22.

32   For details, see Sabrina Petra Ramet, "Slovenia's Road to Democracy," *Europe-Asia Studies* 45, no. 5 (1993).

33   Radio Slovenia Network (Ljubljana), 25 Oct. 1993, trans. in FBIS, *Daily Report* (Eastern Europe), 1 Nov. 1993, 40.

34   Garabed Minassian and Stoyan Totev, "The Bulgarian Economy in the Early 1990s: Will the Way Down Lead Up?," *Russian and East European Finance and Trade* 28, no. 4 (Winter 1992/93): 82.

35   *Neue Zürcher Zeitung*, 29 Jan. 1993, 4.

36   Alfredo Thorne, "Reforming Financial Systems in Eastern Europe: The Case of Bulgaria," in *Creating Capital Markets in Eastern Europe*, ed. John R. Lampe (Washington D.C.: Woodrow Wilson Center Press, 1992), 94–101.

37   See *Anteni* (Sofia), no. 3 (20 Jan. 1993): 8, trans. in FBIS, *Daily Report* (Eastern Europe), 29 Jan. 1993, 6–7.

38   Major General Simeon Petkovski, deputy head of the Military-Economic Sector on Military Issues and Coordination, in interview with *Bulgarska Armiya* (Sofia), 19 Nov. 1992, 1, 3, trans. in FBIS, *Daily Report* (Eastern Europe), 23 Nov. 1992, 11.

39   BTA (Sofia), 23 Sept. 1992, in FBIS, *Daily Report* (Eastern Europe), 25 Sept. 1992, 6; *Financial Times*, 2 Oct. 1992, 2; *Neue Zürcher Zeitung*, 3 Oct. 1992, 16; and *Duma* (Sofia), 19 Nov. 1992, 1, 4, trans. in FBIS, *Daily Report* (Eastern Europe), 25 Nov. 1992, 3.

40   BTA, 23 Sept. 1992, in FBIS, *Daily Report* (Eastern Europe), 25 Sept. 1992, 6.

41   *Wall Street Journal*, 21 Sept. 1992, A6. See also Ognian Hishow, "Struktur und Konjunktur der bulgarischen Volkswirtschaft. Vorhaben der Wirtschaftsreform," *Südost Europa* 40, no. 2 (Feb. 1991); Raina Parwanowa and Iwanka Petkowa, "Die Wirtschaft Bulgariens—der öffnung zugewandt?," *Südost Europa* 40, no. 5 (May 1991).

42   BTA, 25 Jan. 1993, in FBIS, *Daily Report* (Eastern Europe), 25 Jan. 1993, 13; and BTA, 1 Feb. 1993, in FBIS, *Daily Report* (Eastern Europe), 1 Feb. 1993, 12.

43   ROMPRES (Bucharest), 9 Oct. 1990, in FBIS, *Daily Report* (Eastern Europe), 10 Oct. 1990, 41; ROMPRES, 10 Oct. 1990, in FBIS, *Daily Report* (Eastern Europe), 12 Oct. 1990, 47.

44   ROMPRES, 7 Aug. 1991, in FBIS, *Daily Report* (Eastern Europe), 7 Aug. 1991, 26; Radio Romania Network (Bucharest), 24 Aug. 1992, trans. in FBIS, *Daily Report* (Eastern Europe), 25 Aug. 1992, 25; ROMPRES, 6 Apr. 1993, in FBIS, *Daily Report* (Eastern Europe), 8 Apr. 1993, 12.

45   ROMPRES, 2 Feb. 1993, in FBIS, *Daily Report* (Eastern Europe), 2 Feb. 1993, 36.

46   ROMPRES, 4 Feb. 1993, in FBIS, *Daily Report* (Eastern Europe), 5 Feb. 1993, p. 32.

47   *Neue Zürcher Zeitung,* 3 Apr. 1991, 15; Petra Pissulla, "Rumänien auf dem Weg in die Marktwirtschaft," *Osteuropa* 41, no. 12 (Dec. 1991): 1211–14; *Neue Zürcher Zeitung,* 5 May 1993, 13.

48   Re the erection of barriers to foreign investment, see *Financial Times,* 12 Sept. 1990, 4. Re the dismantlement of barriers to foreign investment, see *Financial Times,* 4 Mar. 1993, 3.

49   *Neue Zürcher Zeitung,* 24 Feb. 1993, 16.

50   Re food shortages, see *Süddeutsche Zeitung,* 14/15 Dec. 1991, 34; and ROMPRES, 21 Feb. 1992, in FBIS, *Daily Report* (Eastern Europe), 26 Feb. 1992, 27. Re the cadaver shortage, see *Budapest Week,* 11–17 June 1992, 11.

51   ROMPRES, 9 Sept. 1992, in FBIS, *Daily Report* (Eastern Europe), 9 Sept. 1992, 25.

52   *Financial Times,* 11 June 1992, 3; *Neue Zürcher Zeitung,* 23 Apr. 1992, 3. See also *Financial Times,* 8 Apr. 1993, 21.

53   ROMPRES, 13 Nov. 1992, in FBIS, *Daily Report* (Eastern Europe), 16 Nov. 1992, 29.

54   *Adevarul* (Bucharest), 19 Jan. 1993, 1, 3, trans. in FBIS, *Daily Report* (Eastern Europe), 26 Jan. 1993, 37.

55   For details re Albania, see Ramet, "Balkan Pluralism," 554–56.

56   *New York Times,* 3 Aug. 1993, A3; and letter from Michel Noel of the World Bank, to *The Economist* (London), 7 May 1994, 6. For further discussion of economic stabilization programs in Eastern Europe, see Koji Suzuki, "Economy in Eastern Europe After CMEA System," *Japanese Slavic and East European Studies* 13 (1992): 45–64.

57   *Financial Times,* 11 Jan. 1993, supplement, 5.

58   *Rynki Zagraniczne* (Warsaw), 5 Nov. 1991, 7, trans. in JPRS *Report,* no. EER-91-180 (Eastern Europe), 17 Dec. 1991, 52–53.

59   BTA, 12 Mar. 1992, in FBIS, *Daily Report* (Eastern Europe), 18 Mar. 1992, 5.

60   The price provision expired in Dec. 1992. See BTA, 5 Feb. 1992, in FBIS, *Daily Report* (Eastern Europe), 6 Feb. 1992, 2; BTA, 12 Mar. 1992, in FBIS, *Daily Report* (Eastern Europe), 18 Mar. 1992, 5.

61   Eduardo Borensztein and Manmohan S. Kumar, "Proposals for Privatization in Eastern Europe," *IMF Staff Papers* 38, no. 2 (June 1991): 318; *Neue Zürcher Zeitung,* 21 Feb. 1991, 13.

62   *Vjesnik* (Zagreb), 29 Apr. 1993, 13.

63   For an analysis of alternative strategies of privatization in Eastern Europe, with specific chapters devoted to Hungary, Poland, Czechoslovakia, and Germany, see Michael P. Claudon and Tamar L. Gutner, eds., *Comrades Go Private: Strategies for Eastern European Privatization* (New York: New York University Press, 1992).

64   Third Program Radio Network (Warsaw), 3 Apr. 1992, trans. in FBIS, *Daily Report* (Eastern Europe), 6 Apr. 1992, 17; *Zycie Warszawy* (Warsaw), 7 Apr. 1992, 1, trans. in FBIS, *Daily Report* (Eastern Europe), 14 Apr. 1992, 17; PAP, 1 June 1992, in FBIS, *Daily Report* (Eastern Europe), 2 June 1992, 16; PAP, 5 June 1992, in FBIS, *Daily Report* (Eastern Europe), 10 June 1992, 27; PAP, 19 Sept. 1992, in FBIS, *Daily Report* (Eastern Europe), 24 Sept. 1992, 17.

65   *Zycie Warszawy* (Warsaw), 8 Nov. 1991, 2, trans. in JPRS *Report,* no. EER-91-178 (Eastern Europe), 12 Dec. 1991, 28–29.

66   *The Times* (London), 1 May 1993, 10.

67   *Mainichi Daily News* (Tokyo), 16 Sept. 1993, 5.

68   *Neue Zürcher Zeitung*, 28 July 1992, 8, and 3 Aug. 1992, 13; CSTK (Prague), 18 Nov.
     1992, in FBIS, *Daily Report* (Eastern Europe), 18 Nov. 1992, 20. See also Jiri Kosta,
     "Staat und Wirtschaft der CSFR vor der Spaltung," *Osteuropa* 42, no. 11 (Nov.
     1992), esp. 989–92.

69   Borensztein and Kumar, "Prospects for Privatization," 301, 320.

70   Ibid., 305. For a recent appraisal of the present economic situation in Eastern
     Europe, including discussion of mechanisms of privatization, see Jozef van Bra-
     bant, ed., *The New Eastern Europe and the World Economy* (Boulder, Colo.:
     Westview Press, 1993).

71   *Neue Zürcher Zeitung*, 29/30 Nov. 1992, 16.

72   BTA, 15 Feb. 1992, in FBIS, *Daily Report* (Eastern Europe), 18 Feb. 1992, 5; BTA,
     11 June 1992, in FBIS, *Daily Report* (Eastern Europe), 12 June 1992, 13; BTA, 6 Oct.
     1992, in FBIS, *Daily Report* (Eastern Europe), 8 Oct. 1992, 4; BTA, 3 Nov. 1992, in
     FBIS, *Daily Report* (Eastern Europe), 4 Nov. 1992, 9.

73   Gerd Biro, "Privatisierung in Ungarn," *Südost Europa* 39, nos. 11–12 (Nov.–Dec.
     1992): 676–77.

74   *Financial Times*, 4 Feb. 1993, 3.

75   *Uj Magyarorszag* (Budapest), 2 Apr. 1993, 9, trans. in FBIS, *Daily Report* (Eastern
     Europe), 7 Apr. 1993, 24; *The Hungarian Economy* 20, no. 2 (1992): 1.

76   Pissulla, "Rumänien auf dem Weg," 1210; *Financial Times*, 12 Mar. 1993, 2.

77   *Financial Times*, 4 Feb. 1993, 3.

78   For further discussion of the challenges of privatization in Eastern Europe, see
     Martin Brusis, "Privatisierungskonflikte in Polen, Ungarn und der ehemaligen
     CSFR. Überlegungen zu einer vergleichenden Analyse," *Osteuropa* 43, no. 7
     (July 1993).

79   Interview with Miro Cerar, secretary of the Constitutional Commission of Slo-
     venia, Ljubljana, 18 Mar. 1992.

80   In the east German context, for example, see Dorothy J. Rosenberg, "Shock
     Therapy: GDR Women in Transition from a Socialist Welfare State to a Social
     Market Economy," *Signs* 17, no. 1 (Autumn 1991).

81   Re rumors of a military coup in Bulgaria, see BTA, 25 Feb. 1992, 3, in FBIS, *Daily
     Report* (Eastern Europe), 26 Feb. 1992, 3; BTA, 2 Sept. 1992, in FBIS, *Daily Report*
     (Eastern Europe), 3 Sept. 1992, 2. Re rumors of a military coup in Poland, see
     New York Times, 8 Apr. 1992, A6; Radio Warszawa Network (Warsaw), 11 June
     1992, trans. in FBIS, *Daily Report* (Eastern Europe), 12 June 1992, 31.

82   Expanding the purview, I would also include Croatia and Serbia in the latter
     category.

83   David McQuaid, "The 'War' Over the Election Law," RFE, *Report on Eastern
     Europe* (2 Aug. 1991): 12.

84   Ibid., 26.

85   For further discussion, see Sabrina Petra Ramet, "The New Poland: Democratic
     and Authoritarian Tendencies," *Global Affairs* 7, no. 2 (Spring 1992).

86   As reported in PAP, 13 Feb. 1992, in FBIS, *Daily Report* (Eastern Europe), 18 Feb.
     1992, 22.

87   *Neue Zürcher Zeitung*, 6 May 1992, 3; *Süddeutsche Zeitung* (Munich), 9/10 May
     1992, 2; *Głos Wybrzeza* (Gdańsk), 7/8 Nov. 1992, 1–2, trans. in FBIS, *Daily Report*
     (Eastern Europe), 20 Nov. 1992, 14–15.

88   For an oblique reference to the controversy in Hungary, see Kossuth Radio Net-

work (Budapest), 5 June 1992, trans. in FBIS, *Daily Report* (Eastern Europe),
9 June 1992, 20–21; for Bulgaria, see Stoyan Stalev, "Neuer Anfang in Bulgarien,"
Südosteuropa Mitteilungen 31, no. 3 (1991).

89   *Neue Zürcher Zeitung*, 26/27 Apr. 1992, 3.

90   *Financial Times*, 3 Aug. 1992, 2; Louisa Vinton, "Poland's 'Little Constitution'
Clarifies Wałęsa's Powers," *RFE/RL Research Report* (4 Sept. 1992): 24.

91   *International Herald Tribune* (Tokyo ed.), 29/30 May 1993, 4; 31 May 1993, 2;
2 June 1993, 2. Also *Neue Zürcher Zeitung* (17 Apr. 1993), 3.

92   László Bruszt and David Stark, "Remaking the Political Field in Hungary: From
the Politics of Confrontation to the Politics of Competition," in *Eastern Europe
in Revolution*, ed. Ivo Banac (Ithaca, N.Y.: Cornell University Press, 1992), 51.

93   Othmar Kolar, "Die Politische und Wirtschaftliche Entwicklung in Rumänien
seit dem Dezember 1989," *Österreichische Osthefte* 34, no. 4 (1992).

94   *Neue Zürcher Zeitung*, 27 May 1992, 5.

95   *Duma* (Sofia), 22 May 1992, trans. in FBIS, *Daily Report* (Eastern Europe), 26 May
1992; *Duma* (6 July 1992), 1, 2, trans. in FBIS, *Daily Report* (Eastern Europe),
13 July 1992, 7; BTA, 26 Jan. 1993, in FBIS, *Daily Report* (Eastern Europe), 27 Jan.
1993, 11.

96   Kjell Engelbrekt, "Toward the Rule of Law: Bulgaria," *RFE/RL Research Report*,
3 July 1992, 5–6.

97   Michael Shafir, "Romania's New Institutions: The Constitutional Court," *RFE/
RL Research Report*, 23 Oct. 1993, 47–48.

98   For details and discussion, see Edith Oltay, "The Postcommunist Judiciary," in
RFE/RL Research Institute, *Report on Eastern Europe*, 11 Oct. 1991.

99   *Duma*, 18 Nov. 1992, 6, trans. in FBIS, *Daily Report* (Eastern Europe), 24 Nov.
1992, 5–6.

100   *Polska Zbrojna* (Warsaw), 2 Nov. 1992, 1, 2, trans. in FBIS, *Daily Report* (Eastern
Europe), 9 Nov. 1992, 28.

101   *Polska Zbrojna*, 28 Feb.–1 Mar. 1992, 1–2, trans. in FBIS, *Daily Report* (Eastern
Europe), 6 Mar. 1992, 16.

102   *Magyar Hírlap* (Budapest), 2 Nov. 1992, 3, trans. in FBIS, *Daily Report* (Eastern
Europe), 5 Nov. 1992, 19.

103   Owen V. Johnson, "The Press of Change: Mass Communications in Late Communist and Post-Communist Societies," in Ramet, *Adaptation and Transformation*, 217–18; Kossuth Radio Network (Budapest), 24 May 1992, trans. in FBIS,
Daily Report (Eastern Europe), 27 May 1992, 17.

104   PAP, 12 Feb. 1992, in FBIS, *Daily Report* (Eastern Europe), 14 Feb. 1992, 21.

105   PAP, 19 Nov. 1992, in FBIS, *Daily Report* (Eastern Europe), 20 Nov. 1992, 16.

106   Interview with Andrej Poznić, chief editor of Kanal A (Ljubljana), 20 Mar. 1992.

107   Interview with Boris Bregant, member of the board of directors of RTV Slovenia,
Ljubljana, 26 Mar. 1992.

108   MTI, 10 Apr. 1992, in FBIS, *Daily Report* (Eastern Europe), 13 Apr. 1992, 13.

109   *Neue Zürcher Zeitung*, 26 Sept. 1991, 3.

110   *New York Times*, 9 Jan. 1993, 4; *Neue Zürcher Zeitung*, 11/12 Apr. 1993, 6.

111   Quoted in MTI, 27 Jan. 1993, in FBIS, *Daily Report* (Eastern Europe), 28 Jan.
1993, 18.

112   Kossuth Radio Network, 14 Jan. 1993, trans. in FBIS, *Daily Report* (Eastern
Europe), 15 Jan. 1993, 20.

113 Milan Zitny, "The New Slovak Market of Ideas," *East European Reporter* 5, no. 3 (May–June 1992): 30.

114 Ibid.

115 Quoted in ibid., 31.

116 *New York Times,* 10 Aug. 1992, A3.

117 Jiri Pehe, "The Media: Czechoslovakia," *RFE/RL Research Report* (2 Oct. 1992): 37.

118 *Smena* (Bratislava), 6 Jan. 1993, 2, and CTK, 7 Jan. 1993, both trans. in FBIS, *Daily Report* (Eastern Europe), 12 Jan. 1993, 23.

119 *Demokratsiya* (Sofia), 24 Jan. 1992, 1, 4, trans. in FBIS, *Daily Report* (Eastern Europe), 30 Jan. 1992, 5–6; *24 Chasa* (Sofia), 23 Apr. 1992, 1, 3, trans. in FBIS, *Daily Report* (Eastern Europe), 30 Apr. 1992, 3.

120 Crisula Stefanescu, "The New Press Law," RFE/RL, *Report on Eastern Europe,* 21 Sept. 1990, 27.

121 For details, see Crisula Stefanescu, "Draft Press Law Withdrawn a Second Time," RFE/RL, *Report on Eastern Europe,* 5 Apr. 1991, 21.

122 Crisula Stefanescu, "Information Department Set Up," RFE/RL, *Report on Eastern Europe,* 25 Oct. 1991, 19–20.

123 *New York Times,* 9 Mar. 1993, A14.

124 PAP, 19 Nov. 1992, in FBIS, *Daily Report* (Eastern Europe), 20 Nov. 1992, 16.

125 TVP Television First Program Network (Warsaw), 18 Sept. 1992, trans. in FBIS, *Daily Report* (Eastern Europe), 22 Sept. 1992, 20.

126 Ibid.

127 Re Slovakia, see *Neue Zürcher Zeitung,* 21 Nov. 1992, 2; *Uj Szo* (Bratislava), 4 Jan. 1993, 1, trans. in FBIS, *Daily Report* (Eastern Europe), 3 Feb. 1993, 25; *Süddeutsche Zeitung,* 24/25 Apr. 1993, 7. Re Vojvodina, see Kossuth Radio Network, 30 Oct. 1992, trans. in FBIS, *Daily Report* (Eastern Europe), 2 Nov. 1992, 45.

128 See Michael Shafir, "Toward the Rule of Law: Romania," *RFE/RL Research Report,* 3 July 1992, 37.

129 Re Ruthenes in Slovakia, see *Lidove Noviný* (Prague), 23 Oct. 1991, 3, trans. in FBIS, *Daily Report* (Eastern Europe), 25 Oct. 1991, 10; re Serbs in Hungary, see MTI (15 Nov. 1992), in FBIS, *Daily Report* (Eastern Europe), 18 Nov. 1992, 19.

130 Re Germans and Hungarians in Romanian Transylvania, see *Süddeutsche Zeitung,* 13/14 Mar. 1993, 9.

131 See Konstanty Gebert, "Anti-Semitism in the 1990 Polish Presidential Election," *Social Research* 58, no. 4 (Winter 1991).

132 Education Minister Andrzej Stelmachowski, address to Sejm, 26 Apr. 1992, quoted in *Zycie Warszawy,* 27 Apr. 1992, 1, trans. in FBIS, *Daily Report* (Eastern Europe), 5 May 1992, 20.

133 For further discussion of the abortion issue in Poland, see Małgorzata Fuszara, "Legal Regulation of Abortion in Poland," *Signs* 17, no. 1 (Autumn 1991); Hanna Jankowska, "Abortion, Church and Politics in Poland," *Feminist Review,* special issue no. 39 (Winter 1991).

134 *Neue Zürcher Zeitung,* 9 Apr. 1992, 4.

135 *Süddeutsche Zeitung,* 15 July 1993, 7.

136 Ibid., 29 July 1993, 8.

137 Quoted in MTI, 24 June 1992, in FBIS, *Daily Report* (Eastern Europe), 25 June 1992, 14.

138   ROMPRES, 26 Oct. 1992, in FBIS, *Daily Report* (Eastern Europe), 28 Oct. 1992, 13; and *Süddeutsche Zeitung*, 31 Oct./1 Nov. 1992, 8.

139   *Neue Zürcher Zeitung*, 13 Mar. 1992, 5, and 4/5 Apr. 1992, 3.

140   *Borba* (Belgrade), 6 Apr. 1993, 10.

141   *Frankfurter Allgemeine*, 19 June 1993, 12.

142   As related in the case of Hungary in Bunce and Csanádi, "Uncertainty in the Transition," 257–59.

143   *Romania Libera* (Bucharest), 5 Sept. 1991, 1, 4, trans. in FBIS, *Daily Report* (Eastern Europe), 6 Sept. 1991, 25. See also *Cotidianul* (Bucharest), 14 Oct. 1992, 2, trans. in FBIS, *Daily Report* (Eastern Europe), 20 Oct. 1992, 25.

144   *Süddeutsche Zeitung*, 23 June 1993, 7.

145   TVP Television First Program (Warsaw), 24 Jan. 1993, trans. in FBIS, *Daily Report* (Eastern Europe), 25 Jan. 1993, 30; *Rzeczpospolita* (Warsaw), 25 Jan. 1993, pp. 1, 3, trans. in FBIS, *Daily Report* (Eastern Europe), 27 Jan. 1993, 29.

146   *Süddeutsche Zeitung*, 26/27 June 1993, 7.

147   See ibid., 6 Sept. 1993, 6; *Der Spiegel,* 13 Sept. 1993, 162, 164.

148   See *Der Spiegel,* 6 Sept. 1993, 176.

149   *Mainichi Daily News* (Tokyo), 16 Sept. 1993, 4.

150   *New York Times,* Weekly Review (international ed.), 12 Sept. 1993, 4.

151   *Japan Times,* 21 Sept. 1993, 1.

152   *Reforming the Economic,* 29.

153   *Kontinent* (Sofia), 23/24 Jan. 1993, 4, trans. in FBIS, *Daily Report* (Eastern Europe), 28 Jan. 1993, 6.

154   Bunce and Csanádi, "Uncertainty in the Transition," 272.

17. Yugoslav Breakup and Ethnic War

1   For details, see Ivo Banac, *The National Question in Yugoslavia: Origins, History, Politics* (Ithaca, N.Y.: Cornell University Press, 1984).

2   Robert A. Dahl, *A Preface to Democratic Theory* (Chicago: University of Chicago Press, 1956), 80.

3   *NIN* (Belgrade), no. 1869, 26 Oct. 1986, 14–15. For a detailed discussion of this memorandum, see Ivo Banac, "Historiography of the Countries of Eastern Europe: Yugoslavia," *American Historical Review* 97, no. 4 (Oct. 1992): 1099–1101.

4   Dijana Pleština, *Regional Development in Communist Yugoslavia: Success, Failure and Consequences* (Boulder, Colo.: Westview Press, 1992), 132–33.

5   For details and documentation, see Sabrina Petra Ramet, *Balkan Babel: Politics, Culture, and Religion in Yugoslavia* (Boulder, Colo.: Westview Press, 1992), chap. 3.

6   In February 1991 I predicted the outbreak of civil war in "The Breakup of Yugoslavia," *Global Affairs* 6, no. 2 (Spring 1991). Surprisingly, other Yugoslav-watchers in the West either expressed optimism that everything would be worked out amicably among the republics, or they declared that the entire situation was "uncertain." Both of these approaches represented a misreading of overwhelming evidence of the country's by-then rapid skid to ethnic war.

7   For details and explanation, see Ramet, *Balkan Babel,* chap. 2.

8   Branka Magaš, *The Destruction of Yugoslavia: Tracking Yugoslavia's Break-up 1980–92* (London: Verso, 1992), 268.

9   For details, see Ramet, *Balkan Babel*, epilogue.

10 Magaš, *Destruction of Yugoslavia*, 333.

11 Ibid., 267.

12 Ibid., 311.

13 Ibid., 261.

14 Quoted in ibid., 273.

15 Anton Bebler, "Political Pluralism and the Yugoslav Professional Military," in *The Tragedy of Yugoslavia: The Failure of Democratic Transformation*, ed. Jim Seroka and Vukašin Pavlović (Armonk, N.Y.: M. E. Sharpe, 1992), 124.

16 For details, see Sabrina Petra Ramet, *Nationalism and Federalism in Yugoslavia, 1962–1991*, 2nd ed. (Bloomington: Indiana University Press, 1992), 249ff.

17 Official communiqué from Bosnian-Croatian meeting, Sarajevo, 21 Jan. 1991, "Documents on the Future Regulation of Relations in Yugoslavia," *Yugoslav Survey* (Belgrade) 32 no. 1 (1991): 6.

18 Official communiqué from Serbian-Bosnian meeting, Belgrade, 22 Jan. 1991, "Documents on the Future," 7.

19 Press conference of Croatian-Montenegrin meeting, Zagreb, 23 Jan. 1991, "Documents on the Future," 8.

20 Press conference of Bosnian-Macedonian meeting, Sarajevo, 29 Jan. 1991, "Documents on the Future," 14.

21 Svetozar Stojanović, interview (Feb. 1991), published as "Optimistic About Yugoslavia: Interview with Svetozar Stojanović," *East European Reporter* 4, no. 4 (Spring/Summer 1991): 14.

22 Official communiqué of the SFRY Presidency, Sarajevo, 22 Feb. 1991, "Documents on the Future," 18.

23 From the session of the SFRY Presidency, Belgrade, 12, 14, and 15 Mar. 1991, "Documents on the Future," 19.

24 For further details, see Ramet, *Nationalism and Federalism*, 248–51.

25 For more discussion of this point, see Sabrina Petra Ramet, "War in the Balkans," *Foreign Affairs* 71, no. 4 (Fall 1992): 86.

26 See, for example, Dobrica Ćosić, "Velika obmana srpskog naroda," *Politika* (Belgrade), 20 Jan. 1991, trans. into German as "Der Drang der Serben nach ihrem Staat," *Osteuropa* 41, no. 10 (Oct. 1991): A592–A596.

27 For details, see Ramet, "War in the Balkans," 86–87; Ramet, *Nationalism and Federalism*, 259.

28 Radio Croatia Network (Zagreb), 19 May 1992, trans. in FBIS, *Daily Report* (Eastern Europe), 20 May 1992, 18.

29 Tanjug Domestic Service (4 July 1992), trans. in FBIS, *Daily Report* (Eastern Europe), 6 July 1992, 33; and *Nova Makedonija* (Skopje), 6 July 1992, 4. See also *Vecernji list* (Zagreb), 19 Nov. 1992, 5.

30 That was the lowest estimate. Other estimates ran as high as 350,000.

31 The Slovenian figure was cited originally in my "Slovenia's Road to Democracy," *Europe-Asia Studies* 45, no. 5 (1993); the Macedonian figure comes from "Address by Mr. Kiro Gligorov, president of the Republic of Macedonia, to the Centre for Policy Studies, London, October 15, 1992," *South Slav Journal* 14,

no. 1/2 (nominally Spring/Summer 1991, but actually printed May 1993): 65; the German figure comes from *Der Spiegel* (Hamburg), 7 June 1993, 19; the other figures were cited originally in my "War in the Balkans," 79.

32   Re Serbian and Montenegrin capacity to produce M-84A tanks, see *Politika* (28 Oct. 1992), 8, trans. in FBIS, *Daily Report* (Eastern Europe), 17 Nov. 1992, 28–29.

33   Letter to the editor from Flora Lewis, *Foreign Affairs* 72, no. 3 (Summer 1993): 221.

34   AFP (Paris), 12 Jan. 1993, in FBIS, *Daily Report* (Eastern Europe), 12 Jan. 1993, 1.

35   *Politika* (Belgrade), 19 Apr. 1993, 1–2; *Washington Post*, 27 Apr. 1993, A1.

36   *Denver Post*, 15 Apr. 1993, 8A.

37   *Washington Post*, 28 Apr. 1993, A1.

38   *Los Angeles Times*, 9 May 1993, A1, A9. Clinton had begun making strong statements earlier. See, for example, *Star Tribune* (Minneapolis), 17 Apr. 1993, 1A; *Washington Post*, 29 Apr. 1993, A35.

39   *Vjesnik* (Zagreb), 24 Apr. 1993, 9.

40   *International Herald Tribune* (Tokyo ed.), 29/30 May 1993, 1.

41   *Vjesnik*, 23 May 1993, 5.

42   *International Herald Tribune* (Tokyo ed.), 3 June 1993, 4.

43   *The Times* (London), 27 May 1993, 11.

44   *International Herald Tribune* (Tokyo ed.), 10 June 1993, 1.

45   Ibid., 5/6 June 1993, 2.

46   Re the collapse of the Vance-Owen plan, see Adolf Karger, "Der gescheiterte Vance-Owen Plan und die ethnisch-geographischen Strukturen von Bosnien-Herzegowina," *Osteuropa* 43, no. 8 (Aug. 1993).

47   *International Herald Tribune* (Tokyo ed.), 17 June 1993, 2; *Vjesnik*, 19 June 1993, 7.

48   *The Times* (London), 18 June 1993, 12.

49   Ibid., 21 June 1993, 9.

50   Quoted in *Vjesnik*, 19 June 1993, 7.

51   *Le Monde*, 19 June 1993, 1.

52   *Japan Times*, 22 June 1993, 1, and 23 June 1993, 4.

53   *Vjesnik*, 19 July 1993, 2–3. For a Croatian perspective on peace negotiations, see Marko Barišić, "Hrvatska UN-u nudi novi plan," *Danas* (Zagreb), new series, 14 Sept. 1993, 5–7.

54   Quoted in *Japan Times*, 1 Aug. 1993, 1. The provisions of this document are reported in *New York Times*, 31 July 1993, 1, 4.

55   For details, see Sabrina P. Ramet, "The Yugoslav Crisis and the West: Avoiding 'Vietnam' and Blundering into 'Abyssinia'," *East European Politics and Societies* 8, no. 1 (Winter 1994).

56   *New York Times*, 11 Aug. 1993, A3.

57   *Danas* (Zagreb), new ser., 24 Aug. 1993, 33.

58   *Süddeutsche Zeitung*, 30 Aug. 1993, 1.

59   Ibid., 2 Sept. 1993, 1; *New York Times*, 2 Sept. 1993, A1, A8.

60   *Japan Times*, 23 Sept. 1993, 4.

61   *Der Spiegel*, 27 Sept. 1993, 175.

62   *Süddeutsche Zeitung*, 29 Sept. 1993, 2, 30 Sept. 1993, 8, and 1 Oct. 1993, 9; *Vjesnik*, 30 Sept. 1993, 1.

63   Quoted in *Japan Times*, 9 Oct. 1993, 4.

64   *Neue Zürcher Zeitung*, 14 May 1994, 3; and *Globe and Mail* (Toronto), 1 June 1994, A7.

65   Re the counter-offensive, see *The Times* (London), 25 May 1994, 12. Re arms supplies to the Bosnian Muslims, see *Seattle Times*, 13 May 1994, A3.

66   *The Times*, 25 May 1994, 12; *Globe and Mail*, 1 June 1994, A7; and *Seattle Times*, 19 May 1994, A1, A2.

67   For details, see *Seattle Times*, 12 May 1994, A18; *Corriere della Sera* (Milano), 13 May 1994, 8; *New York Times*, 9 June 1994, A1, A6; *Financial Times*, 10 June 1994, 5; and *Seattle Post-Intelligencer*, 10 June 1994, A2.

68   Cited in Macedonien Information and Liaison Service, MILSNEWS, *Dnevni Vesti Angliski*, 9 Sept. 1993.

69   For further discussion of the question of the possibility of the war spreading to Macedonia, see "Atomwaffen auf dem Balkan? Eine Stimme zur Lage aus Skopje" and "Wird Mazedonian Kriegsschauplatz? Gespräch mit dem makedonischen Politiker Ljupco Georgievski," both in *Osteuropa* 43, no. 6 (June 1993).

70   *Japan Times*, 2 June 1993, 13.

71   Re a Romanian shipment of oil to Serbia on 13 Apr., see a statement by the Bulgarian Foreign Ministry, reported in *Vjesnik*, 16 Apr. 1993, 48.

72   *The Times*, 10 May 1993, 10.

73   *Süddeutsche Zeitung*, 6 Sept. 1993, 2.

74   *Borba* (Belgrade), 23 Apr. 1993, 9; *Japan Times*, 18 June 1993, 10; and *The Times*, 7 December 1993, 12.

75   *Politika* (Belgrade), 5 Nov. 1992, 11.

76   *Süddeutsche Zeitung*, 16 Aug. 1993, 4.

77   *Borba*, 4 Mar. 1993, 10.

78   *Vjesnik*, 8 June 1993, 25.

79   For details, see *Süddeutsche Zeitung* (Munich), 2/3 Jan. 1993, 7; *Vreme* (Belgrade), 22 Mar. 1993, 47–48; *Borba*, 24 Mar. 1993, 10.

80   *Glas Srpski* (Banja Luka), 26 Jan. 1993, 9, trans. in FBIS, *Daily Report* (Eastern Europe), 2 Apr. 1993, 29.

81   *Süddeutsche Zeitung*, 3 Sept. 1993, 7, and 14 Sept. 1993, 8; and *Nedjeljna Dalmacija* (Split), 8 June 1994, 8.

82   *Neue Zürcher Zeitung*, 14 May 1992, 5.

83   *Vjesnik*, 31 July 1993, 10.

84   Vojislav Šešelj, in interview with *Der Standard* (Vienna), 19 Sept. 1991, 2, trans. in FBIS, *Daily Report* (Eastern Europe), 19 Sept. 1991, 41.

85   *Politika*, 30 Mar. 1992, 8. The April 1991 census recorded the presence of 1,686,661 Albanians in the Republic of Serbia, including the provinces of Kosovo and Vojvodina. Almost all of these Albanians live in Kosovo. For figures, see "The National Composition of Yugoslavia's Population, 1991," *Yugoslav Survey* 33 no. 1 (1992): 11.

86   Quoted in *Nedeljna Borba* (Belgrade), 16/17 May 1992, 11, trans. in FBIS, *Daily Report* (Eastern Europe), 28 May 1992, 69.

87   *The Times*, 15 May 1993, 12.

88   Quoted in *New York Times*, 20 Dec. 1992, 4.

89   Quoted in *The Times*, 23 Dec. 1992, 6.

90   Misha Glenny, *The Fall of Yugoslavia: The Third Balkan War* (Harmondsworth, Middlesex: Penguin Books, 1992), 39.

91   Quoted in *Novi Vjesnik* (Zagreb), 12 Oct. 1992.

92 Ibid.

93 Reported and described at length in *Delo* (Ljubljana), 7 Jan. 1993, 5, trans. in FBIS, *Daily Report* (Eastern Europe), 1 Feb. 1993, 67–69.

94 *Politika*, 15 May 1992, 9.

95 Quoted in *Vjesnik*, 1 Apr. 1993, 25, reprinted from *Novi List* (Rijeka).

96 *Vjesnik*, 31 July 1993, 14–15, reprinted from *Slobodna Dalmacija* (Split).

97 See Filip Svarm, "War Crime: Fighting to the Last Booty," *Vreme*, 8 Mar. 1993, 28–31, trans. in FBIS, *Daily Report* (Eastern Europe), 7 Apr. 1993, 45–48.

98 Quoted in *The European* (London), 22–25 Apr. 1993, 11.

99 *Vjesnik*, 2 June 1993, 9. See also *Glas Istre* (Pula), 2 June 1993, 16; and *International Herald Tribune* (Tokyo ed.), 2 June 1993, 2.

100 For more details, see *International Herald Tribune* (Tokyo ed.), 3 June 1993, 1, 4; *Vjesnik*, 4 June 1993, 9.

101 *Glas Istre*, 6 June 1993, 5.

102 *The Times*, 7 July 1993, 12; *Frankfurter Allgemeine*, 8 July 1993, 2; *Süddeutsche Zeitung*, 16 July 1993, 7.

103 Glenny, *Fall of Yugoslavia*, 44.

104 Re the firings, see *Vreme*, 27 Jan. 1992, 24–25; Tanjug Domestic Service, 3 Apr. 1992, trans. in FBIS, *Daily Report* (Eastern Europe), 7 Apr. 1992, 44; *Vreme*, 10 Aug. 1992, 9. Re the attempt to nationalize *Politika*, see *Süddeutsche Zeitung*, 25/26 July 1992, 8; *Politika*, 28 July 1992, 1; *Politika*, 16 Sept. 1992, 6.

105 Slobodan Antonić, "Fighting for the Truth," *East European Reporter* 5, no. 4 (July–Aug. 1992): 62.

106 Vlado Mareš, cited in Petar Hadji-Ristić, "Holding on to the Home Front," *Index on Censorship* 21, no. 9 (Sept. 1992): 11.

107 As reported in *Borba*, 12 Jan. 1993, 9.

108 *Nedeljna Borba*, 9/10 Jan. 1993, 7, trans. in FBIS, *Daily Report* (Eastern Europe), 22 Jan. 1993, 72.

109 From testimony printed in *Index on Censorship* 21, no. 9 (Sept. 1992): 9. Re an attempt to kill Bojan Stojanović, a Serbian photographer whose pictures recorded the atrocities being perpetrated by his countrymen, see *The European*, 22–25 Apr. 1993, 2.

110 *Le Monde*, 21 Nov. 1992, 8, trans. in FBIS, *Daily Report* (Eastern Europe), 10 Dec. 1992, 45.

111 *Politika—International Weekly* (Belgrade), 24 Oct.–6 Nov. 1992, 1.

112 *Vreme*, 16 Dec. 1991, 12–13; Tanjug Domestic Service, 11 June 1992, trans. in FBIS, *Daily Report* (Eastern Europe), 12 June 1992, 54; *Srpska reč* (Belgrade), no. 57, 26 Oct. 1992, 38–41; and *Srpska reč*, no. 58, 9 Nov. 1992, 36.

113 *Globe and Mail* (Toronto) 11 Apr. 1991, A7.

114 Glenny, *Fall of Yugoslavia*, 56.

115 See Douglas E. Schoen, "How Milošević Stole the Elections," *New York Times Magazine*, 14 Feb. 1993.

116 *Politika*, 23 Dec. 1992, 6, trans. in FBIS, *Daily Report* (Eastern Europe), 5 Jan. 1993, 51.

117 *Süddeutsche Zeitung*, 4/5 Sept. 1993, 7.

118 Ibid., 1 Sept. 1993, 7.

119 A conversation recorded by Brian Hall, "A Holy War in Waiting," *New York Times Magazine*, 9 May 1993, 44.

120   Hanna Arendt, *On the Origins of Totalitarianism,* rev. ed. (Boston: Beacon Press, 1963).

121   Elez Biberaj, "Kosova: The Balkan Powder Keg," *Conflict Studies,* no. 258 (London: Research Institute for the Study of Conflict and Terrorism, Feb. 1993): 6–7.

122   *Bujku* (Priština), 14 Sept. 1991, p. 3, trans. in FBIS, *Daily Report* (Eastern Europe), 25 Sept. 1991, 35.

123   Radio Tirana Network (Tirana), 27 Oct. 1992, trans. in FBIS, *Daily Report* (Eastern Europe), 28 Oct. 1992, 30.

124   AFP (Paris), 23 Sept. 1992, in FBIS, *Daily Report* (Eastern Europe), 24 Sept. 1992, 44.

125   Macedonian Information and Liaison Service, MAKNEWS, 8 Sept. 1993.

126   Tanjug Domestic Service, 21 Oct. 1991, in FBIS, *Daily Report* (Eastern Europe), 22 Oct. 1991, 54; *Neue Zürcher Zeitung,* 17 Oct. 1992, 3; Radio Belgrade Network, 25 Aug. 1992, trans. in FBIS, *Daily Report* (Eastern Europe), 26 Aug. 1992, 45; ATA (Tirana), 3 Nov. 1992, in FBIS, *Daily Report* (Eastern Europe), 4 Nov. 1992, 29. Re the continued closure of Albanian-language schools in the autumn of 1993, see *Süddeutsche Zeitung,* 17 Sept. 1993, 8.

127   *Borba,* 6 Apr. 1993, 4. See also *Vjesnik,* 15 July 1993, 8.

128   *Bujku,* 1 Nov. 1991, 4, trans. in FBIS, *Daily Report* (Eastern Europe), 6 Nov. 1991, 40; Radio Croatia Network (Zagreb), 5 Oct. 1992, trans. in FBIS, *Daily Report* (Eastern Europe), 6 Oct. 1992, 44; ATA, 7 Oct. 1992, in FBIS, *Daily Report* (Eastern Europe), 8 Oct. 1992, 45; ATA, 5 Nov. 1992, in FBIS, *Daily Report* (Eastern Europe), 6 Nov. 1992, 42; ATA, 4 Apr. 1993, in FBIS, *Daily Report* (Eastern Europe), 5 Apr. 1993, 58.

129   AFP (Paris), 23 Sept. 1992, in FBIS, *Daily Report* (Eastern Europe), 24 Sept. 1992, 44.

130   *Rilindja* (Zofingen), 7 Oct. 1992, 1, trans. in FBIS, *Daily Report* (Eastern Europe), 16 Oct. 1992, 59.

131   Tanjug Domestic Service, 18 Aug. 1992, trans. in FBIS, *Daily Report* (Eastern Europe), 19 Aug. 1992, 30.

132   *Globe and Mail* (Toronto), 13 May 1993, A9.

133   Tanjug Domestic Service, 16 Sept. 1992, trans. in FBIS, *Daily Report* (Eastern Europe), 17 Sept. 1992, 44.

134   *Borba,* 6 Apr. 1993, 10; and *Politika,* 7 June 1994, 2.

135   Quoted in *International Herald Tribune* (Tokyo ed.), 1 June 1993, 2.

136   Tanjug, 19 Oct. 1992, in FBIS, *Daily Report* (Eastern Europe), 20 Oct. 1992, 45.

137   Ibid.; *Večernji list* (Zagreb), 27 Apr. 1992, 8; *Borba,* 14 Jan. 1993, 10.

138   See, for example, MTV Television Network (Budapest), 28 Feb. 1992, trans. in FBIS, *Daily Report* (Eastern Europe), 28 Feb. 1992, 40; Kossuth Radio Network (Budapest), 27 Sept. 1992, trans. in FBIS, *Daily Report* (Eastern Europe), 30 Sept. 1992, 41.

139   *Večernji list,* 27 Apr. 1993, 8, trans. in FBIS, *Daily Report* (Eastern Europe), 7 May 1992, 36.

140   Quoted in *Borba,* 14 Apr. 1993, 23.

141   Re threatening letters, see *Le Monde,* 16 June 1992, 9, trans. in FBIS, *Daily Report* (Eastern Europe), 30 June 1992, 57–58; Kossuth Radio Network, 30 Oct. 1992, trans. in FBIS, *Daily Report* (Eastern Europe), 2 Nov. 1992, 45. Re barricades, see HTV Television (Zagreb), 19 Nov. 1992, trans. in FBIS, *Daily Report* (Eastern Europe), 20 Nov. 1992, 44. Re purges, see Radio Croatia Network (Zagreb), 8 Dec. 1992, trans. in FBIS, *Daily Report* (Eastern Europe), 10 Dec. 1992, 59. Re the sup-

pression of *Magyar Szó*, see Kossuth Radio Network, 22 Nov. 1992, trans. in FBIS, *Daily Report* (Eastern Europe), 23 Nov. 1992, 59.

142 Quoted in Tanjug, 18 June 1992, in FBIS, *Daily Report* (Eastern Europe), 19 June 1992, 24.

143 Sandar Hodi, interview with *Magyar Nemzet* (Budapest), 13 Oct. 1992, 2, trans. in FBIS, *Daily Report* (Eastern Europe), 21 Oct. 1992, 58.

144 *Neue Zürcher Zeitung*, 12 Sept. 1992, 5.

145 *The Europa World Year Book 1993*, 34th ed. (London: Europa Publications, 1993): 2: 3229–30.

146 *Borba*, 15 Oct. 1992, trans. in FBIS, *Daily Report* (Eastern Europe), 2 Nov. 1992, 38.

147 *Vjesnik*, 15 Apr. 1993, 8.

148 *Borba*, 17/18 Apr. 1993, 6.

149 Dijana Pleština, "Democracy and Nationalism in Croatia: The First Three Years," in *Beyond Yugoslavia: Politics, Economics, and Culture in a Shattered Community* ed. Sabrina Petra Ramet and Ljubiša S. Adamovich (Boulder, Colo.: Westview Press, 1994).

150 Drazen Budiša, president of the Croatian Social Liberal Party, interview with *Globus* (Zagreb), 20 Nov. 1992, 34.

151 *Danas*, 12 Mar. 1993, 16–17, trans. in FBIS, *Daily Report* (Eastern Europe), 6 Apr. 1993, 36–37; *Die Zeit* (Hamburg), 26 Mar. 1993, 2; *Vreme*, 29 Mar. 1993, 35, trans. in FBIS, *Daily Report* (Eastern Europe), 19 Apr. 1993, 50.

152 Jasmina Kuzmanović, "Media: The Extension of Politics by Other Means," Ramet and Adamovich, *Beyond Yugoslavia*.

153 Dubravka Ugrešić, "Zagreb, Autumn 1992," *Granta*, no. 42 (Winter 1992), 243–44.

154 For a discussion of present dilemmas in Macedonia, see Sabrina Petra Ramet, "The Macedonian Enigma," in Ramet and Adamovich, *Beyond Yugoslavia*.

155 The Serbian state is now subsidizing the Serbian Orthodox church.

156 Juan J. Linz and Alfred Stepan, "Political Identities and Electoral Sequences: Spain, the Soviet Union, and Yugoslavia," *Daedalus* 121, no. 2 (Spring 1992): 127.

157 Ibid., 131, emphasis in original.

18. Civil Society and Uncivil Chauvinism

1 Theodor W. Adorno et al., *The Authoritarian Personality* (New York: Harper, 1950).

2 By contrast, they write that "cults are deviant religious movements within a deviant religious tradition." Rodney Stark and William Sims Bainbridge, *The Future of Religion: Secularization, Revival and Cult Formation* (Berkeley: University of California Press, 1985), 26.

3 Ibid., 149, 153.

4 Ibid., 56.

5 Ibid., 315–16.

6 Max Stirner, *The Ego and His Own*, trans. from German by Steven T. Byington (New York: 1845; Libertarian Book Club, 1963), 213.

7 Wolf Oschlies, *Rechtsradikalismus im postkommunistischen Osteuropas. Teil 1: Fallstudien* (Cologne: Bundesinstitut für ostwissenschaftliche Studien, no. 29, 1992), 4.

8 Re organized crime in eastern Germany, see *Neues Deutschland* (Berlin), 29 Mar. 1993, 4. Re organized crime in Slovakia, see CTK (Prague), 12 Jan. 1993, in FBIS,

Daily Report (Eastern Europe), 14 Jan. 1993, 21; and *Wirtschaftswoche* (Vienna), 8 Apr. 1993, 43, trans. in FBIS, *Daily Report* (Eastern Europe), 14 Apr. 1993, 2. Re organized crime in Hungary, see *Nepszava* (Budapest), 31 Dec. 1992, 5, trans. in FBIS, *Daily Report* (Eastern Europe), 6 Jan. 1993, 22. Re organized crime in Serbia, see *Srpska reč* (Belgrade), no. 51, 20 July 1992, 52; *Vreme* (Belgrade), 8 Mar. 1993, 18–19. Re organized crime in the area as a whole, see *New York Times*, 2 Sept. 1993, A13.

9   *Zeri i popullit* (Tiranë), 3 Apr. 1992, 2, trans. in FBIS, *Daily Report* (Eastern Europe), 14 Apr. 1992, 2–3.

10 Douglass W. Bailey, "The Looting of Bulgaria," *Archaeology* (Mar.–Apr. 1993): 26–27.

11 *Vreme*, 22 Mar. 1993, 10–13.

12 Macedonian Information and Liaison Service, MILS-NEWS, *Dnevni Vesti Angliski*, 30 June 1993.

13 Re a Bulgarian-Polish agreement, see BTA (Sofia), 22 Apr. 1993, in FBIS, *Daily Report* (Eastern Europe), 23 Apr. 1993, 3. Re Croatian agreements with Slovenia, Hungary, and Italy, see *Glas Istre* (Pula), 5 June 1993, 5. Re a multilateral agreement involving Poland, Ukraine, Lithuania, Estonia, Latvia, Russia, and Belarus, see *New York Times*, 20 Nov. 1992, A4.

14 *Romania Libera* (Bucharest), 16 Dec. 1992, 1, 2, trans. in FBIS, *Daily Report* (Eastern Europe), 28 Jan. 1993, 30–31.

15 Re the economic slump in Western Europe, see *International Herald Tribune* (Tokyo ed.), 14 June 1993, 1, 9.

16 Thus, for example, nearly 50 percent of the Dutch feel that too many foreigners work and reside in the Netherlands. Re the situation in the Netherlands, see *Japan Times*, 18 June 1993, 6.

17 *The Times* (London), 16 June 1993, 7.

18 Mirjana Kasapović, "Srpski nacionalizam i desni radikalizam," *Naše teme* (Zagreb) 33, nos. 1–2 (1989): 67.

19 For example, in April 1993 Mirko Jović, chair of the Serbian National Renewal party, told a news conference in Belgrade that "currently the most threatened part of the Serb people lives on the territory of the Former Yugoslav Republic of Macedonia." Tanjug Domestic Service, 10 Apr. 1993, trans. in FBIS, *Daily Report* (Eastern Europe), 12 Apr. 1993, 59.

20 See Vladimir Dedijer, *The Yugoslav Auschwitz and the Vatican*, trans. from German by Harvey L. Kendall (Buffalo, N.Y.: Prometheus Books, 1992); Alida Bremer, "Neuere serbische Literatur: Zwischen Geschichte, Mythos und Nation," *Die Neue Gesellschaft. Frankfurther Hefte* 39, no. 5 (May 1992): 459.

21 For details, see Sabrina Petra Ramet, "Yugoslavia and the Two Germanys," in *The Germans and Their Neighbors*, ed. Dirk Verheyen and Christian Soe (Boulder, Colo.: Westview Press, 1993).

22 *Die Presse* (Vienna), 3 Oct. 1991, 1–2, trans. in FBIS, *Daily Report* (Eastern Europe), 3 Oct. 1991, 37.

23 Dobroslav Paraga, chair of the Croatian Party of Right, interview with *Der Spiegel* (Hamburg), 21 Sept. 1992, 246–48, trans. in FBIS, *Daily Report* (Eastern Europe), 22 Sept. 1992, 33. Re Paraga's difficulties at the hands of the Tudjman government, see *Danas* (Zagreb), new ser., 4 June 1993, 5–7.

24 Peter Kenez, "Nationalism on the Rise in Hungary," *New Leader*, 21 Sept. 1992, 7.

25 "Excerpts from Csurka's Theses," originally published in *Magyar Forum*,

20 August 1992, and excerpted in *Nepszabadsag* (Budapest), 27 Aug. 1992, 6, trans. in FBIS, *Daily Report* (Eastern Europe), 3 Sept. 1992, 9.

26   Hannah Arendt, *On the Origins of Totalitarianism*, rev. ed. (London: A. Deutsch, 1963).

27   See, for instance, Mile Paspalj, chair of the assembly of the Republic of the Serbian Krajina, interview with *Borba* (Belgrade), 4 Apr. 1993, 4, trans. in FBIS, *Daily Report* (Eastern Europe), 14 Apr. 1993, 33.

28   *Slovensky Dennik* (Bratislava), 28 Sept. 1992, 4, trans. in FBIS, *Daily Report* (Eastern Europe), 1 Oct. 1992, 11–12; MTI (Budapest), 13 Nov. 1992, in FBIS, *Daily Report* (Eastern Europe), 17 Nov. 1992, 16–17. See also *Süddeutsche Zeitung* (Munich), 2 Sept. 1993, 10; *Frankfurter Allgemeine*, 20 Dec. 1993, 5, and 8 Jan. 1994, 5.

29   *Critianiki*, 19 Dec. 1991, summarized in ATA (Tirana), 8 Jan. 1992, in FBIS, *Daily Report* (Eastern Europe), 9 Jan. 1992, 2–3; MILS-NEWS, *Dnevi Vesti Angliski*, 15 July 1993.

30   See Radio Vilnius Network, 23 Sept. 1991, trans. in FBIS, *Daily Report* (Soviet Union), 24 Sept. 1991, 60–61; *Trybuna Slaska* (Katowice), 24 July 1992, 6, trans. in FBIS, *Daily Report* (Eastern Europe), 31 July 1992, 17–18.

31   See Wolfgang Höpken, "Türken und Pomaken in Bulgarien," *Südosteuropa* 32 no. 2 (1992): 147.

32   MTI, 2 Dec. 1992, in FBIS, *Daily Report* (Eastern Europe), 7 Dec. 1992, 18; confirmed in *Frankfurter Allgemeine*, 23 Mar. 1993, 2; reconfirmed in *Borba*, 2 Apr. 1993, 14.

33   As of August 1994, the United States still had not recognized Macedonia. Re the coat of arms, see *Süddeutsche Zeitung* (Munich), 3/4 April 1993, 7. For further discussion of this controversy, see Sabrina Petra Ramet, "The Macedonian Enigma," in *Beyond Yugoslavia: Politics, Economics, and Culture in a Shattered Community*, ed. Sabrina Petra Ramet and Ljubisa S. Adamovich (Boulder, Colo.: Westview Press, 1994). Re the establishment of diplomatic ties with Macedonia by Britain, France, Germany, Italy, Denmark, and the Netherlands, and the continued refusal of the United States to recognize Macedonia, see *Süddeutsche Zeitung*, 13 Dec. 1993, 6; *The Times*, 17 Dec. 1993, 14; and *Frankfurter Allgemeine*, 17 Dec. 1993, 1–2.

34   MTI, 27 Aug. 1992, in FBIS, *Daily Report* (Eastern Europe), 28 Aug. 1992, 27–28; CTK (Prague), 4 Jan. 1993, in FBIS, *Daily Report* (Eastern Europe), 8 Jan. 1993, 11–12.

35   CTK, 30 Dec. 1992, in FBIS, *Daily Report* (Eastern Europe), 6 Jan. 1993, 16.

36   See Sabrina Petra Ramet, "The Radical Right in Germany," manuscript.

37   *Reporter* (Prague), 20 Nov. 1991, 22, trans. in JPRS *Report*, no. EER-91-180 (Eastern Europe), 17 Dec. 1991, 10–11.

38   *Süddeutsche Zeitung*, 19/20 Feb. 1994, 11.

39   Oschlies, *Rechtsradikalismus, Teil 1*, 15, 18.

40   Ibid., 20–21.

41   Estimate by *Nepszabadsag*, reported in *Süddeutsche Zeitung*, 25 June 1993, 7.

42   Quoted in *Magyar Hirlap* (Budapest), 2 Nov. 1992, 1, 5, trans. in FBIS, *Daily Report* (Eastern Europe), 6 Nov. 1992, 15.

43   See the detailed article in *New York Times*, 15 Jan. 1993, A4.

44   Glyn Ford, *Fascist Europe: The Rise of Racism and Xenophobia* (Boulder, Colo.: Pluto Press, 1992), 40.

45 For specifics, see *Beszelo* (Budapest), 9 Nov. 1991, 17, trans. in JPRS *Report*, no. EER-91-175 (Eastern Europe), 3 Dec. 1991, 21–22.

46 MTI, 17 Nov. 1992, in FBIS, *Daily Report* (Eastern Europe), 20 Nov. 1992, 11; MTI, 7 Dec. 1992, in FBIS, *Daily Report* (Eastern Europe), 9 Dec. 1992, 17.

47 Oschlies, *Rechtsradikalismus, Teil 1*, 22–24.

48 Cited in ibid., 25–26.

49 *The European* (London), 22–25 Apr. 1993, 18.

50 Ibid.

51 Oschlies, *Rechtsradikalismus, Teil 1*, 30.

52 Ford, *Fascist Europe*, 40.

53 See Sabrina Petra Ramet, "Balkan Pluralism and Its Enemies," *Orbis* 36, no. 4 (Fall 1992): 552–53.

54 *Since the Revolution: Human Rights in Romania* (New York: Helsinki Watch, Mar. 1991), 21.

55 Michael Shafir, "The Movement for Romania: A Party of 'Radical Reform,'" *RFE/RL Report*, 17 July 1992, 18, 19.

56 *Cotidianul*, 3 Mar. 1992, quoted in Shafir, "Movement for Romania," 19.

57 *Frankfurter Allgemeine*, 15 April 1994, 1, reporting official estimates of the Federal Office for the Protection of the Constitution.

58 *Der Spiegel*, 7 June 1993, 25; *Die Zeit* (Hamburg), 8 Jan. 1993, 2.

59 *Die Zeit*, 11 Dec. 1992, 21.

60 Quoted in *New York Times*, 2 Dec. 1992, A1.

61 Ibid.; *New York Times*, 3 Dec. 1992, A9. Since then, Böhse Onkelz has experienced a "conversion" and now uses the stage to warn about dangers from the right. On 17 October 1993, for example, Böhse Onkelz was scheduled to play a "Rock Against the Right" concert in the Bremen City Hall. See advance report, *Süddeutsche Zeitung*, 29 Sept. 1993, 6.

62 *New York Times*, 4 Feb. 1993, A4; *Neue Zürcher Zeitung*, 5 Feb. 1993, 3; *Süddeutsche Zeitung*, 8/9 May 1993, 6.

63 *Süddeutsche Zeitung*, 13/14 Mar. 1993, 21.

64 See, for example, William Pfaff, "Will the Clock Keep Ticking?," *Japan Times*, 16 June 1993, 17.

65 George L. Mosse, *Nationalism and Sexuality: Middle-Class Morality and Sexual Norms in Modern Europe* (Milwaukee: University of Wisconsin Press, 1985).

66 Quoted in Renata Salecl, "Nationalism, Anti-Semitism, and Anti-Feminism in Eastern Europe," *New German Critique*, no. 57 (Fall 1992): 58–59.

67 *Süddeutsche Zeitung*, 4/5 Apr. 1992, 6.

68 Christiane Lemke, "Women and Politics in East Germany," *Socialist Review* 15, no. 3 (1985): 129.

69 On this point, see Irene Kaufmann, "Enveristischer Stachanovismus: Die 'Emanzipation' der Albanischen Frau," *Österreichische Osthefte* 34, no. 1 (1992).

70 See Barbara Jancar, "Zur Rolle der Frau in der kommunistischen Gesellschaft," *Osteuropa* 26, no. 7 (July 1976).

71 Quoted in Marlene Nadle, "For Men Only? No!," *World Monitor* (May 1992): 49.

72 Birgit Meyer, "Feminismus und Demokratie," *Die Neue Gesellschaft, Frankfurter Hefte* 39, no. 11 (Nov. 1992): 1005; see also Vivian Gornick and Barbara Moran, eds., *Woman in Sexist Society* (New York: Basic Books, 1971).

73 Meyer, "Feminismus und Demokratie," 1004.

74   Frigga Haug, "Über die Frauenfrage als Systemfrage," *Das Argument* (Berlin) 32, no. 2 (Mar.–Apr. 1990): 263.

75   Ina Merkel, "Ohne Frauen ist kein Staat zu machen," *Das Argument* 32, no. 2 (Mar.–Apr. 1990): 256.

76   Karin Hildebrandt, "Frauen in DDR-Hochschulen," *Das Argument* 32, no. 3 (May–June 1990): 382–83; Barbara Einhorn, "Where Have All the Women Gone? Women and the Women's Movement in East Central Europe," *Feminist Review*, special issue no. 39 (1991): 17.

77   *Welt am Sonntag* (Bonn), 14 Mar. 1993, 2. For a plea for a guaranteed 40 percent minimum in the legislature for each sex, see Anne Phillips, "Must Feminists Give Up on Liberal Democracy?," in *Prospects for Democracy: North, South, East, West*, ed. David Held (Oxford: Polity Press, 1993), 104.

78   "Kongressberichte: 5. Konferenz des Europäischen Forums Sozialistischer Feministinnen," *Das Argument* 32, no. 2 (Mar.–Apr. 1990): 281.

79   Quoted in Nadle, "For Men Only?," 46.

80   Quoted in Slavenka Drakulic, "Feminism Is a Dirty Word in Hungary," *Utne Reader* (Jan.–Feb. 1990): 102.

81   Quoted in ibid.

82   Jirina Šiklová, "Sind die Frauen aus Ost- und Mitteleuropa Konservativ?," *Die Neue Gesellschaft, Frankfurter Hefte* 38, no. 11 (Nov. 1991): 1016.

83   Nadle, "For Men Only?," 46; and Milica G. Antic, "Democracy Between Tyranny and Liberty: Women in Post-'Socialist' Slovenia," *Feminist Review*, special issue no. 39 (1991): 151.

84   Yudit Kiss, "The Second 'No': Women in Hungary," *Feminist Review*, special issue no. 39 (1991): 53.

85   Kaufmann, "Enveristischer Stachanovismus," 33.

86   Małgorzata Fuszara, "Legal Regulation of Abortion in Poland," *Signs* 17, no. 1 (Autumn 1991): 120, 127.

87   PAP (Warsaw), 30 Nov. 1992, in FBIS, *Daily Report* (Eastern Europe), 1 Dec. 1992, p. 30.

88   *Rzeczpospolita* (Warsaw), 8 Jan. 1993, 3, trans. in FBIS, *Daily Report* (Eastern Europe), 14 Jan. 1993, 31.

89   *Japan Times*, 30 May 1993, 5.

90   Gail Kligman, "The Politics of Reproduction in Ceauşescu's Romania: A Case Study in Political Culture," *East European Politics and Societies* 6, no. 3 (Fall 1992): 377.

91   Ibid., 391.

92   Kiss, "The Second 'No,' " 53.

93   Gertrude Schaffner Goldberg, "Women on the Verge: Winners and Losers in German Unification," *Social Policy* 22, no. 2 (Fall 1991): 40; *Süddeutsche Zeitung*, 27/28 Mar. 1993, 7.

94   Mita Castle-Kanerová, "Interview with Alena Valterova, Founder of the Political Party of Women and Mothers (Prague, November 1990)," *Feminist Review*, special issue no. 39 (1991): 163.

95   Einhorn, "Where Have All the Women Gone?," 18.

96   Quoted in Nadle, "For Men Only?," 46.

97   See Susan Faludi, *Backlash: The Undeclared War Against American Women* (New York: Crown Publishers, 1992).

98   Kiss, "The Second 'No,'" 54–55.

99   *The European*, 11–14 Mar. 1993, 46.

100   Kaufmann, "Enveristischer Stachanovismus," 35.

101   Quoted in Hanna Jankowska, "Abortion, Church and Politics in Poland," *Feminist Review*, special issue no. 39 (1991): 180n.

102   *Vjesnik* (Zagreb), 15 June 1993, 3.

103   Ibid.

104   See *The Times*, 23 Dec. 1992, 6; *Süddeutsche Zeitung*, 9/10 Jan. 1993, 1. Also *Vjesnik*, 18 June 1993, 10; *Seattle Times*, 2 June 1994, A9. Re the political aspect of these rapes, see the article by Vesna Kesić, originally published in *Danas*, trans. into German as "Zur Situation von Frauen im ehemaligen Jugoslawien," *Osteuropa* 43, no. 7 (July 1993): A401–A402.

105   See Małgorzata Tarasiewicz, "Women in Poland: Choices to Be Made," *Feminist Review*, special issue no. 39 (1991): 182.

106   *Globus* (Zagreb), 11 Dec. 1992, 33.

107   Quoted in Chris Corrin, "Gendered Identities: Women's Experience of Change in Hungary," in *Women in the Face of Change: The Soviet Union, Eastern Europe and China*, ed. Shirin Rai, Hilary Pilkington, and Annie Phizacklea (London: Routledge, 1992), 179.

108   Ibid.

109   Klára Makara, "A Woman's Place," *New Hungarian Quarterly* 33, no. 126 (Summer 1992): 100.

110   E. Fischer and P. Lux, *Ohne uns ist kein Staat zu machen: DDR Frauen nach der Wende* (Cologne: Kiepenheuer and Witsch, 1990), quoted in Einhorn, "Where Have All the Women Gone?," 25 (Einhorn's insertion).

111   Merkel, "Ohne Frauen," 261.

112   Eva Schäfer, "'Wer sich nicht wehrt, kommt an den Herd!' Zur feministischen Erneuerung in der DDR," *Das Argument* 32, no. 2 (Mar.–Apr. 1990): 279.

113   Kate Soper, "Postmodernism and Its Discontents," *Feminist Review*, special issue no. 39 (1991): 104.

114   For an in-depth discussion, see Sabrina Petra Ramet, "The Serbian Church and the Serbian Nation," in Ramet and Adamovich, *Beyond Yugoslavia*.

115   Sabrina Petra Ramet, "The New Church-State Configuration in Eastern Europe," in *Protestantism and Politics in Eastern Europe and Russia: The Communist and Post-Communist Eras*, ed. Sabrina Petra Ramet (Durham, N.C.: Duke University Press, 1992), 321.

116   *Kana* (Zagreb), Mar. 1992, 37; and *Novi Vjesnik* (Zagreb), 28 Sept. 1992, 4A.

117   PAP, 20 Aug. 1992, in FBIS, *Daily Report* (Eastern Europe), 21 Aug. 1992, 15; *New York Times*, 22 Apr. 1993, A7.

118   Quoted in Ramet, "New Church-State," 321.

119   Re the elections in Croatia, see *Novi Vjesnik* (Zagreb), 5 Sept. 1992, 5A.

120   *Danas* (Zagreb), no. 531 (21 Apr. 1992): 28.

121   Quoted in Graeme Duncan and John Street, "Liberalism, Marxism, and Tolerance," in *Justifying Toleration: Conceptual and Historical Perspectives*, ed. Susan Mendus (Cambridge: Cambridge University Press, 1988), 226.

122   Quoted in ibid., 223.

123   Immanuel Kant, *Grundlegung zur Metaphysik der Sitten* (Leipzig: 1797; Philipp Reclam, n.d.). For a discussion of Kant's thinking about morality, see also my

early essay, "Kantian and Hegelian Perspectives on Duty," *Southern Journal of Philosophy* 21, no. 2 (Summer 1983).

124 See his comments as reported in *La Stampa* (Torino), 4 Oct. 1991, 6; *Japan Times*, 18 June 1993, 6.

125 As summarized in Margaret Canovan, "Friendship, Truth, and Politics: Hannah Arendt and Toleration," in Mendus, *Justifying Toleration*, esp. 182.

19. Propositions About the Future

1 Re this debate, see the self-congratulatory preface to Vladimir Tismaneanu, *Reinventing Politics: Eastern Europe from Stalin to Havel* (New York: Free Press, 1992).

2 Anders Åslund, *Post-Communist Economic Revolutions: How Big a Bang?* (Washington, D.C.: Center for Strategic and International Studies, 1992), 14.

3 Daniel N. Nelson, "Democracy, Markets and Security in Eastern Europe," *Survival* 35, no. 2 (Summer 1993): 159.

4 Robert Moss, *The Collapse of Democracy* (London: Temple Smith, 1975), 269.

5 Three fine preliminary studies are *Reforming the Economies of Central and Eastern Europe* (Paris: OECD, 1992); Åslund, *Post-Communist Economic Revolutions*; and Michael McFaul, *Post-Communist Politics: Democratic Prospects in Russia and Eastern Europe* (Washington, D.C.: Center for Strategic and International Studies, 1993). See also *The Transition to a Market Economy*, 2 vols. (Paris: OECD, 1991).

6 See Sabrina Petra Ramet, "When Systems Fail: Toward a Theory About the Relationship Between System Decay and Civil Strife," in *Adaptation and Transformation in Communist and Post-Communist Systems*, ed. Sabrina Petra Ramet (Boulder, Colo.: Westview Press, 1992).

Selected Bibliography

Sources consulted in connection with the research for this book are cited in the notes. The following is a brief guide for further reading, organized on a country-by-country basis, with subsequent heads for dissent, religion, women, and general discussions. I have deliberately limited myself to no more than four books per category, a limitation that necessarily excludes many noteworthy books, but it will also simplify the use of this bibliography.

Albania. The classic treatment of postwar Albania is still Peter R. Prifti's *Socialist Albania Since 1944: Domestic and Foreign Developments* (Cambridge, Mass.: MIT Press), first published in 1978. Its scope includes both political and social issues, including chapters on religion and women's equality. Also useful is Anton Logoreci's oft-cited volume, *The Albanians* (London: Gollancz, 1977), which includes much material on the labor camp and prison system established under Enver Hoxha. Two studies by Elez Biberaj published more recently are also of note: *Albania and China: A Study of an Unequal Alliance* (Boulder, Colo.: Westview Press, 1986) and *Albania: A Socialist Maverick* (Boulder, Colo.: Westview Press, 1990).

Bulgaria. John D. Bell wrote an excellent history of the Bulgarian ruling party, *The Bulgarian Communist Party from Blagoev to Zhivkov* (Stanford, Calif.: Hoover Institution Press, 1986). It remains one of the best treatments of Bulgaria to date. R. J. Crampton's *A Short History of Modern Bulgaria* (New York: Cambridge University Press, 1987) is a good overview and covers a lot of ground. John R. Lampe's *The Bulgarian Economy in the Twentieth Century* (New York: St. Martin's Press, 1986) is perhaps the most solid Western treatment of Bulgarian economic issues. Not much recent work about Bulgaria is available in English, but a good overall introduction is provided by Robert J. McIntyre, *Bulgaria: Politics, Economics and Society* (London: Pinter, 1988).

Czechoslovakia. No list of books about Czechoslovakia can omit H. Gordon Skilling's mammoth magnum opus, *Czechoslovakia's Interrupted Revolution* (Princeton, N.J.: Princeton University Press, 1976), which discusses the Dubček period. The pres-

1993); Marilyn Rueschemeyer, ed., *Women in the Politics of Post-Communist Eastern Europe* (Armonk, N.Y.: M. E. Sharpe, 1993); and a special issue of *Feminist Review* devoted to women and politics in Eastern Europe and Russia, no. 39 (1991).

General. A useful short history of the region is Robin Okey's *Eastern Europe, 1740–1980* (Minneapolis: University of Minnesota Press, 1982). Joseph Rothschild's mistitled *Return to Diversity: A Political History of East Central Europe Since World War II* (New York: Oxford University Press, 1989) actually devotes one-third of its space to events taking place between the end of World War I and the outbreak of World War II. It is perhaps the best short account of twentieth-century Eastern Europe to date. Zbigniew Brzezinski's *The Soviet Bloc: Unity and Conflict*, rev. and enlarged ed. (Cambridge, Mass.: Harvard University Press, 1967), is still the standard reference for the period from the late 1940s to the 1960s. Misha Glenny's *The Rebirth of History: Eastern Europe in the Age of Democracy*, new ed. (London: Penguin Books, 1993), is a fast-paced, concise story of changes in Eastern Europe since 1989, organized country-by-country.

Index

James Bond Club (Slovakia), 245
Jancar, Barbara, 232
Janik, Leszek, 240–241
Jankowski, Henryk, 188
János Kádár Society (Hungary), 136, 296
Janša, Janez, 307, 365
Japan, 18
Jarocin rock festival (Poland), 236, 241, 243
Jaruzelski, Wojciech, 27, 45, 86–88, 90, 92, 110, 118, 186, 187, 241, 271, 289, 303, 304, 358, 360; does not like punk music, 243; elected "King of Poland," 105
Jaworski, Seweryn, 94
Jazzbulletin (bulletin of the Czech Jazz Section), 128
Jazz Forum (monthly magazine), 242
Jazzpetit, 128
Jazz Section (Czechoslovakia), 128–129
Jazz Stop (Czechoslovak magazine), 133
Jedinstvo (Kosovo daily newspaper in Serbo-Croatian), 212
Jedynak, Tadeusz, 112, 114
Jehovah's Witnesses, 163, 166, 167, 168, 169 (t. 6)
Jelenet (Hungarian independent political weekly), 293
Jesus Christ Superstar, 256
"Jewish conspiracy," 393, 437, 440
Jewish Religious Communities Central Union (Bratislava), 438
Jodkowski, Edmund, 87
Jovanović, Ana, 221
Jovanović, Vladislav, 426
Jović, Borisav, 406
Jowitt, Ken, 22
Judasil (guru), 172
Jugendweihe (East German youth dedication ceremony), 156
Judiciary, independent, 385, 388–389
Junge Welt (official organ of the East German "Free German Youth" organization), 324, 327
Jurczyk, Marian, 94
Jurczyk, Stefan, 114
Jurevičius, Juozas, 171
Justinian, Patriarch, 164

Kádár, János, 291, 296, 311, 323, 355
Kádár, Maria, 296
Kádár, formula, 8
Kadare, Ismail, 341

Kadijević, Veljko, 417
Kafka, Franz, 346
Kamenev, Lev, 319, 320
Kamiński, Tadeusz, 189
Kant, Immanuel, 454
Kantor, Pavel, 339
Karadžić, Radovan, 407; rejects Vance-Owen plan, 409
Karadžić, Vuk, 163
Karakalpak ASSR, 171
Kardelj, Edvard, 201, 318, 417
Karl, Terry Lynn, 5, 12, 16–17
Karl Marx University of Economics (Budapest), 41
Kasapović, Mirjana, 436
Katedra (Slovenian youth newspaper), 307
Katolické noviny (Czech Catholic newspaper), 130
Katunarić, Vjeran: *Female Eros and the Civilization of Death*, 228
Kautsky, Karl Johann, 74
Kempný, Josef, 336
Kerensky, Aleksandr, 320
Keston College, 164
KGB, 320, 323, 347
Khan, Genghis. See Genghis Khan
Khrushchev, Nikita, 74, 288, 315, 320
King, Martin Luther, Jr., 438
Király, Zoltán, 291, 293
Die Kirche (East German Evangelical newspaper), 66
Kirche im Sozialismus (West German monthly journal), 66
Kis, János, 29, 121, 135, 138, 148
Kiss, Yudit, 448, 449
Kiszczak, Czesław, 117, 118, 301–302, 304, 359
Kiuranov, Deyen, 286
Kizyn, Maria, 162
Klier, Freya, 68
Književne novine (Serbian literary newspaper), 310
Koburg, Andreas, 68
Kočab, Michal, 339
Kock, Wilhelm, 68
Kohl, Helmut, 101, 334–335, 353, 410, 436, 454
Kollár, Attila, 257
Kołodziej, Andrzej, 98
Koltay, Gábor, 257
Komárek, Valtr, 315
Kommunist (Soviet official communist party ideological organ), 323

Sabrina Petra Ramet is Professor of International
Studies at the University of Washington. Born in
London, England, she has lived for extended periods of
time in England, Austria, Germany, Yugoslavia, and
Japan, as well as in the United States. She is the author
of four previous books: *Cross and Commissar: The
Politics of Religion in Eastern Europe and the USSR*
(1987), *The Soviet-Syrian Relationship since 1955: A
Troubled Alliance* (1990), *Balkan Babel: Politics,
Culture, and Religion in Yugoslavia* (1992), and
Nationalism and Federalism in Yugoslavia, 1962–1991,
2nd ed. (1992).

Library of Congress Cataloging-in-Publication Data

Ramet, Sabrina P., 1949–
Social currents in Eastern Europe : the sources and
consequences of the great transformation / Sabrina
Petra Ramet. — 2nd ed.
p.   cm.
Includes bibliographical references and index.
ISBN 0-8223-1551-3 (cloth : acid-free paper). — ISBN
0-8223-1548-3 (pbk. : acid-free paper)
1. Europe, Eastern—Social conditions.   2. Europe,
Eastern—Politics and government—1945–1989.   I.
Title.
HN373.5.R36   1995
306'.0947—dc20   94-28352